FOR Dummies
BESTSELLING
BOOK SERIES

Colorado & the Rockies For Dummies, 2nd Edition

W9-CSX-231

Cheat Sheet

Denver Walking Tour

1 Civic Center Park
2 Colorado History Museum
3 Denver Art Museum
4 City and County Building
5 U.S. Mint
6 Denver Pavilions
7 Denver Performing Arts Complex
8 Larimer Square
9 Writer Square
10 Tabor Center
11 D & F Tower
12 16th Street Mall
13 Brown Palace Hotel
14 State Capitol

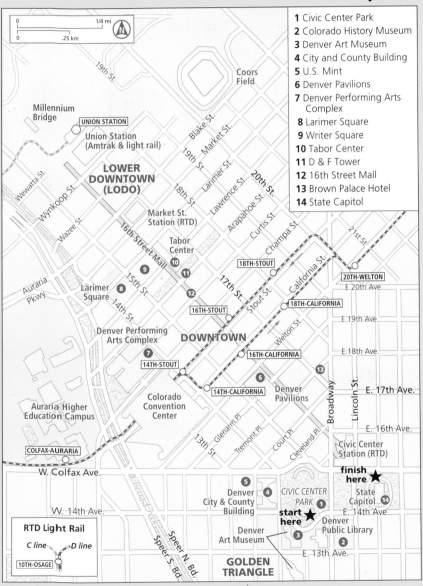

Side Trips from Denver

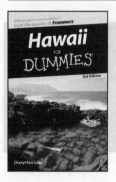

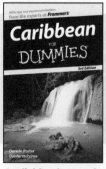
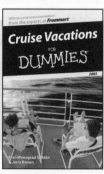

Colorado & the Rockies

FOR DUMMIES®

2ND EDITION

by Nicholas Trotter

WILEY

Wiley Publishing, Inc.

Colorado & the Rockies For Dummies® 2nd Edition

Published by
Wiley Publishing, Inc.
111 River St.
Hoboken, NJ 07030-5774
www.wiley.com

Copyright © 2005 by Wiley Publishing, Inc., Indianapolis, Indiana

Published simultaneously in Canada

For general information on our other products and services, please contact our Customer Care Department within the U.S. at 800-762-2974, outside the U.S. at 317-572-3993, or fax 317-572-4002.

For technical support, please visit www.wiley.com/techsupport.

Wiley also publishes its books in a variety of electronic formats. Some content that appears in print may not be available in electronic books.

Library of Congress Control Number: 2005924068

ISBN: 0-7645-7647-X

Manufactured in the United States of America

10 9 8 7 6 5 4 3 2 1

2B/QV/QX/QV/IN

WILEY

About the Author

Nick Trotter is a writer and cartographer. For the past five years, he has been drawing maps for *Frommer's* travel guides and the *For Dummies* travel series. A Denver native, he graduated from the University of Colorado at Boulder with a degree in geography, and has been perfecting the delicate art of getting lost for a couple of decades. His travel writings have taken him to Brazil, Italy, and the Caribbean; for now (at least), his home base is Brooklyn, New York.

Dedication

This book is dedicated to the living memory of David Lee Bucknam. More than anyone else I know, Dave devoted his life to being outdoors in Colorado; a member of the old Colorado Mountain Club, he became an expert mountaineer in his teens, and formed friendships with other members that lasted his whole life. One of these friends married him; together, Dave and Susan had a partnership that, for me, defined the word *marriage*. As a teenager, I befriended their son, and the family virtually adopted me as one of their own, over time taking me skiing, camping, mountain climbing, and even sailing.

Dave spent most of his working career in the mountains. He served as an employee, and later head, of the Office of Active and Inactive Mines for the State of Colorado, a job that took him all over the state, closing up old, abandoned, dangerous mines, and making the mountains cleaner and safer for adventurers like you and me. And he loved it.

So much of what I know about these mountains, I learned from Dave; without him, I could not have written this book. As a devoted husband, father, and grandfather, he will not be forgotten. As a great Coloradan, he will be forever remembered; Everywhere you travel in this state, whether you know it or not, you will see his legacy.

Author's Acknowledgments

First, I want to thank clan Bucknam for the myriad ways in which they helped with the research for this book: to Alan and Robyn for loaning me their car and their home office; to Peter, Dave, and Susan for their expertise and their libraries; and to little Piper and Sophie for loaning me their parents. I also need to thank Tiffany Shields and Jeff at the Millennium Harvest House in Boulder, and the staff of the Hinsdale County Museum. To my editors, Michael Kelly, Caroline Sieg, and Kathleen Dobie, thanks so much for your guidance, your skillful work, and your encouragement. Thanks also to my parents and Trina for their support and patience; finally, a big tip of the ol' Stetson to Alex Wells, who laid the groundwork for me in the first edition of this book.

Publisher's Acknowledgments

We're proud of this book; please send us your comments through our Dummies online registration form located at www.dummies.com/register/.

Some of the people who helped bring this book to market include the following:

Editorial

Editors: Kathleen A. Dobie, Michael Kelly

Cartographer: Nick Trotter

Editorial Manager: Michelle Hacker

Editorial Supervisor: Carmen Krikorian

Editorial Assistant: Melissa Bennett

Senior Photo Editor: Richard Fox

Front Cover Photo: © Chris Marona/ The Viesti Collection, Inc.

Back Cover Photo: © Robert Mitchell/ The Viesti Collection, Inc.

Cartoons: Rich Tennant, www.the5thwave.com

Composition Services

Project Coordinator: Michael Kruzil

Layout and Graphics: Carl Byers, Lauren Goddard, Denny Hager, Joyce Haughey, Barry Offringa, Julie Trippetti

Proofreaders: David Faust, Leeann Harney, Jessica Kramer, TECHBOOKS Production Services

Indexer: TECHBOOKS Production Services

Publishing and Editorial for Consumer Dummies

Diane Graves Steele, Vice President and Publisher, Consumer Dummies

Joyce Pepple, Acquisitions Director, Consumer Dummies

Kristin A. Cocks, Product Development Director, Consumer Dummies

Michael Spring, Vice President and Publisher, Travel

Kelly Regan, Editorial Director, Travel

Publishing for Technology Dummies

Andy Cummings, Vice President and Publisher, Dummies Technology/General User

Composition Services

Gerry Fahey, Vice President of Production Services

Debbie Stailey, Director of Composition Services

Contents at a Glance

Introduction *1*

Part I: Introducing Colorado *7*

Chapter 1: Discovering the Best of Colorado 9
Chapter 2: Digging Deeper into Colorado 15
Chapter 3: Deciding When and Where to Go 21
Chapter 4: Following an Itinerary: Four Great Options 35

Part II: Planning Your Trip to Colorado *41*

Chapter 5: Managing Your Money 43
Chapter 6: Getting to Colorado 52
Chapter 7: Getting Around Colorado 59
Chapter 8: Booking Your Accommodations 68
Chapter 9: Catering to Special Travel Needs
or Interests 74
Chapter 10: Taking Care of the Remaining Details 80

Part III: The Front Range *87*

Chapter 11: Denver 89
Chapter 12: Side Trips from Denver 134
Chapter 13: Boulder 142
Chapter 14: Colorado Springs 161

Part IV: The High Country *179*

Chapter 15: Rocky Mountain National Park 181
Chapter 16: Middle Park 202
Chapter 17: Summit County 212
Chapter 18: Leadville and the Upper Arkansas Valley 224
Chapter 19: Vail and the Vail Valley 240
Chapter 20: Aspen and the Roaring Fork Valley 251
Chapter 21: Steamboat Springs 274
Chapter 22: Gunnison, Crested Butte,
and the Black Canyon 286

*Part V: The Western Slope and
Southern Colorado* *297*

Chapter 23: Grand Junction and the Western Slope 299
Chapter 24: The Southwestern High Country 312
Chapter 25: The High San Juans and
the San Luis Valley 352

Part VI: The Part of Tens 367

Chapter 26: Ten Signature Colorado Experiences 369
Chapter 27: Beer, Beer, Beer — Ten Breweries
and Their Signature Brews 374

Appendix: Quick Concierge 379

Index...387

Maps at a Glance

· ·

Colorado 22
Driving Times & Distances 60
Denver Neighborhoods 93
Denver Accommodations & Dining 104
Denver Attractions & Nightlife........................114
Boulder 146
Colorado Springs 164
The High Country 182
Rocky Mountain National Park 187
Middle Park..203
Summit County..213
Vail 242
The Roaring Fork Valley 252
Aspen...255
Steamboat Springs..276
The Western Slope..301
The Southwestern High Country 314
The Southern Rockies 354

Table of Contents

Introduction *1*

    About This Book 1
    Conventions Used in This Book 2
    Foolish Assumptions 3
    How This Book Is Organized 4
        Part I: Introducing Colorado 4
        Part II: Planning Your Trip to Colorado 4
        Part III: The Front Range 4
        Part IV: The High Country 5
        Part V: The Western Slope and
            Southern Colorado 5
        Part VI: The Part of Tens 5
        Quick Concierge 5
    Icons Used in This Book 6
    Where to Go from Here 6

Part 1: Introducing Colorado *7*

Chapter 1: Discovering the Best of Colorado 9

    The Best Outdoor Adventures 9
    The Best Old (And New) West Experiences 10
    The Best Ski Areas 10
    The Best Luxury Hotels 11
    The Best Restaurants 12
    The Best Small Towns 12
    The Best Accommodations for Families 13
    The Best Natural Wonders for Kids of All Ages 13

Chapter 2: Digging Deeper into Colorado 15

    History 101: The Main Events 15
    Taste of Colorado: Local Cuisine 17
    Background Check: Recommended
      Books and Movies 19

Chapter 3: Deciding When and Where to Go 21

    Going Everywhere You Want to Be 21
        Traveling the Front Range 24
        Going beyond the Front Range:
            The High Country 25
    Scheduling Your Time 26

Revealing the Secrets of the Seasons 27
Spring 29
Summer 29
Fall 30
Winter 31
Looking at Colorado's Calendar of Events 31
January 32
February 32
March 32
April 32
May 33
June 33
July 33
August 34
September 34
October 34
November 34
December 34

**Chapter 4: Following an Itinerary:
Four Great Options** **35**
Taking In the High Passes (And Higher Peaks) 35
Touring Colorado with Kids 37
Colorado for History Buffs 38
The Ski-'Til-You-Drop Tour 39

Part II: Planning Your Trip to Colorado 41

Chapter 5: Managing Your Money **43**
Planning Your Budget 43
Totaling up your transportation 44
Calculating lodging costs 45
Eating out 45
Budgeting for attractions 46
Pricing activities and tours 46
Shopping for Colorado goods 46
Controlling nightlife costs 47
Cutting Costs — But Not the Fun 47
Handling Money 49
Using ATMs and carrying cash 49
Charging ahead with credit cards 49
Dealing with debit cards 50
Toting traveler's checks 50
Dealing with a Lost or Stolen Wallet 50

Chapter 6: Getting to Colorado **52**

Flying into Colorado 52
    Getting the best deal on your airfare 53
    Booking your ticket online 54
Driving In 55
Arriving by Rail 55
Joining an Escorted Tour 56
Choosing a Package Tour 57

Chapter 7: Getting Around Colorado **59**

Driving around Colorado 59
    Handling the highways 59
    Negotiating road hazards 61
    Getting the best deal on a rental car 64
Winging It 66
Riding the Rails 66
Taking the Bus 67

Chapter 8: Booking Your Accommodations **68**

Lining Up Your Lodging Choices 68
    Booking a B&B 68
    Bunking down at a motel 69
    Staying at historic or luxury hotels 69
    Choosing a chain 69
    Going to a guest ranch or dude ranch 70
    Camping out 70
Finding the Best Room at the Best Rate 70
    Surfing the Web for hotel deals 72
    Reserving the best room 73

**Chapter 9: Catering to Special Travel Needs
or Interests** **74**

Traveling with the Brood: Advice for Families 74
Making Age Work for You: Advice for Seniors 76
Accessing Colorado: Advice for Travelers
    with Disabilities 77
Following the Rainbow: Advice for Gay
    and Lesbian Travelers 78

**Chapter 10: Taking Care of the Remaining
Details** **80**

Playing It Safe with Travel and Medical Insurance ...80
Staying Healthy When You Travel 82
Staying Connected by Cellphone 82
Accessing the Internet away from Home 83
Keeping Up with Airline Security 85

Part III: The Front Range *87*

Chapter 11: Denver **89**
  Getting There 89
    Arriving by air 89
    Arriving by car 92
    Riding in (Not on horseback) 92
  Denver Neighborhoods 92
    Downtown (the Central Business District) 95
    Lower Downtown (LoDo) 95
    The Golden Triangle 95
    Uptown 96
    Capitol Hill 96
    Cherry Creek 96
    Central Platte Valley 96
    Other Denver neighborhoods 97
  Getting Information after You Arrive 97
  Getting Around Denver 98
    By mass transit 98
    By taxi 99
    By car 99
    On foot 100
  Where to Stay 101
  Where to Dine 107
  Exploring Denver 113
    The best things to see and do 113
    Touring historical sites 119
    Other things to see and do 119
  Staying Active 121
  Seeing Denver by Guided Tour 123
    Faux trolley tours 123
    Real trolley tours 123
    Guided tours 124
  Considering One-, Two-, and Three-Day
    Itineraries 124
  Shopping in Denver 125
    The best shopping areas 125
    What to look for and where to find it 126
  Nightlife 128
    Hitting the local clubs 128
    Drinking up 130
    The performing arts 131
  Fast Facts: Denver 133

Chapter 12: Side Trips from Denver 134

Riding through the Golden Circle 134
   Getting there 134
   Exploring Golden, Idaho Springs,
     and Georgetown 135
   Where to stay and dine 138
Following Five Classic Mountain Drives 139
   Guanella Pass Road 139
   Mount Evans 139
   St. Mary's Glacier 140
   The Peak-to-Peak Highway 140
   U.S. 285 to South Park and beyond 140

Chapter 13: Boulder 142

Getting There 143
Getting Around 144
Where to Stay 145
Where to Dine 149
Exploring Boulder 153
   The best things to see and do 153
   Other things to see and do 154
   Staying active 155
   Hitting the slopes 156
   Shopping 157
   Nightlife 157
Fast Facts: Boulder 160

Chapter 14: Colorado Springs 161

Getting There 161
Getting Around 162
Where to Stay 163
Where to Dine 167
Exploring Colorado Springs 169
   The best things to see and do 169
   Other things to see and do 172
   Guided tours 173
   Staying active 173
   Shopping 174
   Especially for kids 174
Nightlife 174
   Hitting the bars and clubs 174
   Enjoying classical music 175
Fast Facts: Colorado Springs 175

Heading Out to Cañon City and Royal Gorge 176
    Getting there 176
    Exploring Royal Gorge 176
    Finding places to stay and dine 177

Part IV: The High Country *179*

Chapter 15: Rocky Mountain National Park **181**
    Choosing a Season to Visit 184
    Getting There 184
        Driving to the park 184
        Busing in to the park 185
    Planning Ahead for Your Park Visit 185
    Learning the Lay of the Land 186
    Arriving in the Park 188
        Paying fees 188
        Getting around 188
        Considering safety 189
    Enjoying the Park 190
        Taking a hike 191
        Roving with rangers 194
        Watching wildlife 194
    Staying Active 194
        Inside the park 194
        In the gateway communities 195
    Where to Stay and Dine in Estes Park
        and Grand Lake 195
        Estes Park 196
        Grand Lake 198
    Fast Facts: Rocky Mountain National Park 201

Chapter 16: Middle Park **202**
    Winter Park and Fraser 202
        Getting there 204
        Getting around 204
        Where to stay 205
        Where to dine 206
        Exploring Winter Park and Fraser 207
    Fast Facts: Winter Park/Fraser 210
    Heading farther into the Parkland 210
        Two classic ranch-resort experiences 210
        Staying active 211
        On the slopes 211

Chapter 17: Summit County 212

Summit County Essentials 212
    Getting there 214
    Getting around 214
    Where to stay 215
    Where to dine 217
Exploring Summit County 218
    The best things to see and do 218
    Especially for kids 219
    Staying active 220
    Hitting the slopes 221
    Nightlife 222
Fast Facts: Summit County 223

Chapter 18: Leadville and the Upper Arkansas Valley 224

What's Where? The Arkansas Valley
    and Its Attractions 224
    Leadville highlights 224
    Buena Vista and Salida highlights 225
Leadville 225
    Getting to Leadville 225
    Getting around 226
    Where to stay in Leadville 226
    Where to dine in Leadville 227
    Exploring Leadville 228
    Staying active in Leadville 230
    Hitting the slopes 231
Fast Facts: Leadville 232
Buena Vista, Salida, and the Upper Arkansas 232
    Getting there 233
    Where to stay in the Arkansas Valley 233
    Where to dine in the Arkansas Valley 234
    Exploring Salida 235
    Staying active in Salida 237
    Hitting the slopes 238
Fast Facts: Buena Vista and Salida 239

Chapter 19: Vail and the Vail Valley 240

Vail Essentials 240
    Getting there 240
    Getting around 241
    Where to stay 241
    Where to dine 244

Exploring Vail 246
    The best things to see and do 246
    Staying active 247
    Hitting the slopes 248
    Shopping 249
    Nightlife and culture 249
Fast Facts: Vail 250

Chapter 20: Aspen and the Roaring Fork Valley 251

What's Where? The Region
    and Its Major Attractions 251
    Aspen highlights 252
    Glenwood Springs, Carbondale,
        and Redstone highlights 253
Aspen 253
    Getting to Aspen 254
    Getting around Aspen 254
    Where to stay in Aspen 256
    Where to dine in Aspen 258
    Exploring Aspen 259
    Shopping in Aspen 263
    Nightlife in Aspen 263
    Culture in Aspen 263
Fast Facts: Aspen 264
The Roaring Fork Valley 264
    Getting there 265
    Getting around 266
    Where to stay 266
    Where to dine 267
    Exploring Glenwood Springs, Carbondale,
        and Redstone 270
    Shopping 272
    Nightlife 273
Fast Facts: The Roaring Fork Valley 273

Chapter 21: Steamboat Springs 274

Getting There 274
Getting Around 275
Where to Stay 275
Where to Dine 278
Exploring Steamboat Springs 280
    The best things to see and do 280
    Other things to see and do 281
    Especially for kids 282

Staying active 282
Hitting the slopes 284
Shopping 284
Nightlife and culture 284
Fast Facts: Steamboat Springs 285

**Chapter 22: Gunnison, Crested Butte,
and the Black Canyon** **286**
Gunnison and Crested Butte 286
Getting to Gunnison and Crested Butte 286
Getting around 287
Deciding where to stay 287
Dining in Gunnison and Crested Butte 288
Exploring Crested Butte and Gunnison 290
Enjoying the nightlife 292
Fast Facts: Gunnison and Crested Butte 292
Black Canyon of the Gunnison National Park 293
Getting there 293
Where to stay 293
Exploring the park itself 294
Other things to see and do 295
Staying active 296
Fast Facts: Montrose and Delta 296

**Part V: The Western Slope and
Southern Colorado** **297**

**Chapter 23: Grand Junction and
the Western Slope** **299**
Grand Junction 300
Getting there 300
Getting around 302
Where to stay 302
Where to dine 303
Exploring Grand Junction 304
Shopping 308
Fast Facts: Grand Junction 309
Taking a Side Trip to Dinosaur and Dinosaur
National Monument 309
Getting to Dinosaur 309
Seeing the sights 309
Where to stay in Dinosaur 310
Where to dine in Dinosaur 311

Chapter 24: The Southwestern High Country 312

What's Where? Southwest Colorado and Its
   Major Attractions 313
      Telluride highlights 313
      Ouray and Silverton highlights 313
      Durango highlights 313
      The Four Corners highlights 315
Telluride 315
      Getting to Telluride 315
      Getting around in Telluride 316
      Where to stay in Telluride 317
      Where to dine in Telluride 319
      Exploring Telluride 320
      Nightlife in Telluride 323
Fast Facts: Telluride 324
Ouray and Silverton 324
      Getting to Ouray and Silverton 324
      Getting around Ouray and Silverton 325
      Staying in Ouray and Silverton 325
      Dining in Ouray and Silverton 327
      Exploring Ouray and Silverton 328
      Shopping in Ouray and Silverton 332
      Finding nightlife in Ouray and Silverton 332
Fast Facts: Ouray and Silverton 332
Durango 333
      Getting to Durango 333
      Getting around Durango 333
      Where to stay in Durango 334
      Where to dine in Durango 336
      Exploring Durango 337
      Shopping in Durango 340
      Nightlife in Durango 340
      Springing off on a side trip
         to Pagosa Springs 340
Fast Facts: Durango 341
Mesa Verde and the Four Corners 342
      Getting there 342
      Getting around 342
      Where to stay 343
      Where to dine 344
      Exploring the world of the Ancestral
         Puebloans 345
      Shopping 351
Fast Facts: Cortez, Dolores, and Mancos 351

Chapter 25: The High San Juans and the San Luis Valley 352

Lake City 353
  Getting to Lake City 353
  Getting around Lake City 353
  Where to stay in Lake City 353
  Where to dine in Lake City 353
  Exploring Lake City 355
Fast Facts: Lake City 357
Creede 357
  Getting to Creede 358
  Getting around Creede 358
  Where to stay in Creede 358
  Where to dine in Creede 359
  Exploring Creede 360
  Staying active in Creede......................................361
  Culture in Creede 361
  Hitting the slopes in Creede 361
Fast Facts: Creede 362
Alamosa and the San Luis Valley 362
  Getting there 362
  Getting around 363
  Where to stay 363
  Where to dine 363
  Exploring Alamosa and the San Luis Valley ...364
Fast Facts: Alamosa 366

Part VI: The Part of Tens *367*

Chapter 26: Ten Signature Colorado Experiences 369

Summitting a Fourteener — on Foot
  or (If You Must) by Car 369
Riding the Ski Train to Winter Park 370
Dropping Trou and Soaking in a Hot Spring 370
Taking in a Concert at Red Rocks 370
Dining on Native Game 371
Cowboy Up at the Stock Show 371
Go from the Sublime to the Ridiculous
  in Glitter Gulch 371
Goooooooo, Broncos!!!!! 372
Sampling a Colorado Microbrew (Or Two) 372
Getting off the Beaten Track —
  without Getting Lost 372

Chapter 27: Beer, Beer, Beer — Ten Breweries and Their Signature Brews 374

The Wynkoop Brewing Company, Denver 375
New Belgium Brewery, Fort Collins 375
Breckenridge Brewery, Denver
  and Breckenridge 375
Odell Brewing Company, Fort Collins 375
Walnut Brewery, Boulder 376
Flying Dog Brewery, Denver 376
Mountain Sun Pub & Brewery, Boulder 376
Golden City Brewery, Golden 376
Ska Brewing Company, Durango 376
Dolores River Brewery, Dolores 377

Appendix: Quick Concierge............................*379*

Colorado A to Z: Facts at Your Fingertips................379
Toll-Free Numbers and Web Sites 383
  Major airlines 383
  Major car-rental agencies 383
  Major hotel and motel chains 384
Finding More Information 385
  Tourist information 385
  Useful Web sites 385
  State guides 385

Index...*387*

Introduction

● ●

*P*hotographs of purple-mountained majesty, roaring rivers, and high alpine lakes don't even come close to capturing Colorado's essence. To do that, the photos would also have to deliver the sweet pungency of pine trees after a rainstorm, the coolness of snowflakes on your cheeks, and the half-rustle, half-rattle of aspen leaves in a fall breeze. They would have to re-create the weightless sensation that powder skiers experience between turns and the icy splash of river water on a spring rafting trip. Then they'd have to dish up a gourmet dinner of native game, a tasty microbrew, and the real-life smile of a friendly server. That's asking way too much of a photograph. And it's one big reason why you should travel to Colorado.

Unfortunately, like most things that are really sensational, Colorado involves a certain element of risk. While you absorb the mountain beauty, the mountain beauty can absorb you as well. If you're not careful, you can easily freeze, crash your car, get lost, or get swept away by snow. There are lesser risks, too: restaurants expensive enough to make Donald Trump blanch, motels with papier-mâché walls, servers who incessantly call you "dude," undersized beers, oversized bears, bad bands, boring boutiques, and black-and-white color televisions.

Luckily, you've done the right thing and bought this book, which can help you avoid any potential pitfalls that could mar your trip. In these pages, you'll find out what you need to know to freely enjoy the majestic mountains, rich history, and diverse cultures of the Rocky Mountain state.

About This Book

Guidebook writers like to think that readers page through their books from cover to cover as if the books were suspense thrillers or Harlequin romances. You're welcome to read *Colorado & the Rockies For Dummies* that way; I, for one, would appreciate your perseverance. Be forewarned, however, that nothing earthshaking will be consummated in the last chapter.

If you're pressed for time, you can read only the chapters or sections that interest you most because the book is set up to read like a reference book. In fact, the chapters on particular regions and cities are close to being guidebooks unto themselves. For example, if you plan to travel to Mesa Verde, you can go straight to Chapter 24. It has the lowdown on the park, hotel and restaurant recommendations, maps, driving tips, area attractions, and curious facts that should inspire and delight you. If Rocky Mountain National Park is your destination, then Chapter 15 is the place to go.

Dummies Post-it® Flags

As you read this book, you may find information that you want to reference as you plan or enjoy your trip — whether a new hotel, a must-see attraction, or a must-try cross-country trail. To simplify your trip planning, mark these pages with the handy Post-it® Flags included in this book.

Other parts of the book provide information that will help you *reach* your destination as efficiently as possible. For example, if you need to fly into Denver and then rent a car to drive to Mesa Verde, go to Chapter 6 for tips on traveling to Colorado. If you want to hit the slopes while you're in town, but you aren't sure when the flakes start flying, see Chapter 3 for suggestions on Colorado's seasonal offerings. Still other chapters offer tips that will make you a better traveler, no matter what your destination.

In order to make the region and city chapters self-contained, I do repeat myself some. For example, you'll find information on the Amtrak train that passes through Colorado in several destination chapters. I repeat this information not because of premature senility but because the train seemed to turn up nearly everywhere I visited. (It was almost creepy.)

Conventions Used in This Book

The hotel and restaurant recommendations in this book are split into two categories: my personal favorites and other places I feel comfortable recommending. Don't hesitate to visit any of the listed establishments. All are pleasant; the bad places have been relegated to other guidebooks. Sure, a little personal bias may have crept in to my selections, but I'm definitely not as bad as an Olympic figure skating judge. And I do try to clarify my reasoning, so you can factor in your own preferences.

I also provide some pricing information that you can use to help keep your trip on budget (or not). The number of dollar signs next to a hotel's name tells you roughly how much the hotel costs for a one-night stay for two people; the number of dollar signs next to a restaurant's name represents the general range of prices for dinner entrees (or, in some cases, fixed-price meals). Here's how to translate the dollar signs.

Dollar Signs	Hotel	Restaurant
$	$75 or less	$10 or less
$$	$76 to $125	$11 to $20
$$$	$126 to $175	$21 to $35
$$$$	$176 or more	$36 or more

After each review, you encounter a host of additional numbers, names, and abbreviations, which at first glance may seem confusing. These are how I condense key facts about the establishment. Keep in mind that phone numbers are listed in bold alongside the telephone icon. I also provide specific pricing information, but remember that the hotel prices are usually the *rack rates* — that is, the double-occupancy rates before any discounts are given — for particular periods. (***Remember:*** By using the tips in Chapter 8, you can often avoid paying the rack rate.) Unless otherwise noted, restaurant prices reflect the price range for dinner entrees.

I also use abbreviations for the credit cards accepted by the establishments I review in this book. I only kept track of the majors, so if your particular card isn't listed here, it may or may not be accepted. The abbreviations, and the credit cards represented by them, are as follows:

> AE: American Express
>
> DC: Diners Club
>
> DISC: Discover
>
> MC: MasterCard
>
> V: Visa

Compared to more densely populated states, Colorado doesn't have many highways. But the ones it does have are important, and they can sometimes be confusing. It's important to remember that highways are built by federal, state, and local governments, all of which have their own numbering and naming systems, and the interstates are another matter entirely. When reading a map or list of directions, make sure that you keep track of which roads are part of which system. If you're getting directions from a local Coloradan, you're likely to just get numbers: "Goin' up to Leadville, are ya? Well, take 70 to Frisco and get off on 91. Take that up to Leadville. Or you can take 285 to where it hits 24 and head north." In order, that's Interstate 70 to Colorado Highway 94, or U.S. Highways 285 and 24. In this book, I try to keep things simple and clear by referring to highways in the same format, such as **I-70, Colorado 91,** and **U.S. 285.**

Foolish Assumptions

In writing this book, I made some assumptions about you and what you may need from a Colorado guidebook:

- ✔ You may be a traveler who is new to Colorado, and you're trying to determine what to see and when to see it.

- ✔ You may have traveled through Colorado in the past, but now you have less time and want insider information that can help you plan the most efficient trip possible. Or you want to plan an adventure or two instead of just driving around looking at mountains.

✔ You don't want a book that lists every restaurant, bar, hotel, and attraction, no matter how bad. You just want accurate descriptions of the best places within a variety of price ranges.

If any of my foolish assumptions prove to be, in your case, not so foolish, you'll benefit from reading *Colorado & the Rockies For Dummies*.

How This Book Is Organized

In order to make this book more useful as a reference guide, I broke it into six logical sections, each one discussing a different aspect of your Colorado trip. Each part is further divided into a handful of easy-to-read chapters. If a particular subject doesn't interest you, skip it and go straight to the chapter that has the information you need. You won't fail Colorado Vacation 101 just because you don't read the whole book. I'm too lazy to write an exam.

Part I: Introducing Colorado

This section identifies the state's treasures — both artificial and natural. It sums up the most interesting regions — from the red-rock canyons of the Four Corners area to the 14,000-foot summits of the southern Rockies — and then digs a little deeper into the history and culture behind the state. And it tells you the best times to go to the area of your choice. I also propose some itineraries, including ones for history buffs, for adventure-seekers, and for people traveling with children.

Part II: Planning Your Trip to Colorado

If you have a question about trip-planning, this section more than answers it. Here you find tips on how to reach Colorado by plane, train, or automobile and advice on how to get around Colorado after you cross the state line. I also discuss the various accommodations choices in Colorado. You can discover when and why to choose different payment methods while traveling, and what to do when your wallet goes skittering down a mountainside (or is otherwise compromised), taking all those payment methods with it. I tell you which tickets and reservations you need to arrange in advance of your trip, and then share information on how to do it. And I offer Colorado-specific travel tips for those with special travel needs or interests, including families, seniors, people with disabilities, and gays and lesbians. There are even a few pointers on packing. By the time you finish Part II, you'll be ready to hit the road.

Part III: The Front Range

This part introduces you to the area of the state you're most likely to encounter first: the Front Range. The name itself has kind of a double meaning to Coloradans, which can be a little confusing: specifically, it refers to the easternmost mountains in the state, stretching from the

Arkansas canyon in the south across the Wyoming border up north, incorporating the smaller spurs of the Medicine Bow range east of North Park, and the Rampart Range west of Colorado Springs, which includes Pikes Peak. Coloradans, though, also use the term Front Range to refer to the urban corridor that now stretches in front of those mountains from Pueblo to Fort Collins, including Colorado Springs, Denver, Boulder, Longmont, and all the old farm-towns-turned-suburbs in between. I direct you to the most exciting experiences and recommend the finest restaurants, the cushiest accommodations, the spiciest nightclubs, the most intriguing neighborhoods, and the best side trips through the region.

Part IV: The High Country

This region is what you probably think of first when you think of Colorado: towering peaks, thick forests of pine and aspen, and wild rivers tumbling through steep, rocky canyons — and oh, yeah . . . lots of skiing! The rivers and glaciers have done a great job of neatly carving the region into valleys and ranges; these are dotted with small mountain towns (including some of Colorado's best ski spots) and open country-side. For each area I cover, I tell you how to get there and get around, and where to stay, play, party, shop, and eat.

Part V: The Western Slope and Southern Colorado

This vast swath of land that circles the High Country is some of the most pristine, beautiful country in the state, graced with smaller surprises such as hot springs, desert canyons, sand dunes, relaxed towns, and ancient Indian dwellings. In this part, I do everything possible to make sure you don't speed past the area's hidden wonders. And, of course, I also tell you where to stay and eat along the way.

Part VI: The Part of Tens

The Part of Tens is, in reality, far more lighthearted than its ominous-sounding title. Each chapter in this fun section showcases a roster of related items, much like one of David Letterman's top ten lists — only, in this case, each list pertains to Colorado, and I'm not half as funny.

Quick Concierge

Imagine a helpful concierge who is an all-around Colorado expert and has the recall of an elephant. The Quick Concierge section on the yellow pages at the back of this book is as close as you'll come to finding that person. It distills key information on subjects ranging from the American Automobile Association to weather. It also has contact numbers and Web sites for major airlines, rental car agencies, and hotel chains; and it lists several outstanding sources for finding more information on current happenings in Colorado.

Icons Used in This Book

I use six different icons in this book to call your attention to different types of information. Here's what each means:

Find out useful advice on things to do and ways to schedule your time when you see the Tip icon.

Best of the Best highlights the best the destination has to offer in all categories — hotels, restaurants, attractions, activities, shopping, and nightlife.

Watch for the Heads Up icon to identify annoying or potentially danger- ous situations such as tourist traps, unsafe neighborhoods, budgetary rip-offs, and other things to beware.

Look to the Kid Friendly icon for attractions, hotels, restaurants, and activities that are particularly hospitable to children or people traveling with kids.

Keep an eye out for the Bargain Alert icon as you seek out money-saving tips and/or great deals.

Colorado is filled with magnificent scenery, and this icon highlights par- ticularly noteworthy spots that showcase the state's natural beauty.

Where to Go from Here

Unlike most states, Colorado sprawls both horizontally and vertically. It has 58 14,000-foot peaks (known as fourteeners), more than any other state, not to mention grasslands, red-rock canyons, and high-desert mesas. This means your travels will involve not only significant dis- tances, but also some major twists and turns. The beauty comes at you from a variety of angles, and there's never enough time to absorb it all. Nor is there time to experience all the activities that go with this turf — everything from hot springs to hiking.

You can smooth out your trip by considering ahead of time what attracts you most in Colorado, and then planning a trip around your interests. That way, fewer distractions come into play, and you'll be able to con- centrate on the magnificence of your surroundings. Be sure, however, to leave a few things to chance! Ideally, this book can help you straddle the divide between practicality and spontaneity; between security and adventure; and between a warm car and the call of the wild. So saddle up or strap on those skis and keep reading!

Part I
Introducing Colorado

The 5th Wave   By Rich Tennant

MT. FLAT TOP
ELEVATOR

COLORADO
RESIDENTS
ONLY

MT. FLAT TOP
5.8 mi.

In this part . . .

So, you're thinking about visiting Colorado, but you aren't really sure where to start. Don't worry! This part introduces you to the state and all it can offer. After discussing the very best things in the state, it gives history and background information, weighs the pros and cons of coming at different times, and provides four great itineraries that help you make the most of your time.

Chapter 1

Discovering the Best of Colorado

In This Chapter

▶ Finding adventures in the Old and New West
▶ Choosing the finest hotels and restaurants
▶ Hitting the best slopes
▶ Singing the praises of little towns
▶ Appreciating Mother Nature

Colorado's vertical landscape — the mountains, and their location between the High Plains and the Great Basin desert — gives the state an incredible range of environments. Lush pine forests, stark alpine tundra, arid plateaus, and the cycle between gentle summers and snowy winters make for a dizzying array of activities. Add in a major metropolitan area, smaller towns ranging from the comfortably urban to the downright tiny, and you'll find that Colorado has quite a lot to keep you busy, whether you're seeking urbane luxury, a real back-country adventure, or something in between.

This chapter outlines a few key categories of things to do in the state, and shows you the possibilities for finding the best of each. Throughout the book, you'll see the "best of the best" icon next to these features and activities. Stick with these, folks, and you won't go wrong.

The Best Outdoor Adventures

Whether on rock, on water, or on snow, Colorado positively brims with opportunities for you to enjoy its great outdoors. This section details the best of the best outdoors that doesn't involve downhill skiing — for that, refer to "The Best Ski Areas," later in this chapter.

> ✔ For **rock climbing,** Boulder (see Chapter 13) and its granite canyons (and indoor climbing gyms) are world-renowned. If you're an expert looking for a classic climb, go for the **Diamond** on Longs Peak in Rocky Mountain National Park.

- ✔ **Whitewater rafting** is at its finest on the **Upper Arkansas River near Buena Vista and Salida** (Chapter 18). This is premier rafting territory for beginner and expert alike.

- ✔ **Fly fishing for trout** doesn't get any better than the Gold Medal Waters of the **Roaring Fork and Frying Pan** rivers (Chapter 20). Anglers should head to the **Taylor Creek Fly Shop** in **Basalt** for everything from flies and gear to tips or guided trips.

- ✔ **Crested Butte** (Chapter 22) and **Fruita** (Chapter 23) offer the best **mountain biking.** The Western Slope in general has great desert and mountain terrain, but these two towns have the best trail systems and fat-tire scenes for serious enthusiasts and novices alike.

- ✔ **Cross-country skiers and snowshoers** will be happy anywhere in the state, but **Middle Park** (Chapter 16) has the best terrain, and the area, except for Winter Park and Fraser, is largely undiscovered.

The Best Old (And New) West Experiences

From prospectors to ranchers and so much in between, Colorado has drawn the best and the brightest (as well as its share of the not-so-bright) citizens looking to prosper from the promise of the West. Much that remains from this era is available for viewing and exploring today.

- ✔ The whole town of **Leadville** (Chapter 18) is a gold mine — literally — for mining history and lore. A visit to the **Matchless Mine** tour is a must, and the **National Mining Hall of Fame and Museum** is a fascinating trip into the past of this incredible industry.

- ✔ The **Durango & Silverton Narrow Gauge Railroad** (Chapter 24) is the most fun way to experience the most spectacular part of the state, and to visit the great small towns of Durango and Silverton to boot.

- ✔ For a working ranch experience, don't miss **Saddleback Ranch** in **Steamboat Springs** (Chapter 21). Ride with the cowboys and eat ranch-style dinners in the beautiful high-range country of the Yampa Valley.

- ✔ The New West lives on (and parties hard) at the **National Western Stock Show & Rodeo** in **Denver** (Chapter 11). Check out the national-circuit pro rodeo, exotic livestock exhibits, a ranch equipment exposition, and great music as cowboys and ranchers descend to Denver every January for this trade show and winter party.

The Best Ski Areas

Skiing is what most people think of when they think of Colorado, though as this chapter alone shows, there's way more going on here than just skiing. But for those of you who really want the champagne powder experience, here are the areas I recommend:

- ✔ **The best all-around skiing is in Aspen** and the surrounding areas (Chapter 20). **Aspen Highlands** and **Aspen Mountain** are great for experts, while **Snowmass** is ideal for intermediate skiers, and **Buttermilk** is perfect for beginners (even the Swiss rave about this place!). And the town itself is a Colorado classic. The downside, of course, is that it's expensive. But a ski vacation in Aspen is one you'll never forget.

- ✔ **For more moderate budgets, head for Winter Park** (Chapter 16). Winter Park offers great skiing for a moderate price; the snow is great until late in the season, and the adjacent **Mary Jane** area offers more challenging slopes for the mogul-hungry. Skiing Winter Park is easily doable as a day trip from Denver, especially if you ride the Ski Train — another classic Colorado experience.

- ✔ **Families will love Keystone** (Chapter 17) for its great instructional slopes and family-friendly atmosphere. This is where I and most of my friends learned to ski, and it's perfect. You can do it as a day trip from Denver, but the resort also has all-inclusive options for accommodations and dining that make it a no-brainer for a family trip. And since transportation in Summit County is so good, more experienced skiers can make easy excursions to **Copper Mountain** or **Arapahoe Basin.**

- ✔ **Extreme skiers** can head straight for **Crested Butte** (Chapter 22) or **Silverton** (Chapter 24). These high-mountain towns are harder to get to, but if you dream of super-steep terrain, these areas are a dream come true.

The Best Luxury Hotels

To treat yourself to the most luxurious of luxury accommodations during your Colorado vacation, these four choices are a good place to start:

- ✔ **The Broadmoor** in Colorado Springs (Chapter 14) has it all, from a grand tradition as a luxury destination to world-class golf on any of three 18-hole courses. The enormous property features hiking, a spa, and easy access to Pikes Peak and the rest of the Rampart Range.

- ✔ Denver's **Brown Palace** (Chapter 11) is where the Beatles stayed, don't you know — also presidents, movie stars, and visiting royalty. The hotel serves an English high tea in the afternoon, and the downtown location puts you near everything that's great about Denver — restaurants, entertainment, museums, and parks.

✔ **The Little Nell** in Aspen (Chapter 20) offers an intimate experience with all the lavish amenities of a world-class ski town such as Aspen. This is where Hollywood moguls come to crash in style.

✔ You'll think you're in Europe at **Sonnenalp** in Vail (Chapter 19). This classy but low-key place is the best place to pamper yourself in this, Colorado's *other* world-class resort town.

The Best Restaurants

Colorado has gone a long way towards forging a culinary identity for itself; the local cuisine focuses on buffalo and game, with a strong Southwestern influence and some international flair. But you find all the great styles here, from Tuscan to Cuban to Szechuan. And with fish flown in daily from the coasts, the sushi ain't half bad, either.

✔ If you're staying in Denver, a trip to **The Fort** or the **Buckhorn Exchange** (Chapter 11) is a must. These excellent restaurants are the best places to experience buffalo in all its glory, as well as appetizers such as rattlesnake and Rocky Mountain oysters. The Fort is definitely a fine-dining experience, while the Buckhorn is a little more laid-back. Both function as Old West museums as much as restaurants; either one will satisfy you.

✔ In Aspen, **Cache Cache** (Chapter 20) has been serving up fine French cuisine with a Rocky Mountain attitude for years. The preparations are outstanding, the presentations are gorgeous, and the portions are hearty. You won't be disappointed. The bar menu offers many of the same dishes for folks on a budget. Don't miss it if you're in Glitter Gulch.

✔ **The Shed** in Winter Park (Chapter 16) offers wonderful food in a great après-ski atmosphere. The menu changes often, and it's very popular with the locals.

✔ **Beau Jo's** in Idaho Springs (Chapter 12) is the all-time classic après-ski pizza joint for Front Range residents. The huge pizzas and original recipes are just the ticket after a long day on the slopes (or hiking, snowshoeing, rafting, rock climbing, shopping, or even just sitting around!).

The Best Small Towns

Colorado is more than metropolises and ski resorts. Check out one (or more) of these quaint little towns for a taste of small-town Colorado:

✔ If you're not on a budget, **Telluride** (Chapter 24) is a fantastic place, winter or summer, for an exciting small-town sojourn. The restaurants are outstanding, the nightlife is spectacular, and local festivals appeal to every interest and temperament — the biggest being the **Telluride Bluegrass Festival,** which is held each year in June.

✔ **Grand Lake,** in Middle Park but very close to Rocky Mountain National Park (Chapter 15), is a very relaxed little place with comfortable lodging, good restaurants, and a number of activities. The town is ideal as a base for excursions into the park, and boating, hiking, fishing, and snowshoeing or cross-country skiing are also within easy reach.

✔ **Salida** (Chapter 18) offers great opportunities for rafting on the Arkansas, as well as a vibrant art scene and access to great skiing, hiking, and even the Great Sand Dunes (Chapter 25).

The Best Accommodations for Families

Traveling with the family shouldn't be a chore. For some hotels that "get it," consider the following:

✔ The **Embassy Suites Downtown Denver** (Chapter 11) is clean, friendly, and casual, and the kids will dig the in-room Nintendo games. All the rooms are suites, too, so *you* won't have to hear all that digital chaos.

✔ Families wanting an all-inclusive resort, winter or summer, that's both affordable and top-notch, will love **Snow Mountain Ranch** in Middle Park (Chapter 16). It's a YMCA facility that's expertly run and offers numerous options for outdoor adventures, including excellent skiing at Winter Park and Mary Jane.

✔ For a hotel that's practically a history lesson in itself (in a spectacular part of the state), check out the **Strater Hotel** in Durango (Chapter 24). The staff dresses in high silver-boom fashion, and the building itself is meticulously preserved. The proximity to the Durango and Silverton Narrow Gauge Railroad and Mesa Verde National Park make this a great family opportunity.

The Best Natural Wonders for Kids of All Ages

If your idea of a good, outdoor vacation is looking at stuff that makes you grab your head and go, "gee *whiz!*" here are a few can't-miss parts of the state that will definitely do the trick:

✔ The **Great Sand Dunes National Park and Preserve** in the San Luis Valley (Chapter 25) is one of my all-time favorite places in the state. The visitor center is very informative, kids will be entertained playing in the creek next to the dunes, and the dunes themselves, nestled up against the towering Sangre de Cristo range, are truly awesome. Unless you're from southern Saudi Arabia, you'll be impressed.

✔ **The Black Canyon of the Gunnison** (Chapter 22) is a ponderous gap in the Earth that will knock your socks off. The powerful Gunnison River, aided only by gravity, has carved such a deep, narrow channel through the sandstone that sunlight rarely reaches the bottom — hence the darkness implied by the name.

✔ Okay, it's not a geological feature, but **Mesa Verde National Park** (Chapter 24) is certainly one of the wonders of *human* nature. These ruins of the ingenious Puebloan civilization are one of the state's top draws, and for good reason. The fascinating artifacts and the history they represent are a great testament to the human spirit and a vital link to Colorado's past — with lessons for its future as well.

✔ **The Rockies,** of course, are the main draw. For the most spectacular views of peaks, check out at least one of these sights: the drive over Trail Ridge Road in Rocky Mountain National Park (Chapter 15); the Collegiate Peaks near Buena Vista, and the drive over Independence Pass to Aspen (Chapters 18 and 20); or the drive to the top of Pikes Peak or Mt. Evans. A great one-hour diversion in Vail is the Gondola ride to the incredible view of the Mount of the Holy Cross.

Chapter 2

Digging Deeper into Colorado

* *

In This Chapter

▶ Perusing a brief history of the Centennial State

▶ Sampling the local cuisine

▶ Wrapping your mind around essential reading and maps

* *

A visit to Colorado is sure to satisfy the most ardent naturalist, challenge the most active skier, or sate the most adventurous diner (and drinker), but there's more to this country than meets the eye. To give you a glimpse of the land underneath all the exciting activities, this chapter mines this state's historical and cultural landscape.

History 101: The Main Events

There have been people living in this region for thousands of years, but most of what we consider to be "Colorado" has a very recent history.

The first civilization within the present state's boundary was that of the **Ancestral Puebloans.** Before them, hunters and gatherers roamed the deserts, mountains, and plains, but the Puebloans built the first permanent settlements and developed the building material *adobe,* still in use today throughout the American Southwest. They also were excellent hydrological engineers and astounding artists whose homes, life, and culture you can explore at **Mesa Verde National Park** (Chapter 24). Their civilization here faded, though, probably due to environmental causes such as drought, and they migrated southward to found the modern-day Pueblos of Acoma, Zuni, and Hopi.

This left the state once again to the hunters and gatherers; in the last few centuries, the predominant tribes have been the Ute in the mountains and Western Slope, and the **Cheyenne, Arapahoe,** and **Comanche** on the Eastern Plains and foothills. The Cheyenne and Arapahoe are Northern Plains Indians with cultural ties to the Sioux; the Comanche migrated south from Wyoming, settling between the Arkansas and Platte rivers on the high plains. The **Navajo,** after they settled northern New Mexico 500 years ago, ventured sometimes into the San Luis Valley.

The first Europeans in the area were the Spanish; Coronado led the first known expedition through the southern part of the state in 1541 and 1542, and later Spanish settlers called this part of New Spain *El Norte.* In fact, many of the families living in the San Luis Valley still live on land granted to their ancestors by the king of Spain! The king lost the territory, though, to **Mexican Independence** in 1821. Eastern and northern Colorado, though, had been claimed by France and became part of the United States with the **Louisiana Purchase** in 1803. **Zebulon Pike** explored the southern part of the Purchase in 1806, and you can see the peak named after him near Colorado Springs from 90 miles away on the plains! For a few decades more, though, the Indians still ruled outside the San Luis Valley.

Gold was discovered, in **Cherry Creek** near Denver and in **Cripple Creek** west of Pikes Peak, in 1858, and the **Gold Rush of 1859** started the following spring, with many hopeful prospectors crossing the plains of Kansas Territory with the banner **"Pikes Peak or Bust!"** painted on their covered wagons (many were to return, however, with the slogan, "Busted, by God!"). The Gold Rush, of course, was short-lived, and little happened in the state until **silver** was discovered higher in the mountains in the early 1870s. The ensuing **Silver Boom** lasted 20 years and built most of the wrecked mining equipment you can see across the state to this day. It also cemented Colorado's economy into the **boom-and-bust cycle** of commodities that continues to this day. The Silver Boom was followed by booms in other minerals such as molybdenum, uranium (in the 1940s) and oil (in the '70s and early '80s.) But it was silver that built the towns of **Leadville** (once by far the largest city in the state), **Aspen, Breckenridge,** and **Telluride.** The pressure of mining and settlement, though, brought conflict with the territory's earliest residents. In 1864, a group of Colorado Volunteers, under the auspices of the Union Army, attacked a sleeping camp of Cheyenne and Arapaho along Sand Creek in eastern Colorado; this shameful event has become known as the Sand Creek Massacre and was the decisive blow in driving the Plains Indians out of the territory. Around the same time, a Union officer named Kit Carson was pursuing a genocidal campaign against the Navajo in the southern part of the territory, eventually driving them into southern New Mexico, before a reservation was established around the Four Corners area. Up in the mountains, a bloody war between the Utes and white settlers took place in the 1870s, ending only with the careful diplomacy of Ute Chief Ouray and the establishment of two small Ute reservations along the New Mexico border. Colorado was made a state in **1876.**

Between the booms and busts, **farmers and ranchers** settled in and eked out their living, though the arid climate and rugged land make it hard. The agricultural industry as a whole still survives here, but family farms and ranches are mostly a thing of the past, unable to compete with corporations and the cheaper land and labor of South America and Asia.

Colorado has been a destination for the health-conscious from the start, as the arid climate was deemed ideal for curing tuberculosis and asthma;

Denver grew prosperous, oddly, as a location for **sanatoriums** for those afflicted with those types of respiratory diseases. The *lungers* who were treated there often settled in the new streetcar suburbs that grew up around the warehouses and smelters downtown. **Boulder,** an old mine camp and farm community, advertised itself as a spa, where one could drink the supposedly pure waters of the **Indian Peaks glaciers;** you can see signs touting this attraction in the **Boulderado Hotel** to this day.

After World War II, veterans of the **Army 10th Mountain Division** who had trained in the Rockies founded the ski resort at **Aspen,** and Colorado found new life as a tourist destination. Athletes and health-nuts continue to make up a huge part of the state's population. World War II also saw the coming of the **military-industrial complex,** largely focused around **Colorado Springs,** with the **U.S. Air Force Academy,** two large military bases, and a number of defense-technology contractors overtaking what had been a tiny resort community. The **Cold War** between the United States and the Soviet Union from the 1940s through the 1980s added **NORAD** under Cheyenne Mountain and led to a uranium-mining boom, which devastated large tracts of land with immensely destructive mining techniques and underground nuclear weapons testing.

After the oil market crashed in the mid-1980s, Colorado went through a recession that affected the whole state; it ended with the high-tech boom of the 1990s, when software and telecommunications brought a massive new population to the Front Range (metropolitan areas of Denver, and Colorado Springs). This seems to have stabilized the economy a bit, as Denver has been pushed over the hump into its present status as a major American urban community. The leisure class has settled deep into the mountains, particularly the valleys around **Vail;** and **Grand Junction** could be the suburb of the telecommuting age. As the 21st century gets underway, it's fascinating to see how Colorado continues to change and grow.

Taste of Colorado: Local Cuisine

Colorado's chefs used to look to the coasts for inspiration and direction, but no more. In the last couple of decades, Colorado has been in the forefront of a revolution in American cuisine emphasizing local foods, grown and served according to their natural seasons and geography.

Like their counterparts elsewhere, Colorado chefs began looking to the land, its history, and the local cultures to design their menus. The rugged landscape and the state's roots in the Old West led directly to what the new cuisine features above all else: wild game. In many of Colorado's finest restaurants, you find elk, rabbit, native trout, quail, venison, and the ubiquitous buffalo (more properly known as American bison). I think you'll find these flavorful meats a welcome respite from the increasingly tired and bland commercially raised beef, pork, and chicken. This being the modern world, of course, most of these game species are raised on ranches (not hunted), but without centuries of

What do you mean, the chili is *green?!?!*

It's time to discuss one of the most confusing (and wonderful) aspects of the local cuisine: In Colorado and New Mexico, chili comes in two colors, red and green. You'll
also find that "chili" is most often spelled "chile" (from the Spanish), though the pro-
nunciation is the same.

Red chile is what you're probably used to just calling "chili." It's ground beef, maybe
with beans, in a thick, tomato-based stew and served in a bowl, like soup, or on hot
dogs. No big surprise here.

The green stuff, though, is what you really should look for: It's a pork stew with green
chiles (usually a combination of Hatches or Anaheims and jalapeños — peppers, that
is) — and you'll find it on burgers and steaks, smothered over burritos or rellenos,
served as a soup with tortillas on the side, in vegetarian versions, and in just about
any other situation you can think of. It's been a staple in this part of the world for centuries; everyone's grandmother has a unique recipe, and it's the real hallmark of New
Mexican and southern Coloradan cooking. One point will ignite furious debate:
Coloradans are known (and ridiculed by New Mexicans) for putting tomatoes in their
chile verde. I've always liked the tomatoes, but I'm from Colorado, so maybe I just don't
know any better. You can find it, both with tomatoes and without, everywhere in
Denver, from greasy-spoon diners to steakhouses.

At various points along the boulevards of Denver and the highways of the state, you
see roadside vendors advertising Hatch chiles; these are the large, mild Anaheim-
style chiles grown near Hatch, New Mexico, which is to chiles what Napa Valley is to
grapes. They sell them fresh, by the pound or even the bushel, and it can be worthwhile
to stop and get some if you have access to a kitchen. You can roast them or freeze
them fresh, and eat them for breakfast, lunch, and dinner. Good stuff.

breeding, they retain the savory character that evokes 19th-century
pioneers cooking over an open fire. Grilling is, naturally, the preferred
method for cooking game.

The proximity of Mexico, New Mexico, and Arizona has had an influence
on the Colorado chefs also, though I wouldn't characterize most of the
food here as Southwestern. You do find the corn, beans, and squash
that are the traditional staples of the Pueblo and Navajo nations, and
Coloradans put chile peppers in darn near everything, from fruit sauces
for game meats to even (incredibly) the beer.

Beer itself is another major aspect of dining in Colorado, as microbreweries and brewpubs are ubiquitous — indeed, I dedicate a whole chapter
to the subject at the end of the book (see Chapter 27)!

The Southwestern influence isn't just restricted to haute cuisine, either;
most diners here serve breakfast burritos and *chile verde* (a spicy sauce
made with green chiles). For a great breakfast anywhere in the state, you
can order *huevos rancheros* and get a big plate of eggs smothered with

chile verde and served with flour tortillas on the side. To eat it like the locals do, tear off pieces of the tortilla and pinch them around the eggs and *chile* with your fingers.

Among the many restaurants that exemplify this new Colorado cuisine are **The Fort** and the **Buckhorn Exchange,** both in the Denver area; the **Craftwood Inn** and the restaurants of the **Broadmoor Hotel** in Colorado Springs; **E. G.'s Country Inn** in Grand Lake; and the restaurants at the **Hotel Jerome** in Aspen.

Wine aficionados will want to check out the burgeoning Colorado wine industry; the town of Palisade in the arid Western Slope, in particular, is turning out some fine wines. One wine expert I spoke to points out that the industry here is very young, and the *terroir* hasn't been fully explored yet; vintners are still figuring out which grape varieties grow best here. You can find some good wines at decent prices, but if you're looking for a stateside version of Tuscany, you may be somewhat disappointed. Do try the beer, though.

Background Check: Recommended Books and Movies

You can find out more about Colorado's history in *Colorado: A History,* by Marshall Sprague, published by W. W. Norton & Company. *A Lady's Life in the Rocky Mountains,* by Isabella Bird, is one of the classics of Old West history. Bird was the first white woman to climb Longs Peak, and her adventures are first rate. James Michener fans will love *Centennial,* a novel that offers a literary look at the history of Colorado, centering around the fictional town of Centennial — at least it was fictional at the time of the novel's publication in 1974. In 2001, a far-flung southeast suburb of Denver incorporated as the city of Centennial; it has no relation to the novel. For more recent history, Hunter S. Thompson's account of his 1970 bid for sheriff of Aspen in *Fear and Loathing in America* is a hilarious classic. Rest in peace, Hunter.

For fiction buffs, Jack Kerouac's account of his journey to Colorado in *On the Road,* of course, is a must for beatniks and aspiring Boulderites. The novel *Angle of Repose,* a story of westward migration that prominently features 19th-century Colorado, won Wallace Stegner a Pulitzer Prize in 1971. And horror fans need look no further than Stephen King's *The Stand* set in Boulder, and *The Shining,* inspired by the Stanley Hotel in Estes Park.

If you're interested in roadside geology (but don't want to spend a few years in Boulder getting a degree, like I did), pick up a copy of *Messages in Stone: Colorado's Colorful Geology,* written and published by the Colorado Geological Survey. It's available in many of the visitor centers in the National Parks, or you can order it directly from the Survey at http://dnr.state.co.us/geostore/. It's extremely well done, with large color photos on every page, excellent digital maps, and

The essential atlas

The *Colorado Atlas & Gazetteer,* published by DeLorme and available in most book-stores in the state, is **absolutely essential** for anyone who wants to venture even a little way off the beaten path. Featuring topographic maps that cover the whole state, this atlas shows every road and most of the trails, as well as National Forests and other public lands. The front of the atlas has an exhaustive listing of great hiking, camp-ing, biking, scenic drives, and other activities that will be a great companion to any travels in the state. In addition to being a travel writer, I'm a cartographer, and I carry this atlas wherever I go; you'll probably want one for your home state, too.

clear descriptions of the geology you'll see — and you don't need an advanced degree to read it. It's truly outstanding.

Travelers who want to see wildlife will love the *Colorado Wildlife Viewing Guide,* by Mary Taylor Gray, published by Falcon. Serious anglers should check out the *Flyfisher's Guide to Colorado* by Marty Bartholomew (Wilderness Adventures Press) for outstanding info on all the rivers and seasons, and strategies for catching trout. Lastly, anyone planning to spend serious time in Rocky Mountain National Park should get a copy of *Frommer's Rocky Mountain National Park,* a must for really in-depth exploring.

Movie buffs also have a lot to choose from. Colorado has a starring role in *City Slickers,* starring Billy Crystal as an Easterner trying to find his smile and a memorable Jack Palance as his dude-ranch guide. The early Woody Allen–classic *Sleeper* was filmed in Colorado: Try to spot the scenes shot at the Denver Botanic Gardens, the National Center for Atmospheric Research (NCAR) in Boulder, and the "flying saucer house" visible from I-70 in Genesee Park, just west of Denver.

Old Western fans will like *Gunfight at the OK Corral* — granted, the movie takes place in Arizona, but the antihero Doc Holliday is buried in Glenwood Springs. Look back on the Cold War and laugh (or shudder) with *War Games,* an early Matthew Broderick movie about a young hacker who taps into the Department of Defense computers at NORAD in Colorado Springs.

For romance fans, the great actress Kathy Bates gives a not-too-flattering portrayal of Denver native Molly Brown in *Titanic.* And last but certainly not least, you'll learn almost nothing about Colorado from *South Park,* the wildly irreverent animated show on Comedy Central, but you'll prob-ably have a lot of fun. There is no actual town of South Park, though there is a large and beautiful valley by that name along U.S. 285; the show's creators went to Columbine High School in the southern suburbs of Denver, and the show's skewed take on life more closely reflects those claustrophobic suburbs than any mountain town.

Chapter 3

Deciding When and Where to Go

In This Chapter

▶ Choosing where to go
▶ Budgeting your time
▶ Understanding mountain weather
▶ Catching the best events on the calendar

*O*nce you choose to visit Colorado, your next major decision involves determining when and where to go. In this chapter, I introduce you to the top cities and the most tourist-friendly regions of the state, and I explain the pros and cons of traveling here at different times of year. I break down the weather by location and season and even provide a calendar of major Colorado events. Mind you, this isn't the part where I really dissect the destinations — you have to check out Chapters 11 through 25 for specific information on Colorado's most popular places.

Going Everywhere You Want to Be

I have a confession to make: Not every place in Colorado is covered in this book. To cover every nook and cranny of Colorado, this book would need to be 20 times larger, and I'd need a stronger pair of legs, a new car, a bigger paycheck, and a transplanted liver.

I don't even cover every single great spot. The state is *big* — it holds a lifetime's worth of secrets. Dozens of canyons and side canyons are etched into every vast mountainside, and every side canyon has a dozen more little hiding places that somebody somewhere dearly loves. Unfortunately, you may have only a week or two to see the state, so I boil down the best Colorado has to offer visitors with a limited amount of time on their hands. That means you won't read about the Great Plains of eastern Colorado, or the ranges of northwestern Colorado. There's just not that much going on out there.

The places I do cover are the top cities (the Front Range) and the other major tourist regions in the state (see the nearby "Colorado" map).

Colorado

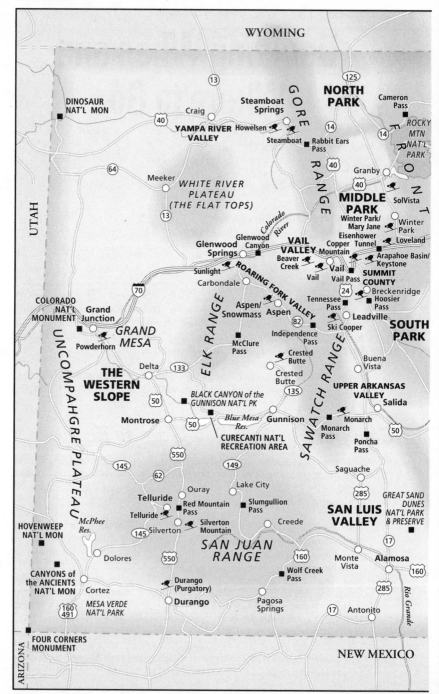

WYOMING

DINOSAUR NAT'L MON

Craig

13

125

NORTH PARK

Cameron Pass

ROCKY MTN NAT'L PARK

Steamboat Springs

YAMPA RIVER VALLEY

Howelsen

Steamboat

14

Rabbit Ears Pass

FRONT

64

40

Meeker

WHITE RIVER PLATEAU (THE FLAT TOPS)

13

Granby

40

MIDDLE PARK

SolVista

Colorado River

Glenwood Canyon

Glenwood Springs

VAIL VALLEY

Beaver Creek

Winter Park/ Mary Jane

Winter Park

Eisenhower Copper Tunnel Mountain

Loveland

Vail

Arapahoe Basin/ Keystone

Sunlight

ROARING FORK VALLEY

Carbondale

Vail

Vail Pass

SUMMIT COUNTY

24

Breckenridge

Hoosier Pass

Tennessee Pass

Ski Cooper

Leadville

SOUTH PARK

70

COLORADO NAT'L MONUMENT

Grand Junction

GRAND MESA

Powderhorn

UNCOMPAHGRE PLATEAU

Aspen/ Snowmass

Aspen

82

Independence Pass

McClure Pass

Crested Butte

Crested Butte

135

Buena Vista

UPPER ARKANSAS VALLEY

Salida

ELK RANGE

THE WESTERN SLOPE

Delta

133

Montrose

50

BLACK CANYON of the GUNNISON NAT'L PK

50

Blue Mesa Res.

Gunnison

CURECANTI NAT'L RECREATION AREA

Monarch

Monarch Pass

Poncha Pass

SAWATCH RANGE

50

550

145

62

149

Saguache

285

Ouray

Lake City

Telluride

Telluride

Red Mountain Pass

Slumgullion Pass

GREAT SAND DUNES NAT'L PARK & PRESERVE

SAN LUIS VALLEY

HOVENWEEP NAT'L MON

McPhee Res.

145

Silverton

Silverton Mountain

Creede

17

SAN JUAN RANGE

CANYONS of the ANCIENTS NAT'L MON

Dolores

550

Wolf Creek Pass

Monte Vista

Alamosa

160

Cortez

160 491

MESA VERDE NAT'L PARK

Durango (Purgatory)

Durango

Pagosa Springs

17

Antonito

285

160

Rio Grande

FOUR CORNERS MONUMENT

ARIZONA

UTAH

GORE RANGE

NEW MEXICO

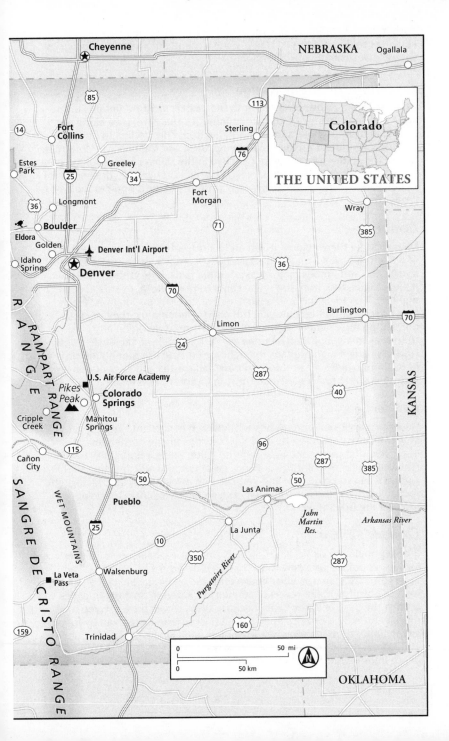

Within these locations, I fill you in on the best attractions to see and activities to do so that you don't waste a minute of your time going anywhere unworthy of your attention.

Traveling the Front Range

The term *Front Range* refers to both the easternmost mountains in the state and the corridor of urban communities that stretches along the prairie in front of those same mountains from Fort Collins to Pueblo, including Boulder, Denver, Colorado Springs, and Cañon City. More than half of the state's 4.3 million people live in the Denver metropolitan area; Colorado Springs is the next largest city, but compared to Denver, parts of Colorado Springs feel like a sleepy little resort, and Boulder feels positively tiny.

Denver

Denver has a thriving downtown and all the entertainment you expect of a major city. It's a major American city, complete with major-league sports and sometimes major-league traffic jams. Everything else is major-league, too, from the restaurants to the cultural events and the nightlife. The town has a youngish, active, healthy population. When these people aren't off enjoying the nearby mountains, they're eating out, shopping, or cheering on their favorite pro team. The city is easy to tour — many major attractions are within a mile of each other downtown, making it a good place for sightseeing. And the mountains start only about 6 miles west of town. I cover all the ins and outs of Denver, including some really cool side trips, in Chapters 11 and 12.

Boulder

Boulder is a vibrant community of high-tech health nuts and university students, situated at the base of the Flatirons in one of the most strikingly beautiful piedmont valleys in the state. Being a university town (the University of Colorado is here), great cultural and sporting events always seem to be on tap, and you can find awesome hiking, biking, and rock-climbing in the canyons just outside of town. More details about Boulder are in Chapter 13.

Colorado Springs

With a population of 350,000, Colorado Springs has taken over Denver's former reputation as a cow town that's a little big for its britches. The downtown area has spacious boulevards and a low skyline. A few miles west of downtown, the resort community of **Manitou Springs** snuggles against the base of **Pikes Peak.** Because these towns have catered to tourists for over a century, they have a host of road-tested, family-friendly attractions, not to mention historic hotels such as the Broadmoor and the Cliff House. And **Cañon City** and the **Royal Gorge** aren't far away. For in-depth information on Colorado Springs, turn to Chapter 14.

Going beyond the Front Range: The High Country

All the regions I cover in this book offer stunning scenery and lively towns. If you decide to go the regional route on your vacation, your best bet is to select one or two adjacent valleys or ranges (see the "Colorado" map earlier in this chapter to find out what's where) and spend a week there. If you have more time, you can then branch out and see more of the state.

Rocky Mountain National Park

Colorado's most popular national park makes seeing the mountains easy. Located within a few hours' drive of Denver, Rocky Mountain National Park is traversed by **Trail Ridge Road,** which goes up and over the tree line, cresting at over 12,000 feet. After a day spent hiking some of the 300 miles of trails, camp inside the park or retreat to one of the gateway communities of **Estes Park, Grand Lake,** or **Granby.** I cover everything you need to know about the park in Chapter 15.

The Parklands and Summit County

This group of valleys just behind the Front Range is famous for its fishing, cross-country skiing, and rafting, and this is also where the downhill skiing and snowboarding gets really good. **Middle Park** (Chapter 16) and the **Upper Arkansas Valley** (Chapter 18) have cool towns with activities for all seasons, while **Summit County** (Chapter 17) is all about skiing and boarding. **Leadville** (Chapter 18) is in a class of its own; once the capital of the Silver Boom, it's now a treasure trove of history and lore. Downstream of Leadville, in a valley warmed by southerly winds, is the artsy, mellow town of **Salida** and the great rafting territory near **Buena Vista.**

The high valleys: Vail, Aspen and the Roaring Fork, and Steamboat Springs

This area is home to the best skiing on Earth (and I'm not just boasting — Swiss skiers have told me that), but there's so much to keep you busy here, winter or summer, you'll never want to leave. Don't forget your wallet, though; premiere resorts aren't the cheapest. **Vail** (Chapter 19) and **Aspen** (Chapter 20) are the toniest of towns, while **Steamboat Springs** (Chapter 21) is a little more of a just-kick-back-and-have-fun kind of place.

The Gunnison Valley and the Western Slope

Gunnison and **Crested Butte** (Chapter 22) are fun mountain towns near the top of stunning **Black Canyon,** a 2,000-foot-deep gorge. This is where the mountains slope downward into the Great Basin, and farther west, near Grand Junction, erosion has isolated the sandstone **Uncompahgre Plateau** and the canyons of **Colorado National Monument.** I detail the major highlights of this region in Chapter 23.

The Four Corners and Mesa Verde

This area plummets from the 14,000-foot peaks of the San Juans to the canyon bottoms of the Four Corners area, which gets its name from the four-cornered meeting point of four states (Colorado, Utah, Arizona, and New Mexico). The towns of **Telluride, Silverton,** and **Ouray** preserve a 100-year-old mining history in addition to offering abundant recreation. Other areas have ancient history. Near **Cortez** and **Durango,** you can explore the remnants of the ancestral Pueblo culture, which flourished here until about A.D. 1300. For more on this historic region, see Chapter 24.

The San Juan Mountains and the San Luis Valley

The highest peaks in the state tower above river valleys in this area just east of the continental divide. High in the mountains, the colorful mining towns of **Lake City** and **Creede** are virtual living museums, showing the life of Colorado 100 years ago. And below Creede, the Rio Grande River helped carve out the broad San Luis Valley, home to farms, geothermal springs, and **Great Sand Dunes National Monument and Preserve.** For detailed information on this region, see Chapter 25.

Scheduling Your Time

One of the great aspects of travel in Colorado is that nature has done a pretty good job of organizing the state into fairly discrete ranges and the valleys between them. I organize this book as much as possible according to these guidelines created by Mother Nature, and for a visual aid, you can study the nearby "Colorado" map, which emphasizes the valleys and the passes between them.

As a general rule, you'll do fine if you pick one town or valley as a base, and then explore adjacent valleys in day trips. Trying to go farther than that, though, is only for travelers who like driving a lot and who would rather see the state through car windows. For example, if you base yourself in Buena Vista (Chapter 18) during summer, you can easily get to the Great Sand Dunes (Chapter 25), Summit County (Chapter 17), and Aspen (Chapter 20). Don't try to get to Steamboat Springs or Durango, though.

Denver makes the most sense as a base for visiting the Front Range, as you can easily take day trips to Boulder and Colorado Springs, as well as Rocky Mountain National Park, Middle Park, and Summit County. Because it's right on I-70, even Vail is doable from Denver, but remember to plan for a two-hour drive.

For skiers, if your plan is to fly into Denver, rent a car, and head straight for the High Country, I don't recommend trying to ski the day you arrive — unless you arrive on a red-eye flight and have a gonzo streak worthy of Hunter S. Thompson. Denver is a long flight from both coasts (as well as the rest of the continent), and you'll save yourself a headache (and possibly other injuries) by taking your arrival day slowly, giving yourself time to acclimate to the high altitude and to deal with the ever-present possibility of inclement weather. This is Colorado . . . you're *supposed* to relax!

Revealing the Secrets of the Seasons

The single most important factor affecting Colorado weather is elevation. One general rule, subject to a few exceptions, is that for every 1,000 feet of elevation, the air temperature drops 3.5 degrees. When air cools, it condenses and forms precipitation that eventually comes down as rain or snow. So the higher up you go, the cooler — and snowier — it usually gets, no matter what the season. Mountain temperatures can be bitterly cold, especially if it's windy, but even at the higher elevations of some of the nation's top ski resorts, you can find plenty of sunshine.

At 5,280 feet, Denver may be known as the Mile High City, but it's much lower than the mountains to its west, 58 of which top 14,000 feet. (Locals refer to these peaks as *fourteeners.*) Whether you're in Denver or higher up in the Rockies, you'll probably notice the (relatively) cool, thin air. But like much of the state, Denver is a dry place that has more than 300 sunny days each year — more than Miami or San Diego! — and it can get surprisingly warm here. Temperatures have been known to climb to 90 degrees and higher during the height of summer.

 The cool, dry, thin air means dehydration and intense sunlight. Be sure to have moisturizer, sun block, and shades, and it's a good idea to keep a bottle of water with you, even in Denver.

If you don't like the weather in Colorado, wait ten minutes or, better yet, drive up or down. It's not unheard of for Coloradans to ski and golf on the same day, simply by changing elevations. Still, you'll definitely want to visit during the ideal season for pursuing your favorite activities. The only place for snow in July is on the highest mountain peaks, so if you want to slalom, your best bet is to show up between late November and early April. But if you're a hiker or a biker, the trails are usually snowless and dry from late May through early October.

 Unless you're traveling with children and are governed by their school schedules, the most convenient times to visit the state are the *shoulder seasons* during early spring and late fall. Not only will you avoid crowds, you'll also save money.

Frozen zones

The air temperature not only affects how you feel when you visit Colorado but also affects the plant and animal species you see in a given area. Atop Colorado's highest peaks are zones of biological life comparable to ones found near sea level as far north as the Yukon. Meanwhile, the low-lying canyons in the southern part of the state bear species that flourish as far south as Mexico.

Along the Front Range, where Denver and Colorado Springs are located, summer days are hot and dry, evenings pleasantly mild. Evenings start to get even cooler by mid-September, but as late as November the days are often warm. Surprisingly, winters here are warmer and less snowy than those in the Great Lakes area or New England.

Most of Colorado is considered semiarid, and overall the state has an average of 296 sunny days a year. The prairies average about 16 inches of precipitation annually; the cities along the Front Range, 14 inches; the western slope, only about 8 inches. Rain, when it falls, is commonly a short deluge — a summer afternoon thunderstorm. However, if you want to see snow, simply head to the mountains, where snowfall is measured in feet rather than inches, and mountain peaks may still be white in July.

In the following sections, I break down Colorado's seasonal score sheet. To get an idea of the average temperatures, rainfall, and snowfall you'll encounter in some of Colorado's cities, see Tables 3-1 and 3-2, which list average temperatures (in degrees Fahrenheit) and precipitation (in inches).

Table 3-1 — Denver's Average Temperatures and Total Precipitation

	Jan	Feb	Mar	Apr	May	June	July	Aug	Sep	Oct	Nov	Dec
High	43	46	52	61	70	81	88	85	76	66	52	44
Low	16	20	26	34	43	52	58	56	47	36	25	17
Rainfall	0.5	0.6	1.3	1.7	2.4	1.8	1.9	1.5	1.2	1.0	0.9	0.6
Snowfall	8.1	7.5	12.5	8.9	1.6	0.0	0.0	0.0	1.6	3.7	9.1	7.3

Table 3-2 — Leadville's Average Temperatures and Total Precipitation

	Jan	Feb	Mar	Apr	May	June	July	Aug	Sep	Oct	Nov	Dec
High	29	31	35	42	53	64	70	68	61	51	38	30
Low	0	0	5	15	25	33	38	37	30	23	12	3
Rainfall	1.5	1.2	1.4	1.4	1.3	1.1	2.0	2.1	1.4	1.1	1.3	1.5
Snowfall	16.8	13.1	16.9	14.7	6.6	2.4	0.0	0.0	3.9	7.4	12.5	23.2

Spring

Depending on when you arrive and where you visit, spring in Colorado can be either a beautiful blessing or a muddy nightmare. Here are some of the season's pluses:

✔ By mid-May, Denver and the other Front Range towns have usually passed their freezing point. Flowers start blooming and the landscape is stunning.

✔ Rafting on mountain rivers, swollen by the winter snows and spring thaw, is an especially thrilling experience this time of year.

✔ No matter where you go in the state, you'll have many tourist destinations, including the national parks, nearly to yourself.

✔ Many resorts offer discounts and drop their rates.

But spring has some serious downsides:

✔ Before all its flowers can bloom, the Front Range is often battered by thunderstorms caused by cold air sliding down from the mountains meeting sun-warmed, damp air surging northward from the Gulf of Mexico. On average, Denver receives over two inches of precipitation during May, its wettest month.

✔ If you make a date with spring in the Rockies, you'll probably get stood up. The sun does shine sometimes, yet much of the high country remains snow-covered, and areas where the snow has melted can stay muddy into June.

✔ Temperatures in areas of high elevation remain cool. For example, in May, the average high temperature in Leadville is a not-so-balmy 53 degrees. So if you want to spend time above the treeline, this is not the time do it.

Summer

Colorado is very popular with visitors and outdoor enthusiasts in summer. The season sizzles because

✔ Denver is usually sunny, warm, and mild.

✔ Summer is beautiful in the Rockies. Clusters of aspen trees bloom one by one, dabbing green across the hillsides. The mountains quickly become lush and fragrant, and when the snow in the high country melts (in mid-July), wildflowers such as penstemon, columbine, fireweed, and dwarf clover illuminate the meadows and tundra.

✔ Temperatures in the mountain regions climb blissfully into the 70s and beyond during the day.

✔ The major attractions are up and running, and the going doesn't get much better in the hiking department.

But summer fizzles because

- ✔ When the sun goes down, the mountainous areas in Colorado can get downright cold. Leadville's low temperature in July is a chilly 38 degrees, and Aspen's nighttime low is a measly 47 degrees. Even cities at lower elevations, such as Denver, can get pretty cool at night. You'll need a jacket!

- ✔ Afternoon thunderstorms can flare up without warning. The wettest months are July and August.

- ✔ The major parks can get uncomfortably crowded in summer, especially if you're unwilling or unable to head too far off the beaten path. Denver, too, buzzes with visitors.

- ✔ Your wallet will take a beating, because most resort and hotel rates climb as high as the Rockies.

Fall

Fall in Colorado starts off with a burst of color, but its end can be a little bleak. It's fabulous because

- ✔ Denver is at its sunniest and driest, and the temperature here remains pretty temperate — 60s in October, 50s in November. And the leaves first start turning colors in early October, so the foliage season lasts longer than in the mountains.

- ✔ Come September, the changing leaves in the mountains can be nearly as extraordinary as the late-summer wildflowers are. Rocky Mountain maple, Gambel oak, and quaking aspen spatter the hills with red, orange, and yellow, respectively, against a backdrop of evergreen trees.

- ✔ The start of the school year means fewer people in the parks and at the major attractions. You won't be alone, but you won't feel cramped either, especially not in late September and October.

- ✔ Prices drop from their stratospheric elevations to more reasonable levels.

On the other hand

- ✔ Fall comes fast and early to the mountains, so the foliage show is over by early October. Miss it and the only leaves you'll see in the Rockies will be the ones on the ground.

- ✔ Temperatures drop, especially in the mountain zones. Snowstorms are guaranteed in the Rockies — although they won't provide enough snow for good skiing — and it can get brutally cold. By late October, even Denver is pretty frosty — growing up, I had to prepare for snow when planning my Halloween costume!

Winter

Winter in Colorado brings most travelers visions of snow-covered mountains, and those visions are pretty true to life. This time of year is wonderful because

- Snow falls, heavily at times, throughout the Rockies from October (and sometimes earlier) through May (and sometimes later). The amount of snowfall varies greatly from place to place and season to season, yet many towns average over 200 inches annually — even without the help of a ski-area marketing department. All that white stuff looks pretty, feels soft, absorbs sound, and is fun to slide around on.

- Because of their southern latitude, the Rockies warm up rapidly on sunny winter days, so you can stay relatively comfortable. Despite being perched at 10,046 feet, Leadville has an average high temperature of 29 degrees during January.

- Storms coming from the west tend to lose moisture over the mountains, so Denver often stays dry in early winter. Denver's average high temperature in January is 43, and the skies are usually sunny. And a lot of the snow that falls during the rest of the winter here tends to melt quickly so you won't get snowed-in, but you can still take advantage of the city's proximity to good recreational opportunities.

But winter does have its downside. Consider the following:

- Nights in the mountain regions, when no clouds trap warm air in the atmosphere, are particularly frosty. Leadville's average low temperature in both January and February is 0 degrees. Towns in mountain valleys where cold air settles can be even more frigid. The communities of Gunnison and Fraser sometimes register the coldest temperatures in the continental United States!

- All that mountain snow may look beautiful, but it can wreak havoc on the roads and make life miserable for drivers.

- You won't be the only one basking in the beauty of the winter mountains. Crowds flock to all the major ski areas as soon as the snow gets deep enough for skiing.

- Hotel and resort rates skyrocket in the major ski towns during Christmas week and they don't start moving downhill until late March.

Looking at Colorado's Calendar of Events

Although I list Colorado's major annual events in this section, dozens of other local and regional events take place around the state every week. To find additional events on the dates you'll be visiting, check the

Colorado Tourism Office Web site (www.colorado.com), the Colorado Festivals & Events Association Web site (www.coloradofestival.com), and the Web sites for individual towns and cities you plan to see.

January

At the **National Western Stock Show, Rodeo & Horse Show** in Denver (☎ 303-297-1166; www.nationalwestern.com), livestock buffs enjoy a first-rate stock show in which more than 15,000 hoofed creatures are displayed and sold. Participants ride and rope some of the more cantankerous animals in 22 rodeo performances, including bull riding. Mid-January.

Aspen hosts **Gay and Lesbian Ski Week,** one of the largest cold-weather gay happenings in the world, attracting upwards of 5,000 people. Attendees participate in ski clinics, costume parades, special shows, and parties. Call ☎ 800-367-8290 for more information or go to www.gayskiweek.com. Late January.

February

Hosted by the Steamboat Springs Winter Sports Club, the **Steamboat Springs Winter Carnival** is the oldest annual Winter Carnival west of the Mississippi. Activities include ski racing, ski jumping, *ski joring* (in which snow skiers are towed, water-ski style, behind running horses), fireworks, and performances by the Steamboat Springs skiing band. Call ☎ 970-879-0880 for details, or visit www.steamboat-chamber.com. Mid-February.

March

Though Denver is not generally known as a hotbed of Irishness, on the Saturday before St. Patrick's Day, Denverites come out in force for the **St. Patrick's Day Parade,** which features floats, thousands of horses, and a Western spin. It's the second largest St. Paddy's Day parade in the country. Call ☎ 303-321-7888 for details. Mid-March.

Representatives of over 70 tribes attend the annual three-day **Denver March Powwow,** one of the largest in the nation. Activities include musical performances and competitions in dancing and drumming. Authentic Native American art and food is also sold. Call ☎ 303-934-8045 or visit www.denvermarchpowwow.org for details. Mid-March.

April

Easter sunrise services have been held in Colorado Springs's Garden of the Gods Park since the 1920s. For years they were broadcast live across America on CBS radio, and by the mid-1900s attendance had swelled to over 25,000. Today, interdenominational Easter services continue at the park, although the crowds are usually smaller. For more information, call ☎ 800-DO-VISIT or go to www.coloradosprings-travel.com.

May

America's largest **Cinco de Mayo** celebration takes place not in Albuquerque, El Paso, or Los Angeles but in downtown Denver. Upwards of 400,000 people flood this annual outdoor gathering in Civic Center Park. While performers ranging from mariachi bands to traditional Aztec dancers entertain the crowd from several stages, hundreds of booths sell Latino food, crafts, and art. Call ☎ 303-534-8342, ext. 106, for details. May 5.

In Boulder, the **Kinetic Conveyance Challenge** is a crowd-pleasing event involving a race of imaginative human-powered vehicles, held every year at Boulder Reservoir. Speed counts in this event, but so do costumes, color, creativity, and all-around joie de vivre. Call ☎ 303-444-5600 for more information. Early May.

Some of the world's fastest runners break away from a very large pack — upwards of 40,000 entrants — in the **Bolder Boulder** (☎ 303-444-RACE; www.bolderboulder.com), an annual 10-kilometer run that is the fourth-largest running race in America. Memorial Day.

June

Some of Telluride's lesser-known festivals are easier to endure and just as much fun as the **Telluride Folk and Bluegrass Festival,** simply known as *Bluegrass,* but this four-day festival is the one everyone talks about. The town hosts talented folk, bluegrass, and rock performers who share a fondness for acoustic music. Past performers include the likes of Ani DiFranco, Lucinda Williams, Bela Fleck, David Grisman, and Peter Rowan. Call ☎ 800-624-2422 or check out either www.planetbluegrass.com or www.visittelluride.com for more information. Mid-June.

The **FIBArk Whitewater Festival** (☎ 877-772-5432; www.fibark.net) is a long-running celebration of whitewater rafting and paddling that takes place on the Arkansas River near Salida. Events include races, skills competitions, demonstrations, and live music. Mid-June.

First run in 1915, the **Pikes Peak International Hill Climb** (☎ 719-685-4400; www.ppihc.com) in Manitou Springs is America's second oldest automobile race. It's also the highest, reaching 14,000 feet in elevation at the finish line. Usually the final Saturday in June.

July

Saddle up for **Cattlemen's Days,** a century-old Western celebration in downtown Gunnison. The bill includes horse races, a parade, a Professional Rodeo Cowboys Association (PRCA) rodeo, cowboy poetry readings, a carnival, a fashion show, and a country dance. For details, call ☎ 970-641-1501. Mid-July.

Over a quarter million people attend the **Cherry Creek Arts Festival** in Denver (☎ **303-355-2787;** www.cherryarts.org). During this three-day arts festival, 200 carefully selected artists display and sell works in media ranging from photography to glass. Musicians and dancers perform throughout the day on several stages. And area restaurants sell a variety of dishes from booths along Culinary Row. Early July.

August

Call it perfect. The **Palisade Peach Festival** (☎ **970-464-7458;** www.palisadepeachfest.com) is timeless. Held in western Colorado's orchard country, it celebrates peach recipes, peach growers, and peach eating. There's also a street dance and an ice cream social. Mid-August.

September

Just when you thought the summer fun was over, Telluride brews up three days of blues (and, lately, jam band) music and beer tasting at the **Telluride Blues & Brews Festival** in Town Park. Past performers include James Brown and Blues Traveler. Call ☎ **888-278-1746** or 970-728-8037 for more information or see www.visittelluride.com. Mid-September.

October

Over 1,700 different beers compete for medals at the **Great American Beer Festival** in Denver, the most prestigious beer festival in the United States. For a fee, you can evaluate beers from throughout the nation yourself, but your vote only counts for you. Be careful: If you have 1 ounce of all the competing brews, you'll end up drinking the equivalent of 108 12-ounce beers. Call ☎ **303-447-0816** or check out www.beertown.org for information. Mid-October.

November

Santa throws the switch at the **Lighting of Christmas Mountain U.S.A.,** illuminating 10,000 bulbs on a mountainside overlooking Salida. The bulbs, which are strung to form the outline of an enormous tree, stay up until New Year's Day. On the day of the lighting, you can also enjoy refreshments and caroling. The day after Thanksgiving.

December

For the entire month of December, the 40,000 lights of the **World's Largest Christmas Lighting Display** illuminate Denver's City and County Building.

Chapter 4

Following an Itinerary: Four Great Options

- -

In This Chapter

▶ Eyeing amazing sights in central and western Colorado

▶ Doing Colorado with youngsters

▶ Finding hot spots for history buffs

▶ Skiing Colorado

- -

*I*tineraries that involve a lot of driving aren't for everyone. One of the best ways to enjoy Colorado is to rent a cabin for a week and then do a different outdoor activity or a new trail every day. Colorado isn't really the kind of place where people tend to go and *look* at stuff, like, say Italy, where the history is amazing but you can't walk up and touch a lot of it. People tend to come to Colorado to *do* stuff — be it hiking, skiing, or just hanging out.

But if you're the type of person who needs to see a lot on vacation, I give you four itineraries designed to cover a string of highlights for people with specific interests. One itinerary details the state's most spectacular drives, involving a number of Colorado's greatest hits. Another identifies family-friendly spots, and ways to get the most out of touring Colorado with kids. The last is for history buffs who want to experience the Old West.

Taking In the High Passes (And Higher Peaks)

This warm-weather tour is designed to show you the most spectacular sights with a minimum of fuss. It takes you over progressively higher mountain passes with hairpin turns and stunning views. Note that not all these roads can handle vehicles longer than 25 feet, and a few are closed during the winter.

Spend **Day 1** in Denver (Chapter 11), getting your bearings. A trip to the
Colorado History Museum will give you a good idea of the history of the
state and the territory you're about to experience. For dinner, feast on
buffalo or game at **The Fort** or the **Buckhorn Exchange,** and catch 40
winks at the **Oxford Hotel** or one of the great bed-and-breakfasts in town.

Get an early start on **Day 2**, and head southwest on **US 285** through
Conifer and Bailey. If you get a really early start, take I-70 up to
Georgetown (Chapter 12) and go over Guanella Pass to Grant. This puts
you on US 285, and you continue south and west over **Kenosha Pass** into
South Park. You traverse this gorgeous high valley and go over **Trout
Creek Pass** into the **Upper Arkansas Valley.** Marvel at the splendor of the
grandiose **Collegiate Peaks.** At the junction with US Highway 24, turn
right and have lunch at **Jan's Restaurant** in **Buena Vista** (Chapter 18).
Continue down through **Salida** and into the **San Luis Valley** (Chapter 25),
where you get an afternoon to explore the **Great Sand Dunes.** Head back
to Salida for dinner and a good night's sleep.

Day 3 takes you back up the Arkansas valley to **Colorado 82
(Independence Pass).** Hold on tight at the top! Spend the rest of the
morning exploring the shops at **Aspen** (Chapter 20) where you'll have
lunch. If you don't want to window shop, go through town and head up
the beautiful road to the ghost town of **Ashcroft.** After lunch, head up
the Maroon Creek road, park at **Maroon Lake,** and take an easy hike
up the valley to see the **Maroon Bells,** some of the most beautiful mountains in the state. Hike back to your car and head down valley to find
dinner and spend the night in **Basalt** or **Carbondale.**

Day 4 starts up the Crystal River Valley (Colorado 133) from Carbondale
to **Redstone.** Tour **Redstone Castle** and keep driving on 133 over **McClure
Pass.** At Hotchkiss, turn onto Colorado 92 and go down through Crawford
to the **Black Canyon of the Gunnison National Park** (Chapter 22). Spend
the afternoon gazing into the abyss and either camp or get yourself to
Gunnison for the night.

You have to do some backtracking on **Day 5,** a long driving day. From
Gunnison, take Monarch Pass (US 50) back over to the Arkansas Valley
and head north. However, don't stop until you get to **Leadville** (Chapter 18). Have lunch there, and take Colorado 91 down into **Frisco and
Silverthorne** (Chapter 17). You can explore this area a bit, or press on;
you'll be going down Colorado 9 along the Blue River to Kremmling,
where you turn east on US 40 and go through Hot Sulphur Springs to
Granby. Turn onto US 34 and make your weary way to Grand Lake where
you'll find a well-deserved dinner and rest for the night.

Spend **Day 6** in **Rocky Mountain National Park** (Chapter 15), hiking,
climbing, and driving over Trail Ridge Road. If you can spend an extra
day here, do so; or bed down in Estes Park and head back to Denver for
Day 7 and your trip home.

Touring Colorado with Kids

Most of the activities in this itinerary — designed for those traveling with kids — work well for youths between the ages of 8 and 16. And they're fun for adults, too. What they aren't, however, is cheap. This trip impresses not just with natural splendor but also with spectacles bought and paid for with cash. If you're on a tight budget — or a tight schedule — you may need to cross off a few of the attractions listed here to save money, time, and energy.

Start **Day 1** in Denver (Chapter 11). If you arrived early in the morning and have at least a half-day, ride the roller coasters and water slides at **Six Flags Elitch Gardens.** Even if you only have a few hours, you have enough time to stroll past the aquariums and watch a simulated flash flood at **Ocean Journey.** Then drive south to **Manitou Springs** (Chapter 14) and spend the night there at the historic Broadmoor or one of the area's many family-friendly motels.

On the morning of **Day 2,** get up and take the **Pikes Peak Cog Railway** to the summit of Pikes Peak. In the afternoon, tour **Cave of the Winds,** or, if you prefer a free attraction, go hike among the immense sandstone slabs in **Garden of the Gods.** Come evening, enjoy the Skee-Ball, kiddy rides, and video games at **Arcade Amusements, Inc.,** in Manitou Springs (Chapter 14), where you should spend another night.

On **Day 3,** sleep late and then drive to the **Royal Gorge Bridge and Park,** near **Cañon City** (Chapter 14). This is high-priced fun, but the bridge over the 1,000-foot-deep gorge is cool. Walk across it, walk back, take some rides, and then continue on to **Salida** (Chapter 18). After dinner in Salida, go swim and soak at the **Salida Hot Springs.** Spend the night in Salida at the Woodland Motel.

Spend most of **Day 4** taking a half-day **raft trip** on the Arkansas River. When you arrive back on dry land, drive north to **Breckenridge** (Chapter 17) and spend the night at the **Breckenridge Mountain Lodge,** which has a game room with a pool table, foosball, and video games.

On **Day 5,** let the kids go wild playing in the maze, on the climbing wall, and on the alpine slide at the **Peak 8 Fun Park** at **Breckenridge Mountain Resort.** Spend another night in Breckenridge.

On **Day 6,** drive a few miles to **Silver Plume** (Chapter 12). Take a ride on the **Georgetown Loop Railroad** and go for a mine tour midway through the ride. Spend the night in Georgetown (Chapter 12) at the **Georgetown Mountain Inn,** where the kids can cool off in the outdoor swimming pool.

On **Day 7,** return to **Denver.** Play around with the hands-on exhibits at the **Museum of Nature and Science** and then stroll through the **Denver Zoo.** Both attractions are within walking distance of one another at City Park.

Colorado for History Buffs

This tour is a hard-charging, weeklong romp across the state. It takes in some of the oddest and most unusual historical sites in the nation, but because of the extensive driving, it's really suitable only for avid drivers who have a strong historical bent.

Welcome to Colorado. If you're like most people flying into the state, you'll probably start out in Denver. Spend **Day 1** in **Denver** (Chapter 11). After settling in at your hotel, visit the **Molly Brown House** and then check out the Colorado history timeline at the **Colorado History Museum.** Have dinner alongside the taxidermy at the **Buckhorn Exchange,** the oldest restaurant in town. By the end of the day, a good night's sleep is in order, and I suggest you bed down at the ornate but relaxed **Oxford Hotel** in LoDo (Lower Downtown), a classic hotel in Denver's historic nightlife district.

On **Day 2,** ascend to **Leadville** (Chapter 18) by car. Visit the **National Mining Hall of Fame and Museum,** and then take a driving tour of the historic mines around town. If you have a few minutes to spare, go hear the chilling story of Baby Doe Tabor at the **Matchless Mine.** Afterwards, walk the catacombs at the **Tabor Opera House.** Wind down your day with a beverage at one of Doc Holliday's old haunts, the **Silver Dollar Saloon,** before spending the night at the **Delaware Hotel.**

On **Day 3,** finish seeing any sights you missed in Leadville, then make the 253-mile drive to **Durango** (Chapter 24) and check into the **Strater Hotel.**

On **Day 4,** take the **Durango & Silverton Narrow Gauge Railroad** (Chapter 24) to the mountain town of **Silverton** (you can park your car at the railway's station). If you have an extra day to spare, get a room at the **Wyman Hotel.** If you're sticking to the seven-day itinerary, return on the train to Durango that afternoon and stay another night at the **Strater.**

On **Day 5,** rise early, and then drive from Durango to **Mesa Verde National Park** (Chapter 24), and take an early morning tour of **Cliff Palace.** Spend a few more hours at the park, and then head from Cortez to **Telluride** (Chapter 24). At twilight, walk Telluride's historic downtown. Spend the night at the **New Sheridan Hotel.**

On **Day 6,** drive from Telluride north to Delta. At Delta, cut off on Colorado 92 to Paonia, and then take Colorado 133 to **Redstone** (Chapter 20). Take an afternoon tour of **Redstone Castle,** built in the early 1900s by one of the richest men in America, John Osgood. Spend the night at the **Redstone Inn,** once part of Osgood's utopian community for miners.

If you don't need to be in Denver on **Day 7,** drive an hour or so to
Glenwood Springs (Chapter 20). Stay in the **Hotel Colorado** and soak
in the **Hot Springs Pool.** If you need to be closer to Denver in order to
catch a flight the next day, explore the mining towns of **Idaho Springs**
and **Georgetown** (Chapter 12). Unwind by soaking at the historic **Indian
Springs Resort** in Idaho Springs.

The Ski-'Til-You-Drop Tour

Okay, for all you serious downhillers who want to shred as much of the
state as possible, this tour is just for you. No guts, no glory, right? If
that's your style, read on. . . .

Fly into Denver for **Day 1,** and take it easy, kid. You'll need all that energy
(and then some) for the week ahead. Get a room for two nights at the
Embassy Suites Downtown Denver or the **Oxford Hotel** (Chapter 11)
and get up bright and early on **Day 2** to catch the **Ski Train** to **Winter
Park** (Chapter 16). The more advanced runs at **Mary Jane** are on the
adjacent mountain and between the two ski areas, so you'll get a good
warm-up for what's to come. Ride the train back down the hill and have
dinner and microbrews at the **Wynkoop Brewing Company** (Chapter 11).
Then hit the hay, cowpokes.

Hit the road early on **Day 3** to drive to **Breckenridge,** the best all-around
mountain in **Summit County** (Chapter 17). If you want more serious backcountry skiing, go to **Arapahoe Basin** instead. Breckenridge has the nicest
town in the area, though, and the **Breckenridge Brewery** will fill you up
with good beer and pub food.

On **Day 4,** drive over the pass to **Vail** or **Beaver Creek.** You could easily
ski here for two or three days and not cover the whole place — it's that
big. This is world-class skiing, though, so savor it. Take an extra day
(or two).

Not tired yet, are you? Good. **Day 6 (or 7)** will find you following the
river down to **Glenwood Springs** — it's not a bad idea at this point to
soak for the morning in the hot springs here, to prepare yourself for the
glory that is **Aspen.** An hour's drive up the Roaring Fork Valley from
Glenwood, the four mountains of this resort — **Aspen Mountain, Aspen
Highlands, Snowmass,** and **Buttermilk** — are also worth two or three
days, so take 'em if you got 'em. And enjoy the legendary nightlife in
town, if your legs can take it.

If you can still operate the pedals on your car, it's time for your final
challenge: On **whatever day this is,** drive back down the valley and
towards Vail again to **Wolcott,** where you'll pick up Colorado 131 north

to **Steamboat Springs.** Ski in the afternoon if you must, or soak in a hot tub and tackle the mountain the next day.

For the certifiably insane only: If you want to end the trip on the steepest note possible, you can skip Steamboat Springs, take a day just for driving and find some way to get to **Crested Butte** or **Silverton.** This will cement your reputation as the craziest skier ever and win the awe and admiration of your friends back home.

If you can get back home, that is. . . .

Part II
Planning Your Trip to Colorado

The 5ᵗʰ Wave   By Rich Tennant

"Yes sir, our backcountry orientation programs are held at the Footblister Visitor Center, the Lostwallet Ranger Station or the Cantreadacompass Information Pavilion."

In this part . . .

So you've decided to go to Colorado. Now you have to climb one small mountain before you embark on a relaxing vacation: trip-planning. This part deals with all the challenges you have to overcome in order to set up your adventure in Colorado. It goes over different ways to travel there (and how to find the best deals for each), transportation options for after you arrive, the types of accommodations available throughout the state, and even last-minute details such as trip insurance. It also provides travel tips for parents, gays and lesbians, people with disabilities, and seniors.

Chapter 5

Managing Your Money

. . . .

In This Chapter

▶ Budgeting your trip costs and avoiding expensive surprises
▶ Saving some dough
▶ Taking care of paying
▶ Handling a lost wallet

. . . .

$\mathcal{C}$olorado may not be as expensive as, say, Manhattan, but it's not cheap either. If you're not careful during your travels, you may end up panning for gold in order to finance your bus ticket back home.

Planning Your Budget

Making a budget for your trip ahead of time always pays, even if you don't necessarily stick to it after you arrive. Start by writing down the cost of transportation to and from the airport and continue adding anticipated costs until you budget for every expense — even the smallest souvenirs you hope to buy. As you work through your budget, consider all the costs described in the following sections. When you have your total, add another 15 percent for unexpected costs.

Tables 5-1 and 5-2 give you an idea of what things typically cost in Denver and Vail, respectively, so you don't end up with sticker shock when you get to Colorado.

Table 5-1	What Things Cost in Denver
Item	**Cost**
Shuttle from Denver International Airport to downtown Denver (1 adult)	$18
Double room at Brown Palace Hotel (expensive)	$235–$315
Double room at Queen Anne Bed & Breakfast (moderate)	$75–$175

(continued)

Table 5-1 *(continued)*

Item	Cost
Lunch at Wynkoop Brewing Company (moderate)	$7–$11
Dinner entree at The Fort (expensive)	$20–$46
Adult admission to Denver Art Museum	$8
Child (age 13–18) admission to Denver Art Museum	$6
Denver Broncos ticket	$30–$311
Greens fees at City Park golf course	$20
Adult ski-lift ticket at Loveland Ski Area	$48

Table 5-2   What Things Cost in Vail

Item	Cost
Shuttle ride from Denver International Airport to Vail (1 adult)	$66
Shuttle from Vail/Eagle County Airport to Vail (1 adult)	$44
Double room at Sonnenalp Lodge (expensive)	$240–$1,085
Double room at Comfort Inn, Avon (moderate)	$79–$199
Lunch at Bully Ranch (moderate)	$10–$17
Dinner entree at Sweet Basil (expensive)	$23–$28
Burrito at La Cantina (inexpensive)	$5–$8
Single adult admission to Colorado Ski Museum	$1
Vail International Dance Festival tickets	$17–$89
Greens fees at Vail Golf Club	$90
Adult ski-lift ticket at Vail	$77

Totaling up your transportation

Transportation is one of the easiest categories to budget for ahead of time because airlines and rental-car companies will quote prices in advance. When you calculate your transportation costs, make sure you consider the taxes on both your rental car and your airfare, and don't overlook the cost of gas.

Some people prefer to avoid mountain driving — especially during winter when roads can be treacherous — and instead fly closer to destinations such as Telluride, Crested Butte, and Aspen. This option is a pricey one, but it may let you get by without renting a car, because many ski towns have excellent, free shuttle systems.

For more on transportation costs, turn to Chapter 7, which has different options for flying inside Colorado and tips on how to keep your rental-car costs down.

Calculating lodging costs

Where and when you stay in Colorado affects your accommodation expenses. The college towns, such as Boulder, are expensive in summer and during special university events (parents' weekends, football games, and so on), but are less expensive at other times. In resort communities, such as Vail and Aspen, the price of a nice hotel room for even one night can rival the cost of airfare from the East Coast. If you want to stay in the fanciest hotels in the trendiest ski towns, be prepared to sell some stock. Downtown Denver is similarly pricey. You may be able to sell fewer shares if you stay in downtown Denver on weekends, and hit the ski towns in late April and early May (after the ski areas close) and November (before the ski areas open).

The good news is that a wide range of other options exists. People sometimes forget that the mountain West has not traditionally been a wealthy region; even today, you can often drive a half-hour from a resort town to a smaller ranching or mining community where lodging is available at a fraction of the price. Pleasant, spare, $50 motel rooms in pretty areas are hardly out of the question, especially during winter and spring.

Eating out

As with lodging, you can spend as much or as little as you want while dining in Colorado. You can eat pretty well for $30 to $40 a day per person if you skip the fanciest restaurants and don't load up on liquor.

The state has lots of charming but cheap small-town cafes that serve hearty meals for under $10. It also has more than its share of gourmet restaurants, most of them concentrated in the cities and resort communities, where a dinner entree can go for upwards of $20. At most good Colorado eateries, you can get a dinner entree for $8 to $20. Watch out for places that bill à la carte — your tab can add up quickly. If you decide to splurge, you can make up the difference by scrimping the next few days. Even in resort communities, you can often eat for $6 or $7 if you're willing to forgo a sit-down meal.

If you're on a strict budget, know that many hotels offer a free continental breakfast as part of the room rate, so ask before you book a room. If a free breakfast is not offered at your hotel, you can usually save a few bucks by going to a local coffee shop or espresso bar instead of dining in the hotel restaurant. Not only will you save money, but you'll get a better feel for the town. And those traveling with children will be happy to know that many Colorado restaurants have special low-priced kids' menus.

Budgeting for attractions

Most Colorado attractions are fairly inexpensive — just make sure you stay around long enough to get to know them. In other words, if you go to four different attractions in a day, it's going to cost you. An adult ticket to the Denver Zoo during high season costs $8; in low season, it's $6. The national parks and monuments in Colorado are the state's best deals. For $15, a carload of people gets admitted to Rocky Mountain National Park for an entire week. Mesa Verde National Park costs just $10 per carload per week, and admission to Black Canyon of the Gunnison National Park runs a mere $7.

If you plan on visiting more than a few national parks and monuments, buy a Golden Eagle pass. For $65, the card admits you and others traveling with you to national parks and monuments for a year from the date of purchase. For more information, go online to www.nps.gov/fees_passes.htm or call ☎ **888-467-2757.**

Pricing activities and tours

Unlike parks and museums, recreation in Colorado can be dauntingly expensive. For example, ski-lift tickets at Colorado resorts can sell for $65 or more. These prices can really hurt your wallet, but most visitors manage to avoid paying them.

You can find discounted lift tickets that let you ride the slope's chairlifts for a day as part of travel packages or by coming during the off season. You can also go to smaller ski areas that offer great skiing but less acreage and fewer amenities. If you plan your trip far enough in advance, you can save on lift tickets another way: season passes. Prices have dropped so low at the ski areas nearest Denver that season passes can be a bargain for visitors planning to spend a week at the same resort. The passes are cheapest early in fall and climb in price as you get closer to prime skiing season.

If you're a golfer, you can find discounts on late-afternoon tee times at many courses.

Shopping for Colorado goods

You can shop for fine art in galleries throughout Colorado. Like the land where they're located, prices at the hottest galleries start mile-high and go up from there. A less expensive option is to browse the quirky crafts and homespun knickknacks in offbeat tourist shops, where you may find something you like for under $20.

Outdoor enthusiasts should watch for maverick companies producing clothing and gear. Although high-quality outdoor goods are pricey, you won't get fleeced if you buy directly from the source.

Another item that can cost a little — or a lot — is Native American art. If you know what you're doing, you can get the best deals by purchasing directly from the artist or from vendors on a reservation. If you don't know your Native American art, you're better off buying from a reputable trading post. I like the Cultural Center at 25 N. Market St. in Cortez (☎ **970-565-1151**), for one.

Controlling nightlife costs

The cost of a night on the town varies widely depending on where you happen to be when the sun goes down. Most of the really expensive options are in Denver, where you can fork over $8 for a martini or up to $130 to take in an opera. But Denver also has some reasonably priced bars and clubs, and even the unreasonable ones offer drink specials and happy-hour deals.

Outside the cities, prices drop. In most ski towns, you can quaff a pint of Colorado microbrew for around $3.50 and hear live music for a cover charge of $8 or less. The really rural towns are even cheaper — a shot and a beer at a cowboy bar will dent your sobriety more than your pocketbook.

Cutting Costs — But Not the Fun

The destination chapters in Parts III, IV, and V all include money-saving tips specific to those regions, but here's some additional free advice to help keep your money in your pocket:

- **Go in the off season.** During nonpeak times, Colorado's hotel prices can be one-third of what they are during peak months. The ski areas slow down during the weeks preceding Christmas, the month of January (when the snow is often excellent), and April. If you simply want to visit the mountains but don't care when, consider going in mid- to late-September, when the leaves change and the rates start falling. In Denver, May and September are often uncrowded, and temperatures can be near-perfect.

- **Travel midweek.** If you can travel on a Tuesday, Wednesday, or Thursday, you may find cheaper flights to your destination. When you ask about airfares, see if you can get a cheaper rate by flying on a different day. For more tips on getting a good fare, see Chapter 6.

- **Try a package tour.** For many destinations, you can book airfare, hotel, ground transportation, and even some sightseeing just by making one call to a travel agent or packager for a price much less than if you put the trip together yourself. (See Chapter 6 for more on package tours.)

- **Rent an economy car, not an SUV.** The amount of money you can save renting, fueling, and insuring a smaller car is often enough to pay for a *very* nice meal or two.

Keeping your phone bills down

Hotels impose a variety of fees for telephone calls. Some allow free local calls; others charge 50¢ or more per call. If you need to make dozens of local calls, look for accommodations where you can make them for free.

No matter where you stay, never, ever direct-dial long distance from your room, where rates can top $2 per minute. And don't count on your cellphone working either, because signals can be weak in the mountains and roving charges often apply. If you expect to make long-distance calls while on the road, your best bet is to shop ahead of time for an inexpensive prepaid calling card. (The ones sold through Costco and Sam's Club cost around 4¢ per minute.) Make your calls via the toll-free number on the card. You still have to pay any fees that apply to local calls if you call from your room, but your total cost will easily beat the tab for long distance. When using a pre-paid calling card, remember that some hotels also start charging for calling-card (and other toll-free) calls after a given amount of time (usually about 20 minutes). If you're worried you'll go over the time limit, find a pay phone and call from there.

✔ **Reserve a room with a refrigerator and coffeemaker.** You don't have to slave over a hot stove to cut a few costs; several motels have minifridges and coffeemakers. Buying supplies for breakfast will save you money — and probably calories.

✔ **Always ask for discount rates.** Membership in AAA, frequent-flier plans, trade unions, AARP, or other groups may qualify you for savings on car rentals, plane tickets, hotel rooms, and even meals. Ask about everything; you may be pleasantly surprised.

✔ **Ask if your kids can stay in the room with you.** A room with two double beds usually doesn't cost any more than one with a queen-size bed. And many hotels won't charge you the additional person rate if the additional person is pint-size and related to you. Even if you have to pay $10 or $15 extra for a rollaway bed, you'll save hundreds by not taking two rooms.

✔ **Try expensive restaurants at lunch instead of dinner.** Lunch tabs are usually a fraction of what dinner would cost at a top restaurant, and the menu often boasts many of the same specialties.

✔ **Get out of town.** In many places, big savings are just a short drive or taxi ride away. Hotels just outside the city, across the river, or less conveniently located are great bargains. Outlying motels often have free parking, with lower rates than downtown hotels offering amenities that you may never use. Sure, at a motel you'll be carrying your own bags, but the rooms are often just as comfortable and a whole lot cheaper. See Chapter 8 for more about hotels.

✔ **Walk a lot.** A good pair of walking shoes can save lots of money in taxis and other local transportation. As a bonus, you'll get to know your destination more intimately as you explore at a slower pace.

✔ **Skip the souvenirs.** Your photographs and your memories could be the best mementos of your trip. If you're concerned about money, you can do without the T-shirts, key chains, salt-and-pepper shakers, and other trinkets.

Handling Money

You're the best judge of how much cash you feel comfortable carrying or what alternative form of currency is your favorite. That's not going to change much on your vacation. True, you'll probably be moving around more and incurring more expenses than you generally do (unless you happen to eat out every meal when you're at home), and you may let your mind slip into vacation gear and not be as vigilant about your safety as when you're in work mode. But, those factors aside, the only type of payment that won't be quite as available to you away from home is your personal checkbook.

Using ATMs and carrying cash

The easiest and best way to get cash away from home is from an ATM (automated teller machine). The **Cirrus** (☎ 800-424-7787; www.mastercard.com) and **PLUS** (☎ 800-843-7587; www.visa.com) networks span the globe; look at the back of your bank card to see which network you're on, then call or check online for ATM locations at your destination. Be sure you know your personal identification number (PIN) before you leave home and be sure to find out your daily withdrawal limit before you depart. Also keep in mind that many banks impose a fee every time your card is used at a different bank's ATM (usually at least $1.50). On top of this, the bank from which you withdraw cash may charge its own fee. To compare banks' ATM fees within the United States, use www.bankrate.com.

Charging ahead with credit cards

Credit cards are a safe way to carry money: They also provide a convenient record of all your expenses, and they generally offer relatively good exchange rates. You can also withdraw cash advances from your credit cards at banks or ATMs, provided you know your PIN. If you've forgotten yours, or didn't even know you had one, call the number on the back of your credit card and ask the bank to send it to you. It usually takes five to seven business days, though some banks will provide the number over the phone if you tell them your mother's maiden name or some other personal information.

Dealing with debit cards

Another way of working with money you have — as opposed to the virtual money of credit cards — is to use a debit card, or check card as they're sometimes called. In many cases, your debit and ATM card are the same piece of plastic. Instead of getting cash, however, the debit card pays for purchases pretty much anywhere a credit card is accepted. The advantage? The money comes out of your checking account rather than pushing up against your credit card limit. Plus, you're not likely to pay an additional fee to use it (though you may end up with some charge if your bank limits, say, the number of debit transactions in a month), and you have less cash to carry around.

Toting traveler's checks

These days, traveler's checks are less necessary because most cities have 24-hour ATMs that allow you to withdraw cash as needed. However, keep in mind that you will likely be charged an ATM withdrawal fee if the bank is not your own, so if you're withdrawing money every day, you may be better off with traveler's checks — provided that you don't mind showing identification every time you want to cash one.

You can get traveler's checks at almost any bank. **American Express** offers denominations of $20, $50, $100, $500, and (for cardholders only) $1,000. You pay a service charge ranging from 1 percent to 4 percent. You can also get American Express traveler's checks over the phone by calling ☎ 800-221-7282; Amex gold and platinum cardholders who use this number are exempt from the 1 percent fee.

Visa offers traveler's checks at Citibank locations nationwide, as well as at several other banks. The service charge ranges between 1.5 percent and 2 percent; checks come in denominations of $20, $50, $100, $500, and $1,000. Call ☎ 800-732-1322 for information. AAA members can obtain Visa checks without a fee at most AAA offices or by calling ☎ 866-339-3378. **MasterCard** also offers traveler's checks. Call ☎ 800-223-9920 for a location near you.

If you choose to carry traveler's checks, be sure to keep a record of their serial numbers separate from your checks in the event that they are stolen or lost. You'll get a refund faster if you know the numbers.

Dealing with a Lost or Stolen Wallet

Be sure to contact all your credit card companies the minute you discover your wallet has been lost or stolen and file a report at the nearest police precinct. Your credit card company or insurer may require a police report number or record of the loss. Most credit card companies have an emergency toll-free number to call if your card is lost or stolen; they may be able to wire you a cash advance immediately or deliver an emergency credit card in a day or two. Call the following emergency numbers in the United States:

- ✔ **American Express** ☎ **800-221-7282** (for cardholders and traveler's check holders)
- ✔ **MasterCard** ☎ **800-307-7309** or 636-722-7111
- ✔ **Visa** ☎ **800-847-2911** or 410-581-9994

For other credit cards, call the toll-free number directory at ☎ **800-555-1212.**

Identity theft and fraud are potential complications of losing your wallet, especially if you've lost your driver's license along with your cash and credit cards. Notify the major credit-reporting bureaus immediately; placing a fraud alert on your records may protect you against liability for criminal activity. The three major U.S. credit-reporting agencies are **Equifax** (☎ **800-766-0008;** www.equifax.com), **Experian** (☎ **888-397-3742;** www.experian.com), and **TransUnion** (☎ **800-680-7289;** www.transunion.com). Finally, if you've lost all forms of photo ID, call your airline and explain the situation; they may allow you to board the plane if you have a copy of your passport or birth certificate and a copy of the police report you filed.

Chapter 6

Getting to Colorado

• •

In This Chapter

▶ Deciding among plane, train, and automobile
▶ Trawling for bargains using the Internet
▶ Finding a package (tour) that delivers

• •

*E*ver since the World Wide Web empowered travelers to search for the cheapest rates and fares, vacation planning has become an exercise in self-reliance, if not an exercise in self-frustration. People often feel duty-bound to find the best deal, even if they grow old in the process. And there's a lot to think about. You can shop for the best airfares and room rates individually, seek the best package deals, or drop the mouse and hire a travel agent. Here are some tips that should help, no matter which course you choose.

Flying into Colorado

More than 100,000 passengers pass through **Denver International Airport,** also known as DIA (☎ **800-AIR-2-DEN;** TDD 800-688-1333; www. flydenver.com) every day, but you can easily fly to Colorado without ever setting foot in DIA. Flights from outside Colorado land in or near Aspen, Colorado Springs, Durango, Grand Junction, Montrose, Steamboat Springs, Telluride, and Vail. Eight airlines, offering 100 flights daily, serve **Colorado Springs** (☎ **719-550-1972;** www.flycos.com) alone.

If you do land in Denver, you can take commuter flights to all the airports listed in the preceding paragraph as well as ones in Alamosa, Cortez, and Gunnison. Denver is, however, the only international airport in the state. In addition to serving 100 destinations in the United States, DIA offers nonstop service to 11 foreign destinations, including ones in Canada, Mexico, and Europe.

Major domestic and international carriers that fly into both Denver and Colorado Springs include American, America West, Continental, Delta, Northwest, and United. Air Canada, Alaska, British Airways, JetBlue, Lufthansa, Mexicana, and U.S. Airways offer service to Denver only.

During winter, the busiest mountain airport, **Vail/Eagle County Airport** (☎ **970-524-9490;** www.eaglecounty.us/airport), has daily nonstop service to Atlanta, Chicago, Dallas, Denver, Houston, Minneapolis, and Newark, with less frequent nonstop flights from six other U.S. cities.

For phone numbers and Web sites of the major airlines, see the appendix. Table 6-1 lists commuter airlines that service various cities in Colorado.

Table 6-1 Commuter and Regional Airlines Serving Colorado

Carrier	Phone	Web Site
Allegiant Air	☎ 877-202-6444	www.allegiantair.com
Frontier	☎ 800-432-1359	www.flyfrontier.com
Great Lakes Airlines	☎ 800-241-6522	www.greatlakesav.com
Mesa	☎ 800-637-2247	www.mesa-air.com

Getting the best deal on your airfare

Competition among the major U.S. airlines is unlike that of any other industry. Every airline offers virtually the same product (basically, a coach seat is a coach seat is a . . .), yet prices can vary by hundreds of dollars.

Business travelers who need the flexibility to buy their tickets at the last minute and change their itineraries at a moment's notice — and who want to get home before the weekend — pay (or at least their companies pay) the premium rate, known as the *full fare.* But if you can book your ticket far in advance, stay over Saturday night, and are willing to travel midweek (Tuesday, Wednesday, or Thursday), you can qualify for the least expensive price — usually a fraction of the full fare. On most flights, even the shortest hops within the United States, the full fare is close to $1,000 or more, but a 7- or 14-day advance purchase ticket may cost less than half of that amount. Obviously, planning ahead pays.

The airlines also periodically hold sales, in which they lower the prices on their most popular routes. These fares have advance purchase requirements and date-of-travel restrictions, but you can't beat the prices. As you plan your vacation, keep your eyes open for these sales, which tend to take place in seasons of low travel volume. In Colorado, the off seasons are the so-called shoulder seasons of late April to Memorial Day and mid-September to mid-November. You almost never see a sale around the peak summer vacation months of July and August, or around Thanksgiving or Christmas, when many people fly, regardless of the fare they have to pay.

Consolidators, also known as bucket shops, are great sources for international tickets, although they usually can't beat the Internet on fares within North America. Start by looking in Sunday newspaper travel sections; U.S. travelers should focus on the *New York Times, Los Angeles Times,* and *Miami Herald.*

Bucket shop tickets are usually nonrefundable or rigged with stiff cancellation penalties, often as high as 50 to 75 percent of the ticket price, and some put you on charter airlines with questionable safety records.

Several reliable consolidators are worldwide and available on the Net. **STA Travel** (☎ **800-781-4040;** www.statravel.com), the world's leader in student travel, offers good fares for travelers of all ages. **ELTExpress** (☎ **800-TRAV-800;** www.flights.com) started in Europe and has excellent fares worldwide, but particularly to that continent. Flights.com also has "local" Web sites in 12 countries. **Air Tickets Direct** (☎ **800-778-3447;** www.airticketsdirect.com) is based in Montreal and leverages the currently weaker Canadian dollar for low fares; it'll also book trips to places that U.S. travel agents won't touch.

Booking your ticket online

The big three online travel agencies, **Expedia** (www.expedia.com), **Travelocity** (www.travelocity.com), and **Orbitz** (www.orbitz.com), sell most of the air tickets bought on the Internet. (Canadian travelers should try www.expedia.ca and www.travelocity.ca; U.K. residents can go for expedia.co.uk and opodo.co.uk.) Each has different business deals with the airlines and may offer different fares on the same flights, so shopping around is wise. Expedia and Travelocity will also send you an **e-mail notification** when a cheap fare becomes available to your favorite destination. Of the smaller travel agency Web sites, **SideStep** (www.sidestep.com) receives good reviews from users. It's a browser add-on that purports to "search 140 sites at once," but in reality only beats competitors' fares as often as other sites do.

Great **last-minute deals** are available through free weekly e-mail services provided directly by the airlines. Most of these deals are announced on Tuesday or Wednesday and must be purchased online. Most are only valid for travel that weekend, but some (such as Southwest's) can be booked weeks or months in advance. Sign up for weekly e-mail alerts at airline Web sites or check megasites that compile comprehensive lists of last-minute specials, such as **Smarter Living** (smarterliving.com). For last-minute trips, **www.site59.com** in the United States and **www.last minute.com** in Europe often have better deals than the major-label sites.

If you're willing to give up some control over your flight details, use an *opaque fare service* such as **Priceline** (www.priceline.com) or **Hotwire** (www.hotwire.com). Both offer rock-bottom prices in exchange for travel on a mystery airline at a mysterious time of day, often with a mysterious change of planes en route. The mystery airlines are all major, well-known carriers — and the possibility of being sent from Philadelphia to Chicago via Tampa is remote. But your chances of getting a 6 a.m. or 11 p.m. flight are pretty high. Hotwire tells you flight prices before you buy; Priceline usually has better deals than Hotwire, but you have to play their "name our price" game. *Note:* In 2004, Priceline added non-opaque service to its roster. You now have the option to pick exact flights, times, and airlines from a list of offers — or opt to bid on opaque fares as before.

 Great last-minute deals are also available directly from the airlines themselves through a free e-mail service called *E-savers.* Each week, the airline sends you a list of discounted flights, usually leaving the upcoming Friday or Saturday and returning the following Monday or Tuesday. You can sign up for all the major airlines at one time by logging on to **Smarter Living** (www.smarterliving.com), or you can go to each individual airline's Web site. Airline sites also offer schedules, flight booking, and information on late-breaking bargains.

Driving In

You can easily drive to Colorado via one of three interstate highways, all of which meet in Denver:

- ✔ **Interstate 70,** which stretches all the way from Baltimore, Maryland, to southwestern Utah, is the primary east-west artery through Colorado.

- ✔ **Interstate 76** branches off of I-80 (which spans from Chicago to San Francisco) in southwestern Nebraska and makes a 190-mile jaunt southwest to its terminus in Denver.

- ✔ **Interstate 25** links Denver with destinations in the north (Casper and Cheyenne, Wyoming) and the south (Albuquerque, New Mexico). As I-25 skirts the eastern slope of the Rockies, this heavily traveled freeway passes through major Colorado cities including Fort Collins, Denver, Colorado Springs, and Pueblo.

Arriving by Rail

 Amtrak's California Zephyr train traverses the entire width of Colorado en route from Chicago to Emeryville, California (near Oakland). Between Denver and Fort Collins, it passes through some spectacular high country, crossing the continental divide just south of Rocky Mountain National Park and paralleling the Colorado River for long stretches in western Colorado. The Zephyr doesn't exactly breeze down the tracks — it takes roughly 12 hours to cross the state — but its fares are fair: In February 2005, one-way coach tickets from Denver to Chicago, Salt Lake City, and Emeryville were $103, $57, and $130, respectively.

A second Amtrak train, the Southwest Chief, clips the southeast corner of Colorado on its way from Chicago to Los Angeles. For complete fare information and scheduling for both of these routes, contact Amtrak (☎ **800-USA-RAIL;** www.amtrak.com).

Joining an Escorted Tour

You may be one of the many people who love escorted tours. The tour company takes care of all the details and tells you what to expect at each leg of your journey. You know your costs up front and, in the case of the tame ones, you don't get many surprises. Escorted tours can take you to the maximum number of sights in the minimum amount of time with the least amount of hassle.

If you decide to go with an escorted tour, I strongly recommend purchasing travel insurance, especially if the tour operator asks you to pay up front. But don't buy insurance from the tour operator! If the tour operator doesn't fulfill its obligation to provide you with the vacation you paid for, there's no reason to think that it'll fulfill its insurance obligations either. Get travel insurance through an independent agency. (I tell you more about the ins and outs of travel insurance in Chapter 10.)

When choosing an escorted tour, along with finding out whether you have to put down a deposit and when final payment is due, ask a few simple questions before you buy:

- ✔ **What is the cancellation policy?** Can they cancel the trip if they don't get enough people? How late can you cancel if you are unable to go? Do you get a refund if you cancel? If they cancel?

- ✔ **How jam-packed is the schedule?** Does the tour schedule try to fit 25 hours into a 24-hour day, or does it give you ample time to relax by the pool or shop? If getting up at 7 a.m. every day and not returning to your hotel until 6 or 7 p.m. at night sounds like a grind, certain escorted tours may not be for you.

- ✔ **How large is the group?** The smaller the group, the less time you spend waiting for people to get on and off the bus. Tour operators may be evasive about this, because they may not know the exact size of the group until everybody has made reservations, but they should be able to give you a rough estimate.

- ✔ **Is there a minimum group size?** Some tours have a minimum group size, and may cancel the tour if they don't book enough people. If a quota exists, find out what it is and how close they are to reaching it. Again, tour operators may be evasive in their answers, but the information may help you select a tour that's sure to happen.

- ✔ **What exactly is included?** Don't assume anything. You may have to pay to get yourself to and from the airport. A box lunch may be included in an excursion, but drinks may be extra. Beer may be included but not wine.

- ✔ **How much flexibility do you have?** Can you opt out of certain activities, or does the bus leave once a day, with no exceptions? Are all your meals planned in advance? Can you choose your entree at dinner, or does everybody get the same chicken cutlet?

Depending on your recreational passions, I recommend one of the following tour companies:

- ✔ In 2005, **Globus Tours** offered an eight-day "Colorado and the Old West" tour for $1,459, which included visits to Rocky Mountain National Park, Vail, and a side trip to Moab, Utah.

- ✔ Also for 2005, **Cosmos** listed a nine-day "Colorado National Parks and Trains" tour for $1,199 that included the Pikes Peak Cog Railway, the Royal Gorge Railway, the Durango & Silverton Narrow Gauge Railroad, and Mesa Verde, Moab, Vail, and Rocky Mountain National Park.

Choosing a Package Tour

For lots of destinations, package tours can be a smart way to go. In many cases, a package tour that includes airfare, hotel, and transportation to and from the airport costs less than the hotel alone on a tour you book yourself. That's because packages are sold in bulk to tour operators, who resell them to the public. It's kind of like buying your vacation at a buy-in-bulk store — except the tour operator is the one who buys the 1,000-count box of garbage bags and resells them ten at a time.

Package tours can vary as much as those garbage bags, too. Some offer a better class of hotels than others; others provide the same hotels for lower prices. Some book flights on scheduled airlines; others sell charters. In some packages, your choice of accommodations and travel days may be limited. Some let you choose between escorted vacations and independent vacations; others allow you to add on just a few excursions or escorted day trips (also at discounted prices) without booking an entirely escorted tour.

To find package tours, check out the travel section of your local Sunday newspaper or the ads in the back of national travel magazines such as *Travel + Leisure, National Geographic Traveler,* and *Condé Nast Traveler.* **Liberty Travel** (call ☎ 888-271-1584 to find the store nearest you; www. libertytravel.com) is one of the biggest packagers in the Northeast, and usually boasts a full-page ad in Sunday papers.

Another good source of package deals is the airlines themselves. Most major airlines offer air/land packages, including **American Airlines Vacations** (☎ 800-321-2121; www.aavacations.com), **Continental Airlines Vacations** (☎ 800-301-3800; www.covacations.com), **Delta Vacations** (☎ 800-221-6666; www.deltavacations.com), and **United Vacations** (☎ 888-854-3899; www.unitedvacations.com). Several big **online travel agencies** — Expedia, Travelocity, Orbitz, Site59, and Lastminute.com — also do a brisk business in packages. If you're unsure about the pedigree of a smaller packager, check with the Better Business Bureau in the city where the company is based, or go online at www. bbb.org. If a packager won't tell you where it's based, don't fly with them.

For some sample prices on packages during the 2005 ski season, **Mountain Vacations** (www.mountainvacations.com) lists a family three-night vacation at Keystone, flying from Chicago O'Hare for $490 per person, and a five-night stay in Vail, flying from Houston for $1,430 per person. Other places to look include the following:

- ✔ **Vacation Together, Inc.** (☎ 800-839-9851; www.vacation together.com) allows you to search for and book packages offered by a number of tour operators and airlines.

- ✔ The **United States Tour Operators Association's** Web site (www. ustoa.com) lets you locate operators that offer packages to a specific destination. A number of Colorado companies are listed here. Travel packages are also listed in the travel section of your local Sunday newspaper.

Chapter 7

Getting Around Colorado

● ●

In This Chapter
▶ Traveling the Colorado roads
▶ Getting a good rental-car deal
▶ Flying, chugging, and bussing around

● ●

*W*hat's the best way to see Colorado? If you have cash to spare,
you may enjoy flying to an airport right near your favorite resort
town, taking a cab into town, and then riding the free buses around the
community. You can easily enjoy Colorado without ever getting behind
the wheel of a car. If you're like most people, however, you'll eventually
get behind the wheel, beginning your trip at either Denver International
Airport or at points farther out.

Driving Around Colorado

The bicycle may be superior and the plane may be faster, but the car
(or SUV) still moves most people around Colorado. If you're driving
in Colorado, these sections — plus the nearby "Driving Times and
Distances" map — offer some advice on getting around the state on
four wheels.

Handling the highways

Mountains make for tricky driving. They lift and cool air, which releases
rain and snow; they unloose rocks that roll onto roadbeds; and in spring,
their snowmelt occasionally floods things. The condition of a Colorado
highway often depends on who mounted the most recent offensive —
the road crew or the mountain. If the mountain happens to be winning
while you're driving in the area, don't blame the road crew — they're
plotting their next move over coffee as we speak!

Certain Colorado roads are especially vulnerable to mountain weather:

> ✔ **Interstate 70** east of Denver usually remains open during winter,
> but chains or four-wheel-drive may be required during storms, and
> weekend traffic can slow to a near standstill.

Driving Times & Distances

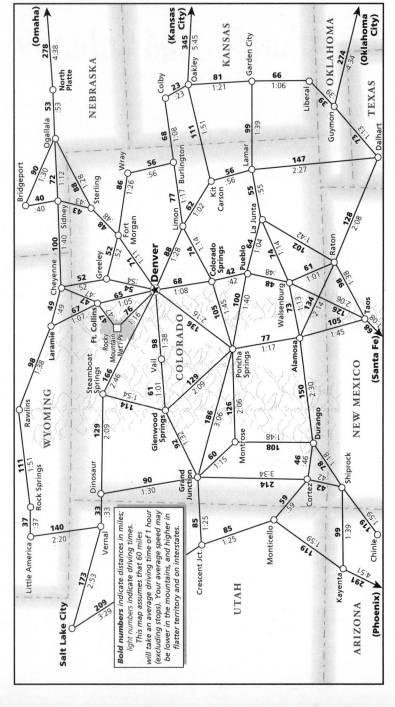

Bold numbers indicate distances in miles; light numbers indicate driving times. This map assumes that 60 miles will take an average driving time of 1 hour (excluding stops). Your average speed may be lower in the mountains, and higher in flatter territory and on interstates.

✔ **U.S. 550** between Ouray and Silverton serves up what is arguably the most frightening winter driving in the state. As it passes over 11,000-foot Red Mountain Pass, this two-lane highway edges across the tops of enormous cliffs yet offers little in the way of guardrails or shoulders for protection. It often closes during and after storms.

✔ Other roads close altogether. **Colorado 82** between Aspen and Leadville shuts down during winter due to heavy snows on 12,095-foot Independence Pass. **U.S. 34,** which crosses the continental divide at 12,183 feet inside Rocky Mountain National Park, also closes during winter.

For recorded updates on road conditions within two hours of Denver, call ☎ **303-639-1111.** For road conditions elsewhere in the state, dial ☎ **303-639-1234.**

Negotiating road hazards

Drivers in Colorado face a unique set of challenges that may phase visitors unused to the state's rugged terrain and weather. For a smooth ride, make certain you read this section, where I discuss climate and other related problems that may crop up while you're on the road.

Keeping pace with the rhythm of the traffic

On the steep inclines of Colorado's mountain roads, it's important to remember that every vehicle has a different size and weight and that different engines have varying degrees of power. It's difficult for any vehicle to accelerate going uphill, and there's also commercial traffic to consider. Trucks and heavy vehicles clog up the right-hand lanes, and often go very slowly, for safety's sake. The trick is to pass them smoothly without cutting off faster vehicles that might be coming up behind you (always keep an eye on your rearview mirror).

Leave plenty of space in front and behind, slow down *before* you get to the turn, and for Pete's sake, stay out of the left lane unless you intend to pass and can do it safely.

Surviving snow and ice

Many Colorado highways traverse mountain passes that receive, on average, more than 200 inches of snow annually. Most of us are ready for snow during winter, but it's easy to get fooled in spring and fall, when valley rains sometimes become snowstorms up high. If you're traveling in spring, fall, and winter, be ready for snowy and icy conditions in the mountains.

Here are some tips on how to prepare for a ride in the frozen stuff:

✔ Check your tires to make sure they have adequate tread and are properly inflated.

✔ If you don't have a four-wheel-drive vehicle with snow tires, carry chains.

- Make sure your brakes, wipers, defroster, and heater all work.

- Carry a small shovel, a bag of sand (for extra weight inside the car and for traction under the tires), a window brush, and a scraper.

- Stow a sleeping bag in your vehicle, just in case you get stranded.

- Keep a powerful flashlight handy so you can signal other drivers in the event of an accident. You also may want to carry an emergency flare for the same reason.

- Watch the weather and try to imagine what may be happening high above. If you suspect bad weather and are ill-prepared, don't go.

- Clean and scrape all your windows so that you have maximum visibility. Shovel off the hood and roof as well, so snow doesn't blow onto your windshield and the cars around you.

- If you have four-wheel-drive, make sure it is engaged. Remember, though, that though four-wheel-drive helps you start, it won't help you stop.

- If you have rear-wheel drive, carry a set of chains.

 When driving on snow and ice, use caution even if your vehicle has four-wheel-drive. Sport-utility vehicles are great on snow, but on ice they're no better than your grandmother's Oldsmobile. Use these helpful tips for winter driving in Colorado:

- **Allow extra time for the trip.** Mountain driving takes longer, especially during winter.

- **Be especially cautious during descents.** There's less margin for error when gravity gives you an extra push from behind. Don't, however, ride the brakes. Carefully shift into a low gear and then let the car's engine limit your speed.

- **Watch for black ice on shadowy corners.** Certain stretches of mountain road receive almost no sunlight in mid-winter. When water trickles from sun-warmed areas onto these frigid, shadowy stretches, look out.

- **Beware of ice on bridges.** Without warm earth to heat them, bridges freeze sooner than the rest of the road when the temperature drops. Bridges that cross mountain streams may also gather condensation from the waters below.

- **Don't cut corners.** Although this holds true in all weather conditions, it is especially important during storms, when snowplows with enormous blades lurk.

Avoiding rockfall

 Rockfall usually happens on warm days during late winter and early spring, when snowmelt permeates and loosens dirt that holds rock in place on hillsides. Other times, it happens when snowmelt seeps into

Driving with chains

Coloradans regard a set of chains as standard equipment for mountain driving; chains are a worst-case-scenario necessity. If you're going to be driving the high country in winter, it's good to at least consider getting a set. Unfortunately, many car-rental companies won't allow you to use them; used improperly, they can be destructive and somewhat dangerous. So if your car is rented and a blizzard moves in, stay inside and have another cup of hot chocolate. The storm will pass, and the snowplows will show up eventually.

If you're using your own vehicle, you can buy chains at most hardware stores, automotive specialty stores, and megamarts. Make absolutely sure that you know the make and model of your *tires* — not just your *car* — so that you get properly sized chains. Read the instructions very carefully, and if you need a tutorial from the store you buy them from, don't be afraid to ask. Installation usually involves laying the chains out in front of the tires, then driving over them and hooking the ends together, but this varies from brand to brand.

Remember that chains are only for driving on *snow,* if you drive them on bare pavement, they'll absolutely *shred* your tires.

cracks in cliffs, freezes, and then expands at night, wedging loose chunks of rock. The rocks careen downhill until they come to rest on relatively flat roads, where they wait around in hopes of destroying rental cars. Be particularly careful when low sunlight or shadows make it difficult for drivers to detect foreign objects on the road. Check the clearance on your vehicle before straddling anything big.

Eluding wildlife

Deer did not evolve to watch out for fast-moving automobiles; nor have they proven themselves quick studies in the century since Henry Ford invented the Model A. Roughly 7,000 of Colorado's half-million deer are hit by cars every year, causing $3 million in damage.

The best way to avoid deer is to slow down considerably at night, when it's nearly impossible to detect their approach. (Deer are most active at dawn and dusk but can be encountered any time.) During winter, watch for groups of them browsing just below the snow line. If a deer crosses the road in front of you, always assume that a second one is trailing.

Deer aren't the only animals to watch out for. At high elevations, you may encounter bighorn sheep and elk. Pronghorn antelope roam the grasslands and valleys. And, though most of the rangeland in Colorado is fenced, cows do sometimes shamble onto the pavement.

Getting the best deal on a rental car

Car-rental rates vary even more than airline fares. The price depends on the size of the car, the length of time you keep it, where and when you pick it up and drop it off, where you take it, and a host of other factors. The following list suggests a few ways to save you hundreds of dollars:

- ✔ Weekend rates may be lower than weekday rates. If you're keeping the car five or more days, a weekly rate may be cheaper than the daily rate. Ask if the rate is the same for pickup Friday morning as it is Thursday night.

- ✔ Some companies may assess a drop-off charge if you don't return the car to the same rental location; others, notably National, don't.

- ✔ Check whether the rate is cheaper if you pick up the car at a location in town rather than at the airport.

- ✔ Find out whether age is an issue. Many car-rental companies add on a fee for drivers under 25; some don't rent to them at all.

- ✔ If you see an advertised price in your local newspaper, be sure to ask for that specific rate; otherwise you may be charged the standard (higher) rate. Don't forget to mention membership in AAA, AARP, and trade unions. These memberships usually entitle you to discounts ranging from 5 to 30 percent.

- ✔ Check your frequent-flier accounts. Not only are your favorite (or at least most-used) airlines likely to have sent you discount coupons, but most car rentals add at least 500 miles to your account.

- ✔ As with other aspects of planning your trip, using the Internet can make comparison shopping for a car rental much easier. You can check rates at most of the major agencies' Web sites. Plus, all the major travel sites — **Travelocity** (www.travelocity.com), **Expedia** (www.expedia.com), **Orbitz** (www.orbitz.com), and **Smarter Living** (www.smarterliving.com), for example — have search engines that can dig up discounted car-rental rates. Just enter the car size you want, the pickup and return dates, and location, and the server returns a price. You can even make the reservation through any of these sites.

In addition to the standard rental prices, other optional charges apply to most car rentals (and some not-so-optional charges, such as taxes). The *Collision Damage Waiver* (CDW), which requires you to pay for damage to the car in a collision, is covered by many credit card companies. Check with your credit card company before you go so you can avoid paying this hefty fee (as much as $20 a day).

The car-rental companies also offer additional *liability insurance* (if you harm others in an accident), *personal accident insurance* (if you harm yourself or your passengers), and *personal effects insurance* (if your luggage is stolen from your car). Your insurance policy on your car at home

Before you rent that SUV . . .

So, you're renting a car and heading for the mountains. Any season of the year, you know you'll be in some of the most rugged country you've ever seen. You're going to need an SUV, right?

Not so fast. Unless you know you're going to spend a lot of time in the most extreme, backcountry, unpaved parts of the state, you just aren't going to need an SUV. The Colorado state government has spent a *lot* of time and money building good roads to all the best parts of the state, and this is especially true for all the major tourist areas. An economy car, wagon, or sedan big enough to comfortably hold you and your stuff will be just fine. In fact, there are many disadvantages to SUVs when compared to smaller cars:

✔ In snow, that four-wheel-drive can help you get going, *but it's not going to help you **stop***. And that's when you really need control. The security that SUVs supposedly give is an illusion, and a snowstorm is no time to discover that you've rented something you can't control.

✔ Take it from someone (me!) who's rolled an SUV on a snowy mountain pass — they're top-heavy and very easy to roll. You're better off with a low center of gravity, front-wheel drive, good tires, and chains.

✔ Gas prices are higher in the mountains, and there's a lot of territory to cover. Don't spend money needlessly filling the tank of some behemoth that only gets 12 miles to the gallon. Remember also that more fuel consumption causes more pollution, and one of Colorado's greatest assets is the clean air.

✔ An SUV with a V-6 won't go appreciably faster over the high passes than a four-cylinder sedan. Those roads are pretty curvy, so you have to carefully control your speed anyway, and the extra torque from a big engine can sometimes be a detriment on dirt roads or snow, especially when turning.

✔ Because you're sitting higher above the pavement in an SUV, you get the illusion that you're moving more slowly than you actually are. It can be really easy to accelerate beyond a safe speed because you're not used to the vehicle.

✔ If, God forbid, you're in a wreck, an SUV will certainly cause a bigger, more dangerous, and much more expensive wreck than a smaller car will. SUVs are also harder for other drivers to see around, and on the mountain roads where you're dealing with blind curves, rockfall, snow, and other hazards, it's critical that everyone on the road be able to see as much as possible.

✔ The money you save renting, fueling, and insuring a smaller car instead of an SUV will buy a *very* nice meal or two. Remember that you can easily rent a Jeep for an afternoon in places like Ouray and Lake City, if you feel like off-roading there, and the cost for that is much lower than renting an SUV for the whole trip.

So play it safe, save money, and keep Colorado's roads safer and cleaner for everyone. Don't rent a car bigger than you really need.

probably covers most of these unlikely occurrences. However, if your own insurance doesn't cover you for rentals or if you don't have auto insurance, definitely consider the additional coverage (ask your car-rental agent for more information). Unless you're toting around the Hope diamond, and you don't want to leave that in your car trunk anyway, you can probably skip the personal effects insurance, but driving around without liability or personal accident coverage is never a good idea. Even if you're a good driver, other people may not be, and liability claims can be complicated.

Some companies also offer *refueling packages,* in which you pay for your initial full tank of gas up front, and can return the car with an empty gas tank. The prices can be competitive with local gas prices, but you don't get credit for any gas remaining in the tank. If you reject this option, you pay only for the gas you use, but you have to return the car with a full tank or face charges of $3 to $4 a gallon for any shortfall. If you usually run late and a fueling stop may make you miss your plane, you're a perfect candidate for the fuel-purchase option.

Winging It

Flying to airports in western Colorado is an appealing option when mountain highways become snow-covered or crowded. Many small Colorado airports offer daily commuter service to and from Denver, and some have nonstop flights to and from destinations outside Colorado. The most active in-state carrier, **United Express** (☎ 800-241-6522; www.ual.com), provides commuter service between Denver and Durango, Grand Junction, Montrose, Steamboat Springs, and Telluride.

The commuter service may be convenient, but it isn't necessarily cheap. Round-trip fares from Denver to Durango in the 2005 ski season averaged $250 per person.

If the southwestern part of the state (the Four Corners, Telluride area) is your only Colorado destination, consider taking advantage of **Southwest Airlines's** (☎ 505-244-7780; www.southwest.com) low fares and flying into Albuquerque, New Mexico, then renting a car and driving up.

If you fly all the way to one of Colorado's mountain towns, you may find that you don't need a car at all. Towns such as Aspen, Telluride, Winter Park, Vail, Crested Butte, and Steamboat all have free bus systems and are very pedestrian-friendly.

Riding the Rails

Amtrak's (☎ 800-USA-RAIL; www.amtrak.com) California Zephyr train works better as a way of getting *to* Colorado than as a way to get *around* it. The train stops in some intriguing locales, including downtown Denver's

Union Station, Fraser (near the Winter Park Resort), Glenwood Springs, and Grand Junction. But if you want to keep your costs down, you'll probably have to choose a single destination when traveling by rail, and then drive or figure out another way to get around from there.

Taking the Bus

Greyhound/Trailways (☎ **888-454-7277;** www.greyhound.com) provides bus service to most Colorado destinations, though some remote places aren't served. Greyhound also sells a **Discovery Pass** entitling users to unlimited bus travel in the U.S. for periods ranging from seven days (cost: $219) to 60 days (cost: $589). Pass holders can get off the bus and sightsee for a day, and then catch a bus passing through later. The passes can be bought through a travel agent or online at Greyhound's Web site.

Before splurging on a Discovery Pass, however, you should ask yourself two questions: First, given the comfort level, shouldn't they be paying *you* to ride the bus? And second, given some of the tough neighborhoods where these buses tend to stop, are you sure you want to get off?

Chapter 8

Booking Your Accommodations

· ·

In This Chapter

▶ Choosing your lodgings
▶ Avoiding the rack rate
▶ Browsing the Internet for a better rate
▶ Booking the best room

· ·

The good news is that Colorado has a number of accommodations selections for you to choose from, no matter what your budget or interests. This chapter sums up a few of your lodging options in Colorado and then goes over a few different ways to save money when you're ready to book, no matter where you choose to stay.

Lining Up Your Lodging Choices

In Colorado, the accommodations you choose can set the tone for your vacation. You can have a Western experience at a ranch, simplify life at a mom and pop motel, luxuriate in one of the fancy hotels, or immerse yourself in history (and sometimes acquire a temporary family) at a B&B. I give you the lowdown on the major types of accommodations available to Colorado visitors in these sections.

Booking a B&B

Colorado has dozens of B&Bs, many of which offer surprisingly good value. If you take a room with a shared bath — and these are often great rooms — you can usually stay at a B&B for less than the price of a chain hotel. You stay in cozy (and often historic) surroundings, enjoy a full complimentary breakfast, and get to know your hosts and some fellow travelers. Some B&Bs have ultraluxurious rooms and modern amenities such as steam showers, jetted baths, and TV/VCRs; others have hardly changed in a hundred years.

Not all B&Bs allow kids on the premises, so ask about this if you're planning your family vacation. You should also avoid B&Bs if you or your kids are rowdy, if you're on a tight schedule that means arriving late or leaving early, or if you simply want some downtime alone.

But if these exceptions aren't an issue, then bed-and-breakfasts are a great deal. Many of the state's B&Bs are written up in this book; others can be located through the **Bed & Breakfast Innkeepers of Colorado** (☎ **800-265-7696;** www.innsofcolorado.org).

Bunking down at a motel

The privately owned mom and pop motels in Colorado are often bright, clean, and reasonably priced. And they're only slightly less historic than the state's many Victorian B&Bs. Many Colorado motels date to the 1920s and 1930s, when car travel first became popular in the West. Because they're old, and because every owner is different, ask to see a room before settling in. After you're in, however, you can enjoy the solitude and convenience that a motel provides. Carry your bags a few yards from your trunk to your room, fetch some ice cubes and a soda, turn on the TV, and float downstream.

Staying at historic or luxury hotels

Colorado has two world-famous, historic luxury hotels. **The Brown Palace** in Denver and **The Broadmoor** in Colorado Springs have turned lodging into an art form. Elsewhere in Colorado are many less-expensive historic hotels that provide equally memorable experiences for travelers.

One caveat: At the most luxurious hotels, whether they're historic or not, you not only pay an expensive room rate, but you also have to tip for the many services provided. At some places, you can't even get ice cubes on your own, and you're discouraged from carrying your own bags. For people with bulging bank accounts, this can be paradise, but it may not feel that way if you're on a more modest budget.

Choosing a chain

Chain hotels are like your favorite pair of socks; they offer comfort with few surprises. If you've stayed often enough at a particular chain, then you'll probably know ahead of time what color scheme and amenities to expect inside your room (although some chains do offer unique properties). In general, I like staying at chains. They wouldn't be such a popular option if their rooms weren't pleasant. And they're really great for control freaks. Yet, they do have their limitations. Colorado offers many other options that will color your experience in ways that chain hotels won't, and it would be a shame not to experience at least a few of these less-predictable properties. For the Web sites and phone numbers of the most popular chains in the U.S., see the appendix.

Going to a guest ranch or dude ranch

With at least 40 officially recognized guest and dude ranches, you could say that Colorado has made a cottage industry of ranches. Other than their both being out in the sticks, guest ranches and dude ranches have little in common. Guest ranches tend to operate more like motels: You can often pay by the night, and few services are included in your room rate. Dude ranches are more likely to charge a set amount for an all-inclusive week that includes accommodations, meals, activities that may range from a gentle hay ride to robust whitewater rafting, and sometimes even your own horse (for the requisite horseback riding found at most ranches). Some dude ranches are ultraluxurious; others are rustic working ranches where you can help with roundups and other chores (the complete *City Slickers* works). For more information on dude and guest ranches in Colorado, contact the **Colorado Dude & Guest Ranch Association** (☎ **970-887-3128;** www.coloradoranch.com).

Camping out

Although I don't cover many Colorado campgrounds in this book, you should know that they're great options if you have the right gear. Campgrounds can be found in Colorado's national forests, national parks, state parks, and on private land. Most have drinking water and toilets; some have showers, too. You can make reservations for some, but most are first-come, first served. The going rate for a tent site at most campgrounds is $10 to $15, making this a fabulous option for those on a shoestring budget. You can also camp for free inside any of the national forests in Colorado, provided you follow a few simple regulations. Stop by any Forest Service office for details or surf the Internet to www.fs.fed.us.

Finding the Best Room at the Best Rate

The **rack rate** is the maximum rate a hotel charges for a room. It's the rate you get if you walk in off the street and ask for a room for the night. You sometimes see these rates printed on the fire/emergency exit diagrams posted on the back of your door.

Hotels are happy to charge you the rack rate, but you can almost always do better. Perhaps the best way to avoid paying the rack rate is surprisingly simple: Just ask for a cheaper or discounted rate. You may be pleasantly surprised.

In all but the smallest accommodations, the rate you pay for a room depends on many factors — chief among them being how you make your reservation. A travel agent may be able to negotiate a better price with certain hotels than you can get by yourself. (That's because the hotel often gives the agent a discount in exchange for steering his or her business toward that hotel.)

Reserving a room through the hotel's toll-free number may also result in a lower rate than calling the hotel directly. On the other hand, the central reservations number may not know about discount rates at specific locations. For example, local franchises may offer a special group rate for a wedding or family reunion, but they may neglect to tell the central booking line. Your best bet is to call both the local number and the toll-free number and see which one gives you a better deal.

Room rates (even rack rates) change with the season, as occupancy rates rise and fall.

In this book, I use dollar signs to help you quickly determine a price range for a hotel you're interested in. Table 8-1 shows you what you can expect in each price category. Prices are based on double occupancy for one night during high season.

Table 8-1	Key to Hotel Dollar Signs	
Dollar Sign(s)	**Price Range**	**What to Expect**
$	$75 or less	These accommodations are relatively simple and inexpensive. Rooms are likely to be small, and televisions are not necessarily provided. Parking is not provided but rather catch-as-you-can on the street.
$$	$76–$125	A bit classier, these mid-range accommodations offer more room, more extras (such as irons, hair dryers, or a microwave), and a more convenient location than the preceding category.
$$$	$126–$175	Higher-class still, these accommodations begin to look plush. Think chocolates on your pillow, a classy restaurant, underground parking garages, maybe even expansive views of the water.
$$$$	$176 and up	These top-rated accommodations come with luxury amenities such as valet parking, on-premise spas, and in-room hot tubs and CD players — but you pay through the nose for them.

Although rates for accommodations in Denver and the rest of the Front Range remain fairly consistent year-round, the High Country seasons are summer (Memorial Day through Labor Day) and winter (mid-November through early April). In between are the **shoulder seasons,** and these are the times to get the best rates, the least crowds, and the most tranquility. Your outdoor recreation options may be spotty, though, because it's usually too cold for anything but skiing, but there's not much snow. See Chapter 3 for more information about the seasons and weather in Colorado.

But even within a given season, room prices are subject to change without notice, so the rates quoted in this book may be different from the actual rate you receive when you make your reservation. Be sure to mention membership in AAA, AARP, frequent flyer programs, or any other corporate rewards programs you can think of — or your Uncle Joe's Elks lodge in which you're an honorary inductee, for that matter — when you call to book. You never know when the affiliation may be worth a few dollars off your room rate.

Package tours and escorted tours can be great ways to save on lodging, as well; see Chapter 6 for more information.

Surfing the Web for hotel deals

Shopping online for hotels is generally done one of two ways: by booking through the hotel's own Web site or through an independent booking agency (or a fare-service agency such as Priceline). These Internet hotel agencies have multiplied in mind-boggling numbers of late, competing for the business of millions of consumers surfing for accommodations around the world. This competitiveness can be a boon to consumers who have the patience and time to shop and compare the online sites for good deals — but shop you must, for prices can vary considerably from site to site. And keep in mind that hotels at the top of a site's listing may be there for no other reason than that they paid money to get the placement.

Of the major travel Web sites, **Expedia** offers a long list of special deals and *virtual tours,* or photos of available rooms, so that you can see what you're paying for (a feature that helps counter the claims that the best rooms are often held back from bargain booking Web sites). **Travelocity** posts unvarnished customer reviews and ranks its properties according to the AAA rating system. **Orbitz** features a handy tool to let you search for specific amenities you may be interested in. Also reliable are **Hotels.com** and **Quikbook.com**. An excellent free program, **TravelAxe** (www.travelaxe.net), can help you search multiple hotel sites at once, even ones you may never have heard of — and conveniently lists the total price of the room, including the taxes and service charges. Another booking site, **Travelweb** (www.travelweb.com), is partly owned by the hotels it represents (including the Hilton, Hyatt, and Starwood chains) and is therefore plugged directly into the hotels' reservations systems — unlike independent online agencies, which have to fax or e-mail reservation requests to the hotel, a good portion of which get misplaced in the shuffle. More than once, travelers have arrived at the hotel only to be told that they have no reservation. To be fair, many of the major sites are undergoing improvements in service and ease of use, and Expedia will soon be able to plug directly into the reservations systems of many hotel chains — none of which can be bad news for consumers. In the meantime, it's a good idea to get a confirmation number and make a printout of any online booking transaction.

In the opaque Web site category, **Priceline** and **Hotwire** are even better for hotels than for airfares; with both, you're allowed to pick the neighborhood and quality level of your hotel before offering up your money. Priceline's hotel product even covers Europe and Asia, though it's much better at getting 5-star lodging for 3-star prices than at finding anything at the bottom of the scale. On the down side, many hotels stick Priceline guests in their least desirable rooms. Be sure to go to the Biddingfor-Travel Web site (www.biddingfortravel.com) before bidding on a hotel room on Priceline; it features a fairly up-to-date list of hotels that Priceline uses in major cities. For both Priceline and Hotwire, you pay upfront, and the fee is nonrefundable. *Note:* Some hotels do not provide loyalty program credits or points or other frequent-stay amenities when you book a room through opaque online services.

Reserving the best room

After you make your reservation, asking one or two more pointed questions can go a long way toward making sure you get the best room in the house. Always ask for a corner room. They're usually larger, quieter, and have more windows and light than standard rooms, and they don't always cost more. Also ask if the hotel is renovating; if it is, request a room away from the renovation work. Inquire, too, about the location of the restaurants, bars, and discos in the hotel — all sources of annoying noise. And if you aren't happy with your room when you arrive, talk to the front desk. If they have another room, they should be happy to accommodate you, within reason.

Chapter 9

Catering to Special Travel Needs or Interests

. . . .

In This Chapter

▶ Meeting the travel needs of families
▶ Uncovering tips for seniors
▶ Breaking down barriers for travelers with disabilities
▶ Navigating Colorado: Tips for gays and lesbians

. . . .

*W*hen I talk about people with special interests, I don't mean opera buffs or model-airplane builders. I'm referring to people for whom travel presents some unique challenges and opportunities that other travelers may not face. In this chapter, I offer some valuable travel-specific advice for families traveling with children, older travelers, persons with a disability, and gay and lesbian travelers.

Traveling with the Brood: Advice for Families

If you have enough trouble getting your kids out of the house in the morning, dragging them thousands of miles away may seem like an insurmountable challenge. But family travel can be immensely rewarding, giving you new ways of seeing the world through smaller pairs of eyes.

Your family can have fun anywhere in the state, but if you want a little help with your kids now and then, the ski towns are among the best places to be. In the past 20 years, the ski areas have shifted their focus from attracting rowdy baby-boomer partiers to luring responsible baby-boomer families. All the resort areas offer reduced-price lift tickets for children, and many allow young children to ski and snowboard for free.

The ski zones also have family-friendly activities off the slopes. Most resort towns now have ice-skating, tubing, and sleigh rides, among other options. And in summer, certain ski areas become full-on fun centers for kids, complete with mazes, alpine slides, mountain biking, horseback riding, and trampolines.

You also benefit from strong support systems for families, such as learn-to-ski programs for small children, high-quality day care, and baby sitting. None of it is cheap, but it is generally reliable. Day care at a ski area usually costs around $80 per day (8:30 a.m. – 4:30 p.m.). All-day children's supervised skiing programs, including lessons and lift tickets, average around $80; add $20 or so for programs that include equipment.

People of all ages get dehydrated, sunburned, and tired much faster in the mountains. You'll feel the effects yourself if you don't drink enough water, wear sunscreen, and conserve energy. However, your kids are far more likely than you are to air their discontent. Use these tips to help keep the kids happy when traveling in the mountains:

- ✔ Protect them from dehydration by giving your kids water bottles and making sure they drink a lot.

- ✔ Keep them slathered in sunscreen when you're spending any time outdoors, even in winter — children burn far more easily than adults. Give them floppy hats and sunglasses with 100 percent UV protection — and encourage them to keep them on. And remember that most of the skin-cancer-causing sun exposure happens before age 12.

- ✔ Make sure your kids eat regularly when engaged in active pursuits. Pack healthy snacks such as fruits, vegetables, and trail mix.

- ✔ Dress them in layers of synthetic fabrics such as polypropylene and polar fleece during cold weather. Avoid cotton, which provides no insulation when wet.

- ✔ Set aside an hour or so in the afternoon for resting, whether it's in your room or at a scenic, quiet, natural setting.

- ✔ Let your kids pick many or most of the activities your family engages in. Because Colorado has so many activities that are enjoyable for both parents and kids, this isn't as painful as it may sound.

- ✔ Plan a few Colorado-specific car activities. For example, buy a field guide and encourage your kids to check off animal species they see during the trip.

- ✔ Take advantage of the kid-friendly activities and programs in many of the national parks and set aside some time to let your kids experience some of them.

Familyhostel (☎ **800-733-9753**; www.learn.unh.edu/familyhostel) takes the whole family, including kids ages 8 to 15, on moderately priced domestic and international learning vacations. Lectures, field trips, and sightseeing are guided by a team of academics.

You can find good family-oriented vacation advice on the Internet from sites such as the **Family Travel Forum** (www.familytravelforum.com), a comprehensive site that offers customized trip planning; **Family Travel Network** (www.familytravelnetwork.com), an award-winning site that offers travel features, deals, and tips; **Traveling Internationally with Your Kids** (www.travelwithyourkids.com), a comprehensive site that offers customized trip planning; and **Family Travel Files** (www.the familytravelfiles.com), which offers an online magazine and a directory of off-the-beaten-path tours and tour operators for families.

Making Age Work for You: Advice for Seniors

Though Colorado is plenty rugged, senior travelers won't have a difficult time here. Driving in the mountains can be grueling and dangerous for anyone, regardless of age, but it's something seniors will want to take into consideration when planning their vacation here; luckily, trains, busses, shuttles, and cabs make things worry-free, and many, especially shuttles, have discounts for seniors.

Mention the fact that you're a senior citizen when you make your travel reservations. Although all the major U.S. airlines except America West have cancelled their senior discount and coupon book programs, many hotels still offer discounts for seniors. In most cities, people over the age of 60 qualify for reduced admission to theaters, museums, and other attractions, as well as discounted fares on public transportation.

Members of **AARP** (formerly known as the American Association of Retired Persons), 601 E St. NW, Washington, DC 20049 (☎ **888-687-2277** or 202-434-2277; www.aarp.org), get discounts on hotels, airfares, and car rentals. AARP offers members a wide range of benefits, including _AARP The Magazine_ and a monthly newsletter. Anyone over 50 can join.

The **U.S. National Park Service** offers a **Golden Age Passport** for a one-time processing fee of $10. The passport gives seniors 62 years or older lifetime entrance to all properties administered by the National Park Service — national parks, monuments, historic sites, recreation areas, and national wildlife refuges. You must make the purchase in person at any NPS facility that charges an entrance fee. Besides free entry, a Golden Age Passport also offers a 50 percent discount on federal-use fees charged for such facilities as camping, swimming, parking, boat launching, and tours. For more information, go online to www.nps.gov/fees_passes.htm or call ☎ **888-467-2757.**

Elderhostel (☎ **877-426-8056;** www.elderhostel.org) arranges study programs for those aged 55 and over (and a spouse or companion of any age) in the United States and in more than 80 countries around the world. Most courses last five to seven days in the United States (2–4 weeks abroad), and many include airfare, accommodations in university dormitories or modest inns, meals, and tuition.

Recommended publications offering travel resources and discounts for seniors include: the quarterly magazine _Travel 50 & Beyond_ (www.travel50andbeyond.com); _Travel Unlimited: Uncommon Adventures for the Mature Traveler_ (Avalon); _101 Tips for Mature Travelers,_ available from Grand Circle Travel (☎ **800-221-2610** or 617-350-7500; www.gct.com); *The 50+ Traveler's Guidebook* (St. Martin's Press); and *Unbelievably Good Deals and Great Adventures That You Absolutely Can't Get Unless You're Over 50* (McGraw-Hill), by Joan Rattner Heilman.

Accessing Colorado: Advice for Travelers with Disabilities

Most disabilities shouldn't stop anyone from traveling. There are more options and resources out there than ever before.

Alas, the backcountry is pretty inhospitable to wheelchairs, but there has been a major effort in recent years to create wheelchair-accessible trails. The national parks here (Rocky Mountain National Park, Mesa Verde National Park, and Great Sand Dunes National Park & Preserve, to name the biggest) all have activities and facilities for the disabled. Also, Web sites such as Achievable Concepts (www.achievableconcepts.us) sell adaptive devices for fishing, hiking, and even water- and snow-skiing! So don't discount an active vacation here.

The U.S. National Park Service offers a **Golden Access Passport** that gives free lifetime entrance to all properties administered by the National Park Service — national parks, monuments, historic sites, recreation areas, and national wildlife refuges — for persons who are visually impaired or permanently disabled, regardless of age. You may pick up a Golden Access Passport at any NPS entrance fee area by showing proof of medically determined disability and eligibility for receiving benefits under federal law. Besides free entry, the Golden Access Passport also offers a 50 percent discount on federal-use fees charged for such facilities as camping, swimming, parking, boat launching, and tours. For more information, go online to www.nps.gov/fees_passes. htm or call ☎ **888-467-2757.**

Many travel agencies offer customized tours and itineraries for travelers with disabilities. **Flying Wheels Travel** (☎ **507-451-5005;** www.flying wheelstravel.com) offers escorted tours and cruises that emphasize sports and private tours in minivans with lifts. **Access-Able Travel Source** (☎ **303-232-2979;** www.access-able.com) offers extensive access information and advice for traveling around the world with disabilities. **Accessible Journeys** (☎ **800-846-4537** or 610-521-0339; www. disabilitytravel.com) assists wheelchair travelers and their families and friends.

Avis Rent a Car has an Avis Access program that offers such services as a dedicated 24-hour toll-free number (☎ **888-879-4273;** www.avis.com) for customers with special travel needs; special car features such as swivel seats, spinner knobs, and hand controls; and accessible bus service.

Organizations that offer assistance to disabled travelers include
MossRehab (www.mossresourcenet.org), which provides a library of
accessible-travel resources online; **SATH (Society for Accessible Travel
and Hospitality)** (☎ 212-447-7284; www.sath.org; annual membership
fees: $45 adults, $30 seniors and students), which offers a wealth of
travel resources for all types of disabilities and informed recommendations on destinations, access guides, travel agents, tour operators, vehicle rentals, and companion services; and the **American Foundation for
the Blind** (AFB) (☎ 800-232-5463; www.afb.org), a referral resource for
the blind or visually impaired that includes information on traveling with
guide dogs.

For more information specifically targeted to travelers with disabilities,
the community Web site **iCan** (www.icanonline.net/channels/
travel/index.cfm) has destination guides and several regular columns
on accessible travel. Also check out the quarterly magazine **Emerging
Horizons** ($14.95 per year, $19.95 outside the U.S.; www.emerging
horizons.com)*;* **Twin Peaks Press** (☎ 360-694-2462; http://
disabilitybookshop.virtualave.net/blist84.htm), which
offers travel-related books for travelers with special needs; and *Open
World Magazine,* published by SATH (subscription: $13 per year,
$21 outside the United States).

Following the Rainbow: Advice for Gay and Lesbian Travelers

Colorado, contrary to its reputation as a so-called "red state" that's dominated by the activities of conservative Christian groups, is a very gay-
friendly place. Denver has an enormous gay population centered around
the Capitol Hill and Baker neighborhoods; the bi-weekly *H ink Magazine*
(☎ 303-752-4300) is a prominent news and lifestyle publication for
Denver's gay and lesbian community. Boulder and Aspen are also traditionally very friendly places — Aspen has a great Gay and Lesbian Ski
Week. In the more remote parts of the state, you may find a little hostil-
ity, but in any of the established ski towns you will feel quite comfortable. Colorado as a whole has a proud libertarian tradition that
emphasizes neighborliness over philosophical differences, and all travelers should feel at home here.

The International Gay and Lesbian Travel Association (IGLTA) (☎ 800-
448-8550 or 954-776-2626; www.iglta.org) is the trade association for
the gay and lesbian travel industry, and offers an online directory of gay-
and lesbian-friendly travel businesses; go to their Web site and click on
Members.

Many agencies offer tours and travel itineraries specifically for gay and
lesbian travelers. **Above and Beyond Tours** (☎ 800-397-2681; www.
abovebeyondtours.com) is the exclusive gay and lesbian tour operator

for United Airlines. **Now, Voyager** (☎ 800-255-6951; www.nowvoyager. com) is a well-known San Francisco–based gay-owned and -operated travel service. **Olivia Cruises & Resorts** (☎ 800-631-6277 or 510-655-0364; www.olivia.com) charters entire resorts and ships for exclusive lesbian vacations and offers smaller group experiences for both gay and lesbian travelers.

The following travel guides are available at most travel bookstores and gay and lesbian bookstores, or you can order them from **Giovanni's Room** bookstore, 1145 Pine St., Philadelphia, PA 19107 (☎ 215-923-2960; www.giovannisroom.com): *Frommer's Gay & Lesbian Europe,* an excellent travel resource (www.frommers.com); *Out and About* (☎ 800-929-2268 or 415-644-8044; www.outandabout.com), which offers guidebooks and a newsletter ($20/yr; ten issues) packed with solid information on the global gay and lesbian scene; *Spartacus International Gay Guide* (Bruno Gmünder Verlag; www.spartacusworld.com/gay guide/) and *Odysseus,* both good, annual English-language guidebooks focused on gay men; the *Damron* guides (www.damron.com), with separate, annual books for gay men and lesbians; and *Gay Travel A to Z: The World of Gay & Lesbian Travel Options at Your Fingertips* by Marianne Ferrari (Ferrari International; Box 35575, Phoenix, AZ 85069), a very good gay and lesbian guidebook series.

Chapter 10

Taking Care of the Remaining Details

· ·

In This Chapter

▶ Insuring your bundles, bags, and body

▶ Handling health problems on the road

▶ Staying in touch by phone and by Internet

▶ Knowing what to expect at the airport

· ·

*T*his chapter deals with the little things that people tend to put off until the last minute before leaving on a trip, such as buying trip insurance, preparing for illness on the road, making sure you stay connected (if you absolutely need to), and even what to expect should your trip take you through the airport security maze.

Playing It Safe with Travel and Medical Insurance

Three kinds of travel insurance are available: trip-cancellation insurance, medical insurance, and lost luggage insurance. The cost of travel insurance varies widely, depending on the cost and length of your trip, your age and health, and the type of trip you're taking, but expect to pay between 5 and 8 percent of the cost of the vacation itself. Here is my advice on all three:

✔ **Trip-cancellation insurance** helps you get your money back if you have to back out of a trip, if you have to go home early, or if your travel supplier goes bankrupt. Allowed reasons for cancellation can range from sickness to natural disasters to the State Department declaring your destination unsafe for travel. (Insurers usually won't cover vague fears, though, as many travelers discovered who tried to cancel their trips in October 2001 because they were wary of flying.)

A good resource is **Travel Guard Alerts,** a list of companies considered high-risk by Travel Guard International (www.travelguard.com). Protect yourself further by paying for the insurance with a credit card — by law, consumers can get their money back on goods and services not received if they report the loss within 60 days after the charge is listed on their credit card statement.

Note: Many tour operators, particularly those offering trips to remote or high-risk areas, include insurance in the cost of the trip or can arrange insurance policies through a partnering provider, a convenient and often cost-effective way to obtain insurance. Make sure the tour company is a reputable one, however: Some experts suggest you avoid buying insurance from the tour or cruise company you're traveling with, saying it's better to buy from a third-party insurer than to put all your money in one place.

✔ For domestic travel, buying **medical insurance** for your trip doesn't make sense for most travelers. Most existing health policies cover you if you get sick away from home — but check before you go, particularly if you're insured by an HMO.

✔ **Lost luggage insurance** is not necessary for most travelers. On domestic flights, checked baggage is covered up to $2,500 per ticketed passenger. On international flights (including U.S. portions of international trips), baggage coverage is limited to approximately $9.07 per pound, up to approximately $635 per checked bag. If you plan to check items more valuable than the standard liability, see if your valuables are covered by your homeowner's policy or get baggage insurance as part of your comprehensive travel-insurance package. Also, many policies purchased through Travel Guard International include access to its baggage-tracking service. Don't buy insurance at the airport, as it's usually overpriced. Be sure to take any valuables or irreplaceable items with you in your carry-on luggage, as many valuables (including books, money, and electronics) aren't covered by airline policies.

If your luggage is lost, immediately file a lost-luggage claim at the airport, detailing the luggage contents. For most airlines, you must report delayed, damaged, or lost baggage within four hours of arrival. Airlines are required to deliver luggage, once found, directly to your house or destination free of charge.

For more information, contact one of the following recommended insurers: **Access America** (☎ 866-807-3982; www.accessamerica.com); **Travel Guard International** (☎ 800-826-4919; www.travelguard.com); **Travel Insured International** (☎ 800-243-3174; www.travelinsured.com); and **Travelex Insurance Services** (☎ 888-457-4602; www.travelex-insurance.com).

Staying Healthy When You Travel

Getting sick will ruin your vacation, so I *strongly* advise against it (of course, last time I checked, the bugs weren't listening to me any more than they probably listen to you).

Talk to your doctor before leaving on a trip if you have a serious and/ or chronic illness. For conditions such as epilepsy, diabetes, or heart problems, wear a **MedicAlert identification tag** (☎ **888-633-4298;** www. medicalert.org), which immediately alerts doctors to your condition and gives them access to your records through Medic Alert's 24-hour hotline. Contact the **International Association for Medical Assistance to Travelers (IAMAT)** (☎ **716-754-4883** or, in Canada, 416-652-0137; www. iamat.org) for tips on travel and health concerns in the countries you're visiting, and lists of local, English-speaking doctors. The United States **Centers for Disease Control and Prevention** (☎ **800-311-3435;** www.cdc.gov) provides up-to-date information on health hazards by region or country and offers tips on food safety.

Staying Connected by Cellphone

For travelers visiting Colorado from other parts of the United States, keep in mind that just because your cellphone works at home doesn't mean it'll work elsewhere in the country (thanks to our nation's fragmented cellphone system). It's a good bet that your phone will work in major cities. But take a look at your wireless company's coverage map on its Web site before heading out — T-Mobile, Sprint, and Nextel are particularly weak in rural areas. If you need to stay in touch at a destination where you know your phone won't work, **rent** a phone that does from **InTouch USA** (☎ **800-872-7626;** www.intouchglobal.com) or from a rental-car location, but beware that you'll pay $1 a minute or more for airtime.

Cellphones are darn-near useless in the mountains, except in wealthier towns such as Aspen and Vail. If you get a signal at all, you'll probably be roaming, so think about that when you're budgeting for your trip.

If you're venturing deep into national parks or the backcountry, you may want to consider renting a **satellite phone (satphone),** which is different from a cellphone in that it connects to satellites rather than to ground-based towers. A satphone is more costly than a cellphone but works where there's no cellular signal and no towers. Unfortunately, you'll pay at least $2 per minute to use the phone, and it only works where you can see the horizon (that is, usually not indoors). In North America, you can rent Iridium satellite phones from **RoadPost** (☎ **888-290-1606** or 905-272-5665; www.roadpost.com). InTouch USA offers a wider range of satphones but at higher rates. As of this writing, satphones are very expensive to buy.

If you're not from the U.S., you'll be appalled at the poor reach of our **GSM (Global System for Mobiles) wireless network,** which is used by much of the rest of the world. Your phone will probably work in most major U.S. cities; it definitely won't work in many rural areas. (To find out where GSM phones work in the U.S., check out www.t-mobile.com/ coverage/national_popup.asp). And you may or may not be able to send SMS (text messaging) home — something Americans tend to do less than the rest of the world anyway, for various cultural and technological reasons. (International budget travelers like to send text messages home because it's much cheaper than making international calls.) Assume nothing — call your wireless provider and get the full scoop. In a worst-case scenario, you can always rent a phone; InTouch USA delivers to hotels.

Accessing the Internet away from Home

Travelers have any number of ways to check their e-mail and access the Internet on the road. Of course, using your own laptop — or even a PDA (personal digital assistant) or electronic organizer with a modem — gives you the most flexibility. But even if you don't have a computer, you can still access your e-mail and even your office computer from cyber-cafes.

It's hard nowadays to find a city that *doesn't* have a few cybercafes. Although there's no definitive directory for cybercafes — these are independent businesses, after all — places to start looking are www. cybercaptive.com and www.cybercafe.com.

Aside from formal cybercafes, most **youth hostels** nowadays have at least one computer you can get to the Internet on. And most **public libraries** offer Internet access free or for a small charge. Avoid **hotel business centers** unless you're willing to pay exorbitant rates.

Most major airports now have **Internet kiosks** scattered throughout their gates. These kiosks, which you also see in shopping malls, hotel lobbies, and tourist information offices around the world, give you basic Web access for a per-minute fee that's usually higher than cybercafe prices. The kiosks' clunkiness and high price mean they should be avoided whenever possible.

To retrieve your e-mail, ask your **Internet service provider (ISP)** if it has a Web-based interface tied to your existing e-mail account. If your ISP doesn't have such an interface, you can use the free **mail2web** service (www.mail2web.com) to view and reply to your home e-mail. For more flexibility, you may want to open a free, Web-based e-mail account with **Yahoo! Mail** (http://mail.yahoo.com). (Microsoft's Hotmail is another popular option, but Hotmail has severe spam problems.) Your home ISP may be able to forward your e-mail to the Web-based account automatically.

If you need to access files on your office computer, look into a service called **GoToMyPC** (www.gotomypc.com). The service provides a Web-based interface for you to access and manipulate a distant PC from anywhere — even a cybercafe — provided your target PC is on and has an always-on connection to the Internet (such as with Road Runner cable). The service offers top-quality security, but if you're worried about hackers, use your own laptop rather than a cybercafe computer to access the GoToMyPC system.

If you're bringing your own computer, the buzzword in computer access to familiarize yourself with is **Wi-fi** (wireless fidelity), and more and more hotels, cafes, and retailers are signing on as wireless hot spots from where you can get a high-speed connection without cable wires, networking hardware, or a phone line. You can get a Wi-fi connection one of several ways. Many laptops sold in the last year have built-in Wi-fi capability (an 802.11b wireless Ethernet connection). Mac owners have their own networking technology, Apple AirPort. For those with older computers, you can purchase an 802.11b/**Wi-fi card** (around $50) to plug into your laptop. You sign up for wireless access service much as you do cellphone service, through a plan offered by one of several commercial companies that make wireless service available in airports, hotel lobbies, and coffee shops, primarily in the United States (followed by the United Kingdom and Japan). **T-Mobile Hotspot** (www.t-mobile.com/hotspot) serves up wireless connections at more than 1,000 Starbucks coffee shops nationwide. **Boingo** (www.boingo.com) and **Wayport** (www.wayport.com) have networks in airports and high-class hotel lobbies. IPass providers also give you access to a few hundred wireless hotel lobby setups. Best of all, you don't need to be staying at the Four Seasons to use the hotel's network; just set yourself up on a nice couch in the lobby.

The companies' pricing policies can be byzantine, with a variety of monthly, per-connection, and per-minute plans, but in general you pay around $30 a month for limited access — and as more and more companies jump on the wireless bandwagon, prices are likely to get even more competitive.

There are also places that provide **free wireless networks** in cities around the world. To locate these free hot spots, go to **www.personal telco.net/index.cgi/WirelessCommunities.**

If Wi-fi is not available at your destination, most business-class hotels throughout the world offer dataports for laptop modems, and a few thousand hotels in the United States and Europe now offer free high-speed Internet access using an Ethernet network cable. You can bring your own cables, but most hotels rent them for around $10. **Call your hotel in advance** to see what your options are.

In addition, major Internet service providers (ISP) have **local access numbers** around the world, allowing you to go online by simply placing a local call. Check your ISP's Web site or call its toll-free number and ask how you can use your current account away from home, and how much it costs. If you're traveling outside the reach of your ISP, the **iPass** network has dial-up numbers in most of the world's countries. You'll have to sign up with an iPass provider, who will then tell you how to set up your computer for your destination(s). For a list of iPass providers, go to www.ipass.com and click on Individuals Buy Now. One solid provider is **i2roam** (☎ **866-811-6209** or 920-235-0475; www.i2roam.com).

 Wherever you go, bring a **connection kit** of the right power and phone adapters, a spare phone cord, and a spare Ethernet network cable — or find out whether your hotel supplies them to guests.

Keeping Up with Airline Security

With the federalization of airport security, security procedures at U.S. airports are more stable and consistent than ever. Generally, you'll be fine if you arrive at the airport **one hour** before a domestic flight and **two hours** before an international flight; if you show up late, tell an airline employee and he or she can probably whisk you to the front of the line.

Bring a **current, government-issued photo ID** such as a driver's license or passport. Keep your ID at the ready to show at check-in, the security checkpoint, and sometimes even the gate. (Children under 18 do not need government-issued photo IDs for domestic flights, but they do for international flights to most countries.)

In 2003, the Transportation Security Administration (TSA) phased out **gate check-in** at all U.S. airports. And **E-tickets** have made paper tickets nearly obsolete. Passengers with E-tickets can beat the ticket-counter lines by using airport **electronic kiosks** or even **online check-in** from your home computer. Online check-in involves logging on to your airline's Web site, accessing your reservation, and printing out your boarding pass — and the airline may even offer you bonus miles to do so! If you're using a kiosk at the airport, bring the credit card you used to book the ticket or your frequent-flier card. Print out your boarding pass from the kiosk and simply proceed to the security checkpoint with your pass and a photo ID. If you're checking bags or looking to snag an exit-row seat, you can do so using most airline kiosks. Even the smaller airlines are employing the kiosk system, but always call your airline to make sure these alternatives are available. **Curbside check-in** is also a good way to avoid lines, although a few airlines still ban curbside check-in; again, call before you go. (The appendix has airline phone numbers and Web site addresses.)

Security checkpoint lines are getting shorter than they were during 2001 and 2002, but some doozies remain. If you have trouble standing for long periods of time, tell an airline employee; the airline will provide a wheelchair. Speed up security by **not wearing metal objects** such as big belt buckles. If you have metallic body parts, a note from your doctor can prevent a long chat with the security screeners. Keep in mind that only **ticketed passengers** are allowed past security, except for folks escorting disabled passengers or children.

Federalization has stabilized **what you can carry on** and **what you can't.** The general rule is that sharp things are out, nail clippers are okay, and food and beverages must be passed through the X-ray machine — but that security screeners can't make you drink from your coffee cup. Bring food in your carry-on rather than checking it, as explosive-detection machines used on checked luggage have been known to mistake food (especially chocolate, for some reason) for bombs. Travelers in the United States are allowed one carry-on bag, plus a personal item such as a purse, briefcase, or laptop bag. Carry-on hoarders can stuff all sorts of things into a laptop bag; as long as it has a laptop in it, it's still considered a personal item. The TSA has issued a list of restricted items; check its Web site (www.tsa.gov/public/index.jsp) for details.

Airport screeners may decide that your checked luggage needs to be searched by hand. You can now purchase luggage locks that allow screeners to open and re-lock a checked bag if hand-searching is necessary. Look for Travel Sentry certified locks at luggage or travel shops and Brookstone stores (you can buy them online at www.brookstone.com). These locks, approved by the TSA, can be opened by luggage inspectors with a special code or key. For more information on the locks, visit www.travelsentry.org. If you use something other than TSA-approved locks, your lock will be cut off your suitcase if a TSA agent needs to hand-search your luggage.

Part III
The Front Range

The 5th Wave   By Rich Tennant

GOLFING COLORADO

© RICHTENNANT

In this part . . .

The term "Front Range" refers both to the first large chain of mountains you encounter when traveling from the east; more often, though, it refers to the urban communities along the foothills of those mountains. Chances are this is where you'll start exploring the state. This part tells you how to get to Denver, Boulder, and Colorado Springs, and all the fun you're going to have there. I also throw in a few cool side trips to some of the state's former boomtowns, where you can still pan for gold, and some gambling zones, where you can also try to strike it rich.

Chapter 11

Denver

In This Chapter

▶ Getting there without a hitch
▶ Moving around the city
▶ Finding a room that fits your budget
▶ Experiencing the taste of Denver
▶ The sights and sounds of the city

· ·

*I*f your knowledge of Denver includes the phrase "overgrown cow town," then let this chapter direct you to the modern metropolis that the city is today. Old mining towns up in the high country have turned into multisport resort towns, and Denver is the gateway to all the outdoor adventure you can dream of, winter or summer. Denver gets more days of sunshine per year (over 300) than even San Diego, so you can play outdoors year-round. (Dress warmly in winter, though; the sun might be shining, but it does get cold.) If the weather inside is more to your liking, world-class orchestras, museums, and opera and theatre companies will keep you busy, and touring rock acts, jazz combos, and Broadway shows are always in the mix. This chapter offers details on much of what Denver has to offer — in addition to my recommendations for places to stay and eat.

Getting There

Although Denver's airport is a good distance from the city's downtown core, flying into Denver remains the most efficient manner of getting there. Of course, having a car to help you navigate the city is a good idea, so if driving to Denver is an option for you, you can save on rental-car costs.

Arriving by air

After a rocky beginning, **Denver International Airport** (☎ **800-AIR-2-DEN** [800-247-2336]; www.flydenver.com) — popularly known as **DIA** — now earns accolades for both efficiency and capacity. Located 23 miles northeast of downtown Denver, the $4.3 billion airport has 94 gates and 5 runways in a 53-square-mile area. Nearly all the major domestic airlines fly into DIA, including Alaska, America West, American, Continental, Delta, JetBlue, Northwest, United, and US Airways. A handful of international airlines also offer flights in and out of Denver, including Air Canada, British Airways, and Qantas. (See the Quick Concierge appendix for contact information for these airlines and more.)

The airport's centerpiece is the 1.5-million-square-foot Jeppesen Terminal, whose roof consists of 15 acres of Teflon-coated, woven fiberglass that allows 10 percent of visible light to pass through it. From above, the terminal looks like a city of white tents, though its profile was designed to echo the peaks of the Front Range on the western horizon. The terminal's interior, during daylight hours especially, feels light, spacious, and comfortable.

From Jeppesen Terminal, passengers travel to three concourses, two of which are accessible only via an underground train. (You can also reach Concourse A via a pedestrian bridge that actually passes over a runway.) The train runs every two minutes, and the longest ride lasts under five minutes. The train does, however, get crowded. And if you're late for a flight or trying to make a close connection, it can be disconcerting to take an escalator downstairs and then have to wait around on a platform.

When flying out of DIA, allow a little extra time both for the train and for the trip on foot — or via moving walkway — across one or more airport concourses, the longest of which is 3,300 feet. Also, if you get claustrophobic, bear in mind that the middle car on each train is usually less crowded than the end cars.

Despite having one of the world's most technologically advanced baggage-handling systems, DIA is simply too big for the airlines to instantly produce the baggage you check. You usually have to wait a bit at the carousels, which are located on Terminal Level 5, right across from the hotel and ground transportation information boards. If you're taking commercial transportation to your hotel, grab your bags and then head out the doors on Level 5 to the curbside pick-up areas. If someone in a private vehicle is picking you up, go to Level 4.

Assistance is readily available, and you should have no problems getting answers to questions while at the airport: In addition to DIA information booths in the main terminal and on all three concourses, the Denver Metro Convention and Visitors Bureau has its own information booths in the main terminal and on Concourse B.

For general airport information, call the **Denver International Airport Information Line** at ☎ **800-AIR-2-DEN,** 800-688-1333, or 303-342-2200. For **ground transportation,** the number is ☎ **303-342-4059.** When you have your bags and your bearings, you can choose from a number of options to get you from DIA to your accommodations.

Renting a car

All the major rental-car companies are represented at DIA, so you're bound to find your favorite here. The list includes **Advantage, Alamo, Avis, Budget, Dollar, Enterprise, Hertz, National, Payless,** and **Thrifty.** For information on contacting individual car-rental agencies, see the Quick Concierge appendix.

To reach the downtown Denver area, exit the airport onto Trussville Street and go southwest for about ¼ mile. Bear left onto Pena Boulevard and go southwest for another 10 miles. Continue on the ramp and go southwest for 1¼ miles. Follow I-70 west for 9 miles, and take the exit that brings you closest to your destination.

Taking a shuttle or cab

Dozens of private companies provide shuttle service from DIA to points throughout Colorado. One reliable service linking DIA with Denver's downtown area is **SuperShuttle** (☎ **800-525-3177** or 303-370-1300; www. supershuttle.com). You don't need a reservation to take SuperShuttle from the airport to your hotel. Tell the representative at the Super Shuttle desk near baggage claim that you'd like a ride. You'll probably have to wait 20 to 30 minutes, and the driver may drop off other passengers before you, but the per-person cost to most downtown hotels is a reasonable $18. For your return trip to the airport, make sure to call SuperShuttle for a reservation at least 24 hours in advance.

Three taxi companies are licensed to operate out of Denver International Airport: **Freedom Cab** (☎ **303-292-8900**), **Metro Taxi** (☎ **303-333-3333**), and **Yellow Cab** (☎ **303-777-7777**). All three charge a flat fee of $46 (including a $3 gate fee) to go from DIA to the downtown area. If you're traveling with a group of three to five people (the maximum that most companies will take), a cab affords you a per-person price second only to the skyRide public bus.

Hopping a bus

The cheapest way to reach many destinations in Denver and Boulder is via a public **skyRide** bus (☎ **303-299-6000** and then speed dial **1-2-1;** www.rtd-denver.com/skyRide). Between 4 a.m. and midnight, skyRide buses — part of the city's public **Regional Transportation District (RTD)** system — depart DIA's Level 5 (outside doors 506 or 511) at least once every hour. From DIA, the buses service 28 skyRide stops throughout the Denver metropolitan area, including 18 free park-and-ride lots, and provide links to other RTD buses and light-rail.

At a cost of $6 to $10, skyRide may work for you if you're on a tight budget, have time to spare, and are traveling light. (At DIA, skyRide drivers may assist you with luggage, but don't count on this service if you transfer to another RTD bus.) If you're considering using RTD, you can get more information by visiting the skyRide counter in the ground-transportation area of Level 5, or by going to the RTD's Web site. If you do decide to take skyRide, bring plenty of small bills and quarters, because drivers cannot make change.

Arriving by car

Interstate 70, which passes within a few miles of Denver International Airport, is the principal east-west corridor through both Denver and Colorado. En route from St. Louis to southern Utah, it passes a few miles north of Denver's downtown and then climbs into the Colorado high country, passing Golden, Summit County, Vail, Glenwood Springs, and Grand Junction, among other towns, before crossing the Utah border. Interstate 25, which slices through the west side of the city, travels north and south between New Mexico and Wyoming. Take I-25 to reach Denver from the major Front Range cities of Colorado Springs and Fort Collins. To get to Denver from Boulder, head southeast to I-25 on U.S. 36. U.S. 285 goes northeast to Denver from Salida.

Riding in (Not on horseback)

With more than 60 daily arrivals and departures at its Denver terminal at 19th and Arapahoe streets, **Greyhound** (☎ **800-231-2222;** www.grey hound.com) provides a variety of options for reaching destinations both inside and outside Colorado. This terminal, located in the Central Business District, is convenient to city bus and light-rail service. You'll also find taxis readily available outside the station.

If you choose to come into Denver via train, Amtrak runs two routes — both go from Chicago to various destinations in California — that pass through Denver. With such massive distances between Denver and points east or west, delays are frequent and can be frustrating, but this remains, by far, the most relaxing and civilized way to travel. The Amtrak trains stop at historic Union Station, at 17th and Wynkoop streets (☎ **800-USA-RAIL** or 303-825-2583; www.amtrak.com) in Lower Downtown.

Denver Neighborhoods

If you get lost in Denver, look for the Rocky Mountains, visible 14 miles west of town. As long as some of the city's taller buildings don't block your view, you should always be able to figure out which way is west. Denver's street grid can be confusing, especially going to or from the downtown area: The original streets of the Denver City Mining Camp par-alleled Cherry Creek; later, when it became clear that the town was no flash-in-the-pan, city planners designed newer neighborhoods around the same north-south-east-west grid that exists in Chicago and most other western cities (see the nearby "Denver Neighborhoods" map).

Denver Neighborhoods

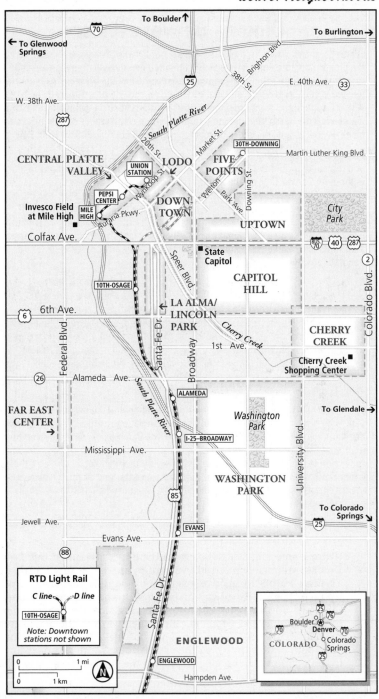

Digging Denver's history

When gold was discovered along the banks of Cherry Creek in the summer of 1858, the plains along the Front Range were inhabited mostly by buffalo and a sea of grass that stretched across Kansas Territory to Missouri. The Cheyenne and Arapaho nations followed the buffalo herds, and in the mountains, the Ute tribes hunted and gathered. A few trappers and frontiersmen crossed through the area, but winters on the high plains were so harsh, and the land so dry, that no one thought of trying to settle the place — that is, until the glitter of gold took hold and precipitated the Gold Rush of '59.

A couple of hardscrabble camps were assembled at the confluence of Cherry Creek and the south fork of the Platte River: Auraria was considered the more respectable of the two; Denver City, on the eastern side of Cherry Creek, was believed to be one of the most dangerous towns in America, with speculators, gamblers, and other unsavory types collecting there to take advantage — any way they could! — of the new-found, largely unregulated wealth hidden in the creeks trickling down from the mountains. Through a shady, back-room deal, Denver City was granted a stagecoach stop, and the resulting economic advantages allowed it to swallow Auraria and become the boomtown of Denver.

No one foresaw, of course, the skyscrapers that now dominate the Platte River Valley and the suburbs that stretch literally to every horizon. Denver's spectacular growth has been accomplished in fits and starts, though, and its history provides the very definition of a boomtown. The Gold Rush was short-lived, and Denver actually dwindled in population during the 1860s. The 1870s, though, brought a silver boom that lasted for 20 years, oversaw the building of the mighty mansions of Capitol Hill, and established the names of Moffat and Tabor as local royalty. When the silver market crashed in the 1890s, though, Denver again had to stop growing and just survive, while the mining camps in the mountains turned to ghost towns.

World War II brought a new boom: air transportation and the military-industrial complex, which stretched the population eastward and began the urban sprawl that now blankets the valley. In the 1970s, oil became the commodity of the day and built the giant towers in the downtown area, until the market crashed in 1984. The ensuing recession lasted ten years, but was followed by the high-tech bubble of the 1990s when the Lower Downtown area, decaying since the end of the silver boom, was reborn as LoDo, the nighttime playground of the hipsters who came to work in software and telecommunications.

Historic areas such as the **Auraria Campus, Downtown,** and **Lower Downtown** (locally referred to as **LoDo**) are on the older, angled grid. The **Five Points** area is situated on the old grid's northeast corner. **Uptown** starts at Broadway, just east of Downtown, and stretches east to City Park. The west side of Denver's central downtown area is bordered by Speer Boulevard, which parallels Cherry Creek (the actual creek, not the neighborhood). Many other intriguing neighborhoods are located just south of Downtown, on the newer, north-south grid. Heading south from Downtown, zigzagging slightly to the east and west, you'll pass through the **Capitol Hill, Cherry Creek,** and **Washington Park** neighborhoods, each with its own unique personality. The neighborhoods don't have perfect dividing lines, and Denverites sometimes disagree as to where one begins and another one ends. Still, the descriptions in this section should give you some idea where you're going, and what to expect when you get there.

Downtown (the Central Business District)

To find this area, head for the skyscrapers on 16th, 17th, and 18th streets between Broadway and Lawrence. Built primarily in the 1970s and 1980s, these tall buildings define the Denver skyline and make it easy to forget that this is also one of the oldest parts of town. Be sure to see the district's remaining 19th-century buildings, including the Brown Palace Hotel and the Trinity Methodist Church, as well as Larimer Square, as you tour the area.

On weekends, business travelers vacate the area's many luxury hotels, only to be replaced by tourists arriving for shows in the Denver Performing Arts Complex, shopping in the 16th Street Marketplace, and games at Coors Field, all of which are within walking distance of this section of town. In spite of the tourist influx, the area becomes less crowded and more relaxed on weekends.

Lower Downtown (LoDo)

Once a blighted area of abandoned warehouses, LoDo's modern heyday began with the opening of the Wynkoop Brewing Company in 1988 and exploded soon after Coors Field was completed, at a cost of $215 million, in 1995. Parking for this redbrick, state-of-the-art ballpark was scattered throughout the LoDo area, so fans of the Colorado Rockies baseball team began wandering through the neighborhood, pausing for food, drink, and entertainment along the way. LoDo, which runs from Speer Boulevard northeast to 20th Street and from Market Street northwest to Wynkoop Street, is the center of the city's nightlife and now houses dozens of bars, brewpubs, restaurants, and galleries. Many of these businesses occupy restored brick warehouses with high ceilings, hardwood floors, and (sometimes) rooftop seating. The area has 127 historic structures, including Union Station. Many date back to the 1870s, when the railroad first reached Denver. LoDo is definitely a nightlife destination, though — if you're looking for serious window-shopping and cafe hangouts, head for Cherry Creek instead.

The Golden Triangle

This once-derelict neighborhood just south of Downtown, bounded by Colfax Avenue, Broadway, and Speer Boulevard, has undergone a facelift and is being transformed into a loft community, popular with urban hipsters, and thus is now home to some of the hottest new restaurants and clubs. Recent and ongoing additions to the Denver Public Library and Denver Art Museum make this the most architecturally interesting and vibrant neighborhood in the city.

Uptown

The highlights of this neighborhood, stretching from Broadway east to York Street and from 23rd Street south to Colfax Avenue, are its lovely homes. Before the price of silver crashed in the 1890s, the city's first millionaires built ornate Victorian and Queen Anne–style homes in this area west of Denver. The area became run down in the 1950s, but many of its houses have been lovingly restored. New restaurants, bars, and coffee shops popped up to serve this recently gentrified area, particularly along 17th Street. The west side of Uptown borders City Park, home to the Denver Zoo and Denver Museum of Nature and Science. The southern border of this neighborhood is a gritty but interesting strip of Colfax Avenue, where you can get tattooed, buy vinyl records, load up on incense, and practice kung fu.

Capitol Hill

Capitol Hill, which spans from Broadway east to York Avenue and from Colfax Avenue south to Sixth Avenue, has impressive Victorian homes like the ones in the Uptown neighborhood to its north. It serves as the center of the city's gay and lesbian community, as well as Denver's bohemian scene — with lots of funky shops and cafes along 13th Avenue and down Broadway, and counter-cultural hipsters living in the cheap apartments nearby. Capitol Hill also is home to some of Denver's best-known landmarks, including the State Capitol, whose gold dome is visible for miles, and the expansive Civic Center Park, which has a symmetrical, European-style design. Along the park's edges are the Denver Public Library, the Denver Art Museum, and the Colorado History Museum. The U.S. Mint, recently closed to tourists due to security issues, is a block away from the park.

Cherry Creek

Fifty years ago few people would have foreseen Cherry Creek, which runs from East First Avenue north to East Eighth Avenue and from Downing Street east to Colorado Street, encompassing Denver's wealthiest neighborhoods. Located near the city dump, it was the place where returning World War II veterans built bungalows and quietly raised families. Today, most of those bungalows have been replaced by glitzy prefab condominiums; the Denver Country Club, which counts some of the city's financial elite among its members, is located nearby; and the chic stores in the Cherry Creek Mall attract shoppers from throughout the region. Just north of the mall, in Cherry Creek North, you find tree-lined streets with expensive galleries, boutiques, spas, and restaurants. Recently, on-street parking here ceased to be free: Parking is by permit only in the residential areas, and you must look for the kiosks or electronic pay stations in the shopping district.

Central Platte Valley

After a flood destroyed what was left of the railyards in the 1960s, the Central Platte Valley languished in decay. Over time, though, the city built a system of parks and greenways that make this an oasis of green among the concrete canyons. From the kayaking course in Confluence Park and the newer Commons Park nearby, you can walk, bike, or jog via the Platte River and Cherry Creek greenways to many other city parks, and even to Waterton Canyon in the foothills. Some of Denver's biggest attractions have sprouted alongside the river, including the Pepsi Center, a 20,000-seat arena for the city's pro hockey and basketball teams; Invesco Field at Mile High, a 76,000-seat football stadium for the Denver Broncos (just west of I-25); the Six Flags Elitch Gardens theme park; and Colorado's Ocean Journey, a $93 million aquarium.

Other Denver neighborhoods

The neighborhoods described in the preceding sections tend to attract the most attention from tourists, but they're just a few of the many intriguing downtown spots. Some others that merit attention are

- **Far East Center,** a strip of Federal Boulevard between West Alameda and West Mississippi avenues, has a large Asian-American population and some fine Vietnamese and Thai restaurants.

- **Five Points,** which runs west from Park Avenue to Downing Street and southeast from 38th to 23rd streets, is a center for Denver's African-American population and home to the Black American West Museum and Heritage Center.

- Denver's Latino population operates many shops, restaurants, and stores in the **La Alma/Lincoln Park Area,** on Santa Fe Drive between West Colfax and West Sixth avenues.

- The **Washington Park** area is alive with young professionals of all ethnicities who have bought homes around Denver's largest park. The area, known to locals as Wash Park, spans from Broadway east to University Boulevard, and from Alameda Avenue south to Evans Avenue. Washington Park itself is a glorious piece of greenspace with two large lakes (popular with local fishers) and is *the* place to rollerblade, sunbathe, and play soccer and volleyball.

Getting Information after You Arrive

The best source for area information is the **Denver Metro Convention and Visitors Bureau,** 918 16th Street Mall at Champa Street (☎ 800-233-6837; www.denver.org). It's open Monday through Friday from 8 a.m. to 5 p.m. and, from May to September, on Saturday from 9:30 a.m. to 1:30 p.m.

The Visitors Bureau also operates information booths in the main terminal and in Concourse B at Denver International Airport. You can also get information during business hours inside the **State Capitol** (☎ 303-866-2604), at the corner of Broadway and Colfax Avenue. The public entrance to the capitol is at street level on the building's south (14th Street) side.

If, for some reason, you lose your bearings at **Cherry Creek Mall,** 3000 E. First Ave. (☎ **303-388-3900**), you can stop at an information booth there.

Getting Around Denver

No matter how you choose to travel, Denver is a fairly user-friendly city. Of course, any major city always has a few tie-ups. Whether you're traveling by car, bus, train, or even on foot, here's how to avoid the ones in Denver.

By mass transit

An immense bus and light-rail system known as the **Regional Transportation District (RTD)** serves Denver, Boulder, and other communities.

Bussing it

With 179 bus routes going to 41 municipalities, the system can be tricky to figure out if you're using it for the first time. You can try using the route planner on RTD's Web site (www.rtd-denver.com), but you stand a better chance of sorting things out if you talk to a warm-blooded information specialist at the RTD hotline (☎ **800-366-7433**). Printed bus and rail schedules are available at **Market Street Station,** on the corner of Market and 16th Street; **Civic Center Station,** on the corner of Broadway and 16th Street; and at many area King Soopers and Safeway supermarkets.

Running between Civic Center Station and Union Station is the 16th Street Mall, the anchor and center of the entire transportation system. The free shuttle buses along the Mall are far and away the best way to get around Downtown and LoDo, and they connect all the other bus and light-rail lines. During peak hours, you seldom have to wait more than a minute or two for a bus; at off hours, the wait can be a little longer. By using these buses, which run from 6 a.m. to 1 a.m. daily, you can shorten your walking distance to many of the prime attractions in the downtown area while sparing yourself parking headaches.

Also, the RTD-operated **B-Line** runs between Downtown and the Denver Tech Center along Colorado Boulevard, stopping in Cherry Creek along the way and saving you the hassle of dealing with traffic in the busiest parts of the metro area. It's a no-brainer, especially if you have business in the Tech Center.

If you plan to take in cultural attractions throughout the downtown area, pay $16 for a daylong pass on the **Cultural Connection Trolley** (☎ **303-289-2841**). Every hour between 8:30 a.m. and 5:30 p.m. (last trolley departs at 3:30 p.m.), the Gray Line–operated trolley stops at Denver's prime tourist attractions, including Cherry Creek Shopping Center, Ocean's Journey, Union Station, and Larimer Square. The trolley operates only from Memorial Day through Labor Day.

If you're staying in Denver but want to visit Boulder, the regional **B** bus (not related to the just-mentioned B-Line) runs from Market Street Station or Union Station to the Boulder Station in downtown Boulder in less than an hour, passing near all the attractions in the University of Colorado/Chatauqua Park area. At rush hour it's packed with commuters, but lots of buses run during those times, and it's the only way to avoid the often hellish traffic on U.S. 36 and I-25. Pay attention to the schedule, though, especially if you're barhopping on Boulder's Pearl Street Mall — the last bus leaves Boulder at 1 a.m.

Riding the light-rail train

Also worth trying is the light-rail train into the Platte Valley. From Union Station, you can take the train to stations at Invesco Field at Mile High, the Pepsi Center, Six Flags Elitch Gardens, and Colorado's Ocean Journey. This line makes nearly all the major downtown attractions easily accessible, via mass transit, from downtown hotels. In general, the light-rail route is easier to grasp than the bus lines. The color-coded routes are posted at the stops, and they're relatively easy to decipher.

The cost for local light-rail or bus routes is $1.25 for adults, 60¢ for seniors and youths ages 6 to 18. Express routes cost $2.75 for adults, $1.35 for seniors and youths. Regional buses are $3.75 for adults, $1.85 for seniors and youths. If you're taking the train, bring plenty of quarters and $1 bills for the ticket machines at each stop. The machines provide no more than $1 in change.

After buying your ticket, you need to validate it before getting on the train. If you're taking the bus, put your exact fare into the box next to the driver, and ask for a free transfer slip if you need to change buses. The light-rail lines operate from about 6 a.m. to midnight, depending on where you board the last train.

By taxi

Taxi drivers in Denver charge an initial drop-flag fee of $1.80, plus $1.60 per mile. You're allowed to hail a cab in Denver, but unless you're downtown and have some luck, the attempt could be a Hail Mary. This is especially true on weekends, after the bars have shut down for the night. You can find a reliable taxi stand at the Westin Tabor Center, though, on Lawrence Street between the Mall and 17th Street. Cab companies with large fleets are **Freedom Cab** (☎ 303-292-8900), **Metro Taxi** (☎ 303-333-3333), **Yellow Cab** (☎ 303-777-7777), and **Zone Cab** (☎ 303-444-8888).

By car

You can walk and use mass transit to reach the major attractions in the downtown area — indeed, it's much cheaper and easier for you to do so — but you need a car if you hope to take in all the sights in the outlying communities and the mountains.

Driving is surprisingly manageable in LoDo and the Central Business District, which are on Denver's oldest grid. This grid consists of numbered streets running northwest and southeast, intersected at right angles by named arteries such as **Market Street** (one-way northeast), **Lawrence Street** (one-way northeast), and **Larimer Street** (one-way southwest). Traffic usually moves well, especially on weekends. **Speer Boulevard** is far and away the best way to get from Downtown to Cherry Creek (see the "Denver Accommodations & Dining" map later in this chapter), and in the Uptown area, the one-way thoroughfares of **17th** and **18th avenues** are much faster and easier to travel than the clogged, two-way **Colfax Avenue.**

Most streets in the downtown core are one-way, so you may have to go around a block or two in order to get to your destination.

The drawback to driving in the downtown neighborhoods is trying to find inexpensive parking. Daily parking usually costs between $5 and $10, with hourly rates sometimes running $2.50 or more. Some hotels charge upwards of $15 per night for valet parking. If you manage to find a parking space on the street, the meter usually costs 25¢ for every 15 minutes, with a two-hour maximum in effect. If you must park here, bring quarters for meters and small bills for the self-pay lots.

You'll have an easier time parking, but you can expect to encounter more intense traffic as you leave the downtown area and move from the old grid to the new grid. The new grid consists of numbered avenues that run east and west, intersected by named streets and boulevards that run north and south.

If an address is on a numbered road, check out whether the road is a street or an avenue, so you know which grid it's on. Numbered streets are on the old grid; numbered avenues are on the new one. Population growth has been poorly managed over the last ten years, and some of the main streets on the new grid, such as Colorado Boulevard and Colfax Avenue, get extremely clogged during rush hour. All the downtown area turns into a parking lot after baseball games, and, as in most major cities, freeway traffic can slow dramatically during rush hour.

A highway construction project known as T-Rex will slow traffic on I-25 until 2006. Traveling south on I-25 from Central Downtown to the Tech Center area can be particularly agonizing during peak periods.

On foot

By and large, Denver is a great place to walk. Hundreds of miles of bike and walking paths wend their way through the city, with the majority of these in the parks and on old rail grades paralleling the city's waterways. If you're walking for pleasure only, the trails along the South Platte River and Cherry Creek are especially nice. They're mostly below street level, along rivers that, except for the occasional bobbing vodka bottle or half-submerged shopping cart, are remarkably clean. If transportation

What's up with the diagonal crosswalks?

Downtown Denver has something you don't see in most American cities: diagonal crosswalks. These are known as "Barnes Dances," after Henry Barnes, the Denver traffic engineer who invented them in the late 1940s. Basically, car traffic in all directions is stopped, allowing pedestrians to cross in any direction they choose. Go ahead, try it; it's not jaywalking, and it's perfectly safe. Not coincidentally, the Barnes Dance led to another Denver innovation that caught on around the world: timed traffic lights.

is your goal, you can easily reach the popular tourist destinations in the Central Business District, LoDo, and Capitol Hill areas on foot, especially if you occasionally jump on a free bus on the 16th Street Mall to shorten the distances. However, you need a car to reach most other areas in and around the city.

As for problem areas, don't go too far east on Colfax Avenue — but don't shun Colfax, either. The stretch between Broadway and University has some lively music venues (including the revamped Ogden Theater and Fillmore Auditorium) and restaurants, and it passes between the Capitol Hill and Uptown neighborhoods, which boast many of the city's historic homes. The crime-riddled spots on Colfax are east of Colorado Boulevard, where there are few tourist attractions.

Where to Stay

As in most major cities, staying in downtown Denver on a weeknight is expensive. The Central Business District and LoDo areas (see the map, "Denver Accommodations & Dining") are long on luxury hotels for business travelers and short on budget accommodations for families. Weeknight prices often run $175 to $225, including parking. On Friday and Saturday nights, however, business travelers vacate the Central Business District, and you can usually find a luxurious room for under $100. The lower end of the rack rates I list in this section tend to be weekend rates, while the higher end is what you pay on a weekday.

If you have to be in downtown Denver on a weeknight, look for a small room at one of the area's bed-and-breakfasts. These often cost under $100 and include free breakfast. Plus, they're nice. Prices for rooms drop as you move farther from Downtown. Accommodations in the Cherry Creek area, roughly ten minutes from Downtown by car, cost about $20 to $30 dollars less than Downtown and have free parking. If you need a motel or hotel room in the $70 range, your best bet may be to surf the Internet for deals at the many chain hotels in the suburbs. (See Chapter 8 for more information on getting good hotel deals and for an explanation of the dollar signs that indicate the price ranges.)

Brown Palace Hotel
$$$$ **Central Business District**

The Brown Palace has always been *the* place to stay in Denver, attracting guests as varied as Dwight Eisenhower and the Beatles. The atrium inside the hotel is one of those rare architectural masterpieces that are nearly as breathtaking as a natural wonder. A skylight illuminates eight stories of balconies with cast-iron grillwork; floors and columns of white onyx; and a tea area where either a piano or lute player provides music daily. The hotel is shaped like a triangle, and it's old (opened in 1892), so the rooms come in a variety of shapes and sizes. That said, the rooms are quite comfortable and decorated in either a Victorian or Art Deco style. The hotel promotes itself not only to wealthy and expense-account travelers but also to regular people hoping to create their own memories, and a number of weekend package deals bring the hotel's prices into the lower reaches of the earth's atmosphere. But if you can't stay here, definitely peek inside at the lobby — or better yet, stop by between noon and 4 p.m. during the week for afternoon tea in the lobby's tea room.

See map p. 104. 321 17th St. ☎ 800-321-2599 or 303-297-3111. Fax: 303-312-5900. www.brownpalace.com. Valet parking: $24. Rack rates: $235–$315 double; $315–$985 suite. AE, DC, DISC, MC, V.

Castle Marne Bed & Breakfast
$$–$$$$ **Uptown**

One of Denver's most famous architects, William Lang, designed this 1889 stone mansion, which looks and feels like a living museum (it's a registered National Landmark). Everywhere you look, you'll find something stunning, whether it's the circular stained-glass window on the stairs, wainscoting of Honduran mahogany, floors of quarter-sawn oak, or the specially textured walls in the dining room (which are protected by the U.S. Department of the Interior). The guest rooms are equally beautiful and several rooms have private balconies with hot tubs. Fortunately for the guests, all the beauty doesn't make things seem stuffy or tense — innkeepers Jim and Diane Peiker somehow keep things down-to-earth, making this a winning experience in every way. *Note:* The inn is entirely nonsmoking, so if you like to light up, look elsewhere. Children age ten and under are not permitted, making this a lousy choice for families but a great one for couples looking for a more tranquil atmosphere.

See map p. 104. 1572 Race St., at 16th Avenue. ☎ 303-331-0621. Fax: 303-331-0623. www.castlemarne.com. Free parking. Rack rates: $85–$250 double; $100–$250 suite. Rates include full breakfast and afternoon tea. Children under 10 not permitted. AE, DC, DISC, MC, V.

Embassy Suites Downtown Denver
$$$–$$$$ **Central Business District**

Of all the luxury hotels in the Central Business District, this 19-story building, located just two blocks from the 16th Street Marketplace, may be the best for families. Kids in particular seem to enjoy the suite rooms, the in-room Nintendo games, and the pool and spa. All accommodations here are one- or two-bedroom suites, with separate living areas (with pullout sofas, refrigerators, and microwaves) and sleeping areas. Because the hotel's complimentary breakfast combines buffet and table service, you can locate a few favorite items for your kids, then leave the rest of the work to a professional server. For an extra $10, you can use the 65,000-square-foot Denver Athletic Club attached to the hotel.

See map p. 104. 1881 Curtis St., at 18th Street. ☎ *800-733-3366 or 303-297-8888. Fax: 303-298-1103.* www.esdendt.com. *Valet parking: $19 Sun–Thurs; $15 Fri–Sat. No RVs or roof racks. Rack rates: $139–$259 double. Rates include full breakfast and evening cocktail reception. AE, DC, DISC, MC, V.*

The Holiday Chalet
$$–$$$ **Capitol Hill**

This oasis of Victorian propriety amid the neon on Colfax Avenue is one of the best deals in Denver. Built as a mansion in 1896, the B&B now offers 12 comfortable and family-friendly minisuites. The minisuites were added in the 1950s and are starting to feel historic themselves — especially the kitchens, which have tile floors and gas stoves. The rooms also have antiques, desks, and TVs with VCRs; a few rooms have sunrooms and two have fireplaces. Ice cream socials are held in summer and barbecue grills are available for guests' use. If you plan to stay a while, bring your pet (for an extra $5 a day), your kids (baby-sitting can be arranged), and your food, and take advantage of a $500 weekly rate. If traffic noise bothers you, ask for a room on the side away from Colfax.

See map p. 104. 1820 Colfax Ave. ☎ *800-626-4497 or 303-321-9975. Fax: 303-377-6556.* www.bbonline.com/co/holiday. *Free street parking. Rack rates: $94–$160 double. AE, DC, DISC, MC, V.*

Hotel Monaco Denver
$$–$$$$ **Downtown**

This hotel, which oozes 1990s excess, sports lavishly decorated rooms, whose amenities include CD stereos, terrycloth robes, and Starbucks coffee. And if you're lonely, the hotel will send up a free "companion gold-fish," although at these rates, they should send a dolphin. The location is great, though, for both downtown business trips and casual travelers look-ing for LoDo nightlife. And the bar on the ground floor is top-notch.

See map p. 104. 1717 Champa, at 17th Street. ☎ *800-397-5380 or 303-296-1717. Fax: 303-296-1818.* www.Monaco-denver.com. *Rack rates: $100–$199 double; $200–$500 suite. AE, DC, DISC, MC, V.*

JW Marriott
$$–$$$ **Cherry Creek**

Finally, Cherry Creek has an upscale hotel to call its own. This swanky new place opened in the summer of 2004 and has been packing them in ever

Denver Accommodations & Dining

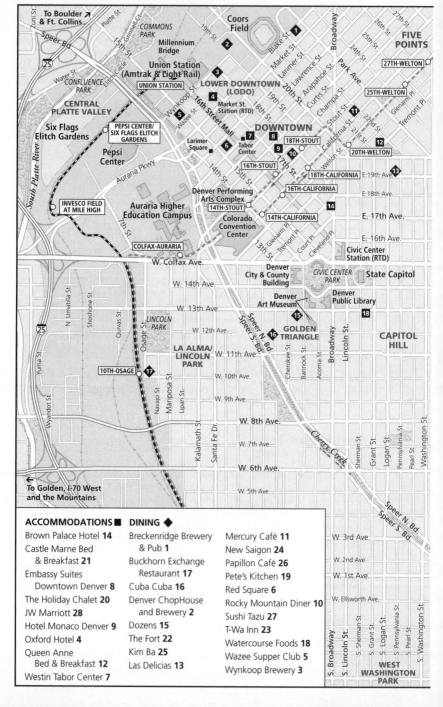

ACCOMMODATIONS ■

Brown Palace Hotel **14**
Castle Marne Bed
  & Breakfast **21**
Embassy Suites
  Downtown Denver **8**
The Holiday Chalet **20**
JW Marriott **28**
Hotel Monaco Denver **9**
Oxford Hotel **4**
Queen Anne
  Bed & Breakfast **12**
Westin Tabor Center **7**

DINING ◆

Breckenridge Brewery
  & Pub **1**
Buckhorn Exchange
  Restaurant **17**
Cuba Cuba **16**
Denver ChopHouse
  and Brewery **2**
Dozens **15**
The Fort **22**
Kim Ba **25**
Las Delicias **13**

Mercury Café **11**
New Saigon **24**
Papillon Café **26**
Pete's Kitchen **19**
Red Square **6**
Rocky Mountain Diner **10**
Sushi Tazu **27**
T-Wa Inn **23**
Watercourse Foods **18**
Wazee Supper Club **5**
Wynkoop Brewery **3**

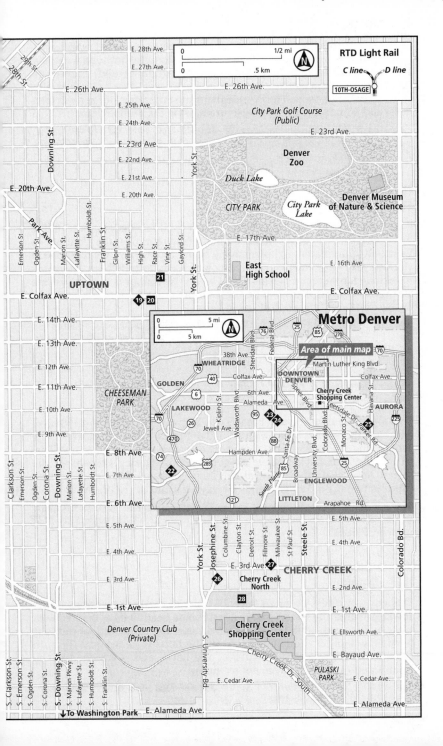

E. 28th Ave.

E. 27th Ave.

E. 26th Ave.

E. 26th Ave.

E. 25th Ave.

E. 24th Ave.

E. 23rd Ave.

E. 22nd Ave.

E. 21st Ave.

E. 20th Ave.

E. 20th Ave.

UPTOWN

E. Colfax Ave.

E. 14th Ave.

E. 13th Ave.

E. 12th Ave.

E. 11th Ave.

E. 10th Ave.

CHEESEMAN PARK

E. 9th Ave.

E. 8th Ave.

E. 7th Ave.

E. 6th Ave.

E. 5th Ave.

E. 4th Ave.

E. 3rd Ave.

E. 1st Ave.

Denver Country Club (Private)

To Washington Park

RTD Light Rail

C line   D line

10TH-OSAGE

City Park Golf Course (Public)

E. 23rd Ave.

Denver Zoo

Duck Lake

CITY PARK

City Park Lake

Denver Museum of Nature & Science

E. 17th Ave.

East High School

E. 16th Ave.

E. Colfax Ave.

Metro Denver

Area of main map

WHEATRIDGE

38th Ave.

GOLDEN

Colfax Ave.

Martin Luther King Blvd.

DOWNTOWN DENVER

LAKEWOOD

6th Ave.

Alameda

Cherry Creek Shopping Center

Colfax Ave.

AURORA

Jewell Ave.

Hampden Ave.

ENGLEWOOD

LITTLETON

Arapahoe Rd.

E. 5th Ave.

E. 4th Ave.

CHERRY CREEK

E. 3rd Ave.

Cherry Creek North

E. 2nd Ave.

E. 1st Ave.

Cherry Creek Shopping Center

E. Ellsworth Ave.

E. Bayaud Ave.

PULASKI PARK

E. Cedar Ave.

E. Cedar Ave.

E. Alameda Ave.

since. It's located in the beautiful new Clayton Lane development, across First Avenue from the Cherry Creek shopping center and easy walking distance from all the retail and dining that make the neighborhood what it is. The rooms are all sumptuously appointed with dark wood, granite surfaces, enormous flat-screen TVs, and, on higher west-side floors, stunning views of the mountains. The Presidential suite is designed for serious business, and Mirepoix, a hot new restaurant, is on the ground floor.

See map p. 104. 150 Clayton Lane ☎ **303-316-2700.** *Fax: 303-316-4697.* www.marriott.com. *Valet parking: $22. Rack rates: $125–$200 double; $350–$450 suite. AE, DC, DISC, MC, V.*

Oxford Hotel
$$–$$$ Lower Downtown

If you want to stay in LoDo, look no farther than this historic hotel in the heart of it all. The silver-boom building is sumptuously decked out in Victorian appointments, though many of the rooms have been redone in glorious Art Deco. The Deco rooms, in fact, have recently been renovated to include large-screen plasma TVs. Oh, my. Next door is the Oxford Spa and Salon (for first class pampering) and the ground floor is home to the Cruise Room, still the coolest bar in LoDo.

See map p. 104. 1600 17th St. ☎ **800-228-5838** *or 303-628-5400.* www.theoxfordhotel.com. *Valet parking: $21. Rack rates: $125–$200 double; $350–$450 suite. AE, DC, DISC, MC, V.*

Queen Anne Bed & Breakfast Inn
$–$$$ Downtown

This award-winning bed-and-breakfast, which occupies adjacent 19th-century Victorian homes laden with art and antiques, offers excellent service with a personal touch. Some rooms offer canopy beds, jet tubs, and TVs; all the accommodations have air-conditioning. During ski season, the Queen Anne features a special Ski Train package ($295 double) that includes two nights' lodging and one-day Ski Train tickets for two.

See map p. 104. 2147–51 Tremont Place. ☎ **800-432-4667** *or 303-296-6666. Fax: 303-296-2151.* www.queenannebnb.com. *Rack rates: $75–$165 double; $155–$175 suite. AE, DISC, MC, V.*

Westin Tabor Center
$$$$ Downtown

This cool, business-oriented hotel has one of the best locations in the downtown area and features large guest rooms beautifully appointed with modern European-style furnishings. Drift upstairs to the indoor-outdoor swimming pool on a fourth floor deck. The hotel is convenient for both business and pleasure in Downtown and LoDo, and is attached to the Tabor Center mall for convenient shopping.

See map p. 104. 1672 Lawrence St. ☎ **303-572-9100.** *Fax 303-572-7288.* www.westin.com. *Rack rates: $269 double. AE, DISC, MC, V.*

Where to Dine

Dining in Denver is a richly textured experience: You can eat as down-home, way-out-west, or cosmopolitan as you want (sometimes even within a single meal!). Finer restaurants across Colorado have worked hard over the last few years at developing a true regional cuisine — they no longer look to the coasts for guidance — and Denver's eateries have led the way. This movement has focused on western game, and the proximity of Mexican and Southwestern food cultures has had an impact as well. The diners and burger joints lean heavily on the Southwestern style; if you've never had a breakfast burrito, here's your wake-up call! Of course, all the top-flight European and Asian styles are well represented; fresh seafood is flown in daily, so there's plenty of good sushi if you're jonesing for it. Latin American cuisines (besides just Mexican) are also well represented, and a sizeable Vietnamese population has contributed a number of restaurants over the years that are now Denver traditions.

If meat-and-potatoes is your thing, I can't emphasize enough the incredible experience of local game, especially buffalo and elk. If you want a steak, Denver has the usual chains — Ruth's Chris, Gallagher's, Morton's — but you're selling yourself short if you don't try the buffalo. Compared with beef, it's more tender, much leaner, and more flavorful by a mile. You find it here in the form of burgers and even meatloaf, but you owe it to yourself to head over to the Buckhorn or the Fort and try a tenderloin or porterhouse. Trust me on this one.

Check out the "Denver Accommodations & Dining" map, earlier in this chapter, to locate the restaurants listed here.

Breckenridge Brewery & Pub
$–$$ LoDo   PUB FARE

One of Denver's best breweries, its location across from Coors Field makes it very popular before and after baseball games. It's casual and sports-oriented without being a grungy, sweaty sports bar. Menu offerings include fajitas, sandwiches, salads, pub fare, and entrees such as grilled salmon and homemade pork tamales.

See map p. 104. 2220 Blake St. ☎ *303-297-3644. Reservations accepted. Main courses: $11–$17. AE, DISC, MC, V. Open: Daily 11 a.m. to midnight.*

Buckhorn Exchange Restaurant
$$–$$$$ Near Downtown   STEAKS/GAME

For an unforgettable experience, hop on the RTD light-rail and ride to the Buckhorn (it's at the 10th Avenue/Osage station), which stands — barely, it seems — right next to the train tracks in a forgotten area near Denver's downtown. The oldest restaurant in Colorado, the Buckhorn was founded by one Henry H. Zietz, who befriended Chief Sitting Bull, hunted with

Teddy Roosevelt, and accepted the sword of the vanquished General George Custer from the Blackfeet Sioux. You'll believe these seemingly far-fetched tales when you peek inside the restaurant at the 500-odd pieces of taxidermy on the walls and — in the spaces where nothing stares back at you — at the historic photos and antique guns. The restaurant serves items that would have been available in Colorado when it opened in 1883, such as elk, steaks, pheasant, grouse, and buffalo. Don't forget to ask about the Rocky Mountain oysters. Vegetarians should definitely head elsewhere.

See map p. 104. 1000 Osage St., at 10th. ☎ *303-534-9505.* www.buckhorn.com. *Reservations strongly recommended. Main courses: $18–$42. AE, DC, DISC, MC, V. Open: Mon–Fri 11 a.m.–2 p.m.; Mon–Thurs 5:30–9 p.m., Fri–Sat 5–10 p.m., Sun 5–9 p.m. Bar open all day.*

Cuba Cuba
$–$$$ Golden Triangle   CUBAN

This new restaurant brightens up the Golden Triangle neighborhood with its light, tropical atmosphere, breezy mojitos, and some truly heavenly food. The adventurous wine list focuses on Latin America, Spain, and Portugal; your server can help you match your food and wine orders. The ceviche de tuna is a perfect warm-up for the savory entrees, many of which feature the signature of Cuban cuisine, the mojo — a blend of various spices and vegetables, ground into a sort of paste and featured like a sauce. I recommend the puerco con yuca with black bean mojo or the camarones habanero — shrimp in a fiery sauce. Among several options for dessert, try the traditional tres leches (three-milk cake) — don't argue, just order it; resistance is futile.

See map p. 104. 1173 Delaware St. ☎ *303-605-2822.* www.cubacubacafe.com. *Reservations not accepted. Main courses: $9–$21. Open: Mon–Thurs 5–10 p.m., Fri–Sat 5–10:30 p.m.*

Denver Chophouse and Brewery
$$–$$$ LoDo   RED MEAT

This dark, old-fashioned joint is part of the same company as the Walnut Brewery in Boulder; the brewmasters are different, though, so the beer is a slightly different experience, and the food is on another level entirely. No pub fare here, this is the place for steaks, chops, and surf-and-turf. Vegetarians, I apologize. Reputedly, it's a popular hangout for victorious Broncos and Avalanche players after home games, so if you want to rub shoulders with large, sweaty millionaires, this is the place to go. Make reservations, especially on game days.

See map p. 104. 1735 19th St. ☎ *303-296-0800. Reservations recommended. Main courses: $11–$29. AE, DISC, MC, V. Open: Mon–Thurs 11 a.m.–11 p.m., Fri–Sat 11 a.m. to midnight, Sun 11 a.m.–10 p.m.*

Dozens
$ Golden Triangle   BREAKFAST

You can only get breakfast at this Denver institution. Tucked behind the Denver Art Museum, this place has been packing them in for decades with outstanding and original omelets, French toast, and pancakes. You may not get the humor of the '80s-era cultural references on the menu, but don't let that stop you from ordering.

See map p. 104. 236 W. 13th Ave. ☎ *303-572-0066. No reservations. MC, V. Open: Daily 6:30 a.m.–2 p.m.*

The Fort
$$$$ Morrison   COLORADO GAME

Don't come to The Fort to eat the usual steak and potatoes while sitting in a 1962 adobe reproduction of Historic Bent's Fort (a trading post in southeastern Colorado), even though you can. And don't come here for the panoramic views of southeastern Denver, even though the place does have them. Come here for the restaurant's native game dishes such as braised buffalo leg in oatmeal stout gravy, elk tenderloin with huckleberry sauce, and farm-raised rattlesnake. There is a filet mignon on the menu, but beef really isn't the point here. Buffalo steaks are always on the menu, and once you've tried it, you'll never look at a cow the same way again.

See map p. 104. Located in Morrison on Colorado 8, just north of Highway 285. ☎ *303-697-4771.* www.thefort.com. *Reservations recommended. Main courses: $20–$46. AE, DC, MC, V. Open: Mon–Fri 5:30–9:30 p.m., Sat–Sun 5–9:30 p.m. Call for special holiday hours.*

Las Delicias
$–$$ Downtown   MEXICAN

If you want traditional Mexican food without a lot of frou-frou, postmodern, Fusion nonsense, this should be your fist stop. Las Delicias is a very casual, family-run restaurant where the ambience is relaxed, the service prompt and friendly, and the food is *spectacular.* You find the usual array of burritos, enchiladas, and fajitas, but let me point you toward the carne adobada, steak ranchero, or carnitas estilo michoacan for other delicious options.

See map p. 104. 439 E. 19th St. ☎ *303-839-5675. No reservations accepted. AE, DISC, MC, V. Open: Mon–Fri 11 a.m.–9:30 p.m., Sun 9 a.m.–9 p.m.*

Mercury Café
$ Downtown   HEALTHY SOUL FOOD

This artsy, bustling cafe has performance spaces upstairs and two large dining areas downstairs. Upstairs, you can take in shows ranging from poetry slams to belly dancing, usually for a fee; downstairs, you can hear free live music while tasting food that's made with mostly organic ingredients. The best selections on the eclectic menu are the pasta dishes. Many vegetarian options are available.

See map p. 104. 2199 California St. ☎ 303-294-9258 (reservations) or 303-294-9281 (information). Reservations accepted. No credit cards. Open: Tues–Sun 5:30–11 p.m.; Sat–Sun 9 a.m.–3 p.m.

Papillon Café
$$ Cherry Creek   FRENCH/ASIAN FUSION

If you're browsing the chic stores in Denver's Cherry Creek North, plan on coming to this upscale restaurant to experience the colorful creations of chef Radek R. Cerny, who likes adding Asian oils, curries, and spices to what might otherwise be French food. Cerny's lobster ravioli has been earning raves for years, but the best items are sometimes the daily specials, which may include tuna with sesame, wasabi, and soy. You eat in a stylish dining room graced with a long bank of windows and huge planters of fresh-cut flowers. Make sure to reserve your spot in advance. After seven years here, Cerny is still packing in the well-to-do of Denver.

See map p. 104. 250 Josephine St. ☎ 303-333-7166. Reservations recommended. Main courses: $9–$12 lunch; $14–$22 dinner. AE, DC, DISC, MC, V. Open: Mon–Fri 11 a.m.–3 p.m.; Mon–Sat 5–10 p.m., Sun 5–9 p.m.

Pete's Kitchen
$ Capitol Hill/Uptown   DINER FARE

This old Colfax Avenue landmark still packs them in, especially for late-night snacking after a night on the town. If you head here during the bar rush, be ready to wait, and to wait outside (even in winter!). Waits are usually nonexistent for breakfast and lunch, though. Once you get inside, you're in for a treat: classic American diner food with Greek and Southwestern twists. The burgers are great, but go for the souvlaki and eggs or one of the enormous breakfast burritos smothered in green chili. And if you're here after the bars have closed, remember to drink lots of water.

See map p. 104. 1962 E. Colfax Ave. ☎ 303-321-3139. Reservations not accepted. Main courses: $4.45–$15. AE, DC, DISC, MC, V. Open: Mon–Thurs, 6 a.m.–11 p.m., Fri–Sat 24 hours.

Red Square
$$–$$$ Downtown   FUSION

This elegant, urban bistro serves up European Fusion cuisine with a decidedly Russian cast. Start with a bowl of borsht and the yazyk (veal tongue); or go less traditional with the Dungeness crab strudel served on a bed of aromatic greens with an orange vinaigrette. The entree menu features lots of fish. I had a perfectly grilled walnut-crusted rack of lamb with baby bok choi in a grape reduction. The beef stroganoff is a contemporary spin on a classic: It's a New York strip steak with mashed potatoes and a house variation on the traditional mushroom sauce. The wine list is varied and inventive, balances beautifully with the menu, and contains some exceptional values; the vodka list (with many house-flavored varieties) is exhaustive. The kitchen closes at 9 p.m., but then the bar takes on a life of its own.

See map p. 104. 1512 Larimer St. (in Writer's Square). ☎ *303-595-8600.* www.red squarebistro.com. *Reservations recommended. Main courses: $13–$20. AE, DC, DISC, MC, V. Open: Mon–Thurs 5–9 p.m., Fri–Sat 5–10 p.m.*

Rocky Mountain Diner
$–$$ Downtown AMERICAN

Take your basic American diner, elevate it to casual dining status, add a western flavor with a healthy dose of cowboy kitsch, and you have the Rocky Mountain Diner. It's all in good fun, but the food is serious stuff. Starters include venison chili and Yuppie-I-O dip (warm and rich, with cream cheese, artichoke hearts, and spinach). The house specialty is a huge portion of pan-fried chicken and mashed potatoes, but the real attractions are the buffalo meatloaf and the duck-and-havarti enchiladas. There's a great selection of local microbrews on tap, and the service is friendly and fast. If you have any room left, go for the white chocolate, black-bottom, banana cream pie — and waddle home carefully.

See map p. 104. 800 18th St. ☎ *303-293-8383.* www.rockymountaindiner.com. *Reservations accepted. Main courses: $7.50–$19. AE, DC, DISC, MC, V. Open: Mon–Thurs 11 a.m.–10 p.m., Fri–Sat 11 a.m.–11 p.m., Sun 11 a.m.–9 p.m.*

Sushi Tazu
$–$$ Cherry Creek JAPANESE/SUSHI

At this very popular sushi joint, the individual chefs all have signature creations with names such as "Volcano Roll" and "Charlie Brown." The sake selection is excellent, and familiar Japanese teriyaki and noodle preparations are available if you're not in the sushi groove.

See map p. 104. 300 Fillmore St. ☎ *303-320-1672. Reservations accepted. Sushi: $5–$15; Entrees: $12–$19. AE, DC, MC, V. Open: Mon–Fri 11:30 a.m.–2:30 p.m. and 4:30–10 p.m., Sat 11:30 a.m.–11 p.m., Sun 11:30 a.m.–10 p.m.*

Watercourse Foods
$ Capitol Hill VEGETARIAN

Okay, vegetarians, I haven't forgotten you completely. This place sets the standard for vegetarian and vegan food in the area, so if tempeh scaloppini and Caribbean jerk tofu are what you're after, look no further. The folks at Watercourse make their own granola, and the buckwheat pancakes are awesome. Naturally, the restaurant also has an excellent selection of salads — check out the fig salad with wilted spinach, feta, and balsamic

Nuoc mam, anyone?

One of the coolest aspects of Denver's ethnic mix is the large Vietnamese population, which has firmly entrenched itself in the local cuisine. Start by heading over to Federal Boulevard, and the strip south of the Far East Center to **T-Wa Inn** (555 S. Federal Blvd.; ☎ 303-922-2378; $–$$), the oldest of the great Vietnamese restaurants, for crispy roasted duck and Tai Chanh, a cold salad of beef and vegetables in a spicy mint-lemon marinade. You can also go across the street and a block down to **New Saigon** (630 South Federal Blvd.; ☎ 303-936-4954; $–$$) for Pho Tai Nam (a variation on the traditional Vietnamese *Pho*, or soup) or Ca Tim Mu Hanh, fried eggplant in a home-recipe sauce.

For my money, though, the best Vietnamese food in Colorado is at **Kim Ba** (2495 S. Havana St., Unit F31, Aurora; ☎ 303-745-1637; $–$$), way out in Aurora, but worth the drive. Chef Ba Forde, a scion of the family that opened T-Wa Inn, has produced highly original versions of traditional dishes, and the results are stupendous. Start with Dungeness crab in a rich buttery sauce, or Goi Cuon, shrimp spring rolls with a spicy peanut sauce. For dinner, go for the sea scallops in a sweet red pepper sauce, or the marinated pork that comes served over noodles or in a roll-it-yourself preparation with cucumber, cilantro, and mint. Everything comes with nuoc mam, the fish sauce that's often called the "Vietnamese ketchup." Finish with Ba's unique take on flan, a sweet, coconut-laced custard — and tell her Nick sent you.

vinaigrette. A great wine and microbrew list complements the dinner menu.

See map p. 104. 206–214 E. 13th Ave. ☎ *303-832-7313.* www.watercoursefoods. com. *Reservations recommended. Main courses: $4.95–$7.95 breakfast; $7.50–$8.25 lunch; $6.95–$10 dinner. AE, MC, V. Open: Tues–Sun 8 a.m.–10 p.m.*

Wazee Supper Club
$–$$ LoDo   PIZZA AND PUB FARE

Offering bar food with a difference, this place is another Denver landmark. It was a dinner destination among the old warehouses before LoDo was a glint in a developer's eye. The atmosphere is classic; it has a 20th-century Old West feel that's definitely not faked. Burgers, salads, and great pizzas are the stars here, with plenty of vegetarian options. Lots of beers on tap — mostly familiar imports with a few choice microbrews.

See map p. 104. 1600 15th St. ☎ *303-623-9518.* www.wazeesupperclub.com. *Reservations recommended. Main courses: $4.75–$8.95. Pizzas: $6.25–$20. AE, DC, DISC, MC, V. Open: Mon–Sat 11 a.m.–2 a.m., Sun noon to midnight.*

Wynkoop Brewery
$–$$ LoDo   NEW AMERICAN

This is the place that inaugurated the LoDo era in Downtown; its founder, John Hickenlooper, is so influential and widely admired that he is now

Denver's *mayor.* Seriously. His brainchild, this brewery and grill with full-size billiards tables upstairs, is the epitome of modern Colorado nightlife. Burritos and burgers are on the menu, but so are a buffalo rib-eye steak and elk medallions (some enlightened vegetarian options are also available). The real stars, though, are the rotating selection of hand-crafted beer, of which there are 15 or so on tap at any given time. RailYard Ale is the flagship of the fleet, but the Sagebrush Stout makes great cold-weather sipping, and try Patty's Chile Beer — infused with Anaheim chiles — with your Mexican food. The servers are casual but professional, knowledgeable, and happy to educate you about the brewing process. Fine cigars are sold and smoked upstairs in the pool hall, and the Impulse Theater takes over the basement with outstanding improv entertainment.

See map p. 104. 1634 18th St. at Wynkoop St. ☎ *303-297-2700.* www.wynkoop.com. *Reservations not accepted. Main courses: $7.25–$11 lunch; $7.25–$19 dinner. AE, DC, DISC, MC, V. Open: Daily 11 a.m.–2 a.m.*

Exploring Denver

Whether it's a museum of miniatures or a mile-high football stadium, you can find an attraction that interests you in Denver. The city's many top sights are conveniently clustered (see the nearby map, "Denver Attractions & Nightlife"), so you can see a lot of them in a few short days. This section tells you which ones are worth seeing.

The best things to see and do

Colorado History Museum
Civic Center Park

Even if the mere idea of a diorama makes you drowsy, you should check out the meticulously detailed ones at this museum. Using paper, cardboard, matchsticks, and wood veneers, artists in a Depression-era work relief program created tiny renderings of Colorado's history, which are displayed today in this museum. You can also view exhibits on pioneers, miners, ranchers, and Native Americans, and read a timeline tracing the major events of the past 150 years in the state's history. Memorabilia of a more recent vintage is also on display, including a gondola car from Steamboat Ski Area and a Denver Nuggets warm-up suit.

See map p. 114. 13th Street and Broadway. ☎ *303-866-3682.* www.colorado history.org. *Open: Mon–Sat 10:00 a.m.–4:30 p.m., Sun noon to 4:30 p.m. Admission: $5 adults, $4.50 seniors 65 and up and students 13–18, $3.50 children 6–12.*

Denver Art Museum
Civic Center Park

One of America's premier art museums sits right next to Civic Center Park in a startling, fortresslike building. The building's architecture is certainly fitting; the Geo Ponti–designed museum is the protective home of many

Denver Attractions & Nightlife

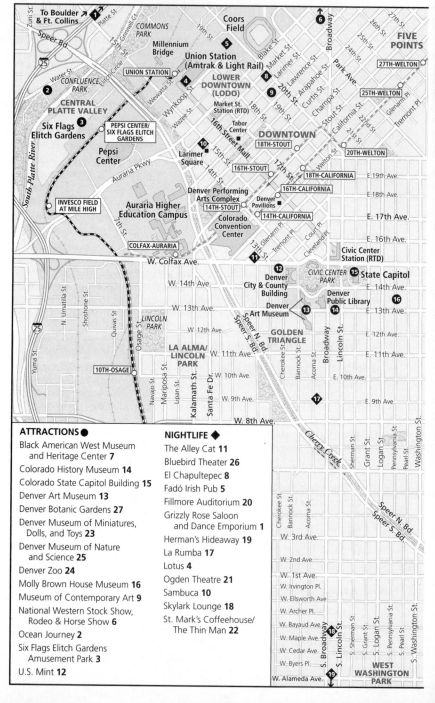

ATTRACTIONS ●

Black American West Museum
  and Heritage Center **7**
Colorado History Museum **14**
Colorado State Capitol Building **15**
Denver Art Museum **13**
Denver Botanic Gardens **27**
Denver Museum of Miniatures,
  Dolls, and Toys **23**
Denver Museum of Nature
  and Science **25**
Denver Zoo **24**
Molly Brown House Museum **16**
Museum of Contemporary Art **9**
National Western Stock Show,
  Rodeo & Horse Show **6**
Ocean Journey **2**
Six Flags Elitch Gardens
  Amusement Park **3**
U.S. Mint **12**

NIGHTLIFE ◆

The Alley Cat **11**
Bluebird Theater **26**
El Chapultepec **8**
Fadó Irish Pub **5**
Fillmore Auditorium **20**
Grizzly Rose Saloon
  and Dance Emporium **1**
Herman's Hideaway **19**
La Rumba **17**
Lotus **4**
Ogden Theatre **21**
Sambuca **10**
Skylark Lounge **18**
St. Mark's Coffeehouse/
  The Thin Man **22**

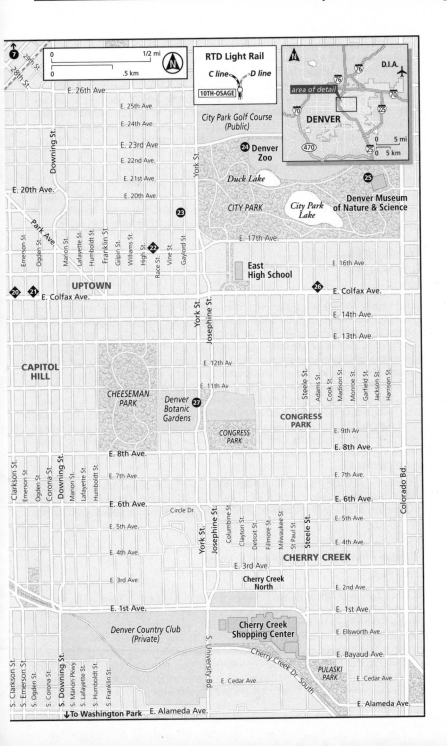

treasures. The museum houses an immense collection of Native American art; a Western gallery that has Remingtons and Russells; and pre- and post-Colombian works from Latin America. The Asian and African exhibits are also excellent. Works by Degas, Matisse, Picasso, and others are on display, though European art is not this museum's forte. The fall of 2006 will see the opening of the Frederic C. Hamilton building, another shocking piece of postmodern architecture designed by Daniel Libeskind that dramatically alters the skyline of the Golden Triangle, and doubles the size of the museum itself. The museum has a kids' corner where children can make art, and it schedules special kids' activities, too. Call ☎ 720-913-0049 to find out what will be on tap during your visit.

See map p. 114. 13th Street and Acoma. ☎ *720-865-5000.* www.denverart museum.org. *Open: Tues–Sat 10 a.m.–5 p.m., Wed 10 a.m.–9 p.m., Sun noon to 5 p.m. Admission to permanent collection: $8 adults, $6 seniors over 65 and youths 13–18, 12 and under free. Free admission for Colorado residents on Saturdays.*

Denver Botanic Gardens
Cherry Creek

On the 23 acres of the Denver Botanic Gardens, scientists nourish, breed, and study 15,000 plant species from around the world, including many threatened varieties. The individual plants are like brush strokes on a living canvas; each of the 30 or so gardens qualifies as a work of art. Highlights include a Japanese garden replete with pools, carefully placed granite, and aggressively pruned trees; an alpine garden that features high-alpine species from around the world; and a water garden with more than 400 types of aquatic plants. There's also a warm, misty, tropical conservatory, where you can forge through the fronds of jungle plants. Each year, the Summer Concert Series brings several world-renowned classical, folk, and pop music acts to the open-air stage at the center of the gardens; bring a picnic dinner or order one from the on-site caterer (many people bring wine and pâté, and generally show off). You sit on the grass, though, so bring a blanket.

See map p. 114. 1005 York St. ☎ *720-865-3500.* www.botanicgardens.org. *Open: May–Sept Wed–Fri 9 a.m.–5 p.m., Sat–Tues 9 a.m.–8 p.m.; Oct–Apr daily 9 a.m.–5 p.m. Admission: $8.50 adults 16 and over, $5.50 seniors 65 and over; $5 students and youths 4–15.*

Denver Museum of Nature and Science
City Park

Colorado's geological history makes it one of the best places in the world to find dinosaur fossils, and this museum takes full advantage of that situation. The fourth largest natural history museum in the United States, this museum has dioramas of wildlife from around the globe; mounted butterflies and insects; mummies; gems and minerals; and plenty of dinosaur skeletons. But the place is hardly musty. Almost everywhere you turn, you can try an interactive activity, whether it's prospecting for mineral pockets inside a simulated mine, comparing the densities of rocks, or smelling the odor that attracts a doe to a buck (not as bad as you'd expect). The museum also has a large hall that houses popular touring exhibits, an IMAX theatre, and the world-class Gates Planetarium. If you want to take in a very large movie at the adjoining IMAX Theater, you can buy combination tickets for both the museum and the show at a considerable discount — only a few dollars more than the price of museum admission.

See map p. 114. 2001 Colorado Blvd. ☎ *303-322-7009.* www.dmnh.org. *Open: Daily 9 a.m.–5 p.m. Closed December 25. Museum admission: $9 adults, $6 seniors 60 and over and kids 3–18. Museum and IMAX or planetarium combination tickets: $13 adults, $9 seniors and kids 3–18. Museum, IMAX, and planetarium combination tickets: $16 adults, $12 seniors and kids 3–18.*

Denver Zoo
City Park

The nation's fourth most popular zoo and Colorado's number-one cultural attraction, the zoo has a marvelous array of critters, including rhinos (one of whom paints — I kid you not) and hippos; lions, tigers, and jaguars; a large bird population that includes a rare Andean condor; a group of rare Komodo dragons; and 29 species of primates, including Brazilian monkeys that wander freely through the zoo (with zoo employees close behind). Not only do the 3,500 animals appear healthy, the zoo also seems determined to teach visitors about the destruction of animal habitats around the planet. Numerous information panels discuss threats to animals and explain how zoos protect endangered species through conservation and breeding programs. The zoo offers eight free admission days annually. The dates change, so call before you go or visit their Web site to find out whether a free day will occur during your visit. Keep in mind, though, that the zoo tends to be *very* crowded on these days.

See map p. 114. 23rd Avenue between Colorado and York. ☎ *303-376-4800.* www.denverzoo.org. *Open: Apr–Sept daily 9 a.m.–6 p.m. (gates close at 5 p.m.); Oct–March daily 10 a.m.–5 p.m. (gates close at 4 p.m.). Admission: $11 adults summer, $9 adults winter; $9 seniors 62 and over summer, $7 seniors winter; $7 children 3–11 (accompanied by an adult) summer, $5 children winter; free for children under 3.*

Ocean Journey
Platte River Valley

Two distinct journeys are offered at this $93-million aquarium. One traces a river as it flows from an Indonesian rain forest to the Pacific Ocean; the other follows the Colorado River from the Rockies to the Sea of Cortez. Each journey features aquariums housing the plant and animal species that the river would have at different points. For example, the first tanks in the Colorado River journey show trout and other species that may inhabit a mountain brook; the last tanks show seahorses, eels, and puffer fish (among many other species) in the Sea of Cortez, below the river's delta. Watching the Pacific Ocean tanks, where sharks and colorful reef fish swim all around you, even underfoot and overhead, is the most fun.

Where the Old West meets the new: The National Western Stock Show, Rodeo & Horse Show

If you're in Denver in mid-January, this can't-miss event offers a bunch of different family-pleasing options, from first-class professional rodeo to an exhibition and sale of ranching and farming equipment. The rodeo is what most people come out for; with competitions throughout the two weeks of Stock Show events featuring barrel races, saddle bronc riding, and, of course, bull riding. A special treat is the Mexican Extravaganza, two shows usually near the beginning of the two-week event that showcases the Mexican roots of both rodeo and, actually, all of North American western culture. These shows are more about showmanship than the subjugation of farm animals, and they're quite a spectacle. There's also a world-class horse show, exhibits of exotic livestock, a petting zoo, and an exposition of farming and ranching equipment, which is well worth the trip for home gardeners. The whole shebang happens in a complex north of Downtown, just off I-70 and east of I-25. Call ☎ **303-297-1166** or visit www.nationalwestern.com for schedules, tickets, and information.

The most breathtaking display, however, is a simulated flash flood in the red rock desert of Utah. The price of admission is steep, but you'll enjoy what you get, even if it only lasts a few hours.

See map p. 114. 700 Water St. ☎ ***303-561-4450.*** www.oceanjourney.org. *Daily 10 a.m.–6 p.m. Admission: $14.95 adults, $12.95 youths 13–17 and seniors 65 and up, $6.95 children 4–12, free for children under 4.*

Six Flags Elitch Gardens Amusement Park
Platte River Valley

This Six Flags–owned amusement park, which opened in the Platte Valley in 1996, takes its name from an 1889 theme park in another, leafier part of town. With 48 thrill rides on the premises, the newer incarnation is more about defying gravity than gardening. Highlights include Boomerang, which drops you 125 feet, throws you for a few twists and flips, and then replays the whole ordeal in reverse; and Mind Eraser, a suspended roller coaster that hits speeds over 60 mph. The park also has gentler rides for kids too little and adults too big to enjoy nausea. Admission to Island Kingdom Water Park, which has a wave pool and giant waterslides, is included in the price.

See map p. 114. 2000 Elitch Circle. ☎ ***303-455-4771.*** www.sixflags.com. *Open: Daily 10 a.m.–10 p.m. during summer. Usually open 10 a.m.–8 p.m. on weekends during May, Sept, and Oct. (call for low-season hours). Admission: $38 for people over 48 inches tall; $22 for people under 48 inches tall, seniors 55–69, and the disabled; free for children under 4 and seniors over 69.*

Touring historical sites

Built over the course of 30 years beginning in 1886, the **Colorado State Capitol Building** can't help but command attention. It has 4-foot-thick granite walls, immense pillars, and a 272-foot-high, gold-coated dome visible from miles away. Inside, the capitol has wainscoting of rare Colorado onyx, stained-glass windows, murals, paintings, chandeliers, and an 80-foot rotunda. Free 40-minute tours depart every half hour from 9:00 a.m. to 3:30 p.m. during summer and every 45 minutes from 9:00 a.m. to 2:30 p.m. the rest of the year. The tour guides are thorough — and then some. If you're short on time, pick up a free guide to the capitol at the tour desk and walk around on your own. And don't worry about doing something wrong — if you're about to violate protocol, a very large guard will let you know. For more information on tours, call ☎ 303-866-2604. The capitol is at the corner of Broadway and Colfax Avenue. The public entrance is at street level on the building's south (14th Street) side.

Molly Brown not only survived the _Titanic_ disaster, she was also a philanthropist, suffragist, fashion plate, activist, mother, social matron, and sometime yodeler who lived in Denver's Capitol Hill neighborhood. You can almost sense Brown's unsinkable presence at the **Molly Brown House Museum,** 1340 Pennsylvania St. (☎ 303-832-4092; http://molly brown.org), an 1888 Victorian mansion where Brown lived in the early 1900s. Some of Brown's personal effects are here, including alabaster sculptures, a Tiffany lamp, and a Mother of Pearl tray from Japan. And the house itself has been lovingly restored. The only way you can go inside is on a 45-minute tour, offered from 10:00 a.m. to 3:30 p.m. Tuesday through Saturday, noon to 4:30 p.m. on Sunday. (During summer, tours are also offered from 10:00 a.m. to 3:30 p.m. on Monday.) Cost is $6.50 for adults, $3 for children ages 6 to 12, and $5 for ages 65 and up.

The free walk-in tours of the **U. S. Mint,** located at West Colfax Avenue and Cherokee Street, were suspended after the terrorist attacks of September 11, 2001. At press time, visitors couldn't enter the mint unless they prearranged a visit through a member of Congress. To check on the status of the tours, call ☎ 303-405-4761.

Other things to see and do

Like a lot of cities, Denver brims with small, diverse attractions that can momentarily (and sometimes permanently) change your perspective. Around Denver, you can

- **Recognize long-overlooked cowboys.** As many as a third of the cowboys on the great cattle drives of the 19th century were African American. The **Black American West Museum and Heritage Center,** 3091 California St., at 31st Street (☎ 303-292-2566; www.blackamericanwest.org), celebrates the often-overlooked role of African-Americans in pioneering and settling the American West. It also tells the stories of other early black settlers, including physicians, legislators, miners, and teachers. Open since 1971, the museum is in the three-story, 1,800-square-foot home of Justina Ford, the first African-American female doctor in Denver. It's right across from the Downing Street light-rail stop. Hours: May through September daily 10 a.m. to 5 p.m.; October through April Wednesday through Friday 10 a.m. to 2 p.m. and Saturday and Sunday 10 a.m. to 5 p.m. Admission: $6 adults, $5 seniors 65 and over, $4 children 5 to 12.

✔ **Look closely at small things.** The **Denver Museum of Miniatures, Dolls, and Toys,** 1880 Gaylord St. (☎ 303-322-1053; www.dmmdt.com), exhibits miniatures, including some tiny, highly detailed dollhouses; dolls from around the globe; and toys ranging from 17th-century antiques to modern action figures. It's in the 1899 Pearce-McAllister Cottage. Hours: Tuesday through Saturday 10 a.m. to 4 p.m., Sunday 1 to 4 p.m. Admission: $5 adults, $4 seniors and children 2 to 16.

✔ **Shrink your art world.** There's no reason to run through the 3,500-square-foot **Museum of Contemporary Art,** 1275 19th Street, in Sakura Square (☎ 303-298-7554; www.mcartdenver.org). Go slowly and absorb the full impact of the paintings, sculptures, and installations, because the space is small, the concepts are thought-provoking, and the art will never be here again. (There is no permanent collection; the exhibitions change every few months.) If you're a film buff, call and inquire about experimental film nights, which showcase works from the Modern Art Library in New York. In 2006, the museum expects to open in a brand-new building in LoDo. Open: Tuesday through Saturday 11:00 a.m. to 5:30 p.m. Admission: $5 adults, $3 students and seniors, free for children 12 and under.

✔ **Chase butterflies.** The main attraction at the **Butterfly Pavilion and Insect Center,** 6252 W. 104th Ave., at U.S. 36 in Westminster (☎ 303-469-5441; www.butterflies.org), is a conservatory housing 1,200 butterflies from around the world. If you're used to visiting museums where displays are fixed in place, you'll need to get used to this place, where butterflies flutter all around you and sometimes disappear altogether. When you get in the habit of scanning the tropical vegetation for resting butterflies, however, you'll be able to admire more of them up close, and you may even come to enjoy the search. In the museum's Crawl-A-See-'Em, kids can pet a tarantula and examine other creepy-crawlers such as giant centipedes, black widow spiders, and cockroaches. If they still feel like eating afterward, there's a snack shop, too. Open: Daily 9 a.m. to 5 p.m. (until 6 p.m. in summer). Admission: $7.95 ages 13 to 61, $5.95 seniors 62 and up, $4.95 children 4 to 12.

✔ **Get small.** About 30 miles west of Denver, brake fast and you'll find yourself at **Tiny Town,** 6429 S. Turkey Creek Rd., off U.S. 285 5 miles west of Colorado 470 (☎ 303-697-6829; www.tinytownrailroad.com). All 100 buildings in this historic Wild West town are to ⅙

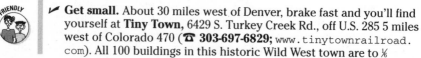

scale — even the windows, doorknobs, and doorways. The buildings are too small for adults or anyone else who is not to ⅙ scale,
but small kids fit inside and adults will appreciate the detail work.
A miniature steam locomotive circles a ⅜-mile track through the
grounds (cost: $1). Built by a father for his daughter in the early
1920s, Tiny Town became a popular tourist attraction in the late
'20s, but after a flood made it a tiny disaster area, it became a tiny
ghost town in the early 1970s. In the late 1980s, the owners
restored the site and it's now a great place for kids. There's also an
open-air playground, snack bar, picnic area, and gift shop. Open:
10 a.m. to 5 p.m. on weekends in May, September, and October;
daily 10 a.m. to 5 p.m. from Memorial Day through Labor Day.
Admission: $3 ages 12 and up, $2 children 2 to 12.

Staying Active

Denver residents are an active bunch — statistically the thinnest city
dwellers in the United States. When they get serious about exercising,
they often make a beeline for the mountains surrounding the city. But
there's plenty to do around town as well. While you're in Denver, you
can take a break from sightseeing for any of the following:

- **Biking:** Denver's extensive trail system makes this a fun place to
  ride a bike. You can't go everywhere on a bike (safely), but you can
  pedal and run on over 400 miles of paved designated trails. My
  favorite places for biking are the trails alongside **Cherry Creek** and
  the **South Platte River.** You can access these trails at many downtown locations. For more information, contact **Bicycle Colorado**
  (☎ **303-417-1544;** www.bicyclecolo.org).

- **Boating/rafting:** At the confluence of Cherry Creek and the South
  Platte River is a short stretch of whitewater in a man-made park
  where you can practice your kayaking during peak flows. The park
  is near **REI,** 1416 Platte St. (☎ **303-756-3100**). Use the designated
  parking area near the park or else feed one of the meters on the
  street.

- **Golfing:** The City of Denver operates seven public golf courses,
  and there are many more in the suburbs. The one most convenient
  to the downtown core is at **City Park,** E. 25th Ave. at York Street
  (☎ **303-295-4420**). Greens fees are $20 for 18 holes, $12 for 9 holes
  ($24 and $14, respectively, on weekends). Reservations are available for residents seven days in advance; for nonresidents, five
  days in advance.

- **Hiking:** If you're interested in hiking (as opposed to walking), head
  for **Denver's Mountain Parks,** a system of 31 parks totaling 14,000
  acres in the foothills and mountains west of town. Far and away the
  best for short hikes is **Red Rocks Park,** on Colorado 74 between
  Evergreen and Morrison. For more on the mountain parks, surf the
  Internet to www.denver.org or call ☎ **303-697-4545.**

✔ **Running:** You can run in any number of Denver City parks. **Washington Park,** at Downing Street and Virginia Avenue, has long been the outdoor workout ground of choice. There's a crushed-granite jogging path around the mile-plus perimeter, and a paved ring road for bikes and rollerblades.

✔ **Playing tennis:** The Denver Department of Parks and Recreation (☎ 303-964-2500) manages or owns close to 150 tennis courts, more than a third of them lit for night play. For $3 an hour, you can rent one of the 12 courts at **City Park,** E. 25th Avenue at York Street. Go to the **Denver Parks and Recreation Permitting Office,** 2300 15th St. (☎ 303-964-2522), to purchase some court time.

Taking in a pro sports event

Anyone who has seen Denver Broncos fans smeared with orange and blue body paint knows that the town takes its sports *very* seriously. It's a big-league city, with pro teams in all the major sports. All these teams sell tickets through **Ticketmaster** (☎ 303-830-TIXS; www.ticketmaster.com). Here's the roster that spurs the city's sport-minded faithful:

✔ The **Colorado Avalanche** (☎ 303-893-6700; www.coloradoavalanche.com) captured the National Hockey League's Stanley Cup in 1996, the first season after the franchise moved to Denver from Quebec City. The team won the championship again in 2001 and has challenged for the Cup most years since then. Tickets to Avalanche games at the **Pepsi Center** (corner of Speer Boulevard and Auraria Parkway) are the second most difficult to obtain in Denver (behind Broncos tickets). Even if you can find a seat at face value, it won't come cheap. Prices range from $25 for the upper-end balconies to $224 for the front row behind the glass.

✔ Because of Denver's thin air, baseballs that are walloped at **Coors Field** (in LoDo) tend to carry out of the park easily. All this adds up to runs and action galore, which may be one reason that the **Colorado Rockies** (☎ 800-388-7625 or 303-762-5347; www.coloradorockies.com) regularly sell most of their 50,000 seats. Prices for Rockies games range from $5 to $45, with the leftover cheap seats, in an area known as the Rockpile, going for $2 and $5 on game day — one of the best deals in baseball.

✔ The **Denver Broncos** (☎ 720-258-3333; www.denverbroncos.com) play their home National Football League games at **Invesco Field at Mile High,** a $360 million, 76,000-seat stadium that was completed in 2001. Played from September through December, the eight regular-season home games always sell out, but if you order your tickets right after they go on sale in early summer, you should be able to obtain seats. Prices range from $30 to $311.

✔ The other pro football name in town belongs to the **Colorado Crush** (☎ 720-258-3400; www.coloradocrush.com) of the indoor Arena Football League. Co-owned by Denver Bronco–legend John Elway, the squad's home games take place at the **Pepsi Center,** and ticket prices range from $7 to $46.

✔ The **Denver Nuggets** have been popular whipping boys during most of their time in the NBA, but recent management changes and the addition of Carmelo Anthony have made the team competitive in the tough Western Conference. They play at the striking new **Pepsi Center** (☎ 303-405-1100; www.nuggets.com), at the corner of Speer Boulevard and Auraria Parkway. The place seats up to 19,309, and the season runs from late October through mid-April. Tickets range in price from $10 to $325.

✔ The **Colorado Rapids** (☎ 800-844-7777 or 303-299-1599; www.colorado rapids.com) compete in Major League Soccer from late March through early September at **Invesco Field at Mile High.** Tickets cost $14 to $40.

✔ If lacrosse is more your speed, check out the **Colorado Mammoth** (☎ 303-405-1101; www.coloradomammoth.com). This National Lacrosse League franchise plays at the **Pepsi Center** from January through April. Tickets run from $5 to $38.

Seeing Denver by Guided Tour

If Denver seems like too much of a load for you to tackle alone, you can choose from a number of guided walking, bus, and trolley tours. I offer a few good options here.

Faux trolley tours

During summer, the **Cultural Connection Trolley** (☎ 303-289-2841), which strongly resembles a bus, makes hourly stops at each of Denver's prime tourist attractions, including Cherry Creek Shopping Center, Ocean Journey, Union Station, Larimer Square, and Coors Field. Most major hotels have brochures with the trolley's schedule. Just pay the driver $16 per adult, $8 per child under 12 (MasterCard and Visa are accepted), upon boarding, and you can ride all day between 8:00 a.m. and 5:30 p.m. A recording triggered by a global positioning system highlights the major sights you pass, and you can get on and off at any of the stops and catch the next bus, er, trolley.

Real trolley tours

The **Platte Valley Trolley** (☎ 303-458-6255; www.denvertrolley.org) parallels a scenic stretch of the Platte River while passing Invesco Field at Mile High, Six Flags Elitch Gardens, and Ocean Journey Aquarium. Unlike the Cultural Connection Trolley, this trolley actually travels on tracks. It operates from May 25 through September 8 from 11 a.m. to 4 p.m. daily. Cost for the half-hour ride is $3 for adults, $1 for seniors and children. To get there, take I-25 to 23rd Avenue (Exit 211). Turn east onto Water Street and follow the signs.

Guided tours

Half- and full-day bus tours of Denver and the nearby Rockies are offered by the ubiquitous **Gray Line** (☎ **800-348-6877** for information only, 303-289-2841 for reservations and information; www.coloradogray line.com). Prices range from $25 to $75 depending on the tour and include entry fees but usually no food; children 12 and under pay half the adult price. Tours depart the Cherry Creek Shopping Center at First Avenue and Milwaukee Street, as well as local hotels and hostels on a reservation basis.

Another company offering guided tours in and around Denver is **The Colorado Sightseer**, 6780 W. 84th Circle, Suite 60 (☎ **303-423-8200;** www.coloradosightseer.com). Prices range from $35 to $75 and include entrance fees to some of the destinations, which include locations outside Denver such as Rocky Mountain National Park and Boulder.

The **LoDo District** (☎ **303-628-5484;** www.lodo.org) offers guided walking tours of the historic area. Tours depart from Union Station (17th and Wynkoop streets) on Saturday at 10 a.m.; the cost is $5 per person. Two certified paranormal investigators conduct a variety of tours given by **Gunslingers, Ghosts & Gold** (☎ **303-860-8687**). As the name implies, the emphasis is on haunted houses and history, with some humor thrown in. Tours cost around $10 to $15 per person.

Considering One-, Two-, and Three-Day Itineraries

If you don't add a trip to a remote destination, the sightseeing in Denver breaks down neatly into a three-day itinerary. None of the daylong itineraries is clearly superior to the others. If you're only in town for a day or so, you'll just have to choose which itinerary you (or your kids) like best. If you have a few extra hours in the evening, LoDo and the 16th Street Mall are always fun options.

On **Day 1,** concentrate on the **Capitol Hill** area. Take in some of the works at the **Denver Art Museum.** From there, look at the tiny dioramas at the **Colorado History Museum.** If you're hungry for lunch, stop at one of the cafes near 13th Avenue and Pearl Street. In the afternoon, tour the **Molly Brown House.** Allow a little extra time to stroll past the historic homes near the Molly Brown House, and then accompany a group through the **State Capitol Building.** Finish by cruising three blocks north on Broadway to the ornate **Brown Palace Hotel** for a cold beverage.

The Denver Art Museum has taken pains to make itself kid-friendly, but children still may not enjoy this day as much as Days 2 and 3, so if you have young children, you may want to skip this plan and go straight to Day 2.

Start **Day 2** by venturing a few miles west of the downtown area to **City Park.** Visit the **Denver Museum of Nature and Science,** then walk across the park to the **Denver Zoo.** After observing the animals, make the short drive to the **Cherry Creek North** area. Have a late lunch, and then browse the shops and galleries there. In the soft light of late afternoon, wind down with a stroll in the **Denver Botanic Gardens.** If you're heading back into the downtown area from here, detour past some of the historic homes in the **Uptown** neighborhood. Consider dining at one of the fine restaurants on 17th Avenue.

On **Day 3,** drive or take a light-rail train into the **Platte River Valley** and visit **Ocean's Journey.** Lunch at **Zang Brewing Co.,** 2301 Seventh St. (☎ 303-455-2500), a historic brewery that now houses a popular sports bar and restaurant. Then head for **Six Flags Elitch Gardens.** You can kill the better part of a day at the park, but you may want to save some time and energy to really visit LoDo on your way back Downtown. If you're taking the light-rail into town, stop at or near **Union Station** and stroll the galleries in **LoDo.** Use the free buses on 16th Street to take in other parts of the 16th Street Mall. Enjoy dinner at one of the dozens of restaurants in this area.

Shopping in Denver

Store hours in Denver tend to vary from place to place. Generally, stores are open Monday through Saturday, with many open on Sunday, too; department stores usually stay open until 9 p.m. at least one evening a week. Discount stores and supermarkets are often open later than other stores, and some supermarkets are open 24 hours a day.

The best shopping areas

Denver's most lively shopping district is the **16th Street Mall,** a downtown street that's been converted into a pedestrian-only walkway and has free bus service running its entire mile-long length. The mall's clientele includes everyone from office workers to tourists, and the businesses are as diverse as the shoppers. Nestled into the mall between Welton and Tremont streets is the glittery new, $100 million **Denver Pavilions,** home to trendy chains such as Niketown, Wolfgang Puck's Café, and Virgin Megastore. Besides the big stores, the 16th Street Mall features discount outlets such as T.J. Maxx and Ross Dress For Less as well as dozens of locally owned shops, T-shirt stores, brewpubs, and cafes. During warm weather, you can sit at one of many sidewalk cafes, people-watch, and soak in the colors from some of the 25,000 flowers planted annually. Also located on the mall is the **Tabor Center,** home to ESPN Zone and other restaurants.

When you're walking the 16th Street Mall, make sure to detour south two blocks on Larimer Avenue. Follow the street as it takes you past **Writer Square,** 1512 Larimer (☎ 303-628-9056), a block of jewelry stores, gift shops, galleries, and restaurants, and on to **Larimer Square** (☎ 303-534-2367), where quirky businesses are tucked into nooks and crannies of historic Victorian buildings. If you tire of shopping, walk over to the Larimer Square information booth and get a free brochure describing a walking tour of the area. And if you feel like wandering the galleries of **LoDo,** venture in either direction off of 16th Street onto Wynkoop, Wazee, or Blake streets.

Don't come to **Cherry Creek Mall,** 3000 E. First Ave. (☎ 303-388-3900), for bargain hunting. Located 3 miles southeast of Downtown, this thriving, upscale mall is one of the largest and most popular attractions in Denver, and the prices reflect the high demand. Premium retailers such as Saks Fifth Avenue, Neiman Marcus, Lord & Taylor, and Foley's anchor the 160 shops and restaurants. Parking is free and usually easy. If it isn't, you can valet park for $7 for the first three hours, $1 for each additional hour. The mall is open Monday through Friday from 10 a.m. to 9 p.m., Saturday from 10 a.m. to 8 p.m., and Sunday from 11 a.m. to 6 p.m.

Across the street from Cherry Creek Mall, along First, Second, and Third avenues between University Boulevard and Steele Street, the leafy suburban shopping district of **Cherry Creek North** (☎ 303-394-2903), is home to 330 shops, 50 spas and salons, and 25 high-end art galleries. Around here, it's easier to find a large gem than a polished rock and much easier to find a priceless antique than cool junk. Even if you're not buying, come here to admire the galleries, many of which feature museum-quality work. Plan on staying for a meal — some of the city's finest restaurants are in this area. Most stores are open Monday through Saturday from 10 a.m. to 6 p.m., Sunday from noon to 5 p.m.

What to look for and where to find it

You can find everything from A to Z in Denver, provided you have enough time for all the letters. The following sections offer information on some places with character where you can start your Denver-area shopping.

Art

Earthzone Mineral and Fossil Gallery, 1411 Larimer St. (☎ 303-572-8198), offers art, jewelry, home decorations, and gifts made partly or entirely of fossils and minerals. The stones aren't as precious as gems or diamonds, but they're nearly as pretty after the gallery's featured artists finish with them.

If you want to find that perfect oil painting of a cowboy at sunset, start your search at **Mudhead Gallery** at the Hyatt Regency, 555 17th St. (☎ 303-293-0007). As one of Denver's main trading posts for Southwestern and Western art, Mudhead offers paintings and bronze sculptures by Western artists, as well as Native American pottery, baskets, fetishes, and rugs.

The **Camera Obscura Gallery,** 13th Avenue and Bannock Street (☎ 303-623-4059), is the place to go for great photography, past and present. **David Cook/Fine American Art,** 1637 Wazee St. (☎ 303-623-4817), specializes in Native American art and trades for premium items.

Books

If it starts raining during your visit, head for either of two **Tattered Cover Bookstores.** The employees at these stores actually want you to sit around and read. You can settle into an overstuffed chair near a reading lamp, then leaf through a magazine or book without worrying about whether the pages become dog-eared. Eventually, as payment, you should consider purchasing one of the more than 150,000 available titles or at least get some coffee to stay alert. The older and larger store is in Cherry Creek, at the corner of First Avenue and Milwaukee Street (☎ 303-322-7727; www.tatteredcover.com); the other occupies a historic mercantile building at the corner of 16th and Wynkoop streets (☎ 303-436-1070) at the LoDo end of the 16th Street Mall.

Imports

For clothes by the hottest designers from New York, Rome, and Paris, shop the big stores and boutiques at **Cherry Creek Mall,** 3000 E. First Ave. (☎ 303-388-3900). For clothes by the hottest designers in Nepal, Tibet, and India, go to **Mount Everest Import,** 707 16th St. (☎ 303-573-8451), in the 16th Street Mall. The shop also carries fabrics, weavings, and musical instruments.

Maps

The **Tattered Cover Bookstores** (see the previous "Books" section) have great map departments, and even better departments with books detailing the sights, history, geology, and any other aspect of the Colorado region you can imagine. If you're heading to the high country, **REI,** 1416 Platte St., next to Confluence Park in the Central Platte Valley (☎ 303-756-3100), will have most of what you're looking for; better, though, is to get United States Geological Survey (USGS) maps directly from the source at the **Earth Science Information Center (ESIC)** on the grounds of the Denver Federal Center. Take 6th Avenue west to Kipling Street, head south to Gate #1 and tell the guards at the gate you want the map store. They'll point you in the right direction, and you won't find better prices (or better maps) anywhere else.

Music

Seasoned record collectors recognize **Jerry's Records,** 312 E. Colfax Ave. (☎ 303-830-2336), as a world-class phenomenon: It has thousands of LPs in stock, along with plenty of CDs and alternative music publications, and the prices here are legendarily low. If digging through stacks of vinyl or finding that cool CD is your bag, Jerry's is a must.

If you don't find what you're after there, head around the corner to **Wax Trax,** 638 E. 13th Ave. (☎ **303-831-7246**), Denver's established alternative-culture headquarters. They have a great poster and novelty shop next door, and awesome blues and jazz collections on both CD and vinyl.

Sports equipment/gear

Denver's **REI Flagship,** 1416 Platte St. (☎ **303-756-3100;** www.rei.com), occupies a parklike setting near the confluence of Cherry Creek and the South Platte River. The gargantuan store features a climbing wall, an outdoor bike-testing area, and a "cold room" to try out outerwear and sleeping bags. You can load up on the gear of your dreams, then go running or bicycling on paved paths alongside the river or, better still, kayak in a nearby whitewater park on the South Platte River.

The **Gart Sports** store at Tenth and Broadway (☎ **303-861-1122;** www.gartsports.com) was the outdoor retailer's first huge Sportscastle and is the largest sporting goods store in the country. Since then, Gart has opened another 17 Denver-area stores. Unlike REI, which concentrates more intensely on backcountry endeavors, Gart covers a wider variety of sports, including old standbys such as basketball, baseball, and football. The store's five stories feature a range of fun activities for the sports-minded, including a driving cage for golfers and ball courts on the roof.

Gart Sports's annual Sniagrab (that's *bargains* spelled backwards), offers rock-bottom prices on ski equipment every Labor Day weekend.

Nightlife

Denver has some 30 theaters, more than 100 cinemas, and dozens of concert halls, nightclubs, discos, and bars. Clubs offer country-and-western music, jazz, rock, and comedy. A good online resource for local music is www.coloradomusic.org.

Current entertainment listings appear in special Friday-morning sections of the two daily newspapers, the *Denver Post* and *Rocky Mountain News. Westword,* a weekly newspaper distributed free throughout the city every Wednesday, has perhaps the best listings: It focuses on the arts, entertainment, and local politics. *The Denver Post* (☎ **303-777-FILM;** www.777film.com) provides information on movie showtimes and theaters.

The "Denver Attractions & Nightlife" map earlier in this chapter includes locations for many of the hot spots mentioned here.

Hitting the local clubs

It may not be renowned for its underground, but Denver has an active club scene and you usually won't have to go far to find a place that suits your taste. There are lounges, dance halls, music clubs, and even a few genuine dives. Following is a sampling of the best clubs around town.

Country

Touring country acts sometimes park their buses at the **Grizzly Rose Saloon and Dance Emporium,** 5450 N. Valley Hwy. (☎ **303-295-2353**). Near Downtown most nights, the place to be is **Skylark Lounge,** 140 Broadway (☎ **303-722-7844**), which hosts the best alternative-country bands in the area.

Dance

The most popular dance club in town, as of this minute, is **The Alley Cat** (☎ **303-571-4545**), located at 1222 Glenarm Place behind the Diamond Cabaret strip club. On weekends it has a $15 cover charge, gets thronged with young people who are half-dressed to the nines, and features cage dancers who look as if they just got off work next door. DJs spin music in the main chamber; a smaller lounge has trance music.

If salsa is more to your liking, head for **La Rumba,** 99 W. Ninth St. (☎ **303-572-8006**).

Jazz

Jazz enthusiasts should not miss the legendary **El Chapultepec,** 1962 Market St. (☎ **303-295-9126**). This small club has offered free nightly jazz since the 1950s. One long wall is covered with photos of jazz legends who have played this tiny room, including Tony Bennett, Ella Fitzgerald, and Frank Sinatra. Despite having such an illustrious past, the bar still charges no cover and has just a one-drink minimum per set. Just make sure you get there early.

Sambuca, 1320 15th St. (☎ **303-629-5299**), is an ultraswank new club that revives the supper-club scene of the Swing era. You'll definitely want reservations here, and whatever you do, don't dress down. There's live music most nights of the week — swing, jazz, and blues — and an excellent kitchen.

Rock, funk, and R&B

For the past 20 years, **Herman's Hideaway,** 1578 S. Broadway (☎ **303-777-5840**), has helped launch the careers of Colorado's up-and-coming bands. Herman's keeps its prices reasonable even when the most popular acts are playing: $4 on most weekend nights, and $7 on most Fridays and Saturdays.

The most rockin' local and regional bands can be heard at the **Ogden Theatre,** 935 E. Colfax Ave. (☎ **303-830-2525**). If you want to catch a national touring act, check the listings at two theatres on Colfax Avenue: the **Bluebird Theater,** 3317 E. Colfax (☎ **303-322-2308**), and the larger **Fillmore Auditorium,** 1510 Clarkson, at Colfax (☎ **303-837-1482**), an all-ages ballroom that has limited seating and a large dance floor.

A clean, well-lighted place, indeed . . .

If you're looking for something nonintoxicating — especially if you're staying in the Uptown neighborhood — check out **St. Mark's Coffeehouse,** 2019 E. 17th Ave. (☎ 303-322-8384). This family establishment has been caffeinating the local counter-culture for years. The homemade brownies, pies, and pastries are legendary, and it's a good place for a light and inexpensive lunch, too, with panini and a rotating selection of soups. In the summer, the front windows are raised by a garage-door opener, making the whole place as open-air as the sidewalk tables out front. Excellent local artists display their work on the walls.

For those who want a beer or cocktail without the downtown scene, head next door to **The Thin Man,** owned by the same folks, who present a serious range of microbrews and house-flavored vodka.

Drinking up

More beer is brewed in Denver than in any other U.S. city, and foamy, frothy beverages flow liberally at establishments throughout town. No matter what your preferred poison — be it a Bond-style martini or a microbrew — you're sure to find a place that serves it.

Lounges/martini bars

Lotus, 1701 Wynkoop St. (☎ 303-718-6666), next to Union Station in LoDo, boasts velvet ropes, burly doormen, expensive martinis . . . what more could a hipster want? For a slightly different experience, **Fadó Irish Pub,** 1735 19th St., next to the Denver Chophouse and Brewery (☎ 303-297-0066), runs the gamut of Irish pub experiences, from leaded-glass-and-wainscoting Dublin elegance to the earthy, sawdust-on-the-floor country inn — all under one roof! It feels a bit overproduced, but honestly, it's the only place outside of County Cork I've ever had a properly poured pint of Guinness.

Brewpubs

Wynkoop Brewing Company, 1634 18th St. (☎ 303-297-2700; www.wynkoop.com), gave birth to the modern American brewpub, and many still consider it Denver's best. Along with its great beer, Wynkoop may serve the tastiest food of the area brewpubs, and an added attraction is a large upstairs pool hall, which generally attracts a more party-hearty crowd than the bar.

Breckenridge Brewery, 2220 Blake St. (☎ 303-297-3644; www.breckenridgebrewery.com), has a convenient location kitty-corner to Coors Field and boasts some of the hottest selling microbrews in the west. **Rock Bottom Restaurant and Brewery,** 1001 16th St. (☎ 303-534-7616), usually has around 18 beers on tap, including one named for the brewery's cat, Splatz. It's a popular stopping point for shoppers in the

The red menace

Unless you're from Michigan, think twice before setting foot in **Tin Lizzie,** 1410 Market St. (☎ 720-932-0181). As the official home to displaced Detroit Red Wings fans, this sports bar is as repulsive as a leper colony to most Denverites. It's an especially loathsome place when the Red Wings defeat their archrivals, the Colorado Avalanche. Three words that will win you friends in Denver: Red Wings suck!

16th Street Mall, especially when its large patio is open. And the Coors-owned **Sandlot Brewing Company,** inside Coors Field, sells handcrafted beers with baseball-inspired names. It doesn't open onto the field, but you can hear the crowd while watching the game on TV.

Many local brewpubs — including Breckenridge and Rock Bottom — offer free tours of the brewing process. Call ahead if you're interested.

Sports bars

Denver, being one of America's premier sports cities, hardly lacks for sports bars. The biggest and best known of them is **ESPN Zone,** 1187 16th Street (☎ 303-595-3776), a place with more television sets (130) than many underdeveloped nations. ESPN often does live feeds from the bar during sporting events. The Zone also has food and lots of games that simulate athleticism.

The performing arts

Denver may be best known as a sports town, but its performing-arts scene is pretty active and has a loyal following. A Tony-winning theater company, a symphony orchestra, a ballet, and a modern dance company, among other groups, can all be found in town. And when the big Broadway productions go on tour, they always come out to Denver, attracting theatergoers from throughout the Midwest and the mountains.

Tickets to some of the big shows are available through Ticketmaster (☎ 303-830-TIXS). The Denver Center for the Performing Arts box office (☎ 800-641-1222 or 303-893-4100; www.denvercenter.org) handles other attractions.

Performance venues

The hub of Denver's arts community is the **Denver Performing Arts Complex,** 14th and Curtis streets (☎ 303-640-PLEX; www.denvercenter.org). Also known as "The Plex," the Performing Arts Complex covers four city blocks and has nine theaters totaling 10,000 seats. A walkway under a giant glass arch connects the four theater buildings, which range in age from 11 to 94 years.

The oldest venue, **The Auditorium Theatre,** hosted the 1908 Democratic National Convention and is now home to the Colorado Ballet and touring Broadway musicals. Completed in 1978, **Boettcher Concert Hall** was the nation's first in-the-round symphony hall, with seating for 2,750. The Colorado Symphony Orchestra and other performers take advantage of the superb acoustics, which are adjusted by moving discs suspended from the ceiling. The 2,800-seat **Temple Buell Theater** is the stomping (and leaping) grounds of the Colorado ballet. And the **Helen Bonfils Theatre Complex** houses five small performance venues, the smallest being the 200-seat Source Theatre. A wide variety of productions are staged in the complex each year.

Ballet

The **Colorado Ballet** (☎ 303-837-8888; www.coloradoballet.com) leaps into action from October through May. Tickets range from $19 for rear balcony seating to $101 for the prime spots.

Modern dance

The **Cleo Parker Robinson Dance Company** (☎ 303-295-1759), a multi-cultural dance ensemble, celebrates "the universal language of movement" in productions in fall, winter, and spring. It also has a year-round dance school and outreach programs, including an intervention program for troubled kids. They perform at both the Auditorium Theatre and the Space Theater at the Plex. Tickets are $15 to $38.

Opera

Founded in 1981, **Opera Colorado** (☎ 303-778-1500; www.opera colorado.org) performs three operas between February and May every year. World-class performers often assume the leading roles. Tickets range from $25 to $130.

Symphony

The **Colorado Symphony Orchestra** (☎ 303-893-4100; www.colorado symphony.com) performs over 100 concerts a year, including classical, pops, and family concerts. From September through June, they usually play at the Boettcher Theater in Denver. Tickets cost $15 to $70.

Theater

The **Denver Center Theater Company** (☎ 303-893-3272 events line, 800-641-1222 or 303-893-4100 for tickets) won the 1998 Tony for best regional theater company. It's a very active company, staging 11 plays between October and June every year. Offerings run the gamut from Shakespeare to world premieres. Tickets cost $29 to $34.

If you like theatre on the edgier side, head down to the Acoma Center in the Golden Triangle for a performance by the **Curious Theatre Company** (☎ 303-623-0524; www.curioustheatre.org). They've been producing excellent repertory plays and new works for several years, and are keeping Denver's cultural edge pretty sharp. Tickets cost $20 to $26.

Fast Facts: Denver

American Express

The American Express office at 555 17th St. (☎ 303-383-5050) is open weekdays from 8 a.m. to 5 p.m. Call ☎ 800-528-4800 if you lose your American Express card or ☎ 800-221-7282 if you lose your traveler's checks.

Area Code

Denver's area codes are **303** and **720**. You must dial all ten digits of a phone number even when making local calls.

Emergencies

Dial **911**.

Hospitals

St. Joseph Hospital, 1835 Franklin St. (☎ 303-837-7111), and Children's Hospital, 1056 E. 19th Ave. (☎ 303-861-8888), each provide 24-hour emergency care.

Internet Access and Cybercafes

Many downtown hotels offer business centers for guests and Internet access from guest rooms. At Common Ground Coffee Shop, 17th Street and Wazee (☎ 303-296-9248), you can get online for 10¢ a minute.

Maps

Mapsco Map and Travel Center, 800 Lincoln St. (☎ 800-456-8703 or 303-623-4299), has USGS maps, state maps, globes, and other navigational aids.

Newspapers/Magazines

Denver has two daily papers, *The Denver Post* and *The Rocky Mountain News,* and an alternative newsweekly, *Westword.* National papers such as *The New York Times* and *The Wall Street Journal* are also available.

Pharmacies

Two chain drugstores — Walgreens (☎ 800-WALGREENS or 800-289-2273; www.walgreens.com) and Longs (☎ 800-865-6647; www.longs.com) — have a strong presence in Denver. Call to find the local branch nearest to your location.

Police

Dial ☎ **911**.

Smoking

Denver prohibits smoking in restaurants that don't have separate, well-ventilated areas for smokers, and it limits smoking to designated areas in public venues such as airports and sports arenas.

Weather and Road Updates

Call ☎ 303-337-2500 for recorded weather forecasts and ☎ 303-639-1111 for road conditions.

Chapter 12

Side Trips from Denver

* *

In This Chapter

▶ Touring a trio of boomtowns
▶ Finding a slot machine you can call your own
▶ Navigating five classic Front Range mountain drives

* *

*J*ust a few miles west of Denver, the terrain becomes rugged and the towns are steeped in mining history. Even if you feel most comfortable in a big city, don't pass up the chance to take a day trip into the foothills of the Rockies and beyond.

Riding through the Golden Circle

Golden, Idaho Springs, and Georgetown — collectively known as the *Golden Circle* — boomed during Colorado's first gold rush in 1859. Since then, Golden has grown into a small city of 13,000, thanks in part to the Coors Brewing Company, which operates the world's largest brewery there. Golden works hard to retain a Western flair, partly in honor of Buffalo Bill Cody, who is buried outside the town. Idaho Springs has flourished as a tourist hub, capitalizing on its mining past, its historical hot springs, and its prime location on I-70 west of Denver. Georgetown is the quietest town of the three, but it's the most picturesque. It has a neighborhood of well-preserved Victorian homes, a slow-paced but colorful downtown, and, during the summer months, a historic railroad.

Georgetown has great shopping, if you're looking for art glass, mining memorabilia, geological specimens, or other unique souvenirs. If tchotchkes are your thing, skip the tourist traps on the 16th Street Mall in Denver and head up here for the good stuff.

Getting there

Golden is 15 miles west of downtown Denver. You can get there by exiting off I-70 onto either U.S. 6 or Colorado 58. Idaho Springs is 32 miles west of Denver on I-70, and Georgetown is 13 miles west of Idaho Springs on I-70.

Exploring Golden, Idaho Springs, and Georgetown

 The grave of William "Buffalo Bill" Cody — the long-haired Pony Express rider, buffalo hunter, soldier, and showman — sits atop the aptly named **Lookout Mountain** (I-70, exit 256), between Interstate 70 (to the south) and Golden (to the north). After paying your respects at the grave and absorbing the views of Denver and the Plains, walk a few steps to the **Buffalo Bill Memorial Museum**, 987½ E. Lookout Mountain Rd. (☎ 303-526-0747; www.buffalobill.org). Established soon after Cody's death in 1917, the museum is loaded with colorful memorabilia from Cody's famous Wild West Show. There's also a short video about the show, which traveled the country for nearly 30 years before closing in 1913. The museum is open daily from May through October 9 a.m. to 5 p.m.; November through April, it's open Tuesday through Sunday from 9 a.m. to 4 p.m. Admission is $3 adults 16 and over, $2 seniors 65 and over, and $1 for children ages 6 to 15.

The **Colorado Railroad Museum,** 17155 W. 44th Ave. in Golden (☎ 800-365-6263 or 303-279-4591; www.crrm.org), exhibits thousands of historic photos and documents relating to Colorado's past and present railroads. You can rest your eyes by looking at larger antiques from Colorado's railroads or by clambering around on some of the 60 historic locomotives and rail cars outside. Downstairs, put a quarter in the slot and watch a large, painstakingly decorated model railroad in action. It's fun to see, even if you're not a model-train buff. The museum is open daily from 9 a.m. to 5 p.m. (until 6 p.m. in summer); admission is $7 adults, $6 seniors over 60, $4 for youths under 16, and $16 per family.

The **Georgetown Loop Railroad,** 1106 Rose St. in Georgetown (☎ 800-691-4386 or 303-569-2403; www.georgetownloop.com), follows tracks that are as interesting as the steam engine pulling the cars. In 1877, a railroad company wanted to extend an existing narrow gauge (3-foot-wide) rail line 2 miles from Georgetown to Silver Plume, 600 feet higher than Georgetown but just 2 miles away. To keep the grades manageable, the engineers needed to add as much distance as possible to the line, so they built a 100-foot-high, 300-foot-long trestle where the track finishes an ascending circle by crossing over itself. Today, the train completes the 9-mile round-trip in an hour and ten minutes. Rides are offered daily from mid-May through mid-September. You can catch the train in either Georgetown or Silver Plume, 2 miles west of Georgetown on I-70. If you depart from Silver Plume, you can also take a 70-minute mine tour as part of the package. Trains depart every 80 minutes, daily, from late May to early October. Tickets for just the train ride cost $14.50 adults, $9.50 for children ages 3 to 15. The train-and-mine tour package costs $20.50 adults, $13.50 children.

Indian Springs Resort, 302 Soda Creek Rd. in Idaho Springs (☎ 303-989-6666; www.indianspringsresort.com), has indoor private baths, a swimming pool, outdoor Jacuzzis, and mud baths, but what sets the

Gambling in Central City and Black Hawk

In 1990, a statewide referendum legalized gambling in Black Hawk, Central City, and Cripple Creek (west of Pikes Peak). At the time, Black Hawk and Central City were dilapidated remnants of what was once called "the richest square mile on Earth." Today, a few casinos have moved into the historic brick buildings in downtown Black Hawk and Central City, and other buildings have been revamped and repaired.

Central City and Black Hawk are 34 miles west of Denver. Take I-70 west to exit 243 to Central City Parkway. This new, four-lane road makes the trip to this region much safer and faster than ever. You can self-park in the lots at some of the casinos; others require valet parking. Free 24-hour shuttles regularly run between the two towns. Some of the casinos also run buses to Denver. If you take a casino bus, you usually get your fare back in vouchers for free food and drink and gambling tokens.

A Black Hawk city employee told me there was nothing to do in town but gamble. A closer look reveals that there are, in fact, many activities: You can eat, drink, smoke, stare, walk around, and, if you're lucky enough to get a room, sleep. The town's 24 casinos range from small rooms to sprawling, multistory complexes. Some offer poker and blackjack tables; others have only slot and video machines. Most provide free cocktails if you're playing, and some have even exhumed Las Vegas lounge acts such as Tony Orlando and Sha Na Na. Following are a couple of casino options to consider:

- ✔ The **Mountain High Casino,** 111 Richman St. (☎ **303-567-1234**), boasts the most impressive room. It's decorated in the Colorado Rustic motif, replete with antler lamps, fake logs, lamps that resemble rawhide, and murals of mountain scenes — only, in this case, the rustic look is accompanied by dazzling lights and a bar with televisions the size of drive-in movie screens.

- ✔ If a tropical motif is more to your liking, go to **Isle of Capri Casino,** 401 Main St. (☎ **800-THE-ISLE;** www.isleofcapricasino.com/Black_Hawk). It has a real, live tropical bird, a three-story waterfall, and fake palm trees — as well as the most rooms in town.

place apart are its geothermal caves. Segregated by gender, each cave has its own pools fed by geothermal hot springs. The pools are an intense 104 to 112 degrees, and the air temperature inside the caves is in the 90s, so you can really get roasted (if not toasted). Built in 1905, the main resort building looks its age, and the men's changing area resembles a high-school locker room, but the caves make it worthwhile. The caves are open 7:30 a.m. to 10:30 p.m. daily; admission (you must be at least 13 years of age) costs $16.50 Monday through Thursday and $18.50 Friday through Sunday and holidays. The resort offers other bathing options (indoor and outdoor), each with a separate price of admission. If you're too zapped to go anywhere after getting out of the caves, rent a rustic room in the lodge or a room in newer buildings across the street. Rooms at the resort range from $59 to $88 double.

Taking a tour

If the wait isn't too long, the free **Coors Brewery Tour** (☎ 303-277-BEER) is a winner: Just follow the signs to the parking area at 13th and Ford streets in downtown Golden. Shuttles pick you up and take you to the brewery entrance. Inside, you can look at displays on the history of Coors; watch dewy commercials starring the company chairman, Pete Coors; go on a 40-minute brewery tour; and then quaff 24 ounces of free beer. Oddly enough, the tour is most interesting for what is *not* going on. The brewery, the world's largest, is so thoroughly mechanized that few employees are visible and almost nothing moves until you reach the packaging area. The wait can be long on summer afternoons, and it may not always be worth it (except, of course, for the free beer).

If your main goal at the Coors Brewery is to down a couple free beers, tell the people in front that you want to go on a short tour or beer tasting. They'll point you to the taps. Tours run Monday through Saturday from 10 a.m. to 4 p.m. Admission is free.

The best mine tour in the Front Range is the **Phoenix Mine Tour** (☎ 303-567-0422; www.phoenixmine.com), a small operation just outside Idaho Springs on Trail Creek Road (off Stanley Road). As part of the tour, you get a hard hat and then get to accompany a real miner on foot into a working gold mine. After the tour, you can pan for gold in a nearby creek; you can keep whatever you find. The cost is $9 for adults, $8 for seniors, and $5 for children under 12. It's open 10 a.m. to 6 p.m. daily, even during winter if the road is passable. To reach the mine, follow Colorado Boulevard west through Idaho Springs, go under the bridge, and follow the signs.

Hitting the slopes

Travelers heading west from Denver on I-70 may catch a glimpse of a few runs near the base of **Loveland Ski Area** (☎ 800-736-3SKI or 303-571-5580; www.skiloveland.com) just before disappearing into Eisenhower tunnel, which crosses the continental divide by going directly *under* the hill. What they don't see is a beautiful ski area, particularly when the weather is calm and fair. Much of the skiable terrain is above the tree line, in a vast, horseshoe-shaped basin that sits flush against the east side of the continental divide. Loveland allows skiers of all ability levels to sample the joy of skiing at high elevations on open faces where the air is so thin and fresh it seems to hum. The best skiing is off Lift 9, the highest four-person chairlift in North America, which unloads you atop the continental divide at 12,700 feet in elevation. From there, you can head in either direction, eventually dropping in wherever the terrain intrigues you. Lift lines here are usually short, and the base area, which has ample parking, tends to be relaxed. The main drawback to this mountain is its potentially ferocious storms. But that same weather contributes to the 400-inch annual snowfall here, which allows the resort to stay open into May.

For $38, Loveland offers a four-hour lift ticket that goes into effect the moment it is sold, no matter what time of day it is. Buy this $38 ticket, ski four hours straight, and then call it a day. You'll save money, enjoy a great day of skiing, and quit before your legs get too tired.

For the vital facts and figures on Loveland Ski Area, see the chart on the inside back cover of this book.

Where to stay and dine

Each of the 72 rooms at the faux-adobe **Table Mountain Inn,** 1310 Washington Ave. in Golden (☎ 800-762-9898 or 303-277-9898; www. tablemountaininn.com), has its own, unique Southwestern décor, and most rooms have a private deck with a view of the town and the surrounding hills. The location at the edge of Golden's historic downtown is even better, and the prices are best of all. The rates — $132 to $214 double — are fixed year-round, so what seems like a fair price on a fall weekday becomes a steal on a summer weekend. During peak season, the inn often sells out a month or more in advance, so be sure to book early.

The **Georgetown Mountain Inn,** 1100 Rose St. in Georgetown (☎ 303-569-3201; www.georgetownmountaininn.com), is just 11 miles from the Loveland Ski Area and has some of the most reasonable rooms near Denver. All have ceiling fans and tables, and the upgraded rooms have log furniture, wood-paneled walls, refrigerators, microwaves, and oversized bathrooms. In-season rates run from $61 to $100. For an extra $8, it's worth getting an upgraded room. The inn also has an outdoor swimming pool and hot tub, and offers free coffee and pastries every morning.

Make your dinner reservations early for **Hilltop Café,** 1518 Washington Ave. in Golden (☎ 303-279-8151), because it sometimes fills up days in advance. Perched in a historic home near Golden's downtown, Hilltop Café happily dishes up traditional dishes that have been enhanced for the new millennium. The chef, Ian Kleinman, changes the menu regularly

The Front Range's best pizza

New York thin-crust aficionados and Chicago deep-dish fans beware: The best pizza experience in America awaits you in Idaho Springs. **Beau Jo's** (1517 Miner St.; ☎ 303-567-4376; $6.50–$19) has set the standard for post-skiing, appetite-sating bliss since 1973. They call their pizzas "Mountain Pies" — and the pies certainly live up to the name. From toppings as traditional as pepperoni to as exotic as fontina cheese or giardiniera peppers, and offering several different crusts and sauces, Beau Jo's fashions pizzas that put California Pizza Kitchen to shame. Beau Jo's has plenty of salads and vegetarian options for the pizza, as well. Denverites long ago made a habit of stopping here while heading down from the slopes, so on Saturday or Sunday, get here early or be ready to wait.

to use the freshest ingredients and is known for his ever-evolving soups. The room, with large windows and widely spaced tables, is as pleasing as the fare. Main courses at dinnertime will set you back $15 to $25.

The **Red Ram & Rathskeller,** 606 Sixth St. in Georgetown (☎ 303-569-2300), has very normal dinner fare such as burgers, fried chicken, and steaks, not to mention oversized (but still normal) salads and a handful of Mexican dishes. What makes this restaurant noteworthy is its atmosphere — a historic 1876 building replete with vintage signs, photos of old Georgetown, and a hand-carved bar that is said to have been dragged here by horse and buggy from Oregon. Great for families. A dinner entree at the restaurant costs between $5.95 and $15.

Georgetown's best meals are at **Café Prague,** 511 Rose St. (☎ 303-569-2861), where hearty portions of central European soul food warms you up fast on cool summer mountain days, and makes for great après-ski on your way down from the slopes. Schnitzel, sausages, and wonderfully flavorful red sauerkraut dominate the menu. The décor is not fancy; it features stock photos of — you guessed it — Prague, and of Avalanche star Milan Hejduk and other Czech hockey greats.

Following Five Classic Mountain Drives

From April through early November, the mountains and foothills of the Front Range are great for just wandering around in. Early September, in particular, makes for great driving: The aspen are turning, the air is crisp, and the sky is the deepest blue. Shocking waves of gold and crimson cascade down the slopes, framed by the deep green of the Douglas firs and the bright, puffy white clouds caught in the autumn winds. High drama, indeed. New England can keep her maple trees; I'll take the stark beauty of the West any day.

Guanella Pass Road

Officially designated a National Scenic and Historic Byway, this 22-mile long road takes you up to 11,669 feet above sea level, with gorgeous views and fun mountain driving along the way. Start in Georgetown and follow the signs to the steep road out of town; you'll pass the old Silverdale mining camp, and some of the best aspen-viewing country in Colorado along the way. Pavement gives way to gravel toward the top, but it's an easy drive for any car (not so easy for RVs) and sets you down in Grant, on U.S. 285. Head back to Denver via Bailey and Conifer.

Mount Evans

The road to the summit of this *fourteener* (a local term for mountains that top 14,000 feet in elevation), also a National Scenic and Historic Byway, is open only during summer, from Memorial Day to Labor Day. From Idaho Springs, follow the signs for the Mount Evans road (Colorado 103) at exit 240 from I-70. Just past Echo Lake, turn right on Colorado 5 and continue up past the tree line to the 14,264-foot summit and the incredible views — on a clear day, you can see nearly to Kansas. Seriously! And you can say you bagged a fourteener (just don't tell anyone you did it in a car). Summit Lake, on the way up, is the highest wheelchair accessible lake in the United States. After Labor Day, stay on Colorado 103 and go over Squaw Pass and down into Bergen Park. This has been a favorite Sunday morning aspen-viewing drive in my family for years.

St. Mary's Glacier

Alaskans will get a good belly laugh out of what Coloradans call a glacier, but we think it's pretty cool nonetheless. This year-round ice deposit is all that remains of one of the glaciers that carved out the Front Range during the last ice age, about 12,000 years ago. Two miles west of Idaho Springs, take exit 238 off I-70 onto Fall River Road and follow it all the way up to the glacier area. The road is steep and curvy — so watch out in winter — but it's a lot of fun, and the hiking is great if you decide to get out of the car. The snowshoeing and cross-country skiing are phenomenal in winter, and it's all doable in a half-day trip from Denver.

The Peak-to-Peak Highway

This combination of Colorado highways 119, 7, and 72 runs from Black Hawk to Estes Park, through more spectacular aspen-viewing territory over Rollins Pass, through old mining camps, and along the southeastern flank of Rocky Mountain National Park. For the full experience, I recommend starting in Golden and taking U.S. 6 up through Clear Creek Canyon to Black Hawk and heading north from there. You go through the towns of Nederland, with its rock shops and aging hippies, and Ward, with its famously misanthropic residents, past great hiking in the park along St. Vrain Creek on the Ouzel Falls Trail outside Allenspark, and down into Estes Park. A good day's itinerary would start early and aim for lunch in Estes Park and dinner in Boulder later on. You can also skip Estes Park entirely and go down beautiful Boulder Canyon from Nederland on Colorado 119.

U.S. 285 to South Park and beyond

This is my favorite, and one of the all-time great Colorado experiences. Hampden Avenue, running across southern Denver and Englewood, becomes a freeway and heads southwest through Turkey Creek Canyon past Aspen Park and Conifer, down Crow Hill into Bailey and the Platte Canyon, and up past Grant and the southern end of Guanella Pass Road. Then it curves up and around Kenosha Pass, and here you have to be careful: Don't let go of the steering wheel when the jaw-dropping sight of South Park comes into view. The road works its way south, past Fairplay and Route 9 to Breckenridge, through the great ranching country of South Park. You could make a day's trip out of fishing the valley's two big artificial lakes, Spinney Mountain Reservoir and Antero Reservoir, or along the banks of the South Platte River and its tributaries. Or you can continue on 285 over Trout Creek Pass and head down into the Upper

Where to get your kicks

It's not Route 66 exactly, but head down to Evergreen for some classic mountain culture. For years, famous musicians such as Leon Russell, Dave Mason, Greg Allman, and Jerry Jeff Walker have played the **Little Bear Saloon,** 28075 Colorado 74 (☎ **303-674-9991;** www.littlebearsaloon.com). It's a great old mountain roadhouse, complete with lingerie — donated on-the-spot by audience members — hanging from the ceiling.

If you're looking for elegance and sophistication, look elsewhere, but if you want to say you've got friends in low places, this is one of Colorado's traditional places to start. And you're likely to catch some legendary music in the process.

Arkansas Valley. This is where you move from the Front Range into the heart of the high country — you see the forest change from ponderosa pine and Douglas fir to piñons and junipers, and hold onto the steering wheel again when the Collegiate Peaks of the Sawatch Range come into view. Turn right at the bottom of the valley, and you'll be in Buena Vista, where you can lunch if you set out by 8 or 9 a.m. From here, Colorado is your Rocky Mountain oyster, as you can head north to Leadville, west to Aspen, or south to the San Juans or the San Luis Valley. Or stay in Buena Vista and have an afternoon of whitewater rafting (see Chapter 18.)

Chapter 13

Boulder

• •

In This Chapter
▶ Getting to Boulder and finding your way around
▶ Finding the best lodging and eats in Boulder
▶ Drinking in Boulder's variety of outdoor activities

• •

*L*ooking for a fun town with multiple-personality disorder? Look no
further. Originally a mining camp, Boulder has been a quiet farming
hub, a rowdy college town, a cauldron of space-age technology, a health-
nut's paradise, and a nexus of new-age spirituality — all rolled into one.
The town and its personality are unquestionably dominated by the
University of Colorado, a school of 25,000 known for attracting both the
most talented aerospace engineers *and* the most dedicated ski bums.
But the cutting-edge science pursued by the university and government
institutions are balanced by such touchy-feely and left-brained organizations as the Rolf Institute and Naropa University (the nation's only four-
year Buddhist college). In recent years, Boulder's high-tech sector has
produced much of the software that powers the Internet age; at the
same time, though, the town has worked hard to maintain the open
space surrounding it as a nature preserve and as one of the best networks for hiking, biking, and rock-climbing in the country.

Boulder has its share of microbreweries, and the Pearl Street Mall that
anchors the Downtown area is a vibrant shopping-and-dining district
where you can feast on Tibetan food or deep-dish pizza and buy anything
from African masks to kites and yo-yos. For nightlife, the local arts community is large and prolific, and the local audience is sophisticated: The
university houses the Colorado Shakespeare Festival in the summer, and
draws world-class performers throughout the year to its various stages
and concert halls. Venues such as the Boulder Theatre, Chautauqua
Auditorium, and Fox Theatre bring in the best touring acts, and you can
always find a local jam-band or two playing somewhere if you want to
relive your Deadhead days.

Face it: If you're in the mood to climb a canyon wall, take in a Buddhist
tea ceremony, check up on the latest global warming research, quaff
some local brew, and see some world-class Shakespeare — *all in the
same day* — then Boulder is clearly the place for you. The towering
Flatirons (enormous slabs of sandstone stabbing upward above the city)
say it all: This place has rugged beauty to burn, and the sky's the limit.

Getting There

Denver International Airport (DIA), 40 miles southeast of Boulder, is the closest airport with commercial service. Most major domestic carriers and a few international ones fly into DIA, and major rental-car companies have desks at the airport. For details about navigating DIA (and which airlines fly in and out of DIA), check out Chapter 11. You can find information on contacting individual airlines and car-rental agencies in the appendix at the back of this book.

Between 3 a.m. and 9 p.m. daily, Denver's **Regional Transportation District (RTD; ☎ 303-299-6000;** www.rtd-denver.com) provides hourly bus rides to Denver International Airport (and other Denver locations) from the Boulder main transit terminal at 14th and Walnut streets. Service from DIA to Boulder runs from 6 a.m. to 11 p.m. (Call for the exact schedule.) Known as skyRide, the service costs $10, and exact change is required in either bills or coins. To catch the skyRide buses leaving DIA, go to Level 5 of the main terminal.

RTD's regional **B-Line** between Boulder and Denver can be a great way to visit both cities without switching accommodations. The line runs from Boulder's Walnut Street Station to Union Station and Market Street Station in LoDo, where you can connect with the 16th Street Mall shuttle or Denver's light-rail system. The B-Line trip takes less than an hour, and it's a great way to avoid the hellish commuter traffic on U.S. 36. Do pay attention to the schedule, though; buses run every 15 minutes during rush hour, but slow to once an hour during off-peak times. The last bus leaves either terminal at 1 a.m.

SuperShuttle Boulder (☎ 800-BLUE-VAN or 303-227-0000; www.yellow trans.com) offers van service between Boulder and DIA. The drivers make regular stops at major hotels, and they detour to residences upon request. To go from Boulder to the airport, make your reservation at least 24 hours in advance. Coming from Denver to Boulder, just go to the SuperShuttle desk on Level 5 of the main terminal. Cost for the trip to a regular SuperShuttle stop is $20 for adults and $10 for kids ages 8 to 16; there's no charge for children under 8. The fare to an unscheduled stop is $25 for the first person, $10 for each additional person. (Children under 8 are still free.)

A more expedient — and expensive — way to go from DIA to Boulder is in a cab. Just go to the taxi stand and ask for a ride. To go from Boulder to DIA, call **Boulder Yellow Cab (☎ 303-777-7777),** which charges a $70 flat rate for up to five passengers.

To drive from Denver to Boulder, take I-25 north and then head northeast on the Boulder Turnpike (U.S. 36). From Fort Collins and points north, take I-25 south and then head southeast on Colorado 119. Boulder is 55 miles south of Fort Collins.

Getting Around

Boulder's north–south streets are numbered, with Third Street flush against the foothills and the numbers increasing as you head from west to east (see the nearby "Boulder" map). Foothills Parkway (Colorado 157) is the main north–south artery on the east side of town. However, U.S. 36 brings you closer to the downtown area. Heading northeast from Denver, it veers north in Boulder and becomes 28th Street. From U.S. 36 you can reach the heart of the downtown by turning west on Canyon Boulevard (Colorado 119 and 7) and then north on Broadway (Colorado 7). Two blocks north of Canyon Boulevard on Broadway, you cross Pearl Street, the hub of downtown Boulder. If you continue west on Canyon Boulevard, you'll head up into the mountains via Boulder Canyon.

Driving in Boulder is fairly easy, though not always expedient. Certain roads get congested, and parking spaces can be hard to find. In the downtown area during the day, you usually have to pay for a spot. The curbside meters take nickels, dimes, and quarters. Every 5¢ buys just four minutes of liberty, so empty out your piggybank before going to town. During summer, you can find free parking in the residential neighborhood of The Hill just west of the campus of the University of Colorado (locally known as CU — Colorado State University alums, insert your own joke here); if you want to explore the campus and take in the funky shops and bars on The Hill, this is the way to go, then take the HOP or SKIP (see the next paragraph) into downtown.

Boulder has a highly efficient bus system that serves destinations throughout the city and travels as far away as Denver. Many routes run at ten-minute intervals during peak periods, making the bus a great way to get around. The City of Boulder operates the **HOP** line, which makes 40 stops on a loop through the downtown area. Call ☎ **303-447-8282** for information on HOP service. Another useful line, **SKIP,** goes north and south on Broadway. Denver's **Regional Transportation District** oversees SKIP and other Boulder County routes. For information on those lines, call ☎ **800-366-7433** or 303-299-6000, or surf the Internet to www.rtd-denver.com. You can also pick up an RTD Boulder County bus map at locations throughout town. HOP and SKIP fares are 75¢, 25¢ for seniors 60 and over. Most other local RTD routes cost $1.10 for adults, 55¢ for seniors over 60. Exact change is required.

If the bus doesn't show up, you can always call **Boulder Yellow Cab** (☎ **303-777-7777**) or **Metro Taxi** (☎ **303-666-6666**). The taxi companies don't have a strong presence on the streets, so you'll almost certainly need to pick up a phone and dial.

You can easily ride a bike through much of Boulder. Many roads have bike lanes, and you can also use the Boulder Creek Path, which extends 16 miles on a general east–west course through town and is popular among local cyclists, rollerbladers, joggers, and walkers. **University**

Bicycles, Ninth and Pearl (☎ **303-444-4196**), rents town bikes ($20 for one day, $30 for two) and mountain bikes ($25 for one day, $45 for two). Locks and helmets are included in the price.

Where to Stay

Lodging in Boulder costs a lot (Chapter 8 includes an explanation of the dollar signs used here to indicate price ranges). You can save a few dollars by staying in a chain hotel on the east side of town, but the best way to find an affordable room is to time your visit carefully. Besides its busy summer season, Boulder's hotels fill up during college events, such as parents' weekends, graduation, and home football games. If you want to visit Boulder on a budget, schedule around these events — and, if possible, at times other than July and August.

Boulder University Inn
$–$$ Boulder

This two-story 1960s-era motor lodge, just two blocks from Pearl Street, has rooms that look older than those at the Quality Inn, and it's near a busy intersection. But dozens of shops and restaurants are within walking distance, the rooms are clean, and the prices are fair.

See map p. 146. 1632 Broadway. ☎ **303-417-1700**. *Fax: 303-442-8100.* www.boulder universityinn.com. *Rack rates: $59–$119 double. AE, DISC, MC, V.*

Colorado Chautauqua Association
$$–$$$$ Boulder

Anyone who has a cultural bent should spend a few days in one of the 60 cottages rented out by the Colorado Chautauqua Association. Situated on 26 acres at the base of the Flatiron Mountains, these clean, rustic, Arts and Crafts–style dwellings date back to the early 1900s. They have hardwood floors, screened-in porches, and gas stoves, but no TVs. Rather than watch Regis, you're supposed to become part of a community that's engaged in intellectual and cultural endeavors. This isn't as daunting as it may sound. In between naps, you just go to any concerts, forums, classes, and films that interest you; during summer at least, you have many options to choose from. (For more on cultural offerings at Chautauqua, check out the hotel's Web site.) As for food, you can cook in your room or eat in the Chautauqua Dining Hall, which is fancier than the name implies. Chautauqua borders a large mountain park, so you can start hiking right outside your door.

See map p. 146. 900 Baseline Rd. ☎ **303-442-3282**. *Fax: 303-449-0790.* www. chautauqua.com. *Rack rates: $102–$109 efficiency, $122–$129 1-bedroom cottage, $129–$224 2-bedroom cottage. MC, V.*

Boulder

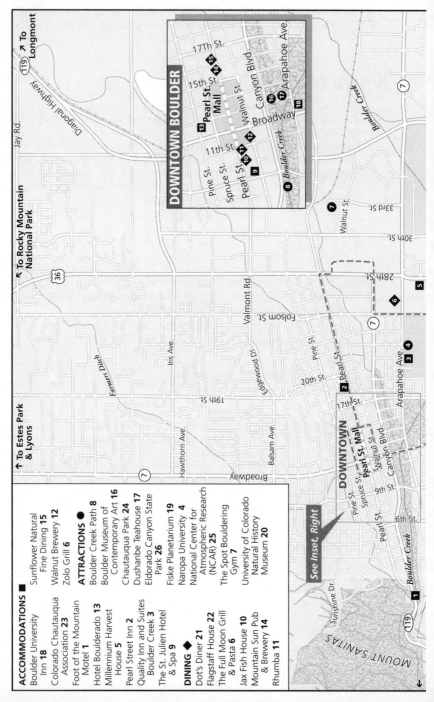

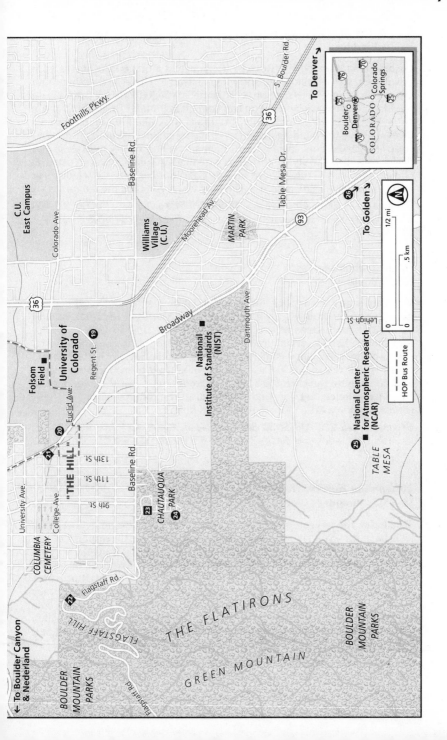

Foot of the Mountain Motel
$–$$ **Boulder**

Located near the mouth of Boulder Canyon, this motel is nine blocks from downtown, so the walk to the shopping district is a little farther than from other area lodges. The trade-off is the motel's wooded location across from the Eben G. Fine Park, where you can cool off in Boulder Creek. Built in the early 1930s, the one-story motel buildings look like lodging for Santa's elves. They — the buildings, that is — have rough-hewn pine exteriors, red trim, and green roofs. Inside the 19 rooms, you find knotty pine walls and desks, as well as old-style bathrooms with medicine cabinets and (usually) showers instead of tubs. There's no air-conditioning, but two windows in each room help create a draft, especially when you turn the fan on.

See map p. 146. 200 W. Arapahoe Ave. ☎ **866-773-5489** *or 303-442-5688. Fax: 303-442-5719.* www.footofthemountainmotel.com. *Rack rates: $70–$85 double. AE, DISC, MC, V.*

Hotel Boulderado
$$$$ **Boulder**

You can easily recognize this Boulder landmark by the bright green canopies on the building, by its imposing five stories of red brick, and by its location mere steps from the Pearl Street Mall. Built in 1909, its sumptuous lobby has Victorian furniture, a cherry-wood staircase, and colorful rugs, all under a ceiling of Italian stained glass. You can stay in the historic hotel, where the rooms are old and full of antiques, or in a more recent addition, where the rooms are full of reproductions. For the most memorable experience, ask for a corner room in the older building — these rooms provide a little more light, air, and history.

See map p. 146. 2115 13th St. ☎ **800-433-4344** *or 303-442-4344. Fax: 303-442-4378.* www.boulderado.com. *Rack rates: $195–$275 double; $315–$365 suite. AE, DC, DISC, MC, V.*

Millennium Harvest House
$$–$$$$ **Boulder**

This hotel, the largest in Boulder, is a great bet for weekend getaways, or as a base for exploring the Boulder area and the northern parts of the Front Range. The rooms are tastefully furnished with Art Nouveau accents in rich wood and copper; wall-to-wall windows face the mountains on one side of the building (ask for a west-facing room). And the staff provides small luxuries, including nightly turndowns and three complimentary morning newspapers. If you want to exercise, you can use the pool, tennis courts, or fitness room, or you can jog on the Boulder Creek Path, which skirts the edge of the property. The hotel also has a good restaurant and room service.

See map p. 146. 1345 28th St. ☎ **866-866-8086** *or 303-443-3850. Fax: 303-443-1480.* www.millennium-hotels.com. *Rack rates: Mid-Oct–mid-March $89–$149* *double; rest of year $135–$200 double; University of Colorado graduation and parents' weekends $245 double. AE, DC, DISC, MC, V.*

Pearl Street Inn
$$$ Boulder

This bed-and-breakfast has a prime location near the action on Pearl Street but is surprisingly quiet. The rooms have such amenities as quilts and antiques, and all but one have a wood-burning fireplace. The prices could be lower, but this really is a prime spot.

See map p. 146. 1820 Pearl St. ☎ ***888-810-1302*** *or 303-444-5584. Fax: 303-444-6494.* www.pearlstreetinn.com. *Rack rates: $159 double; $209 suite. AE, MC, V.*

Quality Inn and Suites Boulder Creek
$$ Boulder

This inn is tucked into a mostly residential neighborhood at the southeast edge of downtown. Most of the rooms are distanced from Arapahoe Avenue, so they're quiet even though the Boulder Creek Path passes nearby, and the heart of Boulder's downtown is only about five blocks away. Rooms have furniture made from pine branches, watched over by framed photographs of the owner's dog, and all of them have refrigerators and microwaves. There's also a workout room, hot tub, pool, and guest laundry. A hot breakfast is included in the rates.

See map p. 146. 2020 Arapahoe Ave. ☎ ***888-449-7550*** *(outside Colorado only) or 303-449-7550. Fax: 303-449-1082.* www.qualityinnboulder.com. *Rack rates: $79–$150 double; $89–$160 suite. AE, DC, DISC, MC, V.*

The St. Julien Hotel & Spa
$$$$ Boulder

Just opening at press time, this brand-new hotel is promising great things for Boulder, including modern luxury accommodations and a first-class spa. The location is fantastic: very close to downtown and right next to the Boulder Creek bike path and greenway. The hotel features a 24-hour concierge and an evening turndown service, and it aims to pamper guests in every way imaginable.

See map p. 146. 900 Walnut St. ☎ ***800-323-7500*** *or 720-406-9696. Fax: 720-406-9668.* www.stjulien.com. *Rack rates: $245–$285 double. AE, DC, DISC, MC, V.*

Where to Dine

Boulder restaurants don't allow smoking, tend to be health-conscious, and have great chefs, many of whom have come here for the lifestyle. As you'd expect in a college town, Boulder has plenty of cheap ethnic places and pizza joints, plus a few brewpubs. Near the Pearl Street Mall, you can also find brightly decorated, trendy, expensive restaurants, much like the ones in Denver's LoDo area (see Chapter 11 for more about Denver). Many of these restaurants have popular bars that border the regular seating. If you give them a try, you may end up eating gourmet food in an environment that's surprisingly festive.

To find out what the dollar signs in the following listings refer to in actual dollars, check out the introduction of this book.

Dot's Diner
$ The Hill   DINER FARE

This greasy-spoon, best at breakfast time, has been filling up CU students for over a decade. It's tucked inside a strip mall, and you may have to wait a bit, but it's worth it for the pancakes, grits, and *huevos rancheros* (eggs with green chili). You can enjoy plenty of vegetarian options, too.

See map p. 146. 1333 Broadway. ☎ 303-449-1323. Reservations not accepted. Main courses: $4–$7. No credit cards. Open: Mon–Fri 7 a.m.–2 p.m., Sat–Sun 8 a.m.–2 p.m.

Flagstaff House
$$$$ Flagstaff Hill   NEW AMERICAN

Half the locals I interviewed loved this pricey Boulder landmark; the other half expressed disappointment. Yet everyone could appreciate the sweeping views of the plains through the mostly glass walls, and all agreed that the service stands out. Owned and operated by the same family since 1971, the elegant and romantic dining room sets the stage for a regularly changing menu that specializes in seafood and Rocky Mountain game. Starters may feature rabbit, pheasant, quail, scallops, or even lobster. And don't be surprised to find Colorado buffalo or venison on the entree list, right there next to Alaskan halibut or Hawaiian big eye tuna.

See map p. 146. 1138 Flagstaff Rd. ☎ 303-442-4640. Reservations recommended. Main courses: $28–$59. AE, DC, DISC, MC, V. Open: Sun–Fri 6–10 p.m, Sat 5–10 p.m.

The Full Moon Grill & Pasta
$$–$$$ Village Shopping Center   NORTHERN ITALIAN

If you love fresh seafood served with handmade pasta, head for the Full Moon Grill before the opportunity wanes. Succulent dishes such as the freeform ravioli (housemade pasta, scallops, fennel, fresh fish, and tomatoes in a saffron-chardonnay broth) and the linguini alla sardegna (swordfish, tomato, garlic, saffron mint, and white wine) may be gone tomorrow. Dip your bread in olive oil and balsamic vinegar, and wax eloquent over a bottle from the immense wine list. Unlike other Boulder eateries, you don't have to howl to be heard here. Once a hamburger joint, the sun-splashed, octagonal dining room takes on ambience when the sun's last glow gives way to candlelight — and moonlight, too.

See map p. 146. 2525 Arapahoe Ave. (inside the Village Shopping Center). ☎ 303-938-8800. Reservations accepted. Main courses: $13–$25. AE, DISC, MC, V. Open: Mon–Fri 11:30 a.m.–2 p.m.; Sun–Thurs 5:30–9 p.m., Fri–Sat 5:30–10 p.m.

Jax Fish House
$$–$$$ **Downtown**   SEAFOOD

Along with the best martinis in town, Jax has some of the freshest fish. The restaurant has fresh oysters, clams, and mussels flown in daily, and its nearly living "filet mignon of tuna" has a devoted following. (The filet is a 2-inch-thick slab of tuna, barely seared and served with scallion hash browns, sweet soy, and pickled ginger.) Because Jax serves seafood, it covers its tables with paper. And because it covers its tables with paper, it gives crayons to customers. The restaurant learned too late that customers who have crayons and martinis in hand can be trouble; that's why the brick walls in here look like a coloring book. If you're looking for a quiet, romantic evening, forget Jax. This place rocks on the weekends, especially when the bar at the front of the room fills up.

See map p. 146. 928 Pearl St. ☎ *303-444-1811. Reservations not accepted. Sandwiches $8–$17; main courses $16–$25. AE, DC, MC, V. Open: Daily 4–9 p.m.*

Mountain Sun Pub & Brewery
$ **Downtown**   TEX-MEX /PUB FARE

The menu here is '70s–style healthfood with a nod toward Mexico; the burritos and burgers are standard, but hearty. Plenty of vegetarian options are on hand, and for lunch or an early dinner, it's a great family choice. Again, this being a brewpub, the beers are the stars, with a large number of house brews and a rotating cast of guest beers from other regional and national microbreweries. The Colorado Kind Ale is rich and *extremely* hoppy, if you're into that sort of thing; the Raspberry Wheat, by contrast, is very light and fruity. After hours on weekends features live music — mostly jam bands and world beat.

See map p. 146. 1535 Pearl St. ☎ *303-546-0886. Reservations not accepted. Main courses: $4.75–$8.75. No credit cards accepted. Open: Mon–Sat 11:30 a.m.–1 a.m., Sun noon–1 a.m.*

Rhumba
$$ **Downtown**   CARIBBEAN

On certain summer nights, this place becomes a huge party. Servers in tropical shirts push through crowds of singles to make sure the people on the patio get their rum drinks in time. The enthusiasm swells when those potent drinks take hold, and the crowds from the bar spill over into the seating area. During my meal here, I couldn't help feeling as if my gourmet dinner and I had together parachuted into a Club Med. With so much activity, it's easy to overlook the delicious food, which has sweet Caribbean ingredients such as mango, coconut, and pineapple. Among the many options, you can get half jerk chicken over black beans with coconut rice, or simplify things (sort of) by ordering a cheeseburger with boniato french fries and banana guava ketchup.

See map p. 146. 950 Pearl St. ☎ *303-442-7771. Reservations accepted sometimes. Main courses: $9–$23. AE, DC, MC, V. Open: Daily 4–9 p.m.; Fri 11:30 a.m.–4 p.m., Sat–Sun 1–4 p.m.*

Sunflower Natural Fine Dining
$$ **Downtown GOURMET NATURAL FOODS**

The Sunflower's menu announces that the restaurant shuns preservatives, additives, and artificial ingredients; that it seeks organically grown ingredients free of synthetic chemical fertilizers, herbicides, and pesticides; and that it uses only aluminum-free cookware, non-irradiated herbs and spices, and Celtic sea salt. That part of the menu has about as much charm as your average corporate mission statement, but the food itself is surprisingly flavorful. Naturally enough, the restaurant serves many vegetarian dishes, but you can also order meaty items such as buffalo steak, seafood cioppino, and fresh Alaskan halibut.

See map p. 146. 1701 Pearl St. ☎ 303-440-0220. Reservations accepted. Main courses: $15–$26. AE, MC, V. Open Tues–Fri 11 a.m.–2:30 p.m.; Tues–Sat 5–10 p.m., Sun 5–9 p.m.

Walnut Brewery
$$ **Downtown PUB FARE**

Boulder's first brewpub, the Walnut's great range of brews and imaginative takes on pub food make this place stand out. Start with the chicken quesadillas, served with chipotle sour cream, then move on to the buffalo fajitas, alder-smoked salmon, or one of several steaks. You may also choose from a variety of fish dishes or, for somewhat clearer arteries, one of the many vegetarian options. The wine list is pedestrian — focus on the beer! The menu makes great suggestions for food/beer pairings, but let me point out the St. James Irish Red, great with most of the food here, or the Devil's Thumb Stout, an extremely dark, rich, full-bodied beer that goes down very, very smoothly. Careful, now. . . .

See map p. 146. 1123 Walnut St. ☎ 303-447-1345. Reservations accepted. Dinner entrees: $7.75–$20. AE, DISC, MC, V. Open daily 11:30 a.m.–2 a.m.

Zolo Grill
$$ **Village Shopping Center CONTEMPORARY SOUTHWESTERN**

This trendy restaurant presents a spicy, smoky, gourmet version of Southwestern food. Key ingredients include habanero and chipotle peppers, strong cheeses, and succulent meats such as duck, ahi tuna, and pulled pork. The tough part is deciding which way you'd like to be overpowered. Choices include the likes of barbeque duck tacos, blackberry habanero pork chops (served with goat cheese), and wild mushroom enchiladas. The room, which is mostly red and yellow, feels just as warm and rich as the food.

See map p. 146. 2525 Arapahoe Ave. (in the Village Shopping Center). ☎ 303-449-0444. Reservations not accepted. Main courses: $11–$20; brunch $6.50–$12. AE, DC, MC, V. Open: Mon–Fri 11 a.m.–9 p.m., Sat–Sun 11 a.m.–3 p.m. and 4–9 p.m.

Exploring Boulder

In Boulder, you don't have to do much to have a good time. You just have to be there and see what happens. Sometimes it's best not to even judge what's good and bad.

The best things to see and do

Okay, some of us get paid to judge things. If fate smiles upon you, you will get to judge some of the following for yourself:

✔ **Sip tea in paradise. Dushanbe Teahouse,** 1770 13th St. (☎ 303-442-4993; www.boulderteahouse.com), looks like something the deep subconscious might unveil in an enlightened state. A gift from the city of Dushanbe, Tajikstan, it took 40 artisans three years to hand carve and hand paint the teahouse. When they finished, they shipped it in crates to the United States, where it sat for several years before being reassembled next to Central Park in downtown Boulder. Under a large skylight at the center of the room sits the Fountain of the Seven Beauties, whose name pretty much describes the scene. The teahouse serves hundreds of teas; on a hot day, a Hibiscus Cooler is just the ticket. The menu is decidedly non-Tajik; it's best described as a fusion of Mexican, Asian, and European peasant cuisines. If you don't feel like eating, come for tea between 3 and 5 p.m. Or simply look around; you're encouraged to visit even if you buy nothing. Admission is free. It's open Sunday through Thursday from 8 a.m. to 9 p.m., and Friday and Saturday from 8 a.m. to 10 p.m.

✔ **Watch human tricks.** Shopping is anything but dull at **Pearl Street Mall,** on Pearl between 11th and 15th streets (☎ 303-449-3774). During summer, you pass street vendors, sidewalk cafes, and, best of all, street performers, including balloon-artists, escape masters, contortionists, opera singers, and tightrope-walkers. The performers yell in order to be heard over the crowds, single out audience members for special attention, and aggressively pass the hat when they're done. Together they make the place more medieval than mall-like. The shops are fun, too (I highlight a few of them in the "Shopping" section later in this chapter), with independent bookstores dotting the area and stores selling everything from kites to CDs.

✔ **Hide out near the Boulder Creek Path.** Like Boulder itself, this paved pedestrian path connects the mountains and the plains. It parallels Boulder Creek downstream for 16 miles, beginning 4 miles up Boulder Canyon and ending on the east side of town, within mooing distance of the plains. The path crosses no streets and has many small, leafy parks alongside it. Starting from the west end, you pass Elephant Rocks, a rock-climbing and bouldering (that is, boulder climbing) hot spot. Just below the mouth of the canyon, you go through shady Eben G. Fine Park, perfect for picnicking, soaking, and cooling off. Another mile or so to the east, behind the

A perfect day in Boulder

A warm spring, summer, or fall day in Boulder means you need to be outdoors. Start at the Pearl Street Mall and get yourself a kite at **Into The Wind** (see the "Shopping" section later in this chapter for details). On a Saturday, walk two blocks west to the **Boulder Farmer's Market** (open Apr–Nov 8 a.m.–2 p.m.; www.boulderfarmers. org) and check out the amazing, locally grown organic produce and food. There's always live music, a food court, and kids' activities, in addition to a once-a-month crafts fair. Hang out and have lunch, or pick up some fresh food and head over to **Chautauqua Park,** have a picnic, and fly your kite! Finish off with dinner at a great restaurant downtown, and watch the buskers on the mall (and don't forget to give them a buck when they've blown your mind.)

Millennium Hotel, you can look at trout through small, murky windows into the creek. Speed-walkers, inline-skaters, runners, and cyclists all blaze down the path, yet many others use the area as a giant natural sedative. On summer afternoons, if you peek through the foliage at the water-smoothed boulders and the creekside park benches, you'll see dozens of people relaxing. It doesn't matter how you use the path, just make sure to spend some time there.

Other things to see and do

Boulder has a host of smaller museums, libraries, and galleries, including venues on two local campuses:

✔ When a Tibetan meditation master, Chogyam Trungpa Rinpoche, founded Boulder's Naropa Institute in 1974, he envisioned a place "where East meets west and sparks . . . fly" — and fly they did, especially when free-thinkers such as Allen Ginsberg and Ann Waldman were teaching there. Today, **Naropa University** (☎ 800-603-3117 or 303-245-4819; www.naropa.edu) still merges Western scholarship and Eastern contemplation. The college is home to Ginsberg's personal library and one of the country's most important spoken-word archives. The institute opens certain workshops, classes, and performances to the public. And its library is a must-see for people interested in Eastern religion and alternative therapies. For information on performances, call ☎ 303-245-4715.

✔ The **Boulder Museum of Contemporary Art,** 1750 13th St. (☎ 303-443-2122; www.bmoca.org), displays cutting-edge work by nationally known artists. The exhibits change every three months and include paintings, collages, mixed media, ceramics, and installations. There's also an area for readings, performances, and discussions. Admission is $4 for adults, $3 for students and seniors 55 and up. The museum is open Tuesday through Saturday from 11 a.m. to 6 p.m.

✔ If you went to the universities of Nebraska, Oklahoma, or Michigan, think twice before blindly wandering where the Buffalo roam. **The University of Colorado at Boulder** (www.colorado.edu) has 25,000 students, and like most big state schools, football rivalries are taken *very* seriously here. So leave the sweatshirt with the big red "N" in the car! The campus can be a little confusing; most of the buildings are built of the same yellow-and-pink sandstone, which comes from a quarry in nearby Lyons. You can avoid getting lost by going straight to the information desk at the University Memorial Center, 1669 Euclid (at Broadway), and picking up a campus map. Then you'll be able to locate attractions such as **The University of Colorado Natural History Museum, The Heritage Center** (dedicated to the history of the university), and **The Fiske Planetarium,** all of which are open to the public.

Campus tours for prospective students are offered weekdays at 9:30 a.m. and 1:30 p.m. and Saturdays at 10:30 a.m., but first you need to make a reservation by calling ☎ **303-492-6301,** option 2. The university discourages regular visitors from taking them, but if you're curious, go ahead. Tours leave from the University Club on the southeast corner of Broadway and Euclid.

Staying active

The national media regularly lauds Boulder as one of the most fit, healthy, and recreation-friendly towns in the country. Some of the praise goes to the town's abundant water, rock, and forest, including more than 30,000 acres of open space. The rest goes to the townspeople themselves, who make a point of getting out and enjoying their resources. When in Boulder, set aside a few hours for the following:

✔ **Cycling and mountain biking:** Bicycling isn't just a sport here; it's the main form of transportation for many residents, even in winter. On 100 miles of bike lanes and multiuse paths, you can pedal most places in Boulder without risking your neck. Alas, the mountain biking in Boulder could be better. To avoid conflicts between cyclists and hikers, the city closed many of the hiking trails nearest town to bicycling. Most of the best off-road cycling is a few miles farther out — or uphill — from the city limits. One prime place to pedal is in **Eldorado Canyon State Park** (see the sidebar, "At the end of your rope? Start climbing!").

✔ **Hiking:** The hiking in Boulder starts right at the west edge of town, where you can hike into city-owned open space in the foothills of the Flatiron Range. You find great trail-running and hiking in **Chautauqua Park,** just south of Baseline Road. Take Baseline Road west from town and park near Chautauqua. From the Ranger Cottage, climb the obvious fire road up the long grassy hillside. The road takes you to the trailhead for the **Mesa Trail,** which undulates through ponderosa pine forest and meadows for 6 miles along the base of the Flatirons. If you want to do a loop hike through this area, go to the ranger station and pick up the free *Circle Hikes Guide* (also available online), published by the **City of Boulder Open Space and Mountain Parks** (☎ 303-441-3440; www.ci.boulder.co.us/openspace). It describes two loop hikes in Chautauqua Park and four others a short drive away.

✔ **Running:** Boulder has a huge population of joggers and runners who take advantage of the elevation, clean air, and hilly terrain to get in top shape. You can run trails all around town, but if you want to test yourself against some maniacally fast Boulderites, go to the busy **Boulder Creek Path,** which parallels Boulder Creek through downtown Boulder.

Hitting the slopes

Given its location about 20 miles west of Boulder, **Eldora Mountain Resort** (☎ 303-440-8700; www.eldora.com) gets skied hard throughout winter. Its 12 lifts can deposit plenty of skiers in a relatively small, 680-acre area, nearly half of which has snowmaking capability in case Mother Nature's supply falls short. Skier traffic and manmade snow often combine to create ice and moguls; as you descend the Eldora's 1,400 vertical feet, you may encounter either of the two (and tortuous combinations thereof), especially if it hasn't snowed in a while. On the upside, you won't have to battle traffic on I-70 to get there, and the place is low-key and has a few challenging spots. It's great if you only have a half-day to ski but are jonesing for a few runs.

At the end of your rope? Start climbing!

Because of the deep, narrow canyons of smooth pink granite west of town, Boulder is renowned as one of the planet's best climbing towns. One hot spot is **Elephant Rocks,** in Boulder Canyon. At **Eldorado Canyon State Park** (☎ 303-494-3943), 8 miles southwest of town in Eldorado Springs, climbers creep up 800-foot canyon walls. There are also great climbs on the Flatirons near Chautauqua Park. For gear, guidebooks, maps, and information, the best place (maybe on Earth) is **Neptune Mountaineering,** 633 South Broadway (☎ 303-499-8866; www.neptunemountaineering.com).

If you've never tried climbing, I recommend it highly; it's a thrill at any level, and looking down at the cliff you just scaled gives quite a sense of accomplishment. But you will want some training: Head over to **The Spot Bouldering Gym,** 3240 Prairie Ave. (☎ 303-447-2804; www.thespotgym.com), for lessons.

Climbing enthusiasts should check out www.climbingboulder.com for the latest news and climbing-related information.

If you're visiting Boulder during winter, don't discount the climbing possibilities — ever scaled a *waterfall?* Dress warmly and do it here!

Shopping

Even unenthusiastic shoppers should browse the stores on Pearl Street. You'll be constantly entertained as you walk, and you'll find products ranging from Tibetan imports to kites. Starting from the top of Pearl Street and working your way down, here are a few interesting stops:

- ✔ **Belle Star,** 385 Pearl St. #7 (☎ **303-249-6958**), will analyze your auric field photograph for $20. The digitally enhanced photograph reveals blotches of color and light around your head. The color and light may not mean much to you — to the ungifted, it just looks like you're at a disco. That's where Belle Star comes in. She can read these photographs to reveal things about you. For example, you may find out that you're a healer, mystic, or teacher. The entire process takes just a few minutes.

- ✔ With 100,000 books on three floors, **Boulder Book Store,** 1107 Pearl St. (☎ **800-244-4651** or 303-447-2074; www.boulderbookstore. com), is the largest of the local independents. Open since 1973, it resembles a downsized version of Denver's popular Tattered Cover Book Store. Chairs and tables are tucked into corners on the different floors, making it easy to hunker down and browse.

- ✔ If it can fly, float, soar, or spin in the wind (without carrying humans along with it), you can probably find it at **Into the Wind,** 1408 Pearl St. (☎ **800-541-0314;** www.intothewind.com). The store sells human-controlled floaters such as boomerangs, kites, and flying discs, as well as yard decorations such as windmills, mobiles, and twisters. The store even sells hats with propellers.

- ✔ Since 1971, the **Boulder Arts and Crafts Cooperative,** 1421 Pearl St. (☎ **303-443-3683;** www.boulderartsandcrafts.com), has represented local artists. Right now the co-op has 50 members, including painters, sculptors, and jewelry-makers. Most of the artists charge reasonable prices for their work, making this a great place to shop for gifts.

- ✔ If you're impressed by goatees and bongo drums, check out the **Beat Book Shop** (☎ **303-444-7111**). Its proprietor, Tom Peters, has amassed a sizeable collection of used books by Beat writers and poets, as well as other vintage paperbacks, LPs, CDs, and magazines. This time capsule of the '50s and '60s occupies a tiny space at 1713 Pearl St.

Nightlife

Even when the students are out of town, Boulder has a vigorous nightlife. The hottest restaurants — Jax, Rhumba, and The Med, to name a few — have bars that are popular with young professionals. In addition to these trendy mingling spots, the town has basement dives, brewpubs, and places specializing in live music. Boulder attracts some great pickers who turn up solo for jam sessions as well as in formal gigs alongside their own groups.

Hitting the clubs and bars

Generally speaking, bars and clubs usually heat up around 11 p.m. and close around 2 a.m. Pick up the latest copy of *Boulder Weekly* to find out who's playing where. If nothing captures your fancy, poke your head into some of these bars, cafes, and clubs:

- ✔ Popular national touring acts gravitate to the **Boulder Theater,** 2032 14th St. (☎ 303-786-7030; www.bouldertheater.com). Offerings include everything from jam bands to comedies and community forums. Most shows at this 1906 Art Deco–style venue are open to all ages.

- ✔ Big-name acts that don't go to the Boulder Theater often turn up at the **Fox Theatre,** 1135 13th St. (☎ 303-447-0095; www.foxtheatre. com). With its location close to the University of Colorado, the Fox Theatre attracts more students than the shows downtown, and the place can get a little rowdy.

- ✔ If you're hungry for blues, check out **The Catacombs,** 2115 13th St. (☎ 303-443-0486), which consists of a maze of underground chambers, including poolrooms, smoking rooms, lounging areas, and a music room. Blues bands often play the music room. It's hard to pinpoint who hangs out here, because every room is different. Cover charges vary.

- ✔ **Tulagi,** 1129 13th St. (☎ 303-443-3399), books some noisy, rowdy acts plus the usual Colorado jam-band fare. It also has cheap drink specials. Cover charges vary.

- ✔ For jazz and R&B, try **Trios Wine and Martini Bar,** 1155 Canyon Blvd. (☎ 303-442-8400). The bar has live music Wednesday through Sunday, usually for no cover.

- ✔ **Penny Lane,** at the corner of 18th and Pearl streets (☎ 303-443-9516), isn't a bar but it does have some quirky entertainment. A coffee shop, Penny Lane has an open mike two nights a week, as well as readings, drop-in jams, and folk singers. There's something every night, usually starting at around 8:00 or 8:30 p.m. No cover.

Looking for culture

The auditorium at the **Chautauqua Institute** is one of the neatest music venues going. Erected in 1898, it's like a huge, rickety barn, but with comfortable seating and a large stage. Daylight peeks through cracks in the walls; the air smells as fresh as if you were outside. During silences in performances, you may hear the rain and wind. Because of the superb acoustics and unusual setting, musicians love playing here. Every summer, two major music festivals are based here.

Several nights a week from late June to mid-August, the **Colorado Music Festival** takes over the auditorium for classical music performances. The festival has its own orchestra, which often plays alongside visiting musicians. It also has a chamber series. Every performance is different, and the offerings include everything from Bernstein to Dvorak. The least expensive tickets always cost $10; prime seats go for $33 to $37. Tickets for each upcoming season go on sale May 1. To find out more about the Festival, visit the **Colorado Music Festival Box Office,** 900 Baseline Rd. (☎ **303-440-7666;** www.coloradomusicfest.org).

When it's not hosting the Colorado Music Festival, Chautauqua has its own summer festival, which brings dance troupes, folk singers, intellectuals, comedians, and other entertainers. Recent performers have included John Hiatt, Joan Baez, the Cleo Parker Robinson Dance Ensemble, and the essayist Andrei Codrescu. Prices for the **Chautauqua Summer Festival** range in cost from free (for the season-ending show) to $35 or more for the most popular acts. Surf the Internet to www.chautauqua.com for more information.

Tickets for both the Colorado Music Festival and Chautauqua Summer Festival are available through the **Chautauqua Box Office** (☎ **303-440-7666**), open Monday through Friday from 10 a.m. to 4 p.m., Saturday from noon to 4 p.m., and 90 minutes before show time. It's on the Chautauqua grounds between the auditorium and the dining hall. **TicketsWest** carries tickets to these shows at area King Soopers stores. You can order online at www.ticketswest.com or call ☎ **866-464-2626.** Tickets to the Chautauqua Summer Festival only are available at the **Boulder Theater Box Office,** 2032 14th St. (☎ **303-786-7030**).

Chautauqua also hosts lower-profile events, including forums, concerts, classes, and film screenings. For information on these events, surf the Internet to www.chautauqua.com or call ☎ **303-442-3282,** ext. 24.

The **Colorado Shakespeare Festival** takes place at the Mary Rippon Outdoor Theater on the University of Colorado campus from late June through mid-August every summer. This talented company does three Shakespearean plays every year, including at least one tragedy. A few students and graduate students take part, but most of the performers are seasoned pros. Best of all, you can picnic (without glassware) beforehand, and then take in the evening sky during the performance. Tickets cost $10 to $46. No children under five are admitted. Order tickets by phone (☎ **303-492-0554**) or by visiting the box office in the basement of the Dance and Theater Building on the University of Colorado Campus, near the intersection of Broadway and Euclid. For more on the festival, surf the Internet to www.coloradoshakes.org.

Fast Facts: Boulder

Emergencies

For all emergencies, dial **911**.

Hospital

Boulder Community Hospital, 1100 Balsam Ave., at North Broadway (☎ 303-442-4521), has 24-hour emergency care.

Information

Boulder Convention and Visitors Bureau, 2440 Pearl St. (☎ 800-444-0447 or 303-442-2911; www.bouldercoloradousa.com), is open 8:30 a.m. to 5 p.m. Monday through Thursday and 8:30 a.m. to 4 p.m. on Fridays.

Internet Access

The Boulder Public Library, 11th and Arapahoe (☎ 303-441-3099), provides free Internet access.

Pharmacies

King Soopers Supermarket, 1650 30th St. (☎ 303-333-0164), fills prescriptions.

Post Office

There is a local branch at 15th and Walnut streets. Call ☎ 800-275-8777 for hours and other Boulder post office locations.

Road Conditions

Call ☎ 303-639-1111.

Weather

Call ☎ 303-494-4221.

Chapter 14

Colorado Springs

● ●

In This Chapter

▶ Staying at Colorado's grandest resort
▶ Pikes Peak or bust for family fun
▶ Visiting a divine, red-rock garden

● ●

*I*f you like orderly, clean-cut, traditional towns, you'll enjoy Colorado Springs. The Air Force Academy is nearby, along with several military installations. The international Christian organization Focus on the Family has its headquarters in town, and the first U.S. Olympic Training Center still conditions athletes here. Even the town's layout feels disciplined — a neat grid centered around a wide boulevard known as Pikes Peak Avenue. Within that grid, the downtown buildings barely obstruct the mountain views. The town and county have 158 nicely maintained parks, including the spectacular Garden of the Gods, where red sandstone slabs seem to have erupted out of the earth at the base of the mountains.

Colorado Springs has been a resort since the 1870s (though many early "guests" were people with tuberculosis, who came for the fresh air). Flush with mining profits from nearby Cripple Creek, millionaires built several grand hotels in and around Colorado Springs in the early 1900s. Visitors flocked here not only for the weather and the mountain views, but for attractions such as the Pikes Peak Cog Railway, the Garden of the Gods, Cave of the Winds, and later, the Pikes Peak Highway. These same attractions still lure throngs of visitors to the area. Colorado Springs isn't too expensive for most families, yet a certain formality remains: This is one of a handful of places in the state where men need a jacket and tie to dine in the finest restaurants.

Getting There

Eight commercial airlines together offer about 100 flights daily to **Colorado Springs Airport (CSA).** The airport has only three runways and a small terminal, so negotiating it is easy. You can get your bearings quickly by stopping at the **ground transportation booth** (☎ **719-550-1930**) on the terminal's lower level, open from 7 a.m. to midnight daily. **Avis, Dollar, Hertz,** and **National** all have desks and return areas at the airport. Other companies, including **Advantage, Budget, Enterprise,** and

Thrifty do business nearby in Colorado Springs. For information on contacting individual airlines and car-rental agencies, see the appendix.

Downtown Colorado Springs is 12 miles from the airport. Coming from the airport, go right (north) on Powers Boulevard, and then take a left (west) onto Colorado 24 (Platte Avenue). Follow Platte Avenue into the downtown area.

A few hotels offer free shuttle services for guests. If yours doesn't, call one of three taxi companies — **Express Airport Taxi** (☎ 719-634-3111), **Fremont County Cab** (☎ 719-784-2222), or **Yellow Cab** (☎ 719-634-5000) — for a ride into town. The cheapest company, Express Airport Taxi, bills $2 plus $1.50 per mile. The trip downtown usually costs around $18.

You can drive into Colorado Springs via Interstate 25, which crosses the west side of town along its route between Denver (70 miles north) and Pueblo (40 miles south). If you're heading west on I-70 and shooting for Colorado Springs, exit onto U.S. 24 in Limon, and then follow that highway southwest for 70 miles into the city. If you're heading east on I-70, take Colorado 9 south for 53 miles to U.S. 24, then follow U.S. 24 east for 66 miles into Colorado Springs.

Getting Around

Colorado Springs (see the nearby map of the same name) is a pedestrian-friendly city. And its citywide bus service, **Springs Transit** (☎ 719-385-5974; www.springsgov.com), is easy to navigate and inexpensive to ride — $1.25 for adults and 60¢ for seniors and kids 6 to 11. Keep in mind, though, that the system operates year-round Monday through Saturday only and is closed Sundays and holidays. Even so, you need a car to reach many of the most popular attractions, because they're scattered around town and in the mountains.

U.S. 24 borders the south edge of the downtown, and I-25 skirts the west side. The major north-south arteries in the downtown are Nevada Avenue and Cascade Avenue. The main east-west roads are Colorado Avenue and Platte Avenue (U.S. 24). The intersection of east-west Pikes Peak Avenue and Nevada Avenue marks the center of town. Street addresses prefaced with *North* or *South* indicate their location relative to Pikes Peak Avenue; ones prefaced with *East* or *West* describe their location relative to Nevada Avenue.

If you follow Colorado Avenue northwest out of the downtown, you soon pass through **Old Colorado City,** between 21st and 31st streets. The oldest part of Colorado Springs, Old Colorado City was a supply stop for gold miners heading west in the late 1850s. It became Colorado's first territorial capital in 1861 but degenerated into a saloon and red-light district. The 1970s saw the area become run-down, though much of it has since been restored into a quaint redbrick shopping area. Farther west, Colorado Avenue becomes Manitou Avenue and enters **Manitou Springs,** where some of the first resort hotels were built. Manitou Springs has a large historic district, including many Victorian homes. It's closer to the mountains, more compact, and more colorful than Colorado Springs. The Pikes Peak Cog Railway, which takes tourists up the steep slope to the top of Pikes Peak, has its depot at the edge of town. West of town, Manitou Avenue joins U.S. 24, which continues west into the mountains.

Where to Stay

You can stay in historic digs in Colorado Springs in every price range. Famous historic hotels such as the Broadmoor and The Cliff House are pricey. Less expensive, but hardly spartan, are a dozen or so area bed-and-breakfasts, including some in Victorian homes. Least expensive are the many historic motor lodges and motels around Manitou Springs, many of which date to the 1920s and 1930s, when tourists began traveling here by car. Some of these lodges and motels are fine; others need work. Ask to see a room before settling in. If you want a chain hotel, you can find one along I-25 in Colorado Springs.

The Broadmoor
$$$$ Colorado Springs

The ultraluxurious Broadmoor is almost a city for the rich and famous. On its 2,400 acres are 11 restaurants and lounges, 45 golf holes, 12 tennis courts, a 300-seat movie theater, 16 massage rooms, and 700 guest rooms. During high season, 1,700 employees cater to needs you didn't even know you had. That level of service has been maintained for over 80 years, so it's not really news. The best new thing here is the outdoor swimming pool. Like a seashore, the bottom of the pool slopes gradually into a deep end that seems to disappear into the hotel's man-made body of water, Cheyenne Lake. A barely visible wall separates pool from lake. The effect is cool and perfect. Of course, there's a price for all this luxury. Even if you can't or won't pay it, you should still walk through the original 1918 hotel. A recent renovation spruced up the fountains, chandeliers, frescos, marble floors, ceiling murals, and ornate plasterwork, making the entire building a work of art.

See map p. 164. 1 Lake Ave., at Circle Drive. ☎ *800-634-7711 or 719-577-5775. Fax: 719-577-5700.* www.broadmoor.com. *Rack rates: Summer $350–$525 double, $585–$750 suites; winter $250–$375 double, $425–$565 suite. AE, DC, DISC, MC, V.*

Eagle Motel
$ Manitou Springs

Come here when you're ready to rediscover those special motel joys: parking outside your door, free local calls, cable television, and soda pop

Colorado Springs

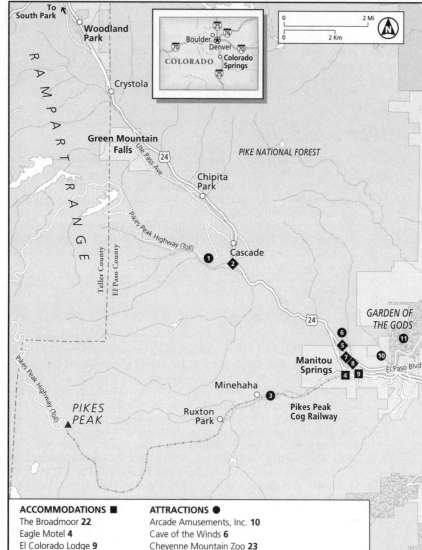

ACCOMMODATIONS ■

The Broadmoor **22**
Eagle Motel **4**
El Colorado Lodge **9**
The Hearthstone Inn **15**
Old Town Guest House **20**

DINING ◆

The Cliff House Dining Room **7**
Craftwood Inn **8**
Dutch Kitchen **5**
Jake and Tellys Restaurant
and Bar **19**
Saigon Cafe **16**
The Wines of Colorado **2**

ATTRACTIONS ●

Arcade Amusements, Inc. **10**
Cave of the Winds **6**
Cheyenne Mountain Zoo **23**
Colorado Springs Fine Arts Center **13**
Garden of the Gods **11**
Museum of the American Numismatic Association **14**
Pikes Peak Cog Railway **3**
Pikes Peak Highway **1**
Pro Rodeo Hall of Fame and Museum of the
American Cowboy **17**
United States Air Force Academy **12**
United States Olympic Complex **18**
World Figure Skating Museum & Hall of Fame **21**

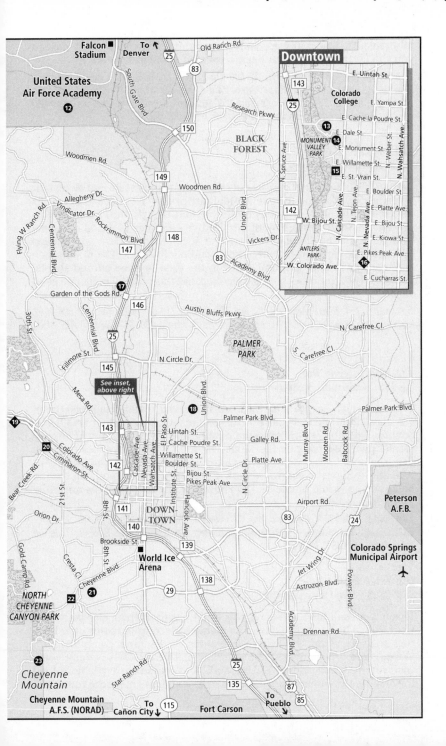

cooled by hollow ice cubes — not to mention a complimentary continental breakfast. The staff vigorously cleans this 1950s motel every day, so you can live the joy without being reminded of the last guests.

See map p. 164. 423 Manitou Ave. ☎ *800-872-2285 or 719-685-5467. Fax 719-685-0542.* www.eaglemotel.com. *Rack rates: Mid-Sept–late May $49–$59 double; late May–mid-June and mid-Aug–mid-Sept $59–$69 double; mid-June–mid-Aug $79–$89 double. Rates include continental breakfast. AE, DISC, MC, V.*

El Colorado Lodge
$–$$ **Manitou Springs**

Built in 1927, this motel consists of real adobe cabins scattered along four acres next to Manitou Avenue in Manitou Springs. The thick adobe walls help muffle the noise of nearby traffic. Not surprisingly, the cabins are decorated in a Southwestern motif, with Native American rugs and art; some even have working fireplaces. The larger accommodations — which sleep up to six people — have refrigerators and microwaves. The El Colorado claims to have been the first lodge in the area to have offered sheets. Fortunately for us, other places caught up, but this one still remains a good value.

See map p. 164. 23 Manitou Ave. ☎ *800-782-2246 or 719-685-5485. Fax: 719-685-4699.* www.pikes-peak.com/ElColorado. *Rack rates: $69–$111 cabin. AE, DISC, MC, V.*

The Hearthstone Inn
$$–$$$ **Colorado Springs**

This inn, which occupies an 1885 mansion and a neighboring 1900 tuberculosis sanitarium, feels more formal and reserved than other area B&Bs. Some of its antiques are museum quality, and reproductions of impressionist paintings hang on the walls. The rooms and suites lack the frilly décor found at other B&Bs — you'll find only comfortable antique furniture and well-preserved woodwork, floors, and trim. If you can't stand being offline, you'll be pleased to know that accommodations are wired for high-speed DSL.

See map p. 164. 506 N. Cascade Ave. ☎ *800-521-1885 or 719-473-4413. Fax: 719-473-1322.* www.hearthstoneinn.com. *Rack rates: $69–$199 double. Rates include full breakfast. AE, DISC, MC, V.*

Old Town Guest House
$$$–$$$$ **Old Colorado City**

This inn doesn't have a long history, but it has everything else you could want from a bed-and-breakfast. The uniquely decorated rooms offer luxuries such as steam showers, CD players, VCRs (and complimentary videos), and private decks. The waterbed mattresses are so comfy, you'll wish you were bed-ridden. And tea, soda, and snacks are available around the clock in the common areas. Thick walls and doors make the rooms feel private, especially for a B&B. When you're ready for a gourmet breakfast or driving directions, innkeepers Kaye and David Caster are right there to help.

See map p. 164. 115 S. 26th St. ☎ 888-375-4210 or 719-632-9194. Fax: 719-632-9026. www.oldtown-guesthouse.com. Rack rates: $99–$237 double. Rates include full breakfast. AE, DC, DISC, MC, V.

Where to Dine

This is one of two Colorado cities where you can dine in semiformal attire without feeling goofy. Dust off that blazer, knot that tie if you know how, and then head for The Cliff House or one of many restaurants at the Broadmoor in search of that perfect meal. Of course, the experience doesn't have to be stodgy. Even the fancy hotels have places where you can dine casually, and plenty of mid-priced restaurants are also in the area. Here are my best dining choices.

The Cliff House Dining Room
$$–$$$$ **Manitou Springs   NOUVEAU CONTINENTAL**

The Cliff House Dining Room is my favorite Colorado Springs eatery and darn near my favorite in the state. Never mind the Broadmoor and its huge reputation. Never mind the price — until your credit-card bill arrives. Just enjoy the Victorian surroundings and the French-influenced fare. Seek advice from one of the six licensed sommeliers on staff, then choose one of the 5,000 bottles of wine. The salmon here is so fresh, it can be eaten nearly raw; like most of the other entrees it's cooked — but not over-cooked — and topped with a buttery sauce. And don't pass up the cheese appetizer plate. For dessert, wash down the soufflé with a sip of port. Above all, enjoy. Suit coats are suggested, but if you don't feel like dressing up, you can dine casually in the cocktail area on the porch.

See map p. 164. 306 Canon Ave. ☎ 888-212-7000 or 719-685-3000. Reservations recommended. Main courses: $19–$36. AE, DC, MC, V. Open: Daily 6:30–10:30 a.m., 11:30 a.m.–2:30 p.m., and 5:30–9 p.m.

Craftwood Inn
$$–$$$$ **Manitou Springs   GAME**

Located in a 1912 Arts and Crafts–style mansion on a hillside above Manitou Springs, the Craftwood Inn is the best place to go if you're hungry for game. The choice of meats reads like a who's who of the local wildlife. Menu items include elk, trout, roast duck, noisettes of caribou, and grilled loin of wild boar. There's an extensive wine list, and the window and deck seating afford views of Pikes Peak.

See map p. 164. 404 El Paso Blvd. ☎ 719-685-9000. Reservations suggested. Main courses: $18–$50. AE, DC, DISC, MC, V. Open: Daily 5:30–10 p.m.

Dutch Kitchen
$ Manitou Springs AMERICAN

The same family has run this tiny hole-in-the-wall on Manitou Avenue for over 40 years. They make most of their food from scratch, ring up orders on a 1930s cash register, and close on Fridays, which makes sense only to them. You can have one of their famous corned beef sandwiches, a burger, or a straightforward dinner entree such as golden fried shrimp or Italian spaghetti. You can dine here for under $10 even if you sample the award-winning pie.

See map p. 164. 1025 Manitou Ave. ☎ 719-685-9962. Reservations for large parties only. Main courses: $6–$12. No credit cards. Open: Sat–Thurs 11:30 a.m.–3:30 p.m. and 4:30–8 p.m. Closed Thurs in spring and fall. Closed Dec–Feb.

Jake and Tellys Restaurant and Bar
$$ Old Colorado City GREEK

Two Greek brothers serve the old-world recipes of their grandmother at this quirky restaurant in Old Colorado City. If you'd like to try a collection of her traditional Greek dishes, order the sampler plate. It has *dolmadaki* (grape leaves with meat stuffing), spanakopita, and other delicacies whose names are too long for a guidebook this size. If the food doesn't transport you back to the Old World, maybe the murals of Greece and mounted ocean fish will.

See map p. 164. 2616 W. Colorado Ave. ☎ 719-633-0406. Reservations accepted. Main courses: $15–25. AE, DC, DISC, MC, V. Open: Sun–Thurs 11 a.m.–9 p.m., Fri–Sat 11 a.m.–10 p.m.

Saigon Cafe
$ Colorado Springs VIETNAMESE

Most of Saigon Cafe's dishes have plenty of fresh vegetables and only a modest amount of meat, served over rice or rice noodles. The best may be the noodle specialties — the meat of your choice served with rice noodles, bean sprouts, cucumber, mint, lettuce, peanuts, and sauce. The restaurant uses linen tablecloths, but if you insist on eating carryout, Saigon Cafe can rustle up a box for your food.

See map p. 164. 20 E. Colorado Ave. ☎ 719-633-2888. Reservations accepted. Main courses: $8–$14. AE, DISC, MC, V. Open: Mon–Sat 10 a.m.–8:30 p.m.

The Wines of Colorado
$ Cascade AMERICAN

This restaurant is the only place in the state where you can sample and purchase wines from all of Colorado's 35 wineries. If this sounds like a painful task, taste the wines! You can sample a half-dozen or so for free, then purchase any of 200 bottled varieties or simply order a glass with dinner. As for the food, you can get salads, sandwiches, wine-marinated hamburgers, and entrees such as grilled ahi and chicken pot pie. The deck overlooking the confluence of two creeks is a pretty place to dine. If you do sit down to dine, don't expect your server to hand over a wine list — you're supposed to have chosen during the tasting process. (Duh.)

See map p. 164. 8045 W. Hwy. 24 (at turn-off to Pikes Peak Highway). ☎ 719-684-0900. Reservations for parties of six or more only. Main courses: $5–$11. MC, V. Open: Summer daily 10:30 a.m.–8 p.m.; closed Mon the rest of the year.

Exploring Colorado Springs

Some of the tourist attractions in Colorado Springs have been operating for so long, they've become historical sites, too. If they weren't worth seeing, most of them wouldn't have lasted so long.

The best things to see and do

Cave of the Winds

Many years ago, on a hillside above present-day Manitou Springs, slightly acidic rainwater flowed through cracks in limestone and gradually dissolved some of the rock, eventually forming a mazelike network of caves — and, as fate would have it, a major tourist attraction. At Cave of the Winds, you can choose between two tours. The mellow, 45-minute Discovery Tour (cost: $16 adults; $8 children ages 6 to 15) is the tour for duffers. It follows paved routes down lighted corridors where tour groups have been going for over 100 years. This tour may not, um, rock your world, but it's still lots of fun, especially if you get a guide who can make light of a script that mixes the right amounts of science, hokum, and humor. On the more demanding Lantern Tour (cost: $20 adults, $12 children ages 6 to 15, children under 6 not allowed), you carry your own lantern into an otherwise dark cave, walk uneven dirt floors, and follow a guide into chambers smaller and more pristine than the ones on the Discovery Tour. For the Lantern Tour, call ahead for reservations. The cave's natural temperature is always 54 degrees, so remember to dress warmly.

See map p. 164. Six miles west of I-25 on U.S. 24, Manitou Springs. ☎ 719-685-5444. www.caveofthewinds.com. *Open: May–Aug, daily 9 a.m.–9 p.m.; Sept–Apr, daily 10 a.m.–5 p.m.*

Cheyenne Mountain Zoo

The people who named Cheyenne Mountain Zoo weren't kidding about the "mountain" part. It sits on a mountainside at 6,800 feet, with steep forest floors above it. The zoo animals suited to this environment wander large, forested plots of land on the hillside. They often seem more comfortable than the zoo-goers, many of whom can't handle the steep climbs. If the climbing wears you out, you can ride on the zoo shuttle (cost: $1 for a full day) alongside other weary Homo sapiens. The zoo has 146 species from around the world, including rarely seen Southwestern animals such as gray wolves and mountain lions. If you bring your kids, be sure to visit the 1920s-era carousel, which costs $2 a ride.

See map p. 164. 4250 Cheyenne Mountain Zoo Rd. (above the Broadmoor). ☎ *719-633-9925.* www.cmzoo.org. *Admission: $12 adults 12–64, $10 seniors 65 and over, $6 children 3–11. Open: Summer, daily 9 a.m.–6 p.m. (8 p.m. on Tues); rest of year, daily 9 a.m.–5 p.m.*

Garden of the Gods

When colliding tectonic plates uplifted the most recent incarnation of the Rocky Mountains, a few massive sandstone slabs were pushed out of the earth at the base of the mountains. In 1,300-acre Garden of the Gods Park, erosion has carved this sandstone into fantastic shapes; it's interesting to note that this is the same geological formation that created the Flatirons in Boulder and the giant natural amphitheatre at Red Rocks outside of Denver. Admission is free, but with 1.7 million visitors annually, it can be hard to find a parking space, let alone a quiet place. If the park is busy, look for a spot at the Garden of the Gods Visitor Center. Many spectacular rocks line the 1½-mile Perkins Central Garden Trail, which is accessible from this area. If you're curious about the rocks, watch the 12-minute, laser-enhanced video (cost: $2 for adults, $1 for kids 12 and under) at the visitor center, which explains how they were formed.

See map p. 164. Ridge Road (off I-25 Exit 146). ☎ *719-634-6666.* www.gardenof gods.com. *Admission: Free. Open: Memorial Day to Labor Day daily 8 a.m.–8 p.m.; rest of year daily 9 a.m.–5 p.m.*

Pikes Peak Cog Railway

Unlike many other historic railroads in Colorado, this 1891 railway has always catered to tourists, and today it carries more than a quarter-million people annually from Manitou Springs (elevation: 6,571 feet) to the summit of Pikes Peak (elevation: 14,110 feet). It's a straight, steep, 9-mile climb, with grades of 25 degrees in places. Ordinary trains can't get enough friction to climb this steeply; that's why this one has a cog that grabs onto a toothy center track. The train passes waterfalls, wildlife, and lakes before finally opening onto views that span all the way to Kansas. It takes 1 hour and 15 minutes to reach the windswept summit, where you linger for 40 minutes in or near the gift shop before making the 40-minute trip back down. Sometimes, discount coupons are offered on the Web site, so if this is definitely on your itinerary, check online to find out what discounts may be available the month you plan to be in the area.

See map p. 164. 515 Ruxton Ave., Manitou Springs. ☎ *719-685-5401.* www.cog railway.com. *Tickets: $29 adults; $17 children under 12. Open: Late April–Dec 29. Train departs every 80 minutes during midsummer, less often during slower periods. Reservations requested.*

A stunt becomes a tradition

The second oldest auto race in America, the **Pikes Peak International Hill Climb** (☎ **719-685-4400;** www.ppihc.com) started as a publicity stunt. In 1916, Spencer Penrose, owner of the Broadmoor Hotel, organized the race as a way of letting the world know about a new toll road he'd just bankrolled. Today, racers in motorcycles and sports cars still careen up the last 12.4 miles (the gravel portion) of the Pikes Peak Highway every year. The road probably would have been paved long ago if local officials hadn't feared ruining the race.

You can find out more about the history of the race and see old cars and motorcycles from past races at the **Pikes Peak Auto Hill Climb Educational Museum,** 135 Manitou Ave., Manitou Springs. The museum is open daily from 9 a.m. to 7 p.m. during summer (call for off-season hours). Admission is $5 adults, $4 seniors, and $2 for children ages 6 to 12.

Pikes Peak Highway

The road up Mount Evans, nearer to Denver, goes higher, costs less, and is just as pretty. But this is the more famous road, the one where race cars race every summer. If you plan on driving the 20 miles to the top, remember that a 14,000-foot peak is a serious undertaking, even in an automobile. Make sure you have at least half a tank of gas, because your round-trip will take 2 hours or more, as well as grippy brakes for the trip down. As for the road, it's wide enough for two city buses to pass each other, but it lacks guardrails and becomes gravel after 7 miles, which makes it plenty scary for flatlanders. And the weather on top is changeable, to say the least. One advantage to the road (over the train, see the preceding listing) is that it lets you set your own pace and pause at overlooks. In winter, the road stays open but is usually only plowed to around the 13-mile mark.

See map p. 164. Turn off U.S. 24 at Cascade (10 miles west of Manitou Springs). ☎ 800-318-9505 or 719-385-PEAK. www.pikespeakcolorado.com. *Admission: $10 per adult (16 and over), $5 per child (6–15), or $35 per carload. Open: May 19–Sept 5, daily 7 a.m.–7 p.m.; Sept 6–30, daily 7 a.m.–5 p.m.; rest of year, daily 9 a.m.–3 p.m.*

United States Air Force Academy

The U.S. Air Force Academy is huge. It encompasses 18,000 acres along the foothills of the Rockies, and the drive from the north to the south gates of the academy covers 14 miles. To get your bearings after arriving, follow the signs to the visitor center, which has Air Force videos, displays, gifts, and an information desk. It also has maps for a self-guided driving tour. From there, you can walk a ⅓-mile paved trail to the popular Cadet Chapel. Afterwards, allow at least two hours for the driving tour. During daytime, you can break up the drive by enjoying some of the open space. It's not exactly Woodstock in there, but you can still mountain-bike or hike on the Santa Fe Trail, road bike, play golf, or picnic. Just make sure you have a photo ID.

See map p. 164. 12 miles north of Colorado Springs, off I-25 Exit 156B (follow signs to the visitor center). ☎ *719-333-8723.* www.usafa.af.mil. *Admission: Free. Visitor Center hours: Summer daily 9 a.m.–6 p.m.; winter daily 9 a.m.–5 p.m.*

United States Olympic Complex

Unfortunately for the likes of you and me, this 36-acre complex is set up to train world-class athletes and not to entertain bored, frumpy tourists. Still, if you love the Olympics, you'll probably enjoy the one-hour tour. After watching a short, unsubtle video highlighting American Olympic achievements, you walk through facilities where athletes train for sports such as volleyball, judo, shooting, swimming, and boxing. If you go during mid-morning or late afternoon, you'll probably see at least a few athletes enduring the repetitive, boring, torturous work that you always hear about, after the fact, during the Olympics. If you don't take the tour, you're still allowed to wander the grounds, visit the gift shop, and stop at the U.S. Olympic Hall of Fame (which has changing displays). You may not, however, enter the buildings, so you're better off taking advantage of the tour.

See map p. 164. 1 Olympic Plaza, corner of Boulder Street (entrance) and Union Boulevard. ☎ *719-866-4618 (visitor center) or 719-866-4656 (reservations). Admission: Free. Open: Mon–Sat 9 a.m.–5 p.m. Last tour leaves at 4 p.m.*

Other things to see and do

In addition to the big draws, Colorado Springs may have more small, quirky attractions than any other Colorado town. While in Colorado Springs, you can

- ✔ **Get thrown.** The **Pro Rodeo Hall of Fame and Museum of the American Cowboy,** 101 Pro Rodeo Dr. (☎ **719-528-4764**), overflows with trophies, hats, boots, spurs, and chaps belonging to famous rodeo cowboys. So many cowboys have been inducted into the hall, you can't help but wonder who's left. It's open daily from 9 a.m. to 5 p.m. (except holidays). Admission costs $6 adults; $5 seniors 55 and over; $3 children 6 to 12; and is free for kids under 6.

- ✔ **Russell up some art.** The **Colorado Springs Fine Arts Center,** 30 W. Dale St. (☎ **719-634-5581;** www.csfineartscenter.org), has a large collection of fine regional art, including pieces by Charles Russell, Georgia O'Keefe, and Albert Bierstadt. My favorite gallery showcases pre- and post-Colombian Native American and Hispanic work. There's also a tactile gallery. It's open Tuesday through Saturday from 9 a.m. to 5 p.m., Sunday from 1 to 5 p.m. Admission is $5 for adults, $3 for seniors, and $2 for kids 6 to 16.

- ✔ **Study sequins.** The **World Figure Skating Museum and Hall of Fame,** 20 First St. (☎ **719-635-5200;** www.worldskatingmuseum.org), isn't so much about skating as about the trappings of the sport — the sequined outfits, polished skates, buttons, trophies, and medals. Seeing these showy historical items up close may pique your curiosity about the people behind the glitter. The museum is open Monday through Saturday from 10 a.m. to 4 p.m. Admission costs $3 adults, $2 for children ages 6 through 17 and seniors over 60.

✔ **Get sprung.** At the **Manitou Springs Chamber of Commerce,** 354 Manitou Ave. (☎ **800-642-2567** or 719-685-5089), you can pick up a map identifying ten mineral water springs in the downtown area. In the late 19th century, the town promoted the mineral water as a cure-all. It's a fun way to tour the downtown. Bring a cup so that you can fill up and drink if you get thirsty.

Guided tours

Pikes Peak Tours/Gray Line, 3704 W. Colorado (☎ **800-345-8197** or 719-633-1181; www.coloradograyline.com), will pick you up at your hotel and take you on a bus tour of Pikes Peak. The four-hour round-trip tour costs $35 for adults over 12, $20 for children 11 and under.

Staying active

With so many full-blown tourist attractions in and around Colorado Springs, you may not spend as much time on the trails as you would in other parts of the state. If you do want to exercise in the backcountry, consider the following activities:

✔ **Biking and hiking:** Trails lace the foothills above Colorado Springs. One especially popular and scenic area is North Cheyenne Canyon. Starting high up in the canyon, an 8-mile stretch of the **Gold Camp Road** is closed to motor vehicles. Once a railroad grade, the wide, gradual trail is ideal for family rides and walks. If you want a more challenging ride, you can branch off the Gold Camp Road onto a single-track trail. To reach the trailhead, take Cheyenne Boulevard past Seven Falls and Helen Hunt Falls. The trailhead is at the High Drive parking lot, where the road turns from pavement to dirt. **Criterium Bicycles,** 6150 Corporate Dr. (☎ **719-599-0149**), rents full-suspension mountain bikes for $35 per half-day, $50 per whole-day. **Challenge Unlimited,** 204 S. 24th St. (☎ **800-798-5954** or 719-633-6399), will set you up with bikes and help you coast down all 20 miles of the Pikes Peak Highway. Cost for that excursion is $93 per person in the morning, $80 in the afternoon (when storms are more likely).

✔ **Golfing:** The preferred public course in Colorado Springs is the 27-hole **Patty Jewett Golf Course,** 900 E. Espanola St. (☎ **719-385-6950**). Nonresident greens fees are $27 for 18 holes, $13.50 for 9 holes. If you're a serious duffer, though, and want one of the world's best golf vacations, the **Broadmoor Hotel** (see "Where to Stay" earlier in this chapter) has three championship-grade courses and several options for golf-and-accommodation packages.

✔ **Rafting:** See "Heading Out to Cañon City and Royal Gorge," later in this chapter.

Shopping

The Bookman, 3163 W. Colorado Ave. (☎ 719-636-0055), specializes in vintage paperbacks (think '50s-era pulp) and old reference books, and it even has some old manual typewriters. Antiques lovers and book geeks will love it.

At **Nevada Village Antiques,** 405 S. Nevada Ave. (☎ 719-473-3351), eight dealers share a 7,000-square-foot mall. Upwards of 50,000 articles are for sale.

Kitsch-lovers and serious collectors alike will love the dolls and figurines at **Simpich Character Dolls,** 2413 W. Colorado Ave. (☎ 719-636-3272; www.simpich.com). Elves, angels, and fairies make up the bulk of the collection, but the studio also specializes in historical and Christmas characters.

Van Briggle Art Pottery, at the corner of 21st Street and U.S. 24 (☎ 719-633-7729; www.vanbriggle.com), has been a working gallery since 1899. The artisans here make a style of pottery that was first created by Artus Van Briggle, who's famous in pottery circles. Some pieces are cast, others are hand-thrown. The studio sells bowls, vases, and lamps, at prices ranging from $20 to $1,500. Free tours are available. It's open Monday through Saturday from 8:30 a.m. to 5:00 p.m.

Especially for kids

Arcade Amusements, Inc., 930 Manitou Ave. (☎ 719-685-9815), in Manitou Springs, has old-fashioned, analog amusement games such as pinball and Skee-Ball for grown ups. It also has kiddie rides for, um, kiddies. And its state-of-the-art video games are sure to please teenagers. Some of the attractions are in the open air, so you won't feel claustrophobic. It's open daily from 10 a.m. to midnight during summer; 11 a.m. to 7 p.m. (and sometimes later) in other months.

Nightlife

Colorado Springs isn't known for its nightlife, but in recent years the night scene has expanded along with the city.

Hitting the bars and clubs

Most of the hottest nightspots are within walking distance of one another in the heart of Colorado Springs, but there are also a few fun roadhouses and pubs outside of downtown. Your options include the following:

✔ Arguably the most popular gathering place in Colorado Springs, **Phantom Canyon Brewing Company,** 2 E. Pikes Peak Ave. (☎ 719-635-2800), has billiards, handcrafted beers, and a menu that's heavy on comfort food. It's owned by the folks who built the Wynkoop Brewery in Denver, so you know the beer is topnotch.

✔ **Rum Bay,** 120 N. Tejon St. (☎ 719-634-3522), is the city's hot dance club, and it fuels the fire with 200 different rums. Cover varies.

✔ Strangely enough, the best jazz bar in Colorado Springs is in a Chinese restaurant: **Genghis Khan,** 30 E. Pikes Peak Ave. (☎ 719-328-1582), has local jazz and blues acts on Wednesday, Friday, and Saturday nights. Cover varies.

✔ Five nights a week, **Acoustic Coffee Lounge,** 5152 Centennial Blvd. (☎ 719-268-9951), books an eclectic lineup of musical acts — everything from folk to jazz. You can get coffee or a smoothie there, or dip into a full bar. No cover.

✔ **The Underground,** 130 E. Kiowa St. (☎ 719-633-0590), offers alternative and modern music, sometimes live and sometimes not. Cover varies.

Enjoying classical music

The **Colorado Springs Philharmonic** (☎ 719-226-9130; www.cs philharmonic.org) performs Saturday evenings and Sunday afternoons at the acoustically suburb, 2,000-seat **Pikes Peak Center,** 190 S. Cascade Ave. Tickets to performances run between $12 and $50, with discounts available for seniors and the military.

Fast Facts: Colorado Springs

AAA

The American Automobile Association has an office at 3525 N. Carefree Circle (☎ 800-283-5222 or 719-591-2222).

Emergencies

Dial **911.**

Hospitals

Memorial Hospital, 1400 E. Boulder St. (☎ 719-365-5000), has a 24-hour emergency room and offers all critical-care services.

Information

Colorado Springs Convention and Visitors Bureau (☎ 800-DO-VISIT or 719-635-7506; www.coloradosprings-travel. com) operates a Visitor Information Center at the corner of Cascade and Colorado avenues. For an update on weekly events,

call ☎ 719-635-1723. In Manitou Springs, the Chamber of Commerce (☎ 800-642-2567 or 719-685-5089; www.manitou springs.org) is at 354 Manitou Ave.

Newspapers

Colorado Springs has its own daily paper, the *Gazette Telegraph.* It also tolerates the two Denver dailies, the *Denver Post* and the *Rocky Mountain News.* For a quirkier approach to the news (and for strong arts and entertainment coverage), pick up the *Springs* magazine or the *Independent,* both of which are free tabloids. Many newsstands also sell national newspapers such as the *Wall Street Journal* and *The New York Times.*

Pharmacies

Walgreens Drug Store, 920 N. Circle Dr. (☎ 719-473-9090), fills prescriptions.

Taxes

State tax is 3%, local sales tax is 7%, and lodging tax is 9% for Colorado Springs and slightly higher in Manitou Springs.

Taxis

Call Express Airport Taxi (☎ 719-634-3111), American Cab (☎ 719-637-1111), or Yellow Cab (☎ 719-634-5000).

Transit Information

Contact Colorado Springs Transit (☎ 719-385-7433).

Weather Updates

Call ☎ 719-475-7599.

Heading Out to Cañon City and Royal Gorge

A quick 43-mile drive from Colorado Springs puts you in Cañon City and near the mouth of Royal Gorge, a 1,200-foot-deep canyon cut by the Arkansas River. Royal Gorge is the area's big tourist attraction, but the highest concentration of visitors is usually found at the nearby Colorado State Penitentiary, which is not even so much as a runner-up hotel in this book.

Getting there

To reach Cañon City from Colorado Springs, take Colorado 115 south for 33 miles, and then follow U.S. 50 west for 10 miles to Cañon City. Cañon City is 39 miles west of I-15 at Pueblo.

Exploring Royal Gorge

Royal Gorge formed when the Arkansas River cut downward through very hard Precambrian rock. It's one of the deepest and most scenic canyons in the state. You'd do well to bypass most of the tourist traps near the gorge, but three attractions are worth checking out:

✔ To see the gorge from the top, go to **Royal Gorge Bridge and Park** (☎ **888-333-5597** or 719-275-7507; www.royalgorgebridge.com), where you can walk (or catch a ride) across the gorge on the world's highest suspension bridge. Built in 1929, the bridge is 880 feet long and more than 1,100 feet above the Arkansas River. Standing on it and staring straight down at the river, feeling the whole structure sway in the wind, is exciting. The admission price also covers rides across the gorge on an aerial tramway, trips up and down a canyon wall on the "world's steepest incline railway," a rim-side mini-railroad, a petting zoo, and live entertainment. A well-marked turnoff for the park departs from U.S. 50 8 miles west of Cañon City. It's another 4 miles to the park. The park is open daily from 8:30 or 9:00 a.m. to dusk. Admission costs $15 adults, $13.50 seniors 60 and up, and $12 children ages 4 to 11.

✔ To see the gorge from the bottom, take the **Royal Gorge Route** (☎ **303-569-2403;** www.royalgorgeroute.com) out of Cañon City. Don't be fooled into riding either of the two miniature trains on the rim of the gorge. If you want to take the real train along the bottom of Royal Gorge, you have to drive into Cañon City and follow the signs to the Santa Fe Depot (on Third Street south of U.S. 50). You'll be rewarded with close-up views of the Arkansas River and the steep canyon walls. The ride goes out and back from Cañon City, lasts two hours, and covers 24 miles round-trip. From May 28 to October 9, the train departs at 9:30 a.m., 12:30 p.m., and 3:30 p.m. daily. The rest of the year, it leaves at 12:30 p.m. on Saturday and Sunday only. Admission is $28.95 adults, $18.50 children ages 3 to 12.

✔ The third and most exciting way to experience the gorge is on a raft floating down the Arkansas River. Because the gorge has some angry (Class 4) whitewater, this trip isn't for everyone, and kids under 15 aren't even allowed. But if you're strong enough to paddle in real rapids and prepared for an adventure, contact **Arkansas River Tours (ART)** (☎ **800-321-4352;** www.arkansasrivertours.com). From mid-May through mid-September, ART offers half-day Royal Gorge paddle trips for $54 and full-day trips for $89. If you've never helped paddle a boat in whitewater before, you'll need to take the full-day trip so that you have time to practice before entering the gorge. ART also offers a handful of oar trips. On oar trips, a guide rows the boat solo, using oars mounted in a metal frame (as opposed to the passengers and guide paddling together).

Finding places to stay and dine

In 1885, two years after the **St. Cloud Hotel,** 631 Main St. (☎ **800-405-9666** or 719-276-2000; www.stcloudhotel.com), was completed, the owners dismantled it brick by brick and moved it from Silvercliff to Cañon City. Since then, it's been the state headquarters for the Colorado Ku Klux Klan, a bus stop, a long-abandoned eyesore, and an asset seized by the state for back taxes. The new ownership has worked hard to restore it to its short-lived glory. Some rooms look Victorian; others look like sets from *The Big Sleep.* On the upside, it's as solid as a pyramid, it has a convenient downtown location, and the prices — $85 to $95 double — are reasonable. However, the hotel is closed for renovation until the fall of 2005, so those prices may be, well, adjusted.

If you want a place without a history, consider the **Comfort Inn Cañon City,** 311 Royal Gorge Blvd. (☎ **800-228-5150** or 719-276-6900; www.choicehotels.com). Rates (which include breakfast) run from $65 to $170, depending on the type of room you get and the season.

A neon sign outside **Merlino's Belvedere,** 1330 Elm Ave. in Cañon City (☎ **800-625-2526**), nearly always alerts this restaurant's incoming customers that there is immediate seating available — no surprise, since the place maxes out at around 500. Inside, most of the dining rooms feel Denny's-casual, with pastel colors and booths along the walls. This third-generation family-run business appears about as intimate as the Coors family business, but the food tastes homemade. The kitchen staff cooks spaghetti sauce three times a week in batches of over 60 gallons, bakes bread, and whips up gelato with fresh seasonal fruit. If you don't feel like pasta, you can choose steak, seafood, chicken, or a burger. A dinner entree sets you back anywhere from $9 to $26. Open for lunch and dinner daily.

Part IV
The High Country

In this part . . .

By the time you reach this region, you may have visited the bigger cities of the Front Range, and you may have acclimated yourself to Colorado's thin air. So it's time to go higher, up into the mountainous country the state is most famous for. In this part, I introduce you to the alpine beauty of Rocky Mountain National Park, the high valleys of the parklands just beyond the Front Range, and to some of the best ski towns that the United States, never mind Colorado, has to offer. Take a deep breath, throw on an extra layer, drink a glass of water, and keep reading.

Chapter 15

Rocky Mountain National Park

• •

In This Chapter

▶ Picking a time to go
▶ Hiking, climbing, and finding other cool things to do
▶ Staying at a classic lodge in the gateway towns

• •

*S*o, maybe by now you've checked out the urban scene along the Front Range; chances are, though, what you're *really* looking for in Colorado is a bit higher up. The true glory of this state is found up in the Rocky Mountains — what we natives tend to call the High Country. This enormous part of the state is divided into several major mountain ranges, all of them with their own rugged charms. Most are made of enormous chunks of granite that pushed up through the crust of the earth millions of years ago, though some (like the San Juans in the southwest and the Rampart Range west of Colorado Springs) are actually extinct volcanoes! All of them have been slowly eroded by the rivers that flow between them and the glaciers of the last ice age that carved out the huge U-shaped valleys above 8,000 feet. And this unique combination of geology, history, and climate makes these mountain ranges among the best outdoor playgrounds in the world, winter or summer. See the nearby map, "The High Country," for a layout of the whole region.

The High Country has a lot going for it. But the 416 square miles of Rocky Mountain National Park merit special attention, and deserve to be your gateway to the rest: the spectacular scenery, excellent resorts, prime camping, and wide range of outdoor activities make the park a perfect microcosm of the High Country as a whole. The main road through the park — Trail Ridge Road — crosses the continental divide at over 12,000 feet. It's the highest continually paved highway in America and probably the easiest way to experience high-alpine tundra, vibrant with life and color for a few short months every summer. With 147 mountain lakes, the park holds more water naturally than most other regions of the state. Countless waterfalls and creeks drain high alpine snowfields and glaciers and feed these languid pools. The peaks themselves aren't the highest in Colorado — Longs Peak, at 14,255 feet, is the park's only

The High Country

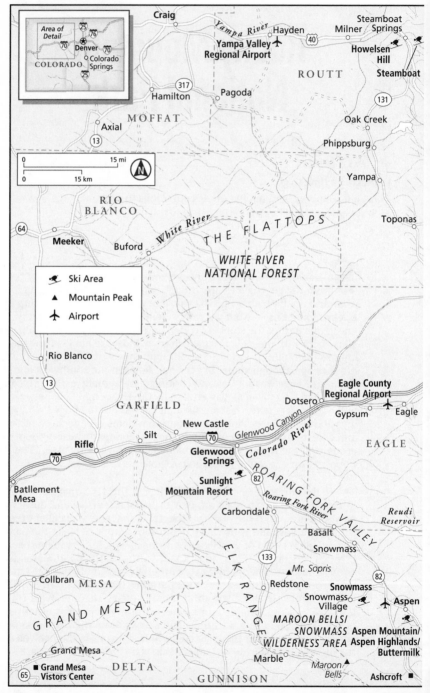

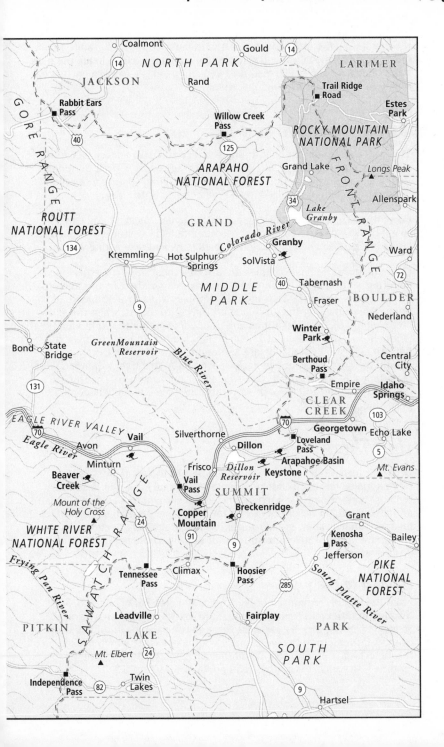

fourteener (local term for a mountain that rises above 14,000 feet) — but they're among the most spectacular, with massive walls of granite looming over immense valleys, all sculpted by ancient glaciers. In all, the park has 114 peaks over 10,000 feet. And you can be at the eastern entrances only two hours after arriving in Denver.

Choosing a Season to Visit

The park's combination of stunning scenery and easy access has contributed to overcrowding and parking shortages during peak periods. Rocky Mountain's visitation in 2004 was 2.9 million, slightly more than Yellowstone National Park — in an area one-eighth the size.

 Don't drive through the park on a July or August weekend and expect to get back to nature. To enjoy these mountains in solitude, you need to come in the off-season or else don a backpack and take a long walk.

Unfortunately, the busiest times are also the most opportune periods for covering ground here. If you want to cross the park by car, you need to visit between Memorial Day and mid-October, when Trail Ridge Road is open. The prime months for hiking are July and August, when the snow melts off the highest elevations and uncovers wildflowers in bloom. Summer doesn't last long at 11,000 feet. In May and June, you may still have to hike snowy trails. In late September and October, the trails should be mostly dry, but an early-season snowstorm may dampen your experience. In winter, most park roads stay open, some of the trails are marked for skiing and snowshoeing, and the area suddenly becomes very quiet.

Getting There

Denver International Airport (DIA), 80 miles to the southwest, is the closest major airport to Rocky Mountain National Park. DIA is served by most major domestic carriers and rental-car companies. For details about navigating DIA, check out Chapter 11. For information on contacting individual airlines and car-rental agencies, see the appendix. After you arrive in the state, your options for getting to the park definitely involve wheels.

Driving to the park

From the city of Denver, it's only 71 miles to Estes Park. Take U.S. 36 through Boulder and then continue on to Estes Park. In Estes Park, U.S. 36 meets U.S. 34, which goes west through the park to Grand Lake and Granby. Coming from the west, make your way to I-40, which passes through Granby en route from I-80 (near Park City, Utah) to I-70 (at Empire, Colorado). In Granby, head north and east on U.S. 34.

From Denver and other points south, the most scenic route is the Peak-to-Peak Scenic Byway, from Central City via Nederland, and along the southeast edge of the park. The byway starts at Colorado 119 north from I-70, picks up Colorado 72 just south of Nederland, and joins Colorado 7 north to Estes Park, where the byway meets up with U.S. 36. Heading west on U.S. 36 leads to the two eastern entrances of the park (see "Learning the Lay of the Land," later in this chapter).

Busing in to the park

From May 16 through October 1, the **Estes Park Shuttle and Mountain Tours** (☎ **970-586-5151**) makes four round-trips daily to Denver International Airport. The shuttle picks up and drops off passengers at most Estes Park locations. One-way fare is $39 per person; a round-trip costs $75. Charter service is also available.

Planning Ahead for Your Park Visit

Call or write **Rocky Mountain National Park,** Estes Park, CO 80517-8397 (☎ **970-586-1206**) for information. You can also get information off the Web at www.nps.gov/romo.

Backcountry permits are required year-round for overnight stays in the park's backcountry. There's a $15 charge for backcountry permits issued for hikes May through October; the rest of the year, they're free.

Permits for spring, summer, and fall go on sale March 1. If you're set on a particular hike, buy your permit well in advance. On summer weekends in July and August, the most popular areas fill up. Backcountry offices are located at the **Kawuneeche Visitor Center,** outside the park's Grand Lake entrance; and on U.S. 36 near the **Beaver Meadows Visitor Center.** For more information, call ☎ **970-586-1242** or write to Backcountry Office, Rocky Mountain National Park, Estes Park, CO 80517.

Three of the park's five campgrounds are always first-come, first-served. Reservations are accepted for the other two for dates during peak season (late May through mid-September). To make a reservation for the **Moraine Park** or **Glacier Basin** campgrounds, call ☎ **800-365-2267** or surf the Internet to http://reservations.nps.gov.

To find out more about the towns bordering the park, contact the following:

✔ The **Estes Park Area Chamber of Commerce,** P.O. Box 3050, Estes Park, CO 80517 (☎ **800-443-7837** or 970-586-4431)

✔ The **Grand Lake Area Chamber of Commerce,** P.O. Box 57, Grand Lake, CO 80447 (☎ **800-531-1019** or 970-627-3372)

✔ The **Greater Granby Chamber of Commerce,** P.O. Box 35, Granby, CO 80446 (☎ **970-887-2311**)

Learning the Lay of the Land

The continental divide goes right through the heart of Rocky Mountain National Park (see the nearby map). The main route through the park and across the divide is **Trail Ridge Road,** which meanders 49 miles from a spot near Estes Park on the east side of the park to Grand Lake on the west. On the way, it snakes for 12 miles across alpine tundra, cresting at 12,183 feet near Fall River Pass. Completed in 1932, Trail Ridge Road is the highest continually paved highway in America, and has some of the most breathtaking views you ever see through the window of a car.

Trail Ridge Road isn't the only way to climb from the area close to Estes Park to the loftier reaches of the park. Beginning in mid-summer (and sometimes earlier), you can also take **Fall River Road.** The first 2 miles of the road are paved and two-way, but near the Endovalley Picnic Area it becomes a one-way dirt road ascending 9 miles to Fall River Pass. This was the first major road in the park when it was completed in 1920, and it doesn't seem to have changed much since then. It's narrow, is exposed to steep drop-offs, and has switchbacks that are too sharp for vehicles longer than 25 feet. It ends at Trail Ridge Road, next to the Alpine Visitor Center. Together with Trail Ridge Road, it makes for a fun loop drive when it's open, but if you've never been to the park before, take Trail Ridge out of Estes Park first; the driving is easier, and the views are so much better.

Rocky Mountain National Park has three main entrances. From the west, U.S. 34 enters the park near Grand Lake and becomes Trail Ridge Road. On the east, U.S. 34 and U.S. 36 enter the park a few miles apart near Estes Park and then meet at Deer Ridge Junction. You can use either U.S. 34 or U.S. 36 to reach Trail Ridge Road. However, U.S. 34 also provides access to Fall River Road, and U.S. 36 takes you closer to the hiking trails in Moraine Park and Glacier Basin.

Other park roads are spurs leading to trailheads in alpine basins. On the east side of the park, **Bear Lake Road** branches south off of U.S. 36 and provides access to two large campgrounds and some of the park's most popular hiking trails. Because the parking areas near popular trailheads often fill up, the park operates two shuttle-bus routes in this area. You can catch either shuttle at the Visitor Transportation System parking area across from the **Glacier Basin Campground.** (For more on the shuttles, see "Getting around," later in this chapter.)

In the southeast corner of the park, a road goes 2 miles east from Colorado 7 to the **Wild Basin Trailhead.** Just north of there, a spur road off of Colorado 7 goes east to a campground, ranger station, and the parking area for the **Longs Peak Trailhead.** The highest mountain in the park, 14,255-foot **Longs Peak,** is located nearby.

Rocky Mountain National Park

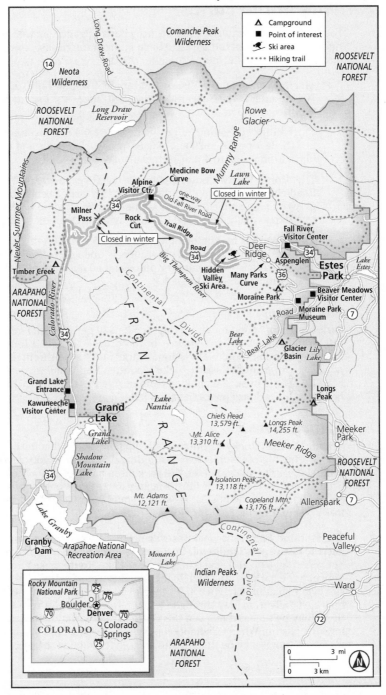

Campground
Point of interest
Ski area
Hiking trail

Comanche Peak Wilderness

ROOSEVELT NATIONAL FOREST

(14) Neota Wilderness

Long Draw Road

ROOSEVELT NATIONAL FOREST

Long Draw Reservoir

Rowe Glacier

Mummy Range

Lawn Lake

Medicine Bow Curve

Alpine Visitor Ctr.

one-way
Old Fall River Road

Closed in winter

Milner Pass

Never Summer Mountains

(34)

Rock Cut

Trail Ridge

Closed in winter

Road (34)

Big Thompson River

Fall River Visitor Center

(34)

Lake Estes

Deer Ridge

Aspenglen

Estes Park

Hidden Valley Ski Area

Many Parks Curve

(36)

Timber Creek

Colorado River

Continental

Divide

FRONT

Moraine Park

Beaver Meadows Visitor Center

Moraine Park Museum

(7)

ARAPAHO NATIONAL FOREST

(34)

Bear Lake

Bear Lake

Road

Glacier Basin

Lily Lake

Longs Peak

Grand Lake Entrance

Kawuneeche Visitor Center

Grand Lake

Lake Nantia

RANGE

Chiefs Head 13,579 ft.

Longs Peak 14,255 ft.

Meeker Park

Meeker Ridge

Mt. Alice 13,310 ft.

ROOSEVELT NATIONAL FOREST

Grand Lake

Shadow Mountain Lake

(34)

Isolation Peak 13,118 ft.

Mt. Adams 12,121 ft.

Copeland Mtn. 13,176 ft.

Allenspark (7)

Lake Granby

Granby Dam

Arapahoe National Recreation Area

Monarch Lake

Indian Peaks Wilderness

Continental

Divide

Peaceful Valley

Ward

Rocky Mountain National Park

(25)

(76)

Boulder

(70)

Denver

(70)

COLORADO

Colorado Springs

(25)

ARAPAHO NATIONAL FOREST

(72)

0   3 mi
0   3 km

N

Arriving in the Park

You find a visitor center at each primary park entrance, as well as one right in the middle of the park. All have information desks, interpretive displays, and park literature.

- ✔ The **Beaver Meadows Visitor Center** (☎ 970-586-1206) is on U.S. 36 just outside the Beaver Meadows entrance. It's open daily from 8 a.m. to 4:30 p.m.

- ✔ The **Fall River Visitor Center,** just outside the Fall River entrance on U.S. 34, opened in 2000. Open Saturdays, Sundays, and most holidays from 9 a.m. to 4 p.m., it has displays on wildlife.

- ✔ The **Alpine Visitor Center** sits where Fall River Road and Trail Ridge Road converge. Located on the tundra, this visitor center has displays on high-alpine plant and animal life. It's open from 10:30 a.m. to 4:30 p.m. daily, Memorial Day through mid-October.

- ✔ The **Kawuneeche Visitor Center** (☎ 970-586-1206), on U.S. 34 just outside the Grand Lake Entrance, is open daily from 8 a.m. to 4:30 p.m. It has a backcountry office and an auditorium that shows a 20-minute video on the park.

Paying fees

Park admission, good for seven days, costs $20 per week per vehicle, $10 for individuals on foot, bicycle, or motorcycle. A $50 **National Parks Pass** covers admission to all National Parks for one year from the date of purchase. An **Annual Pass** to Rocky Mountain National Park costs $35. For $10, people over 62 can buy a **Golden Age Pass,** which entitles the holder to free admission for life at all federal fee areas.

Getting around

Driving through Rocky Mountain National Park isn't difficult; the hard part, during high season at least, is finding parking near your favorite trailhead. During mid-summer, the park often has more cars than it can accommodate. The busiest time is in July and August between 10 a.m. and 3 p.m. One of the busiest areas is 10-mile **Bear Lake Road,** where many popular hiking trails are located.

The **Moraine Park** route makes seven stops between the parking area and the **Fern Lake Trailhead.** Buses on that route run every 20 minutes between 7:30 a.m. and 7:30 p.m. The **Bear Lake Route** makes three stops between the parking area and Bear Lake. Buses on the Bear Lake Route run every 30 minutes between 5 a.m. and 10 p.m. The shuttle service operates daily from May through October. During absolute peak periods, there may be times when even the Visitor Transportation System parking area fills up. When this happens, try the Moraine Park Museum lot. If that's full too, it may be time to find an activity outside the park. The road to Bear Lake recently underwent extensive reconstruction, and is open again year-round.

Considering safety

Although Rocky Mountain National Park isn't an especially dangerous place, it does sport a few hazards that could sour your visit. Take the proper precautions and you should be fine. Check out the following hazards and tips for dealing with or preventing them:

- ✔ **Animal encounters:** Most bear encounters happen because people aren't careful with food. When car-camping inside Rocky Mountain National Park, stow your food in airtight containers inside your vehicle, out of sight, and never, ever in your tent. Mountain lion encounters are rare, but a lion did attack a child inside the park in 1997. When they do attack, cougars usually go after children or small adults, often when the victims are running. If you encounter a large cat in the forest, do your best to act like something other than a deer — seriously. Stand up tall, talk, walk backwards slowly, and toss a few rocks in the general direction of the cat. Whatever you do, don't bound away through the underbrush. As for elk and moose, a general rule is to keep your distance, especially during the fall mating season or if calves are present. Elk and moose often bluff charges, but real attacks do happen.

- ✔ **Falls:** Surprisingly, falls are the leading cause of death in the park, and not because there are so many technical climbers here. Most falling deaths are caused by unspectacular tumbles onto rocks. So watch your step.

- ✔ **Hypothermia:** A summer rain sounds innocent enough, but above 10,000 feet, the water is usually icy enough to make you hypothermic. Even on warm, seemingly clear days, carry insulating layers of synthetic fabrics such as polypropylene and polar fleece — cotton sweatshirts won't do — as well as a water-resistant shell. And eat and drink regularly. Hydration is a key factor in preventing hypothermia.

- ✔ **Altitude sickness:** Headaches, nausea, and fatigue are common when people move rapidly from sea level to high elevations. The best way to avoid altitude sickness is to acclimate and take it easy for a few days at lower elevations before climbing any mountains. Drink plenty of water, and avoid alcohol and caffeine. If you have a headache or nausea, the symptoms should subside if you descend 2,000 to 3,000 feet. Seek immediate medical attention if you experience vomiting, coughing, or a loss of coordination.

- ✔ **Avalanches:** In general, stay off steep snowfields in the backcountry if you don't know about snow safety. During late spring and summer, watch for rapidly warming snow. If you're sinking in deeper than your boot tops in soggy snow and your route crosses steep slopes, it's time to switch to another activity.

✔ **Slab avalanches:** Colorado leads the nation in avalanche fatalities. Most of these deaths result from *slab avalanches,* in which a slab of snow shears off of the snow underneath it, then rides a super-lubricated cushion of air down to the bottom of the valley. Imagine tilting a layer cake until the top part slides off, and you'll have a good picture of what a slab avalanche looks like. Now picture that top layer accelerating to 200 miles per hour in five seconds, and picture yourself trying to run away. . . .

At a critical angle, it may take a little prodding to make the top layer slide, but in an unstable snowfield, the weight of one person can sometimes trigger a large avalanche that's been close to happening. This is no joke: If you're unfamiliar with the rules of snow safety, hire a guide before traveling the backcountry in winter and spring.

✔ **Lightning:** Afternoon thunderstorms are common in summer. If a storm approaches while you're in the park, the best thing to do is vacate exposed peaks and ridgelines until it passes. While heading into heavily forested areas is a good idea, *do not stand under an isolated tree during a lightning storm!*

Enjoying the Park

Most people explore Rocky Mountain National Park by driving some or all of Trail Ridge Road, which tops out at 12,183-foot Fall River Pass. Before starting your drive, stop at a visitor center and pick up a *Trail Ridge Road Guide* (cost: 25¢). This self-guided driving tour provides descriptions of 12 numbered sites along Trail Ridge Road. Even if you don't want to make all the stops, don't miss the following:

✔ **Never Summer Ranch:** Located on the west side of the park, this well-preserved homestead is one of the best places in the West to find out how the ranch families of a century ago lived. The ranch house and outbuildings are full of the belongings, tools, and furniture of the original inhabitants. And the ranch is nestled in a forest near the Colorado River, a half-mile away from the parking lot. (It's a 1-mile round-trip hike.) During summer, volunteers guide free tours of the ranch and outbuildings, open daily from 10 a.m. to 4 p.m.

✔ **Alpine Visitor Center:** One of the subtle delights of Rocky Mountain National Park is its tundra. Many well-insulated plants and animals survive above 11,000 feet, enduring a frost-free season of only eight to ten weeks. To find out more about them, stop at the Alpine Visitor Center, and then drive a few miles east to **Rock Cut** and hike a mile round-trip on the **Tundra Communities Trail.** (For more on this trail, skip ahead to "Taking a hike.")

✔ **Moraine Park Museum:** Located on the **Bear Lake Road,** this may be the best place in Colorado to learn about mountains. Its exhibits on mountain-building clarify the effects of glaciers, volcanoes, weather, movements in the Earth's crust, and other influences. Don't miss it. It's open daily from 9:00 a.m. to 4:30 p.m. from mid-April through mid-October.

Taking a hike

The best way to explore Rocky Mountain National Park is by hiking some of its 350 miles of trails. In the following sections, I suggest areas with great hiking and offer descriptions of prime trails.

If you start your hike early in the morning, you'll have an easier time parking, and you'll also avoid afternoon thunderstorms, which are common during the summer months.

East side (Bear Lake area)

With high-alpine lakes, immense snowfields, views of Longs Peak, and thundering waterfalls, Bear Lake is one of the most scenic areas anywhere. As you may expect, the Bear Lake area lures people by the shuttle-load. Even after hiking a mile or so down a trail here, you can still expect company.

Bear Lake Trail

This wide, gravel trail circles Bear Lake and has benches along the way. The trail is considered handicap-accessible, but there are a few steep climbs. (A sign at the trailhead provides detailed information on gradients and widths.) Always busy, the trail opens onto views of Longs Peak and Hallet Peak.

Distance: 0.5 mile round-trip. Level: Easy. Access: At Bear Lake. Follow Bear Lake Road 9.7 miles off of U.S. 36.

Bear Lake to Lake Haiyaha

As you climb 745 vertical feet over 2.1 miles (one-way) from Bear Lake to Lake Haiyaha, you pass a string of mountain lakes, each with its own unique splendor. First there's Nymph Lake (0.5 mile), a tiny mirror flecked with green lilies and golden flowers. Then comes Dream Lake, flush against mountainsides on which immense, hanging snowfields dribble waterfalls. A few of your fellow hikers may drop out if you continue to Lake Haiyaha. There, you have to clamber across boulders to reach the edge of a lake so clear, you can see fish 30 feet away.

Distance: 4.2 miles round-trip. Level: Moderate. Access: At Bear Lake. Follow Bear Lake Road 9.7 miles off of U.S. 36.

East side (Longs Peak area)

Among the dozens of immense peaks in the park, the park's lone four-teener, Longs Peak, attracts the most attention. Thousands of people climb to the top every year; for some, it's the experience of a lifetime.

Bear in mind that if you're willing to walk far enough to climb Longs Peak, you could also climb a smaller, equally scenic peak in near solitude.

Keyhole Route up Longs Peak

Unless you're a technical climber, take the Keyhole Route to reach the summit. The first 6 miles are on a rocky but clearly defined hiking trail. Where the trail ends in a boulder field, the 2-mile route to the summit begins. You alternately clamber across boulder fields and traverse ledges to reach the top. Bull's-eyes on the rocks help you stay on course. You need good hiking boots in order to grip on steep, slippery rocks. And you need to prepare carefully by bringing lots of food and water, insulating layers, a wind- and water-resistant shell, and a headlamp. The window for summiting via the Keyhole Route is usually mid-July to early September.

Because the round-trip usually takes 12 to 15 hours, many hikers break up the climb by spending the night at a mid-mountain campsite. Call the **Backcountry Office** (☎ **970-586-1242**) several months in advance in order to procure a Backcountry Permit for a campsite on Longs Peak.

Distance: 16 miles round-trip, 4,855 vertical feet from trailhead to summit. Level: Strenuous. Access: Longs Peak Ranger Station, 1 mile off Colorado 7, 7 miles south of Estes Park.

Southeast corner (Wild Basin area)

Trails in Wild Basin are less crowded than ones around Bear Lake — yet still busy during high season. The area is lower and warmer than Bear Lake.

Wild Basin Trail to Ouzel Falls

This trail follows North St. Vrain Creek and then crosses two of its tributaries, climbing gradually for about 900 feet en route to Ouzel Falls. The prettiest sight along the way may be Calypso Cascades, where water dances over boulders as smooth as marble, passing under logs jammed helter-skelter like pick-up sticks. The trail crosses an area where wild-flowers have spruced up a scar left by a 1978 forest fire. Then comes Ouzel Falls, where the creek arcs off a ledge and into a pool below.

Distance: 5.4 miles round-trip. Level: Moderate. Access: Across from Wild Basin Ranger Station. To reach the station, follow Colorado 7 for 13.5 miles south of Estes Park; turn off at the Wild Basin Ranger Station sign and follow the signs.

West side

There's a lot of hiking on the west side of the park, including some trails near Grand Lake. Two prime trailheads are right across from each other on Trail Ridge Road, between Farview Curve and Timber Creek Campground. The less strenuous option, **Colorado River Trail,** is on the west side of the road, and **Timber Lake Trail** is on the east side. For a short hike, try **Tundra Communities Trail,** which is east of the continental divide but on the west side of the park.

Tundra Communities Trail

This paved, half-mile trail gradually climbs across alpine tundra to some craggy rocks. I like it because it makes you feel the raw, unfettered elements in the high mountains. The plants here are so low and tiny, they seem to vibrate in the breezes instead of swaying. You can see where the saturated and oft-frozen earth has squeezed broken rocks onto its surface. And on a clear day, there are smatterings of color everywhere: yellow and purple flowers, greenish lichens, and a cornflower blue sky.

Distance: 1 mile round-trip. Level: Easy. Access: At Rock Cut parking area on Trail Ridge Road.

Colorado River Trail to Lulu City

The National Park Service calls this a moderately difficult trail, but the trail is difficult only because it's 3.7 miles (one-way) to Lulu City. As it follows the Colorado River upstream through forests and meadows, this wide, dusty boulevard climbs only about 350 feet. After 2 miles, you pass an old mine and two cabins in Shipler Park. Another 1.7 miles takes you to the deserted mining town of Lulu City — which is hardly a lulu of a city. (Seems that after the miners left, the ranchers who followed carted away most of the wood from the buildings.) The trail continues on to the headwaters of the Colorado River, 8 miles from the trailhead.

Distance: 7.4 miles round-trip. Level: Moderate. Access: Well-marked parking area for trailhead, on west side of Trail Ridge Road between Farview Curve and Timber Creek Campground.

 ### Timber Lake Trail

You have to work hard to reach the high-alpine lakes on the west side of the park, but the extra effort makes the lakes seem more stunning when you get there. (On the east side, you can drive right up to many of them.) This trail steadily climbs 2,060 feet over the course of 4.7 miles to Timber Lake, cupped between Jackstraw Mountain and Mount Ida. The trail is long, but smooth and not particularly steep — most of the grades are user-friendly. Even so, you should set aside most of a day to go up and back. Most of the way, pine forest shelters you. As you near the lake, the trail becomes more rugged and the forest thins, eventually giving way to alpine meadows alongside Timber Creek.

Distance: 9.6 miles round-trip. Level: Strenuous. Access: Well-marked parking area for trailhead, on east side of Trail Ridge Road between Farview Curve and Timber Creek Campground.

Roving with rangers

Ranger programs are scheduled throughout the year, with a full schedule offered from June through September. Programs include short walks, talks, and guided hikes of up to four hours. For a full schedule, consult the park's free newspaper, *Rocky Mountain National Park High Country Headlines.*

Watching wildlife

It's hard *not* to see wildlife in and around the park. About 3,000 **elk** range from the tundra near the continental divide all the way down to the meadows around Estes Park. They're especially numerous on the eastern side of the park. Look for **bighorn sheep** on the tundra and near Sheep Lake in Horseshoe Park, on the eastern side of the park. The park no longer has grizzly bears, but it does have a healthy population of **black bears.** Black bears often turn up near campgrounds, residences, and businesses where people have not been careful with food or trash. Watch for them in the forest. **Coyotes** prefer open areas but can be found anywhere in and around the park. They look like lanky reddish-brown dogs, only, unlike dogs, they carry their tails low between their legs. **Moose** gravitate to damp, boggy lakes, river bottoms, and forests. Most moose sightings occur on the west side of the park.

Staying Active

With mountains, rivers, lakes, trails, and sheer rock walls, Rocky Mountain National Park attracts a range of athletes and outdoor enthusiasts. Outside the park, you find still more places to recreate, including less pristine settings such as golf courses and reservoirs.

Inside the park

Hiking isn't the only activity you can do inside the park. Check out some other options:

- ✔ **Biking:** Mountain biking is prohibited inside Rocky Mountain National Park. However, road cyclists often cross the park on Trail Ridge Road. The road is narrow, steep, and high. Traffic can be heavy, and the sightlines for drivers are poor. Experienced cyclists will probably enjoy the ride on weekdays; on weekends, however, you're better off avoiding the crush of traffic.

- ✔ **Fishing:** The park's lakes and streams have four species of trout, but most of the fish are small. Only artificial lures and flies are allowed inside the park, and fishing is prohibited in certain lakes and streams. Before entering the park, pick up a Colorado fishing license (cost: $5.25 for one day) at **Estes Park Mountain Shop** (☎ 970-586-6548), 358 E. Elkhorn Ave., in Estes Park; or at **Budget Tackle** (☎ 970-887-9344), 255 E. Agate Ave., in Granby. And check at a visitor center about park-specific regulations.

✔ **Horseback riding:** Riding is allowed on 260 miles of trails (also used for hiking) inside the park. **Hi Country Stables** keeps horses near **Glacier Creek** (☎ 970-586-3244) and **Moraine Park** (☎ 970-586-2327) inside the park boundaries. A walking ride, through forest and across streams costs $40 for two hours.

✔ **Mountaineering:** Skilled mountaineers often attempt challenging routes inside Rocky Mountain National Park. The park presents tests ranging from glacier travel to ice climbing to multiday ascents of rock walls. If you'd like to try your hand at technical mountaineering, contact the **Colorado Mountain School (CMS),** P.O. Box 1846, Estes Park, CO 80517 (☎ 888-CMS-7783 or 970-586-5758; www.cmschool.com). The lone guide service in Rocky Mountain National Park, CMS guides half-day excursions ($170 for one or two people) and full-day excursions ($230 for one person, $320 for two people), in addition to offering a variety of classes. Experienced rock climbers won't want to miss a chance to scale the Diamond, the magnificent east face of Long's Peak. The various routes range from grade IV to grade VI, so they're definitely for experts; maps and information are available through **Neptune Mountaineering,** 633 South Broadway, in Boulder (☎ 303-499-8866; www.neptune mountaineering.com).

In the gateway communities

The mountain scenery doesn't end at the park boundaries. There's a lot to do on both sides of the park, including the following:

✔ **Cross-country skiing:** You can *skate-ski* (cross-country skiing with a skating technique) on 95 kilometers of track at **Snow Mountain Ranch** (☎ 970-726-4628), 9 miles south of Granby on U.S. 40. Snow Mountain has 5 kilometers of dog-friendly trails and illuminates another 1.5 kilometers of track for night skiing. Daily trail passes cost $12 for adults, $5 for ages 6 to 12.

✔ **Golfing:** West of the park, near Granby, championship golf courses are popping up faster than you can say "bogey." The course nearest the park is the 18-hole, par-72 **Grand Lake Golf Course** (☎ 800-551-8580 or 970-627-8008). Greens fees are $65 for 18 holes, $40 for 9 holes. The 18-hole **Estes Park Golf Course,** 1080 S. St. Vrain Street (☎ 970-586-8146), often hosts herds of deer and elk, so you may have company. Greens fees are $36; $22 after 3 p.m.

Where to Stay and Dine in Estes Park and Grand Lake

There's no lodging, and precious little that can really be called "dining," inside Rocky Mountain National Park. However, the park does have five campgrounds totaling 587 sites. The **Timber Creek, Aspen Glen,** and

Longs Peak campgrounds are always first-come, first-served. Reservations are accepted for the **Moraine Park** or **Glacier Basin** campgrounds for dates during peak season (late May through mid-September). To reserve a spot, call ☎ 800-365-2267 or surf to http://reservations.nps.gov. The cost per site is $20. Although you can't stay in the park, accommodations and restaurants abound in the gateway communities of Estes Park, Grand Lake, and Granby.

Estes Park

Most of the lodging east of Rocky Mountain National Park is in the rather crowded, tourism-happy town of Estes Park. Estes Park seems to have more candy stores, T-shirt shops, and ice-cream parlors per capita than anywhere else in the state, but it's also pretty, and very convenient to Denver and the rest of the Front Range. All around town, elk and deer wander grassy hillsides amid greenish, lichen-stained rocks and ponderosa pines. When it comes to lodging, you'll find everything from tiny riverfront cabins to immense historic hotels.

Accommodations

Chalet at Marys Lake Lodge
$$–$$$$ **Estes Park**

Built between 1919 and 1925, this immense log building sat abandoned for more than two decades after half the structure burned down in 1978. The original windows remain, but the floor plan of the lodge has been reconfigured. Instead of having 300 rooms, the place now has 13 suites and 3 studios, all of which have replicas of Country Victorian antiques. The studios are compact and have limited views, but the suites have sitting rooms and plenty of floor space, and they overlook Marys Lake and the Mummy Range. Perhaps because the inn didn't reopen until 2001, the prices are down-to-earth. Like the nearby Stanley Hotel, it's rumored to be haunted.

2625 Marys Lake Rd. ☎ *877-442-6279 or 970-586-8958. Fax: 970-586-5308.* www.maryslakelodge.com. *Rack rates: $89–$129 studio, $119–$199 suite. AE, DISC, MC, V.*

Olympus Motor Lodge
$$ **Estes Park**

Saying that Estes Park has a lot of motels would be an understatement. Still, this motel is a little different. Each room has a unique quilt, and the walls are painted to match the colors in the quilt. (Whatever you do, don't spill.) The owners deliver fresh-baked muffins to the rooms every morning, and they serve tea and espresso in the 1922 lodge building. Perched on a hillside with distant views of Longs Peak, every room has a patio complete with old-style metal lawn furniture.

2365 Big Thompson Ave. ☎ *800-248-8141 or 970-586-8141. Fax: 970-586-8142.* www.estes-park.com/olympus. *Rack rates: June 16–Sept 14 $88–$102 double; Sept 15–June 15 $65–$85 double. AE, DC, DISC, MC, V.*

A shining inspiration

In 1973, a stay at the Stanley Hotel helped inspire Stephen King to write *The Shining.* King was experiencing what must have been a rare case of writer's block when he heard about Trail Ridge Road — the road that runs through Rocky Mountain National Park — closing for the winter. An idea took root. In King's book, the haunted Overlook Hotel is a dead ringer for the Stanley. Parts of the original film version show Timberline Lodge in Oregon, but the made-for-TV remake was set at the Stanley Hotel, and King himself oversaw the production.

Stanley Hotel
$$$–$$$$ Estes Park

The Stanley Hotel may have inspired Stephen King's horror story *The Shining,* but the place is more picturesque than ominous. It's a wide, symmetrical building, four stories high, with a white exterior and a red roof. Fanlights in the windows, Corinthian columns, and a bell tower together give it a classical appearance, and its position on a hillside lends it extra prominence. The hotel's rooms have recently been renovated and all are bright and full of either genuine antiques or reproductions. The superior rooms, which look south to the peaks along the continental divide, cost $20 more than the standard rooms, which look north toward the hotel's courtyard gardens and smaller hills.

333 Wonderview Ave. ☎ *800-976-1377. Fax: 970-586-3673.* www.stanleyhotel. com. *Rack rates: $149–$209 double; $269–$299 suite. AE, DC, DISC, MC, V.*

YMCA of the Rockies Estes Park Center
$$ Estes Park

Families and groups come here to experience a wholesome, summer-camp-style atmosphere. Situated on 860 acres, the YMCA of the Rockies has huge playing fields, hotel rooms for 450, and vacation homes and cabins for 210 (the small, rustic cabins are especially good values). You can swim in an indoor pool; play horseshoes, basketball, or volleyball; ride horses; or shoot archery. There's a restaurant on the premises, plus three other dining rooms for groups. It's a family-oriented place, but anyone can come here. For $5 per day, you can buy a temporary YMCA membership that allows you to rent a room.

2515 Tunnel Rd. ☎ *970-586-3341, ext. 1010. Fax: 970-586-6078.* www.ymcarockies. org. *Rack rates: $74–$105 lodge room (sleeps 4–6); $84–$289 cabin (sleeps 4–10). MC, V.*

Dining

Notchtop Bakery & Cafe
$–$$ **Estes Park   NATURAL FOODS**

Expect here the type of fresh, light, creative food that's popular in Boulder and all too rare in Estes Park. To supplement its gourmet baked goods, the Notchtop cooks omelettes and home fries every morning, and serves sandwiches, salads, and burgers at lunch and dinner. Among the delicacies: deep-fried mahimahi on a bun; fire-roasted green chiles stuffed with herbed mashed potatoes; and a tuna melt on focaccia bread. On Friday nights, folk singers croon to small but enthusiastic crowds.

459 E. Wonderview (in upper Stanley Village). ☎ *970-586-0272. Reservations accepted after 4:30 p.m. Main courses: $6.25–$11. DISC, MC, V. Open: Daily 7 a.m.–7 p.m.*

Poppy's Pizza & Grill
$–$$ **Estes Park   PIZZA**

Like other restaurants in the heart of downtown Estes Park, Poppy's gets slammed in summer. Waves of tourists wash over the place and then ebb away, leaving pizza crusts, dropped silverware, and napkins behind. Yet Poppy's does a good job of turning tables, and it serves fare that's consistently palatable. The restaurant has pizza, but you can also get sandwiches, burgers, and salads. During warm weather, it's worth waiting the extra 15 to 30 minutes for creekside seating.

342 E. Elkhorn Ave. (on the Riverwalk in Barlow Plaza). ☎ *970-586-8282. Reservations not accepted, but you can call ahead to put your name on the waiting list. Sandwiches and burgers: $5–$7; large pizza $12 plus $1.85 per topping. DISC, MC, V. Open: Daily 11 a.m.–10 p.m.*

Sweet Basilico
$–$$ **Estes Park   SOUTHERN ITALIAN**

During summer, you need to plan ahead to get a table at Sweet Basilico. Because the restaurant charges little, seats only 32, and serves flavorful Italian food, it often sells out two weeks in advance (though a few tables are set aside for walk-ins). Sweet Basilico's marinara sauce tastes gourmet on pasta. You can also order chicken, veal, seafood dishes, and pizza. Try the chicken Marsala sautéed with mushrooms, wine, garlic, and sweet basil. If you forget to book ahead, you can order to go and then take your food onto a table on the roof of the restaurant.

401 E. Elkhorn Ave. ☎ *970-586-3899. Reservations highly recommended. Main courses: $8.95–$15. AE, DISC, MC, V. Open: Summer daily 11 a.m.–8 p.m.; rest of year Wed–Mon 11 a.m.–8 p.m.*

Grand Lake

Located just outside the west entrance to the park, **Grand Lake** mirrors the touristy surroundings of Estes Park (on the park's east side), with a few differences. Grand Lake is more remote and, with a year-round population of around 400, much smaller. It's built on the shores of the largest natural lake in Colorado. For lodging, Grand Lake has a historic lodge, lakeside cabins, and motels. For less expensive lodging, drive 12 miles southwest on U.S. 34 to the ranching town of **Granby.**

Accommodations

Grand Lake Lodge
$–$$ **Grand Lake**

Built in 1920, this lodge sits on a hilltop high above Grand Lake. Because Rocky Mountain National Park surrounds the lodge on three sides, guests can hike out of their cabins and keep going into the park. On the lodge's forested acreage, you can choose among activities such as basketball, volleyball, or horseshoes, or best of all, recline next to a pool that seems to hover over the lake. Most cabins sleep two to six people, and the larger units have fully equipped kitchenettes; the smallest cabins look like standard motel rooms and only sleep two. The setting of the lodge is stunning, and some of the rooms offer great views of the lake.

15500 U.S. 34, just outside the west entrance to Rocky Mountain National Park. ☎ *970-627-3967. Fax: 970-627-9495.* www.grandlakelodge.com. *Rack rates: $85–$175 cabin. AE, DC, DISC, MC, V. Open June to early Sept.*

Lemmon Lodge
$$–$$$$ **Grand Lake**

Lemmon Lodge rents out 19 cabins and houses on or near the shore of Grand Lake (the water) and a short walk from Grand Lake (the town). Privately owned, they range from luxury homes with lake views to a rustic cabin. All of them have full kitchens or kitchenettes. The lodge employees do their best to honestly describe the different offerings. No matter what you choose, you'll be in a nice spot.

1224 Lake Ave. ☎ *970-627-3314 (summer) or 970-725-3511 (winter).* www.lemmon lodge.com. *Rack rates: Late May–late June and Labor Day–late Sept $80–$245 cabin; late June–Labor Day $110–$355 cabin. Closed late Sept to late May. MC, V.*

Trail Riders Motel
$ **Granby**

This is the little 1930s motel that could — and can. After 70 years or so, it's still tidy, well maintained, and thick walled. In addition to old-time features such as knotty wood paneling, nooks with wooden benches and tables, and steam heat, the rooms also have modern amenities such as microwaves, refrigerators, and coffeemakers. Ask for a spot away from Grand Avenue — the rooms nearest the road look noisy, though one employee begs to differ. Because it charges up to $20 less for one person than for two people, the motel is an attractive option for single travelers.

On U.S. 40 (215 E. Agate Ave.). ☎ *970-887-3738. Rack rates: $55–$65 double. DISC, MC, V.*

Dining

EG's Garden Grill
$–$$ Grand Lake   STEAK, CHOPS, SEAFOOD

This restaurant has a chef who knows what he's doing. The décor is casual, with a comfortable mountain spareness (and some typical country kitsch), but the food is spectacular. Start things off with the French onion soup, made with smoked Provolone. Frog Legs Piccatta are on the menu (oh, my!), but I had the country-fried pork loin chops, which definitely bring Tuscany to mind, not Iowa. The wine list is large but tame; beers from the Grand Lake Brewery are served, though, and you know I'll point you to those. There's a kids' menu, and several pizza choices, and the bar is popular with locals.

1000 Grand Ave. ☎ *970-627-8404. Reservations accepted. Main courses: $9.50–$23. AE, DISC, MC, V. Open: Summer daily 11 a.m.–10 p.m.; rest of year Mon–Sat 11 a.m.– 9 p.m.*

Grand Lake Lodge
$–$$ Grand Lake   AMERICAN

The grandiose reputation accorded Grand Lake Lodge doesn't seem to prevent the place from putting out a tasty spread at a fair price. The lunch menu has burgers, soups, salads, and sandwiches. At dinner, the prime rib is the main attraction, but you can also get steak, fish, chicken, and pork dishes. Vegetarians may enjoy the linguini with sun-dried tomatoes, capers, artichoke hearts, and kalamata olives. Families traveling with small children will appreciate that children under 5 eat free at the breakfast buffet. You pay a few dollars more than you would in Grand Lake, but the lake views make it worthwhile. The best vantage point, by far, is on the porch. Starting at the beginning of the season, you can make dinner reservations for the end of the season. Make your reservations far in advance and ask for a porch seat when you do.

15500 U.S. 34, just outside the west entrance to Rocky Mountain National Park. ☎ *970-627-3967. Reservations required for dinner and Sunday brunch. Main courses: $16–$28. AE, DC, DISC, MC, V. Open: June to early Sept Mon–Sat 7:30– 10 a.m., 11:30 a.m.–2:30 p.m., and 5:30–9 p.m.; Sun 9 a.m.–1 p.m. and 5:30–9 p.m.*

Pancho and Lefty's Restaurant
$ Grand Lake   MEXICAN/AMERICAN

Pancho and Lefty's looks like a fish place, sort of. In the bar, a stuffed blue marlin is mounted on the wall, across from a tropical plant and a rowboat that dangles, upside down, below the ceiling. Huge windows overlooking Grand Lake give you an eyeful of water. Given the atmosphere, the place should serve bluefish, but instead it cooks up Tex-Mex items such as rellenos, enchiladas, and burritos, many of them smothered in chili. Other options include steaks; burgers; and baskets of deep-fried fish, chicken, and onion rings.

1120 Grand Ave. ☎ 970-627-8773. Reservations not accepted. Main courses: $6.25–$14. AE, DISC, MC, V. Open: Sun–Thurs 11 a.m.–8 p.m., Fri–Sat 11 a.m.–9 p.m.

Fast Facts: Rocky Mountain National Park

Emergencies

Dial ☎ 911.

Hospital

East of the park, the Estes Park Medical Center, 555 Prospect Ave. (☎ 970-586-2317), provides 24-hour emergency care. West of the park, you can get 24-hour emergency care at Granby Medical Center,

480 E. Agate Ave. (☎ 970-887-2117), in Granby. For a full-service hospital, go to Kremmling Memorial Hospital District, 214 S. Fourth Street (☎ 970-724-3442), in Kremmling.

Road Conditions

Dial ☎ 877-315-7623 or 303-639-1111.

Chapter 16

Middle Park

● ●

In This Chapter

▶ Venturing to the playground and the icebox (and back again): Winter Park and Fraser

▶ Seeking adventure farther out in the parkland

● ●

*L*ike its neighbors, South Park and North Park, Middle Park is a wide, flat valley tucked in between the Front Range and the large ranges that fill up the heart of the high country. These high valleys, called *parks* for their open expanses of treeless ground, are the heart of Colorado's ranching country (it's hard to raise cattle up on the ridges, you know), and in their own quiet way may be the southern Rockies' most distinctive feature. Their ancient post-glacial lakes and streams offer great fishing; their expanses of open range make for the best snowshoeing and cross-country skiing; and the mountains, with hiking, skiing and everything else, are never far away. I'll always feel that watching the sun rise or set over the jagged skyline of these quiet, grassy valleys is one of the finest experiences Colorado has to offer.

Note that the town of Grand Lake is one of the highlights of Middle Park (see the nearby "Middle Park" map); its proximity to Rocky Mountain National Park, though, makes it a logical partner of that park in Chapter 15. So be sure to take a peek at that chapter when you plan your trip to Middle Park.

Winter Park and Fraser

For years, these two side-by-side towns were best known for their coldness. Fraser, which is usually a degree or two frostier than Winter Park, registers the lowest temperature in the lower 48 states more days per year, on average, than any other town, earning it the title of "The Nation's Icebox." The daylight hours aren't bad. But on clear nights, the warm air dissipates and cold air plummets from the surrounding mountains onto the 9,000-foot-high valley floor.

Fraser mostly functioned as a ranching community, while Winter Park was the town base for the Winter Park ski resort, owned by the city of Denver as one of its mountain parks. The main strip along U.S. 40 was

Middle Park

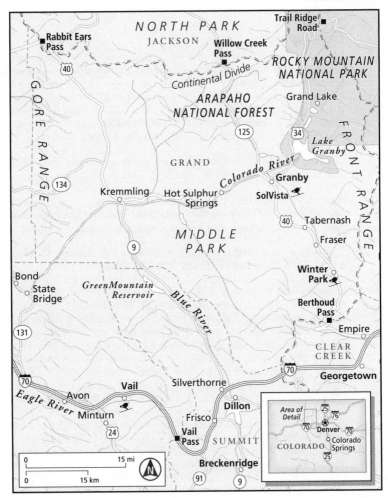

lined with hotels and restaurants that mimicked the Swiss Chalet style of architecture, as Colorado tried to market itself as the new Switzerland.

Lately, though, the towns have become more fashionable and self-assured. The management of Winter Park Resort has contracted with a big-money developer to revitalize and expand its base; several large new lodges decorated in the popular Colorado Rustic look have sprung up. Yet there's something endearing about the town's remaining old-style functionality. Area businesses don't look so perfect as to make you nervous. Folks are very friendly. And the surrounding mountains have a close, cozy atmosphere that's perfect for snuggling with someone special on a cold winter's night.

Getting there

Winter Park is 67 miles northwest of Denver and 85 miles from **Denver International Airport** (DIA; see Chapter 11). Most large domestic carriers serve DIA, and major rental-car companies have desks there. For information on contacting individual airlines and car-rental agencies, see the appendix. To arrange a shuttle ride to Winter Park from DIA, call **Home James Transportation** (☎ 800-359-7503 or 970-726-5060; www. homejamestransportation.com). Cost is $44 per person.

To drive to Winter Park from Denver, go 44 miles west from Denver on I-70, then take U.S. 40 north over Berthoud Pass and into Winter Park.

Amtrak's (☎ 800-USA-RAIL or 303-825-2583; www.amtrak.com) California Zephyr stops in **Fraser** when traveling between the San Francisco Bay Area and Chicago (and vice versa). Call for fares and schedules.

Car rentals are available through **Avalanche Car Rental** (☎ 888-437-4101 and 970-887-3908) and **Hertz** (☎ 970-726-8933).

 If you're staying in Denver and want to travel to Winter Park for a day of skiing, consider using the **Ski Train** (☎ 303-296-4754; www.skitrain. com), a Denver tradition since 1940. Every Saturday and Sunday from mid-December through early April (and on Fridays during February and March), the 17-car, quarter-mile-long train departs Denver's Union Station at 7:15 a.m., climbs into South Boulder Canyon and the Flatiron Range, and then crosses the continental divide through the 6-mile-long Moffat Tunnel. It emerges from the tunnel at the base of the ski area, 4,000 vertical feet above its starting point, and deposits as many as 750 passengers at 9:30 a.m. The return trip leaves at 4:15 p.m. About 40 percent of the train's passengers are nonskiers who take the train as a sightseeing excursion (a trend that one Winter Park resident affectionately calls "Throw Mama *on* the train"). Round-trip coach fare is $44 for adults, $34 for seniors and kids. A limited summer schedule also exists; fares are $40 for adults, $35 for seniors and kids. Check the Web site for summer schedule details.

 The Ski Train has one drawback: In order to avoid over-packing the train on Saturday morning and Sunday afternoon, your return ticket is valid only on the same day that you travel to Winter Park, so you won't be able to use that ticket if you plan an overnight stay.

Getting around

These towns aren't great for walking, because the businesses are pretty spread out. They are, however, perfect for bicycling. You can take a paved bike path all the way from Winter Park Resort to Fraser.

The Lift (☎ 970-726-4163) provides regular, free shuttle service linking Winter Park Resort, Winter Park, and Fraser. During ski season, the shuttles run every half-hour from 7:30 a.m. to midnight. From the Fourth of July to Labor Day, there's hourly service between 9:30 a.m. and 4 p.m. The shuttles don't operate during spring and fall.

Home James Transportation (☎ 800-359-7536 or 970-726-5060) offers taxi service at a cost of $4 for the first mile, plus $2 for each additional mile.

Where to stay

Fraser Valley, home to Winter Park and Fraser, has a hodgepodge of lodging. New condos, old condos, luxury hotels, family lodges, B&Bs, guest ranches, and chain motels all vie for your business.

Arapahoe Ski Lodge
$$–$$$ **Winter Park**

Run by the same family since the mid-1970s, this rustic lodge has a Bavarian exterior and a mostly wooden interior with an intimate, British-style pub. Knickknacks such as steins, baskets, and ski memorabilia clutter shelves that seem to have been nailed up on an as-needed basis. Near the lobby you can hang your skis on hooks, or tune them on a table. The 11 guest rooms are spare but comfortable. They don't have televisions, so guests spend more time in the tiny indoor hot tub and swimming pool, around the shared television room, and in the pub. They get to know each other even better over breakfast and dinner, which are included in the wintertime rates. During slow periods, the place calls itself a B&B and serves breakfast only. It's as old-school as they come.

78594 U.S. 40. ☎ *800-754-0094 or 970-726-8222. Fax: 970-726-8222.* www.arapahoe skilodge.com. *Winter rates (includes breakfast and dinner for two): Dec 20–31 and Feb 1–Mar 31 $220; Jan $190. Winter B&B rates (includes full breakfast only): Nov 15–Dec 19 and Mar 30–Apr 12 $105. Summer B&B rates (includes full breakfast): June–Sept $89. Closed rest of year. AE, DISC, MC, V.*

Iron Horse Resort
$$–$$$$ **Winter Park**

Come to this large condominium hotel at the base of Winter Park Resort if you want to get serious about skiing. The resort's privately owned condos range in size from sport studios with Murphy beds to two-bedroom, three-bath units. No matter what size you choose, you get a full kitchen, a gas-log fireplace, and a private balcony. You also have access to the hot tubs, heated outdoor pool, steam rooms, and exercise room. If you cook a few meals yourself, you can offset the extra dollars you'll spend for this ski-in, ski-out location.

101 Iron Horse Way. ☎ *800-621-8190 or 970-726-8851. Fax: 970-726-2321.* www.iron horse-resort.com. *Rack rates: Nov–Apr, $99–$259 studio, $139–$399 1-bedroom; May–Oct $69–$189 studio, $99–$329 1-bedroom. AE, DC, DISC, MC, V.*

The Pinnacle Lodge at Winter Park
$–$$$ **Fraser**

This new two-story motel has perfect paint, sharp edges, large windows, and lots of space. Not much about the place will surprise you. All the rooms have 28-inch TVs, coffeemakers, refrigerators, microwaves, dataports, and ironing boards. Continental breakfast appears every morning inside a bright, sunny breakfast area. There's also a small indoor swimming pool and spa. The only surprise — and it's a modest one — is that the place is in Fraser and not Winter Park, as the lodge's name would seem to indicate.

108 Zerex St. ☎ *970-722-7631. Fax: 970-722-7632. Rack rates: June–Sept; $89–$99 double; ski season $149–$219 double; late Apr–May and Oct–Nov, $69–$79 double. AE, DC, DISC, MC, V.*

Where to dine
In Winter Park, dining usually costs a little less than in other ski towns. And most of the town's restaurants are fine for children.

Fontenot's Cajun Café
$–$$ **Winter Park   CAJUN**

This restaurant's owner and chef, Chris Moore, likes to go on food-tasting trips to the backwoods restaurants and food stands in rural Louisiana. He brings the best recipes home to chilly Winter Park, where the spicy food tastes especially heartwarming. I loved the gumbo — a soup of crawfish, chicken, peppers, okra, tomatoes, and Cajun spices, served over rice. Being a transplanted New Englander who fusses over fish, the owner is partial to the Tilapia Lafayette — blackened tilapia with crawfish tail meat sautéed in garlic, capers, tomatoes, and basil.

78711 U.S. 40 (in downtown Winter Park). ☎ *970-726-4021. Reservations for large groups only. Main courses: $7.95–$20. AE, DC, MC, V. Open: Daily 11 a.m.–9 p.m.*

Hernando's Pizza Pub
$ **Winter Park   PIZZA/PASTA**

Using magic markers that the restaurant keeps on hand for the express purpose of defacing currency, customers of Hernando's Pizza have colored and then donated a total of 13,000 one-dollar bills to the restaurant. Rather than open a Swiss Bank account, restaurant employees tape the bills to the walls, posts, beams, and ceiling of the establishment, making the place look like a combination rathskeller, gallery, and U.S. mint. No one around here seems to know the value of a buck, but they do know their pizza — Hernando's bakes one of the best pies in the Rockies. For your sauce, you can choose between white, white with extra garlic, and traditional red. Top it with anything from almonds to jalapeños.

78199 U.S. 40 (at the north end of Winter Park). ☎ *970-726-5409. Reservations not accepted. Pizzas: $7.50–$18. Pasta dishes and sandwiches: $6.75–$7.50. AE, DISC, MC. Open: Mon–Thurs 5–10 p.m., Fri–Sun 4–10 p.m. Closed mid-Apr–early June.*

Randi's Irish Saloon
$–$$$ Winter Park   IRISH/AMERICAN

The many high chairs inside the front door of this restaurant indicate how popular the place is — or could be — among families. Every generation should appreciate the menu. Offerings include Irish pub fare such as shepherd's pie and fish and chips, salads, burgers, and entrees such as filet mignon and salmon with blue cheese. Portions are large, and the desserts seem even larger.

78521 U.S. 40 (in downtown Winter Park). ☎ *970-726-1172. Reservations for large parties only. Main courses: $12–$24. AE, DISC, MC, V. Open: Mon–Fri 4–10 p.m., Sat–Sun 11 a.m.–10 p.m.*

The Shed
$$ Winter Park   SOUTHWESTERN FUSION

This Winter Park landmark changes its entire menu every six months. The owner says that some of his regulars try all the items on every new menu, then wait around for the next one. When I was here, they would have had to eat their way through the likes of corn and chipotle chowder, Cajun chimichangas, Portobello mushroom stacks, and lobster and mango fajitas. The bar's enormous margaritas attract locals by the score, especially during the late-afternoon happy hour.

78762 U.S. 40, Winter Park. ☎ *970-726-9912. Reservations not accepted. Main courses: $9–$22. AE, DC, DISC, MC, V. Open: Daily 4–9:30 p.m. Closed mid-Apr–Memorial Day.*

Exploring Winter Park and Fraser

For a long time, there was little to do around here except ski. Now, though, the focus has opened up a lot and you can find plenty to do, winter or summer. Read the "Heading farther into the Parkland" section later in this chapter for more activities just a short drive away.

The best things to see and do

If you visit here, plan on spending time exploring the mountains. But if you need some rest, you can try the following:

- ✔ **Hit the old community center.** Built in 1876, **Cozens Ranch House,** 77849 U.S. 40, between Winter Park and Fraser (☎ **970-726-5488**), was the first homestead in the Fraser Valley and later served as a post office, stagecoach stop, and chapel. The house has displays on area history, including one on World War II–era POWs who worked in the local timber industry. It's open in the summer Tuesday through Saturday from 10 a.m. to 5 p.m., and Sunday from

1 to 5 p.m. Other months, it's open Wednesday through Saturday from 10 a.m. to 4 p.m., and Sunday from 1 to 4 p.m. Admission is $5 for adults, $4 for seniors 62 and up, and $2 for students.

✔ **Be a-mazed.** Kids in particular will enjoy the summer activities at the base of **Winter Park Resort** (☎ **970-726-5514;** www.skiwinter park.com). Options include an alpine slide, mini golf, the Amaze'n Human Maze (a life-sized outdoor maze), indoor and outdoor climbing walls, and gravity-defying bungee and zip-line activities. You can pay for activities individually, at prices ranging from $4 to $10, or get a half- or full-day park pass (cost: $34 and $40, respectively). Winter Park Resort is open daily from 10:00 a.m. to 5:30 p.m., from early June to early September.

If you do pay for activities at Winter Park individually, you can run up a big tab in a hurry.

Staying active

If you come to Middle Park on a weekday, you can often enjoy the backcountry in near solitude; on the weekends, expect company from Denver. Some of the best recreation choices include the following:

✔ **Hiking:** On foot, you can use all the same trails (550 miles' worth) that the mountain bikers do, or you can drive a little higher in the mountains and hike in the **Vasquez, Byer's Peak,** and **Indian Peaks** wilderness areas. You can reach two premier trails by taking County Road 73 out of Fraser and then following the signs: The **St. Louis Lake Trail** goes 3.4 miles to St. Louis Lake, and the rugged **Byer's Peak Trail** rises 2,000 vertical feet over 3.7 miles to the 12,804-foot Byer's Peak, affording panoramic views of the Fraser Valley. Allow 30 minutes to drive to these trailheads from Fraser. You need a high-clearance vehicle (and no trailer) to get there. The **Arapahoe National Forest Sulphur Ranger District Office,** off U.S. 40, ½ mile south of Granby (☎ **970-887-4100**), has maps and information on these areas.

✔ **Mountain biking:** Over 500 miles of trails thread their way through the Fraser Valley, supplementing the 50 miles of lift-served paths at **Winter Park Resort** (☎ **970-726-5514**). Because many Fraser Valley trails are on relatively smooth forest floors, this is an ideal place to learn how to mountain bike. You can get free trail descriptions and maps at the **Winter Park Visitor Center** (78841 U.S. 40; ☎ **800-903-7275**). Intermediate and advanced riders will enjoy the **Creekside Trail,** which parallels St. Louis Creek. To find the trailhead, pedal 3 miles west out of Fraser on County Road 73 and then go left at the turnoff for the **St. Louis Creek Campground.** Starting on the Creekside Trail, you can access intermediate and advanced single-track trails known as **Flume, Zoom,** and **Chainsaw,** plus many others. The trails have a few rocky, technical spots but mostly travel through gently undulating forest. Take your map, because you may have to improvise on your return. If you're pedaling with small children or just want to relax, try the **Fraser River Trail,** which parallels the Fraser River between Winter Park and Fraser. **Beaver's Sport Shop,** 79303 U.S. 40 in Winter Park (☎ **970-726-1092**), rents full-suspension and front-suspension mountain bikes all day for $30 and $18, respectively.

Hitting the slopes

Dollar for dollar, pound for pound, this is my favorite resort in the state. For a megaresort that ranks among the nation's busiest mountains, **Winter Park Resort** (☎ **970-726-5514;** www.skiwinterpark.com) feels like a throwback. It's still owned by the city of Denver, which established it as a park in 1939. Many skiers arrive here on the Ski Train, via a historic rail line that passes within yards of the base area (see "Getting there," earlier in this chapter). And because of cold temperatures and a storm-trapping location just west of the continental divide, the snowpack (the actual amount of snow on the ground) here usually ranks among the deepest in the state, calling to mind the days, etched in every aging skier's memory (or imagination), when it really did snow.

It's the closest full-service mountain resort, mileage-wise, to the Mile High City, so you can get here easily and enjoy the area's mix of terrain. Winter Park serves up a pleasing variety of mogul runs, cruisers, and beginner runs, sometimes in close proximity to one another. If you want to concentrate on expert runs, you can bounce down long, steep mogul runs on Mary Jane, the most challenging of Winter Park's three mountains. For more on the resort, see the chart on the inside back cover of this book.

Novices will appreciate the Galloping Goose chairlift, which serves fenced-in, beginner terrain. Tickets for this chairlift cost just $5, making it an ideal place to teach children how to ski.

The Fraser Tubing Hill

If, after a long day of skiing, you're still intrigued by the combination of snow and gravity, get yourself over to the **Fraser Tubing Hill** (behind the Alco Shopping Center in Fraser; ☎ **970-726-5954**) and keep sliding. It's probably the most fun thing a family can do in the evening here: a specially designed tow rope hauls you up the well-lighted, groomed slope, and you ride your specially designed inner tube down in any position you want. Tube rental is $14 per hour for adults, $12 for kids ages 7 to 15. The hill is open Tuesday through Thursday 2 to 10 p.m., Friday and Saturday 10 a.m. to 10 p.m., and Sunday 10 a.m. to 9 p.m. (closed Mon).

It's a blast. I've even done it with friends as an afternoon trip from Denver, followed by dinner at Beau Jo's in Idaho Springs (see Chapter 12).

Fast Facts: Winter Park/Fraser

Emergencies

Dial ☎ 911.

Hospital

In most cases, you can obtain treatment at 7-Mile Medical Clinic, at Winter Park Resort (☎ 970-726-8066). Kremmling Memorial Hospital, 214 S. Fourth St. (☎ 970-724-3442), has a 24-hour emergency room.

Information

Winter Park Visitor Center, on U.S. 40 in downtown Winter Park (☎ 800-903-7275 and 970-726-4118; www.winterpark-info.com), and Fraser Visitor Center, 120 Zerex Ave. (U.S. 40) in Fraser (☎ 970-726-8312), can handle your questions about the area.

Pharmacy

Fraser Drug Store, next to Alco on U.S. 40 in Fraser (☎ 970-726-1000), can fill your prescriptions.

Post Office

The Fraser Post Office (☎ 970-726-5578) is at 520 Zerex Ave. (U.S. 40). The Winter Park Post Office (☎ 970-726-5578) is at 78490 U.S. 40.

Road Conditions

Call ☎ 877-315-7263 or 303-639-1111.

Heading farther into the Parkland

Beyond Winter Park and Fraser, Middle Park opens up to incorporate some beautiful rangeland, as well as the upper reaches of the mighty Colorado River.

Two classic ranch-resort experiences

Winter or summer, ranch resorts sometimes represent the best Colorado has to offer. Here are two Middle Park favorites:

✔ **Snow Mountain Ranch:** Operated by the YMCA of the Rockies, **Snow Mountain Ranch** (1101 County Road 53, Granby; ☎ 970-887-2152; www.ymcarockies.org) has accommodations ranging from campsites ($20 per night) to two-bedroom rustic cabins ($143) and four-bedroom cabins ($243). The ranch has a dining hall for all meals, and a cafe that's open during ski season. Among the vast array of amenities and activities are an indoor pool, climbing wall, sauna, craft shop, hiking, cross-country skiing, and snowshoeing. Lodging-and-ski packages are available in conjunction with Winter Park Ski Resort, and outdoor education packages for both adults and kids are available. Conference groups and family reunions are welcome as well. If you're staying elsewhere, you can drop in and snowshoe or ski cross-country in some of the best terrain in the state; they have equipment rental and guided day trips available as well. For families and the budget-minded, it's one of the best all-inclusive resorts in Colorado.

✔ **Devil's Thumb Ranch:** The largest Nordic center in Middle Park, **Devil's Thumb Ranch** (☎ **800-933-4339;** www.devilsthumbranch. com) grooms 100 kilometers for skate and classic skiing and also has marked trails for snowshoers. But it doesn't stop there: This is another premiere all-inclusive ranch, and one that doesn't skimp on the finer points of the experience. Accommodations range from lodge rooms (winter only $89–$129) to one- to four-room cabins ($159–$750) and come with continental breakfast and a daily wine and cheese sampling. Facilities include an indoor pool, sauna, hot tubs, video rental, ice skating rink, and sleigh rides. The bar and restaurant are casual but elegant, and provide a cozy après-ski environment. If you want to drop in for cross-country skiing, trail fees are $15 for a full day, $10 after 12:30 p.m. The ranch is at 3530 County Rd. 83, off U.S. 40 south of Tabernash.

Staying active

The **Pole Creek Golf Club** (☎ **800-511-5076** or 970-887-9195; www.pole creekgolf.com) boasts 27 holes at 8,600 feet above sea level. It consistently ranks among the top public courses in America, and in 1985 it won *Golf Digest*'s award as the best new public course in America. Greens fees are $80 during high season, $59 during low season. To get there, take U.S. 40 11 miles west from Winter Park to County Road 5.

On the slopes

SolVista Golf and Ski Ranch, near Granby (☎ **800-757-7669;** www. solvista.com), spans two hills amid gently undulating rangeland where, come spring, sagebrush pokes through melting snow. The 33 mostly gentle trails funnel down to a single base area, so rounding up the kids here is easy.

In the mid-1990s, SolVista's ownership theorized that this environment could be as pleasant for humans as it had been for cows in years past. After trading for 1,000 acres of Bureau of Land Management land near the old Silver Creek Ski Area, they laid plans for a year-round resort with recreation options ranging from cross-country skiing on a groomed, 40-kilometer trail system, to golf on a 7,200-yard, championship golf course. The development is in its fledgling stage — during the next 20 years, SolVista hopes to build as many as 5,000 single-family homes and condominiums. If the resort can complete this build-out without disrupting what today is a remarkably serene place — no easy task — SolVista will remain a nice place for family ski vacations.

See the chart on the inside back cover of this book for technical data on SolVista.

Chapter 17

Summit County

In This Chapter

▶ Discovering the best family skiing in Colorado
▶ Taking on some of Colorado's more challenging slopes
▶ Relaxing in cool towns with great après-ski for everyone

*F*irst, the bad news: Summit County is not the most pristine part of the Rockies. In the heart of the county, a large reservoir stalls water before diverting it to Denver via a tunnel through the continental divide. Not far away, I-70 burrows through the divide and emerges in Summit County, where it's soon engulfed by chain restaurants, retail outlets, and some bona fide sprawl. Many historic buildings dot Frisco and Breckenridge, but condominiums and newer communities have sprouted up all around them. Even the river channels have been altered by dredge mining.

Nevertheless, this semideveloped mountain setting has some real advantages, not least of which is its proximity to Denver. In ideal conditions, you can get to Summit County (see the nearby "Summit County" map) from the Mile High City in an hour and a half. Once you're here, you can use free mass transit to reach all four ski areas and the major towns. You can choose from an array of lodges throughout the county, ranging from slopeside condos to chain hotels near the interstate. And during summer, you can pedal on 55 miles of paved bike paths. If you do need to escape civilization, the 315,000 acres of national forest awaits.

Summit County Essentials

A historic mining town, **Breckenridge** is the largest and best-known community in Summit County. Located alongside I-70, **Frisco** has a relaxed Main Street and a number of quirky lodges and restaurants. Two other towns, **Dillon** and **Silverthorne,** are on the east side of the reservoir, opposite Frisco. This chapter doesn't devote much space to the last two spots, but you should know that Dillon and Silverthorne have many chain hotels and are viable choices for travelers on a budget.

Summit County

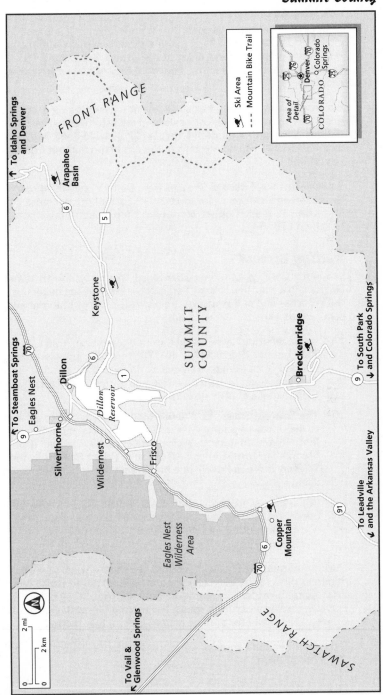

Getting there

Denver International Airport (DIA) is your best bet if you want to fly close to Summit County. Most major airlines serve DIA, and the biggest rental-car companies have desks at the airport; see Chapter 11 for details. For information on contacting individual airlines and car-rental agencies, see the appendix.

Because Summit County has an excellent mass-transit system, many people bypass the rental-car desks and take shuttles to their accommodations. **Colorado Mountain Express** (☎ 800-575-6363 or 970-926-9800; www.cmex.com) will take you from the airport to Summit County for $56 per person.

If you're driving, **Frisco** is 58 miles from Denver on I-70. To reach **Breckenridge**, exit on Colorado 9 at Frisco, and drive 9 miles south into town. To reach **Copper Mountain,** keep going 14 miles west of Frisco on I-70.

Getting around

In Summit County, it's often easier to get around by shuttle than by car. By riding the shuttles, you can spare yourself parking headaches near the ski areas and in downtown Breckenridge. Three different shuttle services operate in Summit County:

- ✔ In Breckenridge, you can get around town year-round on the **Free Ride** buses (☎ 970-547-3140). The busiest routes operate from 6:30 a.m. to midnight. You can avoid paying for parking during peak winter periods by using the free lots at the north end of town and then taking a shuttle downtown.

- ✔ **The Summit Stage** (☎ 970-668-0999) provides free transportation to major towns and resorts in Summit County, including Copper Mountain, with hourly service between 6:30 a.m. and 10:30 p.m. All the town-to-town routes pass through **Frisco Station,** behind the Safeway store in Frisco, one block west of the junction of Colorado 9 and I-70.

- ✔ When the ski areas are open, **KAB Shuttle** (☎ 970-496-4200) offers regular, free service between Breckenridge and Keystone, where connecting service to A-Basin is available. Call for hours of operation.

During summer, the cleanest and most enjoyable way to travel Summit County is by bicycle. Fifty-five miles of paved paths link Frisco, Breckenridge, Copper Mountain, and Vail. Many of these paths travel in forests away from roads. For more on bicycling in Summit County, skip ahead to "Staying active" later in this section.

If the shuttles don't show or your bike breaks its chain, contact **453Taxi** (☎ 970-453-TAXI).

A condo of your own

Central reservations agencies handle most of the bookings for the many condominiums in Summit County. Agencies can search for accommodations by price range, size, and location. Upon arriving, however, you may not always get the attentive service you expect of a luxury hotel. Still, it's your best (and sometimes only) option if you want to stay next to the chairlifts. Here are some places to start your search:

✔ **Copper Mountain Resort** (☎ 800-458-8386; www.coppercolorado.com) handles the lodging at its base, in three villages linked by a free shuttle service. Accommodations range from studios ($118–$344) to four-bedroom condos ($330–$499). All are close to the lifts and, from what I saw, most seemed comfortable. If you're single (or simply rowdy), the main drawback to Copper is the lack of nightlife. Most restaurants and bars close by 10 p.m., even during high season. This could change in the next year as Copper continues a large base-area expansion.

✔ **Keystone Central Reservations** (☎ 800-842-7417 or 970-496-4242; www.keystoneresort.com) owns or manages 1,600 condominiums near the ski area's base, with a standard slopeside studio that sleeps four costing between $288 and $368. Keystone prides itself on being family-friendly and schedules a lot of activities for kids and parents.

✔ **Breckenridge Central Reservations** (☎ 888-697-7834 or 970-453-7238; www.gobreck.com) oversees 3,100 rooms and condos in Breckenridge, including some near the base of the mountain. A standard slopeside studio at Breckenridge generally costs between $200 and $365.

Where to stay

You can find almost every type of lodging in Summit County, but condominiums far outnumber hotel rooms.

Most of Summit County's chain hotels are concentrated along I-70 near Frisco, Dillon, and Silverthorne, a few miles from the ski areas. Options include the **Best Western Lake Dillon Lodge,** 1202 N. Summit Blvd., in Frisco (☎ 970-668-5094); **Days Inn,** 580 Silverthorne Lane, in Silverthorne (☎ 970-468-8661); **Holiday Inn-Summit County,** 1129 N. Summit Blvd., in Frisco (☎ 970-668-5000); and **Super 8,** 808 Little Beaver Trail, in Dillon (☎ 970-468-8888).

You may save a few dollars by staying at a chain hotel, but if nightlife is important to you, pay a bit more and get a room or condominium in Breckenridge. For proximity to the slopes, consider the base areas at Breckenridge, Keystone, and Copper Mountain.

Frisco Lodge Bed & Breakfast
$–$$ **Frisco**

Some of the Frisco Lodge's rooms are in a creaky (but charming) 1885 boarding house; the rest are in a solid, two-story 1965 motel. All are clean, compact, and decorated in flowery patterns. If you want festive surroundings, try the boardinghouse. It has a big TV area where guests gather and watch movies along with the lodge dog, Sugar. The motel rooms feel more private. Unlike some of the lodge rooms, all the motel rooms have their own bathrooms. When you factor into the rate the free breakfast you get here, the price is hard to beat.

321 Main St. ☎ *800-279-6000 (reservations) or 970-668-0195. Fax: 970-668-0149.* www. friscolodge.com. *Rack rates: Spring and fall $50–$80 double; summer $55–$100 double; winter $165–$215 double. Rates include buffet breakfast. AE, DC, DISC, MC, V.*

Hunt Placer Inn B&B
$$$–$$$$ **Breckenridge**

The keepers of this nine-year-old home baked a chocolate cake that won the Golden Pig award at a local chocolate-cooking contest. If you stay here, you can have your cake and afford it, too. This inn has high ceilings, low prices, and immense three-course breakfasts. The rooms are each sumptuously decorated in a different motif. In the next few years, you should be able to ski right to the lodge, because the ski area is planning to build a chairlift and cut new trails through the forest above the inn. For now, however, you'll have to catch a shuttle outside and ride the full two minutes to the mountain.

275 Ski Hill Rd. ☎ *800-472-1430 or 970-453-7573. Fax: 970-453-2335.* www.huntplacer inn.com. *Rack rates: $149–$207 double; $189–$270 suite. A 5-night minimum stay is required during high-season. AE, DC, DISC, MC, V.*

Main Street Station
$$–$$$ **Breckenridge**

Forget about the kitchenettes, fireplaces, and washer/dryers in the guest units of this new condominium hotel. And never mind the fact that the place offers all the amenities you'd expect of a big-city luxury hotel (free newspapers, underground parking, a business center, and a concierge, to name a few). Finally, ignore the location within walking distance of both downtown Breckenridge and the lowest chairlift at Breckenridge Ski Resort. There's only one thing that most of us need to know: In the guest rooms, you'll find complimentary Dove Bars in the freezers.

505 S. Main St. ☎ *970-453-5995. Fax 970-547-5909.* www.mainstreetstation. com. *Rack rates for studio & 1-bedroom suite: summer $200–$245, fall $135–$180, winter $220–$655, spring $135–$180. AE, DISC, MC, V.*

Where to dine

Summit County pulls a lot of visitors from heartland states such as Texas, Oklahoma, and Kansas, so it should come as no surprise that many restaurants here serve family-friendly American fare such as steaks and barbeque. When you pay for dinner, however, you'll find out you aren't in Kansas anymore. But you're not in Aspen, either.

Blue Spruce Inn
$$ Frisco   AMERICAN

Before Dillon Reservoir submerged the old town site of Dillon, this 1944 inn was trucked in pieces to Frisco. Today the interior feels earthy yet homey, like a log cabin run by a Cub Scout Den Mother. The restaurant serves standbys such as ribs, steaks, trout, and roast pork, as well as some creative pasta dishes. If you want to dine in your flip-flops, you can order the same food in the barroom, where there's a historic Brunswick bar that was trucked here in pieces from a condemned building in Black Hawk.

20 Main St. ☎ 970-668-5900. Reservations recommended. Main courses: $15–$28. AE, DC, DISC, MC, V. Open: Daily 5–10 p.m.

Boatyard Pizza & Grill
$–$$ Frisco   AMERICAN/PIZZAS

This place was called Uptown Bistro until the owners decided that the name implied something fancy. Truth is, there *could* be fine dining here: The eclectic menu has some delectable pasta and fish dishes, and the dining room looks as if it aspires to be upscale. Yet the owners have gone the other way, preferring to make people aware of the pizzas, big portions, huge selection, and relaxed atmosphere. The restaurant sometimes closes in the late fall, so call before you go if you plan on coming here during that time of year.

304 Main St. ☎ 970-668-4728. Reservations for large parties only. Sandwiches and burgers: $7.25–$10; main courses: $11–$19. AE, DISC, MC, V. Open: Daily 11 a.m.–10 p.m.

Breckenridge Brewery & Pub
$–$$ Breckenridge   PUB FARE

These days, Breckenridge Brewery produces most of its beer in Denver, but the staff still whips up a few batches on the premises of this restaurant, as it has since 1990. Two huge vats loom behind the bartender, a sight that beer drinkers may find strangely reassuring. Along with four staple beers and two seasonal brews, the brewery serves appetizers, soups, salads, sandwiches, ribs, and Southwestern fare. It's a popular place among both tourists and locals, so you're sure to fit in.

600 S. Main St. ☎ 970-453-1550. Reservations not accepted. Main courses: $10–$18. AE, DC, DISC, MC, V. Open: Daily 11 a.m. to midnight. Closed early May and late Oct.

Café Alpine
$$–$$$ Breckenridge   UNIQUE AMERICAN

Café Alpine's offerings change daily, but they may include anything from tortilla-crusted tofu with vegetable, bean, and green mole chili to grilled ono with wild mushrooms, wilted spinach, Brussels sprouts, toasted couscous, and cranberry demi. If you think ono and demi belong on the E! Channel and not the Food Channel, take a seat at the tapas bar and ask the chefs behind the counter to explain who's who, or what's what (for the record, *ono* is a Hawaiian fish, and *demi* is a food glaze). While you're there, order some wine from one of the most extensive wine lists in town.

106 E. Adams Ave. (½ block east of Main Street). ☎ *970-453-8218. Reservations recommended. Main courses: $15–$28. AE, DISC, MC, V. Open: Daily 5–9 p.m.; open for lunch daily June–Oct.*

Hearthstone Victorian Dining
$$–$$$ Breckenridge   AMERICAN

Located in a 19th-century home, the Hearthstone feels more formal than other area restaurants. Most dishes combine comfort food and contemporary elements; but there are also traditional favorites such as crab legs, prime rib, and filet mignon. Locals seem divided about the Hearthstone, saying it's (a) overrated, (b) the best restaurant in Summit County, or (c) unaffordable. One person argued for (d) "all of the above." Still, the Hearthstone has enough local support to have been named Breckenridge's business of the year for 2002.

130 S. Ridge St. ☎ *970-453-1148. Reservations accepted. Main courses: $18–$32. AE, MC, V. Open: Daily 5–9 p.m.*

Exploring Summit County

With ski areas, historic towns, and mountains, you can always find something to do in Summit County. If nothing is happening in the town where you're staying, check on the ski areas, which promote special events most weekends during summer and early fall. To catch up on happenings around the county, pick up a copy of *Summit Daily News* upon arriving, or surf the Internet to www.summitdaily.com.

The best things to see and do

In Breckenridge and Frisco, you can throw a little history into your shopping, and vice versa. Afterwards, look for a cultural event, concert, or show. Here are a few options:

  ✔ **Shop 'til you need oxygen.** Breckenridge's downtown shopping district is home to about 200 shops, many of them tucked into small spaces on the town's Main Street. Frisco's downtown is smaller, but, like Breckenridge, it has fun stores and character.

✔ **Breathe your money's worth.** If you get winded from the intense, high-elevation shopping, stop at **The O2 Lounge,** 500 South Main St., in Breckenridge (☎ 970-453-6262), where ten minutes of pure oxygen costs $10. You can breathe as fast as you want. The lounge also has aromatherapy, smoothies, and herbal drinks.

✔ **Make a balloon payment.** Colorado Rocky Ballooning (☎ 888-468-9280 or 970-468-9280; www.coloradoballoonrides.com) offers the highest commercial balloon flights in the United States. The one-hour, sunrise flights take off near Breckenridge at 9,600 feet and, under ideal conditions, ascend another 2,000 feet from there. The $195 per-person cost includes a photograph and a champagne breakfast.

✔ **Absorb some sounds.** Dillon, Frisco, and Breckenridge all offer free music during summer. Breckenridge hosts a high-caliber classical music festival (☎ 970-453-9142; www.breckenridgemusic festival.com) during July and August.

✔ **Brake for history.** The **Frisco Historic Park,** 120 Main St., in Frisco (☎ 970-668-3428), comprises 11 historic buildings surrounding a 1911 schoolhouse that now serves as a museum. You can stroll through an 1881 jail, a 1941 log chapel, and an 1890 ranch house, among other options. It's open Tuesday through Sunday from 11 a.m. to 4 p.m. during summer, and Tuesday through Saturday from 11 a.m. to 4 p.m. the rest of the year. Admission is free.

✔ **Seek out Breckenridge history.** The **Summit Historical Society** (☎ 970-453-7798 for recorded information; ☎ 970-453-9022 for tour reservations) can direct you to some of the most intriguing of Breckenridge's 170 historical sites. You can visit some spots alone; to see others, you have to sign up for guided tours ($6 adults, $2 children 2 to 12). To get started, stop at the **Free Museum** at 111 Main St., in Breckenridge. Open daily from 10 a.m. to 8 p.m., the museum houses rotating displays on area history. While you're there, you can get information about the other Summit Historical Society sites, including a placer mining gulch, where water was used to blast hillsides to extract gold; an underground gold mine; and the former home of Edwin Carter, whose collection of taxidermy ended up at the Denver Museum of Nature and Science. For more about that museum, see Chapter 11.

Especially for kids

Peak 8 Fun Park at Breckenridge Ski Resort (☎ 800-789-7669 or 970-453-5000; http://breckenridge.snow.com) has three different alpine slides ($10 per ride, $8 kids ages 7 to 12), miniature golf ($6 per round), a mountain-bike park ($10 per lift ride, $8 kids), scenic chairlift rides ($8 adults, kids $4), a human maze ($5 adults, $4 kids), a climbing wall ($6 per climb), and kids' center.

If you want to keep the kids busy for more than an hour or so, it's worth it to throw down for a half-day ($45) or full-day ($60) pass that lets junior go wild on all the above. It's open daily from 9 a.m. to 5 p.m. from mid-June to early September.

Staying active

With four ski areas, three Nordic centers, three ice rinks, four golf courses, the state's second-largest body of water, a whitewater park, and 315,000 acres of national forest, there's a whole lot for an outdoorsy person to do in Summit County. You can scratch the surface by:

- ✔ **Biking and hiking:** For starters, you can cover 40 miles of paved bike/hiking paths, including one path that climbs 1,500 feet over 14 miles from Frisco to Vail Pass. **Avalanche Sports,** 540 S. Main St., in Breckenridge (☎ 970-453-1461), rents a variety of bicycles at costs ranging from $20 to $38 per day and has copies of the free *Summit County Bike Trail Guide,* which describes all the paved paths as well as 27 more rugged rides in the area. The **Arapahoe National Forest Dillon Ranger District Office,** 680 Blue River Parkway, in Silverthorne (☎ 970-468-5400), can help you locate prime areas for high-alpine hiking and mountaineering.

- ✔ **Boating and sailing:** At 3,200 acres, **Dillon Reservoir** is the second-largest body of water in the state and plenty big for boating and sailing. However, because it holds drinking water for Denver, you can't swim or use a personal watercraft. You can, however, rent fishing boats, pontoon boats, and sailboats at either of two marinas. **Dillon Marina,** on Lake Dillon Drive in Dillon (☎ 970-468-5100), would be my first choice for renting a sailboat or taking sailing lessons. It also has a tiki bar and a large public boat ramp. **Frisco Bay Marina,** 900 E. Main St., in Frisco (☎ 888-780-4970), is the better choice for paddle sports. It rents one-, two-, and three-person canoes, sea kayaks, and paddleboats, and offers kayaking lessons.

- ✔ **Cross-country skiing:** With four Nordic centers, Summit County offers just as many options to cross-country skiers as to downhillers. The largest area, the **Frisco Nordic Center** (☎ 970-668-0866), south of Frisco on Colorado 9, has a groomed 43-kilometer trail system alongside Lake Dillon. **Breckenridge Nordic Center,** 1200 Ski Hill Rd. (☎ 970-453-6855), sets 32 kilometers of track in meadows and forests at the base of the Breckenridge Mountain Resort. Both areas also have ungroomed trails for snowshoeing. A day pass good at both centers costs $14 for adults, $10 for seniors 55 to 69 and kids 7 to 16. You can also find groomed Nordic trails at Keystone (☎ 970-486-4275) and Copper Mountain (☎ 970-968-2882).

- ✔ **Golfing: Breckenridge Golf Club,** 200 Clubhouse Dr. (☎ 970-453-9104), has three distinct, Jack Nicklaus–designed nine-hole courses. You can reserve tee times up to four days in advance. During peak periods, greens fees are $120. On certain days, however, you can pay $75 for unlimited play after 3:30 p.m.

✔ **Kayaking:** After a few whitewater kayaking lessons at Frisco Bay Marina (see the previous bullet item on boating and sailing), you'll be ready to tackle the **whitewater park** on the Blue River in downtown Breckenridge. You can walk there from the **Breckenridge Recreation Center,** 0880 Airport Rd. (☎ **970-547-3125** for recorded information, or 970-547-3125), which is off Colorado 9 at the north end of town.

Hitting the slopes
Arapahoe Basin

Local snowboarders have numerous reasons for adoring the steep little mountain they call A-Basin. The **Arapahoe Basin Ski Area** (☎ **888-ARA-PAHOE** or 970-468-0718; www.arapahoebasin.com) has free parking right near the base, so you won't need a travel agent to get from your car to the chairlift. The 13,050-foot summit — the highest inbounds terrain of any North American ski area — leaves flatlanders breathless but lets the area stay open into summer for die-hard boarders. And, finally, the terrain is a hoot. A-Basin is less than one-tenth the size of Vail yet has as much really steep terrain as you'll find in Vail's entirety. When not hiking the chutes on the area's East Wall, skilled boarders gravitate to the steep gullies and glades below the Pallavinci Lift. Intermediates can cruise the gentle bowls nearer the summit. Beginners are relegated to the lower mountain — or Keystone. Even the trail map seems relaxed and familiar, as befits an area for locals. It advises that the message boards at the bottom of the hill "are especially helpful if your friends are flaking out" and recommends that skiers "use sunscreen by the gallon." For more on the resort, see the inside back cover.

Breckenridge

For the past few years, **Breckenridge Ski Resort** (☎ **800-789-SNOW** or 970-453-5000; http://breckenridge.snow.com) has rivaled and sometimes bypassed Vail as the most popular ski area in North America. Visitors seem most enthusiastic about the easy access, the fun town, the abundant intermediate terrain, and the multiday lift tickets, which are also good at Vail, Keystone, and Beaver Creek. As for the mountain, it's big: 139 trails slice through pine and aspen forest on the flanks of four side-by-side peaks (numbered 7, 8, 9, and 10). Higher up, Breckenridge has nearly 800 acres of ungroomed bowl skiing, some of which are accessible only by hiking. This terrain is exhilarating on a powder day, but because of the resort's popularity, the powder often gets tracked quickly. Breckenridge also enjoys preferred status among snowboarders. Readers of *Snowboard Life* voted Breckenridge's SuperPipe number-one in the nation and judged its terrain park number-two. Check out the technical information on the resort on the inside back cover.

Copper Mountain

Part of a project that has grown steadily since opening in 1972, **Copper Mountain Resort** (☎ 866-841-2481; www.coppercolorado.com) now ranks among the busiest resorts in Colorado. Because of its proximity to I-70, you can watch tractor-trailers rumble past while standing in line for the High Point chair. And the base area, though pleasant for families, lacks the character (and *characters*) found in nearby mining towns. But that's all at the bottom. After hopping on a chairlift, you'll discover terrain that a Forest Service researcher once called "the most nearly perfect ski mountain in the U.S." Intermediates have two huge areas of the mountain to themselves. Beginners can ski from near the summit to the base and even have access to a very gradual bowl. Advanced riders make out best of all. They can choose from mogul runs such as Triple Threat or look for untracked powder in any of four 12,000-foot bowls. This mountain was the biggest surprise during my tour of Colorado ski areas — fun, varied, and challenging. See the inside back cover for further details on Copper Mountain.

Keystone

This is where I and most of my friends learned to ski. Most families who go on ski vacations aren't looking to appear in a Warren Miller movie. They just want to be safe, be comfortable, and have fun. For them, there's **Keystone** (☎ 800-344-8878 or 970-496-4589; www.keystone resort.com), the third-most-popular resort in Colorado. Keystone offers specially priced packages for families and throws in passports good for activities away from the slopes (anything from Nordic skiing to yoga). As for the skiing, a high intermediate could handle about 80 percent of the runs on Keystone Mountain and North Peak. A few expert skiers have ventured to Keystone in recent years to attack the glades and chutes in the Outback, the highest and most challenging part of the resort. Because most expert riders thumb their noses at Keystone, the powder tends to last longer here than at other Summit County ski areas. Keystone also illuminates 17 trails for night skiing. See the inside back cover for more info on this great resort.

Nightlife

Breckenridge jumps on the weekends, when young professionals from Denver check into condos and then check out the scene. A lot of them go to **Cecilia's,** 500 S. Main St., in Breckenridge (☎ 970-453-2243), which has a large dance floor, a big selection of martinis, and a walk-in humidor where you can pick your own cigar. DJs usually generate the sounds, which vary from night to night.

For live music, go to **Sherpa & Yeti's,** 318 S. Main St. (☎ 970-547-9299), a basement barroom that books bands ranging from punk to reggae. The best historical bar in the area is the **Gold Pan Restaurant,** 105 N. Main St., in Breckenridge (☎ 970-453-5499). In Frisco, **Moosejaw Pub,** 208 Main St. (☎ 970-668-3931), is a friendly neighborhood tavern.

Fast Facts: Summit County

Emergencies

Dial **911**.

Hospital

Summit Medical Center, Highway 9 at School Road in Frisco (☎ 970-668-3300), offers 24-hour emergency care.

Information Centers

In Frisco, stop at the Summit County Visitor Information Center, 916 N. Summit Blvd. (☎ 970-668-2051). Breckenridge Resort Chamber (☎ 970-453-2913) has an office at 309 N. Main St.

Pharmacy

The Breckenridge Drug Store, 111 Ski Hill Rd., in Breckenridge (☎ 970-453-2362),

can fill your prescription. There are numerous other drugstores scattered throughout Summit County.

Post Office

The Breckenridge Post Office is at 300 S. Ridge St. In Frisco, go to 35 W. Main St. Call ☎ 800-275-8777 for hours and other information.

Road Conditions

Call ☎ 970-668-1090 for the latest road conditions.

Chapter 18

Leadville and the Upper Arkansas Valley

● ●

In This Chapter

▶ Touring history-, mineral-, and mountain-rich Leadville

▶ Looking for off-the-beaten-path skiing

▶ Art-shopping and river-running in Buena Vista and Salida

● ●

*W*arm winds blow north from New Mexico into the river valleys of South Central Colorado. Flanking those valleys are some of America's highest, frostiest mountains — and a mother lode of mining history.

What's Where? The Arkansas Valley and Its Attractions

Entering Leadville, you may first notice mine tailings, broken-down machinery, dilapidated trailers, and other reminders of the town's mining life, but if you drive a few more miles and look again, you find what may be the best-preserved historic district in the state. Buena Vista is the start of many a mountaineer's journey into the Sawatch. And if you're driving through Salida on U.S. 50, the town looks like the type of place where you'd gas up and keep moving, but a detour downtown puts you at the heart of a thriving arts community.

Leadville highlights

The highest incorporated town in the nation, Leadville also sits within striking distance of the state's highest peak, Mount Elbert. The town's outskirts were mined as hard as any place in America, so Leadville has plenty of history. When you're here, check out the following:

✔ **Mining history** at the Matchless Mine, at the National Mining Hall of Fame and Museum, and in the historic mining district

✔ The **Mineral Belt Trail,** a 12½-mile hiking and biking loop that passes pines, mountains, and mines

✔ The buildings in the town's historic district, including the 120-year-old **Silver Dollar Saloon**

Buena Vista and Salida highlights

These mellow towns along the Arkansas River may not look the part, but they host the best whitewater rafting in Colorado, and are the gateway to the Sawatch Range, the highest mountains in the Rockies. Check out these things to do:

✔ A **river trip** on the Arkansas River

✔ The serenity of **Cottonwood Lake,** and the savage beauty of the mountains beyond

✔ The many **studio galleries** in Salida, where artists create and sell their work

✔ The **Monarch Crest Trail,** atop the continental divide

Leadville

At one point, during the silver boom of the 1880s, Leadville was the largest city in Colorado. The silver market crash changed all that, of course, and now it's known mostly for being old — and cold. At 10,000 feet and higher, Leadville sits just below the tree line, in a limbo between the warm river valleys below and the 14,000-foot peaks above, including the state's highest — 14,433-foot Mount Elbert. Its elevation means that Leadville can get frosty at night, and its summers aren't exactly torrid. People drawn to the highest peaks find this a perfect base camp; others may feel uncomfortably exposed.

Meanwhile, history buffs gravitate to the historic mines around town. Many of these mines date to the early 1880s, when the prospectors uncovered some of the richest silver reserves in the nation and the town grew to have as many as 30,000 residents. Yet hard-rock mining also left tailings and toxins that taint the experience for some visitors. Personally, I love this town and its clutter of tailings, trailers, shacks, and Victorian homes. It feels and looks like a time capsule of Colorado's past.

Getting to Leadville

The closest commercial air service to Leadville is **Vail/Eagle County Airport** (see Chapter 19), 68 miles to the northwest, but it's cheaper to fly to **Denver International Airport** (DIA), 113 miles away. Most major airlines fly into DIA, and major rental-car companies have desks at the airport. For details about DIA, see Chapter 11; for information on contacting individual airlines and car-rental agencies, see the appendix.

To drive to Leadville from Denver, take I-70 west to Exit 195 (Copper Mountain), then go south on Colorado 91 for 24 miles. If you're coming from Aspen during summer and early fall, take Colorado 82 east for 44 miles (crossing Independence Pass), then go north on U.S. 24 for 15 miles. Independence Pass is closed in late fall, winter, and spring. If you're coming from the west on I-70, take Exit 171 (Minturn) and follow U.S. 24 South for 33 miles to Leadville.

Getting around

U.S. 24, the main route through Leadville, enters town from the south as Harrison Avenue. The historic part of town lines Harrison Avenue between Second and Ninth streets. At the north end of the historic district, U.S. 24 jogs east for a block on Ninth Street, then continues north as Poplar Street. A number of museums and historic attractions are near the point where the highway jogs east. Finding parking in Leadville is easy, especially on the side streets. Public transportation isn't an option in Leadville, but after parking your car, you can easily cover the historic part of town on foot.

Where to stay in Leadville

Leadville has a number of Victorian B&Bs and one 19th-century brick hotel. The historic accommodations are the best places to stay in the town, which also has some unspectacular older motels for travelers on a budget.

Delaware Hotel
$$ Leadville

Open since 1886, the Delaware Hotel became a flophouse in the 1970s before being fully renovated in 1992. Fortunately, much of the oak woodwork survived the lean years, and today this antique-filled hotel comes close to reproducing its silver-boom opulence. It's not as cozy as the nearby B&Bs, but it has more activities, including regular murder-mystery weekends.

700 Harrison Ave. ☎ 800-748-2004 (reservations) or 719-486-1418. Fax: 719-486-2214. www.delawarehotel.com. Rack rates: Mid-Dec through Mar and Memorial Day through Oct $99–$139 double, $159 suite; Apr to Memorial Day and Nov to mid-Dec $89–$125 double, $139 suite. Rates include continental breakfast. Children under 12 stay free (with some restrictions) in parents' room. AE, DISC, MC, V.

Leadville Country Inn
$$–$$$ Leadville

This cozy B&B has nine rooms in an 1892 home and its carriage house. The rooms are individually decorated; some feel more historic than others, but my favorites are in the home itself. Polly's Room has a sunroom with a cushy area where you can curl up, catlike, and nap in the window. Built into the home's turret, Lillian's Room has bay windows, a brass-and-iron queen-size bed, and a claw-foot tub in the bathroom. Stay in either for quiet, comfort, and lots of light when you want it.

127 E. Eighth St. ☎ *800-748-2354 or 719-486-2354. Fax: 719-486-0300.* www.leadville bednbreakfast.com. *Rack rates: $70–$158 double. Rates include breakfast. AE, DISC, MC, V.*

Where to dine in Leadville

Leadville has some great lodges, but its cuisine doesn't compare to food in the fancy mountain towns. Even so, you'll probably enjoy the places listed here.

Boomtown Brew Pub
$–$$ Leadville PUB FARE

There's less oxygen in the town's atmosphere, so your body absorbs alcohol more quickly. But if you think that Boomtown's brewmeister has cut back on the alcohol to compensate, have another pint. Along with its seasonal brews, Boomtown offers four power-packed regular brews, the most potent being the Poverty Flats Malt Liquor, which weighs in at a whopping 7.1 percent alcohol. If you remember to eat after visiting Poverty Flats, you can choose among burgers, steaks, and chicken dishes — or go for the owner's favorite: the blackened tuna sandwich with "nuclear" mayonnaise.

115 E. Seventh St. ☎ *719-486-8297. Reservations for large groups only. Main courses: $6–$16. AE, DISC, MC, V. Open: Daily 11 a.m.–11 p.m.*

Manuelita's Restaurant
$ Leadville TRADITIONAL MEXICAN/SEAFOOD

This isn't the most popular Mexican place in town, but the food here is the most authentic. The menu favors fresh seafood over Tex-Mex. Among the offerings are chicken and steak fajitas, grilled octopus, shrimp with hot sauce, deep-fried fish, and Veracruz-style red snapper, as well as Mexican-style sandwiches of marinated pork, shrimp, beef, or chicken. Don't be surprised if your server speaks little English, or if he or she asks for a personal check or cash instead of plastic.

311 Harrison Ave. ☎ *719-486-0292. Reservations not accepted. Main courses: $2–$14. No credit cards. Open: Daily 10 a.m.–9 p.m.*

Quincy's Steak and Spirits
$ Leadville STEAKS

Sometimes it's nice to find a restaurant where you don't have to think too much; Quincy's serves only filet mignon Sunday through Thursday, and has only prime rib on Friday and Saturday. Each dinner comes with a roll, salad (with house dressing), and baked potato. You just have to choose the size of your portion: filets range from 6 to 15 ounces, and prime rib from 8 to 20 ounces. If you insist on having something less meaty, the restaurant will defrost some lasagna for you.

416 Harrison Ave. ☎ 719-486-9765. Reservations for large parties only. Filet mignon dinners: $5.95–$13; prime rib dinners: $7.95–$15. MC, V. Open: Daily 5–9 p.m.

Exploring Leadville

Leadville is heaven for history buffs. The town had the most lucrative silver mines in the country for a time, and the land around town yielded minerals from silver to molybdenum until the 1980s. Leadville's mining history remains right in plain view, unadorned, and there's a lot to explore. In addition to those looking for historical offerings, Leadville also attracts mountaineers, who can climb to the heavens near town.

The best things to see and do

Instead of visiting all Leadville's museums in succession, you're better off mixing up your activities in order to absorb the town's history as many ways as possible. The suggestions in this section can get you started.

National Mining Hall of Fame and Museum

A trip to this museum helps you understand the mine buildings and machinery you see all around Leadville. It has exhibits on all types of mining, ranging from ancient Egyptian gold mines to modern strip mines. There are dioramas of local mining history, re-creations of tunnels (built to scale), and miniatures of historic mines. The Gold Rush Room and the Crystal Room hold samples of gold and crystal, respectively, and the top floor houses a Hall of Fame honoring legendary figures in mining.

120 W. Ninth St., Leadville. ☎ 719-486-1229. www.mininghalloffame.org. *Admission: $6 adults, $5 seniors 62 and over, $3 children 6–12; free for children 5 and under. Open: May–Oct daily 9 a.m.–5 p.m.; Nov–Apr Mon–Sat 10 a.m.–4 p.m.*

Matchless Mine (Baby Doe Tabor Museum)

At the Matchless Mine, you pay to hear a storyteller recount a heart-breaking tale in the very place where its sad ending played out. It's the story of Baby Doe Tabor and Horace Tabor, a married couple who struck it rich in silver and for years lived lavishly, holding extravagant parties and building sumptuous opera houses, homes, and hotels. Suffice it to say that the story ends poorly for the couple. While you're here, you can look down into the mine shaft that helped enrich Horace and visit the shack where Baby Doe spent her last years, but it's the story, told right, that makes this experience special.

Located 1¼ miles east of Leadville on E. Seventh St. ☎ 719-486-4918 or 719-486-8578. Admission: $4 adults, $1 children 6–12. Open: Summer daily 9 a.m.–5 p.m.; rest of year Tues–Sun 10 a.m.–4 p.m.

Leadville, Colorado & Southern Railroad

Pulled by diesel engines, this train rumbles away from a historic depot in downtown Leadville, then climbs scenic forested hillsides high above U.S.

91. After 11½ miles, it approaches the Climax Mine, the world's largest molybdenum mine, which operated through 1986. Soon after the mine-scarred mountainside comes into view, the train reverses direction and returns to Leadville on the same track, arriving in town about two and a half hours after departing. Ongoing commentary about Leadville history accompanies the nonstop journey.

326 E. Seventh St., Leadville. ☎ *719-486-3936.* www.leadville-train.com. *Departures: Late May to mid-June daily 1 p.m.; mid-June to mid-Aug daily 10 a.m. and 2 p.m.; mid-Aug to early Oct weekdays 1 p.m.; two Sept weekends 10 a.m. and 2 p.m. Cost: $26.50 adults, $15 children 4–12.*

Another cool thing to do

Even in a two-wheel-drive car, you can easily cruise through the heart of Leadville's 20-square-mile historic mining district, passing the remains of former mining operations, including tailings, piles, head frames, rusting machinery, and abandoned buildings. Before you go, pick up a free *Route of the Silver Kings* pamphlet at the **Chamber of Commerce Visitors Center,** 809 Harrison Ave. (☎ **888-LEADVILLE** or 719-486-3900; www.leadvilleusa.com). The pamphlet has maps and directions for three self-guided driving tours of area mines. Each drive covers roughly 10 miles and takes one to two hours. The pamphlet explains major landmarks, which are numbered both on the map and in person.

Touring Leadville's historic downtown

Leadville's downtown area is one of the largest National Historic Districts in the U.S. At the **Chamber of Commerce Visitors Center,** 809 Harrison Ave. (☎ **888-LEADVILLE** or 719-486-3900; www.leadvilleusa.com), you can get a printed *Leadville Walking Tour* identifying 73 landmarks in Leadville's National Historic District. Besides some of the other lodges and museums I recommend in previous sections, consider these other stops:

- ✔ **Heritage Museum and Gallery,** 102 E. Ninth Street (☎ 719-486-1878). This museum has a Victorian Room; a display on the 10th Mountain Division; and folksy, big-hearted exhibits that pay tribute to Leadville's past. It's open mid-May to mid-October from 10 a.m. to 6 p.m. daily. Admission is $3.50 adults, $3 seniors 62 and over, and $2.50 kids ages 6 to 16.

- ✔ **Tabor Opera House,** 308 Harrison Ave. (☎ 719-486-8409). Built in 1879, the 880-seat opera house was once part of the Silver Circuit that brought famous actors and singers west to perform for the newly minted millionaires and miners. For $4 ($2 for kids under 12), you can walk through the opera house while listening to an audio-taped history play over the theater's speakers. It's fun to see the catacombs, dressing rooms, and stage, but for $4, it'd be nice to see a movie, too. It's open Monday through Saturday in summer from 10 a.m. to 5 p.m.

✔ **Silver Dollar Saloon,** 315 Harrison Ave. (☎ **719-486-9914**). When you're finished walking, cool off at this saloon. The Brunswick back-bar has been here ever since the place opened for business in 1883. The walls are plastered with darn near everything a bar can accumulate in 120 years, including serving trays, musical instruments, historic photos, and masks.

Staying active in Leadville

The two highest peaks in the state are near Leadville in the Sawatch Range. At 14,433 feet, Mount Elbert is the second highest in the lower 48 states, behind 14,494-foot Mount Whitney in California. Yet it's only 12 feet higher than nearby Mount Massive. You can climb mountains here, but there are a host of other activities to engage in as well. Here are your options:

✔ **Biking/walking:** The **Chamber of Commerce Visitors Center,** 809 Harrison Ave. (☎ **888-LEADVILLE** or 719-486-3900; www.leadville usa.com), publishes a free guide called *Mountain Bike and Recreation Trails.* If you're not interested in the area's rugged trails and forest roads, try the **Mineral Belt Trail,** a paved 12½-mile loop around the outskirts of town. The trail passes old mines, meadows, and thick forest while serving up mountain views. It's closed to motorized vehicles. At the visitor center, you can pick up a free guide that explains the many landmarks along the trail. **Bill's Sport Shop,** Third and Harrison (☎ **719-486-0739**), rents mountain bikes for $25 per day, or $8 for an hour.

✔ **Cross-country skiing:** Located near Tennessee Pass, **Piney Creek Nordic Center** (☎ **719-486-1750**) grooms 25 kilometers of track in gently rolling meadows. Track passes cost $10 for adults, $8 for seniors and kids.

✔ **Golfing:** At 9,800 feet, the nine-hole **Mount Massive Golf Course,** located 3½ miles west of town at 259 County Rd. 5 (☎ **719-486-2176**), is the highest in North America. The strokes you gain by driving in thin air you may lose when putting with 14,000-foot peaks as a backdrop. Greens fees cost $16 for 9 holes, $28 for 18.

Those hooks really carry

Because of the thin air at Colorado's higher elevations, golf shots carry about 5 percent farther on Denver's courses and 10 to 15 percent farther in the mountains than they do elsewhere. But before you rush off to pack your clubs, you should also know that high handicappers seldom score better in the highlands. The thin air allows for added *lateral* movement on shots as well as added distance (though balls do spin more slowly). And people from the flatlands often get confused when they try to read greens against a mountainous backdrop.

Training the 10th Mountain Division

In the early 1940s, the U.S. Army erected Camp Hale just north of the current location of the **Ski Cooper** ski area to house a special division of American servicemen whose mission was to study technical mountaineering, alpine skiing, and mountain survival. (Think Outward Bound with artillery.)

The men at Camp Hale, also known as the 10th Mountain Division, trained at Ski Cooper and on the larger nearby peaks, and proceeded to win critical battles in Italy during World War II. A monument to the 10th Mountain Division is at Tennessee Pass, just outside the ski-area entrance. If you continue past the ski area toward Vail, you pass roadside markers identifying the old location of the encampment, but there's not much left to see.

✔ **Hiking/mountain-climbing:** Three nontechnical hiking trails go to the summit of 14,433-foot **Mount Elbert.** The easiest one, **South Main Elbert,** climbs more than 4,000 vertical feet over 5½ miles (one-way) to the summit. To safely reach the top, you need to prepare carefully, start early, and use common sense. If you start before dawn, you can summit and then make your way back down before the afternoon thunderstorms spark. For additional information on these trails, contact the **San Isabel National Forest Office,** 2015 Poplar St. (☎ **719-486-0749**). Surprisingly, there's no guide service in Leadville, but the climbs I describe don't require technical mountaineering skills; most fit people should be able to do them if they take a few days to acclimate, start early, and keep an eye on the weather.

Hitting the slopes

Ski Cooper (☎ **719-486-2277;** www.skicooper.com) may have played a historic role in preparing soldiers for World War II (see the nearby sidebar "Training the 10th Mountain Division"), but you don't have to be a warrior to conquer its slopes. (In fact, bunnies do quite well here.) Ski Cooper sits on a long hillside that's gradual enough for all but the most wobbly beginners. Its snow, which is seldom skied and entirely natural, tends to stay soft and fresh. It's a great place to learn, relax, save money, and simplify the skiing experience.

For those who crave more exciting terrain, Ski Cooper offers Snowcat Tours on nearby **Chicago Ridge.** The daylong tours usher skiers to seldom-skied runs of up to 1,400 vertical feet on 2,500 acres of terrain — more than six times the acreage inside the ski area. Cost is $234 per day (including lunch), and reservations are required. For more on Ski Cooper, see the chart on the inside back cover.

Fast Facts: Leadville

Emergencies

Dial ☎ 911.

Hospital

St. Vincent's General Hospital, 822 W. Fourth St. (☎ 719-486-0230), handles medical emergences 24 hours a day.

Information

Go to the Chamber of Commerce Visitors Center, 809 Harrison Ave. (☎ 888-LEADVILLE or 719-486-3900; www.leadvilleusa.com).

Pharmacy

Sayer-McKee Drug, 615 Harrison Ave. (☎ 719-486-1846), fills prescriptions in downtown Leadville.

Post Office

The post office is one block west of Harrison, at the intersection of West Fifth and Pine streets. Call ☎ 800-275-8777 for additional information about post office locations and hours.

Road Reports

Contact the Lake County Sheriff's Office (☎ 719-486-1249).

Buena Vista, Salida, and the Upper Arkansas

Buena Vista (the locals pronounce it *byu*-na, or just shorten the whole name to "Byunie") sits at the base of the spectacular Collegiate Peaks, whose principal summits (Mt. Harvard, Mt. Yale, and Mt. Princeton) were first summited — and therefore named — by the mountaineering clubs of those universities toward the end of the 18th century. The sleepy little town has anchored the few farms and ranches up here since the silver boom played out in the 1890s. Now, it's the base for the best rafting in the state.

Salida came of age in the late 1800s as a railroad hub linking the mines and mine camps of the southern Rockies to Denver. Eventually the rails shut down, as did the smoke-belching foundry just east of town. Even the surrounding ranches took some hits. By the 1980s, much of the downtown had been shuttered, but Salida transformed itself. Inspired by the lovely scenery and cheap rent, artists began opening studios and galleries in the storefronts. Today, splashy handmade signs mark the dozens of art and sculpture galleries in Salida's downtown. During warm-weather months, the artists share the town with boaters and river guides who come here for the whitewater on the Arkansas River, which flows along the northeast side of town. Everyone here seems to enjoy the slow pace, the warm banana-belt weather, and the views of the surrounding 14,000-foot peaks.

Getting there

If you're coming by car, the easiest way to get to both towns from Denver is via U.S. 285; it meets up with U.S. 24, which comes down from Leadville, 2 miles south of Buena Vista. Continue on 285 south to Salida, which is also on U.S. 50 between Gunnison (66 miles to the west) and Pueblo (96 miles to the east). In Pueblo, U.S. 50 meets I-25, Colorado's primary north-south thoroughfare.

If you want to fly to near Salida, your best bets are **Denver International Airport** (DIA) (140 miles northeast; see Chapter 11) and **Colorado Springs Airport** (CSA) (105 miles to the east; see Chapter 14). Nearly all the major domestic carriers fly into DIA. Eight commercial airlines serve CSA.

In Denver, you can choose from among all the major rental-car companies. At Colorado Springs Airport, your choices are **Avis, Dollar, Hertz,** and **National.** For information on contacting individual airlines and car-rental agencies, see the appendix.

Where to stay in the Arkansas Valley

Buena Vista has one good hotel, and Salida offers a great selection of bed-and-breakfasts. If you have an aversion to enormous stacks of pillows, however, you may want to look into a privately owned motel downtown or a chain hotel along U.S. 50. Choices include the **Comfort Inn,** 315 E. U.S. 50 (☎ 719-539-5000); the **Econo Lodge,** 1310 E. U.S. 50 (☎ 719-539-2895); and the **Holiday Inn Express,** 7400 W. U.S. 50 (☎ 719-539-8500). The prices are reasonable in this area, especially during winter.

Best Western Vista Inn
$–$$ **Buena Vista**

New to Buena Vista, and a great base for rafting trips, the Vista Inn has the clean (if normal) rooms that you expect from a Best Western, plus an indoor pool and spa, and two outdoor hot tubs open in the summer. A full buffet breakfast is included with each room, and each room comes with high-speed Internet access. The hotel is located on the north end of town, so you won't get to the heart of Buena Vista without a walk (or a car).

733 Hwy. 24 North. ☎ *800-809-3495 or 719-395-8009.* www.bwvistainn.com. *Rack rates: Mid-May through Sept $119–$129 double; Oct to mid-May $64–$92 double. Rates include breakfast. AE, DISC, MC, V.*

Gazebo Country Inn Bed and Breakfast
$$–$$$ **Salida**

The guest rooms in this 1901 home are fluffy even by B&B standards. They come complete with quilts, vintage furniture, robes, extra-plush towels, large bathtubs, and pillows galore. My favorite may be the Rainbow Room, which offers a private door and a spiral staircase to the hot tub. Guests in other rooms have to go around the side of the house. The Rose Room is the most romantic, with pink-and-white striped wallpaper, rose-colored carpeting, and a king-size bed that seems particularly imposing.

507 E. Third St. (at B Street). ☎ *800-565-7806 or 719-539-7806.* www.gazebo countryinn.com. *Rack rates: $70–150 double. Rates include breakfast. AE, MC, V.*

River Run Inn
$$ Salida

This inn occupies an 1895 building that once served as the Chaffee County poor farm. If anything can make you wish you'd been born into a destitute family a century ago, a night here may do it. The seven guest rooms are airy and spacious, with four-poster beds, huge windows, and lace curtains that billow in the afternoon breezes. You can walk a few hundred feet from the inn down to the Arkansas River or simply porch-sit and take in the silence — the inn is on a spacious 5-acre plot 3 miles outside Salida. If you want to save a few dollars, choose the group room with a shared bath; it's a bit hostel-like, but it costs quite a bit less.

8495 County Rd. 160. ☎ *800-385-6925 or 719-539-3818.* www.riverruninn.com. *Rack rates: $90–$125 double; group room $30–$40 per person. Rates include full breakfast and evening sherry. AE, MC, V.*

Woodland Motel
$ Salida

This family-owned motel has snug, immaculate rooms, each with Southwestern décor, 27-inch TVs, air-conditioning, and coffeemakers. The prices are usually among the lowest in town, and the innkeepers do everything possible to put you at ease — even if it means lugging a minirefrigerator or a microwave to your room. The cheapest rooms come with a single queen-size bed, but others have two queens. Ask for a spot away from the road, and bring your dog if you want, too.

903 W. First St. ☎ *800-488-0456 or 719-539-4980.* www.woodlandmotel.com. *Rack rates: $40–$78 double. AE, DC, DISC, MC, V.*

Where to dine in the Arkansas Valley

Salida has just enough good restaurants to see you through a long weekend, and none of them will bust your bank account. If you're at a loss for where to dine next, you can always repeat one of your favorites.

Amicas
$ Salida BREW PUB/PIZZA

Amicas's 14 varieties of thin-crust, wood-oven pizza perfectly complement its award-winning beers. The restaurant also serves calzones, panini sandwiches, lasagna, and salads. It occupies a streamlined room with hardwood floors, a brick wall, and paintings of peppers and tomatoes. The experience is probably worth twice the cost, which, for an entree, is usually around $7.

136 E. Second St. ☎ *719-539-5219. Reservations not accepted. Main courses: $5.25–$7.95. MC, V. Open: Sun–Thurs 11:30 a.m.–9 p.m., Fri–Sat 11:30 a.m.–10 p.m.*

Dakota's Bistro
$$ Salida CONTINENTAL

You can tell that the chef loves food from different regions when you look at his menu. Offerings include such seemingly unrelated entrees as buffalo stroganoff, blackened catfish, and lasagna. On Friday and Saturday nights, he gets even more creative and whips up traditional dishes from a new global region each week.

122 N. F St. ☎ *719-530-9909. Reservations accepted. Main courses: $10–$18. AE, DISC, MC, V. Open: Tues–Thurs 11:30 a.m.–8:30 p.m., Fri–Sat 11:30 a.m.–9 p.m.*

Jan's Family Restaurant
$ Buena Vista DINER

Jan's is the *absolute classic* mountain diner. My friends and I all eat here on day trips from Denver. They offer great chicken-fried steak (with eggs, for breakfast), good burgers, and friendly, down-home service. They carry a rotating selection of hot sauces — some of which seem to exist more for laughs than subtlety of flavor — and there's a dance floor in back for weekend nightlife, when the cowboys come out and step a little.

304 Hwy. 24 South, Buena Vista. ☎ *719-395-6490. Reservations not needed, or accepted. Main courses: $3.45–$9.95. AE, DISC, MC, V. Open: Daily 6 a.m.–9 p.m.*

Laughing Ladies Restaurant
$$ Salida AMERICAN

This is the most popular restaurant in Salida, a funky cafe with rotating art displays, nontraditional American food, and servers who shun uniforms. The place is known for its great salads and appetizers. For starters, try the grilled polenta, Portobello mushrooms, and blue cheese. The honey-grilled pork chop with poblano chile is the most popular entree. Over a dozen wines are available by the glass.

128 First St. ☎ *719-539-6209. Reservations accepted. Main courses: $11–$15. DISC, MC, V. Open: Thurs–Mon 11 a.m.–2:30 p.m. and 5–9 p.m.; Sun brunch 9 a.m.–2 p.m.*

Exploring Salida
If town life is what you're after, you're definitely better off in Salida. Before you go to town, though, take a river trip. Then wind down by strolling through the galleries in the downtown Salida area. When you're done, you're only a few miles' drive from Monarch Pass and the continental divide.

The best thing to do – art shopping

If you want to *look at* art, go somewhere like Aspen, where the galleries have works by the likes of Picasso, Chagall, Warhol, and others whose names ring a cash-register bell. But to *buy* art, go to Salida, where many artists create their pieces right where they sell them. The prices are low, and a lot of the work will move you. Many of my favorite studios are on or near First Street in downtown Salida. Don't miss the following:

- ✔ **Brodeur Art Gallery,** 151 W. First St. (☎ 719-221-1272; www. brodeurart.com). Paulette Brodeur works in a variety of media, but her most recognizable works may be her contemporary paintings of musicians, cafes, and other Bohemian scenes. Her art is sold internationally and this is where it's made.

- ✔ **BroadMinded,** 132 W. First St. (☎ 719-539-3122). The gallery has ceramics, paintings, and sculptures by some really talented women.

More cool things to see and do

You won't get soaked when you shop for art in Salida, so you should have a few dollars left over to spend on other activities you can partake of in the area including the following:

- ✔ **Soak inside.** The Works Progress Administration (WPA) erected a building around the **Salida Hot Springs** (☎ 719-539-6738; www. salidapool.com) in 1937, thereby creating the largest indoor hot springs pool in the state. Under one roof is a six-lane, 25-yard lap pool where the water is a temperate 90°; a four-foot-deep, 110° pool; a wading pool for toddlers; and four toasty, private, 113° tubs that you can rent by the hour for $6 per person. The springs are at 410 W. Rainbow Blvd. (U.S. 50). Admission is $6 adults, $4 ages 6 to 17, $2 kids 5 and under. In summer, it's open daily from 1 to 9 p.m.; the rest of the year, it's open Tuesday through Sunday from 4 to 9 p.m., and Friday through Sunday from 1 to 9 p.m.

- ✔ **Soak outside.** At **Mount Princeton Hot Springs,** 15870 County Rd. 162 (☎ 719-395-2361; www.mtprinceton.com), you can soak outside in geothermal water at the base of white cliffs. The springs are open 9 a.m. to 9 p.m. daily. Admission is free for guests of the attached Mount Princeton Resort; for nonguests, admission is $8 adults, $5 children 12 and under.

- ✔ **Visit a ghost town.** Established in 1880, St. Elmo used to be a railroad way station, moving ore from Aspen and other mountain towns down the east slope of the continental divide. Then it became a ghost town, with a short main street lined by well-preserved buildings. A few year-round residents live there now, and sometimes you can shop at the general store. To reach St. Elmo, drive to Nathrop, 17 miles north of Salida, then head west on County Road 162 for 15 miles to St. Elmo.

The Continental Divide

The continental divide meanders on a general north–south course through the Rocky Mountains just west of the center of Colorado. If you drive to a point on the divide, get out of the car, and then spill a very large cup of coffee, half of your java will flow into the rivers that empty into the Mississippi River, Gulf of Mexico, and the Atlantic Ocean. The other half will pour into rivers that feed the Colorado River and head for the Sea of Cortez and the Pacific Ocean.

Staying active in Salida

Air currents from the south keep Salida warm even during winter. Yet it's also in Chaffee County, home to 15 of Colorado's fourteeners — the highest concentration of peaks over 14,000 feet in the nation. This unusual environment lets you bicycle in winter and cool your feet on mountain snow (or melted snow) during summer. While you're here, think about the following:

✔ **Hiking and biking:** Salida's wintertime zephyrs let you bicycle around town even during the coldest months. However, the classic trails are higher up near the continental divide. For a great hike or mountain bike ride, drive to the parking area at Monarch Pass and get on the **Monarch Crest Trail.** To pick it up, follow the dirt road that begins just left of the lower tram station. About a quarter-mile up this road, the trail branches off on the right. It's a surprisingly smooth terrain, given its perch near the divide. You can do a long (12 miles each way) out-and-back or descend off the ridge on other trails. For maps and detailed directions, consult the free *Monarch Bike Guide,* available at **Absolute Bikes,** 330 W. Sackett (☎ **888-539-9295** or 719-539-9295; www.absolutebikes.com). Absolute Bikes rents full-suspension bikes for $35 a day; front-suspension bikes cost $25. For information on hiking trails, stop by the **San Isabel National Forest Office,** 325 W. Rainbow Blvd. (☎ **719-539-3591**), in Salida.

✔ **Fishing:** Head west on Cottonwood Pass road from Buena Vista. Eight miles out of town is the turnoff for **Cottonwood Lake,** a beautiful little trout hole between Mount Princeton and Mount Yale. Or continue over Cottonwood Pass to **Taylor Park Reservoir.** If you want to leave the fish alone, this is a great mountain drive with hairpin turns and gorgeous scenery.

✔ **Golfing: Salida Golf Club,** at the corner of Crestone and Grant Street (☎ **719-539-1060**), charges $15 for nine holes or $25 to play this city-owned course twice.

✔ **Rafting:** A half-day trip down the Arkansas River costs about as much as a day at an amusement park, and it's a lot more rewarding. You experience both the force of the mountains (via snowmelt) and the peacefulness of a scenic river canyon. You can run rivers throughout Colorado, but the best one for commercial rafting is the Arkansas, a river known for having a long season (usually May through August) and stretches of water perfect for everyone from novices to experts. More than 60 companies are licensed to run the Arkansas, so it's easy to get on a trip. Remember that rafting can be strenuous exercise, especially in the spring and early summer when the river becomes ferocious with snowmelt. If you've never rafted before, consider trying a half-day trip before you commit to a whole day.

Families with children ages 12 and up will love the half- and full-day trips through **Brown's Canyon.** These trips have stretches of calm water where you can scan the craggy canyon walls for bighorn sheep, interrupted by rapids with names such as Pinball, Staircase, and Zoom Flume. Any beginning rafter will be happy here, and most rafting companies in the area offer half- and full-day trips to this stretch of the river.

Brown's Canyon is genuinely exciting, but not as wild (and potentially abusive) as **The Numbers,** which features continuous Class IV/V waters. Trips down The Numbers are for fit, experienced rafters only.

You can usually choose one of two kinds of boat: Paddle boats, where you help the guide paddle, or oar boats, where the guide does all the rowing using oars mounted on a metal frame. I recommend paddling, because it involves you in the action. One experienced company is **Four Corners Rafting** (☎ **800-332-7238** or 719-395-4137; www.fourcornersrafting.com), in Nathrop. Four Corners has been in business since the mid-1970s, and offers half- to three-day trips on different sections of the Arkansas. Half-day trips cost $39 for adults and $33 for kids under 15, and full-day trips go for $71 for adults and $61 for kids.

Hitting the slopes

I'd love to be at **Monarch Ski and Snowboard Area** (☎ **888-996-7669** or 719-530-5000; www.skimonarch.com) during a January storm. Situated against the continental divide on the east side of Monarch Pass, the mountain receives 30 feet of snow annually — one of the state's higher totals. The area's 670 acres include lots of open, ungroomed terrain that's perfect for powder skiing. Because it sells inexpensive lift tickets and is farther southeast than most Colorado ski areas, Monarch lures a lot of gung-ho skiers from heartland states such as Kansas, Oklahoma, Texas, and Arkansas. For some reason, these skiers tend to gravitate to the run known as Lower Christmas Tree, leaving the rest of the area unpopulated — and untracked. Even if you're a novice, you can still enjoy the view from the top of the aptly named Panorama chair, which takes in peaks in the Sangre de Cristo, Uncompahgre, Sawatch, and Collegiate ranges. For a rundown of the resort's technical information, see the inside back cover.

Fast Facts: Buena Vista and Salida

Emergencies
Dial ☎ **911**.

Hospital
24-hour emergency service is available at Heart of the Rockies Medical Center, 448 E. First St., Salida (☎ 719-539-6661).

Information
Visit the Heart of the Rockies Chamber of Commerce, 406 W. Rainbow Blvd., Salida (☎ 877-772-5432 or 719-539-2068; www.salidachamber.org).

Pharmacy
To fill a prescription, try Lallier Pharmacy, 147 F St. (☎ 719-539-2591).

Post Office
Buena Vista's post office is at 110 Brookdale Ave., just off Hwy 24. Salida's post office is at 310 D. St. Call ☎ 800-275-8777 for additional information about post office locations and hours.

Road Conditions
Call ☎ 719-539-6688.

Chapter 19

Vail and the Vail Valley

• •

In This Chapter

▶ Basking in the ultrachic resort town that is Vail

▶ Discovering Avon, Beaver Creek, and activities farther down the valley

• •

*V*ail as we know it didn't exist before 1962, when a former member of the 10th Mountain Division started a small ski area with a lodge and restaurant at the base. He and his friends fashioned the buildings after the mountain villages they had seen in Europe during World War II. They named the area for the highway engineer who designed the road into the area, and the place took off from there. Like Aspen, Vail is now beyond expensive, but it still welcomes thousands of skiers who drive up from Denver on weekends, not to mention many destination travelers. Some of the people who helped build the town have stuck around, helping preserve Vail's sense of tradition. Forty years after it started, Vail still feels as much like a town for hardy skiers as it does a retreat for the very rich. And it still retains its European flavor.

Twelve miles west of Vail is the resort of Beaver Creek, which is a more secluded version of Vail. Like Vail, it has a pedestrian-friendly, European-style village, and it costs a lot to stay there. Unlike Vail, it's a couple of miles uphill from the freeway, and you have to pass through a guardhouse to drive up there. Most visitors gravitate to Vail.

Vail Essentials

Don't be put off by your first glimpse of the community. The town extends down a river canyon alongside I-70, but the downtown villages feel less like an off-ramp than you may think. The heart of the town — two adjoining enclaves known as Vail Village and Lionshead — bans most car traffic and seems remote from the freeway. In places, the splashing of Gore Creek is all you hear. And lush mountainsides border the south side of the community.

Getting there

Part of Vail's allure is its accessibility. It's right on I-70, 109 miles west of Denver and 150 miles east of Grand Junction.

During ski season, **Vail/Eagle County Airport** (☎ **970-524-9490;** www. eaglecounty.us/airport), 35 miles west of town, has daily nonstop service to Atlanta, Chicago, Dallas, Denver, Houston, Minneapolis, and Newark, with less frequent nonstop flights from six other U.S. cities. **American, Continental, Delta, Northwest, United Airlines,** and **US Airways** all fly into Eagle County. Call **Colorado Mountain Express** (☎ **800-525-6363** or 970-926-9800; www.cmex.com) for a shuttle ride (cost: $44 per person) into town. **Hertz, Avis, Enterprise,** and **Budget** all have desks at the airport. For information on contacting individual airlines and car-rental agencies, see the appendix.

Vail is a two-hour drive from Denver, so you can also fly into **Denver International Airport (DIA),** served by most major domestic carriers (see Chapter 11). Numerous companies offer shuttle services between Vail and Denver, including **Colorado Mountain Express,** which charges $66 a person for a shared, one-way ride to Vail from DIA.

Getting around

You can get by without a car in Vail (see the nearby "Vail" map). The town has an outstanding transit system, with **free shuttles** serving Vail Village, Lionshead, East Vail, and West Vail from 6 a.m. to 2 a.m. daily during ski season. (Hours of operation are shorter the rest of the year.) During winter, you seldom have to wait more than ten minutes for a bus. For local shuttle-bus schedules, call ☎ **970-477-3456. ECO Transit** (☎ **970-328-3520** or 970-477-1606) provides regular bus service (for $2 to $3) to outlying areas such as Avon, Edwards, Beaver Creek, and Leadville.

For a cab, call **Vail Valley Taxi** (☎ **970-476-TAXI**).

Where to stay

Lodging costs a lot in Vail. If you're a skier, you can save by shopping for package deals or by coming before Christmas or in April — periods when the snow can be hit-or-miss. Some lodges also discount rooms in mid-January, when the snow tends to be light and fluffy and the coverage is more reliable. If you're not a skier, consider visiting during spring, early summer, and late fall, when the town empties and many lodges sharply discount their rooms. If the rates still seem too expensive, look for lodging in the nearby towns of Avon or Edwards.

 Even during high season, visitors can sometimes find last-minute lodging deals in Vail by calling the **Vail Visitor Center** (☎ **970-479-1394**) or checking www.vailonsale.com.

Hotel-Gasthof Gramshammer
$$–$$$$ Vail Village

One of the original three buildings in town, this hotel is a bargain by Vail standards. During winter, its 35 rooms cost about $100 less than near by accommodations, and they're pleasant. Guests stay in the lodge that

Vail

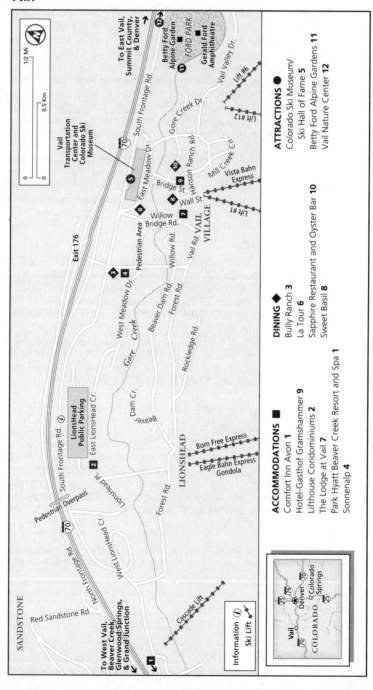

ATTRACTIONS ●
Colorado Ski Museum/
Ski Hall of Fame **5**
Betty Ford Alpine Gardens **11**
Vail Nature Center **12**

DINING ◆
Bully Ranch **3**
La Tour **6**
Sapphire Restaurant and Oyster Bar **10**
Sweet Basil **8**

ACCOMMODATIONS ■
Comfort Inn Avon **1**
Hotel-Gasthof Gramshammer **9**
Lifthouse Condominiums **2**
The Lodge at Vail **7**
Park Hyatt Beaver Creek Resort and Spa **1**
Sonnenalp **4**

Information ⓘ
Ski Lift ⛷

Pepi Gramshammer, a former Austrian ski racer, and his wife, Sheika, have run since 1964. They live on the premises and do their best to make you feel like family. Accommodations range from a standard hotel room to a deluxe apartment with a full kitchen. You can unwind in the two Jacuzzis, in Pepi's Bar, or on Pepi's Deck, where you can eat goulash and other Austrian dishes.

See map p. 242. 231 E. Gore Creek Dr. ☎ *800-610-7374 or 970-476-5626. Fax: 970-476-8816.* www.pepis.com. *Rack rates: Summer and fall $105–$198 double, $150–$650 suite; winter high season (Christmas/New Year's weeks and mid-Feb to early Apr) $245–$350 double, $275–$760 suite; winter low season (balance of ski season) $195–$275 double, $225–$760 suite. During winter, self-parking costs $12 a night. AE, DC, DISC, MC, V. Closed mid-Apr–June.*

Lifthouse Condominiums
$$–$$$$ Lionshead

Built in 1965, the hotel consists entirely of studio condominiums; each with a queen-size bed, rollaway bed, gas fireplace, kitchenette, and dining area. The rooms aren't very roomy, but no space goes to waste. Four very close adults could stay and eat in each studio in something like comfort, and the price is almost right. The hotel's literature says it's only "73 seconds" from the Gondola base but doesn't say who's walking. It is pretty close though.

See map p. 242. 555 East Lionshead Circle. ☎ *800-654-0635 or 970-476-2340. Fax: 970-476-9303.* www.lifthousevail.com. *Rack rates: Apr–May and Oct–mid-Dec $75–$91 double; June–Sept $109–$155; late Dec–Mar $244–$357. During winter, self-parking costs $13 a night. DISC, MC, V.*

The Lodge at Vail
$$$$ Vail Village

The first hotel at Vail, this lodge claimed a prime location mere steps away from the Vista Bahn chairlift. It's considered to be among the finest hotels in the world, with two gourmet restaurants, an exercise room, a swimming

Avon: Vail's cure for sticker shock

No, it's not a makeup factory, it's a town. If the price of lodging is prohibitive to you, but you want the Vail skiing experience (some of the best on the planet), head for the rapidly suburbanizing Avon, 9 miles down the valley from Vail, at the turnoff to Beaver Creek. Here among the strip malls you'll find a number of hotels: One that offers reasonable rates for decent lodgings is the **Comfort Inn,** 161 W. Beaver Creek Blvd. (☎ 970-949-5511; www.comfortinn.com). Nothing too fancy here: straightforward rooms, with continental breakfast in the morning. The outdoor pool and hot tubs make après-ski a bit more glamorous. Rates vary from $79–$199 depending on season and availability, so you'll have a little more green to keep you from feeling like a pauper in Vail, and you're a short drive from the slopes of both Vail and Beaver Creek.

pool, four hot tubs, and a history of luxury and class. The prime location and attentive service help make up for the smallish rooms. Golf and bed-and-breakfast packages are available.

See map p. 242. 124 E. Gore Creek Dr. ☎ *877-LAV-ROCK or 970-476-5011. Fax: 970-476-7425.* www.lodgeatvail.rockresorts.com. *Rack rates: Winter $529–959 double; summer $249–$799 double. Valet parking: $15–$20. AE, DC, DISC, MC, V.*

Park Hyatt Beaver Creek Resort and Spa
$$$$ Beaver Creek

Situated right at the base of Beaver Creek's ski runs, this immense hotel offers luxuries ranging from in-room computers to six roaring whirlpools. The rooms, big enough for a Shriners convention, have been recently redecorated at an inordinate cost in a Western motif. Downstairs, at the feng shui–influenced spa, ultracontent guests drift around in robes, read magazines, or simply relax. If all the deep relaxation and comfort puts you under, you may need to drive into Vail for some nightlife.

See map p. 242. At Beaver Creek Resort, Avon. ☎ *970-949-1234 or 800-55-HYATT (reservations only). Fax: 970-949-4164.* www.beavercreek.hyatt.com. *Rack rates: Dec 20–April 5, $380–$655; rest of year, $120–$345. Add $75 to $150 per night for a room with ski-area views. AE, DC, DISC, MC, V.*

Sonnenalp
$$$$ Vail Village

This hotel, my favorite in Vail, has European-mountain touches such as arched entryways and stonework framing heavy wooden doors. At times, there are so many German and Austrians on duty, you can be sure that the guest-to-European ratio is the lowest in town. The rooms come with gas fireplaces, balconies, windows that open, and heated marble bathroom floors. A single switch shuts off all the lights in the room when you leave. After you're done swimming in the creek-side indoor-outdoor pool, you can relax in the full-service spa.

See map p. 242. 20 Vail Rd. ☎ *800-654-8312 or 970-476-5656. Fax: 970-479-5449.* www.sonnenalp.com. *Rack rates: Late Nov to mid-Dec and early Apr $350–$665; mid-Dec to early Jan $680–$1,085; early Jan to early Apr $605–$1,000; mid-Apr to mid-June and late Sept to late Nov $240–$390; mid-June to late Sept $350–$625. AE, DC, DISC, MC, V.*

Where to dine

Like the town itself, Vail's dining scene seems to have a spoon in Europe and a fork in the United States. Many of Vail's best restaurants serve traditional French, German, Swiss, or Italian food, and most of the rest bring European elements to American fare. The town's list of chefs reads like a reunion of James Beard House nominees. Naturally, dinners cost a lot, but a few places do serve affordable fare, and many bars have specials on food and drinks.

Bully Ranch
$–$$ Vail   AMERICAN

This place is a smart choice for a group of friends who can't agree on what type of food to eat. The menu has salads and wraps for light appetites; chops and salmon for big eaters; and pub fare (including baby-back ribs, fish and chips, and fisherman's stew) for everyone else. The dining room has a relaxed Western feel, from the antler lamps on the ceiling to the weathered wooden floor underfoot. A lot of locals come here just for the famous *mudslides* (a mixed drink made up of vodka, kahlua, and Irish cream), which seem to go hand in hand with overgrazing.

See map p. 242. 20 Vail Rd. ☎ 970-476-5656. Reservations not accepted. Main courses: $7.50–$28. AE, DC, DISC, MC, V. Open: Daily 11 a.m.–11 p.m.

La Tour
$$$–$$$$ Vail   FRENCH/AMERICAN

When Vail's chefs go out for a delectable meal, they often order the latest creations of La Tour's owner, Paul Ferzacca. Ferzacca mastered French cooking at some of Chicago's finest restaurants. When he took over La Tour in 1998, he began subtly tinkering with traditional French fare. The result hardly qualifies as "French lite," but the sauces are a little less creamy than in Paris (or so I'm told), and Asian ingredients have turned up in certain dishes. Plan on staying for a while; this is the place to have a leisurely dinner. The menu is broken down into three courses plus dessert; you may as well shoot for the moon. For a main course, try the Dover sole in brown butter sauce.

See map p. 242. 122 E. Meadow Dr. (across from the west end of the Vail Village parking structure). ☎ 970-476-4403. Reservations preferred. Main courses: $9–$36. AE, DC, DISC, MC, V. Open: Daily 5:30–10 p.m. Closed May 10–Memorial Day.

Sapphire Restaurant and Oyster Bar
$$$ Vail   INNOVATIVE AMERICAN

This restaurant's press kit says that one owner, Joel Fritz, has been "married for 35 years to the same person and never a cross word." It says the other owner, Susan Fritz, has been "raising great kids and well-mannered dogs." The Fritz's miracles carry over into their restaurant, which has delicious food, attentive servers, and, if the pattern holds, charming prep cooks. Dinner fare consists primarily of steaks and seafood; at lunch, options include fish tacos, salads, burgers, and sandwiches. You can sit on the creek-side deck or go inside to the dining room and oyster bar, where tiny ceiling lights sparkle like stars.

See map p. 242. 223 Gore Creek Dr. ☎ 970-476-2828. Reservations recommended. Main courses: $18–$28. AE, MC, V. Open: Summer daily 11:30 a.m.–3 p.m. and 5:30–9:30 p.m.; rest of year daily 5:30–9:30 p.m.

Sweet Basil
$$$ Vail CREATIVE AMERICAN

Sweet Basil is my first choice for a meal out in the mountains. This isn't exactly a bold choice — this bistro-style restaurant has been earning raves for 25 years. Ask for a table with views of Gore Creek, then choose between the fish, steak, chicken, and veal dishes, all with creative sauces. The saffron linguini with lobster, bay scallops, shrimp, and cream has been on the menu forever, and it's delicious. For dessert, try the hot sticky toffee pudding cake.

See map p. 242. 193 E. Gore Creek Dr. ☎ 970-476-0125. Reservations recommended. Main courses: $23–$28. AE, DISC, MC, V. Open: Daily 11:30 a.m.–2:30 p.m. and 5:30–10 p.m.

Exploring Vail

Vail doesn't have a lot of must-see attractions, so you can relax and drift from place to place. During summer, you may drift past gardens, mountain trails, people fishing on Gore Creek, a few galleries, and lots of interesting shops. Go slowly and you'll have energy to spare for the cultural events around town, including outdoor concerts at the amphitheater.

The best things to see and do

Colorado Ski Museum/Ski Hall of Fame

Being a nerd for old ski stuff, I love this museum. It has timelines showing major developments in skiing and snowboarding, along with gear and memorabilia from the different periods. It displays uniforms and equipment from each winter Olympics. And it devotes an entire room to the 10th Mountain Division. I'm partial to the vintage posters advertising ski areas and ski movies, and the old-time footage of powder skiers shown on the TV.

See map p. 242. 231 S. Frontage Rd. E. (in Vail Transportation Center, Level 3), Vail. ☎ 970-476-1876. www.skimuseum.net. Open: Tues–Sun 10 a.m.–5 p.m. Closed May and Oct. Admission: $1 adults; free for children under 12.

Betty Ford Alpine Gardens

The Betty Ford Gardens isn't a rehab center like that other Betty Ford place. Still, your head will feel better when you see the waterfalls, pools, and 2,000 different kinds of high-alpine plants, ranging from bristlecone pines to alpine poppies. Almost anything that legally grows at 8,200 feet is here, including many exotics. It's especially lovely in midsummer, when the flowers are in full bloom.

See map p. 242. In Ford Park, east of Vail Village, Vail. ☎ 970-476-0103. www.bettyfordalpinegardens.org. Open: Daily from dawn to dusk when not under snow. Admission: Free.

Staying active

During winter, the activity in Vail centers around the big — make that enormous — ski area. During the rest of the year, Vail just concentrates on big fun. While you're here, think about going:

- **Fishing:** Even during the peak runoff months, you can usually wade and fish in Gore Creek right in downtown Vail. When the flows drop in midsummer, you'll fare better if you travel below the confluence of Gore Creek and the Eagle River. **Fly-Fishing Outfitters** (☎ **800-595-8090** or 970-476-FISH; www.flyfishingoutfitters.net) can help you find the best holes. Guide service for wade trips costs $200 for a half-day, $300 for a full day. Guided float trips start at $275 for a half-day.

- **Hiking: Vail Mountain** publishes a map showing summer hiking and biking trails on the ski area. You can find those maps in the same boxes that hold ski-area trail maps during winter. The resort has separate hiking and biking trails, so you can go for long walks without having to dodge cyclists. For even less crowded trails, go to Beaver Creek.

  If you want to hike with guides who are knowledgeable in geology, ecology, and history, contact the **Vail Nature Center,** 700 S. Frontage Rd. (☎ **970-479-2291;** www.vailrec.com). The Nature Center schedules guided hikes most weekdays during summer, including mellow half-day strolls near Vail Village and more rigorous all day hikes in the nearby **Holy Cross** and **Eagle's Nest Wilderness Areas.**

- **Golfing:** On the par-71, 7,008-yard **Vail Golf Course,** 1778 Vail Valley Dr. (☎ **970-479-2260**), you can tee off while taking in views of the Gore Range. Don't gawk too much, lest your ball end up in one of many water hazards. You can reserve your tee time 48 hours in advance. On weekdays, greens fees are $105, $80 at twilight; on the weekends, they rise to $115.

  Designed by Arnold Palmer, **Eagle Ranch Golf Course,** 50 Lime Park Dr., in Eagle (☎ **970-328-2882**), is the least expensive course in the area. During summer, greens fees at this par-72, 7,506-yard course are $85 Monday through Thursday and $90 Friday through Sunday.

- **Ice skating:** Here's proof positive that the people at Beaver Creek are not living in the real world: You can ice-skate there, outside, *year-round.* Weather permitting, the rink operates from 6 to 10 p.m. nightly. Cost for skating, including skate rentals, is $9 for adults, $7 for kids. Call ☎ **970-845-0438** for more information. Meanwhile, Vail has a bona fide indoor hockey rink; call ☎ **970-479-2271** for information on open skates in Vail.

- **Mountain biking:** After picking up a free trail map, you can pedal directly onto Vail Mountain at either Vail Village or Lionshead. It's a long grind to gain the ridgeline, where one of the premier rides, the 7-mile **Grand Traverse,** begins. During summer, you can shorten the trip by taking the Eagle Bahn gondola or Vista Bahn chairlift to the top. Lift tickets, valid all day, cost $16 for adults, $10 for children 5 to12 and seniors 65 to 69, and $5 for seniors over 70. You can also find challenging trails on the north side of I-70. **Diamond Ski Shop,** 520 Lionshead Mall (☎ 970-476-5500), can provide directions and also rents full-suspension mountain bikes for $30 a day.

✔ **Rafting: Lakota River Guides** (☎ 800-274-0636 or 970-476-RAFT) has trips ranging from mellow half-day family floats on the Colorado River ($69 adults, $59 ages 6 to 12) to all-day white-knucklers on the Arkansas ($119 for ages 16 and up).

Hitting the slopes

It's hard to overstate the immensity of **Vail** (☎ 970-476-5601; http://vail.snow.com). Its 33 lifts serve 193 trails and five bowls strung across a ridgeline more than 7 miles long. Vail's 5,289 skiable acres make it the largest area in the country by 1,700 acres. It took me most of a day just to ski into every *canyon* in the area boundaries. The terrain includes a pine-covered, north-facing lower mountain with groomed trails as wide as I-80; the famous back bowls, most of which are only moderately steep; and the remote, shady glades of Blue Sky Basin. Beginners have an incredible 35 trails to choose from in Blue Sky Basin alone. Advanced intermediates can drift almost everywhere, even into some of the back bowls. Mogul skiers can test their mettle on the Highline run, where the bumps are bunched like bubble wrap. And powder fanatics can float through an average annual snowfall (348 inches) that ranks among the highest in the state. After a storm, the powder skiers race to make fresh tracks in more than 2,600 mostly open acres in the bowls. A few drawbacks do come to mind: Lift lines inevitably slow skiers who don't know their way around the mountain; parking usually costs $12; and because the back bowls face the sun, the powder quickly warms and condenses after late-season storms. But that's quibbling — this is an awesome mountain. For the technical lowdown on the resort, see the inside back cover.

Compared to Vail, **Beaver Creek Resort** (☎ 800-842-8062; http://beavercreek.snow.com) is a downright intimate place, where everyone seems eager to assist you. The meet-and-greet process starts right after you park your car in Avon. Attendants lift the skis from your hand and load them onto the shuttle bus for the five-minute ride to Beaver Creek Village, where another set of attendants unloads the skis, bucket-brigade style, and places them in a rack. After finally catching up with your skis, you encounter greeters offering trail maps and advice. Then you take two short rides, via sheltered escalator, to the base of the slopes. Everything is ultraluxurious, from the dried flowers in the bathrooms to the heated sidewalks in the base area. When you're on the hill, you finally get to know a delightful mountain that evenly balances beginner, intermediate, and advanced terrain. Beaver Creek has roughly one-third the skiable acreage of Vail, making it large enough to be varied yet small enough to comprehend. A lot of this terrain faces north, so the snow tends to stay cold and soft. Grooming is cherished here, but you can also find some long mogul runs. See the inside back cover for more information on the resort.

Shopping

The shopping in and around Vail varies by neighborhood. **West Vail** has the big grocery stores, liquor outlets, and strip malls. **Beaver Creek,** near Avon, offers high-end boutiques and stores, but it's a little too secluded to qualify as a thriving shopping district.

Vail Village has the most fun and varied offerings, including some nationally known shops. One landmark store is the **Golden Bear** (☎ 970-476-4082), famous for selling its trademarked golden bear pendants. Located on Bridge Street in Vail Village, the store still crafts and sells a full line of bears, ranging from silver starter-bears ($55) to diamond-studded bears (if you have to ask the price, you can't afford them).

Right across the street, at 273 Gore Creek Dr., is the flagship **Gorsuch** store (☎ 970-476-2294). Among other offerings, the store sells ski attire that does more than just keep you dry and warm; it has what the store describes as, ahem, "flawless form . . . and a new sensuality for city, country, and slopes."

American Ski Exchange, 225 Wall St. (☎ 970-476-1477), is the place to go when you need cheap Vail souvenirs for all your gift-greedy cousins and co-workers. Like a Times Square electronics shop, the store always claims to have drastically cut prices. Vail T-shirts have been sharply reduced to two for $15, and Vail fleece vests usually cost around $15, down from $50 or so.

Nightlife and culture

Vail has a diverse nighttime scene, with offerings ranging from dance clubs to cigar bars, sometimes even in the same location.

The Tap Room, 333 Bridge St. (☎ 970-479-0500), seems like a low-key locals' watering hole, but if you walk upstairs to **The Sanctuary,** you may find a ravelike dance party. Cover varies.

Club Chelsea, 2121 N. Frontage Rd. West (☎ 970-476-5600), has a cigar bar, a disco-friendly dance club, and a lounge, all under the same roof. **8150,** 143 E. Meadow Dr. (☎ 970-479-0607), pays real live humans to play funk, rock, and reggae. Cover varies.

Go to **Bully Ranch,** 20 Vail Rd. (☎ 970-476-5656), for mudslides; to **Vendettas Italian Restaurant,** 291 Bridge St. (☎ 970-476-5070), for drafts and late-night pizza; and to the **Red Lion Inn,** 304 Bridge St. (☎ 970-476-7676), for après-ski.

If you want to relax with friends and hear acoustic music, **The Club,** 304 Bridge St. (☎ 970-479-0556), is a good choice. Cover is $5 after 9:30 p.m.

August: Music month in Vail

During July and August, dozens of concerts and performances take place in the Vail Valley, many of them in the Gerald R. Ford Amphitheater, which has a large covered pavilion, an expansive lawn, and a stage from which performers can see the mountains.

From late June to early August, the **Vail Valley Music Festival** (☎ 866-827-5252; www.vailmusicfestival.org) presents more than 60 chamber, pops, and orchestral concerts featuring three major symphony orchestras and 40 soloists of international renown. Tickets range in price from $21 to $59.

The **Vail International Dance Festival** (☎ 970-949-1999; www.vvf.org) schedules performances of contemporary and classical dance in early August. Tickets range in price from $17 to $89.

In late July and early August, some of the world's hottest jazz musicians come to town for the **Vail Jazz Festival** (☎ 888-VAIL-JAM; www.vailjazz.org). In addition to dozens of free outdoor concerts, the festival has intimate club gigs (cover charges vary) and a festival-capping party over Labor Day Weekend. Weekend passes cost $250, and tickets for individual shows cost $40 to $50.

The locals' favorite is probably the **Budweiser Hot Summer Nights Concert Series** — free rock, folk, bluegrass, blues, and reggae performances at the Gerald R. Ford Amphitheater on Tuesday nights during June and July.

Fast Facts: Vail

Emergencies

Dial ☎ 911.

Hospital

Vail Valley Medical Center (☎ 970-476-2451) at 181 West Meadow Dr. (between Vail Road and East Lionshead Circle), has an emergency room open 24 hours.

Information

Vail Valley Tourism and Convention Bureau, 100 E. Meadow Dr., Vail (☎ 800-525-3875 or 970-476-1000; www.visitvailvalley.com).

Pharmacy

City Market, 2109 N. Frontage Rd. W. (☎ 970-476-1621), can fill your prescriptions in Vail.

Post Office

Vail's post office is at 1300 N. Frontage Rd. W. (☎ 970-476-5217), across from Donovan Park.

Road Conditions

Call ☎ 970-479-2226.

Chapter 20

Aspen and the Roaring Fork Valley

· ·

In This Chapter

▶ Festival-going in Aspen
▶ Soaking up Glenwood Springs
▶ Seeing Redstone, a Utopia for the road-weary

· ·

*V*isitors to the mountain towns west of Vail (Chapter 19) and north of Crested Butte (Chapter 22) can find plenty of variety, if not always solitude. Forty miles south of I-70 is Aspen, a historic mining town, cultural hub, and celebrity hot spot. Aspen can be hard to afford for one person, let alone a family, but you can stay in Basalt or Carbondale and save on lodging while exploring the five nearby ski areas. Glenwood Springs, a small city located right on the interstate, is popular with families and known for its enormous Hot Springs Pool.

If you detour onto less-traveled mountain roads, you can choose between two fine destinations: Redstone offers a quiet retreat into nature — and the past. The town has some stunning historic buildings — including an enormous Tudor mansion built in the early 1900s — but the real allure is the quiet setting in the West Elk Mountains. For a truly Western experience, your best bet is Steamboat Springs, a bustling town that happily blends recreation and ranching.

What's Where? The Region and Its Major Attractions

You can have a lot of fun in this region if you set up a base camp in Basalt, Glenwood Springs, or Carbondale and make short excursions to area attractions (see the nearby map, "The Roaring Fork Valley").

The Roaring Fork Valley

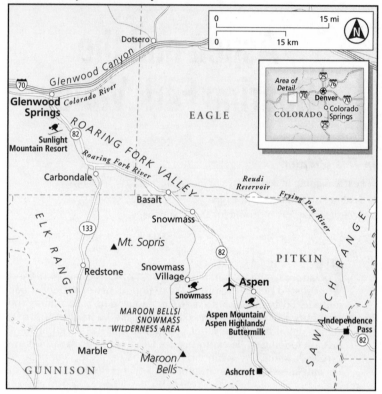

Aspen highlights

Aspen can be snooty, and its prices inspire awe, but at least you get something in return. It has buildings that date to a mining boom in the 1880s and 1890s, it has culture to rival any town of its size in the West, and it has wilderness to spare. Among its finest attractions are

- ✔ **Four ski areas,** including prime choices for beginners **(Buttermilk),** intermediates **(Snowmass),** experts **(Aspen Highlands),** and celebrities **(Aspen Mountain).**

- ✔ The **Aspen Music Festival,** a nine-week summer celebration and school with up to six classical performances daily.

- ✔ Hiking and backpacking in the stunning **Maroon Bells/Snowmass Wilderness Area.**

Glenwood Springs, Carbondale, and Redstone highlights

A popular resort since 1888, Glenwood Springs has some of the most appealing family attractions in the state. Carbondale offers fine restaurants and inexpensive lodging near Aspen. And farther off the beaten path, in the heart of the West Elk Mountains, hides Redstone, an unincorporated town that was once a Utopian community for coal miners. When you're in this area, don't miss

- ✔ **Hot Springs Pool,** the largest public hot springs in the world

- ✔ **Glenwood Caverns,** where two newly opened rooms showcase pristine, ornate limestone formations

- ✔ **Redstone Castle,** a 42-room, lavishly decorated mansion built 100 years ago by one of the world's richest men, John Osgood

Aspen

Aspen has a lot going for it. It's a historic mining community near stunning wilderness. It has traditionally been home to some of the nation's finest skiers and mountaineers, including members of the 10th Mountain Division, who helped develop the ski area on Aspen Mountain after World War II. And since the 1940s, the town's leaders have worked hard to promote recreation, music, culture, and ideas — all of which exist in spades in today's Aspen.

Aspen remains fun, stimulating, and scenic, but don't kid yourself: It isn't for everyone. Prices are high, traffic in and out of town can be heavy, and the locals don't always embrace the common folk.

If you're a Hollywood producer or the permanently elected president of a small Caribbean republic, you should plan a long vacation here. For you, Aspen has designer shops, prestigious galleries, and some of the finest restaurants in the nation. You can tip your mug in historic barrooms where the locals really do get out and party. With four ski areas, Aspen offers plenty of variety on the slopes, and the town's luxury hotels will treat you like royalty (probably because you *are*). If, however, you don't have the do-re-mi or are just plain regular, you may need to consider basing yourself in a satellite town, such as Glenwood Springs or Carbondale or Basalt. All have bus service to Aspen and offer lodging at a fraction of the cost. Plus, they're pretty attractive places themselves.

Getting to Aspen

Aspen is 172 miles west of Denver and 130 miles east of Grand Junction. During winter and early spring, the only way to reach Aspen is by taking Colorado 82 southeast for 42 miles from Glenwood Springs (on I-70). In summer and early fall, you can sometimes shorten the trip from Denver by about 40 miles — and dramatically raise the adventure level — by taking Colorado 91 south to Leadville, continuing south for 17 miles on U.S. 24, and then taking Colorado 82 east over Independence Pass 44 miles. This route stays closed until road crews clear the snow off 12,094-foot Independence Pass in spring.

Don't drive over Independence Pass during stormy weather or if you're tired. Though paved, this stretch of Colorado 82 has only one lane (total) in places and some sobering drop-offs alongside it.

Aspen is far enough from Denver International Airport to make flying closer a good idea. Two airports are within easy striking distance of town. The closest is **Aspen/Pitkin County Airport** (☎ 970-920-5380; www.aspenairport.com), 3 miles northwest of Aspen on Colorado 82. **United Express** offers daily nonstop service from Denver to Aspen; **America West Express** offers a similar service from Phoenix. During winter, you can also fly to Aspen nonstop from Minneapolis/St. Paul on **Northwest Jet Airlink.** Another option is to fly into **Vail/Eagle County Airport,** 70 miles from Aspen on I-70 (see Chapter 19 for information on this airport).

Many hotels offer complimentary ground transfers into town from Aspen/ Pitkin County Airport. If a transfer is unavailable, call **High Mountain Taxi** (☎ 970-925-TAXI). **Avis, Budget, Dollar, Hertz,** and **Thrifty** all have desks at Aspen/Pitkin County Airport. For information on contacting individual airlines and car-rental agencies, see the appendix.

To catch a shuttle to Aspen from Eagle County Airport or Denver International Airport, call **Colorado Mountain Express** (☎ 800-525-6363 or 970-926-9800; www.cmex.com). The one-way trip from Eagle County costs $54 per person; from Denver, it's $106.

Amtrak (☎ 800-872-7245; www.amtrak.com) trains stop at Glenwood Springs Station (☎ 970-945-9563). In Glenwood Springs, you can rent a car through **Enterprise,** 124 W. Sixth St. (☎ 970-945-8360), or **Glenwood Springs Ford-Lincoln-Mercury,** 2222 Devereux Rd. (☎ 877-330-0030 or 970-384-2460). You can also catch a bus (operated by Roaring Fork Transportation Authority) to Aspen; for more information on schedules and fares, contact the **Rubey Park Transit Center** (☎ 970-925-8484; www.rfta.com).

Getting around Aspen

In Aspen, ditch your car and walk or take the bus around this compact city (see the nearby "Aspen" map). Free, regular shuttle buses serve

Aspen

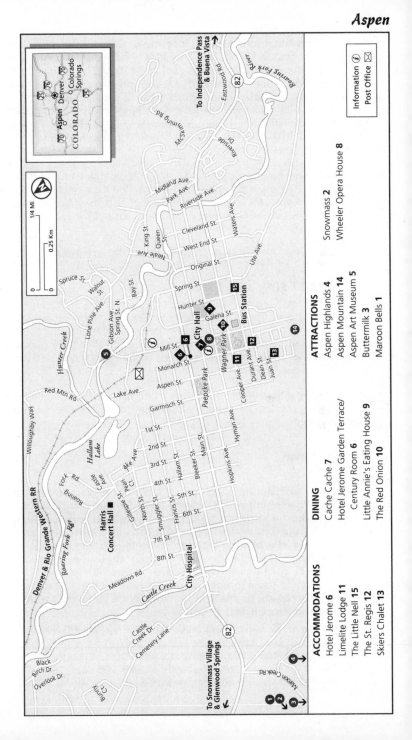

Information ⓘ
Post Office ✉

To Independence Pass & Buena Vista ↑

82

Roaring Fork River

Eastwood Rd.

Riverside Dr.

McSkimming Rd.

Midland Ave.

Park Ave.

Riverside Ave.

Waters Ave.

Cleveland St.

West End St.

Original St.

Ute Ave.

Spring St.

Hunter St.

Galena St.

15

9

City Hall

10

Bus Station

Mill St.

7 8

6 6

ⓘ

6

Monarch St.

11

12

13

5

Cooper Ave.

Durant Ave.

Dean St.

Juan St.

Wagner Park

14

Aspen St.

Papcke Park

Garmisch St.

Hyman Ave.

Hopkins Ave.

Main St.

Bleeker St.

1st St.

2nd St.

3rd St.

4th St.

5th St.

6th St.

7th St.

8th St.

Lake Ave.

ake Ave.

Hallam Ave.

Francis St.

Smuggler St.

North St.

Gillespie St.

Pearl Ct.

Castle Ave.

Roaring Fork Rd.

Harris Concert Hall

Red Mtn. Rd.

Willoughby Way

Hunter Creek

Lone Pine Ave.

Gibson Ave.

Spring St. N.

Bay St.

Spruce St.

Walnut St.

King St.

Queen St.

Neale Ave.

Denver & Rio Grande Western RR

Roaring Fork Rd.

Hallam Lake

Meadows Rd.

City Hospital

Castle Creek

Castle Creek Dr.

Cemetery Lane

82

Black Birch Dr.

Overlook Dr.

Bunny Ct.

Maroon Creek Rd.

To Snowmass Village & Glenwood Springs ↙

4 →

1 2 3 →

1/4 Mi

0.25 Km

Aspen Denver
Colorado Springs
76
25
70
25
COLORADO
70

ACCOMMODATIONS

Hotel Jerome **6**
Limelite Lodge **11**
The Little Nell **15**
The St. Regis **12**
Skiers Chalet **13**

DINING

Cache Cache **7**
Hotel Jerome Garden Terrace/
   Century Room **6**
Little Annie's Eating House **9**
The Red Onion **10**

ATTRACTIONS

Aspen Highlands **4**
Aspen Mountain **14**
Aspen Art Museum **5**
Buttermilk **3**
Maroon Bells **1**

Snowmass **2**
Wheeler Opera House **8**

most popular destinations around Aspen. This includes Aspen Mountain, Aspen Highlands, and Buttermilk ski areas. (Most of the time, rides to Snowmass cost $3 for adults, $2 for kids ages 6 to 16, but during winter, you can take a free skier shuttle during the day.) The local shuttles usually run from around 6 a.m. to 2 a.m. You can also catch rides to far-flung locales such as Carbondale ($5 one-way), Glenwood Springs ($6), and Rifle ($9). A lot of workers reach this parking-deprived community this way. For the latest schedules and fares, stop by the **Rubey Park Transit Center** (☎ 970-925-8484; www.rfta.com), on Durant Avenue between Mill and Galena streets.

 By taking the bus, you can avoid some of the parking challenges around town. Though you can usually find a spot, you have to pay $1 an hour for many downtown spots Monday through Saturday; in other areas, you have to move the vehicle every two hours (or right when you start having fun).

If you need a ride, call **High Mountain Taxi** (☎ 970-925-8294).

Where to stay in Aspen

Over the last 20 years, Aspen has gradually lost most of its affordable lodging. As they opened, the town's big, expensive hotels began sharply discounting their rooms during slow periods, all but wiping out business for the small, cheap motels. As a result, the so-called little guys have closed shop, sold their land, and been replaced by newer and ever-more-expensive hotels.

 If you're on a budget and don't care when you see Aspen, come during late spring and late fall, when you can stay in palatial digs for around $100 a night.

Hotel Jerome
$$$$ Aspen

When he built the Hotel Jerome in 1889, the silver and retail magnate Jerome Wheeler hoped it would rival the famous Ritz Hotel of Paris for luxury. Wheeler seems to have started a trend in Aspen. Nowadays his hotel isn't the only opulent place in town, but it is *the* place if you want your luxury in a historic setting. The hotel's common areas feel more authentic than the rooms do. As you wander these areas, you pass arched hallways, an oak fireplace mantle, tiles colored with gold and cobalt, and the hotel's old paging system and front desk. The 91 guest rooms sport the same feeling of newness as modern luxury units, only with Victorian furniture and eccentric floor plans.

330 E. Main St. ☎ *800-331-7213 or 970-920-1000. Fax: 970-920-2050.* www.hotel jerome.com. *Rack rates: Early Jan–early Apr $600–$635 double, $720–$1,310 suite; early Apr to late May and late Sept to late Nov $255–$290 double, $375–$865 suite; late May to late Sept and late Nov to mid-Dec $460–$495 double, $580–$1,070 suite; mid-Dec to early Jan $835–$870 double, $955–$1,445 suite. AE, DC, DISC, MC, V.*

Limelite Lodge
$$–$$$$ Aspen

If you can afford the rates here, then you can vacation in downtown Aspen. The inn, which has some of the cheapest prices in town, encompasses three motel-style buildings. Don't worry; none is a dump. Rooms are clean and come with refrigerators; a few come with full kitchens. The inn serves a free continental breakfast in a sunny lounge area. The lodge is within walking distance of the gondola at Aspen Mountain.

228 E. Cooper. ☎ **800-433-0832** *or 970-925-3025. Fax: 970-925-5120.* www.limelite-lodge.com. *Rack rates: Apr to mid-Dec $79–$139 double; Christmas week $169–$199 double; New Year's week $290–$349 double; Jan–Mar $169–$299 double. Rates include continental breakfast. AE, DC, DISC, MC, V.*

The Little Nell
$$$$ Aspen

The Little Nell competes directly with The St. Regis for Aspen's ultra-wealthy clientele, but the two hotels have little in common other than luxury. The Little Nell is considerably smaller and more intimate. Owned by the Aspen Skiing Company, it's right at the base of the gondola (which is a short walk away for guests of the St. Regis). It welcomes dogs and even has biscuits at the bell stand. And its rooms, each with a gas fireplace and most with balconies, are generally larger than the ones at the St. Regis. The hotel does not, however, have as many places that invite public lounging, mingling, and star-gazing.

675 E. Durant Ave. ☎ **888-843-6355** *or 970-920-4600. Fax: 970-920-4670.* www.thelittlenell.com. *Jan–Mar $645–$795 double; early–mid-Apr $450–$600 double; mid-May–early June $270–$345 double; early June–Sept $415–$540 double; Oct–late Nov $270–$345 double; late Nov–mid-Dec $450–$600; call for holiday rates. Closed mid-Apr to mid-May. AE, DC, DISC, MC, V.*

The St. Regis
$$$$ Aspen

The St. Regis recently spent $12 million on new décor that one employee described as "Colorado Ralph Lauren." Loosely translated, that seems to mean rocks, leather, wood, rawhide, earth tones, and a higher price tag than "Colorado Wal-Mart." This sprawling luxury hotel, which opens onto splendid views of Aspen Mountain, has everything you'd expect for a small fortune: a swimming pool, spa, health club, enormous bronze sculptures, bellhops, views, a concierge, ultratrendy restaurants, and the occasional celebrity sighting. You can even acquire your own ski butler — someone who will tune your skis, warm your boots, and guide you around the hill.

315 E. Dean St. ☎ **888-454-9005** *or 970-920-3300. Fax: 970-925-8998.* www.stregisaspen.com. *Rack rates: $455–$1,475 double. AE, DC, DISC, MC, V.*

Skiers Chalet
$$$–$$$$ **Aspen**

This budget motel lets you experience the trappings of the old Aspen. Built in 1962 and decorated like a Swiss Chalet, the lodge is right next to the remaining towers on the old Lift 1, which was Aspen's first chairlift and was once the longest lift in America. In the morning, you can easily walk to a modern, functioning chairlift; when you're done skiing, you can glide back to the door. The motel has more character than the Limelite Lodge, but its rooms are darker and older-feeling, and they get noisy when people in ski boots clomp past on the wooden walkways. Ask for a room facing the ski area. It doesn't cost extra, and the views of the skiers and ski hill are spectacular.

233 Gilbert St. ☎ *970-920-2037. Fax 970-920-6504.* www.stayaspensnowmass. com. *Rack rates: $150–$220 double. MC, V.*

Where to dine in Aspen

Within a few square blocks in downtown Aspen are a half-dozen of Colorado's best restaurants — and some of the finest in America. Prices are high, but many gourmet eateries have reasonably priced bar menus, and other places offer early-evening and off-season specials. Choose your spots carefully and you can dine well here without breaking the bank. (Lodging presents the biggest financial challenge in Aspen.)

Cache Cache
$$–$$$ **Aspen**   **FRENCH**

Cache Cache opened with just eight tables 17 years ago and has moved the walls back twice since then. Many locals have been coming here for years when they want a scrumptious meal. Inside the open, relaxed dining area, you can take in the activity around you, study the black-and-white photos of French street life, or simply enjoy the warm colors and candle-light. The offerings include terrines, seafood, meats, and rotisserie-cooked chicken and duck. (Try the rabbit stew.) If you're on a budget, order off the bar menu, which consists entirely of meals costing $12.

205 S. Mill St. ☎ *970-925-3835. Reservations recommended. Main courses: $13–$37. AE, MC, V. Open: Daily 5:30–10:30 p.m. Closed late spring and late fall.*

Hotel Jerome Garden Terrace/Century Room
$$$–$$$$ **Aspen**   **AMERICAN**

For a blowout meal, head for the Hotel Jerome and dine on the Garden Terrace in summer and in the Century Room in winter. Aspen has better-known restaurants than this one and rooms more inviting than the Hotel

Jerome's stodgy Century Room, but no local chef is doing better work than Todd Slossberg. In recent years, Slossberg has twice been nominated by the James Beard Foundation for the honor of "Best Chef in the Southwest." His dishes are symphonies of fresh regional produce and native game such as elk, lamb, and trout. The hotel describes proper attire as "Aspen casual," meaning anything from jeans to furs — and sometimes both.

330 E. Main St. ☎ 800-331-7213 or 970-920-1000. Reservations recommended. Main courses: $24–$38. AE, DC, MC, V. Garden Terrace open May–Sept Mon–Sat 7 a.m.– 2 p.m., Sun 11 a.m.–2 p.m.; daily 5:30–9:30 p.m. Century Room open daily 6–10 p.m.

Little Annie's Eating House
$$ Aspen   AMERICAN

Little Annie's opened its doors in 1972 and has been crammed with customers much of the time since then. During winter, people line up for a chance to eat the restaurant's reasonably priced steaks, salmon, trout, chicken, and burgers. The décor is as all-American as the food: checkerboard tablecloths, wagonwheel lanterns, a yoke, and hundreds of pin flags from golf courses.

*517 E. Hyman Ave. ☎ **970-925-1098**. Reservations not accepted. Main courses: $8–$19. AE, DISC, MC, V. Open: Daily 11:30 a.m.–11 p.m.*

The Red Onion
$–$$ Aspen   MEXICAN

Even if you're not hungry, come here for a beer and a look at the original Brunswick bar, which dates to 1892. Atop the bar, two painted gypsy figures have been perching for even longer than the bar's most devoted patrons. If you dine here, you'll probably sit in a back room that was once a hidden gambling area, surrounded by photos of famous musicians who performed here when the place was a nightclub. The fare consists mostly of Mexican combination plates, and the bar serves unhistoric beverages such as Jell-O shots and Colorado microbrews.

*420 E. Cooper Ave., Aspen. ☎ **970-925-9043**. Main courses: $9–$15. AE, MC, V. Open: Daily 11:30 a.m.–2 a.m. Closed in late Apr and early May.*

Exploring Aspen

In Aspen, you can walk through Victorian neighborhoods left over from the early 1890s, when Aspen was briefly the nation's biggest silver producer. You can attend more high-profile cultural events than in any other mountain town; and you can also escape into some of the tallest and most majestic peaks in the state. To get a well-balanced view of Aspen, do your best to sample each of the town's gifts.

The best things to see and do in Aspen

If you don't feel like spending your day on Aspen's trails, you may enjoy

✔ **Getting the royal treatment.** The 77,000-square-foot **Aspen Club and Spa,** 1450 Crystal Lake Rd. (☎ **866-4VITALITY** or 970-925-8900), has everything you need to exhaust your muscles, including a swimming pool, tennis courts, a large weight room, personal trainers, and group fitness workouts. Afterwards, recover with a massage, a healthy meal, or a treatment at the full-service spa. Three-day club memberships cost $210. No membership is required for the spa.

✔ **Mining for fun.** If you reserve ahead, you can tour two Aspen-area silver mines. One tour goes into the **Smuggler Mine,** 2 miles east of town off Colorado 82, which produced the world's largest silver nugget (1,840 pounds) in 1894 — right after silver lost most of its value. On this 90-minute tour (cost: $22 for adults, $16 for children under 12), you walk 1,200 feet into the mine, usually with a former miner. Tours are conducted by appointment only. Offered on Saturdays during summer, the **Compromise Mine Tour** generates more excitement. You're picked up at your hotel, driven high up Aspen Mountain to the mine entrance, and then are towed more than 2,000 feet underground behind an electric mine-locomotive. The tour takes two hours and costs $32 for adults, $22 for children under 12. Children under 5 are not allowed on either tour. Call ☎ **970-925-2049** for reservations for either tour.

✔ **Visiting the low-rent district.** From Memorial Day through Labor Day, you can go on a guided tour of the mostly abandoned 1890s mining town of **Ashcroft,** 14 miles southeast of Aspen on Castle Creek Road. At 11 a.m. and 2 p.m. daily, one of the ghost town's caretakers will walk you through the eight remaining buildings, including a saloon that's been converted into a museum. The tour costs $3 for ages 10 and over and lasts 20 to 30 minutes. You can also visit the town on your own, free of charge. For more information, call or visit **Heritage Aspen: Aspen's Historical Society,** 620 W. Bleeker St. (☎ **970-925-3721;** www.aspenhistory.org).

If you like Ashcroft, you'll also enjoy the ghost town of **Independence,** 17 miles east of Aspen on Colorado 82.

✔ **Admiring art.** Because Aspen brims with people who have an inordinate amount of wall and floor space — and the means to fill it with fine art — the town has more than 25 galleries, many of which sell museum-quality pieces and even masterpieces. Published by *Aspen Magazine,* the town's *Art Gallery Guide* describes the current galleries and has a map of where to find them. Don't miss the **Aspen Art Museum,** 590 N. Mill St. (☎ **970-925-8050**), which brings world-class art exhibitions to Aspen. The museum is open Tuesday through Saturday from 10 a.m. to 6 p.m.; Sunday from noon to 6 p.m. Admission costs $3 for adults, $2 for students and seniors, and is free for kids under 12.

Wintersköl

Maybe the best time to visit Aspen is the three days of **Wintersköl**, usually in the middle of January. This community love-fest for the season that made it famous incorporates events on all four of the ski mountains, and includes the Canine Fashion Show, the Buttermilk Uphill Race, and the just-like-the-movies Ski Splash, where costumed skiers aim for fame and court the sniffles by launching themselves into a pool of water. There are also fireworks and a parade, but the highlight is definitely the Saturday-night tradition of hundreds of skiers descending Aspen Mountain with torches, which looks like a slow-motion cascade of glowing red lights. It's one of my favorite events of the entire year.

Staying active in Aspen

There are so many ways to pass a day in the mountains near Aspen, it's hard to home in on just a few. The ones listed here are particularly enjoyable:

- ✔ **Cycling:** Hardcore road cyclists should get up early, beat the traffic, and attempt the 4,000-vertical-foot, 20-mile grind to 12,000-foot **Independence Pass.** Other times, consider a more gradual 12-mile climb up the length of the **Maroon Creek Road,** a valley-bottom drive that's closed to most motor vehicles from 8:30 a.m. to 5:00 p.m. daily. If you'd rather avoid cars altogether, you can pedal on paved bike trails throughout the Roaring Fork Valley. The mountain biking is just as much fun — and even more extensive. To rent a bike and obtain area maps, go to **Aspen Velo Bike Shop,** 465 N. Mill St. (☎ 970-925-1495).

- ✔ **Golfing:** At **Aspen Golf Course,** 1 mile west of Aspen on Colorado 82 (☎ 970-925-2145), greens fees are $80 for 18 holes, $45 for 9 holes, with sharply reduced rates late in the day.

- ✔ **Hiking and backpacking:** You can hike straight out of the downtown area, but the most stunning scenery is deep inside the **White River National Forest,** which encompasses the 161,000-acre **Maroon Bells/Snowmass Wilderness Area.** For a fun day in the mountains, visit the ghost town of Ashcroft and then hike the **Cathedral Lake Trail,** located 15 miles southeast of Aspen off the **Castle Creek Road.** The 2.7-mile (one-way) trail climbs 2,000 feet to a small lake. If you want to hike near the two red-brown, pyramid-shaped peaks known as **Maroon Bells,** take a bus ($5.50 adults, $3.50 ages 6 to 16) from the **Rubey Park Transit Center** (☎ 970-925-8484; www.rfta.com) to the end of Maroon Creek Drive and walk 1.8 miles to **Crater Lake.** Backpackers and aggressive hikers sometimes forge onward through the Snowmass/Maroon Bells Wilderness all the way to Crested Butte. Most private vehicles are barred from Maroon Creek Drive between 8:30 a.m. and 5:00 p.m. You can, however, take the drive for a $10 fee between 7:00 and 8:30 a.m. and 5 and 7 p.m. Backpackers and people with disabilities can always drive the road after paying the $10. For maps and information visit the **White River National Forest Aspen Ranger District Office,** 806 W. Hallam St. (☎ **970-925-3445**).

✔ **Horseback riding:** From May 1 through November 15, **Aspen Wilderness Outfitters** (☎ **970-963-0211**) keeps horses in stables at **Snowmass Village** and offers rides ranging from one-hour strolls to multiday trips. Prices start at $40 for one hour. Children under 7 are not allowed.

Hitting the slopes

Lift tickets sold by **Aspen/Snowmass** (☎ **800-525-6200** or 970-925-1220; www.aspensnowmass.com) are good at any of four mountains, linked by a free shuttle system from downtown Aspen. In 2004–05, a high-season, adult, all-day lift ticket cost $74. See the inside back cover for the technical lowdown on each resort.

✔ The low-key mountain for locals is **Aspen Highlands,** an area that boasts some formidable expert terrain and one of the largest vertical drops in the nation. Accessible only by hiking (sometimes with assistance from a Sno-Cat that takes skiers partway to the top) and inbounds at Aspen Highlands, Highland Bowl serves up long, precarious, leg-burning descents, and it also affords stunning views of 14,156-foot Maroon Bells and other immense peaks. If you like skiing steep, classic lines, you need to get to Highland Bowl.

✔ The main advantage to **Aspen Mountain** is its convenience to Aspen's chic downtown area. The Silver Queen Gondola climbs 3,267 vertical feet from the base area in town directly to the 11,212-foot summit. Below the summit, the terrain consists mostly of advanced and intermediate runs — including some steep mogul runs — all of which seem to funnel into gullies brimming with skiers who have a certain élan. If possible, ski this mountain with a local who knows the hidden powder stashes and can steer you away from those gullies. Also, keep in mind that Aspen Mountain has just 673 acres — hardly a lot by Western standards.

✔ **Buttermilk** is a small area catering mostly to beginners. One of its instructors described it as an assembly line churning out new skiers. Former home to the X-Games, Buttermilk also has the largest terrain park at the four resorts. It's more than 2 miles long, with a superpipe for snowboarders and 30 rails.

✔ With 3,010 acres of skiable terrain and the nation's largest vertical drop (4,406 feet), **Snowmass** is the second-largest ski area in the state behind Vail. More than half of its runs are classified as "more difficult" terrain, making Snowmass arguably the single most attractive resort in the state for intermediate skiers.

Shopping in Aspen

Aspen's downtown area is ornamented by designer boutiques with one-word names and cryptic window displays. Every so often the names change, guaranteeing that shoppers can find the very latest of whatever it is that these stores sell.

Meanwhile, at least two Aspen standbys keep doing a brisk business. Since the mid-1970s, **Curious George Collectibles,** 426 E. Hyman Ave. (☎ 970-925-3315), has traded well-preserved relics from the area's recent past — including antique belt buckles, chaps, guns, and native American jewelry. And for over 25 years, **Explore Booksellers,** 211 E. Main St. (☎ 970-925-5336), has carried a thought-provoking selection of contemporary fiction and regional titles. Located in a small Victorian home on Main Street, it has a vegetarian bistro upstairs.

Nightlife in Aspen

For an evening at a historic watering hole that has served cocktails since 1889, try the quietly sophisticated and western saloon–style **J-Bar,** inside the Hotel Jerome, 330 E. Main St. (☎ 970-920-1000).

Among Aspen's top nightspots, **Syzygy,** 520 E. Hyman Ave (☎ 970-925-3700), ranks high with young, high-energy types who appreciate live jazz.

Bentley's at the Wheeler, 328 Hyman Ave. (☎ 970-920-2240), is an elegant English-style pub, good for the older crowd.

And if you want to visit one of the late Hunter S. Thompson's haunts, go to **Woody Creek Tavern,** 0002 Woody Creek Plaza (☎ 970-923-4585), in Woody Creek.

Culture in Aspen

Aspen has been an oasis of culture ever since the 1940s, when an eminent Chicago couple not only bankrolled the first chairlift on Aspen Mountain but also established the Aspen Music Festival and the Aspen Center for Humanistic Studies. Today, the town is particularly rich in classical music, especially from mid-June to mid-August, when the **Aspen Music Festival and School** (☎ 970-925-9042; www.aspenmusic.org) schedules as many as six concerts a day at venues throughout town. The offerings range from free student performances to recitals by virtuosos, for which tickets may cost as much as $65.

Another notable festival is **Jazz Aspen Snowmass** (☎ 970-920-4996; www.jazzaspen.com), which brings top jazz performers to Snowmass Village during June. Herbie Hancock, Roy Hargrove, and Dr. John have performed in recent years. Tickets cost $43 to $48.

From mid-June to late August, you can sit in a partly open tent and take in plays by **Aspen Theater in the Park** (☎ 970-925-9313; www.aspen tip.org). This professional theater company usually does four selections every summer, with tickets costing $30 and $35.

The culture doesn't stop coming in winter. To catch up on happenings in town, stop by the box office inside the **Wheeler Opera House,** 320 E. Hyman Ave. (☎ **970-920-5770;** www.wheeleroperahouse.com). While there, see what film screenings are on tap in the Opera House. **The Wheeler Film Society** (☎ 970-925-5973) regularly screens foreign, independent, and vintage films there. Tickets cost $7.50.

Fast Facts: Aspen

Emergencies

Dial ☎ **911.**

Hospital

Aspen Valley Hospital, 0401 Castle Creek Rd. (☎ 970-925-1120), has a 24-hour emergency room and a Level III trauma center.

Information

You can pick up information in two places in downtown Aspen. The main office for the Aspen Chamber Resort Association is at 425 Rio Grande Place (☎ 970-925-1940; www.aspenchamber.org). The Chamber Resort Association also operates a visitor

center inside the Wheeler Opera House, at Hyman Avenue and Mill Street.

Pharmacy

Carl's Pharmacy, 306 E. Main St. (☎ 970-925-3273), has ample parking and will happily fill your prescription.

Post Office

The main Aspen Post Office is at 235 Puppy Smith Street.

Weather and Road Conditions

Call ☎ 970-920-5454 for the latest road conditions.

The Roaring Fork Valley

The Roaring Fork River wanders northwest from the Continental Divide near Independence Pass to Glenwood Springs, where it empties into the mighty Colorado River. On its way, the Roaring Fork collects water from the Frying Pan River (at Basalt) and the Crystal River (at Carbondale), creating a valley with some of the most spectacular landscapes (and most costly real estate) in the West. As land in Aspen gets more expensive and scarce, the valley has become a defacto suburb for Glitter Gulch, but it has plenty of attractions in its own right: cool mountain towns, glorious vistas, and some of the best trout fishing anywhere.

In the past few years, some of Aspen's millionaires have relocated to the less showy towns of Glenwood Springs and Carbondale, where they're now rubbing elbows with the people who used to wait on them. Each of these towns has a lot going for it.

✔ Back when Aspen residents were still mining silver and not born with it in their mouths, **Glenwood Springs** had already established itself as a world-famous resort. It still has historic hotels, a thriving shopping district, and the largest hot springs pool in the world.

✔ In the past hundred years or so, **Carbondale** profited from coal mining, potato farming, railroads, ranching, and construction; each industry left a mark on this curiously zoned community. The upshot is that it really *is* a community. The townspeople, including many artists and mountain athletes, gather on the town's historic Main Street, which seems relaxed even when most of the Roaring Fork Valley crawls with people.

✔ **Basalt** has profited mightily from the skyrocketing prices of Aspen; notable here is the Frying Pan River, world-renowned for its trout fishing.

✔ The unincorporated community of **Redstone** is the smallest, most remote, and prettiest of the four. Situated on the banks of the Crystal River inside the White River National Forest, it was built around 1900 as a Utopian town for coal miners. Across from a row of historic brick coke ovens is the Craftsman-style Redstone Inn, once a lodge for the unmarried miners. Redstone Castle, a Tudor mansion where the mine's owner once lived, sits atop a grassy hill a mile up the road from the inn.

Getting there

Interstate 70, the Colorado River, and busy railroad tracks all rush down the same corridor through the heart of **Glenwood Springs.** It's 169 miles west of Denver and 84 miles east of Grand Junction. **Carbondale** is 12 miles southeast of Glenwood Springs via Colorado 82. **Basalt** is 20 miles past Carbondale on 82, and **Redstone** is another 17 miles south of Carbondale on Colorado 133. To reach Aspen from Carbondale, continue east for another 30 miles on Colorado 82.

Amtrak (☎ **800/872-7245;** www.amtrak.com) trains stop twice daily in Glenwood Springs Station (☎ **970-945-9563**).

In Glenwood Springs, you can rent a car through **Enterprise,** 124 W. Sixth St. (☎ **970-945-8360**), or **Glenwood Springs Ford,** 2222 Devereux Rd. (☎ **877-330-0030** or 970-384-2460).

If you want to fly closer than Denver International Airport, your best bet is **Vail/Eagle County Airport** (☎ **970-524-9490;** www.eaglecounty.us/airport), 31 miles east of Glenwood Springs on I-70. See Chapter 19 for information on flights and rental cars at that airport. You can arrange a shuttle from Eagle County into Glenwood Springs (cost: $46.50) through **Colorado Mountain Express** (☎ **800-525-6363** or 970-926-9800; www.cmex.com).

Getting around

Many locals in Carbondale, Glenwood Springs, and Aspen use buses to travel between towns. The **Roaring Fork Transit Authority** (☎ 970-925-8484; www.rfta.com) serves all three communities, but not Redstone, which has a year-round population of under 100, so you'll have little trouble getting around. To get to Aspen from Glenwood Springs, it costs you $6 one way. Service runs from about 6 a.m. to midnight.

Inside Glenwood Springs proper, **Ride Glenwood Springs** offers bus service between Wal-Mart, in the south part of town, and Roaring Fork Marketplace at the town's west end, for $2 per day. There's ample parking at the ends of town, so this service comes in handy when the downtown lots fill up. The bus usually runs daily from 7 a.m. to 10 p.m. Call ☎ 970-945-2575 to find out more about stops and schedules.

Where to stay

If you stay in Glenwood Springs or Carbondale when skiing Aspen, you can choose between clean family-run motels, chain hotels, and historic digs, usually for about $100 to $200 less per night than you'd pay for a comparable spot in you-know-where. And you save on meals, too. As for Redstone, it's in its own universe, one that I'm dying to revisit soon. You only have a few options there, but they're good ones.

Best Western Aspenalt Lodge
$ Basalt

This is where my family traditionally stays when we visit the Roaring Fork Valley; its low prices and proximity to darn near everything make it the perfect base for almost any excursion in the region. The rooms are spare and furnished with McHotel-style decorations, but they're plenty comfortable, and you can fall asleep to the sounds of the rippling Frying Pan River right outside your door. There's also an outdoor hot tub, open winter and summer.

157 Basalt Center Circle. ☎ *800-528-1234 or 970-927-3191. Fax: 970-927-2921. Rack rates: Winter and summer $85–$120 double, fall and spring $60–$80 double. AE, DC, DISC, MC, V.*

Hotel Colorado
$$$–$$$$ Glenwood Springs

Once one of America's preeminent resorts, this 1889 hotel lost some of its luster when it was converted to a Naval Hospital during World War II. (Its size and proximity to a train station made it an ideal location.) Yet it still has character, partly because of its perch on a hillside above Glenwood Springs's Hot Springs Pool, originally part of the hotel grounds. Styled after an Italian palace, it also has courtyard gardens, two original fireplaces, grand staircases, and a sunny sitting area. The rooms, which are clean and comfortable, have some of the quirks you'd expect at a historic hotel: There's no air-conditioning, and the hot water can be as unpredictable as Amtrak. But I still savored being here.

526 Pine St. ☎ *800-544-3998 or 970-945-6511. Fax: 970-945-7030.* www.hotel colorado.com. *Rack rates: $139–$452 double. AE, DC, DISC, MC, V.*

Redstone Inn
$–$$$ Redstone

I love old Arts and Crafts–style lodges in remote locations, and the Redstone Inn may be my favorite anywhere. It was built by steel and coal baron John Osgood, who was the fifth richest man in America in the early 1900s. Osgood envisioned — or at least advertised — a Utopian community for his coal miners. In 1904, the inn and the surrounding buildings offered miners a theater, dining room, changing area, reading room, electricity, and hot and cold running water. The inn still has a four-sided clock tower just like the ones in European mountain villages. Today, the miners have been replaced by tourists who oversleep, swim, lift weights, play tennis, hike, and fish — all this on or near the grounds of the inn. The property also has two restaurants and a bar. During summer, the dining room and guest rooms fill up far in advance, so be sure to reserve ahead. The inn also manages tours of Osgood's mansion, the nearby Redstone Castle.

82 Redstone Blvd. (18 miles south of Carbondale on Colorado 133). ☎ *800-748-2524 or 970-963-2526. Fax: 970-963-2527.* www.redstoneinn.com. *Rack rates: $46–$155 double; $110–$220 suite. AE, DISC, MC, V.*

Thunder River Lodge
$ Carbondale

This lodge offers basic motel rooms for a reasonable price. Not counting telephones and televisions, the most noteworthy amenity is an unlimited supply of free ice cubes — enough, even, to fill coolers. You'll love the prices, especially if you use copious amounts of ice cubes and also take advantage of ski packages that let you stay here and ski Aspen for just a few dollars more than the price of lift tickets. (Call the inn or visit the inn's Web site for information on ski packages.) All the rooms are pleasant, but I prefer the upstairs ones, which were added in 1999 and still feel brand-new.

179 Highway 133. ☎ *970-963-2543.* www.thunderriverlodge.biz. *Rack rates: $40–$70 double. AE, DISC, MC, V.*

Where to dine

Of the three communities, my favorite place to eat is Carbondale. It has one exceptional restaurant and several good ones, and you can usually find a table right away. Most Glenwood Springs restaurants don't take reservations, and they fill up fast on summer nights.

If you're in Glenwood Springs during July, avoid eating during the 7 p.m. crunch. If you're staying in Redstone, be sure to reserve a table at the Redstone Inn ahead of time, because you don't have many dining options in this community.

Glenwood Canyon Brewing Company
$–$$ Glenwood Springs   PUB FARE

Like most Colorado brewpubs, this one has hardwood floors, high ceilings, ceiling fans, and glass partitions exposing brewing vats (presumably to remind you that the beer wasn't, in fact, brewed by Schlitz). And, as at the other breweries, this one offers salads, sandwiches, pasta, steaks, and some tasty brews. The unique selections here are the soups in bread bowls. My favorite is the Wisconsin cheddar cheese beer soup, which tastes just right after a day on the slopes, especially when washed down with a Shoshone stout.

402 Seventh St. ☎ 970-945-1276. Reservations for large groups only. Main courses: $5.95–$17. AE, MC, V. Open: Sun–Thurs 11 a.m.–11 p.m., Fri–Sat 11 a.m. to midnight.

Juicy Lucy's
$$ Glenwood Springs   STEAKS AND SEAFOOD

Juicy Lucy's is a rarity among Colorado's upscale restaurants — a place where you can picture in advance what your food is going to look like. Entrees include grilled fresh Atlantic salmon, three lamb chops with mint jelly, and chopped sirloin steak with mushroom gravy, as well as steaks of different heft. Top it off with any of 22 wines available by the glass. You eat in a pleasant, historic dining room with split-bamboo floors, copper light fixtures, and a ceiling of molded plaster.

308 Seventh St. ☎ 970-945-4619. Reservations not accepted. Main courses: $12–$29. MC, V. Open: Daily 11 a.m.–9:30 p.m. Closed Nov.

Sapphire Grill
$$ Glenwood Springs   ITALIAN GRILL

Because Sapphire Grill is in an inconspicuous upstairs spot, you can often walk in and get a table when other Glenwood Springs restaurants are jammed. Another plus is that the chef loves garlic. After eating the bulb of roasted garlic that comes with your home-baked bread, order the escargot in garlic butter as an appetizer. Follow it with linguine with spicy garlic shrimp sauce. The Sapphire also serves grilled steaks, salmon, and pork chops, as well as a popular rack of ribs. The dessert list, entirely garlic free, includes homemade tiramisu and crème brûlée.

710 Grand Ave. ☎ 970-945-4771. Reservations accepted. Entrees: $10–$20. AE, MC, V. Open: Daily 5–9:30 p.m.

Six89 Main Kitchen and Wine Bar
$$$ Carbondale   WORLD CUISINE

In 2002, the chef here cooked a meal at the James Beard House in New York, putting this Carbondale eatery in the ranks of America's finest. Yet the place still feels easygoing. Servers in loose-fitting, patterned shirts deliver delicacies such as herb-crusted chicken and apricot-mustard barbeque pork tenderloin without fanfare. The restaurant's sommelier, who loves to fly-fish, offers tips on wines as casually as he may discuss lures during off-hours. On clear summer nights, the patio opens and seating doubles, so you can sometimes walk right in and get a table.

689 Main St. ☎ 970-963-6890. Reservations accepted. Main courses: $16–$25. AE, MC, V. Open: Daily 5:30–10 p.m.

Village Smithy
$ Carbondale   ECLECTIC

Since 1975, the Village Smithy has been Carbondale's spot to enjoy an extended breakfast. Its omelets, pancakes, smoothies, and sunny patio seating have probably cut into the town's productivity, but no one around here seems to mind. At lunch, the restaurant serves big salads, soups, sandwiches, and South-of-the-Border fare. You can eat in an old blacksmith's shop or on the patio, which stays open, thanks to the miracles known as space heaters, even during winter.

26 S. Third St. ☎ 970-963-9990. Reservations not accepted. Main courses: $3–$10. MC, V. Open: Daily 7 a.m.–2 p.m.

White House Restaurant and Bar
$ Carbondale   PIZZA, PASTA, AND BARBEQUE

Despite having an Italian version of Uncle Sam on its menu, the White House seems to belong in New England more than it does in Washington, D.C., Italy, or, for that matter, Colorado. Its low ceilings, intimate barroom, and friendly servers call to mind those East Coast village taverns where everyone thinks they know your name. A locals' favorite in Carbondale, the White House serves above-average pizzas and calzones. Its wine list consists entirely of $10, $12, and $16 bottles.

801 Main St. ☎ 970-704-9400. Reservations accepted Mon–Thurs only. Main courses: $7.75–$11; pizzas: $10–$20. DISC, MC, V. Open: Daily 4–10 p.m.; Fri–Sun 11:30 a.m.–1 p.m.

Zocalito Latin Bistro
$$ Carbondale   SPANISH/SOUTH AMERICAN

Zocalito's chef and owner, Michael Beary, used to cook French food in Aspen. Then his cooking went south — to Guatemala, southern Mexico, and Spain. Now he uses hard-to-find South American ingredients to flavor seafood, beef, pork, and chicken. In the dining room, masks and festival costumes hang on pumpkin-colored walls, and panels of stamped glass sit atop the dividers between the booths.

568 Colorado 133. ☎ *970-963-6804. Reservations accepted. Main courses: $18–$20. AE, MC, V. Open: Tues–Sun 5–10 p.m.*

Exploring Glenwood Springs, Carbondale, and Redstone

Glenwood Springs has endless activities for families. Redstone is an attraction unto itself, especially for historians looking for well-preserved relics from the early 1900s. And Carbondale is the place to get away from tourist attractions, relax, and enjoy being in the mountains.

The best things to see and do

In the Hot Springs Pool, Glenwood Springs has one of the best kid-friendly attractions in Colorado. If you're hurtling down I-70 past Glenwood Springs, make sure to get off the freeway and soak.

Glenwood Caverns

On this tour, you ride a bus up a winding road onto a hillside high above Glenwood Springs and then go deep inside mountain caves. Some of these caverns opened as a tourist attraction known as Fairy Caves in the late 1800s and early 1900s. The operation closed in 1917, and reopened in 1998. The two-hour family tours visit the original Fairy Caves, where many formations have been damaged, and then continue on into two newly opened rooms with nearly pristine formations. These rooms, known as The Barn (for its size, the second largest in Colorado) and Kings Row (for its perfectly preserved stalactites and stalagmites) make this tour a winner. The family tour requires participants to climb 100 stairs, but the three- to four-hour Wild Tour is even harder. It requires you to wear a headlamp and crawl on your hands, knees, and belly in order to squeeze into caves far off the beaten path. It's an unforgettable adventure for families with teenagers.

508 Pine St., Glenwood Springs. ☎ *800-530-1635 or 970-945-4CAV.* www.glenwood caverns.com. *Family-tour admission: $17 adults, $12 children 3–12, under 3 free. Wild Tours: $50 per person; you must be 13 or older to go. Open: Daily 9 a.m.–4 p.m. in May; daily 9 a.m.–5 p.m. June–Oct.*

Hot Springs Pool

At Glenwood Springs's famous Hot Springs Pool, the natural hot spring pools are so huge and hold so many people, that it can take a while to get used to the sheer mass — and believe me, I mean *mass* — of humanity. But you can still have fun. You can swim in a 400-by-100-foot, 90-degree pool, which has lap lanes and diving boards, or soak in a 100-by-100-foot therapy tub, kept at around 104 degrees. Two 300-foot-long waterslides spin you and then send you skittering across a watery run-out. My favorite time to soak is on winter nights, when you can watch the steam rise in something like solitude. As for the pool's history, the Ute Indians once soaked here, but the first official pool was built in 1888.

401 N. River Road, Glenwood Springs. ☎ *800-537-SWIM or 970-945-6571.* www.hot springspool.com. *Admission: Summer $13.50 adults, $8.50 children 3–12; rest of year $11.50 adults, $7.50 children 3–12. Open: 7:30 a.m.–10 p.m. in summer, 9 a.m.– 10 p.m. rest of year. Closed several days each year for maintenance; call for dates.*

Yampah Spa and Vapor Caves

Like the nearby Hot Springs Pool, the vapor caves are fed by 125-degree geothermal springs. Instead of soaking, however, you descend into rock-walled rooms sculpted out of actual caves, sit on marble benches, and inhale the steamy air, which is hottest in the rooms farthest underground. The caves' detractors find the rooms, the air, and the company all a bit too close. But if you enjoy steam baths, you'll love this place. For over a century, a variety of cures and treatments have been offered in the building above the caves, and today a modern spa sells massages, facials, and wraps.

709 E. Sixth St., Glenwood Springs. ☎ *970-945-0667.* www.yampahspa.com. *Vapor-cave admission: $12 (includes one towel); 2-day pass $19.50. Open: Daily 9 a.m.–9 p.m.*

Staying active

Four rivers that flow from towering peaks all meet in this area, providing great boating and fishing. If the water doesn't keep you entertained, you can always climb high into the mountains.

✔ **Fishing:** The Crystal River passes through Redstone and then empties into the Roaring Fork River near Carbondale. The Roaring Fork, in turn, drains into the Colorado River near Glenwood Springs. All have their share of trout, but you have to make sure not to trespass when you go after them. To find out the rules, contact the **Colorado Division of Wildlife,** 50633 U.S. 6 and 24, Glenwood Springs (☎ **970-947-2920**). The **Taylor Creek Fly Shop,** 183 Basalt Center Cir., Basalt (☎ **970-927-4374**), can set you up with tackle and guide you to the best waters.

✔ **Biking and hiking:** The **Glenwood Springs Chamber Resort Association,** 1102 Grand Ave., publishes a free **Trails Guide** to the Glenwood Springs area. Your options include long Forest Service roads, narrow mountain paths, and the 16-mile, paved **Glenwood Canyon Path,** which has stretches right alongside I-70 but also branches off and follows the Colorado River. You can bike up the Glenwood Canyon Path starting at the east end of Sixth Avenue, right next to Yampah Vapor Caves in Glenwood Springs. Because of the proximity to the freeway, it's a better choice for cyclists than for hikers. If you want to take a quick hike or ride in **Carbondale,** park your car in the lot north of the intersection of Colorado 133 and Colorado 82. The trailhead for the **Red Hill System** is about a quarter-mile up the obvious dirt road, on your left. It's less than a half-mile from the trailhead to **Mushroom Rock,** which has views of the surrounding valley. You can go farther by completing one of several possible loops through the area, on trails that are equally popular among hikers, advanced mountain bikers, and dogs.

The **White River National Forest Supervisor's Office,** 900 Grand Ave., Glenwood Springs (☎ 970-945-2521), oversees seven wilderness areas, including the nearby **Maroon Bells–Snowmass** wilderness. The office can provide maps and information on the area hikes as well as on the forest trails near Redstone.

✔ **Golfing: The Ranch at Roaring Fork,** at 14913 Highway 82, Carbondale (☎ **970-963-3500**), has the cheapest greens fees in the Roaring Fork Valley: $15 for 9 holes. **Glenwood Springs Golf Club,** 0193 Sunny Acres Rd., West Glenwood Springs (☎ **970-945-7086**), charges $19 for 9 holes, $29 for 18. Many other courses in the valley are private, with greens fees running up to $250.

✔ **Rafting:** Local raft companies offer half- and full-day trips on the Roaring Fork and Colorado rivers. In this area, neither river makes for a scary trip, but each has enough whitewater to entertain an average American family. **Whitewater Rafting,** 2000 Devereux Rd., Glenwood Springs (☎ **800-993-7238** or 970-945-8477; www.colorado whitewaterrafting.com), can set up a trip for you.

Hitting the slopes

It's hard *not to* like small ski areas such as **Sunlight Mountain Resort** — places with dirt parking lots, roaming dogs, and base areas that seem to belong on *That '70s Show.*

A few of the advantages to **Sunlight** (☎ **800-445-7931** or 970-945-7491; www.sunlightmtn.com) are: A $36 lift ticket, the cheapest in Colorado; equally cheap digs in nearby Glenwood Springs; and free rides (check for the schedule) to and from town in Sunlight's colorfully painted school bus. The ski instructors and the lift attendants greet each other by name, and they'll probably greet you, too. Sunlight's 460 acres include some serious steeps, challenging glades, and an abundance of intermediate runs. Best of all, Sunlight bundles its vacation packages with the world-famous Hot Springs Pool in Glenwood Springs, so that après-ski soaking is included in the cost. If this mountain doesn't relax you, the springs will. If you want to look at the technical data for the resort, see the inside back cover.

Shopping

Carbondale's Main Street has some fun boutiques and galleries. Make sure you stop at **Kahhak Fine Arts and School,** 411 Main St. (☎ **970-704-0622**). The school's proprietor, Majid Kahhak, uses the same studio to teach, create, and sell spontaneous art he calls *essence painting.*

Glenwood Springs has a thriving shopping district along Grand Avenue, just south of the bridge over the Colorado River. One worthwhile stop: **Summit Canyon Mountaineering,** 732 Grand Ave. (☎ 800-360-6994), which sells gear, clothing, coffee, books, and maps.

Redstone has a number of small galleries and boutiques, some of which are in historic cottages once reserved for miners.

Nightlife

A quarter-century ago, the **Black Nugget,** 403 Main St., Carbondale (☎ 970-963-4498), was a notoriously rough bar that catered mostly to coal miners. Today, it's a friendly locals' hangout, with live music Wednesday through Saturday nights year-round. Smoking is allowed only in a back room. In Glenwood Springs, head for the **Glenwood Canyon Brewing Company,** 402 Seventh St. (☎ 970-945-1276), which I review in the "Where to dine" section earlier in this chapter.

Fast Facts: The Roaring Fork Valley

Emergencies

Dial ☎ 911.

Hospital

Valley View Hospital, 1906 Blake Ave., Glenwood Springs (☎ 970-945-6535), has 24-hour emergency care. It's off 19th Street, one block east of Colorado 82.

Information

The Glenwood Springs Chamber Resort Association (☎ 970-945-6589; www. glenwoodsprings.net) has a visitor center at 1102 Grand Ave. For information on Carbondale and Redstone, visit the Carbondale Chamber of Commerce, 569 Main St. (☎ 970-963-1890; www. carbondale.com).

Pharmacy

In Carbondale, you can fill your prescriptions at City Market,1051 Hwy. 33 (☎ 970-963-5727). In Glenwood Springs, go to Downtown Drug, 825 Grand Ave. (☎ 970-945-7987).

Post Office

The Glenwood Springs Post Office is at 113 Ninth St. The Carbondale Post Office is at 655 Main St. Call ☎ 800-275-8777 for hours and other information.

Weather and Road Conditions

Call ☎ 970-920-5454 for the latest road conditions.

Chapter 21

Steamboat Springs

● ●

In This Chapter

▶ Discovering the town and resort of Steamboat Springs
▶ Cowpoking at some classic western Dude ranches

● ●

*T*ourism has long since overtaken ranching as the top industry in and around Steamboat Springs, and new developments continue to crop up on subdivided ranchland. Yet the town still values its cows and cowboys. The town, which markets itself as "Ski Town, USA," has always been as proud of its Western hospitality as it is of the many skiers it has sent to the Winter Olympics.

Of course, it's not a perfect marriage. The area has two different neighborhoods, each with its own personality. The base area of Steamboat Ski Area feels like a modern-day, megaski area such as Vail, with immense hotels, fine restaurants, expensive boutiques, and homes the size of airport terminals. A few miles northwest of the ski area, along U.S. 40, sprawls the redbrick Western town of Steamboat Springs. Here, bike shops and microbreweries share the main drag with Western stores such as F.M. Light and Soda Creek Outfitters. Next to a skate park, across from a network of mountain-bike trails, there's a historic rodeo ground. This older part of town is my favorite — it's a place where a visitor can enjoy the best of both the old and the new West.

Getting There

Steamboat Springs is 158 miles northwest of Denver, 194 miles east of Grand Junction, and 335 miles east of Salt Lake City. If you're driving from Denver, take I-70 68 miles west to Silverthorne, then take Colorado 9 38 miles north to Kremmling. In Kremmling, turn west on U.S. 40 and go 52 miles to Steamboat Springs. If you're coming from the west on I-70, exit at Rifle and go 88 miles north on Colorado 13 to Craig. In Craig, head east on U.S. 40 for 42 miles to Steamboat Springs. Coming from the northwest, you can take I-40 all the way from Park City, Utah, to Steamboat, a distance of about 300 miles.

During winter, **Yampa Valley Regional Airport** (☎ **970-276-3669**), 25 miles west of Steamboat Springs off of U.S. 40 (near Hayden), has daily nonstop service to Denver (on United Express), Dallas-Fort Worth (American), Houston (Continental), Minneapolis-St. Paul (Northwest), Chicago (American), and Newark (Continental).

Upon landing, you can rent a car through **Avis** or **Hertz.** For information on contacting individual airlines and car-rental agencies, see the appendix. **Alpine Taxi** (☎ **800-343-7433** or 970-879-2800) offers round-trip ($44 per adult) and one-way ($27 per adult) shuttle service between the airport and Steamboat Springs. Call ahead for a reservation.

Getting Around

Steamboat Springs Transit (☎ **970-879-3717**) provides free bus service between Steamboat Springs and Steamboat Ski Area. The buses run every 20 minutes during peak hours. From mid-April to mid-December, the buses run from 7 a.m. to 10:45 p.m. The hours are even longer during the ski season.

If you miss the last bus, call **Alpine Taxi** (☎ **800-343-7433** or 970-879-2800) for a lift.

Steamboat Springs is easy to figure out (see the nearby map, "Steamboat Springs"). Most of the activity is along **Lincoln Avenue,** a stretch of U.S. 40. Lincoln Avenue runs northwest and southeast through town, paralleling the Yampa River, which borders the town on the southwest side. A series of numbered streets (3rd through 13th) cross U.S. 40, with the highest numbers being farthest north and west. Across the Yampa River from the downtown area are the town's rodeo grounds, skate park, and softball fields, as well as the historic Howelsen Hill Ski Area.

About 2 miles southeast of downtown, around the base of the ski area, developments feature hotels, condos, luxury homes, and shopping plazas. Most of the buildings are larger and newer than the ones downtown. To reach the ski area base, go about 2 miles southeast of downtown on U.S. 40, then turn east on Mount Werner Road and follow the signs.

Where to Stay

You can save by staying in Steamboat Springs's downtown area and taking the free shuttle to the mountain. On the outskirts of town along U.S. 40 are newer, chain hotels. The downtown has older but well-maintained motels. I like the downtown area's Western feel and reasonable prices. Bear in mind, however, that a motel along U.S. 40 in downtown Steamboat is hardly a retreat to nature. The highway was built extra-wide to accommodate cattle drives, and it holds a lot of traffic at times. The largest, most luxurious hotels are clustered around the base of the mountain.

Steamboat Springs

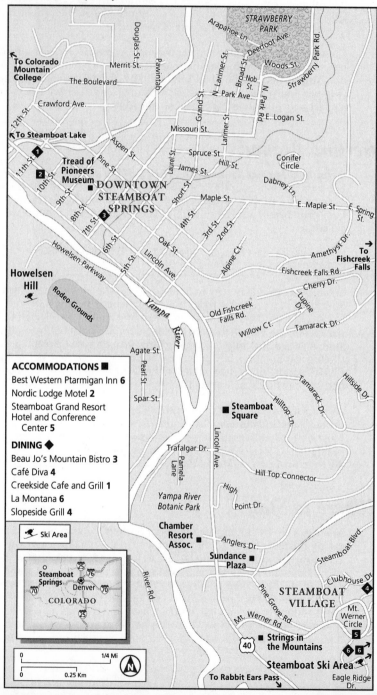

ACCOMMODATIONS ■
Best Western Ptarmigan Inn **6**
Nordic Lodge Motel **2**
Steamboat Grand Resort Hotel and Conference Center **5**

DINING ◆
Beau Jo's Mountain Bistro **3**
Café Diva **4**
Creekside Cafe and Grill **1**
La Montana **6**
Slopeside Grill **4**

🎿 Ski Area

0 _____ 1/4 Mi
0 _____ 0.25 Km

Best Western Ptarmigan Inn
$–$$$$ **Mountain Village**

This ski-in, ski-out hotel at the base of Steamboat Mountain predates the days when luxury hotels dominated the base areas of ski resorts. Built in 1969 (with an addition in 1979), it could as easily be alongside Interstate 80 in Illinois as at Steamboat Ski Area. The smallish basic rooms have gray and tan furnishings. An elevator connects the four levels, but most people just use the stairs. You don't have to dodge any bellhops. (Sometimes, when you ring the front-desk bell, no one hops, period.) But you can ski straight into and out of the hotel, get free newspapers and Internet access, and eat reasonably priced fare at the hotel restaurant. It's cool.

2304 Apres Ski Way. ☎ *800-538-7519 or 970-879-1730.* www.steamboat-lodging.com. *Rack rates: $79–$129 double. Closed mid-Apr–May 24. AE, DC, DISC, MC, V.*

Nordic Lodge Motel
$–$$$ **Downtown Steamboat Springs**

When I asked the front-desk person about this motel's age, she shrugged, said she didn't care and instead offered me a beer. It was the kind of pretzel logic that makes guidebook-writing fun — and dangerous. As it turned out, this lodge, in downtown Steamboat Springs, was built in 1960 but fully refurbished in 2001. Most of the lodge is one story in height, so you can usually lug your belongings straight into your room. The room itself will be clean and comfy, with a small refrigerator and microwave. It will also be convenient to downtown restaurants and shops.

1036 Lincoln Ave. ☎ *800-364-0331 or 970-879-0531. Rack rates: Spring, summer, and fall $44–$75 double; winter, $75–$125 double. AE, DISC, MC, V.*

Steamboat Grand Resort Hotel and Conference Center
$$–$$$$ **Mountain Village**

Developed by the New England–based American Skiing Company, this hotel at the base of Steamboat Ski Area has a stylish Western veneer. The lobby area has waterfalls, cozy leather armchairs, and a flagstone chimney that towers nearly three stories above a gas fireplace. With 328 guest rooms and suites, the Grand is as big as its name and offers more than its share of luxuries, including two restaurants, a fitness center, a spa, a swimming pool, concierge services, and an ardent crew of bellhops. Accommodations start with Deluxe Parlor rooms, each with a full kitchen, dining area, and queen-size sofa sleeper. One caveat: The walls are thin and the noise level pretty high for a hotel in this price range.

2300 Mount Werner Circle. ☎ *877-269-2628 or 970-871-5500.* www.steamboatgrand.com. *Rack rates: Early Apr to late Dec $155–$175 double; Christmas week $339–$475 double; early Jan to early Apr $194–$233 double; President's Day weekend, $299–$419. AE, DC, DISC, MC, V.*

Ranch life

To fully experience Steamboat culture, consider spending some time at a ranch. You can choose among several different experiences, which appeal to different types of vacationers. Choose the one that best fits your style.

Independent types, who prefer to use a ranch as a home base, should head for **Dutch Creek Guest Ranch at Steamboat Lake,** 25 miles northwest of Steamboat Springs on Colorado 62 (☎ **800-778-8519** or 970-879-8519; www.dutchcreek.net). This guest ranch offers accommodations in log cabins or A-frames — both have kitchens — and you're free to enjoy your days as you please. You can try your hand at horseback riding (for an additional fee), Ping-Pong, and horseshoes, or curl up by a fire with some hot cocoa and a copy of *Colorado & the Rockies For Dummies*. Rates, which include breakfast, for the more desirable log cabins run $150 to $175; the A-frames cost $105 to $130.

If you prefer an **all-inclusive experience,** try the **Home Ranch,** 54880 County Rd. 129 (☎ **970-879-1780;** www.homeranch.com). In summer and fall, you have to decide between guided hiking, fly-fishing, or horseback riding. Later on, you can soothe your aching muscles in the pool, sauna, or hot tub. The lodge schedules lots of kids' activities, so you can leave the young ones behind — or not. And after the family-style dinner, join a campfire sing-along or adjourn to your luxuriously appointed room. Accommodations are in cabins and lodge rooms, and prices vary according to how large and luxurious your digs are, but no matter what you choose, you're going to pay big bucks. Prices drop in winter, when you shell out only for your room and your breakfast. Summer and fall double-occupancy rates for seven nights run $4,780 to $5,640; add $1,785 for each additional person. Winter nightly double-occupancy rates (two-night minimum stay required) run from $400 to $500, plus $175 per night for each additional person.

For a true **working vacation,** head for **Saddleback Ranch,** 37350 County Rd. 179 (☎ **970-879-3711;** www.saddlebackranch.net). You can't stay overnight at this 7,000-acre working cattle ranch, but you're welcome to help out with chores. From June through mid-September, you can help round up, move, and tend the ranch's 800 mother cows. Mostly, however, you just ride alongside the cowboys and watch them work. Each ride lasts about four hours, and kids have to be at least 8 years old to go along. Come evening, you can also go for a 1½-hour dinner ride, capped off with a meal of chicken, steak, or fish. The cattle drive costs $65 per adult, $60 per child; a dinner ride is $49 adults, $39 per child.

Where to Dine

Steamboat has more than a few first-rate restaurants and many others providing tasty food at reasonable prices. There are more choices downtown, but my two favorites are at the base of the ski area.

Beau Jo's Mountain Bistro
$$ **Downtown** **PIZZA**

Don't feel like driving to Idaho Springs (see Chapter 12) for Colorado's best après-ski pizza? Don't! Just head over to this new location and find all Beau Jo's crazy toppings, piled high. All the normal pizza toppings are here, plus some exotic ones; soups and salads are also featured. Remember to save your crusts; that bottle of honey on the table is for drizzling over the rich homemade dough and eating as a prelude to (or replacement for) dessert. The beer list is excellent.

704 Lincoln Ave. ☎ *970-870-6401. Reservations not accepted. Pizzas: $10–$25. AE, DISC, MC, V. Open: Daily 11 a.m.–9 p.m.*

Café Diva
$$$ **Torian Plum Plaza** **NEW AMERICAN**

Every night, Café Diva's small staff creates a special experience for diners near the base of Steamboat Ski Area. Both owners are sommeliers, and the chef came here from one of Manhattan's hottest restaurants. Together, they've created the best all-around dining experience in Steamboat Springs. The menu changes seasonally, but you can always order a few standbys. Start with crab and tomato bisque, then, for an appetizer, get the Cajun crab cakes in Creole remoulade. Finish with the elk tenderloin and roasted-garlic mashed potatoes in veal brown sauce. The experience is especially nice in summer, when you can dine on a patio with mountain views.

1875 Ski Time Square Dr. (in Torian Plum Plaza across from Terry Sports). ☎ *970-871-0508. Reservations recommended. Main courses: $16–$35. AE, DISC, MC, V. Open: Daily 5:30–10 p.m.*

Creekside Cafe and Grill
$–$$ **Downtown** **AMERICAN/ECLECTIC**

Creekside Cafe serves three meals most days, but I come here in the morning for the Legendary Creekside Benny's, usually known as eggs Benedict. Creekside serves eight variations on the dish, ranging from *traditional* (poached eggs, English muffin, hollandaise sauce, and black forest ham) to *Yampa* (with smoked trout and tomatoes instead of ham). The staff can be distracted, the coffee is strong, and the creek-side patio gets just the right amount of sunlight. In other words, this is the perfect ski-town breakfast joint. At lunch, the Creekside switches to a diverse menu that includes falafels, gyros, sandwiches, wraps, burgers, and salads. The dinner menu consists mostly of pasta dishes.

131 11th St. ☎ *970-879-4925. Reservations for dinner only. Main courses: $7–$20. MC, V. Open: Daily 7 a.m.–2 p.m. (lunch menu available Tues–Sun only); Wed–Sun 5–9:30 p.m.*

La Montana
$$–$$$ Steamboat Base Area   SOUTHWESTERN/MEXICAN

It's easy to see why this is one of the most acclaimed Southwestern restaurants in Colorado. An old-style tortilla roaster works overtime, throwing heat across the bar patrons and wafting the scent of warm dough throughout the restaurant. One dining room has immense prints of nature photographs taken by the owner; the other room displays masks and traditional Mexican art. It's worth a trip here just to dip a fresh tortilla chip in the tomatillo-and-avocado salsa. The menu has Tex-Mex dishes and fajitas, but there are also creative, gourmet entrees such as coriander tofu with toasted quinoa in black-bean reduction sauce, and grilled elk loin with a cilantro pesto crust.

2500 Village Dr. (off of Apres Ski Way). ☎ *970-879-5800. Reservations recommended. Main courses: $12–$28. AE, DISC, MC, V. Open: Winter daily 5–10 p.m.; summer Tues–Sat 5:30–9:30 p.m.*

Slopeside Grill
$–$$ Torian Plum Plaza   GRILLED ITEMS, PIZZA, PASTA

This is one of those places where the walls seem to be vying with the menu for the title of "Most Eclectic Item on Display." The walls flaunt old signs, ice skates, skis, snowshoes, photos, bridles, and saddles, among other items. Not to be outdone, the menu features everything from peanut butter and jelly sandwiches to *salciccia Ricardo* (red and green bell peppers roasted in olive oil and garlic with Italian sausage and served over fresh fettuccini). You can also buy several flavors of dog food, but only if you and your four-legged friend are on the patio. Best of all, Slopeside offers 11 kinds of handmade pizza for under $10 each, and it keeps serving those pizzas at reduced prices after 10 p.m. in winter, 9 p.m. in summer.

1855 Ski Time Square Dr. (at Steamboat Ski Area base). ☎ *970-879-2916. Reservations suggested. Main courses: $6.45–$17. AE, DISC, MC, V. Open: Daily 11 a.m.–2 a.m.*

Exploring Steamboat Springs

The Yampa Valley has over 150 hot springs, produced by geothermal activity. In Steamboat, soak in the springs first and then figure out the rest of your itinerary — if there *is* a rest of your itinerary. Later on, time permitting, you can shop, absorb history, ride a horse, or pursue almost any kind of recreation known to man (or woman!).

The best things to see and do
First get the soaking out of the way. You can

    ✔ **Soak and exercise.** Kids love the **Steamboat Springs Health and Recreation Center** (☎ 970-879-1828), where the waters are perfect for kinetic young people and adults pursuing active lifestyles.

Located at the east end of town on Lincoln Avenue, this community hub has hot mineral pools (98°–102°), an 82-degree lap pool, a wading pool, and a waterslide, not to mention a weight room, tennis courts, snack bar, and playground. The springs stay open year-round even though they're outdoors. They're open Monday through Friday from 5:30 a.m. to 10:00 p.m., Saturday and Sunday from 8 a.m. to 9 p.m. Admission costs $7.50 adults; $5 students 13 to 17; $3.50 kids 3 to 12 and seniors over 61. The waterslide costs $5 for ten rides, $3 for five rides.

✔ **Soak and — what's exercise?** The **Strawberry Park Hot Springs** (☎ 970-879-0342; www.strawberryhotsprings.com) have little in common with the Health and Recreation Center. Privately owned, they're in a remote, forested canyon and cater mostly to adults who like sitting still in beautiful places. The park has four terraced rock pools, each fed by a mixture of 147-degree mineral water and icy creek water. After sunset, kids are no longer allowed, and the adults may remove their suits. The place is informal: You buy your tickets outside and change in a tipi. There are no lights, so a small flashlight comes in handy after dark. You can camp here or rent a rustic cabin. The road to the springs is rough and often unsuitable for two-wheel-drive vehicles. Call the springs before attempting the drive in winter, no matter what you're driving, but don't pass up a chance to soak here. It's located 7 miles north of town at the end of County Road 36. (Turn east on Seventh Street and follow the signs.) Weekdays before 5 p.m. it costs $5 for adults, $3 for children under 18. Weekdays after 5 p.m., weekends, and holidays it costs $10 for adults, $5 for kids under 18. It's open daily from 10:00 a.m. to 10:30 p.m.

Other things to see and do

When you're done soaking, you can further stimulate your senses by

✔ **Hitting the rodeo.** You can immerse yourself in cowboy culture at the pro rodeos held every Friday and Saturday night from mid-June through August at Romick Arena. The arena is at the base of Howelsen Hill, on the opposite side of the Yampa River from downtown Steamboat Springs. (Use Fifth Street to cross the river.) Live country music kicks off the festivities at 6 p.m., followed by the rodeo, including bull riding, at 7:30 p.m. The cost is $11 for adults, $6 for ages 7 to15, with kids 6 and under free. Call ☎ 970-879-0880 to find out more.

✔ **Treading through the past. The Tread of Pioneers Museum,** 800 Oak St. (☎ 970-879-2214), has the usual artifacts from Victorian life, some of which are displayed in a 1908 Queen Anne–style home. It also has some stunning historic photographs of Native Americans, an exhibit on skiing in Steamboat, and a videotape of a historic hotel burning down. Cost is $5 for adults, $4 for seniors over 62, and $1 for children under 12. It's open Tuesday through Saturday from 11 a.m. to 5 p.m.

Especially for kids

A few places in Steamboat are especially fun for kids:

✔ During summer at **Howelsen Hill,** 845 Howelsen Parkway (☎ 970-871-1104), you can ride a chairlift and then descend 400 vertical feet on the **Alpine Slide.** Howelsen Hill is located across the Yampa River from downtown Steamboat Springs, via Fifth Street. One ride costs $8 for ages 13 and over, $7 for children 7 to12, and $1 for children 3 to 6. It's open June through September on weekdays from 11 a.m. to 6 p.m., and weekends from 10 a.m. to 6 p.m.

✔ A short walk from the alpine slide, check out the town's **skate park** next to Howelsen Hill and the rodeo grounds. It's free and open to the public.

✔ At the base of **Steamboat Ski Area** (☎ 970-871-5252), you (or your kids) can dangle from bungee cords while bouncing on the trampoline. The setup allows people to safely flip, and flip, and flip. The cost is $6 for two minutes. There's also a climbing wall (two climbs for $6).

Staying active

Steamboat may not have the "best" ski area, the "best" mountain biking, the "best" fishing, or the "best" whitewater, but if you want a well-rounded recreation scene, it may be, well, the best. No matter what you want to do, Steamboat has something for you. While you're here, think about:

✔ **Boating:** During years when a lot of snow has fallen, the Yampa River and its tributaries offer some of the most turbulent whitewater in North America. Even if your boat is a half-inflated car inner tube, you're still in luck — certain stretches of the Yampa are so mellow and civilized, you could call AAA to fix a flat. One prime tubing zone starts right in downtown Steamboat Springs. To float the Yampa through town, go to **Backdoor Sports,** at the corner of Ninth and Yampa (☎ 970-879-6249). Rent a tube for $12; and start your 2-mile float trip down the river right there. For people who are more serious about the water, **Backdoor Sports** also gives six-hour kayak lessons for $90, after which you'll be ready to float some of the milder whitewater.

✔ **Golfing:** Picture a golf course with bottomless bunkers, rolling fairways, thick roughs, and lots of water. If the course you imagine is in Scotland and not in hell, then you should go play a round at **Haymaker,** 32500 U.S. 40 (☎ 970-870-1846). Modeled after top Scottish courses, the 18 holes are surrounded by undeveloped land, making the experience even more pure. Greens fees are $79 from June 8 through September 22, $54 after 4:30 p.m. The rest of the season, 18 holes cost $54 at all times. There's also a driving range on the premises.

✔ **Hiking:** On Steamboat Ski Area, your basic easy-to-find hiking trail is the **Thunderhead Trail,** which starts near the base of the Silver Bullet Gondola and climbs 2,180 feet over 3 miles to its terminus at the upper gondola station. The uppermost portions, which skirt rock outcroppings and drift through aspen groves flecked with wildflowers, are the most scenic. To save energy, you can ride the gondola up (cost: $15 adults, $10 kids 13 to 17, and $6 kids 5 to 12) and then hike down.

The most stunning trails near town are at **Fish Creek Falls** (☎ 970-879-1870). For a short hike and picnic, walk ⅛ mile to the falls overlook, where you can sit at picnic tables and watch the falls thunder 165 feet downhill through a mossy gorge. To get closer to the water, take the lower trail (as opposed to the one to the overlook) ¼ mile to the base of the falls. You can continue hiking on this trail and make a 2½-mile (one-way), 1,600-vertical-foot ascent to **Upper Fish Creek Falls.** The trailheads start 4 miles east of town on County Road 32, inside the Routt National Forest. Cost is $3 per vehicle.

Serious hikers and backpackers should drive north of Steamboat Springs and to the edge of the **Mount Zerkel Wilderness Area,** which encompasses parts of the Sawtooth, Park, and Sierra Madre mountain ranges. For more information and maps of this area, go to the **Medicine Bow–Routt National Forest Office,** 925 Weiss Dr., Steamboat Springs (☎ 970-879-1870).

✔ **Horseback riding:** A number of area ranches offer horseback riding. If you want to ride in a pretty spot at the edge of Steamboat Springs, head for **Sombrero Ranches.** Located next to the rodeo grounds at the base of Howelsen Hill, Sombrero Ranches offers one-hour ($25) and two-hour ($40) rides on Emerald Mountain, as well as breakfast ($40) and dinner ($45) excursions by reservation only. Call ☎ 970-879-2306 for more information, or go right to the stables by crossing the river at Fifth Street.

✔ **Mountain biking:** You can access **Steamboat Ski Area's** 50-mile trail system near the base of the Silver Bullet Gondola, or you can start 2,180 feet higher up by riding the gondola (cost: $23 adults, $18 kids 13 to 17, and $14 kids 5 to 12). You can pick up a map of the trails at the base of the resort. There's also prime riding on **Emerald Mountain,** across the Yampa River from the downtown area. Cross the river at 13th Street, then look for the single track trail. The single track meets a rugged road that climbs steadily for 1,550 vertical feet over 3 miles to the top of 8,250-foot Quarry Mountain. This area is warmer than Steamboat Ski Area, so consider hitting it in early morning or late afternoon. The staff at **Sore Saddle Cyclery,** 1136 Yampa St. (☎ 970-879-1675), rents mountain bikes ($35 per day) and town bikes ($15 per day) and can tell you more about area trails. Sore Saddle also sells state-of-the-art titanium bike frames made locally by **Moots Cycles** (☎ 970-879-1676).

Hitting the slopes

Like the town of Steamboat Springs, **Steamboat Ski Area** (☎ 970-879-6111; www.steamboat.com) prides itself on being friendly. Former Olympic medalist Billy Kidd, now the resort's Director of Skiing, often guides complimentary mountain tours, and Nelson Carmichael, the bronze medalist in mogul skiing in the 1992 Winter Games, schedules free bump-skiing clinics for the public. As for the terrain, Steamboat's 2,939 acres make it the third largest area in the state, behind Vail and Snowmass. The 20 lifts efficiently move skiers, and the 142 trails tend to follow fall-line paths down the four linked mountains. More than half the runs are designated as intermediate, so mid-level skiers will relish being here. Advanced skiers will love threading their way through the mountain's seemingly endless aspen glades, which become especially enticing after the resort receives some of its famous dry powder. Beginners have fewer options, since only 13 percent of the terrain is for novices. Still, this is easily one of the top ski areas in the state.

More than 50 Olympians have trained at **Howelsen Hill Ski Area** (☎ 970-879-4300), a winter sports center in Steamboat Springs. At 90 years and counting, this is the oldest continuously operating ski area in Colorado, good for a listing on the National Register of Historic Places. Most visitors come here for the night skiing, but Howelsen Hill also has ski jumps, Nordic trails, and a half-pipe course for snowboarders. The hill hosts about 75 competitions every winter. On most days, it's also open to the public. By Western standards, it's puny — come here for the night skiing, the Nordic trails, or the history. If none of these attracts you, you're better off at Steamboat Ski Area.

For more about both of these resorts, check out the inside back cover.

Shopping

F.M. Light & Sons, 830 Lincoln Ave. (☎ 970-879-1822), has sold Western clothing in Steamboat since 1905. The store has a huge selection of Lee and Wrangler jeans, Stetson hats, and cowboy boots, plus knives, oiled coats, and even stick horses. **Soda Creek Outfitters,** 335 Lincoln Ave. (☎ 970-879-3146), has Western goods that, if anything, are more traditional than the selections at F.M. Light. If, for whatever reason, you ever wanted chaps, spurs, or a new (or used) lasso, this is the store for you.

Nightlife and culture

Slopeside Grill (☎ 970-879-2916), across from the Sheraton in **Ski Time Square,** serves gourmet pizzas at discounted rates after 10 p.m. Slopeside also offers live entertainment every afternoon during ski season and on Sunday afternoons in the summer.

Not far away is the town's hottest club, **Level'z,** 1860 Ski Time Square Drive (☎ 970-870-9090), which has a sprawling dance floor and live entertainment nightly, usually in the form of DJs but sometimes featuring nationally known bands. Cover charges vary. Bands also groove at **The Tugboat Grill and Pub** (☎ 970-879-7070), also located at Ski Time Square. The town's best sports bar is **The Tap House,** 729 Lincoln Ave. (☎ 970-879-2431).

Every summer for the past 15 years, Steamboat's **Strings in the Mountains** music festival has attracted dozens of famous folk, as well as bluegrass, country, world, and classical musicians to a tent near the base of the ski area. Recent performers include Leonard Slatkin, Garrison Keillor, the Colorado Symphony, and Asleep at the Wheel. For more information on Strings in the Mountains, call ☎ 970-879-5056 or surf the Internet to www.stringsinthemountains.org.

Fast Facts: Steamboat Springs

Emergencies
Dial ☎ 911.

Hospital
Yampa Valley Medical Center, 1024 Central Park Dr. (☎ 970-879-1322), has 24-hour emergency service and plenty of experience treating injured knees.

Information
Steamboat Springs Chamber Resort Association runs a visitor center at 1255 S. Lincoln Ave. (☎ 970-879-0880; www.steamboatchamber.com).

Pharmacy
Lyon's Corner Drug & Soda Fountain, 840 Lincoln Ave. (☎ 970-879-1114), can fill your prescription and sell you homeopathic remedies to boot.

Post Office
The Steamboat Springs Post Office is located at 200 Lincoln Ave. Call ☎ 800-275-8777 for hours and other information.

Road Conditions
Call ☎ 877-315-7623 for the latest road conditions.

Chapter 22

Gunnison, Crested Butte, and the Black Canyon

In This Chapter

▶ Finding great skiing and even better mountain biking

▶ Visiting the darkest, deepest canyon in Colorado

*T*his rough and rugged part of Colorado is seldom visited by casual travelers, but it holds some of the best outdoor adventure in the state. The land begins its transition from the peaks and valleys of the High Country to the plateaus of the Great Basin here. The terrain is steep (which makes for great skiing), and the dramatic changes in elevation produce wonders such as the Black Canyon of the Gunnison. Even if you're not looking to get off the grid entirely, these valleys and canyons are far enough removed from civilization to elevate your soul and restore your spirit. And you may have a little fun, too.

Gunnison and Crested Butte

Home to Western States College, **Gunnison** is a low-slung ranching town with a historic Main Street and, around its perimeter, a sprawl of gun stores, liquor stores, motels, and restaurants. It sits in a broad ranching valley at the confluence of the Gunnison River and Tomichi Creek. If you travel more than a few miles to the north or south of town, the scenery gets even better. Eight federally designated wilderness areas are within easy driving distance. In the Elk range to the north, Crested Butte boasts world-class mountain biking, a famously steep ski area, and colorful high-alpine basins.

Getting to Gunnison and Crested Butte

During winter, **Gunnison Crested Butte Airport** (☎ 970-641-2304) has nonstop service to and from Houston on **Continental Airlines.** You can fly to and from Denver year-round on **United Airlines** (see Chapter 11 for details on flying into Denver). **Avis, Budget,** and **Hertz** all have desks at the airport. For information on contacting individual airlines and car-rental agencies, see the appendix.

Alpine Express Shuttle Service (☎ **800-822-4844** or 970-641-5074; www.alpineexpressshuttle.com) provides round-trip transportation between the airport and Crested Butte for $51 per person. There's no taxi service in Gunnison, but some lodges will pick you up at the airport.

The main highway through this area is U.S. 50, which extends all the way from Pueblo, 161 miles east of Gunnison, to Grand Junction, 126 miles to Gunnison's northwest. To reach **Crested Butte,** take Colorado 135 north from Gunnison for 28 miles. Keep going another 3 miles north to reach the ski area, in an area known as Mt. Crested Butte.

Getting around

If you plan on visiting this region, you'll need a car, though in Crested Butte you can survive without one. Crested Butte's free **Mountain Express** (☎ **970-349-7318**) shuttles link downtown **Crested Butte** with **Mt. Crested Butte,** 3 miles to the north. During summer and winter, the buses run from around 7:30 a.m. until 11:30 p.m., with service at least every 20 minutes during peak hours. **Mountain Express** observes a more relaxed schedule in spring and fall. The shuttles can accommodate both bicycles and wheelchairs. Call **Crested Butte Town Taxi** (☎ **970-349-5543**) if you still need a ride.

In Crested Butte, Colorado 135 enters town from the south, becomes Sixth Street and continues to Mt. Crested Butte as Gothic Road. Elk Avenue, the main road through the Crested Butte historic district, intersects Sixth Street in the heart of the downtown area. In Gunnison, U.S. 50 travels east and west through town as Tomichi Avenue. Dozens of businesses are on Tomichi Avenue, but the heart of the downtown is Main Street (Colorado 135), which goes north off Tomichi as Colorado 135.

Deciding where to stay

The most expensive rooms in this area, during winter at least, are at Mt. Crested Butte, at the base of Crested Butte Mountain Resort. The town of Crested Butte costs a few dollars less than Mt. Crested Butte, and Gunnison costs much less.

Cristiana Guesthaus
$–$$ Crested Butte

Completed in 1962, this was the first lodge built expressly for skiers coming to Crested Butte. Today, its low rates still attract avid mountain athletes. The guests usually rise early; consume the strong coffee, cereals, and homemade pastries included with their room rate; and then leave for the day. When, hours later, they finally return to this Swiss-style lodge, they gather and socialize by the fireplace, on the large sundeck, in the television area (the rooms don't have TVs), or in the hot tub. All told, the place has a communal spirit that you seldom find at a lodge. The only drawbacks are the small rooms and a few spots where the building shows its age.

621 Maroon Ave. ☎ *800-824-7899 or 970-349-5326. Fax: 970-349-1962.* www. cristianaguesthaus.com. *Rack rates: Spring, summer, and fall $60–$80 double; winter $75–$95 double. Rates include breakfast. AE, DISC, MC, V.*

Grand Lodge Crested Butte
$$–$$$$ Mt. Crested Butte

This hotel's sturdiness, height (five stories), shops, and attentive employees call to mind a big-city hotel that caters to business travelers. One look out the window, however, and you'll happily remember that you're at the base of Crested Butte Mountain Resort, with the chairlifts just a few yards away. Though the hotel has a restaurant, a coffee shop, and room service, its rooms also have in-room refrigerators, coffeemakers, and microwaves (in the suites only), so you won't feel locked into paying for expensive services. This is one of my favorite luxury hotels near a ski area. It's all business, and the business is skiing.

6 Emmons Rd. ☎ *888-823-4446 or 970-349-8000. Fax: 970-349-8050.* www.grand lodgecrestedbutte.com. *Rack rates: May–Nov $90–$195 double, Dec–Apr $110–$290 double. AE, DC, DISC, MC, V.*

Wildwood Motel
$ Gunnison

To really experience Gunnison (and perhaps Crested Butte) on the cheap, stay at this 1928 motel, located in a parklike setting just outside downtown Gunnison. The rates here top out at $94 during summer; in winter, you can often get a room with a full kitchen for three days for $100. The winter prices make this place a steal if you want to ski for cheap. The rooms are worn around the edges but clean, and they're individually decorated, sometimes in vintage furnishings. Outside, cottonwood trees shade the spacious dirt parking lot and grassy barbeque areas. You can also rent an RV site here, at rates ranging from $17 to $22 per day.

1312 W. Tomichi. ☎ *970-641-1663. Fax: 970-641-7044.* www.wildwoodmotel.net. *Rack rates $55–$94 double. DISC, MC, V.*

Dining in Gunnison and Crested Butte

Garlic Mike's
$$ Gunnison ITALIAN

Mike Busse's credentials as a chef of Italian food are impeccable: New Jersey native, Italian heritage, and culinary school in Atlantic City. Factor in his warm demeanor, and you have a big reason why this is regularly voted the best restaurant in Gunnison by readers of a local publication you've probably never heard of. Look for Mike's specialties, marked by the little garlic-bulb icons on the menu. The best may be the veal with prosciutto, mozzarella, and Madeira wine. During summer, you can dine on a large deck overlooking the Gunnison River.

2674 N. Hwy. 35 (2 miles north of Gunnison). ☎ *970-641-2493. Reservations accepted. Main courses: $10–$24. AE, MC, V. Open: Daily 5–10 p.m.*

Pitas in Paradise
$ Crested Butte   MEDITERRANEAN

The folks behind the counter at Pitas in Paradise dish up cheap, healthy, tasty food faster than you can get through the first article in the town's tabloid newspaper. For under $7, you can get a wrap or pita sandwich crammed with vegetables, rice, and sometimes meat. The choices are mostly Greek, but a Thai wrap (vegetables in a blend of curry and coconut) and a Bombay wrap (creamy spinach sauce with Indian flavors, tofu, vegetables, and ginger) number among the popular offerings. For dessert, have a milkshake or a smoothie. Free Internet access is provided for customers.

214 Elk Ave. ☎ *970-349-0897. Reservations not accepted. Main courses: $5.95–$8.95. MC, V. Open: Daily 11 a.m.–9 p.m.*

The Slogar Bar & Restaurant
$$ Crested Butte Plain   OLD AMERICAN

At the Slogar, your only choices are the best skillet-fried chicken you've ever tasted or a 10-ounce rib-eye steak. Along with your entree, you receive relishes, tomato chutney, sweet-and-sour cole slaw, mashed potatoes, creamed corn, and baking-powder biscuits with honey butter. The servers even throw in some home-style ice cream. One of the owners says the staff needed three years to get the menu down, but for the past 14 years or so everything has run smoothly.

Corner of Second and Whiterock. ☎ *970-349-5765. Reservations recommended. Set meals $14 adults; $7.45 children 2–12. MC, V. Open: Daily 5–9 p.m.*

Soupçon
$$$ Crested Butte   FRENCH

Soupçon occupies a tiny 1916 Miner's Cabin, holds only 30 people, and has just two seatings nightly — at 6 and 8:15 p.m. The menu is about as small as the building: six starters and seven main courses, plus a few dessert choices scratched onto a chalkboard in the dining room. What's huge is the flavor. You'd be hard pressed to find more tender meats than the sashimi tuna, Hudson Valley foie gras, and double-cut grilled lamb chops. And the chef prepares them perfectly. Don't miss this restaurant.

127 Elk Ave. (in the alley behind Kochevar's bar). ☎ *970-349-5448. Reservations requested. Main courses: $21–$38. AE, MC, V. Open: Daily 6–10 p.m.*

Exploring Crested Butte and Gunnison

Most of the best things in this area are outside in the mountains, but there's also a lot of human history in each town. Even if you're not a mountain person, you'll find plenty to do.

The best things to see and do

When you're not in the wilderness surrounding the Gunnison Valley, you can check out one of these museums:

✓ In 2003, the **Crested Butte Mountain Heritage Museum** (www. crestedbuttemuseum.org) and the **Mountain Bike Hall of Fame** (☎ **800-454-4505** or 970-349-1880; www.mtnbikehalloffame.com) opened in their new, permanent location inside an old gas station at 331 Elk Ave. Supplementing the obligatory silver-mining exhibits are displays on more recent local industries such as coal mining and skiing. The Mountain Bike Hall of Fame has trend-setting mountain bikes and the racing jerseys, bikes, and bios of the sport's legends. A $2 donation is suggested; the museum and hall of fame are open daily from noon to 7 p.m.

✓ The **Gunnison Pioneer Museum,** on East Highway 50 in Gunnison (☎ **970-641-4530**), has artifacts and memorabilia scattered through eight buildings, including a 1905 schoolhouse and an 1876 post office. A long-standing institution, this museum costs $7 for adults, $1 for children 6 to 12. It's open Memorial Day through mid-September, Monday through Saturday from 9 a.m. to 5 p.m. and Sundays noon to 4 p.m.

Staying active in Gunnison and Crested Butte

The immense mountains around Crested Butte naturally challenge visitors. This is the place to bike longer trails, ski steeper runs, and catch bigger fish than you ever have. Just don't stretch yourself too far when you're:

✓ **Boating and sailing:** Just west of Gunnison along U.S. 50, the Gunnison River has been dammed three times inside the **Curecanti National Recreation Area** (☎ **970-641-2337**). If you like water sports, get off the highway near **Blue Mesa Reservoir,** the largest and most user-friendly of the three reservoirs — and, incidentally, the largest body of water in Colorado. Blue Mesa Reservoir stretches for 20 miles along the road and has three breezy main basins that are perfect for sailing and windsurfing. Marinas are located at **Elk Creek** (☎ **970-641-0707**), along U.S. 50 midway between the reservoir's west and east ends; and at **Lake Fork** (☎ **970-641-3048**), off U.S. 50 at the west end of the reservoir. The **visitor center** is also at Elk Creek. Before launching a motorboat or a Colorado State–registered boat, you'll need to pay $4 for a two-day user fee. As for swimming, it's the usual reservoir fare: cold water, rocky shores, and no beaches. The recreation area has numerous first-come, first-served campgrounds, with most sites costing $10.

✔ **Fishing:** Near Gunnison you can fish from a raft, rowboat, lakeshore, or streambed. In the **Curecanti National Recreation Area,** federal and state hatcheries stock over 3,000,000 fish every year. Along with brown trout, **Blue Mesa Reservoir** has Kokanee salmon and some immense lake trout. It's a good place for trolling. On the **Gunnison River,** you can spin-fish from a raft for some formidable trout. There's also premier fly-fishing in the **Gunnison, East,** and **Taylor** rivers, among others.

A one-day Colorado fishing license costs $5.25, a five-day license goes for $18.25. To find the best fly-fishing in this area or to get a fishing license, contact **High Mountain Outdoors,** 115 S. Wisconsin St., in Gunnison (☎ **800-793-4243** or 970-641-4243).

✔ **Golfing: The Club at Crested Butte,** 385 Country Club Dr. (☎ **800-628-5496** or 970-349-6131), is one of Colorado's top mountain courses. Greens fees for this 18-hole, Robert Trent Jones course range from $65 to $120, depending on the time of year and the time of day.

✔ **Hiking:** Waterfalls, flower-flecked alpine basins, and immense, craggy cirques surround the trails in the mountains above Crested Butte and Lake City. Some of these trails remain snow-covered until midsummer. During peak snowmelt periods, they may require dangerous (or at least very cold) creek crossings. But what exciting places to get your feet wet! The visitor centers in all three towns can identify popular hikes. For topographical maps and updates on trail conditions, stop at the **Gunnison National Forest Gunnison Ranger District** office, 216 N. Colorado St. in Gunnison (☎ **970-641-0471**). The rangers can tell you about eight wilderness areas, including ones near both Crested Butte and Lake City.

✔ **Mountain biking:** Along with Fruita (see Chapter 23), Crested Butte has some of the most acclaimed mountain biking in North America. Besides the quick and easy rides next to town, you can pedal on an extensive network of single-track and forest roads high in the Elk Mountains.

One legendary ride, **The 401 Trail** via Gothic Road, has a long, snaking single-track descent through hip-high vegetation and flowers — but first, you have to climb to Schofield pass. Before embarking on this 24-mile, advanced ride, stop at **The Alpineer,** 419 Sixth St. (☎ **970-349-5210;** www.alpineer.com), for a detailed trail description and, if needed, a rental bike. When it's too snowy to ride near Crested Butte, you can sometimes pedal on 40 miles of trails at **Hartsman's Rock,** near Gunnison. This arid area has a mixed bag of surfaces, including slickrock, sand, and some craggy, technical stretches. **Tomichi Cycles,** 104 N. Main St., in Gunnison (☎ **970-641-9069**), can tell you more about it and rent you a bike.

Hitting the slopes

Crested Butte Mountain Resort (☎ 800-810-SNOW; www.crested butteresort.com) sits on the flanks of Mt. Crested Butte, an ominous, 12,162-foot shark's tooth that would look right at home in either of two Steven Spielberg movies (*Jaws* or *Close Encounters of the Third Kind*). The mountain appears no less forgiving up close. Its north side has some of the scariest lift-served terrain in the country, including steep glades, steeper chutes, and jagged cliffs. If you want to test your mettle in areas that require you to pass through gates, consult a ski patroller first or sign up for one of the ski school's guided **North Face Tours.** The upshot for everyone else is that this terrain is safely removed from the rest of the runs. While experts tangle with the likes of **The Headwall, Banana Funnel,** and the **North Face,** beginners can tackle **Peanut** and **Yellow Brick Road.** Intermediates can glide down the long groomed slopes and forgiving mogul runs on the mountain's northwest side. Anyone who likes to ski or snowboard will have fun here, but, for talented riders, this is a special mountain. Check out the inside back cover for more on the resort.

Enjoying the nightlife

Being a ski town, Crested Butte has a vigorous party scene during winter. Start your journey on Elk Avenue between Second and Third streets.

- ✔ **Crested Butte Brewery,** 226 Elk Ave. (☎ 970-349-5026), serves handcrafted beers, including the award-winning Red Lady Ale.

- ✔ At **The Eldo,** 215 Elk Ave. (☎ 970-349-9958), you can look out the windows while dancing to live music (a sure-fire way to please your date).

- ✔ Go to **The Last Steep,** 208 Elk Ave. (☎ 970-349-7007), for late-night munchies.

- ✔ For more subdued socializing (not to mention single-malt scotches), head for the **Princess Wine Bar** (☎ 970-349-0210) at 218 Elk Ave.

Fast Facts: Gunnison and Crested Butte

Emergencies

Dial ☎ **911.**

Hospitals

For 24-hour emergency care, go to Gunnison Valley Hospital (☎ 970-641-1456), 711 North Taylor in Gunnison. The Crested Butte Medical Center (☎ 970-349-0321) operates smaller clinics in Crested Butte, at the Ore Bucket Building ½ block north of the Visitors Center on Sixth Street, and in Mt. Crested Butte, in the Axtel Building, at the base of the Silver Queen Chairlift.

Information

In Crested Butte, call or write the Crested Butte-Mt. Crested Butte Chamber of Commerce, P.O. Box 1288, Crested Butte, CO 81224 (☎ 800-545-4505 or 970-349-6438;

www.crestedbuttechamber.com). Or visit the Information Center at the corner of Sixth Street and Elk Avenue or at the Town Center Bus Stop in Mt. Crested Butte. In Gunnison, visit the Gunnison Country Chamber of Commerce, 500 E. Tomichi Ave. (☎ 800-274-7580 or 970-641-1501; www.gunnison-co.com).

Post Office

In Gunnison, the post office is at 200 N. Wisconsin (☎ 970-641-1884). In Crested Butte, go to 215 Elk Ave. (☎ 970-349-5568).

Road Conditions

Call ☎ 877-315-7623.

Black Canyon of the Gunnison National Park

One of the most dramatically beautiful places in the West is the Black Canyon of the Gunnison, where the Gunnison River has cleaved downward for 2,000 feet into a tableland known as Black Mesa. Because the canyon is deeper than it is wide, little sunlight reaches the river. This lack of light, along with the dark walls of Precambrian gneiss (a hard rock formed during a geologic age more than 543 million years ago), makes the canyon mysterious and awe-inspiring. Even if you're just driving by on the way to someplace else, it's worth an hour's stop to peek over the edge near the visitor center.

Getting there

In winter, **Montrose Regional Airport** (☎ 970-249-3203) has daily service to and from Dallas/Fort Worth (on **American**) and Houston (on **Continental**); frequent service to and from Denver (on **United Express**) and Phoenix (on **America West Express**); and Saturday-only service to and from Newark (on **Continental**). During summer, you'll probably have to fly into Grand Junction (see Chapter 23). **Budget, Dollar, National,** and **Thrifty** all have rental desks at the airport. For information on contacting individual airlines and car-rental agencies, see the appendix.

From Grand Junction, the Black Canyon is a gorgeous 75-mile drive southeast on U.S. 50. If you're coming from the east, you can take U.S. 50 all the way from Pueblo, 200 miles away, where the highway dead ends at I-25. If you're coming from the northeast on I-70, get off in Glenwood Springs and follow Colorado 82 south for 12 miles toward Aspen, then take Colorado 133 south to Carbondale. Keep going on Colorado 133 for 90 miles southwest to Delta. This is an exquisite drive. From the south, pick up U.S. 550 in Durango and take it north for 108 miles to Montrose, then take U.S. 50 10 miles east to the canyon.

Where to stay

You can visit the Black Canyon easily from Gunnison or Crested Butte, but the nearby towns of **Montrose** and **Delta** have a number of chain hotels and a few bed-and-breakfasts. In Montrose, there's the **Best Western Red Arrow,** 1702 E. Main St. (☎ 970-249-9641); the **Comfort Inn,** 2100 E. Main St. (☎ 970-240-8000); the **Holiday Inn Express,** 1391

S. Townsend Ave. (☎ **970-240-1800**); and the **Days Inn,** 1655 E. Main St. (☎ **970-249-3411**). In Delta, try the **Best Western Sundance Motel,** 903 Main St. (☎ **970-874-9781**), or the **Comfort Inn,** 180 Gunnison River Dr. (☎ **800-228-5150** or 970-874-1000). During the summer, expect to pay between $70 and $130 per night (double occupancy) for these accommodations.

Exploring the park itself

In the Black Canyon, the Gunnison River falls farther over the course of 48 miles than the Mississippi does over 1,500. Because it had gravity working in its favor, the water was able to saw downward through some of the earth's basement rocks — including incredibly hard gneiss. Because this rock is so hard, rainfall has caused little erosion around the river, and few side canyons have formed. The result is a gorge that's much narrower (as little as 1,300 feet) than it is deep (up to 3,000 feet). Along the river, far below the rims, ponderosa pines cling to rocky shores above the steep, thundering river, but in many places the canyon walls are too steep to hold much vegetation.

Black Canyon of the Gunnison National Park encompasses 15 of the most spectacular miles of the Black Canyon. During late spring, summer, and fall, you can visit either canyon rim. During the warm-weather months, I recommend doing the extra driving, including a few miles on dirt roads, to reach the North Rim. Far fewer people go there, and because the canyon walls are nearly vertical on that side, you can look almost straight down at the river. Being just 7 miles north of U.S. 50 via paved roads, the South Rim can be a quick hit, but it's more crowded and slightly less spectacular.

Here are a few ways to enjoy either rim:

- ✔ **Visit the rangers.** On the South Rim, you can easily spend a half-hour perusing the displays at the modern, full-service Visitor Center (open daily 8 a.m. to 6 p.m. June through September; 8:30 a.m. to 4 p.m. the rest of year). The rangers there can answer your questions about the park. On the North Rim, the Ranger Station is the closest thing to a visitor center. Sometimes there's even a ranger around.

- ✔ **Take a scenic drive.** This is an enjoyable activity on either rim and should take only about an hour. The five overlooks on the North Rim are more stunning (some might say scary) than the twelve South Rim viewpoints. However, the road on the South Rim is paved; the North Rim has gravel roads.

- ✔ **Hike on the rim.** On the North Rim, you can choose between two scenic rim trails. Near the North Rim Campground, there's a short, easy ⅓-mile loop known as the **Cedar Point Nature Trail.** If you're inclined to exercise, I'd skip the Cedar Point Trail and instead walk 3½ miles (round-trip) to and from Exclamation Point on the **North Vista Trail.** The North Vista Trail drifts through a forest of juniper and pine en route to remote Exclamation Point, where you can look far upstream in the canyon. The North Vista trailhead is right next to the Ranger Station.

On the South Rim, your best choice is the 1½-mile (round-trip) **Warner Point Nature Trail.** Located at High Point (the terminus of the South Rim Road), the trail follows a ridgeline with panoramic views south into the Uncompahgre Valley and north into the canyon.

✔ **Hike to the river.** The Park Service doesn't advertise the fact that you can hike deep into the canyon, and with good reason — these descents are really nasty. You need to obtain an inner-canyon permit before going, even if you're only day-hiking. (On the North Rim, you can simply sign the message board at the ranger station.) The routes — not to be confused with trails — are very steep and are covered with loose rock, so it's hard to get traction. If you insist on hiking into the canyon, start with the **Gunnison Route,** which drops 1,800 feet over 1 mile from its trailhead near the South Rim Visitor Center. Free permits for the backcountry campsites along the river are issued on a first-come, first-served basis. I wouldn't take a heavy pack down any inner-canyon route, but when you reach the river, you may relish having the chance to spend the night. So take minimal gear when you head into the canyon.

✔ **Camp on the rim.** There are first-come, first-served campgrounds (cost: $10) on both rims. Both have water and toilets, but some differences exist. The North Rim has a smaller, prettier campground, with a few sites that have partial views of the gorge. It sometimes fills up during spring and fall, when rock climbers flock there to take advantage of the temperate weather and big walls. The South Rim campground is larger and set back farther from the rim. It seldom fills up.

The South Rim is open year-round. The North Rim is open from mid-April through mid-November, weather permitting. To reach the south entrance, drive 8 miles east of Montrose on U.S. 50, and then go 7 miles north on Colorado 347. The north entrance to the park is 11 miles south of Crawford via Colorado 92 and the North Rim Road. Admission, good for seven days, is $8 per car, $4 for individuals on foot, bicycle, or motorcycle. For more information, call ☎ 970-641-2337 or surf the Internet to www.nps.gov/blca.

Other things to see and do

Black Canyon of the Gunnison National Park isn't the only area attraction. In Montrose, you can

✔ **Experience Ute art.** Prior to the arrival of settlers, many members of the Ute tribe wintered in Montrose, then hunted on the Uncompahgre Plateau during summer. Since 1956, the **Ute Indian Museum,** U.S. Hwy. 550 at Chipeta Road in Montrose (☎ 970-249-3098), has preserved artifacts of the tribe. It's worth coming here just to see the beadwork, headdresses, and ceremonial attire. The museum is open Monday through Saturday from 9:00 a.m. to 4:30 p.m., and Sunday 11:00 a.m. to 4:30 p.m. Admission is $3 for adults, $2.50 for seniors, and $1.50 for kids ages 6 to 10.

✔ Located in the former Denver and Rio Grande Railroad depot at the corner of Main and Rio Grande, the **Montrose County Historical Museum** (☎ 970-249-2085), has exhibits on railroads, Victorian life, and a rail yard's worth of antique tools. Its unique displays include a collection of teapots and cast-iron still banks (mainly piggy banks). It's open mid-May through September Monday through Saturday from 9 a.m. to 5 p.m. Admission is $2.50 adults, $2 seniors over 55, $1 students 12 to 18, and 50¢ for kids 5 to 12.

Staying active

After hiking alongside Black Canyon, you may need to wind down with a round of golf in Montrose. The centerpiece of a 445-acre planned community, **Cobble Creek Community Golf Course,** 699 Cobble Dr. (☎ 970-240-9542), is an 18-hole course that fully opened in 2003. Greens fees range from $20 to $34. The **Montrose Golf Club,** 1350 Birch St. (☎ 970-249-GOLF), has an 18-hole course, practice greens, a driving range, and a restaurant. You can play 9 holes for $15, 18 holes for $25. In **Delta,** the 18-hole **Devil's Thumb Golf Club,** 9900 Devil's Thumb Dr. (☎ 970-874-6262), affords views of Grand Mesa and the San Juan and Big Elk ranges. Greens fees for 18 holes are $38.

Fast Facts: Montrose and Delta

Emergencies

Dial ☎ **911.**

Hospital

Montrose Memorial Hospital (☎ 970-249-2211), 800 S. Third St., in Montrose, offers 24-hour emergency care. So does Delta County Memorial Hospital, 100 Stafford Lane (☎ 970-874-7681), in Delta.

Information

Make your way to the Delta County Tourism Council, 310 Main St., in Delta

(☎ 970-874-1616); or the Montrose Visitors Center, 1519 E. Main St., in Montrose (☎ 800-873-0244 or 970-240-1413; www. visitmontrose.net).

Post Office

The Montrose Post Office is at 321 S. First St. (☎ 970-249-6654). In Delta, go to 360 Meeker St. (☎ 970-874-4721).

Weather

For recorded information, dial ☎ 970-243-0914.

Part V

The Western Slope and Southern Colorado

The 5th Wave   By Rich Tennant

"The scenery here is just magnificent. The trees, the plants, and I've never seen so many soaring eagles in one place."

In this part . . .

The ski country may be more famous, but the western and southern reaches of Colorado are home to some of the state's undiscovered treasures. The Western Slope features canyons and mesas famous for their mountain-biking opportunities, and this is where Colorado's wine country is starting to boom. The Four Corners area boasts the largest archaeological preserve in the country at Mesa Verde National Park, and the San Juans include some of the highest and wildest mountains in the state, along with great skiing at Telluride. You should also check out the mysterious Great Sand Dunes in the San Luis Valley. There's no danger of saddle sores on this ride, so start reading.

Chapter 23

Grand Junction and the Western Slope

● ●

In This Chapter

▶ Visiting the Grand Valley, where the mountains meet the desert
▶ Taking in Grand Junction, the region's largest city
▶ Finding the best mountain biking
▶ Unearthing exotic Colorado: From vineyards to fossil beds

● ●

*I*t may not look like much of a slope, but trust me here: Heading west-ward from the Elk Range near Aspen and Crested Butte, you're travel-ing downward from the continental divide into the giant, sunken plateaus and ranges of the Great Basin. The *Great Basin* is a geological formation that covers virtually all of Utah and Nevada and huge parts of New Mexico, Arizona, Idaho, and even Washington and Oregon, as well as the section of Colorado covered in this chapter. The climate here is a cold desert; it qualifies as desert because it receives less than 10 inches of rain per year, and it's cold because unlike the subtropical deserts of southern Arizona and northern Mexico, it snows — but not much — in the winter.

The Colorado and other rivers that descend the Western Slope (the Gunnison, Dolores, and Yampa, among others) have carved through the layers of sedimentary rock to create amazing natural sculptures such as the Book Cliffs and Colorado National Monument near Grand Junction, the canyons of Dinosaur National Monument, and the Uncompahgre Plateau. These rivers are just warming up in Colorado; they go on to create the Arches and Canyonlands of Utah and, eventually, the Grand Canyon itself. Up here in Colorado, though, where it's still high and rela-tively cool, they make the perfect landscape for desert camping, incredi-ble mountain biking, and the country's most exciting new wine country. And all the exposed, ancient sediment makes it one of the world's best hunting grounds for fossils of the dinosaurs and plants that once inhab-ited the Earth.

Grand Junction

Grand Junction is the largest city in western Colorado and has a relaxed downtown graced with many sculptures. But what's really amazing are its immediate surroundings, including the following:

- ✔ **Grand Mesa,** an 11,000-foot, flat-topped mountain with hundreds of small lakes and reservoirs.

- ✔ **Colorado National Monument,** where erosion has sliced four colorful canyons into the edge of the Uncompahgre Plateau.

- ✔ **Orchards and vineyards** east of Grand Junction in Palisade.

From Interstate 70 on a hot summer day, the west side of Grand Junction appears as a bleached sprawl of chain stores and hotels. This isn't a mirage. With a population around 40,000, Grand Junction is the largest town in western Colorado, and people come from all around for shopping, medical care, and entertainment. That's one reason why the west side of town sprawls with malls. If, however, you drive south off the interstate into the downtown, you find attractive homes from the early 1900s, an artsy Main Street shopping district, and a real-world community that evenly balances business and pleasure. When the light softens in the evening, the colors surface in the town's verdant, irrigated parks and golf courses; in the salmon-colored rocks of Colorado National Monument; and in the blue-brown Colorado River, which absorbs the smaller Gunnison River at the south end of town. Water from the rivers, and from the earth itself, helps grow fruit in the nearby valleys and moistens the vineyards of eight area wineries.

Getting there

Grand Junction is in far western Colorado on I-70, 251 miles west of Denver. U.S. 50 enters Grand Junction from the southeast. Montrose (see Chapter 24) is 61 miles southeast of Grand Junction on U.S. 50.

Walker Field, 2828 Walker Field Dr. (☎ 970-244-9100; www.walkerfield.com), has daily service from Phoenix (on America West), Salt Lake City (on Delta) and Denver (on Frontier and United). Upon landing, you can rent cars from **Avis, Budget, Enterprise, Hertz, National,** and **Thrifty,** or call **Sunshine Taxi** (☎ 970-245-TAXI) or **American Spirit Shuttle** (☎ 970-523-7662) for a ride to your hotel (around $15 one-way). For information on contacting individual airlines and car-rental agencies, see the appendix.

Amtrak's California Zephyr train (☎ 800-USA-RAIL; www.amtrak.com), which runs from Chicago to the Bay Area, stops at the station at 331 S. First St. (☎ 970-241-2733) in Grand Junction twice daily, once in each direction.

The Western Slope

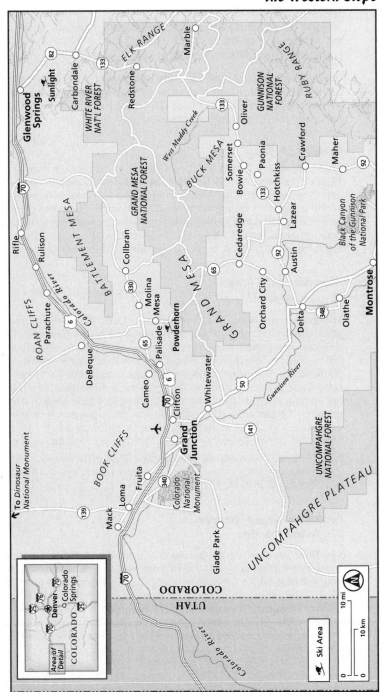

Getting around

Many of Grand Junction's most splendid attractions are in the surrounding countryside, so the best way to get around is by car. Most of the city is between the Colorado River (on the south) and I-70 (on the north).

When driving in town, keep in mind that the town's numbered streets run north and south, perpendicular to Main Street and the named avenues, which go east and west. The downtown borders Main Street between First Street and Seventh Street.

Where to stay

Chain hotels line Grand Junction's Horizon Drive where it crosses I-70. These hotels cater to both passersby and people vacationing in the city, and their rates fluctuate along with the ebb and flow of freeway traffic, which is heaviest during warm-weather months. Scattered through the downtown and surrounding valley are older motels and some pleasant bed-and-breakfasts. An hour southeast of Grand Junction, Grand Mesa has cabins and historic lodges alongside lakes in deep pine forests.

Alexander Lake Lodge
$$ Grand Mesa

The seven cabins on this property overlook one of those perfect little alpine lakes that seem to belong in a sepia-toned movie scene. The cabins sleep anywhere from two to seven people. Some are in almost perfect condition; others need work. Some have full kitchens; others just have microwaves. The owners hired a full-time construction team to add a few cabins and bring the whole place up to snuff. Construction aside, most of the activity is inside the 100-year-old Alexander Lake Lodge, which has an immense fireplace, hanging pelts, and an enclosed porch with lake views. The lodge has a fine, moderately priced restaurant inside that's open for lunch and dinner Thursday through Sunday, year-round.

2121 AA 50 Rd., Cedaredge. ☎ *866-525-ALEX (2539) or 970-856-ALEX. Fax: 970-856-2540.* www.alexanderlakelodge.com. *Rack rates: June–Oct $95–$150 cabin; Nov–May $55–$120 cabin. MC, V.*

Doubletree Grand Junction
$$ Grand Junction

The Doubletree sits right across I-70 from the Holiday Inn — the other major hotel in town — but the two are as different as east and west. The Doubletree is better for couples and business travelers. It costs more, has an upscale restaurant and popular sports bar, and offers amenities such as room service and extra phones in the bathrooms. Because the Doubletree towers eight stories above the vertically challenged town of Grand Junction, it has the most expansive views in the area, including ones of the hotel tennis courts and outdoor swimming pool.

743 Horizon Dr. ☎ ***970-241-8888.*** *Fax: 970-242-7266.* `www.doubletree.hilton.com.` *Rack rates: $89–$169 double. AE, DC, DISC, MC, V.*

Holiday Inn Grand Junction
$–$$ Grand Junction

Close your eyes (briefly) and picture a guest room at an especially nice Holiday Inn. Now that you know what the accommodations look like, I can tell you about the real advantage to this hotel: a HoliDome entertainment zone that will tie up your kids for hours, if not days. Children love the indoor swimming pool, hot tub, pool tables, table tennis, and video arcade. Parents can either suffer the children or suffer on the cardiovascular machines. There's also an outdoor swimming pool and hot tub in a wind-sheltered, sun-splashed courtyard. As at all Holiday Inns, kids stay free, and the hotel restaurant (a Coco's) caters to youngsters. The location, mere yards from I-70, makes this a viable choice even if you're only passing through.

755 Horizon Dr. ☎ ***970-243-6790.*** *Fax 970-243-6790.* `www.holiday-inn.com/grandjunction.` *Rack rates: $89–$119 double. AE, DC, DISC, MC, V.*

Two Rivers Winery
$–$$ Grand Junction

If the words *pitching woo* remind you of Japanese baseball, it's time to rediscover romance by taking your partner to the Chateau at the Two Rivers Winery. Each named for one of the world's prime grape-growing regions, the ten immaculate guest rooms all have French décor and views of the surrounding vineyards. There isn't a HoliDome here to distract you, so you can lavish all your attention on your partner — perhaps even over a bottle of wine. Come morning, you can breakfast on bright-yellow tablecloths in a sunny dining area or take your food onto an outside deck.

2087 Broadway. ☎ ***866-312-WINE*** *or 970-255-1471. Fax: 970-255-0483.* `www.tworiverswinery.com.` *Rack rates: $89–$165. Rates include breakfast. AE, MC, V.*

Where to dine

Grand Junction is only now getting used to the idea of gourmet dining. It has a handful of fine restaurants and many others that serve good eats. Unlike many other Colorado towns, it also has plenty of suburban-style chains.

Fiesta Guadalajara
$–$$ Grand Junction   MEXICAN

Fiesta Guadalajara has tapped into the same successful formula used by chain Mexican eateries across America. In a sprawling, Technicolor dining room, the restaurant serves cheese-heavy, south-of-the-border fare in portions large enough to make you feel as if you've entered an eating contest.

This formula, which also involves flavored margaritas and fried ice cream, seems to play as well in Grand Junction as it does in metropolitan suburbs — which is to say, very well indeed.

710 North Ave. (at Seventh St.). ☎ 970-255-6609. Reservations accepted. Main courses: $5.95–$15. AE, DISC, MC, V. Open: Mon–Thurs 11 a.m.–10 p.m., Fri–Sat 11 a.m.–11 p.m., Sun 11 a.m.–9 p.m. Closed Thanksgiving and Christmas.

Pablo's Pizza
$ Grand Junction PIZZA

On its Spudstacular pizza, Pablo's Pizza dumps roasted potatoes, sour cream, chives, green onions, and cheese; on the Bangkok, it drops Thai peanut sauce, large shrimp, green onions, bell peppers, cilantro, and cheese. The kids' menu even has a Mac 'n' Cheese pizza. Named for Pablo Picasso, the restaurant calls its pizza "a slice of art," but it seems more like pizza underneath a meal. In all, Pablo's offers 14 specialty pizzas as well as made-to-order pies and basic slices. And everything does taste good.

319 Main St. ☎ 970-255-8879. No reservations. Pizzas: $7.25–$12 12-inch; $13–$22 18-inch. DISC, MC, V. Open: Sun–Thurs 11 a.m.–8:30 p.m., Fri–Sat 11 a.m.–9 p.m.

Rockslide Restaurant and Brewery
$–$$ Grand Junction STEAKS AND SEAFOOD

A kayak and hang glider dangle above the smoke-free dining area at this restaurant, making the meals here a potential thrill sport. Rather than worry about things crashing, keep your eyes on the fish, burgers, pizza, pasta, and steaks, as well as on the beer. It's all tasty. The restaurant also has a smoking area and a bar where you can watch televised sports and sip any of the half-dozen or so Rockslide brews available on tap.

401 Main St. ☎ 970-245-2111. Reservations not accepted. Main courses: $7.50–$18. AE, DC, DISC, MC, V. Open: Mon–Sat 11 a.m. to midnight; Sun 8 a.m. to midnight.

Exploring Grand Junction

No matter which direction you go from Grand Junction, you find awesome country. Grand Mesa rises to the southeast, towering 4,000 feet higher than the 7,000-foot Uncompahgre Plateau, which is immediately to Grand Junction's southwest. Vineyards and orchards dot the valley floor east of the city, alongside the Colorado River. And if you drive two hours north from Grand Junction, you end up at Dinosaur National Monument.

A trip to Grand Junction feels most rewarding if you spend time in the surrounding territory. Go to Colorado National Monument for red-rock desert canyons, or make the hour-long drive to Grand Mesa if you prefer alpine lakes. Afterwards, you can enjoy the rewards of the town itself.

Colorado National Monument

Inside 20,000-acre **Colorado National Monument** (☎ 970-858-3617; www.nps.gov/colm), runoff has carved four 800- to 1,000-foot-deep canyons into the northeast edge of the 7,000-foot Uncompahgre Plateau. You can enter the monument from either Fruita or Grand Junction on Colorado 340, but either way, you climb 2,600 vertical feet from the valley floor to the top of the plateau. Inside the National Monument, Colorado 340 becomes Rim Rock Drive, which skirts the northeast edge of the plateau for most of its 23 miles. The drive passes 18 overlooks of the four canyons. From the overlooks, you can see balancing rocks, spires, arches, and other unusual landforms. During breaks from your journey on Rim Rock Drive, try the following:

- ✔ **Go to the Visitor Center.** The Rangers here will answer your questions, and you can purchase maps and books. A 12-minute video flaunts stunning pictures of the surrounding landscape and offers almost no information. (The message seems to be "Feel good about nature.") The visitor center is open daily 9 a.m. to 5 p.m.

- ✔ **Take a short rim hike.** The National Monument has six short, well-marked trails on or near the canyon rim. Start with the **Canyon Rim Trail,** which goes from the Visitor Center along the rim for ½ mile, affording views of Wedding and Monument canyons.

- ✔ **Hike down into a canyon.** Aside from the rim hikes, there are longer, more demanding trails (or routes) that descend into the canyons. Though less panoramic than the rim walks, these trails let you see the rock formations up close, feel the scratchy desert vegetation, and smell the sun-baked soils. Plus, they take you farther away from the crowds. You can walk the **Monument Canyon, Liberty Cap,** and **Ute Canyon** trails all the way to parking areas in Grand Valley or climb back up to the rim.

    Be sure to discuss your plans with a ranger before hiking into a canyon and carry plenty of water.

- ✔ **Camp.** The first-come, first served **Saddlehorn Campground** has sites with picnic tables and grills, and access to drinking water and restrooms. The cost per site is $10.

Colorado National Monument is on Colorado 340 between Grand Junction and Fruita. Admission, valid for seven days, costs $5 per car, $3 for individuals on foot, bicycle, or motorcycle. It's free from October through March.

Drive through the park at sunset for a breathtaking, movie-like display of colorful light and shadow as the reddening sunlight plays on the sandstone, and the sky deepens from azure toward blackness and stars. It's one of those little moments that will illuminate your whole vacation and make it unforgettable.

Other than being flat-topped and near Grand Junction, Grand Mesa and the Uncompahgre Plateau have little in common. With an apex over 11,000 feet, Grand Mesa is higher by more than 4,000 feet. Because of its lofty elevation, it's much wetter. Unlike the mostly arid Uncompahgre Plateau, it has 300-some lakes, ponds, and reservoirs. Grand Mesa's forests of pine and aspen belong to the mountains and not the desert. Even the rock layers are different. Grand Mesa has a cap of erosion-resistant lava atop shale and other soft layers; the Uncompahgre Plateau consists mostly of hard sandstone. You can drive up and over Grand Mesa on Colorado 65 as you go from Cedaredge to Mesa. When you reach the top, stop at the **Grand Mesa Visitor Center** (☎ 970-856-4153; open Memorial Day through Labor Day daily 9 a.m.–5 p.m.). The rangers there can point out places for fishing, picnicking, boating, and hiking. One premier hike is the **Crag Crest National Recreation Trail,** a 10½-mile loop that climbs 1,000 vertical feet to an 11,000-foot razorlike ridge — the highest area on the mesa. You don't have to do the whole loop to reach the ridgeline. Just park at the west trailhead, near Island Lake, and follow Trail 711 to the crest.

Other things to see and do

When you need a break from the hiking, fishing, and boating of Grand Mesa, try one of the many other relaxing and enjoyable activities in Grand Valley.

✔ **Find a perfect peach.** Grand Valley not only has two rivers, it sits atop artesian wells that provide extra irrigation water for fruit and grape growers. The sunny days, dry air, and cool nights also help fatten the fruit. If you're taking I-70 through Grand Valley during summer, check to see what the farmers are selling in **Palisade** (I-70, Exit 42), 13 miles east of Grand Junction. Look for cherries in June, apricots in July, peaches in August, and apples in September.

✔ **Get in the van and start "wining."** Palisade is home to seven of the eight Grand Valley wineries. All offer free tastings and sell wine by the bottle. (The eighth winery, Two Rivers, is in Grand Junction proper.) You can pick up a free guide to area wineries at the **Grand Junction Visitor and Convention Center,** 740 Horizon Dr., in Grand Junction (☎ 800-962-2547 or 970-244-1480; www.visit grandjunction.com).

American Spirit Shuttles (☎ 888-226-5031 or 970-523-7662) offers custom tours of area wineries for a minimum of $130 (or $25 per person for groups of six or more). They also offer regularly scheduled group tours on Wednesdays and Saturdays (cost: $25 per person).

✔ **Brave the Jurassic Robots. Dinosaur Journey Museum,** 550 Jurassic Court (off I-70, Exit 19), in Fruita (☎ 888-488-DINO or 970-858-7282; www.dinosaurjourney.org), has some dinosaur skeletons, but the real attractions are its robotic dinosaurs. They look realistic, move convincingly, and, except for an occasional metallic clunking noise, make all the shrill cries and howls that people in the Age of Spielberg have come to expect of dinosaurs. Later, you can shift your attention to a simulated 5.3 magnitude earthquake. It's open May through September, daily from 9 a.m. to 5 p.m.; and October through April, from Monday through Saturday 10 a.m. to 4 p.m., Sunday noon to 4 p.m. Admission is $7 adults, $6 seniors 60 and over, and $4 children ages 3 to 12.

✔ **Dig it.** The **Museum of Western Colorado** (☎ 888-488-DINO; www.dinodigs.org) lets visitors participate in one-day (cost: $99) and three-day (cost: $695) digs alongside real paleontologists at a site west of Grand Junction. You can get information about these digs at the Dinosaur Journey Museum (see the preceding item).

✔ **Savor sidewalk sculpture.** Long before Denver created its 16th Street Mall, Grand Junction converted its Main Street (between Second and Fifth avenues) into a pedestrian-friendly shopping park. Besides having restaurants and shops, the park is home to **Art on the Corner** — 26 permanent and 28 loaned sculptures that brighten the downtown sidewalks. You can purchase the loaned sculptures at prices ranging from $400 to $30,000. The many whimsical pieces make any trip downtown (and off of the interstate) special. Call the **Downtown Development Agency** at ☎ 970-245-9697 for more details.

Staying active

At less than 5,000 feet, Grand Junction is one of the low spots in western Colorado and a prime area for year-round, snow-free sports. If you're fixing to freeze, you can always drive to Grand Mesa, more than 6,000 feet higher than the Grand Valley. Otherwise, consider these options:

✔ **Cross-country skiing: The Grand Mesa Nordic Council** (☎ 970-434-9753) grooms up to 35 kilometers of track for free skiing on Grand Mesa. Some trails are regularly maintained, others are groomed sporadically. There's also an extensive network of forest roads that are packed down for snowmobiling. For information on winter sports atop the mesa, contact the **Grand Mesa Visitor Center** at ☎ 970-856-4153.

✔ **Golfing:** *Golf Digest* recently named the **Golf Club at Redlands Mesa,** 2325 West Ridges Boulevard, in Grand Junction (☎ 970-263-9270), one of the nation's best new affordable courses. Greens fees for 18 holes are $69.

✔ **Hiking:** Great hikes await both atop Grand Mesa and inside the Colorado National Monument. If you simply want a convenient, pretty place to walk, ride, or inline skate, head for any of four **Colorado Riverfront Trails,** which range in length from ½ mile to 4 miles. One easy one to find is the **Watson Island/Old Mill Bridge Trailhead,** at the intersection of Seventh Street and Struthers, where the city's Botanic Garden is located.

✔ **Mountain biking:** Abundant public lands, a dry climate, and a mixture of forest and desert combine to make this one of the nation's newest mountain-bike hot spots. If you want to go really far, perhaps even with vehicle support, you have two good options. The **Tabeguache Trail,** a mix of double track and some steep, technical single track, drifts 144 miles from Grand Junction south to Montrose, climbing as high as 9,500 feet on the Uncompahgre Plateau. One trailhead is on Monument Road south of Broadway. **Ruby Canyon Cycles,** 301 Main Street, in Grand Junction (☎ 970-241-0141), rents mountain bikes and can tell you more about area trails.

To get your bearings, pick up a free copy of *Biking Guide to the Grand Valley* at visitor centers and bike shops around town.

Hitting the slopes

Powderhorn Resort (☎ 970-268-5700; www.powderhorn.com), on the north face of Grand Mesa, has the closest lift-served skiing to Grand Junction. At just 510 acres, this is one of the smaller ski areas in the state, but it has a respectable 1,650-foot vertical drop, including some direct fall-line skiing off the Take Four Chairlift. Powderhorn doesn't always get enough snow at its base. The ski area's 9,850-foot summit is low by Colorado standards, and the resort isn't in a major snow belt. But the terrain is fine, especially if you can catch it during a big snow year. For more details on Powderhorn, see the inside back cover.

Shopping

In the downtown area, the pedestrian-friendly **Main Street Shopping District** (Main Street between Second and Fifth avenues) has galleries, restaurants, and shops — and more than 50 sculptures. With over 160 stores and restaurants, **Mesa Mall** (☎ 970-242-0008), at the junction of 24 Road and U.S. 6 and 50, is the largest mall between Denver and Salt Lake City. Anchor stores include Target, Sears, J.C. Penney, and Mervyn's.

Fruita's amazing bike trails

For incredible mountain biking in a beautiful high-desert landscape, head over to Fruita, 15 miles northwest on I-70, down the valley from Grand Junction. **Kokopelli's Trail,** a project of the local biking association and the Bureau of Land Management, wends its way from Fruita all the way down Colorado's canyons to Moab, Utah. It's a 142-mile trip, a dream for experienced backcountry riders. Be sure to pick up the map and guide pamphlet at area bike shops or at the Grand Junction Visitor and Convention Bureau (740 Horizon Dr.; ☎ 800-962-2547 or 970-244-1480; www.visitgrandjunction.com). If you want a shorter ride, the **Horsethief Bench Trail** is a short but rugged loop over Horsethief Canyon, easily reachable from Exit 15. From Exit 17, you can take Monument Road south to the trailhead for the **Black Ridge Trail,** which meanders up onto the Uncompahgre Plateau and into the Black Ridge Canyons Wilderness Area. Remember, this is a desert — pack plenty of water!

Fast Facts: Grand Junction

Emergencies

Dial ☎ **911.**

Hospital

St. Mary's Hospital (☎ 970-244-2273), at Seventh Street and Patterson Road, offers 24-hour emergency room services.

Information

The Grand Junction Visitor & Convention Bureau (☎ 800-962-2547 or 970-244-1480;

www.visitgrandjunction.com) is at 740 Horizon Drive, off I-70, Exit 31.

Post Office

The main Grand Junction Post Office is at 241 N. Fourth St. (☎ 970-244-3400).

Road Conditions

Call ☎ 970-245-8800.

Weather

Call ☎ 970-243-0914.

Taking a Side Trip to Dinosaur and Dinosaur National Monument

Surrounded by windswept high desert, the town of Dinosaur is home to 400 people, a handful of motels and restaurants, and not much else. The town has a memorable personality, but the big surprise comes when you visit nearby Dinosaur National Monument: Only a small portion of the monument has anything to do with dinosaurs. The first 80 acres or so were set aside in 1915 to preserve a quarry full of remarkably well-preserved dinosaur fossils; the remaining 210,000 acres encompass scenic desert canyons, including the confluence of the Green and Yampa rivers.

Getting to Dinosaur

Dinosaur National Monument straddles the Utah–Colorado border and has a paved entrance road on each side. The monument's headquarters are on U.S. 40, 2 miles east of the town of Dinosaur, which is 3 miles east of the Utah border and 110 miles north of Grand Junction (about a two-hour drive). To reach Dinosaur from Grand Junction, take I-70 12 miles east to Colorado 139 north. Follow Colorado 139 north for 75 miles, then turn left (west) on Colorado 64 and follow it for 20 miles to the town of Dinosaur. The dinosaur quarry is 7 miles north of Jensen, Utah. To reach Jensen, go 20 miles west of Dinosaur on U.S. 40.

Seeing the sights

The main attraction in this area, sure enough, is **Dinosaur National Monument** (☎ 435-781-7700; www.nps.gov/dino), but you can find many different sights within the monument itself. Two main roads go into the monument, one from the Utah side and one from the Colorado side:

✔ To see dinosaur bones, you need to enter the monument on the **Utah side** and pay a $10-per-car admission fee. Park immediately at the staging area and wait for a free shuttle, which takes you ½ mile to the quarry where you can see the bones. Hours are Memorial Day through Labor Day daily 9 a.m. to 6 p.m.; the rest of year, it's open daily 8 a.m. to 4:30 p.m.

The fossils inside the quarry date to 145 million years ago, when floods swept dinosaur carcasses onto a sandbar, where they were buried by river sediment. Through time, the sediment turned to rock and the bones fossilized. Today, the quarry consists of an exposed rock wall in which hundreds of bones are imbedded. Archeologists removed many bones in the past, then left others for future generations. They even put up a roof to protect the area. Opposite the wall of bones is a two-story viewing area with displays, reconstructed skeletons, and an area for ranger discussions. After seeing the quarry, drive 11 miles on **Cub Creek Road.** You pass 800-year-old rock art, viewpoints above the Green River, hiking trails, a historic cabin, and the most conveniently situated campground in the park. Alongside Cub Creek Road, just inside the entrance gate, you can pick up a brochure that interprets key landmarks along the way.

✔ It costs nothing to enter the National Monument on the **Colorado side.** First, stop at the **Monument Headquarters.** The headquarters has no dinosaur bones, but it does have maps and information as well as a short video about the monument. If you enter from this side, you won't see dinosaur bones, period. Instead, drive **Harpers Corner Road** and climb onto the broad Yampa Plateau, reaching overlooks of the confluence of the Green and Yampa rivers. Twenty-three different geological strata are exposed in the park, and many can be seen in the colorful canyons visible from this road.

I recommend driving all 31 miles to the end of the road and then hiking another mile (one-way) to the end of **Harper's Corner Trail.** This puts you at the tip of a peninsula from which you can see a broad sweep of the canyon carved by the Green River, more than 3,000 feet below, including a massive fin of rock where the Green meets the Yampa. If you have a high-clearance vehicle and the weather is fair, and if you also have a high tolerance for rugged, bumpy roads, you may enjoy a 13-mile detour (one-way) down **Echo Park Road,** which descends to the shady campground near the confluence. En route, it passes more hiking trails, rock art, and a historic cabin. This road becomes impassable when wet, even for four-wheel-drive vehicles, so don't try it if it's been raining.

Where to stay in Dinosaur

Lodging choices are few in Dinosaur. There are a couple of motels, but if you're going this far out into the rangelands, why not camp? The eight campgrounds in the park rarely fill up, except on holiday weekends. Fees range from free to $12 per night. On the Utah side, the **Green River**

Campground, open April to October, has 88 sites with drinking water, modern restrooms and access to the ranger talks at campfire circles. The **Echo Park Campground,** on the Colorado side, has 17 sites and is a more rugged experience, for $8 per night. Call ☎ **435-781-7700** for more camping information.

Where to dine in Dinosaur

At **Miner's Cafe,** 420 E. Brontosaurus Blvd. (U.S. 40; ☎ **970-374-2020**), in Dinosaur, you hear your food before you taste it. Entrees include the likes of chicken-fried steak, hamburger steak, popcorn shrimp, and battered halibut. A hamburger patty on cottage cheese constitutes a "Diet Delight." Nothing costs over $10. The restaurant also sells fossils and tie-dyes, has Christian literature on the tables, and allows smoking. It's open Monday through Saturday for breakfast, lunch, and dinner.

Chapter 24

The Southwestern High Country

. . . .

In This Chapter

▶ The high life in Telluride
▶ The sleepy towns of Silverton and Ouray
▶ Durango, everyone's favorite southwestern town
▶ Mesa Verde and the Four Corners

. . . .

*H*igh peaks, classic Western history, and quiet canyons give way to the arid mesas and sagebrush-lined gullies of the southwestern plateaus. Historic mines still dot the hills around the alpine towns of Telluride, Ouray, and Silverton, left from the silver boom of the 1880s and with gold boom of the 1890s. Not far away, 800-year-old cliff dwellings left by once-thriving Ancestral Puebloan communities fill the openings in canyon walls south of Cortez and Mancos. You can go to this region — my favorite part of the state — to explore remnants of the past or forget the past and go just for the recreation, excitement, and beauty.

Located where the mountains meet the mesas, Durango is the largest and busiest town in the area, and it's central to both the mines of Silverton and the pueblo dwellings of Mesa Verde. If you stay here, you can take the historic Durango & Silverton Narrow Gauge Railroad one day and tour multistory cliff dwellings the next. Telluride is less central, but it's one of the most visually stunning spots in North America. Though trendier than it used to be, it still combines soothing surroundings with an abundance of lodging, recreation, dining, and entertainment. Cortez, Mancos, and Dolores are all down-to-earth communities where you can stay for cheap while you get serious about exploring the world of the Ancestral Puebloans. And if you want to stop exploring and soak your weary muscles in hot springs, head for Pagosa Springs.

What's Where? Southwest Colorado and Its Major Attractions

Don't let nicknames like Derange-O and To-Hell-U-Ride scare you away from southwestern Colorado. Though the mountains are still rugged, the towns have been more or less scrubbed clean for visitors.

Telluride highlights

This 1880s mining town saw its fortunes rise again when Telluride Ski Area opened in 1972. The ski area attracted hippies who saw the beauty here and made the mistake of talking about it. Today the town is far wealthier than it was 20 years ago, but the residents still pride themselves on being relaxed and fun-loving. Make sure you check out the following while you're around:

- ✔ **Telluride Ski Resort:** A mogul-studded ski area that recently developed a family-friendly side.
- ✔ **Bridal Veil Falls:** These 300-foot falls form the headwaters of the San Miguel River, which flows right through town.
- ✔ **Downtown Telluride:** Offers great shops, restaurants, and bars.

Ouray and Silverton highlights

These mountain communities have a few things in common. They both have year-round populations under 800, and, nestled between craggy peaks and crossed by rivers, they're both stunning places with rich histories either as mining or rail towns. Their attractions include the following:

- ✔ **Ouray County Historical Museum:** Former patient rooms in an old hospital now house displays on the town's history.
- ✔ **Hikes around Ouray:** Trek forested hillsides with few roads.
- ✔ **The Old Hundred Gold Mine Tour:** Near Silverton, the mine is worth visiting because much of the machinery still works.

Durango highlights

Built as a rail town to serve the mines in Silverton, Durango sits in a horseshoe-shaped gap in the foothills of the San Juans. Partly because it has a college, a popular railroad line, and abundant recreation, this city of 14,000 stays busy year-round. Highlights include

- ✔ **Durango & Silverton Narrow Gauge Railroad:** A historic rail line that chugs backward in time and upward in elevation.
- ✔ **The Strater Hotel:** You can catch a show, have a meal or a cocktail, or simply admire the ornate woodwork.
- ✔ **Durango Mountain Resort:** A rare ski area that may be more fun in summer.

The Southwestern High Country

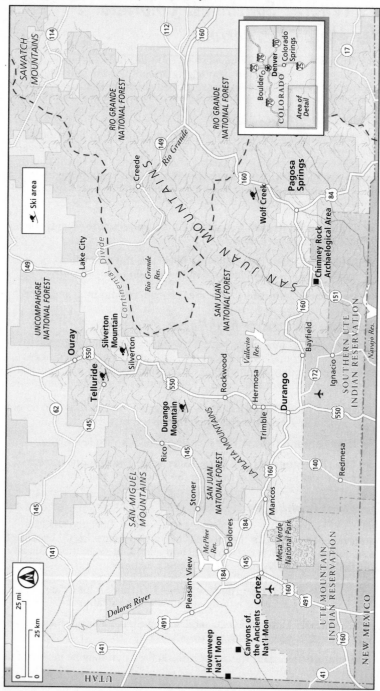

The Four Corners highlights

The Ancestral Puebloans left behind thousands of dwellings and artifacts in this area during the years A.D. 300 to 1300. Today, people come
here to explore the distant past, but towns such as Cortez and Dolores
are fun, too. During your visit, don't miss these stops:

- ✔ **Anasazi Heritage Center** and **Crow Canyon Archeological Center:**
  Two great places to discover the world of the Ancestral Puebloans.

- ✔ **Mesa Verde National Park:** The largest archeological preserve in
  the nation, the park is packed with pit houses, mesa-top pueblos,
  kivas (circular, partly subterranean ceremonial chambers), and cliff
  dwellings.

- ✔ **Ute Mountain Ute Tribal Park:** You can experience amazing cliff
  dwellings and archeological sites while traveling in small groups
  accompanied by Native American guides.

- ✔ **Nighttime programs at Cortez Cultural Center:** Programs include
  Native American dancing, music, and even plays.

Telluride

Telluride locals often use the word *funky* to describe their town, and
somehow it manages to live up to its billing, even though it's hard to be
funky 24/7. This may be the only place where you can hear reggae artist
Burning Spear playing over the stereo inside the grocery store; where
businesses have cheerful (if corny) names such as Sunshine Pharmacy,
Baked in Telluride, and The Magic Market; and where dogs wander about
town with little interference. Old mining shacks and sheds still clutter
the town's muddy back alleys, remnants of the days when Telluride
boomed with immigrants seeking silver.

Still, Telluride is more than just funky. Cradled in a glacier-carved box
canyon with the San Miguel River at its heart, this is one of the most
majestic places in North America. It's also remote. It's not exactly at
Earth's edge — commercial air service reaches the town's airstrip, as
well as the airport at Montrose, 65 miles to the north — but it does take
extra effort to get here, which helps keep it peaceful. If Telluride wasn't
so expensive, most of us would probably be living there right now, and
the town wouldn't feel half as funky, majestic, remote, or peaceful.

Getting to Telluride

Telluride is situated 4 miles up a 6-mile spur of Colorado 145. It's 73 miles
northeast of Cortez on Colorado 145 and 68 miles south of Montrose. To
reach Telluride from Montrose, follow U.S. 550 21 miles south to Ridgway,
go south (right) for 25 miles on Colorado 62. In Placerville, go left on
Colorado 145 and then continue for 17 miles to Telluride, bypassing a
turnoff where Colorado 145 turns right (south) toward Cortez.

To avoid the 335-mile drive from Denver, you can fly directly to **Telluride Regional Airport** (☎ **970-728-5313;** www.tellurideairport.com), 6 miles north of town, either from Phoenix (America West) or Denver (Frontier or United). In winter, **Montrose Regional Airport** (☎ **970-249-3203**) offers daily service to and from Dallas/Fort Worth (American), Denver (United), Houston (Continental), and Los Angeles (Continental), and Saturday-only service to and from Newark (Continental) and Chicago (American).

Some of my friends who regularly attend the Telluride Film Festival take advantage of Southwest Airlines' low fares and fly into **Albuquerque (New Mexico) International Sunport Airport** (☎ **505-244-7780**), then rent a car and drive up — a 350-mile trip.

Budget and **National** have car-rental offices at Telluride Regional Airport. At Montrose Airport, you can choose between **Budget, Dollar, National,** and **Thrifty.** At Albuquerque Sunport, **Advantage, Alamo, Avis, Budget, Dollar, Enterprise, Hertz, National,** and **Thrifty** all have offices. For information on contacting individual airlines and car-rental agencies, see the appendix.

Telluride Express (☎ **888-212-TAXI** or 970-728-6000) offers taxi service between Telluride and both Telluride and Montrose airports. Rides to and from Telluride airport cost $16 per person round-trip. Service to Montrose costs $78 per person round-trip.

Getting around in Telluride

In Telluride, you want to travel on foot as much as possible, if only to best experience the mountains towering above you.

Telluride by car

Driving around town and just outside of town is pretty easy. You can't get lost; Telluride is tiny and surrounded by natural barriers. About 3 miles west of town, Highway 145 becomes Colorado Avenue, Telluride's main thoroughfare. Colorado Avenue travels east and west through the downtown. Most of the cross streets, which run north and south, are named for trees. Continuing east out of town on Colorado Avenue, you pass Town Park — site of numerous music festivals and, in winter, the Nordic center and ice rink. Two miles later you reach Bridal Veil Falls, at the head of the box canyon occupied by Telluride. Bridal Veil and other threadlike falls become the headwaters of the San Miguel River, which curves along the base of Telluride Ski Resort and borders the north side of town.

Telluride by shuttle

During peak periods, parking costs 50¢ an hour on Colorado Avenue and the roads to its south. Look for a spot north of Colorado Avenue. Negotiating the downtown area on foot or by using the free **Galloping Goose** shuttles, which run every 20 minutes during summer and winter, is easier than driving everywhere. During summer, the shuttles only operate on weekdays. Call ☎ **970-728-5700** for 24-hour shuttle information.

A free gondola, which runs from 7 a.m. to midnight daily, links Telluride's downtown with the luxurious Mountain Village development. The gondola makes the trip between Telluride and Mountain Village faster than it is in a car. What's more, you can easily load your bike on it and get off at mid-mountain on the ski area, where some of the best trails are. (You can ride at low elevations even in winter, if there's a warm dry spell while you're visiting.) To reach Mountain Village by car, follow Colorado 145 for 1 mile south from the Telluride turnoff, then go left on Mountain Village Boulevard.

Where to stay in Telluride

Staying in Telluride isn't cheap. You can choose between historic hotels that have lots of character and new hotels that have every imaginable luxury. What you don't find here are a lot of economical lodges that cater to tired skiers on a budget.

The top hotels in Telluride

Hotel Telluride
$$$$ Telluride

Like many other new luxury hotels in Colorado ski towns, the Hotel Telluride has a turreted exterior reminiscent of a European castle, a faux-rustic Western lobby with antler lamps, a flagstone fireplace, and leather sofas; and guest rooms that blend European and Western elements. Even if the formula isn't original, it works well here, mostly because the ownership has enough bucks to create some bang. The plush rooms, for example, feature feather bedding, down comforters, and monogrammed sheets on the beds, as well as Aveda spa products in the bathrooms. All rooms offer mountain views. If you want personal pampering, the hotel's full-service spa offers an array of deluxe treatments.

199 Cornet St. ☎ *866-HOTEL-01 or 970-369-1188. Fax: 970-369-1292.* www.the hoteltelluride.com. *Rack rates: $119–$329 double. AE, DC, DISC, MC, V.*

The Ice House
$$$–$$$$ Telluride

This 1990 lodge feels snug and efficient like a dormitory, but its rooms are luxurious and its location is among the best in town. It's 100 yards from the Oak Street Ski Lift, two blocks from Telluride's lively Colorado Avenue, and flush on the bank of the San Miguel River. The rooms, which are decorated in a Southwestern motif, have private balconies. The deluxe rooms are roughly twice the size of the lodge rooms, and many have balconies right above the river. If you value space, they're probably worth the extra $30 to $50.

310 S. Fir St. ☎ *800-544-3436 or 970-728-6300. Fax: 970-728-6358.* www.icehouse lodge.com. *Rack rates: $195–$305 double. Add $30–$50 for deluxe rooms. AE, DC, DISC, MC, V.*

The Victorian Inn
$$–$$$ Telluride

The year 1976 is carved on the side of the Victorian Inn, as if the building were an architectural landmark that would endure for generations. Truth be told, this inn is still here because it's clean, well maintained, and, above all, among the cheapest in town. Your pocketbook will take a small hit if you stay here, but this is still Telluride's best option for travelers on a budget. For $10 extra, you can get a room with a kitchenette and do a little cooking on your own. The Victorian's Honeymoon Suite is an extra-large room with superlative mountain views. If you're the first to ask for it, you get it for the same rate as for the other rooms.

401 W. Pacific Ave. ☎ *800-611-9893 or 970-728-6601. Fax: 970-728-3233.* www. tellurideinn.com. *Rack rates: Winter $99–$149 double; rest of year $99–$119 double; higher rates during festivals. AE, DC, DISC, MC, V.*

Wyndham Peaks Resort and Golden Door Spa
$$$$ Telluride

Gone are the days when bone-weary skiers gladly settled for a stein of beer, a few bites of summer sausage, and a bug-free bed. Completed in 1992, this six-story, ski-in, ski-out hotel has nearly everything a mortal could want — except maybe character. It has a 42,000-square-foot spa with 44 treatment rooms, a climbing wall, racquetball courts, swimming pools, a water slide, an immense exercise room, a golf course, two restaurants, and a spacious bar. Located in Telluride's tony Mountain Village community, the hotel, easily the largest in town, observes what it calls *seasonality,* which in mortal-speak, that means it's closed from mid-April to late May and again for a time in late fall.

136 Country Club Dr. ☎ *800-789-2220 or 970-728-6800. Fax: 970-728-6175.* www.the peaksresort.com. *Rack rates: $195–$390. AE, DC, DISC, MC, V.*

Camping in Telluride

If you're not averse to pitching a tent, you can camp in the **Town Park Campground** (☎ **970-728-2173**) from mid-May to mid-October. It's a scenic, wooded campground within easy walking distance of town. During music festivals, campsites are sold as part of festival packages, and the place can be noisy. The rest of the season, campsites are available on a first-come, first-served basis, at a cost of $12 per site, or $10 for primitive (meaning no nearby parking) sites. The campground has no hookups and can only accommodate vehicles under 30 feet long. Showers and toilet facilities are available on site.

Where to dine in Telluride

Telluride's food compares with the best on the coasts, probably because some of the best chefs from the coasts fled to Telluride. Far from being cloistered, they return home periodically to check on the latest trends in the industry, and then bring back new discoveries.

Baked in Telluride
$–$$ Telluride   BAKERY

During winter, dogs always seem to be fixating on the door of this Telluride landmark — nearly 30 years old — a place that seems to bake nearly everything possible. Lined up in its glass display cases are bagels, donuts, breakfast pastries, pizzas, calzones, and puff pastries. As for the dogs, they fare best during summer, when the many outdoorsy patrons of Baked in Telluride while away hours on the restaurant's deck, making calls on the pay phones and passing crusts to the canines. If you're just drinking coffee, you can deposit your money in an honor box on the counter.

127 S. Fir St. ☎ *970-728-4775. No reservations. Sandwiches $4.99–$8.49, medium pizzas $16–$21, pasta dishes $6.95–$9.95. AE, DISC, MC, V. Open: Daily 5:30 a.m.–10 p.m.*

The Cosmopolitan
$$–$$$ Telluride   AMERICAN

Located in a sunny room right next to the gondola terminal in downtown Telluride, this is the place to splurge on a first-rate meal with friends. Chef Chad Scothorn, who did a stint at the James Beard House in New York, keeps his prices lower than other establishments of this caliber, and the place stays full even during the off-season. Lately, Scothorn has been tweaking traditional American favorites such as roast duck and pork roast and getting great results. To cap off your meal, try one of the restaurant's homemade sorbets and ice creams.

300 W. San Juan Ave. ☎ *970-728-1292. Reservations recommended. Main courses: spring and fall $17; ski season and summer $20–$31. AE, MC, V. Open: Daily 6–9:30 p.m. Closed mid-Apr–Memorial Day and for one week in November.*

Fat Alley
$–$$ Telluride   BARBEQUE

"Bourbon, beer & BBQ" is the motto of this casual eatery, which lacks table service but dishes up hearty, inexpensive fare that makes it a favorite among locals. Its staples are meaty Southern dishes such as barbeque ribs, fried chicken, and chicken-fried steak, but the restaurant also throws a few non-bones to vegetarians, including a tasty ziti-and-black-bean plate. Side dishes, ordered à la carte, include fried okra; red beans and rice; and sweet potato fries. For your beverage, you're free to order a top-shelf bourbon and take it back to your picnic bench, but if pure trailer-park chic is your goal, throw down $1 for a can of Schlitz.

122 South Oak St. (below Elk's Park). ☎ *970-728-3985. No reservations. Main courses: $6.95–$17. AE, MC, V. Open: Daily 11 a.m.–10 p.m.*

La Cocina de Luz
$ Telluride   MEXICAN

If you don't get to this tiny restaurant before the locals do, they'll take all five tables and linger all night over the fresh — and, by Telluride standards, cheap — fare. If you can't get the other customers to go, get the food to go instead. The restaurant's owner, Lucas Price, does everything possible to support local farmers and to acquire recently harvested ingredients, and the staff rolls tortillas and roasts chiles daily. The freshness permeates a menu that includes *posole* (traditional hominy stew in roasted tomato and guajillo chile broth, with chicken, beef, or veggies) and garlic-roasted veggie burritos. If you want beer or wine, stop at the liquor store next door and bring your own.

123 Colorado St. (behind Telluride Liquors). ☎ *970-728-9355. No reservations. Main courses: $5.75–$10. MC, V. Open: Mon–Sat 9 a.m.–9 p.m.*

Exploring Telluride
If you want to do Telluride like a local on his or her day off, you should party late, sleep in, exhaust yourself on the slopes or trails, seriously relax for a few hours, and then do it all over again. This section offers a few things you may want to pencil into your schedule.

The best things to see and do in Telluride
When you get up in the morning and start moving around, you can choose from among the following:

- ✔ **Find out about the guy who cut out his own appendix.** The **Telluride Historical Museum,** 201 W. Gregory Ave. (☎ 970-728-3344; www.telluridemuseum.com), was the town's hospital from 1888 to 1964. The best exhibits at this newly renovated museum link Telluride's history to the building's past as a hospital. There are displays on mining accidents, causes of death among miners (mostly lung disease and accidents), and the building's onetime claim to fame — the doctor who anesthetized himself and then removed his own, perfectly healthy appendix. It's open Tuesday through Saturday from 11 a.m. to 5 p.m. and is closed from mid-April through mid-May. Admission is $5 for adults, $3 children ages 5 to 17 and seniors over 64.

- ✔ **Walk the historic downtown.** Telluride may look a little more spiffy than neighboring towns, but its mining heritage is just as, uh, unusual. Telluride's *Official Visitor's Guide,* available throughout town, outlines a 14-stop historic walking tour and explains each stop along the way. If you want to hear an audio narration, you can rent a tape and headphones for $7 at the historical museum. During summer, the museum can also arrange 90-minute guided group walking tours, for which a minimum of $40 total is charged.

✔ **Visit Bridal Veil Falls.** To reach the general area of this 300-foot falls, continue east out of town on Colorado Avenue and keep going for 1¼ miles past where the pavement ends. A rugged road goes to the top of the falls. If you have four-wheel-drive and high clearance, you can drive to the top, but there's little room to maneuver or park once you get there. You're better off parking at the bottom and walking the mile or so to the top. If you're walking or pedaling, you can pass the power plant building at the top of the falls and go into the high-alpine **Bridal Veil Basin,** which is a great place to see wildflowers during summer.

✔ **Skate around.** Telluride has a free skateboard ramp in Town Park, open daily from 10 a.m. to 10 p.m. If your kids don't skate and need a place to hang out, they can go to the **Telluride Youth Center,** 233 E. Pacific St. (☎ 970-728-0140), which has a basketball court, games, a big screen TV, and a VCR.

Staying active in Telluride

No matter what your sport, you can probably do it in Telluride's **Town Park** (☎ 970-728-2173), along the San Miguel River at the east end of town. There's a skate park, swimming pool, tennis courts, volleyball courts, and a softball diamond, not to mention a campground. In winter, you can ice skate or Nordic ski here.

Want festivals? We got festivals!

Telluride hosts music, art, and film festivals of world renown, and it seems as if there's one going on every week in the summer. The music festivals are held primarily in Town Park. The best-known one is the **Telluride Bluegrass Festival** (☎ 800-624-2422; www.planetbluegrass.com). Held in mid-June, it draws some of the world's top acoustic musicians, from pickers to singer/songwriters and more. This festival became a must for Colorado music fans back in the 1970s; it's gotten huge, though, and is a bit crowded for some peoples' tastes these days. Nevertheless, you hear the up-and-comers from Austin, Nashville, and beyond, and a rotating collection of music legends that you don't hear anywhere else.

Other notable festivals include **MountainFilm** (☎ 970-728-4123; www.mountainfilm.org) during Memorial Day weekend, which screens films celebrating mountain life and environmental issues; **Telluride Blues & Brews Festival** (☎ 970-728-8037; www.tellurideblues.com) in mid-September; the **Telluride Jazz Celebration** (☎ 970-728-7009; www.telluridejazz.com) in early August; and the **Telluride Film Festival** (☎ 603-433-9202; www.telluridefilmfestival.com) in early September, showcasing mostly independent films. For more on upcoming festivals, surf the Internet to www.visittelluride.com.

Here is a small selection of the many other options you can choose from:

- ✔ **Climbing:** Just a short drive (or walk) east of Telluride is Falls Walls, home to more than 100 climbable pitches. You can also boulder along Bear Creek. The staff at **Telluride Mountaineer,** 219 E. Colorado Ave. (☎ 970-728-6736), can equip you for climbing, mountaineering, and backpacking. If you feel more comfortable climbing with a guide, call **Fantasy Ridge Alpinism** (☎ 970-728-3546).

- ✔ **Fishing:** Kids under 12 can fish for free, without a permit, all summer long at the **Kid's Fishin' Pond** at Town Park. Everyone else has to find a spot on the San Miguel or on one of a half dozen or so nearby alpine lakes. For advice and Colorado fishing licenses, call or visit **Telluride Outside,** 121 W. Colorado Ave. (☎ 970-728-3895; www. tellurideoutside.com).

- ✔ **Golf:** Located at the Wyndham Peaks Resort in the Mountain Village community, **Telluride Golf Club** (☎ 970-728-3458) opens its 18-hole, par-71 course soon after the snow melts. Greens fees are $150 July through Labor Day; $130 the rest of the season.

- ✔ **Hiking:** Hiking trails go into the mountains all around Telluride. The free *Official Visitors Guide,* available throughout town, has information on 15 area trails. If you're looking for one that's rewarding and easy to find, walk to the end of South Pine Street, cross the bridge, and walk 2 miles up the **Bear Creek Canyon Trail.** This easy-to-follow trail ascends 1,040 vertical feet to its terminus at a waterfall. If you want to keep going, you can pick up the more challenging **Wasatch Trail** just below the falls.

- ✔ **Mountain biking:** The mountain biking around Telluride ranges from gradual, wide railroad grades to white-knuckle single track. Beginners often pick up the **San Miguel River Trail** near Town Park and follow it west for 2½ miles. More advanced riders load their bikes onto the free gondola, unload at Station St. Sophia, and then ride trails beginning at midmountain at the Telluride Ski Area. For information, maps, and rentals, contact **Telluride Sports,** 150 W. Colorado Ave. (☎ 970-728-4477).

- ✔ **Nordic skiing:** Among the many trails readily available in and around town, consider the **Telluride Nordic Center** (☎ 970-728-1144), located at the east end of Town Park, which has 3 kilometers of groomed cross-country trails. There's no charge for using the track, and rentals are available. There are also 6 groomed kilometers on the golf course at Mountain Village.

Hitting the slopes in Telluride

In 2002, **Telluride Ski Resort** (☎ 970-728-6900; www.tellurideski resort.com) added three new chairlifts, effectively doubling the amount of lift-served terrain within the ski area to 1,700 acres. Suddenly what had been a mogul-studded, midsized mountain had much more to offer. The mountain now has beginner terrain spanning much of its 3,535 vertical feet. It has several new intermediate runs to supplement the likes of See Forever, which meanders 3¼ miles from summit to base. And it has some exciting new steep terrain around the new Gold Hill chairlift. Telluride still deserves its reputation for being challenging; the mountain's south side, which plummets into the downtown area, continues to sprout Humvee-sized moguls during dry spells. But the resort's new Gorrono Basin area will please skiers for whom bumps are a jarring experience.

The "new" Telluride also prides itself on its family-friendly services. Telluride ski instructors will videotape and critique your skiing for free. Its mountain hosts provide free tours daily. And if your kids have questions about Telluride, they can go straight to a Web site for kids: www.telluridekids.com. Best of all, Telluride almost never has lift lines. For more on the resort, see the inside back cover.

Nightlife in Telluride

Telluride may be a puny little town but it can easily out-party the flashiest big city. A few options for Telluride nightlife follow:

- ✔ At the **Last Dollar Saloon,** 100 E. Colorado Ave. (☎ **970-728-4800**), it's not unheard of for people to get up and dance on the bar. If that's not quite what you had in mind, you can play pool and throw darts. As for décor, you find everything from a stuffed, hanging catfish to a Dollar Rent-A-Car sign. The place is very popular with locals, who call it "The Buck."

- ✔ Please *don't* dance on the counter at **Allred's** (☎ **970-728-7474**), a posh bar and restaurant perched inside the 10,535-foot-high Gondola Station Saint Sophia, but go here anyway to absorb the views from the restaurant nearly straight down 1,800 vertical feet into Telluride.

  Even if you can't afford dinner here (the food is delicious — and *pricey*), order a beverage at sunset and watch the alpenglow illuminate the surrounding peaks. You can ride the gondola to the restaurant for free between 7 a.m. and 11 p.m. A private club at lunchtime, the restaurant opens to the public for après-ski (beginning at 3:30 p.m.) and stays open for dinner.

- ✔ The **New Sheridan Bar,** 231 W. Colorado Ave. (☎ **970-728-3911**), has changed little since opening in 1885. It still boasts a large mahogany bar, chandeliers, and room dividers with lead-glass panels, all of which date back to the days when miners cut loose at the bar. It's also a friendly place, popular with both tourists and locals.

- ✔ For live music, the hot spot is the **Fly Me to the Moon Saloon,** 132 E. Colorado Ave. (☎ **970-728-6666**). Think of any musician who can pick a guitar, mandolin, or banjo, and they've probably played here.

Fast Facts: Telluride

Emergencies

Dial ☎ 911.

Hospital

Telluride Medical Center (☎ 970-728-3848), 500 Pacific Ave., provides 24-hour emergency care.

Information

The Telluride and Mountain Village Visitor Information Center (☎ 970-728-3041;

www.visittelluride.com) is located at 630 W. Colorado Ave.

Pharmacy

Sunshine Pharmacy (☎ 970-728-3601), 236 W. Colorado Ave., can fill your prescriptions.

Post Office

The Telluride post office (☎ 970-728-3900) is at 150 S. Willow St.

Ouray and Silverton

These are a couple of my favorite places on earth. Silverton still has a respectable business district of false-fronted stone and wood buildings, as well as the notorious Blair Street, where warped wooden shacks date back to its days as the town's red-light district. Around it are 13,000-foot peaks streaked with avalanche paths and littered with mine debris. For a few hours every day from May through October, the Durango & Silverton Narrow Gauge Railroad deposits hundreds of oxygen-deprived tourists in this 9,318-foot-high town, but when they're gone, Silverton seems to absorb silence from the surrounding forests.

Ouray (pronounced yuh-*ray,* and named after a great chief of the Ute Nation) fittingly bills itself as the Switzerland of America — it's pinched between cliffs nearly as foreboding as those found in places like Chamonix. Ice climbers love the town's frozen waterfalls, both man-made and natural. Come evening, they thaw themselves in the town's geothermal hot springs, which bubble out of the earth mere yards from the Uncompahgre River.

Getting to Ouray and Silverton

Ouray and Silverton are strung along U.S. 550, which links Durango and Montrose. Silverton lies 47 miles north of Durango on U.S. 550. Ouray is a harrowing 26-mile drive north of Silverton, via the 11,008-foot-high Red Mountain Pass on a stretch of Highway 550 known as The Million Dollar Highway (it was once used to move lots of precious minerals out of Silverton). Ouray is 37 miles south of Montrose.

During winter, **Montrose Regional Airport** (☎ **970-249-3203**), has daily service to and from Dallas/Fort Worth (American), Denver (United), Houston (Continental), and Los Angeles (Continental), and Saturday-only service to and from Newark (Continental) and Chicago (American).

Upon landing, you can rent a car at Montrose Airport from **Budget, Dollar, National,** and **Thrifty.**

America West Airlines and **United Express** serve **Durango(La Plata County Airport (☎ 970-247-8143),** which is 14 miles southeast of Durango on Colorado 172. There, you can rent cars through **Hertz, Avis, National, Budget,** and **Dollar.** For information on contacting individual airlines and car-rental agencies, see the appendix.

During spring, summer, and fall, you can also reach Silverton on the **Durango & Silverton Narrow Gauge Railroad (☎ 970-247-2733;** www. durangotrain.com). For more on the railroad, skip ahead to my review of it in "The best things to see and do in Durango" later in this chapter.

Getting around Ouray and Silverton

These towns are tiny, so you shouldn't have much trouble getting around. Just park your car in the business district (where there's free on-street parking) and start walking. In Ouray, U.S. 550 becomes Main Street and passes right through the heart of town. To locate Silverton's main drag, take Colorado 110 east from U.S. 550. Colorado 110 immediately becomes Greene Street, which is Silverton's main road.

Staying in Ouray and Silverton

These towns are fun places to sleep, with historic hotels and bed-and-breakfasts in a variety of price ranges. Some have every conceivable luxury; at the other extreme is one hotel whose staff names "running water" as an amenity.

The Historic Western Hotel
$ Ouray

Some Victorian hotels — those with large-screen TVs, jetted hot tubs, and steam showers, for example — just don't seem all that Victorian. Well, you won't have any doubts about the authenticity of the 1891 Historic Western, that rare Victorian hotel with historic *plumbing,* few modern amenities, and a traditional floor plan. Fourteen guest rooms are in snug miners' quarters with shared baths down the hall. The floors creak, the doors catch on the doorjambs, and at least one room has its original wallpaper. It feels as if the miners may arrive any minute. Historic Western does have two suites with private baths, but even these aren't what you'd expect. In one, the clawfoot bathtub sits in the middle of the room, mere feet from the bed. I love this place.

210 Seventh Ave. ☎ *888-624-8403 or 970-325-4645.* www.historicwestern hotel.com. *Rack rates: $35–$55 double with shared bath; $70–$105 suite with private bath. DISC, MC, V.*

Riverside Inn and Cabins
$ Ouray

This motel is popular with climbers spending time in Ouray. One look at the rooms and you'll know that climbers aren't slumming as much as they used to. Accommodations are decorated in rich earth tones and are downright luxurious, with large TVs, peeled-log furniture, and, best of all, the soothing whitewater thrum of the Uncompahgre River. If you still want to rough it, you can rent a riverside cabin with a double bed and two bunk beds (but no linens or private toilet) on a nightly, weekly, or monthly basis. The two owners can tell you about the boating, fishing, skiing, and climbing in the area.

1805 N. Main St. ☎ 800-432-4170 or 970-325-4061. Fax: 970-325-7302. www.ouray riversideinn.com. *Rack rates: $33–$50 cabins double; $50–$95 motel rooms double; $65–$160 suite. Rates include gourmet coffee. Minimum stay usually required during holidays. AE, DISC, MC, V.*

Villa Dallavalle Inn
$–$$ Silverton

The Dallavalle/Swanson family has owned this building for over 100 years, and the inn reflects their long history in Silverton. Seven cozy and comfortable rooms are crammed with photos and heirlooms. A narrow upstairs hallway is further constricted by trunks, sculptures, bookcases, and display cases full of memorabilia — not to mention plastic flowers. The innkeepers seem to have set aside a special little corner for everything, including the guests.

1257 Blair St.. ☎ 970-387-5555. Fax: 970-387-5965. www.villadallavalle.com. *Rack rates: $75–$169 double. Rates include breakfast. AE, DISC, MC, V.*

The Wyman Hotel and Inn
$$ Silverton

This luxurious 1902 B&B is best known for its Elevator Room, inside of which a two-person whirlpool tub nestles into the framework of the building's old elevator. (No, you can't go up and down while you soak.) There's also a lavishly decorated guest room inside a caboose next to the hotel. Even if you can't reserve the elevator or the caboose, you can still enjoy the European antiques, mountain views, and a staircase wide enough to accommodate turn-of-the-century ball-goers. Rooms range in size from cozy to cavernous, the largest being a three-room suite that sleeps six comfortably.

1371 Greene St. ☎ 800-609-7845 or 970-387-5372. Fax: 970-387-5745. www.the wyman.com. *Rack rates: $139–$159 double with breakfast, $169–$229 suite with breakfast, $239–$259 double with breakfast and dinner, $269–$329 suite with breakfast and dinner. AE, DISC, MC, V.*

Dining in Ouray and Silverton

Ouray has great food and lots of variety, with a half-dozen or so quality restaurants scattered along Main Street. The options are fewer in Silverton, but you can still find a hearty meal at a reasonable price.

Buen Tiempo Restaurant
$–$$ Ouray   MEXICAN

Buen Tiempo charges muchos pesos for burritos, tacos, fajitas, and the like, but at least the food is fresh and zippy. You dine in a high-ceilinged room that's divided by booths, on the sides of which are colorful carvings of cacti. Once seated, you can crane your neck to see what may be the world's highest television screen. Give your server a dollar bill to stick on the ceiling. It's a stunt worth seeing, and your buck will be taken down eventually and donated to charity.

515 Main St. ☎ 970-325-4544. No reservations. Main courses: $9.50–$16. AE, DISC, MC, V. Open: Daily 5:30–10 p.m.

Coachlight Restaurant and Tavern
$$ Ouray   AMERICAN

Come to the Coachlight when you want a big steak, fish, or chicken dinner with all the fixings, served by a low-key staff. Every dinner comes with salad or soup, choice of potato or wild rice, and fresh brown bread. The most popular dish is the Miner's Filet, a lean steak that's been served here since the 1960s. The dining room has stained-glass windows from a condemned church and some of the most striking historic photos in town. There's also an upstairs tavern with a large deck.

118 W. Seventh Ave. ☎ 970-325-4361. Reservations accepted. Main courses: $8–$26. AE, DISC, MC, V. Open: May–Oct daily 5–10 p.m.

The Pickle Barrel
$–$$ Silverton   AMERICAN

Passengers on the Durango & Silverton Railway flock here at lunchtime when they get off the train. Once inside, they have to let their eyes adjust before they can make out the dark stone walls, hardwood floors, and six-stool backroom bar that has surely witnessed volumes of history. The lunch menu is geared for people who have a train to catch: sandwiches, burgers, and salads. You can still get sandwiches and burgers at dinner, as well as heartier entrees such as top sirloin steak and a black bean burrito with rice and chicken.

1304 Greene St. ☎ 970-387-5713. Reservations accepted. Main courses: $7–$15. AE, DISC, MC, V. Open: Daily 11 a.m.–3 p.m.; mid-May to mid-Oct Thurs–Mon 5:30–9 p.m.

Trail's End Public House
$–$$ **Silverton**   ECLECTIC

Trail's End looks like a barroom, but the food tastes nothing like bar fare. The chef churns out rich, heart-warming entrees such as Jamaican jerk-seared chicken and bacon-wrapped salmon as easily as other bars hand out potato chips. If you just want an appetizer, you won't be disappointed. Among the selections are cheddar-potato-stuffed Anaheim chili rellenos, sweet potato fries, Creole wings, and, yes, pretzels.

1323 Greene St., Silverton. ☎ 970-387-5117. Reservations not accepted. Main courses: $9–$18. DISC, MC, V. Open: May–Oct daily 11 a.m.–9 p.m.

Exploring Ouray and Silverton

In these towns, make sure to immerse yourself in their history — and hot springs.

The best things to see and do in Ouray and Silverton

Old Hundred Gold Mine Tour

The Old Hundred didn't produce many precious minerals, but today it's one of the best mine tours in the state. The mine operated from 1967 to 1972 without turning a profit. Because it's newer than most other area mines, the guides here can fire up and demonstrate fully operational equipment, such as pneumatic drills, slushers, and mucking machines. It's really loud. While learning about mining techniques, you can look around at the tunnels, drifts, and rises, as well as veins of mineral-bearing white quartz. Each tour, or "shift," rides a narrow-gauge train into the mountainside and spends about 40 minutes underground, in air that's around 48 degrees. Dress warmly!

Five miles northeast of Silverton on County Road 4-A. ☎ 800-872-3009 or 970-387-5444. www.minetour.com. Tours depart on the hour from 10 a.m.–4 p.m., May 10–Oct 13. Cost: $14.95 adults, $7.95 kids ages 5–12, $13.95 seniors 60 and over.

Orvis Hot Springs

After paying your $12 entrance fee and showering at Orvis Hot Springs, you don your towel ($1 if rented) and walk a few yards to a 103-degree outdoor pond that's 4 feet deep and about 40 feet across. Once there, you can lose that towel and your worries, too. Wearing a bathing suit here is a little like sporting a tux at Woodstock. Besides, your shape is no worse than the other whales in the pod. Later, you can relax in an indoor tub, broil in the small outdoor pool known as the "lobster pot" (temperature: about 110°), or unwind further with a massage.

You can camp at Orvis for $20 per person, or check into one of six guest rooms available for $89 each (the cost includes soaking for two days). The rooms are spare but comfortable, and they share a bath. Each room has a queen-size bed, a water tank, and plenty of towels, which should remind you where you're supposed to be spending your time.

On U.S. 550, 1½ miles south of Highway 62, Ridgway. ☎ *970-626-5324*. www.orvis
hotsprings.com. *Open: Daily 9 a.m.–10 p.m. Soaking cost: $12 per person, $5 for
kids 4–12.*

Ouray County Museum

Rooms that once housed patients in an 1886 hospital now serve as windows into Ouray's past. From the looks of the place, Ouray not only had a lot of sick and injured people at one time, it also had a lot going on. Today the museum has an old jail cell, a simulated mine, an assay office, a mineral room (illuminated by fluorescent lights), a hospital kitchen, a railroad room, an antique dentist's office, and a huge collection of vintage toys, to name just a few exhibits. Even the hallways brim with memorabilia from Ouray's past, including captivating photographs from the town's mining heyday. If you only go to one county museum in the course of your travels, make it this one.

420 Sixth Ave., Ouray. ☎ *970-325-4075*. www.ouraycountyhistorical
society.org. *Open: Summer daily 10 a.m.–noon, 2–6 p.m.; rest of year, call for
hours. Admission: $5 adults, $1 kids ages 6–12.*

Ouray Hot Springs Pool

The Ouray Hot Springs Pool holds more than a million gallons of geothermally heated, but nonsulfuric, water. A lot of those gallons are in a lap pool and a deep area with a diving board. The swimming areas are usually heated to the 80-degree range, but there are other, hotter sections where you can sit back and poach yourself, including one that runs 102 to 106 degrees. For an extra $2.50, you can also use the cardiovascular machines and free weights in the fitness center.

Located on the west side of U.S. 550 at the north end of Ouray. ☎ *970-325-4638.
Open: June–Aug daily 10 a.m.–10 p.m.; rest of year daily noon–9 p.m. Admission: $8.50
adults, $7 seniors 65 and over, $6 students 7–17, and $4 children 3–6.*

Other things to see and do in Ouray and Silverton

If you start getting water-logged, you can dry off and try some of these other activities:

- ✔ **Go for a walking tour of Silverton or Ouray.** Both these towns have dozens of unspoiled turn-of-the-century Victorian buildings. Ouray's *Visitor's Guide,* available at the visitor center next to the Ouray Hot Springs Pool, maps out a 20-stop walking tour centered around Main Street between Fourth and Eighth avenues. Silverton's walking tour is described in *Silverton Magazine,* available at the visitor center and in businesses around town. There are about 50 stops on the tour, each described in detail that falls just short of providing actual family trees.

- ✔ **Check out the San Juan County Museum.** The museum (☎ 970-387-5838) in Silverton isn't as absorbing as the museum in Ouray, but it does occupy an old jail, so you can wander the cells and mug for photos. The museum displays Derringer guns, minerals, and old mining equipment, among other items. It's behind the San Juan County Courthouse, at the corner of 15th and Greene streets. The museum is open from 9 a.m. to 5 p.m. daily from Memorial Day through mid-September, 10 a.m. to 3 p.m. daily through mid-October. Admission is $2.50 for adults, free for children 12 and under.

✔ **Watch water fall.** It's hard to justify paying to see a waterfall when so many nearby waterfalls are free. But the **Box Canyon Falls Park** (☎ 970-325-4464), located on Oak Street above Third Avenue at the southwest corner of Ouray, is convenient to town and has two hiking trails near a powerful falls, so it may be worth the price. Plan on hiking both trails if you come here. One trail is a 500-foot-long route that crosses ledges dynamited into quartzite walls and goes straight to the falls, which thunder through a slot in a rock wall. The other, less-crowded trail climbs 175 rocky feet over the course of ¼ mile (one-way) to a bridge that crosses the canyon directly above the falls. It's open from May to mid-October, from 8 a.m. to dusk. Admission is $3 adults, $2.50 seniors, $1.50 kids 5 to 12.

Taking Jeep tours in Ouray and Silverton

Over 500 miles of Jeep trails thread across the mountainsides surrounding Silverton and Ouray. Many lead to historic mines, and some eventually connect with other mining towns such as Ophir, Telluride, and Lake City. **Switzerland of America,** 226 Seventh Ave. in Ouray (☎ 800-432-JEEP or 970-325-4484; www.soajeep.com), offers ten different half- and full-day Jeep tours on the roads around Ouray. The best time to go is in late July or early August, when the wildflowers in the high-alpine basins are in bloom. Tours range in cost from $50 to $105. Switzerland of America also rents late-model Jeeps for a full day (cost: $130 per day).

Staying active in Ouray and Silverton

You can find a lot to do in the mountains here. Just make sure you have a detailed map (which you can get from Switzerland of America), especially if you're traveling on the Jeep roads or backcountry trails. Here are some options:

✔ **Fishing:** You can find excellent fishing near both these towns. In Silverton, some great holes are located along the Animas River above town. Stop at **Outdoor World,** 1234 Greene St. (☎ 970-387-5628), for licenses and information. Near Ouray, there's good fishing along the Uncompahgre River, as well as in countless mountain streams and lakes, some of which require hiking. Call the **Riverside Inn and Cabins,** 1805 N. Main St. (☎ 800-432-4170 or 970-325-4061), if you need flies or advice on Ouray-area fishing.

✔ **Hiking:** On two sides of Ouray, trails climb steeply into the forest and up to the tree line. These trails are fairly challenging, but mellower options do exist. If you hike uphill from Main Street on Eighth

Avenue in Ouray, it's only four blocks to **Lower Cascade Falls,** which are just as pretty as the nearby Box Canyon Falls and cost nothing. (Unfortunately, they sometimes dry up during late summer and early fall, so this may be another case of getting what you pay for.) You can also follow a wide, gentle, ½-mile trail alongside the Uncompahgre River on the north end of town. Consult the *Ouray County Trail Guide,* available at the visitor center, for more-detailed information on area trails.

✔ **Ice climbing:** A few years ago, a leaky *penstock* (a water conduit from a now-closed power company) on a canyon wall above the Uncompahgre River south of Ouray became a frozen waterfall — and a popular ice climbing spot. Savvy climbers theorized that more leaks would create more routes, so they built a network of pipes and spigots along the cliffs bordering the Uncompahgre. During cold weather months, the **Ouray Ice Park** (☎ 970-325-4288; www.ourayicepark.com) now offers 150 routes for climbers of all skill levels. There's no charge to climb, but you have to have a helmet and crampons to be on the ice. All guiding in the area is done through the ice park's concessionaire, **San Juan Mountain Guides** (☎ 970-325-4925; www.ourayclimbing.com). The park starts at the junction of Third Avenue and Box Canyon Falls Road and follows the river south to County Road 361. Even if you're not a climber yourself, it's worth driving up there to watch.

✔ **Ice skating:** Ouray has an outdoor hockey rink that has free skating during winter. The rink is at the north end of town alongside U.S. 550. For information on open skating hours and to rent skates, contact the **Ouray Hot Springs Pool** (☎ 970-325-4638). In Silverton, you can skate at **Kendall Mountain Community Center** (☎ 970-387-5522).

Hitting the slopes in Ouray and Silverton

Fashioned after a black-on-yellow highway sign, the logo for **Silverton Mountain** (☎ 970-387-5706; www.silvertonmountain.com) shows the silhouette of a skier somersaulting down a mountainside. Like any effective highway sign, it's both an accurate description and a warning. The slopes at Silverton Mountain plummet at angles ranging from 33 degrees (an expert slope) to 50 degrees (bordering on extreme). Partly because of the challenging terrain, the owners require that all customers be guided. Yet the price is surprisingly reasonable: For $119, you can sign up for a day of guided, lift-served skiing on snow that compares in quality to the seldom-skied fluff in the backcountry. The mountain's staff uses explosives to reduce the likelihood of avalanches, but you also need to carry an avalanche beacon, shovel, and probe (available for rent for a modest fee), just in case. The chairlift operates Thursday through Sunday, and reservations are strongly recommended. If you don't ski often and well, this probably isn't the right place for you. Just look at the sign.

Shopping in Ouray and Silverton

During summer, Ouray's Main Street is a bustling shopping area. When you're there, don't miss the **Salsa Trade Company** (☎ 970-325-4562) at 640 Main Street. It has a wall's worth of little-known hot sauces with names like Third-Degree Burn, Nuclear Waste, and See Spot in Heat. At 520 Main St., you find **Mouse's Handmade Truffles** (☎ 877-7WE-SHIP), a store that fills two critical needs for travelers — gourmet chocolate and inexpensive ($5 per hour) Internet access.

Silverton really has two shopping districts — one on Greene Street, which used to be the respectable part of town, and the other a block away on Blair Street, which was where the brothels, dance halls, and opium dens used to be. To this day, the structures on Blair Street are more ramshackle than on Greene Street, but some intriguing shops and galleries are located there. My favorite shop in Silverton, though, is **Weathertop Wovens,** 1335 Greene St. (☎ 970-387-5257), where two artists weave jackets, pullovers, and other clothing while they look after the store.

Finding nightlife in Ouray and Silverton

No bar will acquaint you with local culture like the **Miner's Tavern/ American Legion Post 14** at 1069 Greene St. in Silverton (☎ 970-387-5560). The bar has been in operation for 54 years, and some of the patrons look like they've been along for the whole ride. Sit down, order an American pilsner, and start playing pull-tabs. If you get bored, you can shoot pool, play darts or shuffleboard, or spin some tunes on the jukebox. Cap it all off with a cup of dangerously black coffee.

Fast Facts: Ouray and Silverton

Emergencies

Dial ☎ 911.

Information

Visit the Ouray Visitor Center (☎ 800-228-1876 or 970-325-4746; www.ouray colorado.com), next to the Ouray Hot Springs Pool. The Silverton Chamber of Commerce (☎ 800-752-4494 or 970-387-5654; www.silvertoncolorado.com) has a visitor center at 414 Greene St. (Colorado 110).

Medical Care

The nearest medical clinic is the Mountain Medical Center, 295 Colorado 62 in Ridgway (☎ 970-626-5123). The nearest hospital to Ridgway and Ouray is Montrose Memorial Hospital, 800 S. Third St. (☎ 970-249-2211). The nearest hospital to Silverton is Mercy Medical Center at 375 E. Park Ave., in Durango (☎ 970-247-4311).

Post Office

The Ouray Post Office (☎ 970-325-4302) is at 620 Main St. The Silverton Post Office (☎ 970-387-5402) is at 128 W. 12th St.

Durango

Nestled in the sun-drenched foothills of the San Juan Mountains, Durango flourished in the late 19th century as a railroad town that helped move minerals mined in Silverton. Today, the same 1881 rail line ferries more than 200,000 tourists a year. The railroad long ago helped pay for the many architectural landmarks in Durango's historic downtown, and today it helps support a bustling row of restaurants, bars, shops, and hotels. A community of 14,000 people also thrives in this active town. Sinewy cyclists career across mountain bike trails in the piñon-juniper and ponderosa-pine forests around town. Kayakers splash through the whitewater of the Animas River, which flows through the community. And, come winter, skiers search for powder on slopes of the nearby Durango Mountain Resort. During the school year, students from Fort Lewis College flood the downtown area on weekends. And ranchers still run cattle on the rangeland south of town. Whether you come here for the history, the recreation, or merely the sight of the red-rock cliffs surrounding town, you'll probably enjoy Durango.

Getting to Durango

Durango sits amid some rugged topography, so the trip to town is often prettier than it is smooth.

Most people who drive through southwestern Colorado land in Durango at some point. It's 5 miles from the easternmost junction of U.S. 160 and U.S. 550, which are two major routes through the region. (The roads join one another for 5 miles, then part ways again at the southwest corner of town.) U.S. 160 links Cortez (to the west) and I-25 (to the east). U.S. 550 joins Farmington, New Mexico (to the south), and Grand Junction (to the north).

America West Airlines and **United Express** serve **Durango/La Plata County Airport** (☎ 970-247-8143), 14 miles southeast of Durango on Colorado 172. After landing, you can rent cars through **Hertz, Avis, National, Budget,** and **Dollar.** For information on contacting individual airlines and car-rental agencies, see the appendix.

Getting around Durango

Durango's roads can be confusing. The main route through town is U.S. 160/550, which parallels the Animas River and, together with the river, defines the southern edge of the community. At the southwest corner of town, highways 160 and 550 part ways, with U.S. 160 continuing west out of town to Cortez. U.S. 550, meanwhile, curves through town on Camino Del Rio and Main Avenue and eventually leaves the north side of Durango en route to Silverton and points beyond.

Durango's downtown area surrounds north-south Main Avenue between College Drive and 15th Street. To get there, take Camino Del Rio north from Highway 160 and then go right (east) on College Drive. Most of the shops are right on Main Avenue, but parking can be scarce. Be sure to carry some nickels, dimes, and quarters for the meters; an hour's parking costs 25¢. If you stay in the historic downtown, you can do most of your shopping and dining without getting in the car. Pedestrians always have the right of way in Durango, so be sure to take advantage of it.

If you prefer public transportation, the **Durango Lift** (☎ 970-259-5438), a local bus system, travels three loops through town, weekdays from 7 a.m. to 7 p.m. year-round. The cost is 50¢ per ride.

Durango's **Main Avenue Trolley Service** goes up and down Main Avenue, hitting stops every 20 minutes or so. It's not a real trolley; rather, it looks like the offspring of a trolley and a bus. When the town is busy, you can park at a lot north of the historic downtown and take the trolley into town. During summer, it operates from 6 a.m. to 10 p.m. During winter, it runs from 7 a.m. to 7 p.m. The cost is 50¢ per ride.

Durango Transportation (☎ 800-626-2066 or 970-259-4818) provides taxi service.

Where to stay in Durango

Durango has three of the best-preserved historic hotels in western Colorado. They're brick-and-stone classics, all with hand-carved wood-work and antiques inside, and all situated, naturally enough, in the historic district, where you can hear the whistle of the Durango & Silverton Railway (even when you don't want to).

General Palmer Hotel
$$–$$$$ Durango

Like the nearby Strater Hotel, the General Palmer is an elegant, well-preserved 19th-century hotel in downtown Durango, but it's smaller and more subdued than its better-known counterpart. Unlike the Strater, there's no old-time saloon or restaurant on the premises, employees dress as if this were the 21st century, and the furnishings include many reproductions. Yet you'll still sense the history here, and the depot for the Durango & Silverton Narrow Gauge Railroad is only a block away. My favorite relic is the hotel's 1910 Otis elevator, with a door that has to be opened and closed by hand. If you plan to use your room mainly for sleeping, go for one of the windowless, inside rooms. Cocooned from street noise, they're surprisingly restful — and a few bucks cheaper, too!

567 Main Ave. ☎ *800-523-3358 or 970-247-4747.* www.generalpalmerhotel. com. *Rack rates: Apr 1–Oct 15 and Dec 20–Jan 1 $98–$180 double; rest of year $75–$125 double. AE, DC, DISC, MC, V.*

Leland House and Rochester Hotel
$$-$$$ Durango

If you love Westerns, saddle up and ride to the 1892 Rochester Hotel, where each of the 15 guest rooms pays homage to a particular film. The Viva Zapata room, for example, holds sombreros and Mexican clay pots; the Butch Cassidy and the Sundance Kid room bears photos of Redford and Newman back when they weren't so long in the tooth. Located across the street, The Leland House — owned by the same company as the Rochester — is a restored 1927 apartment building. Being former apartments, each guest unit has a kitchen, and some have extra rooms and sitting areas. Each unit is named after a different person from Durango's history, someone you've probably never heard of. The kitchens and extra space make Leland House a great place for families, but it's not as much fun as the Rochester Hotel. Check-in for both hotels is at the Leland House.

721 E. Second Ave. ☎ *800-664-1920 or 970-385-1920. Fax: 970-385-1967.* www. rochesterhotel.com, www.leland-house.com. *Leland House rack rates: $129–$159 double; $179–$340 suite. Rochester Hotel rack rates: $131–$199 double; $170–$219 suite. AE, DC, DISC, MC, V.*

Purgatory Village Condominium Hotel
$$$ Durango

At this modern condominium hotel, which offers ski-in, ski-out access at Durango Mountain Resort, your options include compact studios with Murphy beds; one-, two-, and three-bedroom condominiums; and standard hotel rooms with king beds. Shop for a package deal and bring your own food — most rooms have either kitchenettes or full kitchens. Ideally, you'll spend most of your time pursuing an active lifestyle here and little time considering the décor, which varies from unit to unit depending on the whims of the owners. The hotel and resort offer a variety of activities, especially during summer. And with views of both the ski area and the Twilight and West Needle mountains, the backdrop is hard to beat.

1 Skier Place. ☎ *800-693-0175. Fax 970-382-2248.* www.durangomountain resort.com. *Rack rates: $99–$199 studios and standard rooms; $189–$1,100 condominiums. AE, DISC, MC, V.*

The Strater Hotel
$$–$$$ Durango

This four-story hotel of red brick and ornate white stonework still dominates the Durango skyline, much as it did 100 years ago. Just by looking at it, you can tell that the Strater is *the* place to stay. Thanks to a succession of owners who invested in it even during hard times, it never slipped into disrepair and has always been elegant. Today, the hotel even employs a master woodworker to look after its elaborate woods, including a mahogany entryway, a front desk of solid pine, and the world's largest collection of Victorian walnut antiques. The hotel celebrates its history, almost to a fault. Employees in turn-of-the-century period clothing show guests to rooms overlooking Durango's thriving downtown. The guest rooms are more antiquey than posh, but they're comfortable. There's also a saloon with live entertainment, a restaurant, and a theater that presents melodramas during summer.

699 Main Ave. ☎ *970-247-4431. Fax: 970-259-2208.* www.strater.com. *Rack rates: $89–$249 double. AE, DC, DISC, MC, V.*

Where to dine in Durango

I wouldn't say you *couldn't* find a bad meal in Durango because, with over 60 restaurants in town, some chef somewhere must cook a bad meal every once in a while. But I've never had a bad meal here. Because this is a college town that also caters to wealthy tourists, the food choices run the gamut from burrito joints and brewpubs to the finest of fine dining.

Cyprus Café
$$ Durango   WEST COAST/MEDITERRANEAN

At certain times of day, Cyprus Café seems aglow with light emanating from the ceramic masks, castings, and urns, and from the claylike faux finish on the walls. Consisting largely of organic produce and meats, the food, like the surroundings, blends the earthy and the sublime. You can choose from entrees such as *Salmon sto Fourno* (fresh salmon, goat cheese, grape leaves, and olive caper tapenade, baked in parchment paper) and lamb meatball fettuccine, or opt for a creative salad. Cyprus Café is most fun on summer nights when it opens its patio and features live jazz.

725 E. Second Ave. ☎ *970-385-6884.* www.cypruscafe.com. *Reservations accepted. Main courses: $12–$18. AE, DISC, MC, V. Open: Summer daily 11:30 a.m.– 2:30 p.m. and 5–9 p.m.; rest of year Tues–Sat 11:30 a.m.–2:30 p.m. and 5–9 p.m.*

Ken and Sue's Place
$$ Durango   AMERICAN BISTRO

This restaurant's owners have won some major awards in recent years, but for some reason they aren't taking it out on their customers. They still serve inexpensive salads and sandwiches at both lunch and dinner, welcome kids, and leave free jelly beans by the door. The dining room resembles a small-town cafe that has been gussied up a little, and the prices are reasonable. Despite the casual trappings, you can dine on expertly prepared fish, chicken, and steak dishes, including a pistachio-crusted grouper that stands apart.

636 Main Ave. ☎ *970-259-2616. Reservations accepted. Main courses: $11–$19. AE, DC, DISC, MC, V. Open: Daily 5–10 p.m.; Mon–Fri 11 a.m.–2:30 p.m.*

Seasons Rotisserie and Grill
$$–$$$ Durango   NEW AMERICAN

Seasons is a great choice if you're looking for quality upscale dining. You can sit in a yellow dining room with original art, high ceilings, and hardwood floors. Prepared in an open kitchen, the entrees are highlighted by quality meats cooked over an oak-fired, rotisserie grill. The staff here is "99 percent sure" that they have the largest wine list in town. I'm only 50 percent sure that they're credible, but the list is certifiably long.

764 Main St. ☎ 970-382-9790. Reservations recommended. Main courses: $15–$32. AE, DC, DISC, MC, V. Open: Daily 5:30–10 p.m.; Mon–Fri 11:30 a.m.–2:30 p.m.

Sow's Ear
$$–$$$ Near Durango Mountain Resort   STEAKS

Hanging from the high ceiling of this dining room is an extravagant mobile, with components that call to mind a three-way-collision between skier, hiker, and duck. There's a mirrored ball, too. Other than that, the place feels like a country club, with mountain views, hardwood floors, great steaks, strong cocktails, and friendly service. Come here for the elk tenderloin medallions with Portobello-mushroom, red-wine sauce — and for the mobile.

48475 Highway 550 (about 2 miles south of Durango Mountain Resort). ☎ 970-247-3527. Reservations accepted. Main courses: $12–$34. AE, DISC, MC, V. Open: Memorial Day–Labor Day and mid-Dec–Mar daily 5–9:30 p.m.; closed rest of year.

Steamworks
$–$$ Durango   PUB FARE

Located in an old automobile showroom, Steamworks sells copious amounts of homemade beer as well as the many foods that go with beer — soups, salads, Mexican fare, burgers, pasta, a Cajun boil (on weekends only), and pizza, among others. After ordering, the kids can scribble with chalk on the old showroom floor, and you can gaze through windows that open onto the kitchen, brewing vats, and the street.

801 E. Second Ave. ☎ 877-372-9200 or 970-259-9200. Reservations accepted. Main courses: $9–$18. AE, DISC, MC, V. Open: Daily 11 a.m.–11 p.m.

Exploring Durango

In Durango, you can spend a lot of time "training." When you've ridden the Durango & Silverton Narrow Gauge Railroad, you can work out on the trails, on the river, or at the ski area.

The best things to see and do in Durango

Durango & Silverton Narrow Gauge Railroad

Every morning from mid-May through late October, a 1923 coal-fired steam locomotive pulls Victorian-era coaches out of Durango and uphill 45 miles and 3,000 vertical feet to the historic mining town of Silverton. During much of the three-and-a-half-hour trip, the train follows the Animas River upstream, alternately dipping deep into gorges and traversing narrow ledges high above the river. It stops for two hours in Silverton, where most people shop, eat lunch, and get in the way of locals. Then the train returns to Durango. It's one of the prettiest rides you'll ever take, and the history of the train and its surroundings can really make you feel as if you've stepped back in time.

The full ride, however, takes about ten hours, which can seem like ten years when you get tired. Unless you're rabid for rails, I recommend spending the extra $5 to go either to or from Silverton via motor coach. This shortens the trip by two hours and makes it less taxing.

You can choose other interesting ways to break up the trip if you have a little extra time. You can make an overnight layover in Silverton, which has historic hotels and a lively shopping district — not to mention beautiful mountains and old mines all around. Or, you can get off the train at Elk Park or Needleton and hike or backpack in remote areas of the San Juan National Forest, including the Weminuche Wilderness, then flag down the train again that afternoon or even a few days later. For more on hiking in this area, contact the **San Juan National Forest,** 15 Burnett Court, Durango (☎ **970-247-4874**). More trains are added as business picks up, so you can usually find a seat even if you don't book ahead. During fall and winter, a shorter, four-and-a-half-hour round-trip to Cascade Canyon is offered.

Lodging and tour discount packages are available; options and prices vary. For more information, call or check the Web site.

479 Main Ave., Durango. ☎ *888-872-4607 or 970-247-2733.* www.durangotrain. com. *Reservations recommended. Fares: $62 adults, $31 children 5–11, $109 first class (adults only). Cascade Canyon Winter Train: $45 adults, $22 children 5–11, $89 first class (adults only). Parking $7 per day for cars, $9 per day for RVs. Ticket includes admission to the Durango & Silverton Narrow Gauge Railroad Museum.*

Durango & Silverton Narrow Gauge Museum

Even if you don't take a ride on the historic train, this museum tucked behind the depot for the Durango & Silverton Narrow Gauge Railroad is worth exploring. Under one 12,000-square-foot roof, it has one of the largest collections of historic railroad cars, engines, and memorabilia anywhere. Highlights include a combination engine, personnel mover, and ambulance known as a Casey Jones and a luxurious Nomad business car.

479 Main Ave. (in the rail yard for the Durango & Silverton Railroad), Durango. ☎ *970-247-2733. Admission: Free for train passengers; $7 adults, $3.50 kids 6–12 for nonpassengers. Open: Year-round; hours vary seasonally.*

Other things to see and do in Durango

The train isn't the only way to time-travel in Durango. You can step back in history by visiting these area museums:

 ✔ Located in a three-story, 1904 schoolhouse, the **Animas Museum,** 3065 W. Second Ave., at 31st Street (☎ **970-259-2402**), pays homage to the history of Durango and its precursor, Animas City. Its ground floor still houses a century-old classroom, which, if my experience is typical, may look disturbingly similar to the classrooms of your youth. Upstairs are exhibits on Native Americans, European settlers, and the town itself. Next to the museum is a restored, furnished 1876 cabin. Summer hours run Monday through Saturday from 10 a.m. to 6 p.m. Winter hours are Wednesday through Saturday from 10 a.m. to 4 p.m. Admission is $2.50 adults, free for kids under 12.

✔ *Time* magazine is said to have rated the **Diamond Circle Melodrama** (☎ **877-325-3400** or 970-247-3400; www.diamondcirclemelodrama. com) production as "one of the top three melodramas in the U.S." When or why *Time* magazine began rating melodramas, I'm not sure. At any rate, this is fun stuff, and everyone gets to hiss at the villain. It's located at the corner of Seventh and Main streets inside the Strater Hotel. Shows are Monday through Saturday nights from June through August. Admission is $20 for adults, $15 for children under 12.

Staying active in Durango

With mountains above, desert below, and a river through town, Durango is perfect for year-round recreation. Visitors here often end up doing one or more of the following:

✔ **Golfing: Hillcrest Golf Course,** 2300 Rim Dr. (☎ **970-247-1499**), next to Fort Lewis College, is Durango's 18-hole municipal course. This is a good public course with reasonable rates: $20 for 18 holes, $10 for 9. There's also a driving range and putting green on the premises.

✔ **Hiking:** For information on hiking in and around Durango, including some of the more-remote spots, call the **Animas Ranger District** (☎ **970-247-4874**).

✔ **Mountain biking:** This sport may not have been invented in Durango, but it came of age here. And **Mountain Bike Specialists**, 949 Main Ave. (☎ **970-247-4066;** www.mountainbikespecialists. com), has absorbed a lot of the bumps along the way. The Mountain Bike Hall of Fame is in Crested Butte, Colorado, but this store is sort of a satellite version, with bikes and jerseys of famous riders such as Juli Furtado, John Tomac, and Ned Overend mounted across the upper walls. The shop can prepare you — mentally, at least — for the challenging single-track trails surrounding town. It sells trail guides and has maps available for either perusal or purchase. You can rent a full suspension bike for $45 per day.

✔ **River-rafting:** During years when it snows (or rains), Durango has great rafting right in the heart of town. Some of the top-flight kayakers train on the Animas River right next to the town's visitor center. Above town, the Animas makes for extra-challenging boating, with class IV and V rapids. Below town, it's mellow enough to float on an inflatable kayak. **Durango Rivertrippers,** 720 Main Ave. (☎ **800-292-2885;** www.durangorivertrippers.com), offers two-hour ($25) and half-day ($35) trips on the Animas.

✔ **Soaking and swimming:** Located 9 miles north of town, **Trimble Hot Springs**, 6475 County Rd. 203 (☎ 970-247-0111; www.trimble hotsprings.com), has a large, warm swimming pool and even warmer pools for soaking. The cost for soaking during summer is $11 for adults, $7.50 for kids 12 and under; the rest of the year it's $9 for adults and $6.50 for kids.

Hitting the slopes in Durango

The 10,822-foot summit at **Durango Mountain Resort (DMR)** (☎ 800-525-0892 or 970-247-9000; www.durangomountainresort.com) isn't particularly high for a ski area so far south on the map. So the snowfall can be hit or miss, even more so than at other areas. Nor is the mountain enormous. It boasts a respectable 2,029-foot vertical drop, but the thrust of the 1,200 skiable acres is more horizontal than vertical. But if you like lots of warm sunshine, a resort where the bottom of the hill isn't a lifetime away, and rolling intermediate terrain, DMR makes a fine choice. You'll enjoy the relaxed, open people. And if you're a lukewarm skier but a full-blown hedonist, you'll love the resort's Total Adventure Ticket, a program that allows guests holding four- or more day lift-tickets to exchange a day of lift-served skiing for activities such as cross-country skiing, snowshoeing, star-viewing, hot springs, and even massages. See the inside back cover for more information on DMR.

Shopping in Durango

If you want to tour Durango's many art galleries, start at the **Durango Art Center**, 802 E. Second Ave. (☎ 970-259-2606). Open Tuesday through Saturday from 10 a.m. to 5 p.m., it has a large exhibit space that houses traveling shows as well as group shows highlighting local and regional artists. There's also a small gift shop selling local art. When you're done browsing, the art center's staff can help you identify local galleries that have the type of art you like most.

Nightlife in Durango

With over 100 bottled beers and an additional 20 beers on tap, **Lady Falconburgh's Barley Exchange**, 640 Main Ave. (☎ 970-382-9664), boasts one of the largest beer selections in the Southwest. The restaurant also has single-malt scotches and other premium liquors, and it serves a popular Philly cheese steak sandwich. **Scoot 'n' Blues**, 900 Main Ave. (☎ 970-259-1400), books rock 'n' roll, blues, and jazz acts and even has a weekly karaoke night. The hot pickers and jam bands often perform at **Haggard's Black Dog Tavern**, 13544 County Rd. 240 (☎ 970-259-5657).

Springing off on a side trip to Pagosa Springs

In the past few years, folks have been flooding into Pagosa Springs — just 59 miles east of Durango — to live. Archuleta County, where Pagosa Springs is located, ranks among the fastest growing counties in America. I recommend going there as a day trip to soak. Mineral-rich hot springs, rumored to have magical healing powers, bubble out of the earth right across the San Juan River from downtown Pagosa Springs.

Soaking in Pagosa Springs

Besides having therapeutic effects, the geothermal pools have heated many of the buildings on Pagosa's Main Street for almost a century.

To fully appreciate **The Springs at Pagosa,** 165 Hot Springs Blvd. (☎ 970-264-BATH; www.pagosahotsprings.com), you have to soak in most of the 15 outdoor pools, each with its own name and temperature. If you overheat in the 114-degree Lobster Pot, you can immediately cool off by dunking in the San Juan River, which flows right past the springs. While you soak, you can savor the sound of the river and the sight of the landscaped terraces all around you. It's open Sunday through Thursday 7 a.m. to 11 p.m., until 1 a.m. on Fridays and Saturdays (24 hours for overnight guests of the resort). Admission is $13 adults, $12 seniors, and $5 for children under 7 with a paying adult.

Staying and dining in Pagosa Springs

If all that bathing makes you hungry, **Isabel's,** 20 Village Dr. (☎ 970-731-5448), serves excellent fish, meat, pasta, and vegetarian dishes, but the herb-crusted lamb chops are best of all. Main courses at dinnertime cost $13 to $35.

If you order from the early-supper menu (available until 6:30 p.m.), you can eat in style for under $10.

If you want to spend more than a day soaking up Pagosa's atmosphere, many of the rooms at the **Springs Resort,** 165 Hot Springs Blvd. (☎ 800-225-0934 or 970-264-4168; www.pagosahotsprings.com), offer views of the so-called mother spring, which spouts 142-degree water into a pool behind the lodge. Everything around here smells a bit sulfurous, but you won't mind when you start soaking in the adjacent hot springs, included with the room rate. If you tire of the healing waters, you can have your skin moisturized at the spa or take a yoga class. As for the rooms themselves, they're bright, pleasant, and restful. Rates at the inn range from $105 to $189 for a double.

Fast Facts: Durango

Emergencies

Dial ☎ 911.

Hospital

Mercy Medical Center, 375 E. Park Ave. (☎ 970-247-4311), has a 24-hour emergency room.

Information

Contact the Durango Area Chamber Resort Association, 111 S. Camino del Rio (P.O. Box 2587), Durango, CO 81302 (☎ 800-525-8855 or 970-247-0312; www.durango.org), located just south of downtown on U.S. 160/550.

Pharmacy

The Rite-Aid (☎ 970-247-5057) at 28 Town Plaza has a full-service pharmacy.

Post Office

The Durango Post Office (☎ 970-247-3434) is at 222 W. Eighth St.

Road Report

Call ☎ 970-247-3355.

Weather and Ski Conditions

Call ☎ 970-247-0930.

Mesa Verde and the Four Corners

Years ago, the Ancestral Puebloans — ancestors of the modern-day Pueblo people — lived throughout the Four Corners area, including the current location of Cortez. When they departed the area around A.D. 1300, the Puebloans left behind countless ruins and artifacts, the most famous being the cliff dwellings inside Mesa Verde National Park, a few miles southeast of town. Besides being a hotbed for archeologists, the small towns of Cortez, Dolores, and Mancos offer respite from the heat and serve as gateways to the mountains to the north and the deserts beyond. And if you really want to visit the only place where you can stand in four states at once (Colorado, Utah, New Mexico, and Arizona), head for the otherwise-unremarkable Four Corners Monument.

Getting there

The best way to get here from the east or west is via U.S. 160, which spans all the way from I-25 in the east to the Grand Canyon area to the southwest. If you're traveling from the west on I-70, you can take U.S. 191 south to Monticello, Utah, then pick up U.S. 666 to Cortez. If you're coming from the east on I-70, you can pinball south on U.S. 50, U.S. 550, Colorado 62, and Colorado 145. If you're coming from the south, take U.S. 666 north to Cortez from Gallup, New Mexico.

Great Lake Airlines (☎ 800-554-5111) offers service between Denver and **Cortez-Montezuma County Airport** (☎ 970-565-9510), 1½ miles southwest of town on County Road G (via U.S. 160/666). Upon arriving in Cortez, you can rent a car from **Budget** (☎ 800-527-0700), **American Auto Rentals** (☎ 970-565-9168), or **Enterprise** (☎ 800-736-8222).

Getting around

You need to drive to travel in this territory. Most of the activity in **Cortez** is on the east-west U.S. 160, which runs through town as Main Street. At the west end of Cortez, U.S. 160 merges with north-south U.S. 666, or Broadway Avenue, and heads south as U.S. 160/666. On the east side of town, U.S. 160 crosses Colorado 145, which heads 11 miles north to **Dolores** and then continues on to Telluride and Montrose. The entrance to **Mesa Verde National Park** is 10 miles east of Cortez on U.S. 160. The small town of **Mancos** is another 6 miles east of Mesa Verde on U.S. 160.

Mancos is situated just south of the highway. A business loop of U.S. 160 curves off the main highway and goes through downtown Mancos.

Where to stay

Cortez has a strip of chain hotels a few miles west of the entrance to Mesa Verde. The area also has guest ranches, bed-and-breakfasts, and historic hotels. Some lodgings are in the towns; others are in the high desert countryside; and one is deep inside Mesa Verde National Park.

Bauer House Bed & Breakfast
$$ **Mancos**

At this 1890s Victorian mansion, you'll have a hard time deciding whether to spend time inside or out. On the B&B's 1.5 grassy acres, you can find a putting green, a gazebo, and areas for bocce ball and croquet. Inside are four guest rooms, each decorated with a different style of antiques. I like the Wicker Room, full of antique wicker furniture. If you want to feel as if you're outside when you're in your room, rent the third-floor penthouse. Because of its wood paneling and 360-degree views of the Mancos Valley, one recent guest called it a "cabin in the sky."

100 Bauer Ave. ☎ *800-733-9707 or 970-533-9707.* www.bauer-house.com. *Rack rates: $75–$125 double. Open: Apr–Oct. MC, V.*

Enchanted Mesa Motel
$ **Mancos**

The name of this motel sounds nice and the owners are, too. They put out a grill for guests and will even let you use their computer to get your e-mail. Some of the guest rooms have themes, including cappuccino (lots of brown stripes) and cowboy (cowboys and barbed wire stenciled on the walls). Most rooms have refrigerators and microwaves, and all have coffeemakers and cable television.

862 Grand Ave. ☎ *866-533-MESA or 970-533-7729. Fax: 970-533-7758. Rack rates: $50–$65 double. AE, DC, DISC, MC, V.*

Far View Lodge
$$ **Mesa Verde**

The rooms at this motor lodge are old and smallish. Perched on a 9,100-foot hilltop deep inside Mesa Verde National Park, they have private balconies and large windows opening onto views of the surrounding mesas, canyons, and mountains. The views alone make a stay here worthwhile, but there are other advantages to staying inside the national park. If you stay here, you can conveniently drive the Mesa Top Loop Drive right before sunset, when the lighting is perfect and few people are around. You can stargaze at Mesa Verde's crystalline night sky and watch deer and wild horses browse on the vegetation outside your room at dawn. Then, you can take the first — and least crowded — ruins tours of the day.

Mesa Verde National Park. ☎ *800-449-2288 or 970-533-1944. Fax: 970-533-7831.* www.visitmesaverde.com. *Rack rates: $105–$126 double. Closed Nov–Mar. AE, DISC, MC, V.*

Where to dine

A few restaurants in Cortez have borrowed a trick or two from the restaurants a few miles to the southwest in Arizona. In one or two, you may even find a green chili cheese steak. But heartburn is by no means mandatory. You can eat well in this area without spending too much — or paying later.

Dolores River Brewery
$ **Dolores** PIZZA AND SALADS

The smoke from the wood-fired pizza oven here is a better advertisement than any neon sign! Inside, the décor is simple and comfortable, the service casual and very friendly. The pizzas and calzones feature traditional toppings, but with some original twists such as Kalamata olives and Portobello mushrooms. They're all hearty and filling after a long day on the mesas. There's an excellent selection of salads, including a Salmon Caesar, and the beers are top-notch. Try the ESB, an excellent example of the type, or the Schwartz Hacker, and exceptional Oktoberfest-style dark lager.

100 South Fourth St. ☎ *970-882-4677. Reservations not accepted. Main courses: $5.95–$7.50. AE, MC, V. Open: Daily 4–9 p.m.*

Main Street Brewery and Restaurant
$ **Cortez** ECLECTIC

The owners of this microbrewery hope to improve public health through beer consumption. Their motto is "Avoid heart attacks — drink beer." Their dinner menu equates beer with "life itself." And their dessert menu proposes an "amber bock or mild stout" as a "delicious and healthy" substitute for sins such as ice cream. Brewed by a real Bavarian brewmeister, the medicine is hardly bitter; in fact, I recommend an extra dose of the Schnozenboomer Amber Bock. The brewery also has some beer-worthy food, including pasta, fish, steaks, burgers, and salads.

21 E. Main. ☎ *970-564-9112. Reservations for large parties only. Main courses: $6–$20. AE, MC, V. Open: Daily 4–9 p.m.; limited menu later in bar.*

Metate Room (at Far View Lodge)
$$ **Mesa Verde** REGIONAL/AMERICAN

This isn't the only restaurant inside Mesa Verde National Park, but it's the best, hands-down. Unlike the park's cafeterias, where the food brings to mind the stuff you get on airplanes, the fare at Far View tastes gourmet. Even if it didn't, you'd still need to get here to absorb the expansive views out the restaurant windows. The offerings consist of traditional American dishes highlighted by fresh regional ingredients. One winner is the Turkey Roulade, a turkey breast stuffed with mushrooms and pine nuts.

Mesa Verde National Park. ☎ *800-449-2288 or 970-533-1944. Reservations not accepted. Main courses: $12–$26. AE, DISC, MC, V. Open: Apr–Oct Daily 5–9:30 p.m.*

Exploring the world of the Ancestral Puebloans

Most of the ruins in this area were left by the Ancestral Puebloan (or Anasazi) people, who lived in the Four Corners region from around A.D. 300 to 1300. The Ancestral Puebloans may have lived long ago, but they weren't primitive. They built multistory stone dwellings out in the open and, later, under overhangs in cliffs. Plastered in bright colors, the cliff dwellings were shaded in summer and sun-warmed in winter. In addition to being capable architects, the Ancestral Puebloans domesticated animals, hunted for game, foraged for nuts, berries, and other foods, and farmed corn, beans, and squash using sophisticated irrigation systems that gathered water and conserved soils. They even used astronomy. If you're curious about their world, you'll probably enjoy a few days in and near Mesa Verde.

Getting started

Exploring Mesa Verde is more fun if you know a little about the Ancestral Puebloans first. The spots listed here can help you get started:

✔ The **Anasazi Heritage Center,** 27501 Colorado 184 (☎ **970-882-5600;** www.co.blm.gov/ahc), 2 miles south of Dolores, has more than 3 million curated artifacts inside. Some of the most intriguing ones are displayed in a timeline that explains how the culture of the Ancestral Puebloans evolved. The Heritage Center also has a pit house replica; interactive computer programs summing up the findings of different archeological digs; and hands-on activities such as weaving, corn-grinding, and using a microscope.

The Heritage Center serves as headquarters for the newly created **Canyons of the Ancients National Monument.** If you're planning on visiting the monument, make sure to get information and maps while you're here. It's open daily from 9 a.m. to 5 p.m. March through October, and 9 a.m. to 4 p.m. November through February. Admission is $3 adults 17 and over, and free for youths under 17.

✔ After you're done inside the Anasazi Heritage Center, you can hike a paved, ½-mile trail from the parking lot to **Escalante Pueblo,** a 12-room dwelling with panoramic views. There's always something special about the places where the Puebloans built. Escalante Pueblo is a perfect example of this.

✔ If you want to find out even more about the Ancestral Puebloans (and about archeology) before going to Mesa Verde, take a one-day class at the **Crow Canyon Archeological Center,** 23390 Road K, Cortez (☎ **800-422-8975;** www.crowcanyon.org). On Wednesdays and Thursdays during the summer, you can take one-day courses (cost: $50 for adults, $25 for 18 and under) in which you handle and interpret artifacts, tour the center's laboratory, and visit a real dig. You need to reserve a spot ahead of time. When not offering classes, the center is not geared for visitors.

✔ The **Cortez Cultural Center,** 25 N. Market St. (☎ **970-565-1151;** www.cortezculturalcenter.org), in downtown Cortez, has a museum, a gift shop, and a gallery with rotating displays. The best time to visit is on summer evenings, when cultural programs are offered in an outdoor amphitheater. These include Native American dances, music, and even dramas. From June through August it's open daily from 10:00 a.m. to 9:30 p.m.; from September through May, it's open Monday through Saturday from 10 a.m. to 5 p.m. Admission is free.

Mesa Verde National Park

Simply put, this is the best place to view Ancestral Pueblo archeological sites. It's the largest archeological preserve in the country, with 4,000 sites ranging from pit houses to stunning, multistoried cliff dwellings with towers, *kivas* (round, subterranean ceremonial chambers), and terraces. These dwellings, which appear almost as an outgrowth of the earth, justify a special trip to southwest Colorado. The largest and best known of them, Cliff Palace, has 217 rooms, 23 kivas, and a four-story tower. Situated on a relatively pristine 9,000-foot-high mesa, Mesa Verde also lets you absorb some of the natural splendor of the Southwest.

Mesa Verde isn't a quick hit. It takes 45 minutes to get from the park entrance to the **Far View Visitor Center.** The entrance road climbs steadily for 14 miles and has corners too sharp for vehicles longer than 25 feet. From the visitor center, you need to drive another half-hour to reach the park's most popular archeological sites, Balcony House and Cliff Palace, and an hour to reach Wetherill Mesa. Allow a full day to see the park, more if you have time.

Here's how to see the park efficiently:

✔ The only way you can get close to the largest cliff dwellings is by going on a ranger-guided tour. Your first stop should be at the **Far View Visitor Center** (☎ **970-529-5036**) to buy tickets (cost: $2.75 per person), open from 8 a.m. to 5 p.m. from mid-April to mid-October. Try to get there before noon, because the tours sometimes sell out. During spring, summer, and fall, you can go on a guided tour of either **Cliff Palace** or **Balcony House,** but not both on the same day. During summer only, you can also buy tickets for a tour of **Long House,** which is on Wetherill Mesa (a very slow 12-mile drive from the visitor center). All the tours involve walking and climbing. The Balcony House tour is the most strenuous and — some would say — most exciting. On it, you climb 90 vertical feet of stairs, 32- and 20-foot long ladders, and slip through a narrow 10-foot long crawl space.

- After buying your tickets, visit the **Chapin Mesa Archeological Museum** (☎ 970-529-4631). This place is so old, it's a historic building itself. It has an impressive collection of artifacts as well as dioramas showing life in Ancestral Puebloan communities. The museum also has an information desk, and it serves as the park's visitor center during winter. While you're in this area, take a short walk to **Spruce Tree House,** which is the only large cliff dwelling you can visit without going on a guided tour. During winter, it's the only cliff dwelling you can visit, period, open year-round 8 a.m. to 5 p.m. (until 6:30 p.m. mid-April to mid-October). Then, drive to the more remote ruins.

- If you have tickets to a tour of Balcony House or Cliff Palace, drive the **Mesa Top Loop Drive,** which consists of two 6-mile-long lasso-shaped loops. Along these loops are ten parking areas. From each parking area, you can take a short walk to mesa-top ruins or to overlooks of the surrounding canyons. Cliff dwellings and granaries are tucked into openings in the canyon walls, and you can see them if you look carefully. If you have tickets for a tour of Cliff Palace or Balcony House, try to time your drive so that you show up at the tour's meeting place at least ten minutes early. Along the way, don't miss **Square Tower Overlook,** where you can scan the canyon walls for archeological sites, and the mysterious **Sun Temple,** a windowless structure that may have been a prayer to the gods.

- If you have a ticket for a Long House tour, head out to **Wetherill Mesa.** When you're on the mesa, park your car and walk or take a shuttle to the different dwellings and overlooks, including Long House.

Beating the crowds at Mesa Verde

It's hard to contemplate life 1,000 years ago while surrounded by 21st-century people. Mesa Verde can get crowded, but you can do a few things to give yourself a little time alone with the past:

- Visit during May, June, or, best of all, October. During these months, you can still see most of the ruins, but with fewer people around.

- If you come during summer, drive to Wetherill Mesa. Most park visitors don't make this trip, and it's a beautiful area.

- Drive the Mesa Top Loop Drive right before sunset, after most visitors have departed.

- Go on a guided tour of Cliff Palace or Balcony House first thing in the morning. The first tours, at 9:00 and 9:30 a.m., seldom fill up. If you get to the Far View Visitor Center soon after 8 a.m., you should be able to buy tickets and make it to the tour's meeting area on time.

If you have extra time, do the following:

- ✔ Go to places you haven't yet visited. If you've been on the Mesa Top Loop Drive, go to Wetherill Mesa, and vice versa.

- ✔ Go for a longer hike near Spruce Tree House. Two hiking loops begin at Spruce Tree House: the 2¼-mile **Spruce Canyon Trail,** which drops 500 feet to the bottom of Spruce Canyon, and the 2⅛-mile **Petroglyph Point Trail,** which has some rock art alongside it. Before going, you need to register at the trailhead. If you only have time for one, do the Petroglyph Point Trail.

Mesa Verde's entrance is on U.S. 160, 10 miles east of Cortez. For park information call ☎ 970-529-4465 or surf the Internet to www.nps.gov/meve. The park entrance is always open, but you aren't allowed to visit archeological sites after dusk. Admission is $10 per car.

Ute Mountain Tribal Park

If you want to see amazing cliff dwellings with fewer people around than at Mesa Verde, go to the Ute Mountain Tribal Park (☎ 800-847-5485 or 970-749-1452; www.utemountainute.com/tribalpark.htm), a 125,000-acre area bordering Mesa Verde. Located on the Ute Mountain Ute reservation, the park has dwellings that are nearly as large as the grandest ones in Mesa Verde. You can choose between half-day and full-day trips. The half-day trip goes mostly to unexcavated sites littered with thousands of potsherds (pieces of broken pottery). It's much less strenuous than the full-day trip, which goes to the same unexcavated sites and then continues on to at least four well-preserved cliff dwellings.

The full-day tour is the only way to see the most spectacular cliff dwellings, so be sure to take it if you visit the tribal park. The most stunning cliff dwelling, Eagles Nest, is on a 75-foot-high ledge underneath a large overhang. To get there, you need to climb a 30-foot ladder, among other challenges.

Throughout the tour, the Ute guides discuss the Puebloans (who were not related to the Utes) and the history of their tribe. A lot of driving is involved — if you can, try to ride in the same vehicle with the guide, so you can converse while you ride. And bring plenty of sunscreen and water.

Tours meet at Ute Mountain Museum, 20 miles south of Cortez, at the southernmost junction of U.S. 666 and U.S. 160. Tours are offered April through October. The museum is open daily from 7:30 a.m. to 3:30 p.m., from April through October. Half-day tours cost $20 per person; full day tours cost $40 per person. Transportation provided by guide costs $6 extra per person. Reservations are required.

Remote sites

Mesa Verde and the Ute Mountain Tribal Park aren't the only places in southwestern Colorado where you can visit archeological sites. There are thousands of other dwellings and artifacts scattered through the area. Many are unexcavated mounds barely recognizable as past dwellings. At least a few excavated sites are worth seeing if you don't mind taking long, dusty drives in the sticks. Here are two options:

✔ **Hovenweep National Monument** is best known for the remains of towers that the Ancestral Puebloans built in this area between A.D. 1100 and A.D. 1300. These towers may have been used for ceremonies, signaling, storage, defense, living quarters, or observatories. No one knows for certain, and part of the fun is coming up with your own theories. Today, all the towers at Hovenweep have either partly or entirely collapsed, but structures as high as 20 feet remain. Eight obvious ones flank a 1½-mile trail that travels along the rim of **Little Ruin Canyon.** The trail takes one to two hours to hike and has one short, steep stretch where it drops into, and then climbs out of, Little Ruin Canyon. A less strenuous option is the ½-mile **Tower Point Loop,** which takes about 30 minutes and doesn't require much climbing. To reach Hovenweep, take U.S. 160 south 2 miles to County Road G (where the airport is located), and follow the signs. It takes about an hour to get there from Cortez. If you go this way, you'll be on paved roads all the way. The monument grounds are open daily year-round 8 a.m. to 5 p.m. Admission is $6 per vehicle. For more information, call the monument at ☎ **970-562-4282** or surf the Internet to www.nps.gov/hove.

✔ You can also visit widely scattered sites in the new **Canyons of the Ancients National Monument.** Established in 2000, the 164,000-acre monument has more than 5,000 documented archeological sites, and the highest density of sites in the nation. One of the most interesting is **Lowry Pueblo,** the remains of a pueblo-style dwelling that had 40 rooms and 9 kivas. Nearby is a Great Kiva spanning more than 54 feet in diameter — one of the largest ones in this area. Toilets and picnic tables are nearby. Lowry Pueblo is on County Road CC, 9 miles west of Pleasant View, a small community 20 miles northeast of Cortez on U.S. 666. For information on Lowry Pueblo and other sites inside Canyons of the Ancients National Monument, contact or visit the **Anasazi Heritage Center** (☎ **970-882-4811**) at 27501 Colorado 184.

Guided tours of Mesa Verde National Park

Not everyone wants to zoom off into the desert Southwest in search of far-flung archeological sites. For those who prefer extra guidance, **Aramark** (☎ **800-449-2288** or 970-529-4421; www.visitmesaverde.com) offers half-day and full-day motor coach tours of Mesa Verde National Park. The tours stop at some of the most intriguing sites and overlooks, save you from parking hassles, and include a ranger-guided walking tour of a cliff dwelling. Morning half-day tours go to Spruce Tree House, afternoon half-day tours go to Balcony House, and full-day tours go to Cliff Palace.

The actual Four Corners

If you're just *dying* to take a picture of your kid with each limb in a different state, then head southwest from Cortez following U.S. 160 for 40 miles to the very corner of the state. You'll have to go into the Navajo Reservation in New Mexico to get to the entrance, but that's where you find the Four Corners Monument. To be honest, it's an underwhelming experience; there's a brass slab in a bed of concrete marking the actual spot, and not much else. There's no running water at the park, but there are some shacks where Navajo vendors sell jewelry, crafts, and food. Admission is $3, which is steep for what you get. Miss this, and you miss nothing.

 If you're choosing between the two half-day tours, go for the afternoon affair, because Balcony House is more fun to tour than Spruce Tree House. (Besides, you can always do Spruce Tree House on your own.) The motor-coach tours, which run from May to October, leave from Far View Lodge. The morning tour costs $29 for adults, $28 for kids 5 to 17. The afternoon tour costs $38.50 for adults, $27.50 for kids 5 to 17. The full-day tour is $55.75 for adults, $43.75 for kids 5 to 17.

Other things to see and do

The offerings in this area aren't limited to archeological sites. When you're done seeing the ruins, you can do the following:

- ✔ **Relive the pioneer days, and then eat steak. Bartels' Mancos Valley Stage Line** (☎ 800-365-3530 or 970-533-9857; www.thestagecoach. com) will take you for a ride on a replica of the horse-drawn mud coaches used throughout the West in the 1800s. Just like in the old days, the ride is dusty and, despite the leather straps under the coach that serve as shock absorbers, on the bumpy side. Three different tours are offered: The one-hour rides give you a taste of stage-coach travel but not much more. You're better off taking the lunch or dinner tour. Each lasts about three and a half hours and includes a meal at a peaceful old homestead deep inside a canyon near Mesa Verde. The dinner tour costs a little more, but the meal consists of steaks instead of sandwiches, the air is cooler, and you can catch the sunset on the ride home. The rides start and finish at 4550 County Rd. 41, and reservations are required. To get there, continue south on Main Street for 5 miles past Mancos. The rides operate May through September. Prices for the one-hour tour are $35 adults, $17.50 kids 3 to 12; for the lunch tour it's $55 adults, $27.50 kids 3 to 12; and for the dinner tour it's $65 adults, $32.50 kids 3 to 12.

- ✔ **Go for broke. Ute Mountain Casino** (☎ 800-258-8007 or 970-565-8800; www.utemountaincasino.com) offers slot, keno, and video poker machines, as well as blackjack and poker tables. The casino is in Towaoc, Colorado, 11 miles south of Cortez on U.S. 160/666, on the Ute Mountain Ute reservation.

✔ **Soak your feet. McPhee Reservoir,** near Dolores, has 4,470 acres of water and more than 50 miles of shoreline at average water levels. Below the dam is an 11-mile stretch of Gold Medal catch-and-release fly fishing (you need a license). Admission is free. You can float your boat and camp at McPhee Campground (☎ **970-882-2294** or 877-444-6777 for reservations), off Colorado 184 just east of Colorado 145. Camping costs $12 for regular sites, $15 for hookups.

Shopping

Go to Cortez to shop for Native American arts, crafts, and jewelry.

✔ Open since 1961, **Notah Dineh,** 345 W. Main St. (☎ **800-444-2024** or 970-565-9607), carries roughly 250,000 works of art by the Hopi, Navajo, Ute, and Zuni tribes. The store is best known for its rugs, both antique and new, which range in price from $50 to $25,000.

✔ **Mesa Verde Pottery** (☎ **800-441-9908** or 970-565-4492) makes its own line of molded, decorated pottery, which sells for $12 to $200. It also has traditional Native American wares. It's at 27601 Hwy. 160, 1 mile east of Cortez.

✔ The **Cortez Cultural Center,** 25 N. Market St. (☎ **970-565-1151**), has a small but pleasing selection of Native American jewelry at reasonable prices.

Fast Facts: Cortez, Dolores, and Mancos

Emergencies

Dial ☎ **911.**

Hospital

Southwest Memorial Hospital, 1311 N. Mildred Rd., Cortez (☎ 970-565-6666), has a 24-hour emergency room.

Information

For information on the Cortez area, contact the Mesa Verde Country Visitor Information

Bureau, P.O. Box HH, Cortez, CO 81321 (☎ 800-253-1616; www.mesaverde country.com). Upon arriving, visit the Colorado Welcome Center at Cortez, 928 E. Main St. (☎ 970-565-4048).

Post Office

The Cortez Post Office (☎ 970-565-3181) is at 35 S. Beech St.

Chapter 25

The High San Juans and the San Luis Valley

. . . .

In This Chapter

▶ Great hiking and gruesome history in Lake City
▶ Taking in the theater at Creede
▶ Wolf Creek Pass and the Wolf Creek ski area
▶ Checking out Alamosa and the Great Sand Dunes

. . . .

South of I-70, tucked between the continental divide (to the west) and the Front Range mountains, Pikes Peak, and the Sangre de Cristo range (to the east), this region, loosely comprised of the San Luis Valley and the eastern parts of the San Juan Mountains, has three easily overlooked towns, each with its own treasures.

Lake City, a tiny, historic mining town, is 55 miles south of Gunnison in the San Juan range. **Lake San Cristobal,** created when a mountainside slumped into a river, is nearby, and the wildflower-strewn wilderness stretches out, seemingly forever, across the high glacial valleys of this, the most remote and wild part of the state.

When you drive into the tiny mountain town of **Creede,** you know immediately from the rows of Victorian homes and mine shacks that the town has a rich past. Given its population of just 300, you wouldn't expect it to have a top-notch repertory theater, too. The **Creede Repertory Theater** is a risk-taking ensemble that flourishes in the smallest of towns. In a state known more for its outdoor recreation than its indoor culture, Creede Rep is a gem.

Alamosa appears to be just another agricultural community — that is, until you come across the 350-foot-high sand dunes and the geothermal springs a few miles away on the valley floor. Depressed 20 years ago, this former railroad hub has been revitalized, thanks in part to an influx of river runners and artists.

Lake City

In the San Juan range, Lake City's few year-round residents live quietly just downstream of Lake San Cristobal, the second largest natural body of water in Colorado. It's incredibly secluded — a hiker's paradise — and there's some *extremely* colorful local history.

Getting to Lake City

Lake City is 55 miles southwest of Gunnison. From Gunnison, take U.S. 50 west for 9 miles and then go 46 miles south on Colorado 149. If you continue southeast past Lake City on Colorado 149, you'll cross the continental divide and then follow the course of the Rio Grande River down to Creede (46 miles from Lake City) and, beyond that, the San Luis Valley (via U.S. 160 east).

Getting around Lake City

In Lake City, Colorado 149 runs north and south through town as Gunnison Avenue, the town's main road.

Where to stay in Lake City

Lake City can be expensive during July and August, but it's a bargain for most of the rest of the year. The listing below is the best of a small handful in the town proper.

Matterhorn Mountain Motel
$ Lake City

You can tell this motel is a half-century old by looking at its vintage neon sign — it was grandfathered in when Lake City banned other, similar signs. Inside, the rooms have showers instead of tubs, but everything else is modern. Fully remodeled in 2000, all have barn-wood furniture and large windows, and they're inviting. The rooms have either a queen-size bed and full kitchen or two queens and no kitchen. If you're here for a romantic getaway, spend the extra $5 per night for a cottage. They're roomy and private, and sleep two people comfortably — not counting Fido, who's also welcome here. The motel sits on a hillside just above dusty, sleepy, downtown Lake City.

409 Bluff St. ☎ ***970-944-2210.*** *Fax: 970-944-2267.* www.matterhornmotel.com. *Rack rates: June–Sept $89 double, $95 cottages (4-night minimum); Oct–Apr $70 double, cottages closed. MC, V.*

Where to dine in Lake City

Lake City's beauty lures a few skilled chefs who try to cash in on a very short tourist season. You can also find moderately priced, family fare.

The Southern Rockies

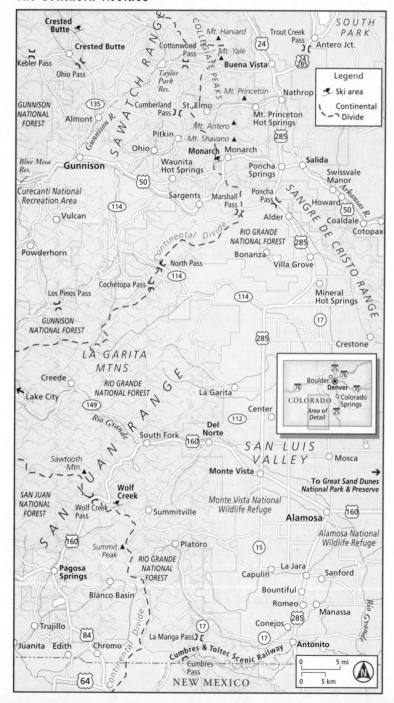

Charlie P's
$ Lake City AMERICAN/TEX-MEX

Charlie P's is in a building that has been a morgue, cigar factory, and bakery. Nowadays it produces barbeque, burgers, five different chicken dishes, and some tasty Tex-Mex fare, among other offerings. The food is consistently palatable, and the low prices attract a stream of (living) locals. The restaurant has a large patio where you can watch the occasional car or pedestrian pass by on Lake City's main drag.

951 N. Hwy. 149. ☎ 970-944-2332. Reservations accepted. Main courses: $5–$17. DISC, MC, V. Open: Mon–Fri 11:30 a.m.–1:30 p.m. and 5:30–7:30 p.m.

The Crystal Inn
$$$ Lake City FRENCH

Chef Bruno, who runs this place, once served as banquet chef at New York City's famous Tavern on the Green. In the twilight of Bruno's career, a friend invited him to cook at this small country inn 2 miles south of Lake City, and, fortunately for us, he's still here. Chef Bruno keeps the menu small. Most nights, he cooks a single veal, pork, fish, and beef dish, each with a classic French sauce. He hopes you'll have some wine, too. You can tell he loves the fermented grape juice — the place overflows with magnums and wine bottles, empty and full, including a few that hold candles. It's a pretty romantic spot.

2175 Hwy. 149 South. ☎ 877-465-6343 or 970-944-2201. Reservations required. Main courses: $20–$30; brunch: $9–$13. MC, V. Open: Thurs–Sat 6–8 p.m.; Sun brunch 10:30 a.m.–1 p.m.

Exploring Lake City

Most of the best things in this area are outside in the mountains, but there's also a lot of human history in each town. Even if you're not a mountain person, you can find plenty to do.

The best things to see and do in Lake City

When you're not in the wilderness surrounding the Gunnison Valley, you can sample the following:

✔ **Spring a lake. Lake San Cristobal,** 3 miles north of Lake City, is dammed like most other lakes in Colorado — only in this case the dam is natural. About 700 years ago, a huge earthflow of partly decomposed volcanic rock slumped into the Lake Fork of the Gunnison River, stalling enough water to create the second largest natural body of water in Colorado (behind Grand Lake, southwest of Rocky Mountain National Park). Come here to camp, picnic, and savor the forested hills around still water. **Wupperman Campground** offers first-come, first-served camping (cost: $10 per car) on County Road 33 on the lake's southeast side. **Lakeview Resort** (☎ 800-456-0170 or 970-944-2401), also on County Road 33 on the lake's east

Alferd Packer, the Colorado Cannibal

Turns out Lake City is famous for its dining, but I don't recommend trying to take part in any "traditions" here. In February of 1874, a man named Alferd Packer and five other men wandered into the San Juans from Montrose, prospecting for silver and gold. Despite warnings about the weather from the Utes who lived nearby, they could not wait to get their hands on a claim, so they headed off into the mountains south of Gunnison with food and supplies for ten days.

Two months later, only Packer returned. He initially claimed that, as the weather worsened, members of the group died one by one; later he changed his story and admitted that things had turned murderous, but that he had only killed in self defense. He did, though, admit to eating his companions' remains in order to survive. His story didn't hold up, though, and in August five bodies were found near the present-day Lake City. Packer managed to escape from the jail in Saguache and was a fugitive for nine years; he was eventually caught, tried and sentenced, tried and sentenced again, and imprisoned for 16 years. With the help of a reporter from the *Denver Post,* he made another impassioned public plea of innocence, became a *cause célèbre*, and was granted clemency. He died in Deer Creek Canyon and was buried in a military cemetery in Littleton, south of Denver.

His legend and the debate about his guilt or innocence continued to grow; the students at Colorado University in Boulder named the cafeteria there the Alferd Packer Memorial Grill and for years had an Alferd Packer Festival, the main event of which was a raw meat-eating contest! In 1981, Governor Dick Lamm stirred up controversy by denying a posthumous pardon; and in 1989 the remains of Packer's victims were found buried two miles south of Lake City, and examined by forensics experts. The results were somewhat inconclusive, but seem to point toward cold-blooded murder, followed by a snowy feast.

You can find out more about Packer at the **Hinsdale County Museum,** 130 Silver St., at the corner of 2nd Street (☎ **970-944-2050**), and visit a memorial for his victims at the site of the alleged murder, 2 miles south of town on Highway 149.

side, rents fishing boats (cost: $45/half-day), pontoon boats ($80/half-day), and sea kayaks ($45/half-day). Personal watercraft (such as jetskis) are forbidden here, because the lake is very small.

✔ **Shop.** Lake City is folksy (think: chainsaw sculptures and quilted wall-hangings).

✔ **Drive a Jeep.** Lake City is one of those places where people who don't mountain bike should rent a Jeep and spend a day bouncing up into the stratosphere. Leaving from the downtown, you can rumble over **12,800-foot Engineer Pass** to Ouray, meander up the San Juan Skyway (U.S. 550) to Silverton, and lurch your way back to Lake City via **12,600-foot Cimarron Pass.** Except for U.S. 550, these roads are part of the **Alpine Loop Backcountry Byway,** which travels 65 miles through the San Juan high country, passing ghost towns and mines but never departing breathtaking scenery. The **Lake City Chamber of Commerce Visitor Information Center,** 800 N. Gunnison Ave. (☎ **800-569-1874** or 970-944-2527; www.lakecity co.com), has information on the loop, open most years from early summer to early October. **Pleasant View Resort,** 549 S. Gunnison Ave. in Lake City (☎ **970-944-2262**), rents Jeeps for $110 per day (gas not included).

Staying active in Lake City

The immense mountains around Lake City naturally challenge visitors. One great hike or mountain-bike ride, which should take you most of a day (pack water and a lunch), is the **Wager Gulch Trail,** which takes you up some pretty challenging terrain, through the **ghost town of Carson,** and to the ridge of the **continental divide.** To get there, take Colorado 149 south from Lake City and turn right on the road to Lake San Cristobal. Follow this road 4 miles; the pavement ends, but you continue 5 more miles to the trail head. Look for the sign for Wager Gulch/Carson on the left. The trail is fairly steep for the first mile and a half, then levels out as you approach Carson, which, you should know, is private property. You can peek around, but don't touch. Continue another mile and a half to the divide, for a total of about 4¾ miles. This is classic glacier landscaping, and you can see the 13,657-foot **Carson Peak** to the west, and the head-waters of the Rio Grande on the other side.

Fast Facts: Lake City

Emergencies
Dial ☎ **911.**

Hospitals
For 24-hour emergency care, go to Gunnison Valley Hospital (☎ 970-641-1456), 711 North Taylor in Gunnison.

Information
The Lake City/Hinsdale County Chamber of Commerce Visitor Information Center, 800

N. Gunnison Ave. (☎ 800-569-1874 or 970-944-2527; www.lakecityco.com), can tell you about goings-on in that community.

Post Office
In Lake City, well, you can't miss it on North Highway 149 (☎ 970-944-2560).

Road Conditions
Call ☎ 877-315-7623.

Creede

If you go over Slumgullion Pass from Lake City, you eventually reach Creede, a former silver-mining town at the mouth of a shadowy *box canyon* (a canyon that's closed on three sides). Above the town, spectacular old mine buildings seem to cling to the dark walls of Willow Creek

Canyon. The Rio Grande passes just below town. It's popular among fishers and boaters, and the surrounding forests lure outdoorsmen and athletes. With just 300 year-round residents, Creede is the type of place where businesses open their doors whenever an employee happens to be around — and that's not very often during the off-season. In summer, however, visitors cram into the tiny downtown area to experience its unspoiled Victorian architecture and one of the West's finest repertory theater companies.

Getting to Creede

United Express (☎ 800-241-6522) offers daily service between Denver and **Alamosa-San Luis Valley Regional Airport** (☎ 719-589-9446), 3 miles south of town on U.S. 285.

Upon landing, you can rent a car through **Budget** (☎ 719-589-0103) or **L & M Auto Rental** (☎ 719-589-4651). For a cab, call **Lil Stinkers Taxi Service** (☎ 719-589-2500).

To reach Creede from Alamosa, drive 47 miles west on U.S. 160, then go 22 miles on Colorado 149 west. If you continue past Creede on Colorado 149, it's 48 miles to Lake City.

Getting around Creede

Colorado 149 makes a giant U-turn in **Creede's downtown** area. It heads straight into town and toward Willow Creek Canyon, then (wisely) doubles back toward the valley carved by the Rio Grande. There's free parking in the small downtown area. There's no mass transit, so you'll have to drive, walk, or ride.

Where to stay in Creede

You won't find chain properties in Creede, but you can choose between guest ranches, historic hotels, B&Bs, and family-run motels. The prices in this area generally run a little lower than in other parts of the Rockies.

Antlers Rio Grande Lodge
$$ Creede

Most of the accommodations at this guest ranch are flush on the banks of the Rio Grande River. They have no phones or televisions, but the splashing of the river more than substitutes. If you cross the Rio Grande via the suspension bridge near the lodge, you're immediately on National Forest land, and you can climb as far and as high into the mountains as you please. You can also fish for trout without leaving the property. I like the cabins best. Rented in one-week blocks during summer, each has a full kitchen, living area, and porch. The motel rooms share a riverside deck, have kitchenettes, and are smaller than the cabins. The ranch also has a fine restaurant that offers dining both indoors and on a riverside deck.

26222 Colorado 149. ☎ *719-658-2423. Fax: 719-658-0804.* www.antlerslodge.com. *Weekly rack rates: 1-bedroom cabins $750–$775, 2-bedroom cabins $780–$925. Daily rack rates: $90 double, $25–$29 RV site. MC, V.*

Creede Hotel
$$ Creede

Located on Main Street, just a few doors down from the **Creede Repertory Theater,** this 19th-century hotel rents out four simple rooms. Each has its original walls and flooring, not to mention spare, tasteful furnishings. The most desirable rooms share a large balcony overlooking Main Street. They don't have phones or televisions, so there's little to distract you from the past. The only real drawbacks are the bathrooms, which look more historic than you may prefer.

120 N. Main St. ☎ *719-658-2608. Fax: 719-658-0725.* www.creedehotel.com. *Rack rates: $80–$95 double. Rates include breakfast during peak season only. AE, DISC, V, MC.*

Snowshoe Lodge
$ Creede

Located a few blocks from Creede's downtown and the repertory theater, this lodge offers some great values. Large families can stay in a homey, two-bedroom suite with a cozy downstairs den for only $95 to $120 during high season. The motel rooms are decorated in themes ranging from John Wayne (the actor once stayed here) to Bear/Moose. They're clean, appealing, and ideal for groups that include kids or pets.

On Colorado 149 at the south edge of town. ☎ *719-658-2315.* www.creede-co.com/snowshoe. *Rack rates: Motel rooms $45–$80, suite $75–$120. AE, MC, V.*

Where to dine in Creede

Many of Creede's restaurants close seasonally, then start fresh the next year. That makes the dining scene less predictable, but it does lend itself to, um, innovation.

Café Ole
$ Creede   PIZZA

Café Ole serves hearty, inexpensive breakfasts and lunches and has pizza on Thursday nights. Locals get fired up about the pizza — a relatively scarce commodity around here. Yet only the boldest order the Slumgullion, with a landslide-sized pile of toppings. Lunch fare includes salads and hot and cold sandwiches.

112 N. Main St. ☎ *719-658-2880. Reservations accepted. Sandwiches $5–$7, pizzas $6–$18. AE, DC, DISC, MC, V. Open: Mon–Sat 7:30 a.m.–4 p.m.; Thurs 5–8 p.m. for pizza only.*

Creede Hotel and Restaurant
$$ Creede   AMERICAN

This restaurant, housed in a 19th-century hotel, packs in theatergoers during the summer months. Once a rowdy bar — the atmosphere still feels like the Old West — it now serves gourmet meals such as merlot-braised lamb shank, New York strip with gorgonzola crust, and free-range pan-roasted chicken. The hotel changed hands in 2002, but its restaurant still enjoys a stellar reputation.

120 N. Main St. ☎ *719-658-2608. Reservations recommended. Main courses: $13–$20. AE, DISC, V, MC. Open: Summer Tues–Sun 11 a.m.–2 p.m. and 5–9 p.m.; rest of year Fri–Sat 5–9 p.m., Sun 11 a.m.–2 p.m.*

Exploring Creede

Creede is world famous for its repertory theatre, but set aside another day or two to explore the nearby mines and mountains.

Underground Mining Museum

Before driving the **Bachelor Historic Tour** (described in the next listing), go to this museum. That way, you'll know what transpired in all the old mine buildings you see on your drive. Located in an old mine tunnel near the mouth of Willow Creek Canyon, this museum displays mining equipment, memorabilia, and the precious rocks that attracted so much attention in the late 1800s. Alongside each display, interpretive panels explain how miners extracted and moved ore. This may not sound riveting on paper, but the underground setting makes the experience more chilling. Most tours are self-guided, but sometimes former miners take groups through the museum.

In Willow Creek Canyon, at the north edge of Creede. ☎ *719-658-0811. Self-guided tours: $6 adults, $5 seniors over 60, $4 kids ages 6–12. Guided tours: $10 for all ages. Hours vary so call ahead for opening times and tour information.*

Bachelor Historic Tour

This 17-mile driving tour, which begins and ends in Creede, passes dozens of 19th-century mine buildings that look as if they were built yesterday. Propped against and perched atop dark cliffs, these wooden structures seem to exist outside both gravity and time.

Before starting out, stop at the **Creede/Mineral County Chamber of Commerce** (☎ 800-327-2102 or 719-658-2374) on Main Street at the north end of town and pick up the 25-page booklet explaining the numbered stops along the road (cost: $1). Then proceed up Willow Creek Canyon at the north end of town. The most impressive structures are in the first 2 miles of the drive.

Even if you don't want to do the full tour, consider driving as far as the **Commodore Mine** (Stop No. 2). Beyond that point, the mines become less spectacular and the mountain scenery steals the show. Allow at least an hour for the whole loop. When dry, the road is passable (barely) for two-wheel-drive vehicles, but steep grades, bumps, and curves slow you down. If the road is wet, consider doing the loop backward — this lets you descend the steepest grades instead of climbing them. You can also rent a Jeep for $115 per day from **Continental Divide Services** (☎ 719-658-2682).

Staying active in Creede

There's great hiking around **Creede. Mineral County** consists of 96 percent public land and has two wilderness areas. For maps and information on area hikes, stop by the **Creede Ranger Station** (☎ 719-658-2556) on South Main Street or duck into **San Juan Sports,** 102 S. Main St. (☎ 719-658-2359).

Culture in Creede

In 1966, the **Creede Repertory Theater,** 124 N. Main St. (☎ 866-658-2540 or 719-658-2540; www.creederep.org), opened shop as part of an economic development project for what was then a depressed mining town. Today this company of around 15 actors is one of the top performing-arts groups in the state. (As for the town, it's doing a lot better, too.) From June through September every year, the company stages eight or more different plays — and as many as five in a single week — spread over two stages. The summer performances are mostly classics, and they sell out during the peak months of July and August. In early fall, the theater switches to riskier material, including regional and world premieres. The company announces its schedule for the next season in the fall of the previous year, and season tickets go on sale January 1.

 If you think you may stay in Creede for a week or more, consider buying a ticket package in order to get the best seats. The least expensive package includes tickets to three Main Stage plays, which you could conceivably use in a week. Individual tickets go on sale May 1. Tickets to Main Stage shows cost $16 to $24. General admission to the more intimate Black Box theater, where the productions are smaller and possibly more experimental, is $19 to $22.

Hitting the slopes in Creede

It's down the road a ways from Creede, on U.S. 160 between Del Norte and Pagosa Springs near the top of Wolf Creek Pass, but there's some good skiing down here. With the entire ski area above 10,000 feet and the summit at 11,900 feet, **Wolf Creek** (☎ 970-264-5639; www.wolfcreek ski.com) averages 450 inches of snow a year, easily the highest total in the state. The abundant snow usually lets Wolf Creek open in mid-November, long before most other resorts get rolling, and it keeps skiers and riders knee-deep in powder for much of the winter. As for the terrain's 1,600 skiable acres, it's a mixed bag, with some nice glades, but there aren't many long, consistently steep slopes.

Fast Facts: Creede

Emergencies
Dial ☎ 911.

Hospital
The San Luis Valley Regional Medical Center, 106 Blanca Ave. (☎ 719-589-2511) in Alamosa offers 24-hour emergency health care.

Information
The Creede/Mineral County Chamber of Commerce (☎ 800-327-2102 or 719-658-2374; www.creede.com) is located in the

County Annex Building, on Main Street at the north end of town.

Pharmacy
The nearest is Jack's Market Pharmacy, 222 Solar Ave. in Monte Vista (☎ 719-852-9894).

Post Office
The Creede Post Office (☎ 719-658-2615) is at 10 S. Main St.

Road Conditions
Call ☎ 719-589-9024.

Alamosa and the San Luis Valley

Alamosa is an agricultural and railroad community that could pass for Anywhere, USA. Yet it sits in the San Luis Valley, one of the most curious spots in the state. Bordered by the San Juan Mountains to the west and the Sangre de Cristo range to the east, the 50-mile-wide, 100-mile-long valley would be steep-walled and deep if tons of sediment hadn't washed into it from the mountains through the ages. Today the sandy valley floor is nearly flat. Through that floor, artesian springs bubble up, creating wetlands and geothermal pools in an otherwise arid area.

The culture in the Valley, like much of the rest of southern Colorado, is very New Mexican in flavor and attitude. This was the northernmost extent of the Spanish colonial conquest in North America — *El Norte* — and many of the area's residents consider themselves *Españoles,* not Hispanic, and certainly not Mexican. You can notice the remnants of Spain's ambitions in some of the place names: Del Norte on the western side of the Valley, and *Salida* — doorway or gateway — at the top of the pass leading north into the Arkansas Valley.

You can watch waterfowl in some of the wetlands or soak in certain pools yourself. When the wind blows, it transports sand from the west side of the valley to the east, adding to the wavelike dunes more than 750 feet high inside Great Sand Dunes National Park, one of Colorado's best treasures.

Getting there

United Express (☎ 800-241-6522) offers daily service between Denver and **Alamosa-San Luis Valley Regional Airport** (☎ 719-589-9446), 3 miles south of town on U.S. 285.

Upon landing, you can rent a car through **Budget** (☎ **719-589-0103**) or **L & M Auto Rental** (☎ **719-589-4651**). For a cab, call **Lil Stinkers Taxi Service** (☎ **719-589-2500**).

If you're driving, Alamosa is at the junction of east-west U.S. 160 and north-south U.S. 285. It's 173 miles north of Santa Fe, New Mexico, via U.S. 285. Denver is another 212 miles northeast of Alamosa via Colorado 17 and U.S. 285. U.S. 160 passes through Alamosa en route from Durango (149 miles to the west) to Walsenberg (73 miles to the east).

Getting around

U.S. 160 takes you into the heart of Alamosa. The town has wide Western-style streets and ample parking.

Where to stay

In Alamosa, you can go to a serene bed-and-breakfast, or choose among a number of chain hotels, including the **Best Western Alamosa Inn,** 1919 Main St. (☎ **719-589-2567**); **Comfort Inn of Alamosa,** 6301 County Rd. 107 (☎ **719-587-9000**); **Days Inn,** 224 O'Keefe Parkway (☎ **719-589-9037**); **Holiday Inn,** 333 Santa Fe Ave. (☎ **719-589-5833**); and **Super 8,** 2505 W. Main St. (☎ **719-589-6447**).

Cottonwood Inn B & B and Gallery
$$ Alamosa

Whether you're sitting on the porch swing, soaking in the hot tub, or lying on a comfy bed, you won't hear much at this B&B. You'd never know that Alamosa's main drag is just two blocks away. Come nighttime, you'll feel yourself cocooned in layers of serenity: valley, town, inn, room, and covers. Before turning off the lights, you can take in the works of local artists, which are on display in the hallways and guest rooms.

123 San Juan. ☎ *800-955-2623 or 719-589-3882. Fax: 719-589-6437.* www.cotton woodinn.com. *Rack rates: Mar–Oct, $90–$119 double; Nov–Feb $75–$105 double. Rates include breakfast. AE, DC, DISC, MC, V.*

Where to dine

In Alamosa, the restaurants stay open year-round and the scene is pretty consistent.

Bullfrog Bar and Restaurant (at Cattails Golf Club)
$–$$ Alamosa   AMERICAN

You can often find Alamosa locals dining at this restaurant next to the pro shop at the local golf club. Bullfrog serves sandwiches, burgers, and salads all day, and has pasta dishes, steaks, and seafood at dinner. Try the green chili pasta — fettuccini noodles topped with creamy sauce spiced with roasted green chilies. The restaurant closes in mid-afternoon and often shuts down for the night by 8 p.m., so if you roll into town late, call ahead to make sure they're open.

6615 N. River Rd. (head north out of town on State Street then turn left ½ mile past the bridge). ☎ 719-587-9999. Reservations accepted. Main courses: $6.95–$19. AE, DISC, MC, V. Open: Daily 11 a.m.–8 p.m.

Taqueria Cal Villo
$ Alamosa MEXICAN

Tucked between a liquor store and gas station, this taqueria serves $5 meals with flavors worth $50. The chefs slow-cook, marinate, steam, dice, and shred their meats, then pair them with fresh vegetables and sauces using family recipes. The *La Gringa* (a large flour tortilla filled with your choice of meat, plus guacamole and refried beans) dissolves into rich juices after you bite into it. It costs under $5 and will more than satisfy your hunger.

119 Broadway. ☎ 719-587-5500. Reservations accepted. Menu items $3–$13; lunch buffet $7.45. Cash only. Open: Sun–Thurs 7 a.m.–9 p.m.; Fri–Sat 7 a.m.–10 p.m.

Exploring Alamosa and the San Luis Valley

Even by Colorado standards, there's a lot to do in this area. Besides the usual (glorious) hikes and fishing holes, you can somersault down a sand dune and feed alligators. Yes, alligators.

The best things to see and do

The can't-miss attraction in this area is Great Sand Dunes National Monument and Preserve. Go to the monument first, then choose some other activities in the San Luis Valley.

Great Sand Dunes National Monument and Preserve

The sight of 750-foot-high sand dunes on the otherwise flat floor of the San Luis Valley is flat-out bizarre. Washed down from the San Juans by the Rio Grande and blown across the valley by steady west-to-east winds, the sand has piled up across a 39-square-mile area at the base of the Sangre de Cristo Mountains, on the east side of the valley. Now the dunes are part of **Great Sand Dunes National Monument and Preserve.** Wind has sculpted them into striking shapes, with gradual ramps on the windward side and steep slopes on the lee side. For finishing touches, it etches delicate ridges, ripples, and waves in the sand.

To enjoy the dunes, stop first at the visitor center to view displays on the area. Then, drive to the Dunes parking area, hike a quarter-mile across the flats to the dunes, and start climbing, preferably when it's not hot or stormy. Wear closed-top shoes on hot days and carry plenty of water. The summit of High Dune is only about 1¼ miles from the parking lot, but the deep sand will slow you. When you reach the top, have fun! You can run, jump, roll, snowboard, or ride a saucer downhill.

If you want to stay longer, camp at **Pinyon Flats Campground,** which has 88 first-come, first-served sites ($10 per car), drinking water, and sunset views.

Located 35 miles northeast of Alamosa on Colorado 150. ☎ *719-378-2312.* www.nps. gov/grsa. *Admission: $3 per adult (children under 17 free). Visitor Center open daily 9 a.m.–7 p.m. in summer; call for hours during the rest of the year.*

Alamosa National Wildlife Refuge

Flanked on the west by the Rio Grande, the wetlands at **Alamosa National Wildlife Refuge** (☎ 719-589-4021) are a sanctuary to mallards, Canada geese, avocets, egrets, herons, and eagles, among other species. The best times to visit are spring and fall, when many migrating birds stop over. You can watch them from an overlook or stroll down a riverside trail. To reach the refuge, go 4 miles east of Alamosa on U.S. 160, then south 3 miles on El Rancho Lane. Visitor center hours are Monday through Friday from 7:30 a.m. to 4:00 p.m. The refuge is open daily from sunrise to sunset. Admission is free.

Especially for kids

Colorado Alligator Farm

The Colorado Alligator Farm is above all a fish farm, raising tilapia in geo-thermal pools on the property. In 1987, the owners bought a few baby alli-gators to eat the fish byproducts. People started coming to see the reptiles, and some began dropping off exotic pets that had outgrown tanks in private homes. Now the place crawls with alligators up to 11 feet and other scary critters like monitor lizards, caiman, and snakes. You can fish for carp (cost: $10, including admission) in pools on the property and then feed the fish to the gators. Adults can also sign up for gator wrestling class, taught by a man with badly scarred arms.

9162 County Rd. 9 North (17 miles north of Alamosa on Colorado 17). ☎ *719-378-2612. Open: Memorial Day–Labor Day daily 7 a.m.–7 p.m.; rest of year daily 9 a.m.–5 p.m. Admission: $6 adults; $4 kids 6–12 and seniors 65–80; free for all others.*

Staying active

While in this area, don't limit your physical activity to an ascent of the dunes.

- ✔ **Golfing: Cattails Golf Club,** 6615 North River Rd. (☎ 719-589-9515), offers 18 holes along the Rio Grande River outside Alamosa. Greens fees are $35 for 18 holes, $20 for 9 holes, and $12 for unlimited play after 5 p.m.

- ✔ **Hiking:** As you drive from **Alamosa** to Great Sand Dunes National Park on Colorado 150, consider a stop at **Zapata Falls.** From its trailhead 10 miles north of U.S. 160, you can walk a quarter-mile to a waterfall in a shadowy canyon. During spring and early summer, you'll have to battle strong, icy currents to approach the falls, but during late summer you can get right up under them. If you feel like going farther, hike past the falls and climb into the **Sangre de Cristo Wilderness** on the 4-mile Zapata Lake Trail. For more information, contact the **Rio Grande National Forest Supervisors Office,** 1803 W. U.S. 160, in Monte Vista (☎ **719-852-5941**).

Fast Facts: Alamosa

Emergencies
Dial ☎ **911.**

Hospital
The San Luis Valley Regional Medical Center, 106 Blanca Ave. (☎ 719-589-2511), in Alamosa offers 24-hour emergency health care.

Information
The Alamosa County Chamber of Commerce (☎ 800-258-7597 or 719-589-4840; www.Alamosa.org) has a visitor center at the corner of Third Street and Chamber Drive.

Pharmacy
You can fill prescriptions at Alamosa Pharmacy, 2111 Stuart Ave. (☎ 719-589-1766).

Post Office
The Alamosa Post Office (☎ 719-589-4908) is at 505 Third St.

Road Conditions
Call ☎ 719-589-9024.

Part VI
The Part of Tens

By Rich Tennant

"Okay—here they come. Remember, it's a lot like catching salmon, only spit out the poles."

In this part . . .

Other parts of this book cover essential Colorado information; this one gives you some hints on how to enrich your trip with a few special experiences and opportunities unique to Colorado (or that aren't the same anywhere else), and points out where to slake your thirst in the process! Chapter 26 is a very personal selection of events or activities you can do to make this a unique, memorable trip for you. Chapter 27 is all about one of the best things going on right now in Colorado: the revival of really good beer.

Chapter 26

Ten Signature Colorado Experiences

● ●

In This Chapter

▶ Actually getting Rocky Mountain high
▶ Soaking au naturel
▶ Experiencing Broncomania and other football madness
▶ Tossing back a beer

● ●

*M*ost people have a pretty good idea of what they're after in Colorado — be it casting flies for trout, taking in the urban hustle of Denver, or laying down a carve in the powder of some back bowl. So I imagine you already have the big picture of what your trip will be like. This chapter lists, in no particular order, a few experiences that can put your trip over the top. Some are broad in scope and can be done in many parts of the state, while others are site-specific. Whatever your itinerary, throw a few of these into the mix, and they'll add that certain something to make your vacation really memorable.

Summitting a Fourteener — on Foot or (If You Must) by Car

Colorado has 58 different points recognized by the United States Geological Survey as topping 14,000 feet above sea level, and you owe it to yourself to get to one of them. This is the elevation at which Katharine Lee Bates wrote "America the Beautiful" (atop Pikes Peak), and when you get there, you'll know why. On a clear day, you can't see forever, but you may see 100 miles or so. The vistas of the high plains or the glacier-carved valleys of the High Country are, in no uncertain terms, breathtaking. Mount Elbert, the highest in Colorado at 14,433 feet, can be easily summitted and descended on foot in a day, if you get an early start and try in late July or August. And plenty of other peaks are waiting to test your mountaineering skills to the max. Remember to be off the peak by early afternoon (when thunderstorms tend to rumble in) and go easy on yourself if you're prone to altitude sickness. And if worst comes to worst, you can just drive: Both Mount Evans and Pikes Peak have good, if popular, roads that go all the way to the top.

Riding the Ski Train to Winter Park

It can be crowded, and the schedule isn't very flexible, but this is far and away the most civilized way to get to my favorite ski area. Let's face it, trains are an anachronism in America these days, so this throwback to the past is like an extended, mellow roller-coaster ride. It's exciting to board the train early at Union Station in Denver's LoDo, and the hypnotic snaking of the train up the snowy canyons of the Front Range is intoxicating. All the while, you're in the good company of fellow powder-seekers looking forward to a day on the slopes. And when the ride's over, you ski! The trip home is relaxing as you peel off your boots and get ready for dinner in downtown Denver. Ah, the life. . . .

Dropping Trou and Soaking in a Hot Spring

Not all of us have spent a lot of time naked around strangers. So you may need to take a minute or two to get used to the idea of being sans clothing at one of Colorado's clothing-optional hot springs. Take that minute or two, then remove your garments — if necessary, do it in a dressing room or tipi when no one's looking — grab a towel, and make your way towards the blissful pool of your choice. Trust me, soaking in the buff won't start you down a slippery slope leading to biker rallies, Steppenwolf medleys, and rowdy sex. When you climb into a natural hot spring au naturel, you realize that there's nothing left to protect you and, better yet, no need to be protected. The springs are there to warm and comfort you, the crystalline air hangs above, and there's nothing to get between you and your own personal bliss.

Taking in a Concert at Red Rocks

The natural sandstone amphitheatre at Red Rocks Park just west of Denver is home to some of the best musical memories of the last two generations. This was where U2 recorded *Under a Blood Red Sky* and where many, many legendary Grateful Dead shows went down. The acoustics are nearly perfect, and the ace sound crew takes care of the rest; it's a Front Range tradition to take the afternoon off, get to the park as early as possible (to get in line for the good general admission seats down front), and let the party begin. If rock 'n roll isn't your speed, the Colorado Symphony plays here regularly, and there's a spectacular Easter sunrise service.

Dining on Native Game

Truthfully, now, how many hamburgers do you really remember? Or for that matter, how many steaks or plates of chicken cordon blah blah blah did you bite into and think, "Now, there's something different!" This state is full of restaurants that want you to try the elk, venison, quail, and pheasant, and if I hear that you read this book and got through Colorado without eating buffalo, well, honestly . . . I don't know what I'll do. But it won't be nice. Seriously, this is what dining in Colorado is all about: a hot plate of savory local game, cooked by someone who knows how to cook it, in a chef's special sauce that will make your taste buds dance to a whole new rhythm. You'll even find rattlesnake and bear on some menus. And for something really unforgettable, ask for the Rocky Mountain oysters.

Cowboy Up at the Stock Show

If you're near Denver in January, don't miss a chance to see the Old and New West rolled into one in the biggest cowboy party you've ever seen. The National Western Stock Show, Rodeo & Horse Show is a great place to see all the ranching traditions — as well as the latest technologies — and catch first-class professional rodeo shows, buy a real Stetson, and see more exotic livestock than you ever dreamed of (and believe me, there are some funny-looking cows out there). The Mexican rodeo performances are an absolute must: They're more colorful, they offer more about showmanship and pomp-and-circumstance than the gringo version, and they show the real cultural roots of the cowboy tradition in North America. It's a can't-miss.

Go from the Sublime to the Ridiculous in Glitter Gulch

If, come January, you find yourself on the other side of the Great Divide, Wintersköl in Aspen is your best bet for some cold, hard fun. From the music performances to the wacky costumed ski-jump competitions, you can find plenty of boisterous fun. And when the sun goes down and it gets dark on the mountainside, the torch-bearers descending the mountain on skis, like volcano lava in a winter wonderland, will leave you breathless but serene. Then you go inside and party some more . . . and get up the next morning and ski the best terrain on Earth. Any questions? I didn't think so.

Gooooooooo, Broncos!!!!!

I admit, it's not quite like the old days, when people would paint their houses orange and blue during the playoffs. (Really. No kidding.) But we Coloradans love our Broncos, even if John Elway has retired and glorious old Mile High Stadium is now a parking lot for the new, high-tech Invesco Field. Season tickets are passed down in wills here, and the season sells out long before you have a ghost of a chance of actually buying a ticket at the box office. But, if you're a pigskin fan, and if you have a friend who knows someone whose boss's sister has a spare ticket, do whatever you have to do to get to a game. Show up hours early for the Gathering of the Tribe (also known as the tailgate party) and get ready for an exciting ride. Denver's fans are the most passionate in America (sorry, Green Bay, but it's true, and by the way — we beat you in the Super Bowl, too), and if the visiting team is the hated Oakland Raiders, look out. You won't be disappointed. Of course, if you can't get tickets and have to see the game at a bar (and you can see the game at darn near any bar, not just the sports bars), you'll be surrounded by faithful fans who scream at the TV as if they were in the first row at the stadium.

In Boulder, of course, Saturdays in fall belong to the CU Buffaloes, while the Colorado State Rams hold sway in Fort Collins, and the Air Force Academy Falcons rule Colorado Springs. They're all good teams with great fans.

Sampling a Colorado Microbrew (Or Two)

Okay, I devote the entire next chapter of the book to this topic, but even if you're not a beer aficionado, you should give yourself a chance to try a beer that's not watered-down and tasteless, like most of the big American megabeers. Colorado has more microbreweries than any other state, and nearly every town has a brewpub; each pub has its own style and range of brews, so there's bound to be something to suit your taste, from the sweet and fruity wheat beers to the dark, rich stouts and porters. Be forewarned, however: The alcohol content usually runs a little higher than in regular beer, and your body won't burn it off as fast, either, when you're high above sea level. So don't be surprised if you find yourself talking a little funny after one or two. Don't worry if you do — you've just picked up a Colorado accent.

Getting off the Beaten Track — without Getting Lost

Colorado has so much wide-open space that even if you come for the skiing or the urban throngs, you'll *still* be able to suddenly find yourself completely, blissfully alone, be it in one of the mountain parks outside Denver or up some unnamed road in the mountains or the Western

Slope. And of course, lots of people come for this purpose only. To just stop moving for a second and simply listen to the wind in the fir trees, the trickle of a canyon stream, or the call of an elk or coyote, while the aspens and columbines waver in the breeze or the sun sets over sagebrush and sandstone — *this* is as much the central Colorado experience as any double-diamond run or crazy football game. Remember to take water, know how to use a map and compass when you need them, and don't let your gas gauge go below a quarter of a tank. If you use common sense and have a healthy taste for adventure, the sky is truly the limit in Colorado.

Chapter 27

Beer, Beer, Beer — Ten Breweries and Their Signature Brews

. . . .

In This Chapter

▶ Recapping a brief history of American beer

▶ Reading about ten companies that are rewriting that history

. . . .

*B*efore Prohibition, every American city was dotted with small, local breweries that produced hand-crafted, old-world style beers that reflected the personalities of their makers and the tastes of the local population. The 18th Amendment, though, changed all that: The art and science of brewing were driven underground, and even into a black market. I have one old friend who grew up on Denver's old North Side whose mother used to brew a small batch every month to help make ends meet during the Depression! In 1933, though, Prohibition was repealed, and large corporations such as Coors and Anheuser Busch were quick to set up shop and dominate the market that smaller brewers could not afford to restart in; they made (and still make) beer the way McDonald's makes burgers. The bland, weak American macrobrew was born. The cheapest and easiest to produce were the very light Pilsner-style lagers, and brewing ales, stouts, and darker lagers became a lost art in this country.

That's all changing, though. Led by regions such as the Rockies and the Pacific Northwest, microbreweries are making a comeback. Today, Colorado has more breweries than any other state (including two big ones: Coors in Golden and Budweiser in Fort Collins). In this state, you'll find every kind of beer you can imagine (and plenty you'd never even dream of). The beers all have colorful labels and even more colorful names, often reflecting local color: Fat Tire, for example, showed up in the early '90s when mountain biking was sweeping the state.

What follows in this chapter is a smattering of the most successful and popular breweries in the state, along with a few that are just personal favorites. Some breweries serve their beers only in their own pubs;

others distribute their brews as widely as possible — you can find many of the beers mentioned here in grocery stores. If you want to taste a number of beers without reliving some college frat-house nightmare, the brewpubs all offer taste sizes and samplers of several different brews. This list is selective, not exhaustive; you can find many other amazing beers throughout the state, and I encourage you to try as many as possible, as long as you're not driving afterward!

The Wynkoop Brewing Company, Denver

Denver's first brewpub, this establishment launched the LoDo revolution. Wynkoop has 15 to 20 beers on tap at any given time, including a home-brewed root beer (for youngsters and designated drivers). The flagship of the fleet is **Railyard Ale**, a rich, malty Oktoberfest–style beer, though the **St. Charles ESB** is my personal favorite here. Also noteworthy are the **Sage-Brush Stout** and **Patty's Chile Beer** (infused with mild Anaheim chiles!) The Phantom Canyon Brewery in Colorado Springs is part of the same organization.

New Belgium Brewery, Fort Collins

New Belgium dominates the Colorado beer scene like no one (except Coors) with the Front Range's favorite microbrew, **Fat Tire Amber Ale.** New Belgium works very much in the Trappist Ale tradition, and you'll say a thankful prayer when you taste the **Trippel Ale** or **Abbey Ale.** **Sunshine Wheat** is a very popular "white" style of beer, brewed with wheat instead of barley, perfect for hot summer days or lighter appetites.

Breckenridge Brewery, Denver and Breckenridge

This brewery and pub started in Breckenridge, but quickly expanded operations to Denver, which offered more room to grow. The main brew, **Avalanche Ale,** is lighter and a bit more bracing than Fat Tire, though it's still full-bodied and malty. My favorite beer here is the **Trademark Pale Ale** — hoppy and refreshing. The **Honey Blonde** is not as sweet as it sounds, and the **Oatmeal Stout** is dark, but dry and smooth.

Odell Brewing Company, Fort Collins

Ah, Odell. Away from home, I dream of you: The **90 Shilling** Scottish-style ale is my favorite beer on the planet. Hands down. Malty, complex, good alone or with food. What more could you ask for? The **Cutthroat Porter** and **Cutthroat Pale** are mighty fine, too; they're both solid English-style beers that appeal to your darker and lighter sides, respectively.

Walnut Brewery, Boulder

The Walnut Brewery makes the popular and ubiquitous **Buffalo Gold** —
look out, Nebraska fans. If you like big American pilsners, try the **Indian
Peaks Pale Ale;** it's very pale, but still way more flavorful than anything
you can get out of a can. The **St. James Irish Red,** though, is the cream
of the Walnut's crop; it's an award-winner, highly carbonated and malty,
and an ideal accompaniment to most of the pub food served here.

Flying Dog Brewery, Denver

This brewery began its life in Aspen, reputedly with the help of Hunter S.
Thompson; his old partner-in-crime, Ralph Steadman, designs the *very*
distinctive labels. The **Doggie Style Pale Ale** is my favorite of the brews
from here, but the **In Heat Wheat** and **Horn Dog Barley Wine** sure are
fun to order. The latter is a very dark, rich beer that ensures you will not
do anything important afterwards. Be careful, here.

Mountain Sun Pub & Brewery, Boulder

For Deadheads and those who love them, Mountain Sun backs up its
cheap Mexican-style food with some really fun beers. The **Colorado
Kind Ale** is *extremely* hoppy, if you're into that sort of thing, and the
Raspberry Wheat beer is a great example of the type; at one point when
I was in college here, every brewery had a raspberry wheat. This is the
best, though, and that's why it's outlasted the fad. The pub has a rotating selection of beers from other local and national breweries, as well,
so come thirsty.

Golden City Brewery, Golden

Billing itself as the "*second* largest brewery in Golden," Golden City made
its reputation with **Golden City Red,** a malty, rich red ale. Golden City
has many seasonal brews and often several fruit beers worth checking
out, especially the **Double Cherry.** The pub is in a residential neighborhood, so dining here is a lot like hanging out in the backyard. And it's
definitely the best beer you'll taste in Golden.

Ska Brewing Company, Durango

Down at the other end of the state, Ska holds its own with its **Pinstripe
Red Ale** and **True Blonde Ale,** either of which are great with burgers —
and the Pinstripe holds up well against the fiery Mexican food you find
in the area. The **Buster Nut Brown Ale** is a fine example of this traditional English style. The beers are available all over the Durango area.

Dolores River Brewery, Dolores

I saved what may be the best for last: This tiny pub, tucked inside the tiny town of Dolores, opened its doors in 2002, and it's a revelation. The **ESB** is an excellent example of the type of brew offered: full-bodied, not too bitter, and very smooth. And the **Schwartz Hacker,** a dark Oktoberfest–style lager, is exceptional. The **Stout** is great for the cool mountain nights, and a rotating variety of cask-conditioned beers have proved to be very popular as well. If you're anywhere near the Four Corners, it's worth a detour to this amazing little pub.

Appendix

Quick Concierge

* *

*T*his handy section condenses all the practical and pertinent information — from crucial phone numbers to ATM locations — you need to have a successful and stress-free vacation. And if you believe there is no such thing as being too prepared, I list a bunch of additional information sources for you to consult. Best of all, you don't need to tip this concierge — although I won't refuse if you insist.

Colorado A to Z: Facts at Your Fingertips

AAA

Members of the American Automobile Association can call ☎ 800-AAA-HELP for 24-hour emergency road service anywhere in the United States. AAA has offices in a half-dozen Colorado cities east of the continental divide. Offices in Durango and Grand Junction serve western Colorado. To get exact addresses, log on to www.aaa.com.

American Express

American Express has a full-service office in downtown Denver at 555 17th St. (☎ 303-383-5050). Additional locations in Denver, Boulder, Centennial, Englewood, Fort Collins, and Steamboat Springs offer select American Express services. For cardholder services and exact office locations, call ☎ 800-528-4800. To report lost or stolen checks, dial ☎ 800-221-7282.

ATMs

Most Colorado banks and large food stores have automated teller machines connected to the major ATM networks; so do many convenience stores. To locate an ATM near your location, contact MasterCard/Cirrus (☎ 800-424-7787; www.mastercard.com) or Visa/Plus (☎ 800-843-7587; www.visa.com). If you withdraw money from an ATM not affiliated with your bank, you're generally charged a service fee.

Business Hours

In Denver, most small stores open by 9 a.m. and operate until 5 or 6 p.m. Stores in Colorado's resort communities start and finish their business day an hour or two later, allowing proprietors to capitalize on the dinner crowd.

Most Colorado banks do business on weekdays from at least 9 a.m. to 5 p.m.; the branches in cities often tack on evening and weekend hours. Similarly, the supermarkets in cities often stay open for 24 hours; small-town grocers generally close around 10 p.m. and don't reopen until 7 or 8 a.m. Small-town restaurants close by 10 p.m. — or five minutes before you get there, whichever comes first.

Credit Cards

If your credit card is lost or stolen, call the issuer of your card immediately. To contact American Express, call ☎ 800-528-4800. For MasterCard, dial ☎ 800-307-7309. And the number for Visa is ☎ 800-847-2911.

Doctors

Colorado's beauty has attracted top-flight physicians to some surprisingly far-flung locales. So, don't assume that the medical care is inferior just because you're in the sticks. If you need to see a physician in a nonemergency situation, check with your insurer about your conditions of coverage. If your hotel has a concierge, he or she may be able to recommend a local physician if you become ill. If the *quality* of care still worries you, go to www.best doctors.com. For $7.95 per month, Best Doctors provides subscribers with referrals to physicians who score high in peer evaluations.

Drugstores

Two chain drugstores — Walgreens (☎ 800-WALGREENS or 800-289-2273; www.walgreens.com) and Longs (☎ 800-865-6647; www.longs.com) — have a strong presence in Colorado. There's a 24-hour Walgreens pharmacy in Denver at 3000 East Colfax Ave. (☎ 303-331-0815).

Large food stores such as Albertsons (☎ 888-746-7252; www.albertsons.com) and King Soopers (☎ 801-974-1400; www.smithsfoodanddrug.com) often have their own pharmacies. And you can still find some independent pharmacies in the state as well.

Emergencies

For fire department, police, or ambulance assistance, call ☎ 911. From hotels and motels, you may need to dial ☎ 9-911.

Fishing

Before you can legally start casting for any of Colorado's 80 fish species, you need to obtain a fishing permit from the Colorado Division of Wildlife. An annual permit costs $40.25 for nonresidents, $20.25 for residents. Five-day and one-day permits cost $18.25 and $5.25, respectively, for residents and nonresidents alike. Permits are available at local sporting goods stores and at Colorado Division of Wildlife (www.wildlife.state.co.us) offices.

Health

Don't be fooled: Colorado has the nation's highest skin cancer rates! If you don't protect yourself in the mountains, you can become sunburned, dehydrated, and hypothermic — sometimes all in the same day. Exposure to the sun's burning rays increases with elevation. When spending time in the mountains, wear sunblock and sunglasses, even when it seems cloudy.

Hydration helps prevent heat-related illness, hypothermia, and altitude sickness alike. In the dry air, you may not realize how much water you're losing, so drink up! If you're coming from sea level, allow yourself a few days (at least) to rest and acclimate before you start exerting yourself in the mountains. Try starting your trip somewhere — Denver's a good choice — that's a little lower in elevation. To avoid hypothermia, wear multiple layers of synthetic fabrics such as polar fleece and polypropylene, plus a water-resistant outer layer, and, of course, take shelter from wind and rain if you do begin shivering.

Information

For Colorado information, start by contacting the Colorado Tourism Office (☎ 800 COLORADO; www.colorado.com). See "Finding More Information" at the end of this chapter for more details.

Liquor Laws

You must be 21 to consume alcoholic beverages in Colorado. If you do imbibe, don't drive. Colorado has some of the nation's strictest standards for drunk driving. If your blood alcohol content tops 0.05 percent, you can be charged with driving while intoxicated; if it passes 0.10 percent, the more serious charge of driving under the influence applies.

Colorado law allows bars to stay open from 7 a.m. until 2 a.m. daily; liquor stores can do business from 7 a.m. to midnight, Monday through Saturday. Liquor stores are the only retail outlets for full-strength beer, wine, and liquor. Grocery stores, gas stations, and convenience stores sell beer and wine coolers, but the alcohol content of these beverages cannot legally exceed 3.2 percent by weight.

Mail

You can call ☎ 800-275-8777 to find the location of the post office nearest you, but first you need to know which zip code you're in. You can receive mail by having it addressed to your name and "General Delivery," care of the post office of your choice. You have one month from the date the post office receives it to claim General Delivery mail.

Maps

For driving directions, go to www.mapquest.com or, if you're a member of the American Automobile Association (☎ 800-541-9902; www.aaa.com), stop by the nearest AAA office.

If you're planning to explore the backcountry, United States Geological Survey (USGS) topographical maps can be a lifesaver. You can usually find these maps (cost: $6 per map, plus $5 handling per order) at local Forest Service offices and sporting goods stores. Or, you can buy directly from the USGS by calling ☎ 888-ASK-USGS or surfing the Internet to www.usgs.gov. Denver, luckily, is actually the source of most of these maps: You can visit the USGS itself at the **Earth Science Information Center (ESIC)** on the grounds of the Denver Federal Center. Take 6th Avenue west to Kipling Street in Lakewood, head south to Gate #1, and tell the guards at the gate you want the map store.

Newspapers

The two major metropolitan daily newspapers in Colorado are the *Denver Post* and *Rocky Mountain News.* Both offer comprehensive coverage of local, state, and national news. Another 18 daily and 31 weekly newspapers report news in smaller cities and towns throughout Colorado. For arts and entertainment coverage, however, you can often do better by picking up an alternative newspaper such as *Boulder Weekly* (www.boulderweekly.com) and *Westword* in Denver (www.westword.com).

Safety

Allow extra time to travel on mountain roads, especially during storms. If you plan on hiking in the mountains, be sure to carry extra clothing, food, water, and a topographical map of the area. As you walk, memorize landmarks and terrain features, including the ones behind you, so that you can find your way back if you get confused. During winter, people unfamiliar with avalanche conditions and terrain should *not go out* unless they hire a guide before venturing into the backcountry.

Smoking

Despite Colorado's reputation for having an active lifestyle (and despite its relative lack of oxygen), over 20 percent of Colorado adults smoke, just 1 percent under the national average. Colorado's state government encourages restaurants to develop separate nonsmoking areas, but doesn't mandate these areas. Many cities and towns, however, have passed ordinances that limit smoking. Denver prohibits smoking in restaurants that don't have separate, well-ventilated areas for puffing, and it limits smoking to designated areas in venues such as sports stadiums and museums. Boulder has banned smoking in all restaurants. Because ordinances vary from town to town, smokers should look for ashtrays before lighting up. And if you want to buy tobacco, you must be 18 years old to do so in Colorado.

Taxes

In addition to Colorado's 2.9 percent state sales tax, you may be asked to pay city sales taxes of up to 4 percent and county sales taxes of up to 5 percent. In most Colorado locales, the total sales tax is between 6 and 9 percent. Some areas levy an additional tax (usually around 2 percent) on hotel rooms. Cars rented at Denver International Airport are subject to a $2.98 per-day usage fee and a 10 percent tax designed to recoup the cost of building the airport.

Time Zone

Colorado is located in the mountain standard time zone, two hours behind New York City and one hour ahead of Los Angeles. From the first Sunday in April through the last Saturday in October, Colorado observes daylight saving time.

Weather Updates

The National Weather Service Web site (www.nws.noaa.gov) provides current weather forecasts and information for every part of America. You need only type in the zip code of the area that interests you.

During winter, the Colorado Avalanche Information Center (☎ 303-275-5360; www.geosurvey.state.co.us/avalanche) provides recorded information on current avalanche conditions and mountain weather. The Colorado Department of Transportation (☎ 303-639-1111) provides recorded updates on road conditions throughout the state.

Toll-Free Numbers and Web Sites

Major airlines

Air Canada
☎ 888-247-2262
www.aircanada.ca

American Airlines
☎ 800-433-7300
www.aa.com

American Trans Air
☎ 800-225-2995
www.ata.com

America West Airlines
☎ 800-235-9292
www.americawest.com

British Airways
☎ 800-247-9297 in U.S.
☎ 0345-222-111 in Britain
www.british-airways.com

Continental Airlines
☎ 800-525-0280
www.continental.com

Delta Air Lines
☎ 800-221-1212
www.delta.com

Frontier Airlines
☎ 800-432-1359
www.frontierairlines.com

JetBlue Airways
☎ 800-538-2583
www.jetblue.com

Mexicana
☎ 800-531-7921
www.mexicana.com

Midwest Express
☎ 800-452-2022
www.midwestexpress.com

Northwest Airlines
☎ 800-225-2525
www.nwa.com

Southwest Airlines
☎ 800-435-9792
www.southwest.com

United Airlines
☎ 800-241-6522
www.united.com

US Airways
☎ 800-428-4322
www.usairways.com

Major car-rental agencies

Advantage
☎ 800-777-5500
www.advantagerentacar.com

Alamo
☎ 800-327-9633
www.goalamo.com

Avis
☎ 800-331-1212 in the continental U.S.
☎ 800-879-2847 in Canada
www.avis.com

Budget
☎ 800-527-0700
https://rent.drivebudget.com

Dollar
☎ 800-800-4000
www.dollar.com

Enterprise
☎ 800-325-8007
www.enterprise.com

Hertz
☎ 800-654-3131
www.hertz.com

National
☎ 800-227-7368
www.nationalcar.com

Payless
☎ 800-729-5377
www.paylesscarrental.com

Rent-A-Wreck
☎ 800-535-1391
www.rentawreck.com

Thrifty
☎ 800-367-2277
www.thrifty.com

Major hotel and motel chains

Best Western International
☎ 800-528-1234
www.bestwestern.com

Clarion Hotels
☎ 800-252-7466
www.clarion.com

Comfort Inns
☎ 800-228-5150
www.choicehotels.com

Courtyard by Marriott
☎ 800-321-2211
www.courtyard.com

Days Inn
☎ 800-325-2525
www.daysinn.com

Doubletree Hotels
☎ 800-222-8733
www.doubletree.com

Econo Lodges
☎ 800-553-2666
www.choicehotels.com

Fairfield Inn by Marriott
☎ 800-228-2800
www.fairfieldinn.com

Hampton Inn
☎ 800-426-7866
www.hampton-inn.com

Hilton Hotels
☎ 800-774-1500
www.hilton.com

Holiday Inn
☎ 800-465-4329
www.basshotels.com

Howard Johnson
☎ 800-654-2000
www.hojo.com

Hyatt Hotels and Resorts
☎ 800-228-9000
www.hyatt.com

ITT Sheraton
☎ 800-325-3535
www.starwood.com/sheraton

La Quinta Motor Inns
☎ 800-531-5900
www.laquinta.com

Marriott Hotels
☎ 800-228-9290
www.marriott.com

Motel 6
☎ 800-466-8536
www.motel6.com

Quality Inns
☎ 800-228-5151
www.choicehotels.com

Radisson Hotels International
☎ 800-333-3333
www.radisson.com

Ramada Inns
☎ 800-272-6232
www.ramada.com

Red Carpet Inns
☎ 800-251-1962
www.reservahost.com

Red Lion Hotels and Inns
☎ 800-547-8010
www.hilton.com

Residence Inn by Marriott
☎ 800-331-3131
www.residenceinn.com

Rodeway Inns
☎ 800-228-2000
www.choicehotels.com

Travelodge
☎ 800-255-3050
www.travelodge.com

Westin Hotels and Resorts
☎ 800-937-8461
www.westin.com

Wyndham Hotels and Resorts
☎ 800-822-4200
www.wyndham.com

Finding More Information

I packed this book with a lot of information, but if you still want more, you can consult the following resources to get more advice and tips on planning your vacation to Colorado.

Tourist information

For planning information, start by contacting the **Colorado Tourism Office,** 1127 Pennsylvania St., Denver, CO 80203 (☎ **800-COLORADO;** www.colorado.com). The office answers questions and mails out free *Colorado Ski Country* and *Official State Vacation* guides.

For a free *Official Visitors Guide* to Denver, contact the **Denver Metro Convention and Visitors Bureau,** 1668 Larimer St., Denver, CO 80202 (☎ **303-892-1112;** www.denver.org). The guide has extensive information on hotels, attractions, and dining in and around Denver.

Useful Web sites

The *Rocky Mountain News* keeps past and present stories on its Web site (www.insidedenver.com), as well as links to what it considers the 100 best Web sites in Colorado. Denver's alternative weekly *Westword* (www.westword.com) has an online calendar of upcoming events.

For information on Denver's cultural attractions and events, surf the Internet to www.artstozoo.org. Click <u>Discounts and Free Tickets</u> for info on cheap last-minute tickets to performances.

State guides

Frommer's Colorado is an excellent complement to this book. If guidebooks were food, this one would be french fries and *Frommer's Colorado* would be a steak. In other words, *Frommer's Colorado* is a lot more beefy and nourishing, and you can chew on it for a lot longer. Ideally, you'll still want some fries with it, just 'cause they're fun to eat. *Frommer's Guide to Rocky Mountain National Park* is a must if you're spending more than a day there.

Index

• A •

AAA, 48, 50, 64, 72, 379
AARP, 48, 64, 72, 76
Absolute Bikes, 237
accommodations
  Alamosa, 363
  Arkansas Valley, 233
  Aspen, 256–258
  bed-and-breakfasts, 68–69
  best for families, 13
  booking online, 72–73
  Boulder, 145–149
  campgrounds, 70
  chain hotels, 69
  Colorado Springs, 163–167
  cost, 2, 3, 45, 70–73
  Creede, 358–359
  Denver, 101–106
  Durango, 334–336
  Estes Park, 196–197
  Golden Circle, 138
  Grand Junction, 302–303
  Grand Lake, 199–200
  guest or dude ranch, 70
  Gunnison and Crested Butte,
    287–288
  historic or luxury hotels, 69
  Lake City, 353
  Leadville, 226–227
  Mesa Verde and the Four Corners,
    343–344
  Middle Park, 205–206, 210–211
  motels, 69
  Ouray and Silverton, 325–326
  Pagosa Springs, 341
  rack rate, 3, 70
  rate, getting best, 70–73
  reserving best room, 73
  Roaring Fork Valley, 266–267
  Rocky Mountain National Park,
    195–197, 199–200
  Steamboat Springs, 275–278
  Summit County, 215–216
  Telluride, 317–318
Acoustic Coffee Lounge, 175
adobe, 15
air travel, 52–55
airlines
  commuter and regional, 53
  contact information, 383
  package tours from, 57
  serving Colorado, 52–53, 66
airports
  Alamosa-San Luis Valley Regional
    Airport, 358, 362
  Albuquerque, 316
  Aspen/Pitkin County, 254
  Colorado Springs, 52, 161–162, 233
  Cortez-Montezuma County, 342
  Denver, 52, 89–90, 184
  Denver International Airport,
    52, 89–90, 143, 184, 204
  Durango/La Plata County, 333
  Gunnison Crested Butte, 286
  Internet kiosks at, 83
  Montrose Regional Airport,
    293, 316, 324
  security, 85–86
  Telluride Regional Airport, 316
  Vail/Eagle County, 53, 225, 241,
    254, 265
  Walker Field (Grand Junction), 300
  Yampa Valley Regional Airport,
    274–275
Alamosa
  accommodations, 363
  attractions and activities, 364–366
  description, 352, 362
  dining, 363–364
  fast facts, 366
  transportation, 362–363
Alamosa National Wildlife Refuge, 365
Alamosa-San Luis Valley Regional
    Airport, 358, 362

Albuquerque (New Mexico) International Sunport Airport, 316
Alexander Lake Lodge, 302
The Alley Cat, 129
Allred's, 323
Alpine Slide, 282
The Alpineer, 291
altitude sickness, 189
American Ski Exchange, 249
American Spirit Shuttles, 306
Amicas, 234–235
Amtrak, 55, 66–67, 92, 204, 254
Anasazi Heritage Center, 315, 345, 349
Ancestral Puebloans, 15, 312, 315, 342, 345–349
Animas Museum, 338–339
Animas River, 339
Antlers Rio Grande Lodge, 358–359
aquarium, 117
Aramark, 349
Arapahoe Basin, 11, 39, 221
Arapahoe National Forest, 208, 220
Arapahoe Ski Lodge, 205
Arapahoe tribe, 15, 94
Arcade Amusements, Inc., 37, 174
Arkansas River, 37, 176, 177, 238
Arkansas RiverTours, 177
Arkansas Valley
  Buena Vista, 225, 232–233, 235, 239
  Leadville, 224–232
  Salida, 225, 232–239
art museums
  Aspen, 260
  Boulder, 154
  Colorado Springs, 172
  Denver, 113, 116, 120, 124
Art on the Corner, 307
art, purchasing, 46–47, 126–127, 236, 272, 351
Ashcroft, 36, 260
Aspen
  accommodations, 256–258
  activities, 261–262, 371
  attractions, 260
  culture, 263–264
  description, 16, 17, 25, 39, 253
  dining, 258–259
  fast facts, 264
  getting around, 254–256
  getting there, 254
  highlights, 252
  map, 255
  nightlife, 263
  shopping, 36, 263
Aspen Art Museum, 260
Aspen Club and Spa, 260
Aspen Golf Course, 261
Aspen Highlands, 11, 39, 262
Aspen Mountain, 11, 39, 262
Aspen Music Festival, 252, 263
Aspen Theater in the Park, 264
Aspen Velo Bike Shop, 261
Aspen Wilderness Outfitters, 262
Aspen/Pitkin County Airport, 254
atlas, 20
ATM, 49, 379
attractions. *See also specific locations*
  budgeting for, 46
  calendar of events, 31–34
The Auditorium Theatre, 132
Avalanche Sports, 220
avalanches, 189–190
Avon, 243

• *B* •

Baby Doe Tabor Museum, 228
Bachelor Historic Tour, 360–361
backcountry permits, 185
Backdoor Sports, 282
backpacking, 261–262
Baked in Telluride, 319
Balcony House, 346, 347, 349–350
ballooning, 219
Barnes Dance, 101
bars. *See* nightlife
Bartels' Mancos Valley Stage Line, 350
Basalt, 36, 252, 253, 264–266
Bauer House Bed & Breakfast, 343
Bear Creek Canyon Trail, 322
Bear Lake Road, 186, 188, 191
Bear Lake Trail, 191
bears, 189, 194
Beat Book Shop, 157
Beau Jo's Mountain Bistro, 12, 138, 209, 279
Beaver Creek Resort, 39, 248–249
Beaver's Sport Shop, 209

bed-and-breakfasts, 68–69
Belle Star, 157
Bentley's at the Wheeler, 263
Best Western Alamosa Inn, 363
Best Western Aspenalt Lodge, 266
Best Western Lake Dillon Lodge, 215
Best Western Ptarmigan Inn, 277
Best Western Red Arrow, 293
Best Western Sundance Motel, 294
Best Western Vista Inn, 233
Betty Ford Alpine Gardens, 246
Bicycle Colorado, 121
bicycling
  Aspen, 261
  Boulder, 144–145, 155
  Middle Park, 204, 208–209
  Summit County, 214
bighorn sheep, 194
biking
  Colorado Springs, 173
  Crested Butte and Gunnison, 291
  Denver, 121
  Durango, 339
  Grand Junction and Fruita, 307–308
  Leadville, 230
  Roaring Fork Valley, 271
  Rocky Mountain National Park, 194
  Salida, 237
  Steamboat Springs, 283
  Summit County, 220
  Telluride, 322
  Vail, 247–248
Bill's Sport Shop, 230
Black American West Museum and
    Heritage Center, 119–120
Black Canyon of the Gunnison
    National Park, 14, 25,
    36, 293–296
Black Hawk, 136, 140
Black Nugget, 273
Black Ridge Trail, 308
B-Line, 98, 143
Blue Mesa Reservoir, 290, 291
Blue Spruce Inn, 217
Bluebird Theater, 129
boating
  Denver, 121
  Gunnison, 290–291
  Lake San Cristobal, 355–356

Steamboat Springs, 282
Summit County, 220
Boatyard Pizza & Grill, 217
Boettcher Concert Hall, 132
Bolder Boulder, 33
The Bookman, 174
books on Colorado, 19–20
Boomtown Brew Pub, 227
Boulder
  accommodations, 145–149
  activities, 155–156
  attractions, 153–154
  description, 142
  dining, 149–152
  fast facts, 160
  getting around, 144–145
  getting there, 143
  map, 146–147
  music, 158–159
  nightlife, 157–158
  shopping, 157
Boulder Arts and Crafts
    Cooperative, 157
Boulder Book Store, 157
Boulder Creek Path, 153–154, 156
Boulder Farmer's Market, 154
Boulder Museum of Contemporary
    Art, 154
Boulder Theater, 158, 159
Boulder University Inn, 145
Boulderado Hotel, 17, 24
Box Canyon Falls Park, 330
Breckenridge
  accommodations, 215–216
  attractions and activities, 218–221
  description, 16, 37, 39, 212, 214
  dining, 217–218
Breckenridge Brewery & Pub,
    39, 107, 130, 217, 375
Breckenridge Golf Club, 220–221
Breckenridge Mountain Lodge, 37
Breckenridge Nordic Center, 220
Breckenridge Recreation Center, 221
Breckenridge Ski Resort, 221
breweries, 137, 217, 372, 374–377. See
    also specific breweries
Bridal Veil Falls, 313, 321
BroadMinded, 236
The Broadmoor, 11, 19, 69, 163, 173

Brodeur Art Gallery, 236
Brown Palace Hotel, 11, 69, 102, 124
Brown's Canyon, 238
Buckhorn Exchange Restaurant,
    12, 19, 36, 38, 107–108
budget
  attractions, activities, and tours, 46
  eating out, 45
  lodging, 45
  nightlife, 47
  planning, 43–44
  shopping, 46–47
  transportation, 44–45
Budget Tackle, 194
Budweiser Hot Summer Nights
    Concert Series, 250
Buen Tiempo Restaurant, 327
Buena Vista
  accommodations, 233
  description, 25, 36, 232
  dining, 235
  fast facts, 239
  getting there, 232–233
  highlights, 225
Buffalo Bill Memorial Museum, 135
Bullfrog Bar and Restaurant, 363–364
Bully Ranch, 245, 249
bus service
  Aspen, 254, 256
  Boulder, 143
  Colorado, 67
  Colorado Springs, 162
  Denver, 91–92, 98–99, 124
  Roaring Fork Valley, 266
  Rocky Mountain National Park,
    185, 188
  Steamboat Springs, 275
business hours, 379–380
Butterfly Pavilion and Insect
    Center, 120
Buttermilk, 11, 39, 262
Byer's Peak Wilderness Area, 208

• *C* •

Cache Cache, 12, 258
Café Alpine, 218
Café Diva, 279
Café Ole, 359

Café Prague, 139
calendar of events, 31–34
Camera Obscura Gallery, 127
Camp Hale, 231
camping
  backcountry permits, 185
  Black Canyon of the Gunnison
    National Park, 295
  Colorado National Monument, 305
  Dinosaur, 310–311
  Great Sand Dunes National
    Monument and Preserve, 365
  Lake City, 355
  reservations and rates, 70
  Rocky Mountain National Park,
    185, 195–196
  Telluride, 318
Cañon City, 24, 37, 176–178
Canyon Rim Trail, 305
Canyons of the Ancients National
    Monument, 345, 349
car rental, 91, 383–384
Carbondale, 36, 252–253,
    264–267, 269–273
Carson, 357
Cascade, 168–169
casinos, 136, 350–351
Castle Creek Road, 261
Castle Marne Bed & Breakfast, 102
The Catacombs, 158
Cathedral Lake Trail, 261
Cattails Golf Club, 365
Cattlemen's Days, 33
Cave of the Winds, 37, 169
Cecilia's, 222
Cedar Point Nature Trail, 294
cellphone, 82
Central City, 136
chains, driving with, 63
Chalet at Marys Lake Lodge, 196
Challenge Unlimited, 173
Chapin Mesa Archeological
    Museum, 347
Charlie P's, 355
Chautauqua Institute, 158
Chautauqua Park, 154, 155
Chautauqua Summer Festival, 159
Cherry Creek, 16, 94, 95, 96, 121
Cherry Creek Arts Festival, 34

Cheyenne Mountain Zoo, 169–170
Cheyenne tribe, 15, 94
Chicago Ridge, 231
children
  advice for family travel, 74–76
  trip itinerary, 37
chili, 18
Christmas Mountain U.S.A.,
    Lighting of, 34
Cinco de Mayo, 33
City Park, 116–117, 121, 122, 125
The Cleo Parker Robinson Dance
    Company, 132
The Cliff House Dining Room, 167, 168
Cliff Palace, 38, 346, 347, 349
climbing
  Boulder, 156
  Leadville, 231
  Ouray, 331
  Rocky Mountain National Park, 195
  Telluride, 322
The Club, 249
The Club at Crested Butte, 291
Club Chelsea, 249
clubs. *See* nightlife
Coachlight Restaurant and Tavern, 327
Cobble Creek Community Golf
    Course, 296
Cody, Buffalo Bill, 134, 135
Collegiate Peaks, 36
Colorado Alligator Farm, 365
Colorado Avalanche, 122
Colorado Avalanche Information
    Center, 382
Colorado Ballet, 132
Colorado Chautauqua
    Association, 145
Colorado Crush, 122
Colorado History Museum,
    36, 38, 113, 124
Colorado Mammoth, 123
Colorado Mountain Express,
    214, 241, 254, 265
Colorado Mountain School, 195
Colorado Music Festival, 159
Colorado National Monument,
    25, 300, 304–305
Colorado Railroad Museum, 135
Colorado Rapids, 123

Colorado River Trail, 193
Colorado Riverfront Trails, 307
Colorado Rockies, 122
Colorado Rocky Ballooning, 219
Colorado Shakespeare Festival, 159
The Colorado Sightseer, 124
Colorado Ski Museum/Ski Hall of
    Fame, 246
Colorado Springs
  accommodations, 163–167
  activities, 173
  attractions, 169–173
  description, 24, 161
  dining, 167–169
  fast facts, 175–176
  getting around, 162–163
  getting there, 161–162
  map, 164–165
  music, 175
  nightlife, 174–175
  shopping, 174
Colorado Springs Airport, 52, 161, 233
Colorado Springs Fine Arts
    Center, 172
Colorado Springs Philharmonic, 175
Colorado State Capitol Building, 119
The Colorado Symphony Orchestra,
    132, 370
Colorado Tourism Office, 381, 385
Comanche tribe, 15
Commodore Mine, 360
Compromise Mine Tour, 260
condominiums, in Summit
    County, 215
consolidators, 53–54
continental divide, 237
Continental Divide Services, 361
Coors Brewery Tour, 137
Coors Field, 122
Copper Mountain Resort,
    11, 214, 215, 222
Cortez, 26, 312, 315, 342–344, 351
Cortez Cultural Center, 315, 346, 351
Cortez-Montezuma County
    Airport, 342
The Cosmopolitan, 319
costs
  activities and tours, 46
  attraction, 46

costs *(continued)*
    cutting, 47–49
    in Denver, 43–44
    eating out, 45
    lodging, 45
    nightlife, 47
    phone bills, 48
    shopping, 46–47
    transportation, 44–45
    in Vail, 44
Cottonwood Inn B & B and
    Gallery, 363
Cottonwood Lake, 225, 237
coyotes, 194
Cozens Ranch House, 207
Craftwood Inn, 19, 167
Crag Crest National Recreation
    Trail, 306
Crater Lake, 261
credit cards, 3, 49, 380
credit-reporting agencies, 51
Creede
    accommodations, 358–359
    attractions and activities, 360–361
    description, 26, 352, 357–358
    dining, 359–360
    fast facts, 362
    transportation, 358
Creede Hotel and Restaurant, 359, 360
Creede Repertory Theater,
    352, 359, 361
Creekside Cafe and Grill, 279
Creekside Trail, 208
Crested Butte, 11, 25, 40, 286–293
Crested Butte Brewery, 292
Crested Butte Mountain Heritage
    Museum, 290
Crested Butte Mountain Resort, 292
Cripple Creek, 136
Cristiana Guesthaus, 287–288
Criterium Bicycles, 173
cross-country skiing
    Grand Mesa, 307
    Leadville, 230
    Middle Park, 210, 211
    Rocky Mountain National Park, 195
    Summit County, 220
    Telluride, 322
crosswalks, diagonal, 101

Crow Canyon Archeological Center,
    315, 345–346
The Crystal Inn, 355
Cuba Cuba, 108
cuisine, local, 12, 17–19, 371
Cultural Connection Trolley, 98, 123
Curecanti National Recreation Area,
    290, 291
Curious George Collectibles, 263
Curious Theatre Company, 132
cybercafes, 83
Cyprus Café, 336

• *D* •

Dakota's Bistro, 235
David Cook/Fine American Art, 127
debit cards, 50
deer, avoiding, 63
Delaware Hotel, 38, 226
Delta, 293, 296
Denver
    accommodations, 101–106
    activities, 121–123
    attractions, 113–121
    description, 24, 37, 38, 89
    dining, 107–113
    fast facts, 133
    getting around, 98–101
    getting there, 89–92
    guided tours, 123–124
    history, 94
    information sources, 97–98
    itineraries, 124–125
    maps, 93, 104–105, 114–115
    neighborhoods, 92–97
    nightlife, 128–132
    pro sports, 122–123
    shopping, 125–128
    weather, 28
    what things cost in, 43–44
Denver Art Museum, 113, 116, 124
Denver Botanic Gardens, 116, 125
Denver Broncos, 122, 372
Denver Center Theater Company, 132
Denver Chophouse and Brewery, 108
Denver International Airport,
    52, 89–90, 143, 184, 204
Denver March Powwow, 32

Denver Metro Convention and
  Visitors Bureau, 385
Denver Museum of Miniatures, Dolls,
  and Toys, 120
Denver Museum of Nature and
  Science, 116–117, 125
Denver Nuggets, 123
Denver Parks and Recreation
  Permitting Office, 122
Denver Performing Arts Complex, 131
Denver Zoo, 37, 117, 125
Denver's Mountain Parks, 121
Devil's Thumb Golf Club, 296
Devil's Thumb Ranch, 211
Diamond Circle Melodrama, 339
Diamond Ski Shop, 248
Dillon, 212, 215, 219, 220
Dillon Marina, 220
dining. *See* restaurants
Dinosaur, 309–311
Dinosaur Journey Museum, 306
Dinosaur National Monument,
  309–310
disabilities, traveling with, 77–78
discounts
  accommodations, 70, 72
  Central City and Black Hawk, 136
  rental car, 64
  saving money with, 48
  for seniors, 76
Discovery Pass, 67
doctors, 380
dollar signs, meaning of, 2, 71
Dolores, 312, 315, 342, 344, 351
Dolores River Brewery, 344, 377
Dot's Diner, 150
Doubletree Grand Junction, 302–303
Dozens, 109
driving
  Denver, 91, 92, 99–100
  Golden Circle, 139–141
  interstate highways, 55, 59, 61
  Mesa Verde, 346
  mountain, 44, 59, 61
  rental cars, 64–66
  rock fall, avoiding, 62–63
  Rocky Mountain National Park,
    184–185, 186, 188–189
  in snow and ice, 61–62, 63

SUV rental, 65
Telluride, 316
times and distances, 60
wildlife and, 63
drugstores, 380
dude ranch, 70
Durango
  accommodations, 334–336
  attractions and activities, 337–341
  description, 26, 38, 312, 333
  dining, 336–337
  fast facts, 341–342
  getting around, 333–334
  getting there, 333
  highlights, 313
Durango & Silverton Narrow Gauge
  Railroad, 10, 38, 312–313,
  325, 337–338
Durango Art Center, 340
Durango Lift, 334
Durango Mountain Resort, 313, 340
Durango Rivertrippers, 339
Durango/La Plata County Airport, 333
Dushanbe Teahouse, 153
Dutch Creek Guest Ranch at
  Steamboat Lake, 278
Dutch Kitchen, 168

• E •

Eagle Motel, 163, 166
Eagle Ranch Golf Course, 247
Eagle's Nest Wilderness Area, 247
Earth Science Information
  Center, 127, 381
Earthzone Mineral and Fossil
  Gallery, 126
Eben G. Fine Park, 148, 153
E.G.'s Country Inn, 19
EG's Garden Grill, 200
El Chapultepec, 129
El Dorado Lodge, 166
Elderhostel, 76
The Eldo, 292
Eldorado Canyon State Park, 155, 156
Eldorado Mountain Resort, 156
Elephant Rocks, 156
elk, 189, 194

Elk Creek, 290
Embassy Suites Downtown Denver,
    13, 39, 102–103
Emerald Mountain, 283
emergencies, 380
Enchanted Mesa Motel, 343
Escalante Pueblo, 345
escorted tours, 56–57
ESPN Zone, 131
Estes Park, 140, 185, 196–198
Estes Park Golf Course, 195
Estes Park Mountain Shop, 194
Estes Park Shuttle and Mountain
    Tours, 185
E-tickets, 85
Evergreen, 141
Explore Booksellers, 263

• F •

Fadó Irish Pub, 130
Fall River Road, 140, 186
falls, 189
family travel, advice for, 74–76
Fantasy Ridge Alpinism, 322
Far View Lodge, 343–345
Fat Alley, 319–320
Fern Lake Trailhead, 188
FIBArk Whitewater Festival, 33
Fiesta Guadalajara, 303–304
Fillmore Auditorium, 129
Fish Creek Falls, 283
fishing
    Gunnison, 291
    license, 380
    Ouray, 330
    Roaring Fork Valley, 271
    Rocky Mountain National Park, 194
    Salida, 237
    Telluride, 322
    Vail, 247
The Fiske Planetarium, 155
Flagstaff House, 150
Fly Me to the Moon Saloon, 323
Flying Dog Brewery, 376
F.M. Light & Sons, 284
Fontenot's Cajun Café, 206
Foot of the Mountain Motel, 148
Forest Service, 70

The Fort, 12, 19, 36, 109
Four Corners area, 25–26,
    315, 342–351
Four Corners Monument, 350
Four Corners rafting, 238
fourteener, 369
Fox Theatre, 158
Fraser, 204–210
Fraser River Trail, 209
Fraser Tubing Hill, 209
Free Museum, 219
Frisco, 36, 212, 214–218, 220–222
Frisco Bay Marina, 220
Frisco Historic Park, 219
Frisco Lodge Bed & Breakfast, 216
Frisco Nordic Center, 220
Fruita, 305
The Full Moon Grill & Pasta, 150

• G •

Galloping Goose shuttles, 316–317
Garden of the Gods Park, 32, 37, 170
Garlic Mike's, 288–289
Gart Sports, 128
Gates Planetarium, 117
Gay and Lesbian Ski Week, 32
gay and lesbian travelers, 78–79
Gazebo Country Inn Bed and
    Breakfast, 233–234
General Palmer Hotel, 334
Genghis Khan, 175
Georgetown, 36, 39, 134–139
Georgetown Loop Railroad, 37, 135
Georgetown Mountain Inn, 37, 138
ghost towns
    Carson, 357
    Independence, 260
    St. Elmo, 236
Giovanni's Room, 79
glacier, 140
Glacier Basin Campground, 186
Glenwood Canyon Brewing
    Company, 268, 273
Glenwood Canyon Path, 271
Glenwood Caverns, 253, 270
Glenwood Springs, 39, 252–253,
    264–268, 270–273
Glenwood Springs Golf Club, 272

Gold Camp Road, 173
Gold Pan Restaurant, 222
Gold Rush of 1859, 16, 94
Golden, 134–138
Golden Access Passport, 77
Golden Age Passport, 76, 188
Golden Bear, 249
Golden Circle
  accommodations, 138
  attractions, 135–137
  getting there, 134
  mountain drives, 139–141
  restaurants, 138–139
  skiing, 137–138
Golden City Brewery, 376
Golden Eagle pass, 46
Golden Triangle, 95
golf
  Alamosa, 365
  altitude effect on, 230
  Aspen, 261
  Breckenridge, 220–221
  Colorado Springs, 173
  Crested Butte, 291
  Denver, 121
  Durango, 339
  Grand Junction, 307
  Leadville, 230
  Middle Park, 211
  Montrose and Delta, 296
  Roaring Fork Valley, 272
  Salida, 237
  Steamboat Springs, 282
  Telluride, 322
  Vail, 247
Golf Club at Redlands Mesa, 307
Gorsuch, 249
GoToMyPC, 84
Granby, 185, 199, 211
Grand Junction
  accommodations, 302–303
  attractions and activities, 304–308
  description, 17, 300
  dining, 303–304
  fast facts, 309
  getting around, 302
  getting there, 300
Grand Lake, 13, 185, 198–201
Grand Lake Golf Course, 195

Grand Lake Lodge, 199, 200
Grand Lodge Crested Butte, 288
Grand Mesa, 300, 306, 307–308
Grand Mesa Nordic Council, 307
Grand Traverse, 247
Gray Line, 124
Great American Beer Festival, 34
Great Basin, 299
Great Sand Dunes National
      Monument and Preserve,
      13–14, 26, 36, 364–365
Greyhound/Trailways, 67, 92
Grizzly Rose Saloon and Dance
      Emporium, 129
GSM wireless network, 83
Guanella Pass Road, 139
guest ranch, 70
Gunnison, 25, 36, 286–293
Gunnison Crested Butte Airport, 286
Gunnison National Forest, 291
Gunnison Pioneer Museum, 290
Gunnison River, 291
Gunnison Route, 295
Gunslingers, Ghosts & Gold, 124

• *H* •

Haggard's Black Dog Tavern, 340
Harper's Corner Trail, 310
Hartsman's Rock, 291
Haymaker, 282
health, 82, 380
The Hearthstone Inn, 166
Hearthstone Victorian Dining, 218
Helen Bonfils Theatre Complex, 132
Heritage Aspen: Aspen's Historical
      Society, 260
The Heritage Center, 155
Heritage Museum and Gallery, 229
Herman's Hideaway, 129
Hernando's Pizza Pub, 206–207
Hi Country Stables, 195
high country, 25, 181–183
High Mountain Outdoors, 291
hiking
  Alamosa, 365–366
  Aspen, 252, 261–262
  Black Canyon of the Gunnison
      National Park, 294–295

hiking *(continued)*
Boulder, 155–156
Colorado National Monument, 305
Colorado Springs, 173
Crested Butte and Gunnison, 291
Denver, 121
Durango, 339
Grand Mesa, 307
Leadville, 231
Mesa Verde, 348
Middle Park, 208
Ouray, 330–331
Roaring Fork Valley, 271
Rocky Mountain National Park, 184, 191–193
Salida, 237
Steamboat Springs, 283
Summit County, 220
Telluride, 322
Vail, 247
Hillcrest Golf Course, 339
Hilltop Café, 138–139
Hinsdale County Museum, 356
The Historic Western Hotel, 325
history
Denver, 94
Leadville, 224, 225, 228
main events, 15–17
Summit County, 219
trip itinerary, 38–39
The Holiday Chalet, 103
Holy Cross Wilderness Area, 247
Home Ranch, 278
horseback riding
Aspen, 262
Rocky Mountain National Park, 195
Steamboat Springs, 283
Horsethief Bench Trail, 308
hot spots, 84
hot springs
Durango, 340
Glenwood Springs, 270–271
Idaho Springs, 135–136
Ouray and Silverton, 328–329
Pagosa Springs, 341
Salida, 236
as signature experience, 370
Steamboat Springs, 281

Hot Springs Pool, 39, 252, 253, 270–271
Hotel Boulderado, 148
Hotel Colorado, 39, 266–267
Hotel Jerome, 19, 256
Hotel Jerome Garden Terrace/ Century Room, 258–259
Hotel Monaco Denver, 103
Hotel Telluride, 317
Hotel-Gasthof Gramshammer, 241, 243
hotels, 11–12, 69, 384–385. *See also specific hotels; specific locations*
Hovenweep National Monument, 349
Howelsen Hill Ski Area, 282, 284
Hunt Placer Inn B&B, 216
hypothermia, 189

• *I* •

ice climbing, 331
The Ice House, 317–318
ice skating, 247, 331
Idaho Springs, 39, 134–140
IMAX theatre, 117
Independence, 260
Independence Pass, 36, 261
Indian Peaks Wilderness Area, 208
Indian Springs Resort, 39, 135–136
information resources, 19–20, 383–385
insurance, 56, 64, 66, 80–81
Internet access, 83–85
interstate highways, 55, 59, 60
Into The Wind, 154, 157
InTouch USA, 82–83
Invesco Field at Mile High, 122, 123, 372
Iron Horse Resort, 205–206
Isabel's, 341
Isle of Capri Casino, 136
itineraries
high passes and peaks, 35–36
history buff, 38–39
with kids, 37
skiing, 39–40

• J •

Jake and Tellys Restaurant and
    Bar, 168
Jan's Family Restaurant, 36, 235
Jax Fish House, 151
Jazz Aspen Snowmass, 263
J-Bar, 263
Jerry's Records, 127
Juicy Lucy's, 268
JW Marriott, 103, 106

• K •

Kahhak Fine Arts and School, 272
kayaking, in Summit County, 221
Ken and Sue's Place, 336
Kendall Mountain Community
    Center, 331
Keystone, 11, 215, 222
Kim Ba, 112
Kinetic Conveyance Challenge, 33
kiva, 346
Kokopelli's Trail, 308

• L •

La Cocina de Luz, 320
La Montana, 280
La Rumba, 129
La Tour, 245
Lady Falconburgh's Barley
    Exchange, 340
Lake City
    accommodations, 353
    attractions and activities, 355–357
    description, 26, 352, 353
    dining, 353, 355
    fast facts, 357
    transportation, 353
Lake Fork, 290
Lake Haiyaha, 191
Lake San Cristobal, 352, 355–357
Lakeview Resort, 355
Lakota River Guides, 248
Las Delicias, 109

Last Dollar Saloon, 323
The Last Steep, 292
Laughing Ladies Restaurant, 235
Leadville
    accommodations, 226–227
    activities, 230–231
    attractions, 228–230
    description, 16, 25, 36, 38
    dining, 227–228
    fast facts, 232
    getting around, 226
    getting there, 225–226
    highlights, 224–225
    weather, 28
Leadville, Colorado & Southern
    Railroad, 228–229
Leadville County Inn, 226–227
Leland House and Rochester
    Hotel, 335
Lemmon Lodge, 199
Level'z, 284
Lifthouse Condominiums, 243
lightning, 190
Limelite Lodge, 257
liquor laws, 381
Little Annie's Eating House, 259
Little Bear Saloon, 141
The Little Nell, 12, 257
Little Ruin Canyon, 349
The Lodge at Vail, 243–244
lodging. See accommodations
Long House, 346
Long's Peak, 9, 181, 186, 192, 195
Lookout Mountain, 135
lost luggage insurance, 81
lost wallet, 50–51
Lotus, 130
Loveland Ski Area, 137
Lower Cascade Falls, 331
Lowry Pueblo, 349
luggage, 86
Lulu City, 193

• M •

mail2web service, 83, 381
Main Avenue Trolley Service, 334

Main Street Brewery and
    Restaurant, 344
Main Street Station, 216
Mancos
  accommodations, 343
  description, 312, 342
  fast facts, 351
Manitou Springs, 24, 37, 163,
    166–171, 173
Manuelita's Restaurant, 227
maps
  Aspen, 255
  Boulder, 146–147
  Colorado, 22–23
  Colorado Springs, 164–165
  Denver accommodations and
    dining, 104–105
  Denver attractions and nightlife,
    114–115
  Denver neighborhoods, 93
  driving times and distances, 60
  The High Country, 182–183
  Middle Park, 203
  Roaring Fork Valley, 252
  Rocky Mountain National Park, 187
  sources of, 381
  southern Rockies, 354
  southwestern high country, 314
  Steamboat Springs, 276
  Summit County, 213
  Vail, 242
  Western Slope, 301
Maroon Bells/Snowmass Wilderness
    Area, 36, 252, 261, 272
Maroon Creek Road, 261
Mary Jane ski area, 11, 39
Matchless Mine, 10, 38, 224, 228
Matterhorn Mountain Motel, 353
McPhee Reservoir, 351
Medicine Bow-Routt National
    Forest, 283
Mercury Café, 109–110
Merlino's Belvedere, 177–178
Mesa Top Loop Drive, 347
Mesa Trail, 155
Mesa Verde and the Four Corners
  accommodations, 343–344
  attractions and activities, 345–351
  dining, 344–345

fast facts, 351
transportation, 342–343
Mesa Verde National Park, 14, 15, 38,
    315, 342–350
Mesa Verde Pottery, 351
Metate Room, 344–345
Middle Park
  accommodations, 205–206, 210–211
  activities, 208–209, 211
  attractions, 207–208
  description, 25, 202–204
  dining, 206–207
  fast facts, 210
  getting around, 204–205
  getting there, 204
  map, 203
  skiing, 209, 211
Millennium Harvest House, 148–149
Mineral Belt Trail, 225, 230
Mineral County, 361
Miner's Cafe, 311
Miner's Tavern, 332
mining
  Aspen, 260
  Creede, 360–361
  Leadville, 224, 225, 228, 229
  Ouray and Silverton, 328
Molly Brown House, 38, 119, 124
Monarch Crest Trail, 225, 237
Monarch Ski and Snowboard Area,
    238–239
Montrose, 293, 295, 296
Montrose County Historical
    Museum, 296
Montrose Golf Club, 296
Montrose Regional Airport,
    293, 316, 324
moose, 189, 194
Moosejaw Pub, 222
Moots Cycles, 283
Moraine Park, 188
Moraine Park Museum, 191
motels, 69, 384–385. *See also specific
    hotels; specific locations*
Mount Elbert, 224, 225, 230, 231, 369
Mount Evans, 139–140, 370
Mount Everest Import, 127
Mount Massive Golf Course, 230
Mount Princeton Hot Springs, 236

Mount Zerkel Wilderness Area, 283
Mountain Bike Hall of Fame, 290
Mountain Bike Specialists, 339
mountain biking
 Aspen, 261
 Boulder, 155
 Colorado Springs, 173
 Crested Butte and Gunnison, 291
 Durango, 339
 Grand Junction and Fruita, 307–308
 Leadville, 230
 Middle Park, 208–209
 Roaring Fork Valley, 271
 Rocky Mountain National Park, 194
 Salida, 237
 Steamboat Springs, 283
 Summit County, 220
 Telluride, 322
 Vail, 247–248
Mountain Express Butte, 287
Mountain High Casino, 136
mountain lion, 189
Mountain Sun Pub & Brewery,
 151, 376
mountaineering, 195, 231, 322. *See
 also* climbing
MountainFilm, 321
Mouse's Handmade Truffles, 332
movies, 20
Mt. Crested Butte, 287
Mudhead Gallery, 126
Museum of Contemporary Art, 120
Museum of Nature and Science, 37
Museum of Western Colorado, 307
museums
 Aspen, 260
 Boulder, 154–155
 Colorado Springs, 172–173
 Creede, 360
 Crested Butte and Gunnison, 290
 Denver, 113, 116–117, 119–121,
 124–125
 Durango, 338–339
 Fruita, 306–307
 Golden Circle, 135
 Lake City, 356
 Leadville, 10, 224, 228, 229
 Mesa Verde, 345–348

Montrose, 295–296
 Ouray and Silverton, 329–330
 Rocky Mountain National Park, 191
 Steamboat Springs, 281
 Summit County, 219
 Telluride, 320–321
 Vail, 246
Mushroom Rock, 272
music
 Aspen, 263
 Boulder, 158–159
 Colorado Springs, 175
 Denver, 127–128
 Evergreen, 141
 at Red Rocks, 370
 Steamboat Springs, 285
 Summit County, 219, 222
 Telluride, 321, 323
 Vail, 249–250

• *N* •

Naropa University, 154
National Mining Hall of Fame and
 Museum, 10, 38, 224, 228
National Parks Pass, 188
National Western Stock Show, Rodeo
 & Horse Show, 10, 32, 118, 371
Navajo tribe, 16, 350
Neptune Mountaineering, 156, 195
Nevada Village Antiques, 174
Never Summer Ranch, 190
New Belgium Brewery, 375
New Saigon, 112
New Sheridan Bar, 323
New Sheridan Hotel, 38
newspapers, 381
nightlife
 Aspen, 263
 Boulder, 157–158
 Colorado Springs, 174–175
 costs, 47
 Crested Butte, 292
 Denver, 128–129, 128–132
 Durango, 340
 Ouray and Silverton, 332
 Roaring Fork Valley, 273
 Steamboat Springs, 284–285

nightlife *(continued)*
  Summit County, 222
  Telluride, 323
  Vail, 249–250
Nordic Lodge Motel, 277
North Vista Trail, 294–295
Notah Dineh, 351
Notchtop Bakery & Cafe, 198
The Numbers, 238

● *O* ●

Ocean Journey, 37, 117–118, 125
Odell Brewing Company, 375
Ogden Theatre, 129
Old Colorado City, 162, 166–167, 168
Old Hundred Gold Mine Tour, 313, 328
Old Town Guest House, 166–167
old west experiences, 10
Olympus Motor Lodge, 196
online booking
  air tickets, 54–55
  package tours, 57–58
  pro sports events, 122–123
  rental car, 64
Opera Colorado, 132
Orvis Hot Springs, 328
The O2 Lounge, 219
Ouray
  accommodations, 325–326
  attractions and activities, 328–332
  description, 26, 324
  dining, 327–328
  fast facts, 332
  getting around, 325
  getting there, 324–325
  highlights, 313
Ouray County Historical
    Museum, 313, 329
Ouray Hot Springs Pool, 329, 331
Ouray Ice Park, 331
Outdoor World, 330
Ouzel Falls, 192
Oxford Hotel, 36, 38, 39, 106

● *P* ●

Pablo's Pizza, 304
package tours, 47, 57–58

Packer, Alferd (cannibal), 356
Pagosa Springs, 312, 340–341
Palisade, 306
Palisade Peach Festival, 34
Pancho and Lefty's Restaurant,
    200–201
Papillon Café, 110
Park Hyatt Beaver Creek Resort
    and Spa, 244
parking, in Denver, 100
parks, 202
Patty Jewett Golf Course, 173
Peak 8 Fun Park, 37, 219–220
The Peak-to-Peak Highway, 140
Pearl Street Inn, 149
Pearl Street Mall, 153
Penny Lane, 158
Pepsi Center, 122, 123
performing arts
  Aspen, 263–264
  Boulder, 158–159
  Colorado Springs, 175
  Creede, 361
  Denver, 131–132
  at Red Rocks, 370
  Steamboat Springs, 285
  Summit County, 219
  Telluride, 321
  Vail, 250
Pete's Kitchen, 110
Petroglyph Point Trail, 348
Phantom Canyon Brewing
    Company, 174
Phoenix Mine Tour, 137
phone bills, 48
The Pickle Barrel, 327
Pikes Peak, 16, 24, 369–370
Pikes Peak Auto Hill Climb
    Educational Museum, 171
Pikes Peak Center, 175
Pikes Peak Cog Railway, 37, 163, 170
Pikes Peak Highway, 171
Pikes Peak International Hill Climb,
    33, 171
Pikes Peak Tours, 173
Piney Creek Nordic Center, 230
The Pinnacle Ledge at Winter
    Park, 206
Pitas in Paradise, 289

Platte Valley Trolley, 123
Pleasant View Resort, 357
Pole Creek Golf Club, 211211
Poppy's Pizza & Grill, 198
Powderhorn Resort, 308
precipitation, 28
Princess Wine Bar, 292
Pro Rodeo Hall of Fame and Museum
    of the American Cowboy, 172
Purgatory Village Condominium
    Hotel, 335

• **Q** •

Quality Inn and Suites Boulder
    Creek, 149
Queen Anne Bed & Breakfast Inn, 106
Quincy's Steak and Spirits, 227–228

• **R** •

rack rates, 3, 70
rafting
    Arkansas River, 37, 177, 238
    Denver, 121
    Durango, 339
    Roaring Fork Valley, 272
    Salida, 238
    Vail, 248
railroads
    Amtrak, 55, 66–67, 92, 204, 254
    Colorado Railroad Museum, 135
    Denver light-rail, 99
    Durango & Silverton Narrow Gauge
        Railroad, 10, 38, 312–313,
        325, 337–338
    Georgetown Loop, 37, 135
    Leadville, Colorado & Southern
        Railroad, 228–229
    Pikes Peak, 163, 170
    Royal Gorge, 176
    Ski Train, 204
    Tiny Town, 121
The Ranch at Roaring Fork, 272
ranches
    Middle Park, 210
    Steamboat Springs, 10, 278
Randi's Irish Saloon, 207

Red Lion Inn, 249
The Red Onion, 259
Red Ram & Rathskeller, 139
Red Rocks Park, 121, 370
Red Square, 110–111
Redstone, 36, 38, 252–253,
    265–271, 273
Redstone Castle, 36, 38, 253
Redstone Inn, 38, 267
Regional Transportation District,
    91–92, 98, 143, 144
REI, 121, 127, 128
rental car, 47, 64–66
restaurants
    Alamosa, 363–364
    Arkansas Valley, 234–235
    Aspen, 258–259
    Boulder, 149–152
    Colorado Springs, 167–169
    costs, 45
    Creede, 359–360
    Denver, 107–113
    Durango, 336–337
    Estes Park, 198
    Golden Circle, 138–139
    Grand Junction, 303–304
    Grand Lake, 200–201
    Gunnison and Crested Butte,
        288–289
    Lake City, 353, 355
    Leadville, 227–228
    local cuisine, 17–19
    Mesa Verde and the Four Corners,
        344–345
    Ouray and Silverton, 327–328
    Roaring Fork Valley, 267–269
    Steamboat Springs, 278–280
    Summit County, 217–218
    Telluride, 319–320
    Vail, 244–246
    Winter Park, 206–207
Rhumba, 151
Ride Glenwood Springs, 266
Rio Grande National Forest, 366
River Run Inn, 234
Riverside Inn and Cabins, 326, 330
road hazards, 61–63
RoadPost, 82
Roaring Fork Transit Authority, 266

Roaring Fork Valley
  accommodations, 266–267
  attractions and activities, 270–273
  description, 264–265
  dining, 267–269
  fast facts, 273
  getting around, 266
  getting there, 265
  map, 252
Rock Bottom Restaurant and
    Brewery, 130–131
rockfall, 62–63
Rockslide Restaurant and
    Brewery, 304
Rocky Mountain Diner, 111
Rocky Mountain National Park
  accommodations, 195–197, 199–200
  activities, 191–195
  attractions, 190–191
  description, 25, 36, 181, 184
  dining, 198, 200–201
  fast facts, 201
  fees, 188
  getting around, 188–189
  getting there, 184–185
  layout, 186
  map, 187
  planning ahead for visit, 185
  safety, 189–190
  season to visit, 184
  visitor centers, 185, 188
  wildlife, 194
rodeo, 281, 371
Royal Gorge, 24, 176–177
Royal Gorge Bridge and Park, 37, 176
Rubey Park Transit Center,
    254, 256, 261
Ruby Canyon Cycles, 308
Rum Bay, 175
running
  Boulder, 33, 156
  Denver, 122

● **S** ●

Saddleback Ranch, 10, 278
safety, 381
Saigon Cafe, 168

sailing
  Gunnison, 290–291
  Summit County, 220
Salida
  accommodations, 233–234
  attractions and activities, 235–239
  description, 13, 25, 37, 232
  dining, 234–235
  fast facts, 239
  getting there, 232–233
  highlights, 225
Salida Golf Club, 237
Salida Hot Springs, 37, 236
Salsa Trade Company, 332
Sambuca, 129
San Isabel National Forest, 231, 237
San Juan County Museum, 329–330
San Juan Mountain Guides, 331
San Juan Mountains, 26, 352, 362
San Juan National Forest, 338
San Juan Sports, 361
San Luis Valley, 26, 36, 362–366
San Miguel River Trail, 322
The Sanctuary, 249
Sand Creek Massacre, 16
Sandlot Brewing Company, 131
Sangre de Cristo Wilderness, 366
Sapphire Grill, 268
Sapphire Restaurant and Oyster
    Bar, 245
satellite phone (satphone), 82
Scoot 'n' Blues, 340
seasons, 29–31
Seasons Rotisserie and Grill, 336–337
seniors, advice for, 76–77
The Shed, 12, 207
Sherpa & Yeti's, 222
shopping
  Aspen, 263
  Boulder, 157
  Colorado Springs, 174
  Cortez, 351
  costs of goods, 46–47
  Denver, 125–128
  Durango, 340
  Grand Junction, 308
  Ouray and Silverton, 332
  Roaring Fork Valley, 272–273
  Salida, 236

Steamboat Springs, 284
Summit County, 218
Vail, 249
shoulder seasons, 27, 71
shuttles. *See specific locations*
signature Colorado experiences,
    369–373
silver boom, 16, 94
Silver Dollar Saloon, 38, 225, 230
Silver Plume, 37
Silverthorne, 36, 212, 215, 220
Silverton
  accommodations, 325–326
  attractions and activities, 328–332
  description, 11, 26, 38, 40, 324
  dining, 327–328
  fast facts, 332
  getting around, 325
  getting there, 324–325
  highlights, 313
Silverton Mountain, 331
Simpich Character Dolls, 174
Six Flags Elitch Gardens Amusement
    Park, 37, 118, 125
Six89 Main Kitchen and Wine Bar, 269
Ska Brewing Company, 376
Ski Cooper, 231
Ski Time Square, 284
Ski Train, 39, 204, 370
Skiers Chalet, 258
skiing
  Aspen, 252, 262
  Boulder, 156
  costs, 46
  Creede, 361
  Crested Butte, 292
  Durango, 340
  family travel, 74–75
  Golden Circle, 137
  Grand Mesa, 308
  Leadville, 231
  Middle Park, 209, 211
  Ouray and Silverton, 331
  recommended areas, 10–11
  Roaring Fork Valley, 272
  Salida, 238–239
  SolVista, 211
  Steamboat Springs, 284
  Summit County, 221–222

Telluride, 322–323
trip itinerary, 39–40
Vail, 248–249
Winter Park, 209
Skylark Lounge, 129
The Slogar Bar & Restaurant, 289
Slopeside Grill, 280, 284
smoking, 382
Smuggler Mine, 260
snow and ice, driving in, 61–62, 63
Snow Mountain Ranch, 13, 195,
    210–211
Snowmass, 11, 39, 262
Snowshoe Lodge, 359
Soda Creek Outfitters, 284
SolVista Golf and Ski Ranch, 211
Sonnenalp, 12, 244
Sore Saddle Cyclery, 283
Soupçon, 289
South Platte River, 121
southwestern high country
  description, 312
  major attractions, 313, 315
  map, 314
Sow's Ear, 337
spas
  Aspen, 260
  Glenwood Springs, 271
  Telluride, 318
The Spot Bouldering Gym, 156
The Springs at Pagosa, 341
Springs Resort, 341
Spruce Canyon Trail, 348
Spruce Tree House, 347, 349–350
Square Tower Overlook, 347
St. Cloud Hotel, 177
St. Elmo, 236
The St. Julien Hotel & Spa, 149
St. Louis Lake Trail, 208
St. Mark's Coffeehouse, 130
St. Mary's Glacier, 140
St. Patrick's Day Parade, 32
The St. Regis, 257
stage coach, 350
Stanley Hotel, 197
Steamboat Grand Resort Hotel and
    Conference Center, 277
Steamboat Ski Area, 282, 283, 284

Steamboat Springs
    accommodations, 275–278
    activities, 282–284
    attractions, 280–282
    description, 25, 40, 274
    dining, 278–280
    fast facts, 285
    getting around, 275
    getting there, 274–275
    map, 276
    nightlife and culture, 284–285
    shopping, 284
Steamboat Springs Health and
        Recreation Center, 280–281
Steamboat Springs Winter
        Carnival, 32
Steamworks, 337
stolen wallet, 50–51
The Strater Hotel, 13, 38, 313, 335–336
Strawberry Park Hot Springs, 281
Strings in the Mountains, 285
Summit Canyon Mountaineering, 273
Summit County
    accommodations, 215–216
    activities, 220–222
    attractions, 218–220
    description, 25, 39, 212
    dining, 217–218
    fast facts, 223
    getting around, 214
    getting there, 214
    map, 213
    nightlife, 222
Summit Historical Society, 219
Sun Temple, 347
Sunflower Natural Fine Dining, 152
Sunlight Mountain Resort, 272
Sushi Tazu, 111
Sweet Basil, 246
Sweet Basilico, 198
Switzerland of America, 330
Syzygy, 263

● T ●

Tabeguache Trail, 308
Table Mountain Inn, 138
Tabor Opera House, 38, 229
The Tap House, 285

The Tap Room, 249
Taqueria Cal Villo, 364
Tattered Cover Bookstores, 127
taxes, 382
Taylor Creek Fly Shop, 10
Taylor Park Reservoir, 237
Telluride
    accommodations, 317–318
    attractions and activities, 320–323
    description, 16, 26, 38, 312, 315
    dining, 319–320
    fast facts, 324
    getting around, 316–317
    getting there, 315–316
    highlights, 313
Telluride Bluegrass Festival,
        13, 33, 321
Telluride Blues & Brews Festival,
        34, 321
Telluride Golf Club, 322
Telluride Historical Museum, 320
Telluride Jazz Celebration Film
        Festival, 321
Telluride Mountaineer, 322
Telluride Nordic Center, 322
Telluride Outside, 322
Telluride Regional Airport, 316
Telluride Ski Resort, 313, 322–323
Telluride Youth Center, 321
temperatures, 28. *See also* weather
Temple Buell Theater, 132
tennis, in Denver, 122
The Thin Man, 130
Thunder River Lodge, 267
Thunderhead Trail, 283
Ticketmaster, 122, 131
TicketsWest, 159
Timber Lake Trail, 193
time zone, 382
Tin Lizzie, 131
Tiny Town, 120–121
toll-free numbers, 383–385
Tomichi Cycles, 291
tourist information, 385
tours
    cost, 46
    Creede, 360–361
    Denver, 119, 123–124
    escorted, 56–57

Golden Circle, 137
Leadville, 229–230
Mesa Verde, 347, 349–350
Ouray and Silverton, 328, 330
package, 47, 57–58
Pikes Peak, 173
Tower Point Loop, 349
Town Park Campground, 318
Trail Riders Motel, 199–200
Trail Ridge Road, 25, 181,
    184, 186, 190
Trail's End Public House, 328
transportation, 44–45. *See also
    specific locations*
Transportation Security
    Administration, 85–86
Travel Guard Alerts, 81
travel insurance, 56, 80–81
traveler's checks, 50
Tread of Pioneers Museum, 281
Trimble Hot Springs, 340
Trios Wine and Martini Bar, 158
The Tugboat Grill and Pub, 285
Tulagi, 158
Tundra Communities Trail, 190, 193
T-Wa Inn, 112
Two Rivers Winery, 303

• U •

Uncompahgre Plateau, 25, 299,
    304, 305
The Underground, 175
Underground Mining Museum, 360
United States Olympic Complex, 172
University Bicycles, 144–145
The University of Colorado at
    Boulder, 155
The University of Colorado Natural
    History Museum, 155
Upper Arkansas Valley, 25, 36
Upper Fish Creek Falls, 283
U.S. Air Force Academy, 17, 171–172
U.S. Mint, 119
U.S. National Park Service, 76, 77
Ute Indian Museum, 295–296
Ute Mountain Casino, 350–351
Ute Mountain Tribal Park, 315, 348
Ute tribe, 15, 16, 94, 348, 356

• V •

Vail
    accommodations, 241–244
    activities, 247–249
    attractions, 246
    description, 17, 25, 39, 240
    dining, 244–246
    fast facts, 250
    getting around, 241
    getting there, 240–241
    map, 242
    nightlife and culture, 249–250
    shopping, 249
    what things cost in, 44
Vail Golf Course, 247
Vail International Dance Festival, 250
Vail Jazz Festival, 250
Vail Mountain, 247
Vail Nature Center, 247
Vail Valley Music Festival, 250
Vail/Eagle County Airport, 53, 225,
    241, 254, 265
Van Briggle Art Pottery, 174
Vasquez Wilderness Area, 208
Vendettas Italian Restaurant, 249
The Victorian Inn, 318
Villa Dallavalle Inn, 326
Village Smithy, 269

• W •

Wager Gulch Trail, 357
Walker Field, 300
wallet, lost or stolen, 50–51
Walnut Brewery, 152, 376
Warner Point Nature Trail, 295
Wasatch Trail, 322
Washington Park, 97, 122
Watercourse Foods, 111–112
Watson Island/Old Mill Bridge, 307
Wax Trax, 128
Wazee Supper Club, 112
weather
    elevation effect on, 27
    fall, 30
    overview, 27–28
    precipitation, 28
    spring, 29

weather *(continued)*
  summer, 29–30
  temperature, 28
  updates, 382
  winter, 31
Weathertop Wovens, 332
Web sites
  for accommodations, 69, 72–73,
    384–385
  airlines, 383
  car rental, 383–384
  family travel, 75–76
  for gay and lesbian travelers, 78–79
  travel agencies, 54
  for travelers with disabilities, 77–78
West Elk Mountains, 252, 253
Western Slope, 299, 301
Westin Tabor Center, 106
Wetherill Mesa, 347
The Wheeler Film Society, 264
Wheeler Opera House, 264
White House Restaurant and Bar, 269
White River National Forest,
    261–262, 272
Whitewater Rafting, 272
Wi-fi (wireless fidelity), 84
Wild Basin Trail, 186, 192
wildlife
  eluding while driving, 63
  Rocky Mountain National Park,
    189, 194
Wildwood Motel, 288
The Wines of Colorado, 168–169
Winter Park
  accommodations, 205–206
  attractions and activities, 207–209
  description, 11, 39, 202–204

dining, 206–207
fast facts, 210
transportation, 204–205, 370
Wintersköl, 261, 371
Wolcott, 39
Wolf Creek, 361
Woodland, 234
Woody Creek Tavern, 263
The World Figure Skating Museum
    and Hall of Fame, 172
Wupperman Campground, 355
The Wyman Hotel and Inn, 38, 326
Wyndham Peaks Resort and Golden
    Door Spa, 318
Wynkoop Brewing Company,
    39, 112–113, 130, 375

• Y •

Yampa Valley Regional Airport,
    274–275
Yampah Spa and Vapor Caves, 271
YMCA of the Rockies Estes Park
    Center, 197
YMCA of the Rockies, Snow Mountain
    Ranch, 210–211

• Z •

Zang Brewery Co., 125
Zapata Falls, 365
Zocalito Latin Bistro, 269–270
Zolo Grill, 152
zoos
  Cheyenne Mountain Zoo, 169–170
  Denver Zoo, 117, 125

BUSINESS, CAREERS & PERSONAL FINANCE

0-7645-5307-0   0-7645-5331-3 *†

Also available:
- Accounting For Dummies †
  0-7645-5314-3
- Business Plans Kit For Dummies †
  0-7645-5365-8
- Cover Letters For Dummies
  0-7645-5224-4
- Frugal Living For Dummies
  0-7645-5403-4
- Leadership For Dummies
  0-7645-5176-0
- Managing For Dummies
  0-7645-1771-6

- Marketing For Dummies
  0-7645-5600-2
- Personal Finance For Dummies *
  0-7645-2590-5
- Project Management
  For Dummies
  0-7645-5283-X
- Resumes For Dummies †
  0-7645-5471-9
- Selling For Dummies
  0-7645-5363-1
- Small Business Kit For Dummies *†
  0-7645-5093-4

HOME & BUSINESS COMPUTER BASICS

0-7645-4074-2   0-7645-3758-X

Also available:
- ACT! 6 For Dummies
  0-7645-2645-6
- iLife '04 All-in-One Desk Reference
  For Dummies
  0-7645-7347-0
- iPAQ For Dummies
  0-7645-6769-1
- Mac OS X Panther Timesaving
  Techniques For Dummies
  0-7645-5812-9
- Macs For Dummies
  0-7645-5656-8
- Microsoft Money 2004 For Dummies
  0-7645-4195-1

- Office 2003 All-in-One Desk
  Reference For Dummies
  0-7645-3883-7
- Outlook 2003 For Dummies
  0-7645-3759-8
- PCs For Dummies
  0-7645-4074-2
- TiVo For Dummies
  0-7645-6923-6
- Upgrading and Fixing PCs
  For Dummies
  0-7645-1665-5
- Windows XP Timesaving
  Techniques For Dummies
  0-7645-3748-2

FOOD, HOME, GARDEN, HOBBIES, MUSIC & PETS

0-7645-5295-3   0-7645-5232-5

Also available:
- Bass Guitar For Dummies
  0-7645-2487-9
- Diabetes Cookbook For Dummies
  0-7645-5230-9
- Gardening For Dummies *
  0-7645-5130-2
- Guitar For Dummies
  0-7645-5106-X
- Holiday Decorating For Dummies
  0-7645-2570-0
- Home Improvement All-in-One
  For Dummies
  0-7645-5680-0

- Knitting For Dummies
  0-7645-5395-X
- Piano For Dummies
  0-7645-5105-1
- Puppies For Dummies
  0-7645-5255-4
- Scrapbooking For Dummies
  0-7645-7208-3
- Senior Dogs For Dummies
  0-7645-5818-8
- Singing For Dummies
  0-7645-2475-5
- 30-Minute Meals For Dummies
  0-7645-2589-1

INTERNET & DIGITAL MEDIA

0-7645-1664-7   0-7645-6924-4

Also available:
- 2005 Online Shopping Directory
  For Dummies
  0-7645-7495-7
- CD & DVD Recording For Dummies
  0-7645-5956-7
- eBay For Dummies
  0-7645-5654-1
- Fighting Spam For Dummies
  0-7645-5965-6
- Genealogy Online For Dummies
  0-7645-5964-8
- Google For Dummies
  0-7645-4420-9

- Home Recording For Musicians
  For Dummies
  0-7645-1634-5
- The Internet For Dummies
  0-7645-4173-0
- iPod & iTunes For Dummies
  0-7645-7772-7
- Preventing Identity Theft
  For Dummies
  0-7645-7336-5
- Pro Tools All-in-One Desk
  Reference For Dummies
  0-7645-5714-9
- Roxio Easy Media Creator
  For Dummies
  0-7645-7131-1

SPORTS, FITNESS, PARENTING, RELIGION & SPIRITUALITY

0-7645-5146-9   0-7645-5418-2

Also available:

- Adoption For Dummies
  0-7645-5488-3
- Basketball For Dummies
  0-7645-5248-1
- The Bible For Dummies
  0-7645-5296-1
- Buddhism For Dummies
  0-7645-5359-3
- Catholicism For Dummies
  0-7645-5391-7
- Hockey For Dummies
  0-7645-5228-7

- Judaism For Dummies
  0-7645-5299-6
- Martial Arts For Dummies
  0-7645-5358-5
- Pilates For Dummies
  0-7645-5397-6
- Religion For Dummies
  0-7645-5264-3
- Teaching Kids to Read
  For Dummies
  0-7645-4043-2
- Weight Training For Dummies
  0-7645-5168-X
- Yoga For Dummies
  0-7645-5117-5

TRAVEL

0-7645-5438-7   0-7645-5453-0

Also available:

- Alaska For Dummies
  0-7645-1761-9
- Arizona For Dummies
  0-7645-6938-4
- Cancún and the Yucatán
  For Dummies
  0-7645-2437-2
- Cruise Vacations For Dummies
  0-7645-6941-4
- Europe For Dummies
  0-7645-5456-5
- Ireland For Dummies
  0-7645-5455-7

- Las Vegas For Dummies
  0-7645-5448-4
- London For Dummies
  0-7645-4277-X
- New York City For Dummies
  0-7645-6945-7
- Paris For Dummies
  0-7645-5494-8
- RV Vacations For Dummies
  0-7645-5443-3
- Walt Disney World & Orlando
  For Dummies
  0-7645-6943-0

GRAPHICS, DESIGN & WEB DEVELOPMENT

0-7645-4345-8   0-7645-5589-8

Also available:

- Adobe Acrobat 6 PDF
  For Dummies
  0-7645-3760-1
- Building a Web Site For Dummies
  0-7645-7144-3
- Dreamweaver MX 2004
  For Dummies
  0-7645-4342-3
- FrontPage 2003 For Dummies
  0-7645-3882-9
- HTML 4 For Dummies
  0-7645-1995-6
- Illustrator CS For Dummies
  0-7645-4084-X

- Macromedia Flash MX 2004
  For Dummies
  0-7645-4358-X
- Photoshop 7 All-in-One Desk
  Reference For Dummies
  0-7645-1667-1
- Photoshop CS Timesaving
  Techniques For Dummies
  0-7645-6782-9
- PHP 5 For Dummies
  0-7645-4166-8
- PowerPoint 2003 For Dummies
  0-7645-3908-6
- QuarkXPress 6 For Dummies
  0-7645-2593-X

NETWORKING, SECURITY, PROGRAMMING & DATABASES

0-7645-6852-3   0-7645-5784-X

Also available:

- A+ Certification For Dummies
  0-7645-4187-0
- Access 2003 All-in-One Desk
  Reference For Dummies
  0-7645-3988-4
- Beginning Programming
  For Dummies
  0-7645-4997-9
- C For Dummies
  0-7645-7068-4
- Firewalls For Dummies
  0-7645-4048-3
- Home Networking For Dummies
  0-7645-42796

- Network Security For Dummies
  0-7645-1679-5
- Networking For Dummies
  0-7645-1677-9
- TCP/IP For Dummies
  0-7645-1760-0
- VBA For Dummies
  0-7645-3989-2
- Wireless All In-One Desk Reference
  For Dummies
  0-7645-7496-5
- Wireless Home Networking
  For Dummies
  0-7645-3910-8